The Noble Savage in the New World Garden

The Noble Savage in the New World Garden:
Notes Toward a Syntactics of Place

Gaile McGregor

University of Toronto Press
Toronto, Ontario, Canada M55 1A6

Bowling Green State University Popular Press
Bowling Green, Ohio 43403

Library of Congress Catalogue Card No. 87-72549

ISBN: 0-87972-416-1 Clothbound
0-87972-417-X Paperback

Published in Canada by University of Toronto Press, Toronto.
ISBN: 0-8020-5791-8

Cover design by Gary Dumm

"I therefore claim to show, not how men think in myths, but how myths operate in men's minds without their being aware of the fact."

Claude Lévi-Strauss,
Overture to *The Raw and the Cooked*

"For the Structuralist, as for the Idealists of a previous day, the culture-system *lives* the individuals and groups caught within its mazes rather than the reverse...Structuralism, as it has been often said, destroys the myth of the transcendental subject, the Cartesian *ego*, which stands over against the world, judges experiences of it, and selectively arranges them for the realization of immanent aims. The only true subject of history is history itself. *It* lives *its life* through us; it is the sole agent of history and we its agencies, even though we do not recognize ourselves as such but persist, at least in the West, in thinking that it is *we* who live *it*."

Hayden White,
"Structuralism and Popular Culture"

Contents

1. Introduction

Social critiques of the last thirty years have been increasingly inclined toward apocalypse. Since the 50s, in both Europe and the United States, as Krishan Kumar points out, conservatives and leftists alike have converged "on the idea that the industrial societies are entering on a new phase of their evolution, marking a transition as momentous as that which a hundred years ago took European societies from an agrarian to an industrial social order." This is far from implying a convergence of visions, of course. There have, in fact, been as many stripes of prognostication as there are prognosticators, with labels for the new age ranging from relatively neutral terms like "post-modern" or "post-industrial" or "post-bourgeois" to value-laden ones like "post-scarcity" or "post-civilized."

There have also, as these last examples imply, been marked differences in the attitudes evinced towards the changes expected to issue from the ostensibly imminent break with the past. Despite this superficial diversity, however, especially in the American corpus one may detect a general trend if not in the substance of the responses at least in the mood of the respondents. During the 50s, writers like Herbert Marcuse touted technology as the great liberator. During the 60s, as science, "taken over" by the military-industrial establishment, became inextricably implicated in "the ideology of domination and manipulation" (Robinson), this technophilia turned into technophobia. Technophobia in turn stimulated neo-primitivism. Neo-primitivism stimulated a cult of "naturalness" which became expressed as a kind of aggressive political and psycho-sexual experimentation. Less appealing in practice than in theory, this, finally, triggered a reactive neo-puritanism.

Here, unfortunately, was where the hangover set in. Unallayed by the prospect of either utopia *or* revolution, the great dis-illusionment of the early 70s was interpreted not as a break*through* but as a break*down*. Post-Vietnam, post-Watergate, post-hopefulness, the 60s vision of personal and political de-repression suddenly seemed naive, facile, even dishonest. Morally exhausted, self-indulgent, and cynical, the new American was clearly neither John Wayne *nor* Che Guevara. This recognition did not, on the other hand, weaken anyone's conviction that the country was undergoing a major socio-political transformation. Whatever their politics, in fact, culture critics like Daniel Bell and Marshall Berman have been almost unanimous in reading 70s social apathy as the endgame in the long, slow, irreversible process by which bourgeois culture

1

has destroyed itself from within. The question that needs to be considered is whether this consensual post mortem is not a premature one.

One point to keep in mind: the post-whateverism scenario, in all its guises, is at root an imported one. As such it carries with it a number of very specific assumptions about the constitution of the world-at-large. One of the more important of these is the obsessive historicity implicit in the European's apparently never-ending battle against the tyranny of the past. It's here that we see most clearly the nineteenth-century roots of twentieth-century Marxism. Despite Sartre's diatribes against the false consolation of conventional narrative form—the "sense of an ending," as Frank Kermode terms it—the fact is that slogans about the "death of history" bespeak, at least as a prior condition, exactly the kind of linearity and closure on which the bourgeois novel has always depended. Just as much as the conservative's concern with continuity, in other words, the Marxist's unshakable faith in fresh beginnings not only reveals but entails an unshakable sense of embeddedness in a rational progression of unrepeatable moments leading irresistibly from *then* to *now*.

It's questionable whether one can say the same of the American. The American in fact neither admits that, nor acts as if, his experience *is* emplotted by the past. Insofar as expectations govern results, there is thus a good deal of difficulty in applying *any* of the implicitly progressive European models. Take this latest phase, for instance. If it was Christopher Lasch who made the culture of narcissism into a cliché, it was Richard Sennett who recognized the true significance of the post-60s inward-turning. Back in the early 50s, he says, David Riesman "contrasted an inner-directed society, in which men pursued actions and made commitments based on goals and sentiments within themselves, to an other-directed society, in which these passions and commitments depend on what people sense to be the feelings of others. Riesman believed American society...was moving from an inner- to an other-directed condition. The sequence should be reversed. Western societies are moving from something like an other-directed condition to an inner-directed condition." The interesting point about this observation lies in the extent to which, tacitly, it explodes the myth of irreversibility. It is only such an "explosion," I would suggest, that can explain the view from the 80s.

What view? Well, it is obvious that there has been another radical shift in communal attitudes. Received opinions notwithstanding, moreover, this shift is adumbrated not merely by the recent popularity of the New Right but even more saliently by changes detectable in the public mood during the decade *preceding* the Reaganite victory by which that popularity was "officially" confirmed. The evidence of mass culture is particularly striking. While the middle class were belatedly busy discovering the "natural look" in clothes and home furnishings, westerns began to rehabilitate the pioneer, TV cops put away their love beads and got out their uniforms, big-bang and mad-machine motifs were edged out by natural catastrophes for the title roles in disaster movies, and the Vietnam vet was transformed first from a villain to a victim and thence to Magnum P.I.

Most significant, perhaps, was the change that took place in communal images of heroism. At the beginning of the 70s the exemplar of the heroic mode tended to be someone like the itinerant warrior-priest of the long-running television show, *Kung Fu*, a gentle peace-loving man who hid beneath his humble exterior an awesome, almost magical martial artistry which enabled him—single-handed and against all odds—to conquer the most invincible villainy. The key characteristic of this figure was not simply his virtual invulnerability, however—*all* true American heroes are invulnerable—but the fact that the power which gave him his victories, consistent with the much decried subjectivity of the period in general, was (a) earned/learned, (b) based entirely on inner resources, and (c) both linked with and sanctioned by an ingrained and self-validating morality.

We see vestiges of the same type as late as the mid-70s in the movie *Star Wars*—but here already the prescription has begun to change. Although Luke Skywalker must achieve some form of personal enlightenment before he can tap the power of the Force, his combat success in practice depends on a good many high-tech trappings. Soon afterwards even the token novitiate is discarded. The hero now becomes Superman, the champion whose strength—*and* whose moral authority for that matter—are simply bestowed by birthright. And beyond this point the ideal splits apart entirely. Authority is vested not in the hero himself but in some paternal, even transcendental principle above or behind him: the President, the Country, capital-S Science, omniscient extraterrestrials— God himself. What happens to the hero once Nobodaddy takes over the reins? *He* becomes something much simpler: Conan the Barbarian, power incarnate, divorced from any responsibility except the responsibility to win. In the 80s, then, the Incredible Hulk (who represents the sinister underside to the Kung Fu hero just as surely as all those Steven King-type nameless-horror stories hint at the flip side to the new Patriarch) has come out of the closet, his brutality no longer deplored but proclaimed.

Does this mean there are no good guys any more? Of course not. Unlike the true hero, however, the new champions are only minimally self-actuated. They are team players. Their women companions are surrogate mothers. They are *domesticated*. They are also profoundly conventional. For all the pretended individualism, lifestyle if not rhetoric reveals the extent to which (albeit covertly) they share establishment goals and establishment values. Co-opted in this way, they lack entirely the true hero's egocentricity and charismatic isolation. Look at the current crop of TV adventurers, for instance. In almost every case their strength depends on extrinsic support: familial, institutional and, especially, technological. Their authority is borrowed—sometimes from the State; often from the Machine. *This brings us right back to Riesman and 1950 again.*

What does it all mean? Actually, there are several ways to interpret this apparent regressiveness. One is to suppose that the revival of old-style Americanism is a sham born of desperation, a last-gasp attempt on the part of old-style Americans to delude themselves that the good old days of innocence and power can simply be willed into existence again. To suggest that Reagan's success is either an anomaly or an illusion is, however, to ignore both economic indicators and public opinion polls. If the 60s people—"the dispersed survivors of the heroic generation," as Clecak, rather disdainfully, characterizes them in a review of Dickstein's *Gates of Eden*—find it impossible to conceive the current president as anything but a patently synthetic and grotesquely inadequate parody of Hollywood's everydaddy, this says much more for their own relict ideals than it does for the views of the majority. For all that Lasch is still talking about "the decline of ideological fervor and political militancy; the growing disrespect for all forms of authority; the weakening of national loyalties," the evidence of fact and fiction alike reveals that America has not only recovered from its binge of self-castigation over the last five years, but in the process of emotional reconstruction managed to resanctify exactly that kind of world view and political philosophy which Vietnam and Watergate purportedly discredited forever. This may be naive, but it is *not* a sham.

Another possibility is to deny that the recent shift involves any "real" regression at all. In this view, Riesman's tradition-directed— inner-directed— other-directed progression would be held to represent the mainstream of American development, with the 60s as merely a temporary aberration traceable to foreign elements imported from abroad during and after the war. The scenario has a good deal to recommend it. Not only does it restore linearity, but it does so in such a manner as to refute the doomsayers. At the same time it saves these same doomsayers—who after all include some of the country's best known scholars—from charges of misrepresentation by de-contextualizing the period which comprises their primary object and source of data. The 60s, at least, was a world event; they were therefore quite correct to elucidate it in world terms.

The problem with this interpretation is that there is considerable evidence that what happened in the United States during the 60s was *not* a generalizable phenomenon. This is not to deny that it influenced and was influenced by many fads and movements spawned in Europe, but the selection, the framing, and the transformation of these elements produced a mood or a meld that was distinctively unEuropean. The combination of similarity and difference makes it tempting but dangerous to apply traditional culture-historical categories or schedules to the American experience. Sennett's attribution of 70s narcissism to a breakdown of distinctions between public and private, for instance, is badly flawed by his unquestioning acceptance that social data drawn from Europe are not merely relevant but equivalent to indigenous data, and his propensity (the reverse of politically oriented Europeans like, say, Perry Anderson) to *read* that foreign data in light of American assumptions. One point should suffice to illustrate. Sennett emphasizes the extent to which, concomitant with the popularization of Romanticism, the nineteenth-century bourgeoisie became torn between the impulse "to flee and to shut themselves up in a private, morally superior realm" and the fear that shunning the "messages" implicit in public experience "might be self-inflicted blindness." What he *doesn't* note, however, are the different ways in which Europeans and Americans chose to "manage" this ambivalence. The solution in Europe was a systematization of the private (Freud, Darwin, even Marx), while in America it was an attempt to subjectivize the public (transcendentalism).

Other writers run into similar problems. Berman, for instance, pins his whole analysis of recent American history on the after-effects of modernism. Even leaving aside Anderson's complaint that the influence of this movement was too "differential" to make it a useful standard ("within the European or Western world generally, there are major areas that scarcely generated any modernist momentum at all"), consensual definitions allow for such a diversity of effects that the label can be made to cover what in psychological terms must be considered as completely discrepant phenomena. Modernism, says Bell, "is the disruption of *mimesis*. It denies the primacy of an outside reality, as given. It seeks either to rearrange that reality, or to retreat to the self's interior, to private experience as the source of its concerns and aesthetic preoccupations." Fine. But as in Sennett's case, this says nothing about how a given individual or people will *respond* to the new orientation.

Protean by nature, the concept of modernism in fact serves better to establish distinctions than to delineate any sort of cross-cultural development. Take the trend toward increasingly non-representational art, for instance. Peter Fuller, adapting D.W. Winnicott's theories of childhood development, identifies the visual version of Bell's "disruption of *mimesis*" with a regression not merely to "magical" thinking but, more specifically, to a "transient phase of development which is *between* that of the 'subjectivity' of the earliest moment, in which even the mother's breast is assumed to be an extension of the self, and the more 'objective' perceptions of later childhood." This phase, Fuller continues, "is characterized by tentatively ambivalent feelings about mergence and separation, about being lost in the near, of establishing and denying boundaries about what is inside and what is outside, and concerning the whereabouts of limits and a containing skin." Far from being "*just* an escape, or a retreat into idealism and 'subjectivity,' " then, the modernist enterprise represents an attempt on the part of the artist to regain that moment of ambivalence "in order to find again, in a new way, his relationship to others and the world." If Fuller is right it makes it all the more interesting that whereas the mid-century American painter typically used the new idiom to explore space, dissolve surface, annihilate all boundaries, his nearest neighbor, the Canadian, produced canvas after canvas re-enacting the inside/outside distinction through images of enclosure, concentricity, and compartmental-ization of psychic spaces (see McGregor, 1985). "Modernism"—if we can even talk about such a thing—obviously triggered something very different in these two cases.

The same problem arises if one tries to tie the social phenomena too firmly to given phases or aspects of economic development. In attributing the twentieth-century "divarication" between art and thought to an exacerbation of class conflict through "the emergence...of the key technologies or inventions of the second industrial revolution," Anderson, for instance, never questions whether the substructures, if not the superstructures, of modern capitalist societies can be treated as if they were homogeneous. In fact, however, if we examine the history of commerce even within Europe itself it becomes apparent that *cultural* factors already present were responsible for considerable differences in the extent and even the way that different countries initially responded to the spur of industrialization. "Under the vigorous patronage of the Junker state," says Kumar, "the business ethos in...Germany was aggressive and expansionist.... By contrast French business, as Landes has shown, remained to the middle of the present century conditioned by a specific set of cultural values that enhanced the importance of the independent family firm, as against the big conglomerates and managerially directed corporations favoured by German and American business." Anderson's generalizations notwithstanding, moreover, political stance in these countries has tended by and large to resolve itself in line with such pre-industrial tendencies as "the Jacobin tradition of...radical...behaviour" and the "Prussian respect for order and authority" (Kumar), rather than following Marx's more idealistic prescription for the development of proletarian consciousness. Like modernism in art, therefore, the techno-economic revolution that Berman calls modernization is so markedly culture-specific that it can hardly be rationalized under a single term, let alone cited to "explain" world trends.

Sources aside, even the manifest data of 60s culture resist an internationalist interpretation. One case in point is the transAtlantic split within the English-language community. No matter how much cross-fertilization there was between youth movements in the United States and Britain, the fact is that both the mood and the content of counterculture were in each case substantially different. The most obvious divergence was in modes of self-imaging. While young Britons tended to draw their iconology from the urban lumpenproletariat "a very economical symbol...[suggesting both] violence and...tribal brotherhood in one neat image" (Martin), the former preferred a much more nature-oriented brand of primitivism. "[A]s he ceases to be beatnik and becomes full hippie," says Leslie Fiedler, "the ultimate Westerner ceases to be White at all and turns back into the Indian." Less obvious was the fact that while the American hippies and yippies represented a fairly homogeneous group in terms of lifestyle, if not in degree of politicization, the British youth movement was deeply fragmented along class lines. More to the point, where the former quite definitely saw themselves as united against the monolithic establishment, the latter were to a large extent self-defined in terms of sub-subcultural divisions. Why? Because in Britain class-consciousness is strong enough not merely to establish standards for conformity but to bias preferences in forms of rebellion. "Working-class youth culture likes to take its liminal excesses in the form of heavy spending, the pursuit of physical excitement, especially through taking risks, and above all in the violation of rigid boundaries, boundaries which nevertheless code identity for individual and group together," says Clare Martin. "Middle-class youth culture, by contrast, explores the possibility of abandoning boundaries and categories in favour of flux and fluidity, in order to achieve constantly shifting identity and expanded inner consciousness."

This last is a key point, not merely in connection with the 60s but with respect to the whole American experience. American sociologists and cultural historians have been criticized for years for ignoring class in their elucidations of national character. Anderson's response to Berman's *All That is Solid Melts into Air* is a typical one. "By and large, it can be said that classes as such scarcely figure in Berman's account at all." Throughout the book, "there is very little between *economy* on the one hand and *psychology* on the other, save for the *culture* of modernism that links the two." While one might stipulate the *letter* of Anderson's complaint, cross-cultural examination of the 60s phenomenon suggests that perhaps such obliviousness to class conflict relates less to the shortcomings of the critic than to the peculiarities of his object. Looking at cultural artifacts well beyond the 60s, quite counter to Anderson's implication that Berman has *missed* something, one would have to say that in the American consciousness there is indeed nothing worth talking about between economy and psychology. Traditionally there has been a tendency to blame this abnormality on the callowness of the country. *And* to decry it. As far back as the nineteenth century, in fact, writers have lamented ostentatiously that America offered neither the historical associations nor the social diversity necessary to provide good raw material for literature. As Richard Poirier points out, however, protestations notwithstanding, the *practice* of these same literati reveals that an asocial bias was in fact a precondition of their world view. "Cooper, Hawthorne, James, and commentators who follow them, all suggest that they would be happier if the social 'texture' of American life were 'thicker' even while they make every sort of literary effort to escape even the supposedly thin 'texture' which American society does provide." The American, it would seem, simply does not conceptualize the world in social terms. More to the point, because of this his world does not *compose itself* in social terms.

The peculiarity has not been generally recognized, even by insiders. Why? Because, as Abner Cohen points out, American "scholars are themselves caught up in the same body of symbols which they try to decode. Most symbols," he continues, "are largely rooted in the unconscious mind and are thus difficult to identify and analyze by people who live under them. As the proverb says: It is hardly a fish that can discover the existence of water." Aware of it or not, on the other hand, it is a rare fish that does not act instinctively in accordance with the constraints of his environment. And so it is with the American. Rooted firmly in his unrecognized ethnicity, he "expresses" much more than he says. Compare Berman's "city" with British critic Raymond Williams's, for example. Where the latter is quite clearly an historical conception tied to specific, broadly contexted, diagnostic economic structures and power relationships ("there is...an ideological separation between the processes of rural exploitation, which have been, in effect, dissolved into a landscape, and the register of that exploitation, in the law courts, the money markets, the political power and the conspicuous expenditure of the city") the former resolves itself into a cosmic psychodrama pitting Robert Moses's steel-and-concrete megalith against Jane Jacobs's pastoral vision of community in the streets. "Ginsberg is urging us to experience human life not as a hollow wasteland but as an epic and tragic battle of giants," he says. "This vision endows the modern environment and its makers with a demonic energy and a world-historic stature that probably exceed even what the Robert Moseses of this world would claim for themselves. At the same time, the vision is meant to arouse us, the readers, to make ourselves equally great, to enlarge our desire and moral imagination to the point where we will dare to take on the giants." In telling the story of the destruction of the Bronx, Berman clearly reveals that Ginsberg's perspective is one that he shares. The city that emerges from this telling is a figment not of history but of myth. As such it is a backdrop rather than a collectivity.

This distinction is critical. The identification of setting as *field* rather than *constituent* of action explains why there are so many curiously isolated figures in American literature: heroes "startlingly different from most of the great heroes of myth or of Marchen" having, as Daniel Hoffman summarizes it, "no parents...no past, no patrimony, no siblings, and no life cycle, because he never marries or has children...[and] seldom dies." It explains why so many of America's best culture critics seem to be writing in a cultural vacuum ("[W]hat is missing from Lasch to an astonishing degree is any direct observation of anything" [Flack]; "Culture appears to have an epidermal, even a cosmetic status in [Bell's] argument" [Abrahams]; "Sennett's book participates in the current revulsion against politics" [Lasch]; "Dickstein's attitude blinds him to the larger currents in American society and culture, not to mention their nuances" [Clecak]). It explains, finally, why Berman, in his rebuttal of Anderson, rather than attempting to counter the charge of political naiveté in so many words, simply offers a number of anecdotes about individuals who epitomize for him the experience not of the city per se but of "the people in the crowd."

Aside from its intrinsic significance, the asociability of the Americans underlines other discrepancies between their and others' experience of the 60s. One element that sets them apart not just from the British but even more clearly from the continental Europeans is a stubborn optimism, an irrational faith in the power of the individual will, that fights tacitly against the most determined doomsaying. It wasn't only the hippy who believed in "doing one's own thing." Look at the image that emerged from American sociology during the 60s of the self-made social actor engaged in constructing his own reality (Meltzer *et al.*). Look at the propensity of artists like Andy Warhol to present not their work but their personalities as their "true[st] and [most] complete creations" (Lucie-Smith). Look at 60s American fiction. Despite its obtrusively ironic tone, its preoccupation with death and disaster, the fact is that this is an oeuvre written from the point of view not of the victim but of the survivor. For all the horrors they take for granted, in other words, most fictional worlds of the 60s are still ones in which—as Jacques Lemieux says of Philip Dick's 1969 science fiction novel, *Ubik*—"the exceptional force of character of the protagonist and his allies permits them to ward off chaos." More to the point, they are also still perceptibly under the control of their creators. Judging from the systemic and structural preoccupations of European theory, one of the most notable intellectual developments since the war has been the general discrediting of the modernist myth of a free, creating subject. Judging from *American* practice, however, with the advent of apocalypse the creating subject becomes more important than ever. Far from subordinating temperament to text, the American in fact tends to view "the poetic act" as first and foremost a "means of self-identification and self-preservation" (Pearce, 1967).

The most obvious demonstration of this oddly anachronistic bias is provided by those writers, like Norman Mailer, who make no distinction between public and poetic acts, for whom creating is performing and "performance is an exercise of power" (Poirier, 1971). Even in the absence of explicit self-display, though, the works themselves almost invariably "give off" unmistakable signs of egocentricity. Gass's hermeticism, Coover's gamesplaying, Capote's blurring of fact and fiction, Sukenik's ostentatious "manhandling of [his] plots" (Glicksberg), the refusal of fable-makers like Pynchon, Barthelme, and Burroughs to pay lip service to either empirical verisimilitude or the reader's need to comprehend—such strategies as these bespeak not so much a loss of faith in the signifying function of art as an incredible confidence in the autonomous activity of the artist. "Underlying it all," says Roger Sale, "is a huge assertion of personal power, which leads to aggressive showmanship...in other words, style used as a badge of personal authority, and personal authority having the ability to invent and master whole worlds." Despite its surficial debt to Europe, then, the covert content of 60s American writing clearly reveals that the 60s American writer is a long way from swallowing whole the anti-individualistic tenets of postmodern aesthetics. Certainly he is a long way from believing that "literature...writes itself" (Kristeva)—*or* that his "unique personal identity" is no more than "a philosophical and cultural mystification" (Jameson).

The 60s, American-style, was not, then, a world event. So much for thesis number two. Which leaves us with the question of how we explain the apparent disruption in the social fabric. Possibility number three would be that there really wasn't a disruption at all. Jesse Battan, for one, suggests that the narcissism that has become almost consensually accepted as the keynote of the period was in fact merely an updated version of an old, ingrained aspect of the American character. "While Lasch maintains that the behavior traits he associates with modern forms of pathological narcissism are far different from those common to the rugged individualist described by Alexis de Tocqueville, R.W.B. Lewis and Quentin Anderson, others argue that they are symptomatic of tensions that have traditionally given shape to the American character. In spite of a shift from a religious to an economic and finally to a psychological orientation, a single underlying impulse—the emphasis on self-scrutiny, self-expression and personal growth—has remained unchanged from the 17th century to the present." Is Battan right? At least in part, I would say. If it is futile to deny that there was any real change of attitudes during the 60s, it *is* true that this period, just like the neo-Rightist 80s, evokes a number of distinct historical echoes. The kind of primitivism we find associated with 60s counter-culture, for instance, is very similar to the primitivism we find in the poetry and romances of post-Revolutionary writers like Washington Irving, William Gilmore Simms, and, especially, James Fenimore Cooper. This *could* mean that what gave the 60s its peculiarly new/old flavor was simply a recurrence of some of the key psycho-social factors operative during the early nineteenth century. It's hard to see, though, how one would set about proving such a postulate, even if it were true. It's even harder to see how one could make any practical use of it. Given the American penchant for recycling its own past as popular culture, on the level at least of the individual artifact there would seem to be no way to distinguish between genuine revivals and what Allison Graham calls commercialized nostalgia. More important, there would also seem to be no way to establish that similar features, similar philosophical and aesthetic biases, actually "mean" the same thing when they turn up in temporally disparate contexts.

Neither Lasch's view nor Battan's, then, could be held to "explain" current history. Indeed, the relations between past and present being above all indeterminate, the question must be raised whether it is even *possible* to arbitrate the kinds of issues we have addressed in this chapter. And that presents a problem. If neither the imported theory nor the home-grown myths of identity provide reliable guidance, we have no way of discriminating between the essential and the ephemeral in the cultural mélange. The structuralist would claim, of course, that it is the substratum *below* the individual artifact that carries the important messages. In general, moreover, I'd be inclined to agree. "By analyzing the indices of attitude embedded in a community's life and language," I say in a recent paper, "we can demonstrate not only that all social phenomena, manifest or propaedeutic, are patterned, but that this patterning...tends to be homologous or at least congruent across any single self-contained—that is, self-defined—system" (McGregor, 1986). Just how, in practice, does one set about this kind of explication, though? How do we get past the apparent fragmentation of the phenomenal surface to grasp "the logic of the totality" that explains and connects such disparate social data as "the distant war, the deodorant advertisement, [and] the soap opera" (Clark)? It's all a question of focus. Where contents may seem to be irreducibly variable, a survey of recurrent formal and formulaic elements within the communal oeuvre will help us to reconstruct the way the American has historically conceptualized his world-at-large. This in turn will enable us to reconstruct the consciousness that produces those conceptions. "Paradoxically," says Edward Hall, "studying the models that men create...tells you more about the men than about the [reality modelled]."

The models that men create. That's what this book is really about. Leaving aside for now the theoretical ramifications of my findings (which only emerged after the fact in any case), what I offer in the following chapters is a working through—*not* simply a demonstration—of a strategy for tackling what we might call the syntactic analysis of culture. Assuming that the landscape will play a key role in any colonial imagination, I began my quest with an examination of the conventions in terms of which the earliest settlers were accustomed to image/structure their relations with nature. By the time this book began to take shape, my focus had zeroed in on the iconic figure whose attributes seemed most saliently to express/mediate/displace the problematic aspects of those relations. What I ended up with is at once a literary history of the Noble Savage in the New World and a metamorphology of the American mind.

2. The Noble Savage in Britain

According to Hoxey Fairchild, "the Noble Savage plays no part in English literature until the restoration of the Stuarts, when he is imported from France as a subtype of the exotic genius of the heroic species." The familiar cognomen was not even coined until 1672, the year in which Dryden's barbaric Almanzor first proclaims himself, in *Conquest of Granada*, to be

> ...as free as Nature first made man,
> Ere the base laws of servitude began,
> When wild in woods the noble savage ran.

The *idea* of noble savagery goes back much further than the seventeenth century, however. Primitivism—for this is the term used to designate collectively the philosophy, attitudes, and assumptions from which the species emerges—has had a long and venerable history in western culture.

A product of "the discontent of the civilized with civilization," as Lovejoy and Boas describe it, primitivism is the expressed belief "that a life far simpler and less sophisticated in some or all respects is a more desirable life." The reference point for this "more" and "less" may, however, be defined in several alternative ways. If it is located in the past—the classical Golden Age or the Christian Garden of Eden—the phenomenon may be called chronological primitivism; if the remoteness is geographical rather than historical—whether in *fact*, like the Americas, or in *myth*, like the legendary Atlantis—it is cultural primitivism. The first of these categories, consonant with either the theory of decadence or the cyclical view of history favored by the ancients, was typical of classical thought, while modern primitivism, under the influence of a Christian view of history as finite, linear, and ultimately progressive, was largely (though hardly exclusively) of the second variety. The one thing both variants have in common is the assumption that primitive cultures provide a viable or at least *instructive* alternative to civilized existence. The primitive man is thought on the one hand to be freer, both physically and emotionally—less inhibited, less oppressed by the necessities of labor, less trammelled with constricting conventions; on the other hand, his simple, austere lifestyle, devoid of luxury and sophistication, is supposed to inculcate both character and morality. The two, somewhat ill-assorted referents latent in this image made the savage an appropriate vehicle for both wish-fulfilling fantasies and moral didacticism.

12

The peasant and shepherd of the pastoral convention as used by Virgil and Spenser right through to Goldsmith and beyond are drawn from a somewhat similar tradition, and to some degree express the same kind of discontent with civilized life. In most of those cases where it is rural rather than "wild" nature that provides the moral standard, though, the social criticism tends to be relative rather than absolute, and the comparison more contrived than spontaneous. The implied relationship between observer and exemplar is slightly different as well. As a result, despite the fact that the two species share many of the same negative virtues—in particular, both are imputed with an enviable immunity to discontent, anxiety about the future, or selfish ambition—when a more exotic image of the savage began to appear in English popular writing its affective content as well as its conventional function were different enough that it can plausibly be considered a new departure—whatever its sources and relations—rather than simply an old convention reworked. Many critics simply subsume all these figures under the pastoral denomination, viewing them as mere stock alternatives for symbolically mediating what Leo Marx terms a "reconciliation between the animal and rational, natural and civilized." A closer look at later developments in the noble savage idea, however, must soon disabuse us of the notion that here is any fit emblem of Marx's moderate "middle landscape." The savage as he is portrayed by the middle of the eighteenth century rather embodies a meeting point for all sorts of extremes. Far from evoking the mild and ordered face of nature as does the well-mannered peasant, this later figure in fact primarily appeals to and expresses the "curious strain of extravagance running through the cult of nature" upon which Marx comments perplexedly: "a seemingly neurotic tendency that...rational theories cannot explain."

From whence did it arise, this streak of irrationality? Certainly there would seem to be little in early versions to explain such a development. With few exceptions, until the advent of full-scale Romanticism the more restrained pastoral perspective tends to dominate not merely the themes but the emotional tone of "primitivistic" literature. In Hans Sach's sixteenth-century poem *Lament of the Wild Men about the Unfaithful World*, for instance, the author's token invocation of Edenic innocence serves as little more than a springboard for his attack on the corruption of court and city. Sach's usage was typical. Notwithstanding, even during this early period the convention was not entirely without its subversive undertones. Long before the eighteenth century, reading between—or behind—the lines, we can find clear if vestigial signs of the savage's essential ambiguity, a covert foreshadowing of the more complex roles which, especially in America, he was later to play. Shakespeare's *The Tempest* is for good reason a key text in the history of literary primitivism. Ariel and Caliban, while only indirectly related to the full-blown noble savage, illustrate vividly the problematic doubleness concealed under the conventional conception of savagery. But this is not really surprising. One thing that has been obscured by the understandable tendency of scholars to focus almost exclusively on formal, literary treatments of cultural stereotypes is the fact that the Renaissance savage had his roots not only, and indeed not primarily, in the positive classical tradition, but rather, in the bestial and degenerate wild man of Hebraic and later Christian tradition. By virtue of his background alone, then, the noble savage was a much more complex character than conventional literary usage would suggest.

The odd ancestry makes it even more intriguing that the savage should have gained so much ascendency over the English imagination. Indeed, invoking the wild man raises more questions than it answers. Why, in the light of such strong negative connotations, should the image of a sanitized savage have crystallized in communal consciousness at that particular point in history? Even more important, *how*? What forces were responsible for reconciling the conflicting associations carried by the original folk version and negotiating what was, in fact, a rather considerable shift in reference. It's easy enough to see the attraction of primitivism in such a period. The cultural crisis precipitated by the breakdown of the medieval social order, far from dissipating in the light of a new day, was in a sense exacerbated when God's retribution for human presumption did *not* materialize. When one is plagued by existential uncertainties, good fortune only intensifies feelings of vulnerability. It is thus quite understandable, as Lois Whitney points out, that the unprecedented economic expansion and national prosperity characteristic of fifteenth and sixteenth-century Britain, by allowing, nay *encouraging*, luxury—by recklessly challenging the "prudential maxims which had been held sacred for countless generations before"—should have catalyzed a reactionary movement which would exploit with unprecedented vigor every weapon offered by historically sanctioned sources in its denunciation of and battle against moral degeneration. At a time when pagan and Christian traditions were being mixed as never before, this reaction inevitably found one of its most appropriate expressions in the noble savage, a figure whose natural innocence could find precedent in both the Bible and Ovid.

Wait, though. We have already intimated that the legendary forebears of the noble savage were *not* entirely positive, especially with respect to Judeo-Christian tradition. Which brings us back to our original question. Even with all the will in the world, how could the savage suddenly divest himself of his ambiguity to emerge as we see him in seventeenth-century letters—a full-blown, morally unequivocal, exemplary type? The answer is: he didn't! To put it plainly, for all the "official" emphasis on the decorous, *reasonable* motifs of pastoral convention, there is ample evidence that it was because of, not despite, his covert ambiguity that the mythic primitive attained his widespread and long-lived popularity in England. And on this level the folk associations were much more important than the literary ones. As Hayden White (1972) points out, the obnoxious medieval wild man exhibited among his generic characteristics a number of features that proved amenable to re-interpretation when the time was right.

[I]f, during the Middle Ages, the Wild Man was an object of disgust and loathing, of fear and religious anxiety, the quintessence of possible human degradation, he was not conceived in general to be an example of *spiritual* corruption... Unlike the rebel angels, the Wild Man did not *know* that he lived in a state of sin, or even *that* he sinned, or even what a "sin" might be. This meant that he possessed, along with his degradation, a kind of innocence... Sin he might, but he sinned through ignorance rather than design. This gave to his expressions of lust, violence, perversion and deceit a kind of freedom that might be envied by normal men, men caught in the web of repression and sublimation that made up the basis of ordinary life. It is not strange, then, that in the fourteenth and fifteenth centuries, when the social bonds of medieval culture began to disintegrate, the Wild Man became gradually transformed from an object of loathing and fear (and only secret envy) into an object of open envy and even admiration. It is not surprising that, in an age of general cultural revolution, the popular antitype of the officially defined "normal" humanity, the Wild Man, should be transformed into the ideal or model of a free humanity.

If it was primarily the conservative bent of primitivism that made it such a useful stock-in-trade for didactically inclined Renaissance and post-Renaissance poets and essayists, the thing that assured its tenacious hold on the popular fancy was a moral ambivalence—an inherent duplicity of reference—that enabled it to satisfy simultaneously both reactionary *and* radical impulses.

Ambiguous parentage, far from undermining the integrity of the image, thus actually must be seen as providing one of the most important psychological bases for the appeal of the noble savage. Carrying such a weight of latent psychological signification, it was perhaps inevitable that this figure should emerge as an important cultural type just when he did. The one final factor that really ensured this emergence, however, was in a sense a pure accident of history. If social upheaval stimulated a general emotional predisposition to primitivism, and if classical sources (obscuring the problematic genetic associations) offered respectable models— especially in the myths of the Golden Age—for literary expression of this predisposition, it was the public excitement about early transAtlantic exploration that provided the immediate impetus which was ultimately to make the noble savage a household word. Why? Even aside from the natural attractions of the novel and the exotic—not to mention the gold, silks, ivory, and spices fondly thought to be forthcoming from the now-immanent "Indies"—the conventions that shaped and colored the language of the voyagers' reports were such as to endow the newly discovered lands with an emotional significance far beyond their foreseeable practical value. This emotional significance in turn enriched those conventions in which it was clothed. "The learned and the popular, the Christian and the pagan, traditions were reconciled by the discovery of America," says Fairchild. "Did not the newly discovered island or continent lie both eastward and westward? And did not the bounty and beauty of that land equal all that was ever said or sung of the blessed Isles? 'I am convinced,' wrote Columbus, 'that there is the terrestrial Paradise.' " The combination was irresistible for a people already attracted by the assumptions of primitivism. One result—Charles Sanford tells us—was that "Renaissance letters became filled, as never before, with allusions to an earthly paradise and a golden age." Another—more important for our present subject—was to provide the savage with a whole new source of numen. "The identification of the Caribbean islands with...Paradise naturally lent prestige to their inhabitants," notes Fairchild. This was all that was needed to complete the rehabilitation of the wild man.

Once enthroned, the noble savage convention demonstrated such a remarkable versatility that it was soon called upon to serve a wide range of different emotional needs and political purposes. As noted above, besides offering the conservatives an appealing vehicle for expressing their fear of decadence, it also provided the pragmatically iconoclastic rising middle class with a convenient means by which to rationalize religious toleration, civil liberty, and economic freedom. As a didactic tool, it could be used to support either the simple, sober morality of ancient Greece and Rome *or* the enthusiastic millennial expectations stimulated by discovery of the Americas. Above all, even before the end of the seventeenth century, the noble savage had come to suggest a personal stance which would have increasingly radical implications in years to come. "The Noble Savage had by this time assumed a bewildering range of disguises," notes Geoffrey Symcox; "he might appear as a subtle Persian, a sardonic Turk living at Paris and reporting on the curious customs of the natives, an agelessly wise Chinese, or a simple and upright Huron. But his message was always the same: man could live justly and well even without the benefit of European culture and religion, if only he practiced what was natural for him."

An improbable mixture? Indeed. The ability of the type—despite the increasing irreconcilability of all these different public images and expectations—to be seen as all things to all people should not surprise us, however. The radical contradictions implicit in the savage's mixed ancestry and cultural associations (remember Ariel and Caliban!) were equally evident in the intellectual background that came to be associated with the idea of primitivism. Again one might point to an essential rupture within the communal vision. Despite what we have said about the excitements of economic expansion and geographical discovery, the Renaissance Englishman was no Romantic. Even aside from the slight, lingering paranoia cited above, neither sixteenth-century Puritanism nor seventeenth-century rationalism—as Fairchild points out—gave much encouragement to "belief in the essential goodness of untutored humanity." To Hobbes, for instance, the stage in savage existence "when the fruits of the earth were common to all" was (in Fairchild's words) just "one long squabble"; "the *state* of nature...[was] in itself lawless, and therefore evil." Hobbes's views were not untypical. At the same time, with the middle classes becoming wealthier and more socially significant—with not merely England but the whole of Europe enjoying an unprecedented prosperity—an optimistic faith in progress was coming to seem more and more "reasonable." There was in consequence a growing resistance to the kind of pessimism implicit in Hobbes's estimate of human nature. The public wanted a new and different model by which to measure themselves. They wanted, in fact, the kind of promise seemingly offered by primitivism. It was predictable, therefore, that during the next two centuries, suppressing if not wholly obliterating their native pragmatism, they seized with alacrity upon the more hopeful and more appealing perspective that could be read into the work of such British and continental philosophers as Montaigne, Locke, and Hume. It was also predictable that the resulting wishful synthesis would eventually founder on its own internal inconsistencies.

Montaigne, the forerunner of this series of thinkers, devoted his autobiographical *Essays* (1580) to an examination and testing of popular prejudices and assumptions against the evidence of personal experience. His modest, good-natured, and mildly sceptical stance asserted common sense over received authority and practical over theoretical knowledge. "How poor is the proficiency that is merely bookish!" he exclaims in his essay "On the Education of Children." It is obvious how such a view could prove conducive to a concept like the noble savage. Montaigne's contribution was more than merely implicit, however. "On Cannibalism," another piece from the same quietly disruptive little collection, in fact proved to be a seminal event in the development of European and British primitivism, influencing both contemporary popular views (Shakespeare, for instance, drew directly on Montaigne for the theme of *The Tempest*) and the philosophic primitivism that was to blossom a century later.

In spite of all this, it would be misleading to imply that Montaigne's attitude toward savage nature was totally positive. He is quite explicit about the hardship of the cannibals' lives and the brutality of some of their customs. Taken as a whole, in fact, the thrust of his argument is clearly relativistic rather than absolute; the essay in question is far closer in tone to the gentle satire of the classical pastoral than to what we would consider primitivism today. "For him the natural is not necessarily the good," says White: "it is certainly preferable to the artificial, especially inasmuch as artificially induced barbarity is much more reprehensible in his eyes than its natural counterpart among savages," *but*—and here is the important point—the solution he would advocate is an attempt to regenerate society along more wholesome lines rather than a desertion of it for a wholly primitive style of life:

> Montaigne wants his readers to identify the artificiality in themselves, to recognize the extent to which their superficial "civilization" masks a deeper barbarism, thereby preparing them for the release, not of their souls to heaven, but of their bodies and minds to nature. By his use of the concept of wildness as a fiction, Montaigne "brackets" the myth of civilization that anchors it to a delibitating parochialism. His purpose is not to turn all men into savages or to destroy "civilization," but to give them critical distance on their artificiality.

Read carefully, then, Montaigne, notwithstanding his reputation as a proto-primitivist, is far from condoning an irresponsible escapist myth.

On what, then, is the reputation based? Actually, considering the *tone* of the essays it is not surprising that Montaigne's ideas had the considerable influence on the history of primitivism that they obviously did. "On Cannibals," for instance, reveals a definite bias toward nature that may easily be overemphasized, and many individual passages, taken out of context, seem to offer an enthusiastic celebration of primitivism unallayed by any reservations at all. "It is not reasonable that art should win the honours from our great and mighty mother nature," he declaims. "With all our efforts we cannot imitate the nest of the very smallest bird, its structure, its beauty, or the suitability of its form, nor even the web of the lowly spider." A rather extreme sentiment for a self-avowed advocate of Leo Marx's "middle landscape"! And what is more suggestive—going far to counter the carefully interpolated demurrers— even those sections of the piece dealing specifically with man *in* nature tend all too frequently to slip into conventional encomium. Whatever they lack, he says, those "barbarous" nations that retain most of their original simplicity, living close to and governed solely by that incomparable nature, surpass "not only the pictures with which poets have illustrated the golden age, and all their attempts to draw mankind in the state of happiness, but the ideas and the very aspirations of philosophers as well." Here, undeniably, whatever Montaigne's own intent, is the prototypical noble savage who would be "taken up" with such enthusiasm by succeeding generations.

Montaigne's contribution to a primitivistic mode of thought was primarily a modern reworking of classical environmentalism: the savage is "good" (whatever this is taken to mean) because his environment makes him or at least allows him to be so. The noble savage was given a whole *new* significance, however, by the associationist psychology of Locke. In *An Essay Concerning Human Understanding* (1690) this philosopher laid the groundwork for a revolutionary epistemology which, according to Whitney, came to comprise such a "radical criticism of induction and scientific generalization" that, save for the fact that it was largely ignored by the scientific community, "would have effectually undermined the whole scientific method." Ignored as he may have been by the scientists, Locke's theories had an enormous long term effect on literature and, among other things, on the increasing popularity of the noble savage convention. By comparing the mind to a *tabula rasa*, and positing the efficacy of natural reason, he gave support to the view that the savage, his intellect unhampered by the stifling and artificial attitudes and habits acquired necessarily in a civilized environment, was more capable of true insight than the educated man. Nor was the operation of natural reason relevant only to mental development. By discarding "native ideas and original characters"— by making sense impressions the *only* source of human knowledge—Locke also discredited the theory of original corruption and revolutionized morality.

Again, these ideas are not totally unambiguous. For one thing, the mechanistic implications of a wholly reflective mind could, and eventually did, lead to a sterile utilitarianism. For the most part, though, Locke's audience picked only what it wanted from the complexities of his thought. "The School of Shaftesbury," for example, Fairchild tells us, "escaped from the meanness of utilitarian ethics by practically identifying God with the ingenious mechanism of the universe. The installation of God in the world spread a divine benediction throughout nature, and...encouraged belief in the doctrine that man is at heart a well-meaning and even rather sensible creature." Even more confusing than the utilitarian undertones, however, was, as Whitney points out, the applicability of Locke's ideas to both primitivism *and* a theory of progress, depending on one's choice among several different interpretive possibilities. If one stressed the negative aspect of the *tabula rasa*—the moral superiority of the naturally *blank* mind, devoid of all artificially acquired and thus unnatural attributes, unspoiled by the corrupting influence of civilization— then the noble savage obviously offered a useful norm. If, on the other hand, one emphasized the potential for improvement through education, the *perfectability* of the undeveloped personality, then the savage was merely raw material. For a while at least the desire for a unified world view easily outweighed such logical quibbles. The predisposition to primitivism clearly favored the former alternative, and for a while at least "learned opinion" seemed to favor that predisposition.

This was the pattern that would characterize the history of philosophical primitivism. Once well launched, the idea of noble savagery—or, rather, the cluster of general sentiments from which this idea emerged—exerted such an allure that it was able to warp to its own ends almost every major development in contemporaneous thought. Another case in point: David Hume's scepticism about "the ability of the mind [meaning the intellect] to arrive at truth, either moral or metaphysical" (Whitney). It might seem that an attitude like this was not really consistent with a positive view of human nature. In that particular intellectual climate, however, Hume's ideas—as Fairchild observes—were taken as pointing directly to the conclusion "that morality, like everything else, must be derived from feeling...no product of utilitarian syllogisms, but an instinctive element in the heart of man." Since any glorification of the emotions and the instincts was even more encouraging to primitivism than the idea of natural wisdom, Hume's influence thus helped to establish the noble savage more firmly than ever. On the whole, Fairchild notes, the logical inconsistencies lurking behind all the optimistic affirmations of natural goodness characteristic of the period being willfully ignored by the majority, or at least skillfully compartmentalized, "the rationalism which dominated England from the middle of the seventeenth to the middle of the eighteenth century was less inimical to the Noble Savage idea than might be supposed." Indeed, however incompatible it might logically seem in the context of other implications of rationalist philosophy, "benevolence" became a key word in eighteenth-century interpretations of human nature.

With all this talk about the influence of popular opinion on scholarly thought, we have not yet mentioned the one philosopher whose name has become almost synonymous with the idea of noble savagery. We are speaking, of course, of Jean-Jacques Rousseau, the eighteenth-century Frenchman whose epoch-making *Discours sur l'origine et les fondemens de l'inégalité parmi les hommes* (1754)—according to Arthur Moore, the "classic exposition of the naturalistic myth"—was to reshape traditional political, social, and religious thought in both Europe and America as no other single document. Despite his undoubted influence, however, it is important to distinguish Rousseau's own position on primitivism from popular assessments. As in Montaigne's case, the text itself contains elements which are obviously inhospitable to an unadulterated theory of noble savagery. While he does indeed, in Moore's words, lavish "uncommon praise on some aspects of savage life," Rousseau's overall estimate of that level of existence is far from enthusiastic. "[N]either the Savage nor the society in which he lived was presented as wholly admirable and flawless," Symcox notes.

Rousseau was ready to admit that even the state of nature which he regarded as least objectionable had serious faults, and in any case was doomed by the irreversible progress of man's intelligence; the clock could not be turned back. [He] was only suggesting that this...stage of social development might have certain lessons which could render civilized life more tolerable. Notably this meant the tempering of reason and its associated quality of *amour-propre* by the more generous emotions... Rousseau was presenting the model of an earlier and a happier time in an effort to humanize the society in which he lived.

Like Montaigne, then, Rousseau's aim was basically relativistic. Judging by the *letter*—if not always the spirit—of the *Discours,* at most he seems to favor a condition which, Fairchild points out, is clearly "not the raw state of nature, [nor] fully evolved society either...[but] a hypothetical intermediate stage combining the physical well-being and natural piety of the savage with the plainer virtues and acquired sociability of civilized man."

Again, predictably, such qualifications were largely ignored by the public. In spite of his real moderation, many of Rousseau's contemporaries preferred to emphasize primarily those aspects of his argument which, as Fairchild describes it, could be made to appear "to confer respectability on libertarianism, to legalize the cult of wildness, and even to sanction blind atavistic impulses." If it is important to note the extent of the retrospective distortion and oversimplification to which this philosopher has been subjected, it is, however, equally important, at least for present purposes, to realize that what he was perceived as saying has just as much relevance to the history of primitivism as what he really did say. In terms of influence exerted, in fact, such popular generalizations probably contributed more to the development of the noble savage convention than the comparatively complex ideas that may be more authentically attributed to the man himself. The ambivalence which is such a significant element in the *Discours* added its own fillip to the subversive undertones which continued covertly to energize this convention, but for eighteenth-century England it was for the most part simply as the champion of "natural goodness" that Rousseau became best known. As such he represents if not the instigator at least the exemplification of a trend: a landmark of no mean significance. By the third quarter of the eighteenth century philosophical primitivism is in its heyday, optimism is to the operative word, and the noble savage has been transformed into what may be seen, for all intents and purposes, as an almost entirely new type. Gone is that stern and stoical embodiment of classical austerity so admired by the Renaissance poet.

In his place is Rousseau's creature of instinct—a gay and colorful child of nature, a spontaneous democrat, a *romantic* savage whose natural "benevolence" could be, and often was, cited by the individual as a convenient authority for him "to realize himself in an excess of emotion" (Moore).

The bandwagon effect of all this should not blind us to the fact that in some ways the development was a most illogical one. As Moore points out, that "rational primitivism should have ultimately furnished an excuse for the satisfaction of rather elemental longings can only be regarded as ironical" when—as we have seen—"philosophers originally conceived the state of nature as relatively free of irresponsible conduct." Such "irony," however, merely reinforces what we have already observed throughout this chapter. Fashions in popular thought have far less to do with logic than with emotional needs. More specifically, fashions in popular thought would seem to reflect less what a community knows than what it wants to believe. This is hardly surprising. There is a sense in which the mythopoeic impulse is entirely predicated upon the individual's inability to live without a coherent world view. Mythopoesis may, in fact, be defined as the means by which old concepts are progressively retailored to accommodate new circumstances. Faced with change, the public simply sorts through its ready-to-hand vocabulary of symbolic forms for ideas and images amenable to appropriate restructuring (Lévi-Strauss, 1966). The evolution of conventional motifs, far from gratuitous, thus provides a mechanism for mediating between cultural development and cultural continuity.

This is where our exemplar comes in. If the traditional literary savage was a long way from his exotic eighteenth-century progeny, he did, as we have seen, contain the seeds that would allow for the particular metamorphosis invited by the mood of the times. Constricted by the narrowness of neo-classical authoritarianism, the eighteenth century (echoing in mood the revolt against feudalism which stimulated the initial impulse toward noble savagery, several centuries earlier) saw a concerted attempt especially by the aristocratic classes in England to emancipate themselves—as Lilian Furst (1969) puts it—"away from the neat, finite, regular schemes of the old system towards a growing appreciation of the irregular beauties of the irrational imagination." This entailed a reorientation toward the "natural and spontaneous not only in the inner realm of the emotions but also in the outer world." The savage provided a convenient focus on both levels. Not only was he conventionally linked with nature but, as we have seen, despite his traditional exemplary function as a pastoral mediator he also exhibited certain subversive associations with a new idea of personal freedom. It was quite predictable, then, that when the time was ripe these particular associations would be picked up and embellished to the detriment of all other features. It was quite predictable, indeed—considering these covert public pressures—that Rousseau's temperate exposition of savagery would be misinterpreted along exactly the lines we have noted. The fact is, despite his carefully iterated personal reservations about primitivism, Rousseau himself—as much as any, a product of inherited cultural predispositions—inadvertently invited such a reading. As Symcox points out,

Rousseau's savage was *not* "just the traditional Savage, the paragon of ideal virtues operating on a lofty plane of reason. Rousseau's Savage in fact harks back to the older, more passionate figure of the Wild Man. Introspection and the use of imagination rather than pure reason led Rousseau to rejuvenate the bloodless figure of the Noble Savage by reendowing him with the passions he had lost." Whatever its overt conclusions, the *Discours* thus clearly provided— or perhaps *activated* would be a better word—the final element needed to complete the charisma of the noble savage.

Once cast in this mold, the figure seemed capable of accommodating the widest imaginable range of associations. When nationalism combined with a taste for the archaic, he turned up as Gray's Bard. When a vogue for the sublime elevated the moral authority of strong, primitive emotion, he became the Celtic warrior of Ossian's pseudo-Welsh epics. Under the banner of sensibility he transformed himself—to an avatar of refinement? But surely we have now gone too far. From any rational perspective it would seem impossible for the late eighteenth-century cult of sensibility to be anything but hostile to primitivism. There is a degree of overlap, in that both of these ideas are conducive to, and even based upon, a celebration of the value of "natural" emotion as an ultimate arbiter of value. The excessive delicacy and the cultivation of taste which were inevitable corollaries to this strange fashion in feeling would seem, however, *necessarily* to rule out any savage worthy of the name. This is to give insufficient credit to the power of an unintellectual and omnivorous public. Instead of casting him off because he is too crude, says Whitney, the popular writer of the eighteenth-century, "attempting to cater to two vogues at once...must needs give the [savage] the same fashionable ultra-refinement of spirit that the most aristocratic heroine suffered under."

This tendency to lump together as many as possible of the ideas currently in vogue, regardless of compatibility, was one of the most distinctive characteristics of eighteenth-century popular culture. If our observations throughout this chapter are accurate, it *had* to be. It was *only* in a period with a strong motivation to suspend critical judgment that such a motley figure as the mature version of the noble savage could exist at all. Transformed and retransformed by three centuries worth of wishful fantasies, he was—quite simply—a logical impossibility. Even aside from the sheer silliness of trying to combine savagery with sensibility, as Whitney points out, the primitivistic ideology implied by the convention was inexorably oriented to the past—"the first stages of society before man had been corrupted by civilization"—while the idea of progress derived from the very same sources "represented a point of view that looked forward to possible perfection in the future." The appetite for excitement in the closing decades of the eighteenth century seemed, however, to be so great that it would swallow even the most ludicrous of mixtures. And this is what counted. Indeed, as long as the emotional predispositions of the public—the same predispositions that welcomed equally the moral grandeur of the sublime and the exotic titilations of the gothic novel, the rude simplicity of archaic culture and the decadent preciosity of orientalism—

were strong enough to sweep aside all the logical inconsistencies inherent in the popular synthesis of widely diverse contemporary ideas, the noble savage, far from foundering on his own inconsistencies, proved capable of focusing a surprising number of attitudes and feelings. As Fairchild observes, "The Noble Savage [became] a convenient example of whatever a writer...wish[ed] to prove." Unfortunately for the durability of this exemplary function, the process was quite capable of working the other way round as well. If popular attitudes, in other words, were enough in themselves to mythicize, willy nilly, a quite unlikely candidate, as soon as the mood changed even slightly, the very same ideas that originally gave the convention its considerable potential for symbolic accretion had the capacity to help discredit it in turn. And did.

The cluster of responses associated with the French Revolution presents an almost paradigmatic example of how this shift took place. In spite of an apparent conflict between the idea of the noble savage and rationalistic philosophy, the former, as Fairchild points out, was not merely accommodated by but broadly identified with "the trend of thought which may be called Jacobin Rationalism." This was partly due to an intellectual confusion: "the tendency to regard reason as instinctive, and uncertainty of the meaning of nature." Even more, however, here as elsewhere there was an element of wishful thinking in the general misapprehension. "By the close of eighteenth century"—in Fairchild's words—"rationalism had long forgotten empiricism. Finding that facts interfere with speculation, it had thrown facts overboard and gone on speculating. That is why revolutionary rationalism and romanticism are so hard to dissociate: philosophy at the height of her pride in cold reason is just on the point of toppling over into the warmest emotionalism." Illogical? Yes. But it was precisely because of this paradox, as Whitney points out, that writers of the period were able to cling to the most popular sentimental formulas while at the same time brandishing the "cant phrases of rationalism and utilitarianism" like a flag. The fact is, she remarks, there were many "to whom the liberty promised by the French Revolution seemed to mean liberty for more indulgence in feeling rather than for the development of reason." Again, then, it is clear that individuals saw only what they wanted to see in current theory.

After the failure of the Revolution, however, and especially in view of the gruesome excesses that characterized its aftermath, the tide of public opinion turned radically against the Jacobin cause and everything associated with it. Rationalism became suspect. Deism became a synonym for godless corruption. Natural reason was discredited. Above all, emotional extremes were now considered dangerous. Too much had been invested in the vision for the disenchantment to be less than shattering. Because most English radicals were Protestant nonconformists, says M.H. Abrams, "the portent of the [French] Revolution reactivated the millennialism of their left-wing Puritan ancestors." This in turn inspired a "chorus of prophets who, [by investing] the political events in France with the explosive power of the great Western myth of apocalypse, [aroused widely] the perfervid expectation that man everywhere was at the threshold of an earthly paradise restored." When paradise didn't materialize, the mythic engrandizement naturally deepened the sense of betrayal. "The hard shocks delivered by the procession of events in France," says Abrams, "led to recantation, or at least to disillusionment and growing fatigue, in all but a few of the most obdurate." The bursting of this bubble was the signal for a general change in the whole emotional climate of the country. Because of its direct ideological links with the Jacobin debacle, the naive primitivism of the eighteenth century was one of the first intellectual fashions to feel the effects of this change.

Once triggered, the fall from favor was accomplished with surprising dispatch. More than merely ambiguous, the noble savage, it now became apparent, had attained his vogue only at considerable cost to his moral authority. Innocent and wise, exotic and austere, primitive and ultra-refined, long before the Jacobins came along to deliver the death blow he had been transformed from a simple, sensuous icon of self-imaging to a symbolic catch-all, a walking contradiction. Augmented into oblivion. No wonder he caught the backlash. As Whitney points out, indeed, that his admirers should *ever* have believed "they could look, Janus-like, both directions at once, hold both their primitive simplicity and evolutionary diversity within the same system, cling to permanence and change at the same time" only testifies to the "hardy digestion" of popular thought. This, of course, was the problem. As soon as the public no longer *wanted* to swallow the monster, such conflicts were bound to become troublesome. The result was predictable. *Especially* when public facts added their own incentive to private misgivings. Times were good as England entered the new century. That same civilized state which was anathema to Rousseau no longer seemed such a bogey. Far from confirming corruption, in fact, advances in the arts and sciences now seemed to establish social evolution and human perfectability as incontrovertible realities. Armed with a whole new sense of his racial potential, in the decades following the French Revolution the Englishman could hardly help but find the idea of progress more comfortable, more patriotic, and especially more *profitable* than primitivism. "The expansion of British Commerce, the establishment of new manufactures in which England was rapidly to gain world-preeminence, the growth of great industrial areas, the beginning of the transfer of the center of economic interest, and of the seat of economic and eventually of political power, from agriculture to machine industry"—all these, Whitney observes, "were manifestly hostile...to those traditional 'virtues' which were most fully expressed in the ideal of the 'simple life according to nature.' "

In strictly logical terms, of course, it is only *chronological* primitivism with its subsidiary implications of historical degeneration that cannot coexist comfortably with progress. *Cultural* primitivism, under the auspices of a theory of cultural relativity perhaps, might easily be accommodated without doing too much violence even to the pragmatic assumptions of the nineteenth century. There are, indeed, certain important features that the two schools have in common. Optimism, for instance. As Irving Babbitt says, if "the Rousseauist hopes to promote the progress of society by diffusing the spirit of brotherhood, the Baconian or utilitarian hopes to achieve the same end by perfecting its machinery... By his worship of man in his future material advance, the Baconian betrays no less surely than the Rousseauist his faith in man's natural goodness." Once the eighteenth century had finished with the noble savage, however—once he absorbed all the diverse characteristics projected on him by the fashionable trends in archaism, exoticism, gothicism, orientalism, and sentimentalism, not to mention taste and sensibility—it was impossible any longer to separate the two types of primitivism in the popular mind. They both stood for the same vague, ill-assorted cluster of ideas centering on different aspects of "nature" and "naturalness." The perceived flaws in one thus inevitably carried over to the other.

Besides this, the turn of the century saw a revival not only of "Baconian" optimism, but also of the same kind of pessimism that had characterized certain aspects of the late Renaissance. In spite of—perhaps even because of—its general enthusiasm, prosperity, and expansiveness, there was an undercurrent of alienation which paradoxically enough reached its most extreme form among some of the most brilliant thinkers of the time; an increasingly obvious "feeling that they did not belong in the intellectual, social, and political milieu of their oppressive and crisis-ridden age" (Abrams). Wordsworth, Coleridge, Arnold, Carlyle, even that child-prodigy of utilitarianism, John Stuart Mill, all experienced, with differing degrees of intensity, the traumatic conviction that their spiritual environment was unbearably impoverished. One of the results of this general feeling was the frequent appearance in the literature of the period of a form which Abrams calls "Crisis-Autobiography." A common version of this, he says, is "the distinctive Romantic genre of the *Bildungsgeschichte,* which translates the painful process of Christian conversion and redemption into a painful process of self-formation, crisis, and self-recognition, which culminates in a stage of self-coherence, self-awareness, and assured power that is in its own reward." Expressions as diverse as Wordsworth's *Prelude* and Carlyle's *Sartor Resartus* may be considered as products of this impulse.

What does this have to do with the noble savage? Quite a bit, indirectly. For one thing it helps explain why, in an era which was, and among a group of writers who were, notorious for an almost religious passion for nature, there was so little enthusiasm for the "child of nature." As Fairchild puts it, the "history of the Noble Savage from 1810 to 1830 is in the main the history of a dying convention." The noble savage thus disappeared just when British Romanticism, a movement which seems to give a final consummate expression to many of the ideas associated with the primitivistic vogue throughout the eighteenth century, was in full swing. Why? Here is where the aforementioned obsessions with psychic health and moral crises comes in. To begin with, the sheer intensity of their commitment meant that the Romantic poets felt a real necessity to work through their *own* relation with "otherness" rather than merely displacing this relation onto a conventionalized mediator. For another thing, their *conception* of "otherness" had changed as well.

The fact is that nature meant something quite different for the Romantics than it had meant for the primitivist of the previous generation. Where the eighteenth-century poet valued the landscape largely because of its power to stimulate wholesome moral or emotional associations in the mind of the observer—for its "collateral accretions," in other words—Romantics like Wordsworth imputed the greatest moral significance to the act of perception itself. One did not merely "appreciate" scenery; one "experienced" it. One experienced it, moreover, less as a reflecting surface than as a self-illuminated lamp. Intrinsically meaningful. The distinction is an important one. It is also predictable. The preoccupation with spiritual values, in combination with a distrust of both authority and superficiality, almost necessarily implied that one should look not merely *in* but *through* nature for inspiration. Nature was hence transformed by the Romantic imagination into a body of symbols. More than a concrete good in itself, more than a moral mirror of some kind, more even than a catalyst for "good thoughts," the Romantic landscape actually came to comprise a cryptic message from some vast reservoir of truth "beyond."

The vivid, even passionate way that nature was treated in Romantic poetry tends to obscure this fact. "[S]ince the symbol often looms as large as the thing it symbolizes, 'nature' was often, for practical purposes taken as synonymous with 'scenery,' " Fairchild says, *but*, he continues, the uninitiated should beware that he is not "deceived by a verbal code which the adept is using with full understanding. Just as the Catholic knows that the efficacy of a relic is derived from God, so Wordsworth knows that natural objects derive their 'power to kindle or restrain' from the 'wisdom and spirit of the universe.' " Nature-as-code does not completely replace the old phenomenal nature, of course. Indeed, as Furst (1969) points out, "few English poets have been more keenly appreciative of the natural world than Wordsworth and Keats. But the Romantic is at the same time also aware of the immanence of the ideal in the real, the Heavenly host as well as the golden guinea of fire when he sees the sun." The result of this duplicity is both a "fundamental tension between the real and the transcendental...which gives the Romantic lyric its particularly haunting quality" *and* a deceptively straightforward sensual surface that often masks an essential tendency toward abstraction. "Some of [Wordsworth's] poems that would seem, to the uninstructed, simple narratives of experience in nature are really half-disguised visionary apostrophes," says James McIntosh, citing "To the Cuckoo" ("Even yet thou art to me/ No bird, but an invisible thing,/ A voice, a mystery") as an illustration of his point. "[H]e will begin by observing a natural object, but this becomes an occasion for his ascending to the haunt of the mind... Thus he uses nature not to achieve a loving relation with it, but to go beyond it."

This trend, not surprisingly, was wholly inimical to the noble savage. Obviously he was far too frivolous to find a place in such an atmosphere of high moral seriousness. Two centuries earlier, with both the dignity of classical morality and the joyful fervor of Protestant millennialism to add weight to his symbolic stature, he had been able to offer an appropriate symbolic defense against the fearful apparition of a world moving too fast for traditional modes of comprehension, but now—vitiated, over-refined, tainted with faddish exoticism, transformed into a toy—the noble savage had lost his power to move his audience in any significant way. More important, in the light of Romantic philosophy even his natural environment, the untamed landscape that he evoked so vividly for his eighteenth-century admirers, could no longer be taken seriously apart from the transforming power of the cultivated poetic imagination. Although the alienated poet still, in a sense, looked to find consolation, an escape from detachment and despair, in some aspects of the natural world, the landscape that the noble savage by definition represented, as overwrought and over-refined as it might have become at the hands of the cultists, was not the same numinous nature to which he addressed himself at all. Despite its supposed moral *associations*, it was a physical realm only: something to see, and hear, and touch, and *feel*. To live in, in fact. Nature for the Romantics, as we have seen, was a much more complicated affair—a kind of surreality quite beyond the power of the simple-minded savage to understand, let alone symbolically mediate.

Whether the new obsession with spiritual questing or the canonization of nature would have been enough to eclipse the noble savage even without the Jacobin disaster is, of course, a moot question. These by no means represented the entire challenge posed to the outmoded epistemology by Romanticism, in any case. There was at least one further element in the new cultural mix which, seeming at first sight a simple extension of eighteenth-century views, turned out to be fatally antipathetic to primitivism. The emphasis placed upon the moral significance of childhood by both the Romantics and the Victorians depended, like the philosophy which assumed the savage to be noble, on a concept of natural goodness. Unlike the savage, who was supposedly a static personality, however, the child could also be made to support a theory of perfectability. Far from representing an end in itself, this new kind of innocence—the true *tabula rasa*—was valuable primarily because, not yet having acquired any negative habits, it was accessible to the positive influence of a healthy, modern, progressive education. Just as much as the savage the child could still be used to symbolize those elements in life which are irrational and spontaneous—both, in a sense, could be seen as reflecting man's "hopeless nostalgia for a lost condition to which [he]...can never return" (Abrams)— but given the choice it is easy to see why the nineteenth century would pick the exemplar whose ambivalent nature could most easily be fitted into its cheerful doctrine of progress.

Like the other trends we have discussed, this last development was perhaps an inevitable one. We already noted the potential utilitarian implications of associationist psychology in our discussion of Locke. And no matter what the sentimental novelists may have pretended in their battle to squeeze everything into their books that the public could possibly want, the concept of the noble savage had been even further undermined by the development of a philosophy of taste which, as Whitney points out, led inexorably "away from primitivism to aesthetic and moral exclusiveness and sophistication." The full-blown glorification of education which perhaps reached its most distinctive form in Matthew Arnold's *Culture and Anarchy* was just a natural outgrowth of the same trend. In the face of what Peter Thorsley describes as "the rise of a Victorian faith in evolution, in progress, and in the benefits of a mercantile and industrial civilization," the views that imputed moral benefits to landscape were doomed to be replaced by the more athletic lessons to be learned on the playing field of Eton. It wasn't *just* a matter of bourgeois materialism, either. The poetic version of the doctrine of perfectability, though not quite as crude as the manufacturers' or the educationalists', was no less hostile to the noble savage, and to the portmanteau primitivism he had come to represent. For all its token nod to nature it depended, in fact, on exactly the same basic social values. Take Blake. Hardly a plausible partner for the utilitarians, one would think. There is, though, some significant overlap in the emphasis on "improvement." The children of Blake's World of Innocence are good, happy, healthy, warm, exuberant, and so on, but to become whole adults they must eventually be initiated into the horrors of the World of Experience. Passive innocence, in other words, is *not* enough. Only by confronting the evils of life—not just the blatant ones like hungry orphans, exploited chimney sweeps, and child prostitutes, but also the more dangerous, seemingly "righteous" sins disguised by frigid systems of man-made morality—can they pass through into what may loosely be called a World of *Higher* Innocence. The Romantic version of the circuitous journey so central to myth and fairy tale thus "fuses the idea of the circular return with the idea of linear progress, to describe...[an] ascending circle, or spiral" (Abrams). Such a return isn't really a return at all. And this, in the end, is what rules out primitivism. The noble savage could be just as much of a positive symbol as those children in Blake's *Songs*— except for one thing: he is a *permanent* resident of the Innocent World; he has none of the potential for learning that was so important to the Romantic poets, no capacity for spiritual change and growth.

The nineteenth century thus marked the virtual end of the British version of the noble savage convention. By the end of the first quarter, that numinous figure who had titillated so many generations of Englishmen had come to seem less a myth than a puerile fantasy. By the end of the third quarter, he had not even nostalgia to sustain him. "For Kipling, at the close of the century," remarks Thorsley, "the collective wild men of the far-flung Empire have become 'the White Man's burden,' the 'lesser breeds without the Law.' " The abrupt decline, however, was played out in terms which, if somewhat ironical, were fully appropriate to our savage's rather chequered career. Just as he originally achieved his eminent position in the life and letters of the English Enlightenment by virtue of his capacity to digest a whole host of mutually incompatible philosophical ideas and cultural trends, transmuting them somehow into an appearance of harmony, he was finally discredited by the joint influence of two of the nineteenth century's strangest bedfellows: on the one hand the Romantic poet with his serious-minded new simplicity and his spiritualization of the landscape, and on the other the prototype of the sane and sober middle-class Victorian gentleman, chock-full of optimism, common-sense, good food, and progressive ideas.

This is not, however, by any means the end. In Fairchild's words, "the Noble Savage, deprived of his philosophical significance, becomes a mere outworn fad...gradually gives place to other aspects of the romantic spirit...[and] dies one of his many deaths in the neighbourhood of 1820." Reversing the order of Fairchild's sentence, we will close this chapter by noting that in spite of his downfall in this time and place, the noble savage remains "as immortal as the phoenix." We will hear from him again.

3. The Noble Savage in America

3.1 The Negative Response

Act two. This brings us to Plymouth Rock. Circa 1650. Enter an Indian—masked. We knew this creature once—but now? Now everything is different. Besides, as Lévi-Strauss (1968) has shown us, myth transplanted only rarely breeds true. Transplanted, *we* find that only fragments of the past are portable. The present is a case in point. If the fortuitous coincidence of certain predispositions in the British popular imagination with the historical facts of transAtlantic discovery made it almost inevitable that the noble savage idea would play an important formative role in the American experience, it was far from determining the *shape* that this idea would take once severed from its roots. The fact is, antecedents notwithstanding, the literary savage—the savage-as-idea—was subjected to an even greater variety and diversity of influences in his New World career than he underwent in Europe from the Renaissance to the nineteenth century. The confrontation with *real* Indians, the typical psychology of pioneers and pilgrims, the unique emotional and social needs implied by a unique environment, the distinctive patterns assumed by the American literary imagination in response to those needs, the reaction *against* and simultaneous continued fertilization *by* European attitudes and conventions, and, finally, a new and somewhat ambivalent response to history—all these elements helped radically metamorphose the symbolic primitive in his new home. A few at least of his more basic associations did, however, remain unchanged. One of the most important of these was his link with the landscape. In the United States as in Britain, the various permutations of the noble savage that appeared over a period of time were closely, perhaps causally, connected with changing attitudes toward "nature." It is in an examination of the complex, shifting love/hate relationship between the American and his natural environment, therefore, that we will find our most appropriate starting point for a discussion of the noble savage in North America.

The first responses to the New World were, of course, inherited ones. Eager to express its sense of momentousness yet incapable of assimilating too much novelty all at once, the Renaissance public was inclined to conceptualize the Americas largely in terms of familiar stereotypes and ready-to-hand stocks of imagery. As a result, as Richard Slotkin points out in his provocative study of American myth, the earliest views of the continent were inevitably set forth "in the conventional terms of utopian treatise-fiction, arcadian poetry, and the chivalric romance-epic." Under the stimulus of great expectations, to these literary conventions were added the paradisial images of Christian tradition, revitalized by the Protestant millennialism which took on such great significance in the context of the religio-patriotic myth of Elizabethan England. The resulting synthesis combined Eden with Arcadia, Elysium, Atlantis, the Hesperides, Tirananogue, and all the other enchanted gardens of antiquity to produce a vision of abundance and felicity such as centuries of human longing could scarcely have conceived. Columbus's own identification of the new World with the terrestrial paradise, far from idiosyncratic, set the tone for the whole period.

An overreaction by the uninformed? Certainly some of the exaggerations were rooted in enthusiastic ignorance. As suggested by the invocation of Columbus, however, the romanticized vision of the New World was not reserved for those utopian dreamers who contemplated its promise only from afar. To such a degree did expectations control perception, Slotkin notes, that "the explorers and conquerers themselves tended to see the landscape of America through lenses colored by their reading of romance epics and pastoral verses." Even first-hand descriptions of the new land were thus most often formulated in the conventional celebratory terms produced by the European imagination. Captains Amadas and Barlow, for instance, reported that when they first entered the coastal waters of North Carolina "we smelt so sweet and so strong a smell, as if we had been in the midst of some delicate garden abounding with all kinds of odoriferous flowers." Later, after landing, they "found the people most gentle, loving, and faithful, voide of all guile and treason, and such as live after the maner of the golden age."

Even the settlers' reports tended to fall into the same pattern—at least for a while. Thomas Morton, that thorn in the side of the Plymouth colony, made frequent, explicit allusions to "paradice," recommending that the colonists emulate Adam and Eve in constructing their new society. Thomas Harriot called America the "paradice of the world," and John Smith, in similar terms, claimed that "heaven and earth never agreed better to frame a place for man's habitation." Daniel Price in 1609 also used the biblical imagery, describing the new continent as "a good land, a land flowing with milk and honey." The keynote to all these descriptions was *abundance*. As if the age-old fantasy recently revived in Europe were truly impervious to reality, the *garden*—whether Edenic or otherwise—was the image most often invoked by newcomers to convey their initial impressions, and the idea most often associated with the garden was *plenitude*. Robert Beverly of Virginia expressed amazement at the "extreme fruitfulness of that Country...[where] no Seed is Sowed...but it thrives." Even the archetypal Puritan, Samuel Purchas, was unable to resist an enthusiastic catalogue of the physical attractions of his new home:

...the heavenly climate and influence, causing such discording concord of dayes, nights, seasons; such varietie of meteors, elements, aliments; such noveltie in Beasts, Fishes, Fowles; such luxuriant plentie and admirable varietie of Trees, Shrubs, Hearbs: such fertilitie of soyle, insinuation of Seas, multiplicitie of Rivers, safetie of Ports, healthfulnesse of ayre, opportunities of habitation, materialls for action, objects for contemplation, haps in present, hopes of future, worlds of varietie in that diversified world.

If this prose, unlike some of the others', falls a little short of an outright paean to nature, it at least demonstrates the impact, especially in the context of traditional paradisial expectations, of seemingly limitless material largess.

To what extent were these early colonists *conditioned* by their own idiom to see this material largess? And how much of the subsequent reaction (the honeymoon, as one might expect, didn't really last very long) was due to the deflating impact of reality on their naive Edenic fantasies? Slotkin, for one, claims that the necessity of "reconciling the romantic-convention myths of Europe to American experience" comprised *the* central problem of colonial adjustment, and certainly the changes that took place in thought patterns and attitudes can be attributed at least partly to a simple process of psychological reorientation. Such a process was after all no more than predictable. The discrepancies between fact and fiction were simply too great to be ignored. *Especially* when it came to the original inhabitants. Even as some voyagers were busy painting the American natives in terms reminiscent of the classical noble savage, others took great delight in detailing their barbarisms. Sometimes, indeed, self-righteous diatribes against specific aspects of Indian conduct could be found side by side with conventional primitivistic panegyrics in a single piece of writing. Such juxtapositions could not help but make the real cultural differences seem even more extreme. In the context of the unrealistic expectations, in fact, it was almost inevitable that the Indians would strike the European observer as much worse than they really were. Simply because they lacked all semblance of the natural delicacy commonly attributed to the *legendary* savage, for instance, the northeastern tribes encountered on Frobisher's second voyage seemed to the explorer (as reported in Hakluyt) not merely culturally inferior but lacking in human sapience altogether.

> If they for necessities sake stand in need of the premisses, such grasse as the Countrey yeeldith they pluck up and eate, not deintily, or salletwise to allure their stomacks to appetite: but for necessities sake without either salt, oyles or washing, like brute beasts devouring the same. They neither use table, stoole, or table cloth for comlines: but when they are imbrued with blood knuckle deepe, and their knives in like sort, they use their tongues as apt instruments to lick them cleane: in doing whereof they are assured to loose none of their victuals.

If this kind of vituperation could be triggered at virtually first sight, it was hardly surprising that the colonists themselves—even those who were enthusiastic about other aspects of the new continent—would tend to react negatively to the aborigines. Purchas was in many ways typical. "On the other side," he says, immediately following the near-encomium quoted above, "considering so good a Countrey, so bad people, having little of Humanitie but shape, ignorant of Civilitie, of Arts, of Religion; more brutish than the beasts they hunt...captivated also to Satans tyranny in foolish pieties, mad impieties, wicked idlenesse, busie and bloody wickednesse." As Roy Harvey Pearce observes in *The Savages of America*, in the experience of many of the newcomers, if "it was a brave new world, Caliban was its natural creature."

The conflict between real and ideal, then, alone provides ample explanation for a considerable degree of backlash. In spite of this, however, there are some features of the characteristic response during this early period which suggest that there may have been other, more covert motives involved than can be compassed under the heading of simple disillusionment. Some of the anxiety we detect may, of course, have been triggered by a disquieting ambivalence of signification inherent in the myth itself. As Slotkin explains it, within the full range of European attitudes towards America were embodied "two antagonistic pre-Columbia conceptions of the West: the primitive belief in the West as the land of the sea, the sunset, death, darkness, passion, and dreams; and the counterbelief in the West as the Blessed Isles, the land of life's renewal, of rebirth, of reason and a higher reality." Any ambiguities turned up in the course of the colonization process, like the gap between the real and the idealized Indian, would naturally tend to activate this essential antithesis—along with its attendent psychic distress.

Such lurking adumbrations, while admittedly disconcerting, only accounted for a small part of the problem, however. Of much greater consequence, there was also a kind of conflict which, though *latent* in the European myths, was transformed by the qualitatively different environment offered by America into something new, something more intense and more potentially corrosive than anything Europe had to deal with. Because of its existential immediacy, this second kind of conflict had the potential to trigger far greater anxiety than any "embedded" linguistic discrepancy, no matter how disturbing the symbolic associations of the latter. Drawing upon J.L. Henderson's Jungian thesis, Slotkin characterizes the new locus as "the basic psychological tension...between 'Moira' and 'Themis'—between the unconscious and the conscious, the dream or impulse and the rational idea, the inchoate desire and the knowledge of responsibility, the gratification-world presided over by the mother and the world of laws and reasons ruled by the father." In the old world and the old myths these contraries were balanced. Tradition and social realities between them provided numerous structures within which the extremes could be mediated, permitting enough input from Moira to keep the culture dynamic but without relinquishing control. In America, though, the equation became unbalanced. The breakdown of authority implied by unmediated nature (Moira), especially when reinforced by the mythic guilt associated with repudiation of the paternal homeland (Themis), seemed to pose a constant threat. Plagued by inarticulable uncertainties, the colonist found that he could not after all be sure whether his environment were benign or hostile, Ariel or Caliban. "On the one hand," says Slotkin, "it led to the execution of good designs; on the other, it stimulated a monstrous ambition against authority, an obscene Faustian lust to satisfy nature by violating all bonds of obedience, religion, and morality. [Moreover,] Even the Ariel face of the New World was somewhat treacherous, tempting the good-willed dreamer into simple, natural willfulness, a delight in the exercise of forbidden...powers...[which would] woo [a] man too far in spirit from the commonday world of human responsibility." The American experience, it seemed, reincarnated not merely the bounties of the original Eden but some of its spiritual dangers as well.

There was thus a deep-seated strain of ambivalence in the American's response, even *before* and *beyond* his pragmatic battle against the inhospitable realities of his demanding new world. And more often than not, exacerbating the disenchantment left in the wake of discarded primitivistic fantasies, this conflict, according to Slotkin, "found an objective correlative in the racial, religious, and cultural opposition of the American Indians and colonial Americans." The Indian lived in the forest. His motives and behavior were as incomprehensible to the European imagination as the forces of nature themselves. His hostility (real or projected) localized the vague and general dangers that they sensed around them. He was Moira personified, in fact. It was therefore natural, having perforce been stripped of his mythic nobility, that he should become a symbolic vehicle for "the emotional difficulties attendant on the colonists' attempt to adjust to life in the wilderness" (Slotkin).

The acquired symbolic overlay was an obstacle to more objective assessments, of course, so the savage, transmuted by the American imagination, while no longer viewed as a moral exemplar, still continued to be more conventional than real. He also continued to play the weathercock, reflecting with remarkable sensitivity the changing tides of public opinion by ritually changing his own public face. Thanks to the environmental association he had at least a few more or less constant character traits, but even these resided largely in the eye of the beholder. These facts have some important corollaries. For one thing, they confirm that the American as much as the European literary savage serves a significant ongoing revelatory function with respect to his cultural context. Conversely—and more to the point—they also suggest that that cultural context not merely illuminates but itself comprises the essential "meaning" of the savage. Not only can good Indians and bad Indians alike— as noted above—be "explained" quite satisfactorily in terms of the American's unstable, inconsistent, and emotionally charged attitude toward nature, then, but—going one step further—we may assume that no image of an Indian in this country can be fully understood *apart* from the nation's historic quest to define for once and for all the meaning and moral significance of the landscape. Turning back to that omnipresent garden image, the three major stages through which this quest has progressed may be identified respectively with the antitheses between the garden and the wilderness, the garden and paradise, and the garden and the city. Before the savage was allowed to become noble again it was necessary for him to play the series of negative roles projected on him by this series of symbolic debates.

3.1.1. The Garden and the Wilderness

Ambivalence about nature is nothing new, to be sure. "Nature" has almost always been an ambiguous term in the history of western thought. There has been a tendency overall to identify the good with that which is "natural" or "according to nature," but there has been very little agreement about what, precisely, is designated by that referent. As Lovejoy and Boas point out, "the sacred word 'nature' is probably the most equivocal in the vocabulary of the European peoples; [and] the range of connotation of the single term covers conceptions not only distinct but often absolutely antithetic to one another in their implications." They themselves isolate at least nine different and often incompatible usages, implying that the list is far from complete. The American experience, with its latent psychic tensions, thus merely intensified a confusion inherent in the term. The resulting vagueness, however, often makes it difficult for us to interpret exactly what a writer thought he was saying about nature. Even at the best of times it is all too easy to slip unconsciously from one meaning to another. And for the American in particular, the tendency to discriminate inadequately between different senses of the term has been aggravated by the fact that attitudes towards nature in this country are typically not only ambivalent but problematic. The necessity of maintaining mental defences has provided a strong incentive for suppressing what Lovejoy and Boas call "the processes of association, or the latent desires, which psychologically explain the substitutions."

The first widely disseminated equivocation about the meaning and value of nature in America was, as stated above, based upon a confusion about whether the environment was, metaphorically speaking, a "garden" or a "wilderness." These terms not only imply two extremely different empirical phenomena but, as Leo Marx points out, they are also "traditionally associated with quite different ideas of man's basic relation to his environment." What really exacerbated the problem for the early colonists, however, was that "in a sense, America was *both* Eden and a howling desert"; that "the actual conditions of life in the New World," in other words, lent "plausibility to both images" (Marx). On the one hand, as already mentioned, the overwhelming fecundity of the landscape initially gave great weight and significance to the garden image. On the other, the novelty that was at least part of this initial enthusiasm soon wore off. As Wilson Clough observes in *The Necessary Earth: Nature and Solitude in American Literature*, "However sharp and novel the first visual impressions, much was inevitably sacrificed in the delay of establishing oneself." More important than the mere loss of aesthetic distance, of course, was the concomitant loss of confidence. Fecundity aside, the physical situation in which the new colonists found themselves was brutally demanding and blatantly precarious. Even apart from the inevitable sense of estrangement, of exile, the most predominant features in their immediate environment were, as Slotkin notes, "the wildness of the land, its blending of unmitigated harshness [with the] tremendous potential fertility; the absence of strong European cultures on the borders; and the eternal presence of the native people of the woods...mysterious, bloody, cruel, 'devil-worshipping.' " Small wonder that they would see the semblance of a wilderness more easily than that of a garden. Small wonder, indeed, that the landscape perceived by these reluctant transplantees should—as one of their own describes it—more often than not show *only* its hostile face:

Being thus passed the vast ocean...they had now no friends to wellcome them, nor inns to entertaine or refresh their weatherbeaten bodys, no houses or much less townes to repaire too, to seeke for succoure...[T]he season it was winter, and they that know the winters of that cuntrie know them to be sharp and violent, and subjecte to cruell and feirce stormes, deangerous to travill to known places, much more to serch an unknown coast. Besids, what could they see but a hidious and desolate wildernes, full of wild beasts and wild men?... Neither could they...have little solace or content in respecte of any outward objects... [T]he whole countrie [being] full of woods and thickets, represented a wild and savage hiew. If they looked behind them, ther was the mighty ocean which they had passed, and was now as a main barr and goulfe to separate them from all the civill parts of the world. [William Bradford, *The History of Plymouth Plantation*, 1620]

Judging by this description, America close-up was not merely somewhat less idyllic than, but almost heartbreakingly inimical to, the paradise it seemed from a distance.

Physical hardships, then, could alone be more than enough to explain the preference for wilderness terminology evinced by the early colonists. No doubt adding its own weight to this spur, moreover, is the fact that the negative designation would have been useful as well as appropriate. As Marx indicates, to "describe America as a hideous wilderness...is to envisage it as another field for the exercise of power [and]...expresses a need to mobilize energy, postpone immediate pleasures, and rehearse the perils and purposes of the community. Life in a garden is relaxed, quiet, and sweet...but survival in a howling desert demands action, the unceasing manipulation and mastery of the forces of nature." *Ipso facto* wildness notwithstanding, given such incentive it seems more ·than likely that "political" factors were fully as instrumental in confirming the "hideous wilderness image of America" as physical ones. Is this the whole answer, though? I think not. Stipulating that all these factors probably *contributed* to the response, Marx's invocation of situation-specific needs hardly scratches the surface of the psychological dimension. Considering the *tone* as well as the substance of surviving documents, it seems obvious that there were other—or at least additional—motives involved in the choice of this particular metaphor than simply a pioneer's natural pragmatism. There is ample evidence that the response was based as much on what these people brought with them as on what they found in America. Indeed, it is possible that certain biases built in to the Puritan world view made the wilderness label almost inevitable. Ursula Brumm, in her study of religious typology in American thought (1970), summarizes some of the more relevant features of the cognitive mode that underlaid these biases.

In [the Puritan's] eyes, world history...is not developing toward something completely new; rather it is developing toward the fulfillment of prophecies and the repetition of exemplary models. In order to prove this he fits his description of events and people into a framework of correspondances taken from ancient, biblical, or Reformation history...

[In this process of rationalization,] the ever-present type [chosen by] the New England Puritans...[to illuminate] their own destiny was the exodus of the children of Israel from Egypt into the wilderness and then to the promised land. This conception...lent the Puritans the strength and endurance necessary for their trials on the story soil of New England in the face of the dangers of the wilderness.

It was no more than predictable, therefore, that the Puritans would be predisposed to the idea of an inimical environment. Cotton Mather, in his "Life of John Winthrop," not only speaks of "the *Noble Design* of carrying a Colony of *Chosen People* into an *American* Wilderness" but even designates Winthrop quite explicitly as "Moses."

If the tendency to scriptural self-identification has important enough ramifications in and by itself for the American's developing vision of his relationship with the new continent, the effects of this *particular* identification were both complicated and intensified by the varied emotional connotations which had been progressively acquired by the term "wilderness" in Christian tradition. The Hebrews, George Williams tells us, originally associated the wilderness with the desert, on a physical level, and with death; there was also an implied connection (through the image of the trackless waste: primordial chaos) with the ocean and/or the "primordial abyss at the beginning of creation and...at the end." In relation to the exile which was so much a formative experience for the people of Israel, however, the wilderness also acquired a very strong positive meaning, which was further reinforced in Christianity by John the Baptist's and Christ's wilderness ordeals. The wilderness was thus paradoxically seen as both a place of spiritual danger—"testing and tutelage," as Williams puts it—and also the setting for "redemptive, convenantal bliss." Both the positive and negative associations were strengthened during medieval times as the symbol was taken up by many reforming, heretical, and monastic sects; renewed, reworked, and—in the end—transformed from a straightforward physical phenomenon to a mystical-cum-mental one. In the course of this process what was originally merely a difference of emphasis was emotionally augmented to such an extent that the duplicity of the concept in a sense came to comprise its greatest source of numen. *And* its most essential meaning. The implications are obvious. For anyone with a typological bent, the wilderness journey, by the power of association, is always going to represent—indeed, literally *stand for*—the conversion experience. Like the conversion experience, therefore, it is always going to be fraught with peril. More important, it is always going to be beyond human comprehension and human control. In the context of Grace not merely the outcome but even the *grounds* of action are by definition ambivalent. The landscape—whether interior or empirical—is thus merely a metaphorical expression of a greater mystery. This, however, is what finally gives it so much power over the Puritan imagination. No matter what mode or mood it may present at any given instant, Janus-like, the wilderness is always ready to reveal another face.

So why did they choose to emphasize only its negative side?

The answer to this is perhaps not as simple as it may at first seem. Part of the explanation is certainly found in the pragmatic considerations pointed out by Marx (above). The wilderness context calls forth much more useful character traits when it is projected as harsh and demanding. On the other hand, the psychological influence of a surrounding wilderness is not as entirely one-sided as Marx's passage might imply. As A.N. Kaul indicates, the wilderness is both "a force for social cohesion" *and* "a temptation to capriciousness and irresponsibility." It brings people together by the necessities of "mutual self-help" in the face of a "vast and unknown or hostile environment," but it *also* provides "an opportunity for the assertion of romantic individual freedom." This double possibility, however, is precisely *why* the Puritans had to put almost the full force of traditional authority behind the image of wilderness as howling waste. For the Puritan "mission" to succeed, the wilderness *had* to be viewed as a deterrent rather than an attraction, and since the weak individual could not be trusted to restrain himself otherwise, it had to be fear that deterred him.

No other response was possible in the context of orthodox Calvinist doctrine. The distinctive Puritan world view emphasized the natural depravity of the unassisted soul. Freedom in a modern sense—and in a sense that the wilderness might imply if it were allowed to—was consequently seen as neither safe nor desirable. Freedom in a modern sense in fact was thought to endanger a man's very capacity to be free. How? Since the reprobate, as Winthrop explains it, is utterly unable to will his own good, personal or "natural" freedom—a man's "liberty to do what he lists...a liberty to evil as well as to good"—being "incompatible and inconsistent with authority," can thus only make him unhappy: to "grow more evil, and in times to be worse than brute beasts." "Real" freedom, in contrast, is that "civil or federal" liberty which, being derived from "the covenant between God and man" is "the proper end and object of authority and cannot subsist without it." The distinction is a subtle but crucial one. It also has some important practical implications. In particular, so construed, "freedom" for the Puritan was not merely compatible but *synonymous* with the voluntary acceptance of social restriction. At utter odds with the invitation potentially offered by the wilderness, therefore, the ideal Puritan community—according to Perry Miller (1956)—was firmly and unambiguously founded on "a social code demanding obedience to external law, a code to which good people voluntarily conformed and to which bad people should be made to conform. It aimed at propriety and decency, the virtues of middle-class respectability, self-control, thrift...dignity, [and] a discipline of the emotions."

This still does not entirely explain the Puritans' response, to be sure. A further question might in fact be raised as to why, if the social ideal was so well internalized and supported by both religious and civil sanctions, it could not exert enough control in and by itself without being set metaphorically against a threatening wilderness. The mere presence of discipline should not have been enough to drive men to rebel in reaction the moment they were permitted to recognize the wilderness as a viable alternative. After all, as Kaul points out, "on the same scene the Indian way of life had for centuries enforced successfully a very severe tribal discipline without mass defection or desertion by individual members of the tribe." The fact was, however, that in the Puritan mind, along with the ideal of social conformity, were already planted the seeds of a rebellion against repression and restraint, and the Puritan elder, while not perhaps capable of articulating his subversive recognitions, was well aware that he had to maintain a constant vigilance against this potential.

The perils were both emotional and intellectual. Mystical or pantheistic yearnings towards a benevolent nature, for instance, were anathema to the whole Puritan commitment, yet these tendencies were both, Miller indicates, fully implicit in Calvinistic doctrine. "Anne Hutchinson and the Quakers commenced as Calvinists," he reminds us: "from the idea of regeneration they drew...the idea that God imparted his teaching directly to the individual spirit. With equal ease others could deduce from the doctrines of the divine creation and providence the idea that God was immanent in nature." The danger of lapsing from orthodoxy was thus inextricably rooted in the most solemn and sacred tenets of Puritan theology. As if this weren't bad enough, it seemed, moreover, that there was a side to the Puritan character that "hungered for these excitements" such that no moderation could be expected once infection touched the weak individual heart. The elders knew full well that "men who imbibed noxious errors from an inner voice or from the presence of God in the natural landscape would reel and stagger through the streets of Boston and disturb the civil peace."

The haunting sense of vulnerability was, of course, why individualism was discouraged so strenuously by the Puritans. It was why the laws of the colony made it illegal for anyone to live alone. As Loren Baritz points out, "everyone had to be or become a member of a household or family. The Daniel Boone type was considered as dangerous to the organic community as were mavericks like Roger Williams and mystics like Mistress Anne Hutchinson." In spite of the strength of their communal convictions, the typical Puritan colony was obsessed with the idea that its people could at any moment—in Slotkin's words—suddenly "emigrate into the woods, beyond the pale of its godly rule."

The Indian became a symbol of this constant threat to peace of mind. To the colonists, as Slotkin tells us, he was "an image of what the Puritan who succumbs to the threat or the promise of the wilderness may become...a symbol of that spiritual, cultural, and racial degradation to which the spiritual thralls of the wilderness are brought." And it was because of this, because the Indian represented something that was *not* totally alien, because he stood for "the Dionysian elements in the English character [which already tended to] weaken or degenerate the power of order, authority, and Christianity," that the Puritan responded to him with such hatred and horror. "[H]e recognized just enough of his own behavior and feelings to be deeply troubled with self-doubt," Slotkin says. "The strangeness of the Indian was a threat to outer man and to Puritan society; [but] the Indian's familiarity, his resemblance to the primitive inner man, was a threat to the Puritan's soul, his sense of himself as English, white, and Christian.''

It is in the context of this double jeopardy that the violent denunciations of the Indian typical of this period must be seen. Fearful of the threatening aspect that the savage had acquired through displacement, and even more fearful lest the displacing mechanism fail, the Puritan felt compelled to cast him irrevocably into a bestial role that would dissociate him from any and all connections with the white, Christian Anglo-American. This compulsion, especially in the context of the Puritan's predisposition to view the world (and himself) in Old Testament rather than the more mystical medieval-Christian terms, reinforced an association already suggested by the Indian's perceived libertinism. Far from evoking the noble avatars of literary primitivism, for the Puritan the American aborigine almost inevitably implied the wild man of earlier Hebraic tradition. Regardless of the behavior of any particular individual—regardless as well of the actual diversity of tribes and types—there was thus a tendency during the early colonial period to conceptualize the Indian primarily in terms of those particular characteristics, physical and temperamental, which this accursed creature was popularly supposed to have exhibited:

The Wild Man is conventionally represented as being always present, inhibiting the immediate confines of the community. He is just out of sight, over the horizon, in the nearby forest, desert, mountains, or hills. He sleeps in crevices, under great trees, or in the caves of wild animals, to which he carries off helpless children, or women, there to do unspeakable things to them. And he is also sly: he steals the sheep from the fold, the chicken from the coop, tricks the shepherd, and befuddles the gamekeeper. In medieval myth especially, the Wild Man is conceived to be covered with hair and to be black and deformed. He may be a giant or a dwarf, or he may be horribly disfigured... He is desire incarnate, possessing the strength, wit, and cunning to give full expression to all his lusts. His life is correspondingly unstable in character. He is a glutton, eating to satiety one day and starving the next; he is lascivious and promiscuous, without even consciousness of sin or perversion... And his physical power and agility are conceived to increase in direct ratio to the diminution of his conscience. [Hayden White, 1972].

Once he was colored by these disquieting associations, it is easy to see why the Indian was suspected and feared by the colonist no matter how unexceptionable his actual conduct. Expectations would necessarily govern what was perceived.

As if this particular habit of attribution weren't troublesome enough, the Indian was not viewed as *just* a wild man, however. Because he was ignorant, the wild man's degradation was in a sense morally neutral, "beyond good and evil"—a feature which, by opening up the possibility of "innocence," invites a more positive interpretation of savagery as a whole. The Puritans could countenance no such suggestion. Not content to identify the savage with merely human degradation, in fact, they were more often than not impelled by the extremity of their abhorrence to impute to him an overtly supernatural or *demonic* role as well. To Cotton Mather he was "a rabid animal, perfidious, bloody, cruel, a veritable devil in the flesh." To Michael Wigglesworth he was a "hellish fiend." And these epithets were mild ones. Edward Johnson and William Hubbard viewed him—quite literally—as an incarnation of evil, characteristically equating such disturbances as the Pequot War and King Philip's War with Satanic plots against God's Chosen People. Michael Saltonstall, with similar implications of a Manichaean battlefield, cited God's will as a justification for destroying mercilessly the brutal, diabolical beasts who were so clearly Satan's creatures. The effect of so many invocations of unhumanity was to make the American aborigine far more fearsome than the poor old wild man. It also enhanced the horrific potential of the natural landscape with which he was identified. The extremism of the rhetoric which quickly became commonplace testifies vividly to the intensity of the Puritans' emotional response to their wilderness situation. The American savage *had* to be repudiated, the more violently the better, not just because he was a real and present danger to the external community but because those tendencies he represented in the New England symbolic equation offered an even greater danger to the Puritan soul.

Once he had been given this character, the "satanic savage," as we might call him, began to function as a useful and versatile cultural symbol in much the same way as did the noble savage in Britain. Two of the most popular semi-literary forms to be produced during the period—and the only two which approach in tone any sort of fictional treatment—are the Indian war tract and the captivity narrative. Both of these genres address themselves to the colonists' relations with the symbolic savage. In doing so, significantly enough, they come far closer, severally and collectively, to expressing a communal myth than any of the other written materials—the numerous sermons, exemplary biographies, personal memoirs, etc.—which document various aspects of the colonial experience. The Indian War tract and the captivity narrative, in other words, demonstrated an unmatched capacity to become metaphoric. Ingenuous for the most part, they yet rose above the adventitious. Although, as Slotkin relates, they originally just "grew out of the fact that many pious and literate New Englanders were continually falling into the hands of the Indians or attempt[ing] to explain their actions in battle," once established as conventional literary forms, like all true myths, they became used widely as vehicles "for justifying philosophical and moral values which may have been extrinsic to the initial experience but which preoccupied the minds of the reading public."

How did this work? The Indian war narrative had at least three distinct functions. On the simplest level, it reinforced the negative aspect of savagery, and provided the rationale of white superiority and self-defense to justify the settlers' treatment of the Indians, both in the immediate context of "brutal recriminations and even...massacres," and also on a long term basis, looking forward to the time when the inferior species would "be forced onto a reservation or pushed farther into the wilderness [as] the land hunger of the whites pressed too heavily on [its] preserves" (Curti).

Secondly, by dramatizing the cosmic nature of the conflict these narratives were able to strengthen community morale and the sense of divine mission. With the Indians as agents of the devil (sometimes they were viewed as instruments of God's deliberate testing and/or chastisement of his people; sometimes simply as natural satanic elements that had to be purged), the Puritan could glorify his heroic role in opposing and withstanding them by whatever means were necessary. Simultaneously, the association between these demonic creatures and the wilderness created a symbolic wall around the community in defense against any tempting/threatening encroachments from disorderly nature.

The third function of the Indian war tracts was both more complex and more deeply buried than these first two, however. These narratives, it would seem, answered a need at the deepest psychological level by justifying the fact that in spite of his firmest resolve the colonist was still forced by his environment into the very modes of response he feared most. As Slotkin puts it, "Fascinated by their opportunity for creating a world, the Puritans were also repelled by...the means necessary to their conquest... In order to convert [or conquer] the Indian, they had themselves to become more like the Indian... [H]ow could they be sure that their immersion in the corrupting element...had not permanently corrupted their vision?" The stories of the Indian fighters provided a structured response whereby this ambiguous behavior could be legitimized. In the terms thus made available, the colonist could claim that he was impelled into the wilderness by the necessities of his mission. It was *not* by free choice, and therefore not to be considered a personal sin. If one of the consequences was "that mysterious sense of identification between hunter and hunted" which Slotkin also identifies with the reconciliation of the individual with his anima, "the hidden part of his male consciousness where feeling subordinates intellect: passive, feminine, essential," then this too was a sacrifice that God required.

The captivity narrative had similar undertones to these, but with a slight change of emphasis. As mentioned above, the position of the colonist, both physically and—especially—psychologically, was perilous. According to the Calvinist doctrines of grace and predestination, the individual—in Slotkin's words—was burdened with the problem "of discovering the will of God with respect to [his] soul, [his] election or damnation." Because there was nothing he could do himself to earn this election, he was perpetually in doubt, and in many ways this constant uncertainty was more unbearable than the actual prospect of damnation. The situation, catalyzing an anxiety that had no tangible object, was a source of considerable psychological stress throughout the community. The captivity narratives, however, "were ideal for expressing this anxiety and for symbolically resolving it." The captive as presented in this model, passive and vulnerable, has had all necessity for decision or choice removed from his or her hands, thus providing a vicarious relief from the Calvinist dilemma.

Above and beyond this, the captivity narrative, like the Indian war tract, also offered a form of ritual drama whereby the colony as a whole could see its fate mirrored in cosmic terms and charged with larger-than-life significance. One function of this drama was purgative. On a communal level as on an individual one, the Puritans were both obsessed with and oppressed by vague but diffuse feelings of guilt for deserting their English parents. The captivity myth embodied both a punishment for this sin and a repudiation of it. On the one hand, according to actual statistics, captivity was "almost certain to result in spiritual and physical catastrophe [since] The captives either vanished forever into the woods, or returned half-Indianized...or converted to Catholicism and stayed in Canada, or married some 'Canadian half-breed' or 'Indian slut,' or went totally savage...[thus becoming] a soul utterly lost to the tents of the English Israel" (Slotkin). It therefore represented a very real threat. On the other hand, it also relieved the stressful aspects of that separation by re-enacting it, but in such a way that free will—and the consequent guilt—was replaced by compulsion.

Above all, like the Indian war narrative, but more so, the captivity tale offered a legitimized occasion for acting out the repressed and horrifying "wish" for reconciliation with the savage that could not be voiced, let alone fulfilled in overt terms. "[O]f all New Englanders, the Indian captives were forced into the closest relationship with the Indians," Slotkin points out. Their "ties to civilization were violently severed, and there was little or no hope of their being restored... Under compulsion they might be forced to attend the rites of savages, even to join them. For their fellows at home this was only a distant temptation, although a present one; for the captives the temptation to accept the Indian way of life was great, since it promised escape from immediate torments." *Under compulsion* is the key phrase. The Puritan, by means of the captivity narrative, could act out his fear/hope of being swallowed by the wilderness while simultaneously punishing the enormity, again vicariously, through the captives' suffering. More important, once "punished" he could also legitimately act out his *absolution:*

> [A] single individual, usually a woman, stands passively under the strokes of evil, awaiting rescue by the grace of God. The sufferer represents the whole, chastened body of Puritan society; and the temporary bondage [is]...the bondage of the soul to the flesh and to the temptations arising from original sin, and [also] the self-exile of the English Israel from England... The captive's ultimate redemption by the grace of Christ and the efforts of the Puritan magistrates is likened to the regeneration of the soul in conversion. The ordeal is at once threatful of pain and evil and promising of ultimate salvation. [Slotkin]

For these myth-like narratives to function effectively, the symbolic savage had to be both enlarged and simplified. Especially, he had to be kept well separated from mere humanity. This is why, contrary to what common sense might suppose, contact with real Indians in America, far from making the conventional European image of the savage more realistic, actually abstracted it even further. In this regard, a significant feature of these narratives is their impersonality. As Slotkin points out, the "lack of human heroes in the King Philip's War tracts is very remarkable. Jehovah is the only hero; of the earthly protagonists, very few individuals and no heroes stand out." Even the actual victims of the ordeals were likely to relate their plight to some great, impersonal, eternal conflict between good and evil, God and His Chosen People. "[O]ur perverse and evil carriages in the sight of the Lord, have so offended him, that instead of turning his hand against [the Indians], the Lord feeds and nourishes them up to be a scourge to the whole Land," says Mary Rowlandson, author of the prototypical captivity tale. There is little evidence here of the egocentric interpretation of events that one would expect in such circumstances. The result of such a perspective, aside from anything else, was to dehumanize the Indians almost entirely. Elemire Zolla's discussion of the captivity narrative in *The Writer and the Shaman*, emphasizing both the graphic, almost emblematic effect of the account and the stark, unidimensional quality of the protagonists and their roles, isolates this characteristic of the genre as being one of its most distinctive marks:

> [H]ere [in Mary Rowlandson's description] is the scene of violent *chiaroscuro* that will become canonical in the new genre: on the one side, "the roaring and singing, and dancing, and yelling of those black creatures in the night" and, on the other, the prisoners, many of them wounded, holding wailing infants in their arms, hungry and utterly dejected.
>
> In Mrs. Rowlandson's book acts of Indian gentleness or kindness are barely mentioned, dismissed as negligible aspects of brute nature, while acts of harshness are exaggerated. And yet do we not see an Indian horseman place a wounded child on his mount in order to help the mother on the long march? Do not others run charitably to bring her food when they see her cry? . . .
>
> In her story these acts become abstract, do not arouse gratitude, do not even appear to have come from human beings. The reiteration of abusive epithets has blunted not only all natural kindness but also any sort of curiosity about the Indians. The colonists wander about among them as though shut up in a transparent and impenetrable sphere, like figures in the paintings of Hieronymus Bosch.

The image of the satanic savage was thus reinforced and intensified with every new appearance.

As time wore on, the physical aspect of the colonists' vulnerability diminished, of course. And as external conditions changed, internal balances shifted as well. As Baritz says, with "the simple existence of Massachusetts Bay made more secure with each passing year, the inhabitants turned away from the energizing piety which had helped their fathers face the terrors of a wilderness. With growing material success, the inhabitants of the Bay turned their gaze from coffins and the afterlife to coffers in this. Wealth made men impatient with a limiting political theology . . . The impressive ecclesiastical and political edifice created by Winthrop and his colleagues began to decay because, in one sense, the Lord had been too bountiful." Was this softening of Calvinistic rigor accompanied by a softening of attitudes towards the Indians? Not at all!—not immediately anyway. The fervent sense of mission of the original colonists had served "to distract [them] from the tempting aspects of wilderness life: from indulgence in sensual pleasures, get-rich-quick schemes, or Faustian rebellions for personal power" (Slotkin). As this internalized factor lost its power to direct and control the colonists' response, the external threats became even more important. As Hayden White (1972) points out, citing the theories of philosopher W.B. Gallie, in "times of socio-cultural stress, when the need for positive self identification asserts itself but no compelling criterion of self-definition appears, it is always possible to say something like: 'I may not know the precise content of my own felt humanity, but I am most certainly *not* like that,' and simply point to something in the landscape that is manifestly different from oneself." At least one element in the reaction to increasing secularization was therefore a resurgence of xenophobia. In the last quarter of the seventeenth century, when "the Puritans began to sense the power of the wilderness working on their minds, hearts, and social institutions," says Slotkin, "their fears that they might degenerate and become 'monstrous' were reflected in a revival of the idea...that the Indians were nonhuman monsters and had been made so by their exotic, un-European environment." The symptoms were misleading. In somewhat the same way that the surprising increase (in both frequency and duration) of Jeremiad-type sermons during this second stage of colonization was, according to Perry Miller (1956), actually an indicator of communal health and vigor in spite of the *overt* implications of pessimism and despair ("The exhortation to a reformation which never materializes serves as a token payment upon the obligation, and so liberates the debtor," he says), the token vituperation of the Indian helped the colonist to hide from himself the actual process of naturalization that was taking place.

Appearances to the contrary, the satanic view of the savage thus continued to be more deeply undermined all the time. This particular version in fact made its last significant bid for recognition around the middle of the eighteenth century during a revival of religious enthusiasm later labelled the Great Enlightenment. One of the most notable products of this movement was a sermon preached by Jonathan Edwards in 1741. Called "Sinners in the Hands of an Angry God," it has since become famous as the prototypical expression of old-fashioned "fire and brimstone" Calvinism. In this sermon Edwards, like his forebears, makes frequent use of allusions to the satanic savage in order to emphasize the spiritual isolation and peril of his listeners. Hidden devils lay in wait all around for the sinful soul, he says, ready to pounce any minute; "the arrows of death fly unseen at noon-day"; God's own wrath is both like a torture fire and like a bow with "the arrow made ready on the string, and justice bend[ing] the arrow at your heart." Counter to this conventionally terrific vision, however, the same man, unlike his ancestors, was *also* capable of a rapturous, semi-mystical communion with god-in-nature such as traditional Calvinism could scarcely have conceived. I had a "kind of vision," says Edwards in his journal, "of being alone in the mountains, or some solitary wilderness, far from all mankind, sweetly conversing with Christ, and wrapt and swallowed up in God." "[H]is wisdom, his purity and love, seemed to appear in everything; in the sun, moon, and stars; in the clouds and blue sky; in the grass, flowers, trees; in the water, and all nature." No matter how fierce the affirmations of traditional values that the period produced, such deviations from orthodoxy in spirit if not in letter illustrate vividly the extent to which the repressed side of Calvinism—the side that invited mysticism, pantheism, and the inner light—was now breaking loose. And in a landscape which, having been irradiated throughout by the divine spirit, was no longer simply an unrelieved and fearful wilderness, a satanic savage could hardly feel at home.

The demythicizing of the satanic Indian did not, it is true, signal the sudden re-emergence of the noble savage. The American was still not ready for the Indian to become a positive symbol again. The eighteenth century in America, however, saw yet another symbolic Indian emerge. This new version, while very different from his European cousin, was also quite distinct from the demonic savage which, though most frequently cited by the Puritans, was more or less typical of general responses among all those early settlers who experienced their new home as a dangerous, hostile place.

3.1.2. Natural versus Cultivated Gardens

During the eighteenth century, America—as distant as she was geographically—could not escape being influenced by developments in European literature and philosophy. Europe, and especially Britain, was still after all her major source of intellectual and cultural stimulation. As the century wore on, consequently, in response to the fashions in thought that filtered across the water there was a discernible shift among the colonists towards a more favorable view of nature. We must be clear, however, on exactly what this shift entailed. More conservative than her highly "civilized" relations, America stopped far short of embracing the emotional and rhetorical extremes characteristic of the mid-century European vogue for primitivism and nature in the raw. "Those few who knew Rousseau's glorification of the savage," says Baritz, "found it laughable" rather than inspiring. The only eighteenth century officially recognized by America, in fact, was the eighteenth century of reason, order, and moderation: Pope's eighteenth century rather than Ossian's. Any increased receptiveness to nature was remarkable only in relative terms. "When Jefferson wrote of men as having the right to assume 'the separate and equal station to which the Laws of Nature and Nature's God entitled them,' " remarks Clough, "or when Joel Barlow predicted that 'as long as we follow nature in politics as in morality, we are sure to be right,' neither...[was] anticipating the semisavage white on the farther frontiers. Instead they were employing the word *nature* in an eighteenth-century manner, with connotations of immutable laws by which the Creator in his benevolence governed men and matter alike, laws uncovered and illustrated by Newton's mathematics and Locke's psychology. They were thinking neither of sunsets and waterfalls nor of uninhibited and bestial man."

In terms of the primitive/pastoral distinction mentioned in Chapter 2, then, eighteenth-century America was clearly oriented towards the latter. "The intelligent agrarian, not the libidinous, unrestrained savage," says Slotkin, "was

[the] type of the ideal American." In spite of this amply iterated official preference, however, the American response—even denuded of Puritan hysteria—continued to be undercut by an inherent conceptual ambivalence rooted once again in the duplicity of the community's favorite icons of self-imaging. The problem this time was the fact that the Edenic myth, with all its accreted associations, tended to imply that the ideal landscape was somehow both natural and cultivated. The key image of the garden—since there is mythic authority for interpreting it in either or both senses—embodied the entire latent conflict microcosmically.

Leo Marx holds up Robert Beverly's *The History and Present State of Virginia* (1705) as a revealing illustration of this confusion. Beverly uses the garden image repeatedly throughout the essay, but his referents are not always made completely clear. In Chapter XXII, "Of the Natural Products of Virginia and the Advantages of Husbandry," for instance, he devotes most of his attention to the capacity of America to support and improve numerous different agricultural products: "The Fruit-Trees are wonderfully quick of growth"; "Peaches, Nectarines, and Apricocks, as well as Plums and Cherries, grow there upon Standard trees"; "Grapes-Vines of the *English stock*, as well as those of their own Production, bear most abundantly"; "All sorts of *English* Grain thrive, and increase there"; "Rice...is found to grow as well, as...in any other part of the Earth"; "Silk-grass is spontaneous"; "The sheep increase well"; "Hogs swarm like Vermine upon the Earth." The standard of reference here is obviously a concept of rural economy. Virginia is a garden, sure enough, and a bountiful one. Its most important characteristic is its yield, its potential to nurture and nourish a community. There is surely nothing ambiguous about that.

Or is there?

If the domesticated landscape were truly so wholesome and health-giving, why then did it have such a bad effect on its inhabitants? Instead of being properly appreciative of all the potential largess so amply remarked upon by Beverly, the settlers there, according to him, "sponge upon the Blessings of a warm Sun, and a fruitful Soil, and almost grutch the Pains of gathering in the Bounties of the Earth." Notwithstanding his catalogue of agricultural *advantages*, in fact, there seems to be some doubt in Beverly's mind whether Virginia *could* validly be identified with a proper garden at all. The distinction becomes almost explicit when he says that although a "Garden is no sooner made than there, either for Fruits, or Flowers...yet *they han't many Gardens in the Country, fit to bear that name*" (italics added). How could Virginia be a garden and yet not fit to be called so? The question is an odd but important one.

Marx claims that Beverly was groping in this essay for the distinction between the two different aspects of the garden metaphor at which we hinted above: on the one side a "wild, primitive, or prelapserian Eden"; on the other a "cultivated garden embracing values not unlike those represented by the classic Virgilian pasture." The respective realities implied by these two images, disastrously enough for Beverly's coherence, were not only different but to some extent incompatible. Marx says both embody something of that timeless impulse to cut loose from the constraints of a complex society, but where the former "conveys an impulse-centered, anarchic, or primitivistic view of life," supported by a bountiful nature, the second state, being a product of human effort, connotes not only "a less exalted estimate of nature's beneficence" but also a more regulated ideal of conduct for man himself. It is because it fails to distinguish adequately between the two versions that Beverly's description of Virginia displays such a curious ambiguity of tone. Actually, reading between the lines, Virginia as Beverly saw it was only *potentially* a cultivated garden. Until this potential was realized by the labor of its settlers it could only offer the advantages of a *natural* garden. And because Beverly was, like Jefferson after him, a product of the rational, neoclassical tradition that blossomed in the eighteenth-century Enlightenment, there was no doubt in his mind as to the relative values of the two alternatives. The more bountiful *uncultivated* nature was, in fact, the more damage it did to the initiative and moral fiber of the settlers. The garden that Virginia *was*, was bad; only the garden that Virginia *could be* was good. Unfortunately, the ambiguity of the current terminology made it almost impossible for a writer to conceptualize, let alone to express this critical distinction with any degree of clarity. The old language was simply not equal to the new task.

Again, of course, the problem went far *beyond* language. Beverly's confusion—which can, I think, be taken as representative—might have remained largely "academic" were it not predicated upon an existential antithesis somewhat more emotionally reverberant than the latent duality—like the double myth mentioned in the last section whereby the west was associated with both death and rebirth—in an inherited rhetorical convention. And again the new environment not merely triggered but *exacerbated* the dormant conflict. The wild garden/cultivated garden dichotomy had in fact always been present in western mythologies, but never before had it become the focal point of a nation-wide identity crisis—perhaps because previous cultures had always been protected by a full range of supportive and adequately internalized value structures such as the fragmentary, disoriented, and vestigial American culture could not offer. In Hebrew tradition, for instance, the countryside was frequently used as a morally positive contrast with the city, while, as Sanford points out, "city cultures became synonymous with sinful backsliding." Throughout all the many references, however—all the Old Testament prophecies of Amos, Hoseah, Jeremiah, and others, which invariably call destruction down upon the evil urban centres—the primary term of the antithesis is quite firmly rural or agrarian rather than primitivistic. The New Testament, too, demonstrates this bias, with its "special veneration [of] shepherds, fishermen...lambs, [and] a manger in the rural village of Bethlehem" (Sanford). The closest it comes to glorifying "nature" as such is the emblematic garden of Gethsemane, a cultivated preserve associated with rest and mediation rather than any sort of primitive spontaneity. A similar stance may also be detected in the classical tradition, as represented by Virgin's *Eclogues*. And jumping ahead fifteen hundred years to the heirs of both these traditions does not reveal any substantial changes of emphasis.

To illustrate this continuity, Marx devotes a chapter to an exposition of the way Shakespeare in *The Tempest* mediated between civilization and nature to image forth a pastoral ideal which may be designated as the "middle landscape." There is an obvious suggestion in the play that the pre-island Prospero, a spiritual failure in spite of his art, had to "renew himself by immersion in the simple, spontaneous instinctual life" before he could triumph over his enemies, but we are still, says Marx, not encouraged to react against the spiritually barren city by embracing uncritically an opposite extreme of primal nature in *any* of its possible aspects: the brutal Caliban, the beautiful but amoral Ariel, even Gonzalo's dream of a "perfect plantation...with its yearning for a soft, passive, and indolent style of life." Instead, Shakespeare offers as a resolution the successful blending of art *and* nature that characterized both classical and biblical pastoral ideals. Represented by Prospero's masque, the preferred landscape "so far from...Eden or the original state of nature, is an idealized version of old England—a countryside that men have acted upon for a long time. It is the traditional domain of Ceres, that is, of *agri-culture* (in the Latin: fields plus culture), an amalgam of landscape and art... This paradise is a product of history in a future partly designed by men."

Shakespeare's strategy here, as Marx points out, is entirely conventional. As such it underlines with particular force something Marx *doesn't* admit, the extent to which America *departed* from its ostensible models. If the wild garden/cultivated garden dichotomy was conceived to comprise a *theoretical* problem in the cultural traditions inherited by the Americans, there is no sign whatsoever in the literary or folk products of those traditions that the distinction ever blurred seriously or that the latent emotional conflict implied by the differential functions and faces of nature became overt. Only in America, apparently, were the additional ingredients available to accomplish this transformation. Why this should be so is somewhat puzzling. One would think that the omnipresent hostility of untamed nature would have assured an even more clear-cut choice. The American forest, as we have seen, was usually not nearly as much like a garden as the conventional wishful fantasies would imply— except perhaps in the single feature of abundance. Even without the satanic character projected on it by the Puritans, in fact, it was clear to any rational observer that it presented both dangers and problems. And, of course, the *general* response reflected this recognition. As Baritz puts it, "For the American, nature in its purest and therefore most dangerous state was the central enemy whose defeat was usually thought to be essential to godliness, prosperity, and progress." The result of this attitude was another American "myth." "The fear of the forest led to a virtual apotheosis of the farmer, who would destroy the enemy and give birth to the [real] garden... [His] symbolic voice now began to resonate in almost all categories of thought. He was *the* American."

But then again—*was* he?

There is considerable reason to suspect that Beverly's simple confusion about the meaning of the two gardens had by the middle of the eighteenth century become a thoroughgoing ambivalence. Although Baritz's description certainly characterizes the *official* view during this period, there are clear— if covert—signs that the emotional appeal of the "other" garden still lingered along the underside of American thought.

Some of the more interesting of these "signs" may be found in Thomas Jefferson. On a conscious level there is no doubt where this famous southerner's loyalties lay. So enthusiastic was his endorsement of the farmer as, in Baritz's words, "*the* American," that his reputation in popular culture has come to rest almost entirely on two issues alone, the Declaration of Independence and "Jeffersonian agrarianism." "Those who labor in the earth are the chosen people of God, if he ever had a chosen people, whose breasts he has made his peculiar deposit for substantial and genuine virtue," he says. "The mobs of great cities add just so much to the support of pure government, as sores do to the strength of the human body." There is nothing equivocal about statements like this.

If, however, Jefferson's heart was so firmly and unambiguously committed to agrarianism, and if, as Marx claims, agrarianism may be considered as merely another version of the traditional pastoral ideal, what are we to make of his complex views of the Indian? Judging by isolated references, one might be inclined to suspect that the noble savage of Europe had sprung up in full bloom upon this stony ground. Certainly his writing contains more than a token nod towards those favorite eighteenth-century philosophic catch-alls, "natural virtue" and "natural wisdom." "Their only controls are their manners, and that moral sense of right and wrong, which, like the sense of tasting and feeling in every man, makes a part of his nature," he says of the Indians in *Notes on Virginia.* "An offense against these is punished by contempt, by exclusion from society... Imperfect as this species of coersion may seem, crimes are very rare among them; insomuch that were it made a question, whether no law, as among the savage Americans, or too much law, as among the civilized Europeans, submits man to the greatest evil, one who has seen both conditions of existence would pronounce it to the last; and that the sheep are happier of themselves, than under care of the wolves."

Marx makes much of the syntax of this statement: "What appears as a preference for the primitive actually is a rhetorical device," he claims, What Jefferson actually meant, in other words, is that "*were* it made a question...he would prefer the Indian way, the whole point being that in the New World such questions need not arise." This is certainly how Jefferson would have *wanted* his readers to interpret the rhetoric; Marx is no doubt correct in pointing out that the savage is really only invoked here to set up an opposition with European corruption in order that the agrarian ideal might stand forth more clearly as the point of healthy moderation between two undesirable extremes. What seems to me more significant than this superficially obvious *intent,* however, is the extent to which praise is lavished upon one of the two alternatives we are meant to reject. The fact is, the Indian way is made to seem appealing enough—both here and elsewhere in Jefferson's writings—that the equation is almost unbalanced. The conclusion is not *seriously* endangered, of course, but there does seem to be a moment there, fleeting perhaps, but unmistakable, when Jefferson's only half-acknowledged admiration for the aborigine almost gets the better of him.

This kind of inconsistency is not uncommon in eighteenth-century American prose and poetry. For all its deep-rooted conservatism, the colonial character seemed unable to resist indulging itself in an oblique dalliance with primitivism. The Rousseauistic flavor is, for instance, a particularly predominant element in Crèvecoeur. More important (perhaps because, being a newcomer, the Frenchman was not as well practiced in rationalizing—that is, repressing, distorting, or displacing—the more problematic aspects of the American experience), so is the deep-seated emotional ambivalence that seems almost always to have covertly accompanied the vestigial romanticism. *Letters from an American Farmer* is an ambiguous enough book to have been very diversely interpreted. Because the ambiguity belongs to the subject as much as to the author, however, it provides an incomparable demonstration of the mental processes we are trying to elucidate in this chapter.

First question: in what, exactly, does this famous ambiguity consist? In his Foreword to the New American Library edition of *Letters*, Albert E. Stone (citing Richard Chase and Marius Bewley) claims that the tensions within Crèvecoeur's work result quite simply from the equal and opposite attraction of irreconcilable values and feelings. What values and feelings? Falling back on the view that any changes manifested by primitivistic conventions after transportation to America must be attributable to the demythicizing influence of empirical evidence, Stone characterizes Crèvecoeur's response as a "conflict between belief and experience" or between "the dream and reality." Crèvecoeur's original attitude, he says, was conditioned by "Romantic stereotypes about the natural world and its admirable natives" but "experience taught a different lesson about America than did Jean Jacques Rousseau." Crèvecoeur's "dilemma," therefore—his susceptibility to "feelings so contradictory as to paralyze effective thought and action"—simply reflected his inability to relinquish his romantic dreams and ideals by honestly recognizing the more unpleasant reality.

Going back a little further, this was D.H. Lawrence's interpretation too. Making the "escapist" aspect of the ambivalence even plainer than in Stone's analysis this critic, indeed, would offer Crèvecoeur as a casebook study of typical artistic schizophrenia. "An artist usually intellectualizes on top, and his dark under-consciousness goes on contradicting him beneath," he says in *Studies in Classic American Literature*. "Crèvecoeur is the first example.... Crèvecoeur the idealist puts over us a lot of stuff about nature and the noble savage and the innocence of toil, etc. etc. Blarney! But Crèvecoeur the artist gives us glimpses of actual nature not writ large...[which] gives the lie to Innocent Nature." Was Crèvecoeur, then, no more than a hypocrite? Despite the weight of critical opinion, if we turn to the essays themselves the answer to this has to be no.

For all its plausibility—for all its undeniable partial truths—as is so often the case in our attempts to unravel the convolutions of the American consciousness, this obvious explanation is not merely insufficient but in some important respects dead wrong. What both of these critics fail to observe is that rather than being simply torn between a comforting dream and a disturbing reality, Crèvecoeur was paralyzed by the tensions generated between two *un*realities.

Stone comes closer to the heart of the matter when he discusses the Old World queries to which the author of the *Letters* presumably addressed himself. "Is Nature in America beautiful *and* beneficient"?, he imagines Crèvecoeur asking. If there is some doubt whether Stone himself realizes the implications of his speculations, in opening up this line of thought he touches on a critical point. Even more than the kingbird anecdote he identifies in his introduction as a recasting of the Jonah myth, revealing nature as "both predatory and beneficient," this casual question tangentially illuminates one of the major sources of the American's confusion about the moral implications of nature. If one of nature's faces were unambiguously predatory, there would be no problem involved in making a symbolic choice between them. *Both* faces, however, have a good *and* a bad aspect. Again, in fact, we come back to the inherent conflict between the cultivated garden and the paradisial garden, and Crèvecoeur, mediating between these two possibilities, offers a choice demonstration of the complexities of the American's emotional reaction to the antithesis.

On an overt level, of course, there is no real doubt as to which hierarchy of values Crèvecoeur professed. For him the American farmer with his "pleasing uniformity of decent competence" provided an exemplary illustration of human nature's most *desirable* state. The "true American freeholders [are] the most respectable set of people in this part of the world," he says in his attempt to define an "American": "respectable for their industry, their happy independence, the great share of freedom they possess, the good regulation of their families, and for extending the trade and dominion of our mother country." Whatever Stone may say of Crèvecoeur's European-bred Romanticism, in fact, pragmatic pronouncements such as this betray far less evidence of primitivism than there is, for instance, in similar statements by Jefferson. And as if to drive home his point with even greater finality, Crèvecoeur spared no pains in his efforts to discredit the alternative. Those men who chose to live in the forest were, he insisted, "ferocious, gloomy, unsociable"; "a mongrel breed half-civilized, half savage," notable mainly for its "lawless profligacy." Why? The reason is quite simple. *Lifestyle.* If a farmer's "manners are not refined, at least they are rendered simple and inoffensive by tilling the earth." Being by both nature and necessity industrious this species has no leisure for misdeeds. Hunters, on the other hand, divide their time "between the toil of the chase, the idleness of repose, [and] the indulgence of inebriation. Hunting is but a licentious idle life, and if it does not always pervert good dispositions, yet, when it is united with bad luck it leads to want: want stimulates that propensity to rapacity and injustice, too natural to needy men, which is the fatal degradation."

This doesn't sound much like a conventional paean to noble savagery, does it? There are plenty of pseudo-primitivistic clichés scattered elsewhere throughout the *Letters*—enthusiastic encomiums on the admirable "economy of...brute creation" and the "perfection of instinct," etcetera, etcetera—but the contrast between the consciously literary qualities of these passages and the more vivid prose that characterizes his discussion of the backwoodsman make it obvious in which viewpoint his emotions are invested. Insofar as it is consciously articulated, it is clearly the pastoral, not the primitive, that comprises Crèvecoeur's ideal.

If we study the *Letters* a little more closely, however, we will find hints of a greater complexity than a superficial reading might indicate. For one thing, if Crèvecoeur was assuredly not a thoroughgoing primitivist, he cannot be dismissed—as Henry Nash Smith and Marx are inclined to do—as a "simple-minded pastoralist." He cannot, in fact, even be considered as a firm or consistent opponent of primitivism. It will be noticed, for instance, that whatever his opinion of the Indianized white man, the denunciation does not carry over to the *natural* inhabitants of the woods, the Indians. Almost every reference made in the *Letters* to the savage, in and by himself, is positive, even verging on adulatory. The negative references to the influence of nature are very specifically related to its effect on the European character. Was his denunciation of the backwoodsman then simply a product of observation, in contrast to his more conventional ideas of the Indians? The liveliness of the relevant passages, as compared to the restrained eighteenth-century tone of much of the rest of the book, suggests that there might be a more personal, more emotional issue involved. Perhaps the key may be found in the twelfth and last letter of the series, "Distresses of a Frontier Man."

This chapter is notorious as the source of Crèvecoeur's famous declaration that henceforth he was going to "revert into a state approaching nearer to that of nature, unencumbered with either voluminous laws or contradictory codes, often galling the very necks of those whom they protect." This is not, however, the part of the chapter that primarily concerns us there. For one thing, as a critical bone, it has already been worried to death. And for another, there is no real evidence that this passage represents any genuine intention or change of attitude on Crèvecoeur's part anyway. It seems much more likely, in fact, that the pose assumed here is just Jefferson's rhetorical opposition carried one step further; the pole of nature, represented by the Indian, dramatically heightened merely so that the author's uneasy disapproval of current developments in the antithetical pole of civilization (the American Revolution) could be more strongly expressed. No—what is more interesting in the section, and much more psychologically revealing, is the quality and quantity of the reservations Crèvecoeur still felt impelled to admit.

These reservations strike an incongruous note almost from the beginning of the chapter. For one thing, they are very poorly integrated into the fabric of the argument as a whole. In terms of rhetorical strategems, in fact, the effectiveness of the author's attempt to condemn the Revolution is actually impaired by the hesitancy and half-heartedness of his endorsement of savage life, at least a a personal alternative, after he has purportedly made his decision to "embrace" it, since the argument would be far more convincing if the antithesis were set forth in completely unambiguous terms. Whatever function (or disfunction) all these qualifications may serve on the superficial level of development, however, Crèvecoeur's emphatic doubts and demurrers in themselves provide a crucial clue to his much-misunderstood inner conflict. Indeed, it is in reviewing these obsessive doubts that we understand for the first time that it is *not* disgust with the brutality and sordidness of raw nature that lies behind his generally negative response to the wilderness but, rather, *a fear that he will find it so attractive that he won't be able to resist it.* In other words, it is not because nature is *predatory* as well as beneficient that he is hesitant to embrace her but because, on the contrary, she *is* beautiful.

The significance of this chapter, as Kaul points out, is easily overlooked or misunderstood. It is ambiguous enough that critics can easily find in it support for whatever view they already entertain. The pro-pastoralists note only his fears about the native lifestyle. The pro-primitivists keep their eyes firmly fixed on what they interpret as a thoroughgoing celebration of noble-savagery. The following excerpt from Crèvecoeur's discussion of the kidnap victims who, after being discovered and offered repatriation, refused even to acknowledge their former families and friends, illustrates the difficulty of discerning either the direction or the limits of this author's true sympathies:

They chose to remain, and the reasons they gave me would greatly surprise you: the most perfect freedom, the ease of living, the absence of those cares and corroding solicitudes which so often prevail with us, the peculiar goodness of the soil they cultivated, for they did not trust altogether to hunting—all these and many more motives which I have forgot made them prefer that life of which we entertain such dreadful opinions. It cannot be, therefore, so bad as we generally conceive it to be; there must be in their social bond something singularly captivating and far superior to anything to be boasted of among us; for thousands of Europeans are Indians, and we have no examples of even one of those aborigines having from choice become Europeans!

Taken out of context such a passage can easily be cited as evidence that Crèvecoeur was expressing a clear preference for the savage state, especially if one interprets the tone of perplexity as a merely conventional device for emphasizing the self-evidence of the inevitable conclusion. To maintain this impression, however, one would have to ignore the other side of the picture. Over and over throughout the chapter Crèvecoeur reiterates his admiration for the primitive condition no less than his fear of it. The phrases recur monotonously: "I am seized by apprehension lest my younger children should be caught by that primitive charm"; "I dread...the imperceptible charm of Indian education"; "Still the danger of Indian education returns to my mind and alarms me much." In fact, to quote Kaul, "Not even the most liberal discounting of his obvious posturing for effect can wholly eliminate the imaginative core of his meaning." The most noticeable feature of this chapter is neither the primitivism *nor* the repudiation of primitivism but, rather, the combination of an emotional *bias toward primitivism* with a considerable concomitant *anxiety about that bias.*

This is merely the old wilderness phobia of the Puritans emerging in a new form, of course. The eighteenth-century version, however, clarifies the real basis of the fear. In the Puritan's mind the wilderness itself became so completely identified with the biblical and/or supernatural analogies which had been formulated to clarify their attitudes towards it that the basic emotional response could rarely be dissociated from all sorts of extrinsic moral/spiritual associations. In Crèvecoeur's case this was no longer so. What is more, on a purely abstract level he was actually predisposed to value the "natural" state. When we see that in spite of this predisposition he, like the typical American of the period, still felt compelled to reject the wilderness and, what is more, to do so almost violently (Crèvecoeur's disgust with the backwoodsman, as we pointed out, provides some of the most striking images in the book), we realize that the real problem is not related to anything specific *in* the wilderness but rather to the American's deep-seated fear that a loss of European manners would inevitably imply a loss of all meaningful identity whatsoever. Far from setting up a thinly veiled primitivistic fantasy, Crèvecoeur's tone of horrified incredulity when he speaks of the whites who went native was undoubtedly quite genuine.

Unfortunately for communal peace of mind, the fear inspired by the primitive did not in any sense eliminate all desire for it. It was because of this paradox, ultimately, that long after the Indian lost his demonic character, the American landscape remained a decidedly ambivalent one. The dichotomy entailed not merely a logical opposition, but also an emotional conflict on numerous levels. The paradisial garden was, as we have seen, colored by very intense and mutually exclusive feelings of attraction and repulsion. The cultivated garden, on the other hand, was simultaneously undermined by the appeal of "real" wildness and magnified as a defense against its dangers. Considering all these diverse pressures it is probable that the farmer—like the captive before him—became a significant symbol at least partly because he embodied a simplified response which *denied* the underlying tensions involved.

Again Crèvecoeur provides an instructive example. For this Frenchman farming necessarily involved attitudes and values which did not so much *conflict* with the tenets of primitivism as simply monopolize all available emotional and psychic energy that might otherwise have been diverted into dangerous pursuits. "I have but one remedy to prevent this great evil" he says, contemplating the danger of his children's assimilation into savage life, "and that is to employ them in the labour of the fields as much as I can... As long as we keep ourselves busy in tilling the earth, there is no fear of any of us becoming wild; it is the chase and the food it procures that have this strange effect." Rather than indulging some frustrated primitivistic impulse, then, it was because pastoralism, for purely pragmatic reasons, would *not* coexist with such fantasies that Crèvecoeur embraced the former. In other cases, the farming model could work quite differently. Jefferson, for instance, employed almost exactly the same rhetoric to an apparently altogether antithetical end. Far from setting the farmer and the Indian at symbolic odds, he clung to the idea that he could both have and eat his emotional cake if the farmer and the Indian could just be fused. "You see then, my children" he says in a speech to a mixed group of Indians in 1808, if you would only take my advice you could "become a numerous and great people":

> Let me entreat you, therefore, on the lands now given you to begin to give every man a farm; let him enclose it, cultivate it, build a warm house on it, and when he dies, let it belong to his wife and children, after him. Nothing is so easy as to learn to cultivate the earth; all your women understand it, and to make it easier, we are always ready to teach you how to make plows, hoes, and necessary utensils. If the men will take the labor of the earth from the women they will learn to spin and weave and to clothe their families. In this way you will also raise many children, you will double your numbers every twenty years, and soon fill the land your friends have given you.

One key point unites these two very different visions. Despite the contrasting emphases, Crèvecoeur and Jefferson in fact found the farmer an attractive exemplar for the same reason: not so much because of any particular fixed symbolic association he might carry as simply because the ambiguity of his stance vis-à-vis "gardens" obscured the ambiguities of their own ill-defined responses. The farmer, like most of the figures who became national symbols in America, was versatile enough to accommodate a wide range of potentially conflicting views.

How did all this affect the image of the symbolic savage, we might ask? On the one hand—as Jefferson in particular demonstrates—it left the door open for the emergence of a more positive version than the satanic savage in the American imagination. On the other hand, the time for that emergence was clearly not yet. If the Indian was not Satan he was still at least Lilith, luring the honest, hardworking American freeholder away from his sturdy self-reliance and self-discipline by dangling before him the unmoral and unAmerican enticements of the frontier. The emotional associations that rendered this ever-present temptation *fearful* rather than just a nuisance could be—and soon would be—virtually eliminated simply by taking away the mystique conferred upon the Indian by the exoticism of his lifestyle. There was, however, a further reason why the negative aspects of the seductive savage (as he might be called during this period)—the disorderly and destructive elements of primitivism—continued to be emphasized at the expense of any positive potential at least for a while. Which brings us to the final and most overt level of the opposition between the two gardens. The American found it necessary to repudiate the whole basic assumption of primitivism *because only by doing so could he continue to rationalize his seizure of Indian lands.*

This side of the American response was not new to the eighteenth century, to be sure. It went all the way back to the earliest colonies. Besides finding in scriptural authority a justification for the convenient denial of all humanity in their basic view of the Indian, the Puritans also utilized theological arguments to support colonial expansion. It was all a matter of conformity to divine order. Or so declared the Reverend Richard Hakluyt in his apologia for the English settlement in Virginia published in 1625. Pearce (1953) summarizes: "Christian Englishmen originally had not the right to despoil heathen Indians of their lands; for ownership of the land is a right in nature, not in God. Hence the Indians cannot be held responsible for not working their land according to God's revealed will; they live only according to the law of nature. Still, the English, as Christians knowing God's will, have an *obligation* to work that land; for it is almost bare of inhabitants and it is rich in all those things which make for 'merchandise.' " Following this reasoning, reclamation of Indian territory for the purposes of agriculture—the lifestyle indicated by biblical models as the only fit foundation for christian society—becomes not simply a matter of practical considerations but also a moral responsibility. As John Cotton wrote in 1630, the Lord commanded His People to "*Multiply, and replenish the earth, and subdue it.* If therefore any soun *Adam* come and finde a place empty, he hathe liberty to come, and fill, and subdue the earth there." The Indians would have kept their title to the land if they *used* it properly, but as shiftless hunters they forfeited their claims. As Slotkin says, they were "a fallen race, a people who. . . failed to realize the arcadian possibilities of the land and their own human capacity for human behavior."

The same line of thought, translated from religious to legal language but still retaining a solid kernel of self-justification through interpretation of man's higher destiny as a function of the process of civilization, continues in evidence well into the nineteenth century. Vattel's classic *Law of Nations,* the standard American authority for international law at that period, approaches the question in the following way:

The whole earth is destined to furnish sustenance for its inhabitants; but it can not do this unless it be cultivated. Every nation is therefore bound by the natural law to cultivate the land which has fallen to its share, and it has no right to extend its boundaries or to obtain help from other Nations *except in so far as the land it inhabits can not supply its needs*. . . Those who pursue this idle [i.e., hunting] mode of life occupy more land than they would have need of under a system of honest labor, and they may not complain if other more industrious Nations, too confined at home, should come and occupy part of their lands. [italics added]

Thus, as Pearce (1953) points out, "Seventeenth-century dependence upon Genesis. . . shifted to nineteenth-century dependence upon natural law[, so that] American progress could be rationalized and comprehended in predominantly naturalistic terms." The impulse, however, was clearly identical in both arguments. The expanding colonies were going to take over the Indian lands in any case—unless they changed radically the whole tissue of goals and values upon which their lifestyle depended, they *had* to—and the hunter/farmer, paradisial garden/cultivated garden antithesis, in whatever particular terms it was expressed, provided them with a comfortable justification for doing so. Pragmatic considerations if nothing else would therefore tend to retain the savage as a negative symbol even after many of the other contributing factors were eliminated. In the later nineteenth century, in fact, this particular negative version of the savage became in some ways more, rather than less, extreme (see the first part of section 5, below).

The overall development from the seventeenth to the nineteenth century can consequently be seen in terms of two inversely correlated but equally negative views. As the psychological reasons for denying the appeal of primitivism declined there was an intensification of the pragmatic reasons for maintaining an adamant stance. The eighteenth century, with its focal opposition between the two gardens was a transition point where both tendencies exerted a considerable influence. With the Vattel quotation, however, we have entered a period that may be characterized by a different antithesis, marking yet another in the American's attempts to define and and redefine his relationship with nature. This particular conflict—both more deeply divisive and more far-reaching in American society, as things turned out, than almost any other—may be expressed as the conflict between the garden and the city.

3.1.3. The Garden and the City

The city metaphor did not suddenly spring up full grown at the end of the eighteenth century. Like most of the various other metaphors that influenced the American's self-image, it was implicit in the assumptions inherited from Europe. Next to the garden, in fact, the symbol used most often by the earliest colonists to typify their aims in the New World was the City of New Jerusalem. In spite of the predominance of agrarian values among the ancient Hebrews, this image had more than enough biblical authority behind it to make it respectable—the city, among other things, was the location of the Temple, and thus the spiritual heart of the nation. Consequently it carried a positive emotional association fully capable of challenging the mythical appeal of a lost paradise. Especially among the Puritans, in fact, the idea of *civilizing*, of creating a millennial City of God in the midst of the wilderness, was far *more* compatible than the idea of untransformed nature in even the most splendid guise. If the country *seemed*, in physical terms, to be an incarnation of Eden, the Puritan knew all too well that it was only an illusion. Since man was corrupt, not innocent, nature could only be viewed as a dangerous threat to the discipline which alone protected him from his inherent degradation. It was hardly surprising, then, that the early Puritan writers would be unanimous in identifying the settler's mission in the New World with the redemption *of*, not *by*, nature—more specifically, with the planting of an exemplary Christian colony which, by virtue of its very presence, would deny everything that nature stood for. If we labor together at this great and sacred task, said

John Winthrop in 1630,

...allwayes having before our eyes our Commission...our Community as members of the same body, soe shall wee keepe the unitie of the spirit in the bond of peace, the Lord will be our God and delight to dwell among us, as his owne people, and will commaund a blessing upon us in all our wayes, soe that wee shall see much more of his wisdome power goodnes and truth then formerly wee have beene acquainted with, wee shall finde that the God of Israell is among us, when tenn of us shall be able to resist a thousand of our enemies, when hee shall make us a prayse and glory, that men shall say of succeeding plantacions: the lord make it like that of New England: for wee must Consider that wee shall be as a Citty upon a Hill, the eies of all people are uppon us.

As with the preceding antitheses, the difference between the city and the garden went far deeper than mere semantics, of course. As Sanford points out, "insofar as the image of a holy city conflicts with that of a primitive paradise, it is a symbol of civilized progress. The sacred city...expresses the buoyant hope of a glorious future paradise rather than a nostalgia for the lost paradise of the past." Implicit in these divergent chronological focuses, moreover, are sharply contrasting life metaphors. As was the case with primitivism and the idea of progress in European philosophy, the garden and the city could not help but suggest different and largely antithetical goals and values. The image of new Jerusalem invited dreams of empire and higher civilization. More to the point, perhaps, for all the salutary rhetoric it *also* invited a kind of self-aggrandizement that could very easily turn into personal ambition. Notwithstanding that first undoubted flush of righteous benevolence, in fact, within a century of their founding the colonies seemed concerned far less with converting than with plundering the natives. If, indeed, one looks to popular rather than public renditions of the rationale for conquest, an inextricably mixed motivation characterized the expectations of actual immigrants right from the beginning. "It takes determined blurring to combine the Eden myth with the earlier pagan stories, blurring reflected in the greed of the conquistadores whose chivalric quest included carrying the word of God to the heathen," notes Richard Ruland. "Return to the Garden of Eden would seem to promise primarily spiritual riches, or at most a pastoral fecundity to sustain the good Christian in his few quotidien needs. But the sand on the Island of the Seven Cities was believed to be one-third fine gold, and in Atlantis there was 'such an amount of wealth as was never before possessed by kings...' Visions such as these provided stern competition for missionary zeal."

The conflict, then, was once more deeply rooted in the first visions of the New World. Until the eighteenth century, on the other hand, the disruptive potential of this third major dichotomy remained largely if not wholly unrecognized. The investment of all possible resources into colonial expansion could be pragmatically regarded as a necessity for survival, purely and simply, without much attention being spared for a debate on the ethical/aesthetic implications of the development. Besides, the full-scale urban/industrial possibilities implied by the word progress in its ultimate form played such a miniscule part in either American thought or American realities up to and beyond the Revolution that Hamilton's championship of financial interests against both Jefferson's agrarianism and Adams' aristocratic conservatism in the post-Revolutionary period seemed something of a novelty in the country's history. Until the nineteenth century there was thus no real counterinfluence to deflect the psychological tendency of the American public to focus upon the problems inherent in different aspects of nature rather than on the nature/civilization debate *per se.*

The problem was further obscured by an essential lack of agreement about what these terms of reference actually implied. Even after the turn of the century, on the conscious level at least, despite the degree to which the *values* of the (idealized) city were already institutionalized as part of the growing nation's sense of self, the *real* city—tainted through its associations with sophistication and corruption in pastoral convention and even more by virtue of its connections, both actual and metaphorical, with European decadence—apparently continued to have, as symbol, more negative than positive connotations. Assorting oddly with their concomitant if largely inadvertent expression of "strong popular hopes for [the] material advantages in urbanization," most works of fiction produced in America during the early nineteenth century, for instance, were quite unequivocal in portraying the city as—in Janis Stout's words—"a basically frivolous, hence morally insecure, place."

Despite the apparent persistence of this particular stereotype, however, the city-as-state-of-mind if not the city-as-place *in fact* became increasingly influential as an arbiter of values and a focus of national identity as America grew up. In the period following the Revolution—ironically, the same period that saw the equation city=Europe=evil asserted most strongly—a number of factors emerged which combined to effect a radical change of emphasis, challenging vigorously the authority of the garden in all its facets. First, there was the not inconsiderable impact of European philosophy. For largely pragmatic reasons—and particularly because the rising middle classes found in them a useful justification for taking advantage of the vast new opportunities for expansion and exploitation made available after Britain's restrictive regulation of industrial/commercial development was brought to an end—the ideas that had already made progress a rallying cry for England were widely disseminated in post-Revolutionary America. Secondly, the increasing self-evidence of this progress—the actual tangible increase in population and wealth—served as an incontrovertible argument in and by itself.

In the face of this undoubted prosperity, so pleasing both to national pride and to the individual pocketbook, the social optimists, who comprised a growing majority at least of the articulate sector of the population, produced vast numbers of essays and orations worthy of the most enthusiastic Rotary Club or Chamber of Commerce in America today. "[I]t is only in the improvements of civil society," says Samuel Williams in his *Natural and Civil History of Vermont* (1794), "that the human race can find the greatest increase of their numbers, knowledge, safety, and happiness." Sentiments such as these provided the refrain for a chorus of adulation for American energy, American industry, American thought. Morgan J. Rhees in 1796, delivering a paean to the stalwart "labourers and mechanics who were the bones and marrow of every community," described the country as a "wide extended empire, whose uncultivated forests and fertile plains, invite the uplifted *ax* and the furrowing *plough*." Tench Cox, in an address to an Assembly of the *Friends of American Manufacturers* (1787), went even further, claiming that the national policy of industrial advance would soon provide the panacea for all human ills.

[Extended manufacturing] will consume our native productions now increasing to super-abundance—it will improve our agriculture and teach us to explore the fossil and vegetable kingdoms, into which few researches have heretofore been made—it will accelerate the improvement of our internal navigation and bring into action the dormant powers of nature and the elements—it will lead us once more into the paths of virtue by restoring frugality and industry, those potent antidotes to the vices of mankind, and will give us real independence by rescuing us from the tyranny of foreign fashions.

If the sentiments here seem extreme, remember that this country had just won a Revolution. In the flush of victory, even the poets turned their talents to a celebration of America as the type and the model of the kind of nation to whom the future would belong:

> All hail, thou western world! by heaven design'd
> Th'example bright, to renovate mankind.
> Soon shall thy sons across the mainland roam;
> And claim, on far Pacific shores, their home:
> Their rule, religion, manners, arts, convey,
> And spread their freedom to the Asian sea.
> Where erst six thousand suns have roll'd the year
> O'er plains of slaughter, and o'er wilds of fear,
> Towns, cities, fanes, shall lift their towery pride;
> The village bloom, on every streamlet's side;
> Proud Commerce' mole the western surges lave;
> The long, white spire lies imag'd on the wave;
> O'er morn's pellucid main expand their sails,
> And the starr'd ensign court Korean gales.

(Timothy Dwight, 1794)

Enthusiasm like this could not help but have its effect on a recalcitrant mythos. Despite—or perhaps even because of—their patently pragmatic motivation, so intoxicating did the ideological platitudes prove to be, that by the second quarter of the century even the city's literary image, for all its antipathetic conventional predispositions, began to show at least some signs of rehabilitation. As Stout points out, the "attitude most characteristic of [fiction of] the period seems to be a strong ambivalence inclining toward fear but open to the possibility that cities (...as in Cooper's late work *New York*) might represent opportunity for the nation as for the individual." This embryonic fictional reorientation toward a more positive city was only a pale reflection, moreover, of some of the contemporaneous cultural movements which, out in the *real* world, were working to dislodge the overt anti-urban prejudice from its long-established grip on the public mind.

One of the most critical developments in this regard comprised a kind of retrospective rationalization for the road already taken. Very soon after the Revolution, in response to all the burgeoning patriotic fervor—as might be expected in a country conditioned to the idea of holy mission—there was a strong drive to align sacred sanction with secular hopes. "The spread of religious awakenings after 1800 convinced clergymen in all parts of the country that the Spirit of the Lord was mightily at work, ushering in the millennium through the hallowing of America," says Timothy Smith. "This conviction sparked the movements for both foreign and home missions, and from 1815 onward sustained all sorts of moral crusades: peace, temperance, Sunday schools, public education, anti-slavery, and concern for the destitute." What is even more important than this generalized enthusiasm, however, was the fact that the religious revival of this time was very largely oriented toward the middle classes, the business and professional elite of the new nation, and the urban environment in which, by and large, they were increasingly based. Weekday bible-study groups for executives were not unusual. Charles Finney, one of the most famous of the evangelists who emerged during this period was, significantly enough, trained as a lawyer, and his ability—along with many of his colleagues—to combine common sense with the mystical, to reconcile the requirements of domestic security and religious duty, above all to legitimize the modern capitalist endeavor by sacralizing instead of condemning both its general aims and the style of life that it generated was eminently gratifying to the emotional needs of an increasingly urbanized and prosperous congregation. As Smith describes it, in fact, the whole bent of the evangelical movement clearly reveals that the spiritual leaders of America at this time "were fully committed to the democratic experiment in government and to the high value that capitalist society placed upon freedom of choice." One of the more notable results of this trend was to reclaim the city, emblem of the new capitalism, from its conventional associations with sin under the general aegis of a new "dream of a Christian society—one in which evangelism, education, social reform, and advancing democracy were all heralds of the approaching rule of Christ on earth" (Smith).

The avalanche of optimism did not, to be sure, sweep the nation entirely unopposed. There were always sceptics. Writing during the Revolutionary period, Tom Paine, for instance, though professing a commitment to progress in its most general sense, clearly recognized the more unsavory aspects of modern life. "Civilization," he said, "or that which is so called, has operated two ways: to make one part of society more affluent, and the other more wretched, than would have been the lot of either in a natural state." Benjamin Rush, similarly, challenged not merely the economic bases of civilization, but its effect on human morality as a whole. "I am not one of those modern philosophers, who derive the vices of mankind from the influence of civilization; but I am safe in asserting, that their number and malignancy increase with the refinements of polished life." In addition to merely sceptical views such as these, moreover, and providing an even greater check to the progressives, there emerged in the culture of the young republic a new and revitalized vision of nature which ironically enough developed side by side with the social enthusiasm noted above. Many factors too complex to explore at this point contributed to this movement, which Miller (1956) calls "a resurgence of the romantic heart against the enlightened head," but the overall result was that increasingly after the turn of the century a more coherent version of the garden threw its emotional weight into the battle against the values of the city. The Transcendentalists, especially Emerson and Thoreau, were naturally in the vanguard of this battle, but what is even more significant is the extent to which, by mid-century, the romanticized view of nature had become commonplace among politicians, historians, and even scientists. Edward Hitchcock, for instance, speaks in *The Religion of Geology and Its Connected Sciences* (1851) of "a world of mountains, bearing the impress of God's own hand" which seemed "to bring the soul into near community with the deity." The religion of nature was well on the way to becoming a cultural cliché.

The emergence of the Transcendentalist and other schools of Romantic thought in America did not, however, signal a resolution of the nature/society conflict in favor of nature, any more than the Puritan's attempt to suppress the positive side of the wilderness image meant that the potential of this image disappeared from the American scene. On the contrary, the nineteenth-century idealization of the landscape merely served to polarize the alternate responses a little more. As intimated above, America was already committed—in fact, if not in imaginative terms—to a program of national expansion and industrial development, and none but the most fanatic nature-lover, one suspects, would have been willing to sacrifice the comfort and prosperity—to say nothing of the patriotic pride—which this program had achieved for the country. George Catlin, in 1841, spoke of "the certain approach of this overwhelming system"— "this splendid Juggernaut," he calls it elsewhere—"which will inevitably march on and prosper." Schoolcraft, ten years later, added quite simply and firmly that "labor, law, and arts, must triumph, and they have triumphed in America as in Europe." As much as Emerson and Thoreau may have appealed to the American heart, it was men like these who came closer to the reality of the American mind.

If the garden could not be truly realized in nineteenth-century America, though, neither could it be forgotten. In spite of the fact that it was obviously not a *real* alternative for the nation, it was still part of the American myth (Americans need *two* homes, says Harbison: "a green one and a brown one, a grown one and a built one"), and if nothing else was responsible for the final shape assumed by many of the attitudes and assumptions which would come to dominate the modern era. One of the more amusing results of this phenomenon, as Perry Miller (1956) describes it, was the way the emotional stature of the garden forced proponents of progress into the most elaborately convoluted rationalizations for the values to which they were already committed—indeed, *impelled*—by the sheer weight of history.

[T]he astonishing fact about this gigantic material thrust of the early nineteenth century is how few Americans would...venture, aside from their boasts, to explain, let alone to justify, the expansion of civilization in any language that could remotely be called that of utility. The most utilitarian conquest known to history had somehow to be viewed not as inspired by a calculus of rising land values and investments, but (despite the orgies of speculation) as an immense exertion of the spirit. Those who made articulate the meaning of this drama found their frames of reference not in political economy but in Scott and Byron, in visions of "sublimity." The more rapidly, the more voraciously, the primordial forest was felled, the more desperately poets and painters—and also preachers—strove to identify the unique personality of this republic with..."romantic Nature."

The trend naturally affected attitudes towards the Indian. If only because of his conventional literary associations it was inevitable that under such circumstances he would at the very least begin to loom somewhat larger in the public imagination. The *kind* of attention he received during this period was, however, rarely as unequivocally positive as we might be led to expect by the increasing popularity of the primitivistic idiom. As always in America his vestigial subversiveness both focussing and reflecting the "officially" unspeakable aspects of communal experience, the nineteenth-century symbolic savage in fact came to embody the most ambiguous elements of post-Revolutionary thought. This latest version of the Indian, in other words, was— as always— a problem. Why? Because he was near to nature he had the potential for once to become a truly positive symbol, but at the same time, as David Levin points out in his study of the nineteenth-century philosophy of history, in the context of a camouflaged progressivist commitment this very nearness was embarrassing. "[L]acking the corrupt motives of George III and Parliament for opposing American progress, the Indian [still] stood squarely in the path of the English colonies, which were growing according to natural law. He was an incorrigible pagan. Nearer to Nature than the simple Greeks had been, he had almost nothing to show for his opportunity: no Homer, no 'gentle philosophers,' no simple architects and sculptors. He was deficient in the faculty of abstraction, and his knowledge of architecture [was] surpassed both in strength and durability by the skill of the beaver." There seemed to be no way around it. The Indian's primitivism just could not be reconciled with dreams of national advancement.

On the other hand, he could no longer simply be dismissed offhand either. For one thing, in association with the new romantic view of nature, he had acquired a kind of sanctity that could not be violated without upsetting the sensibilities of the age. This was the emotional problem. Beyond this, even on a purely intellectual level it seemed impossible to repudiate the Indian and what he represented without repudiating certain important corollaries to those same philosophical assumptions that helped to rationalize a theory of progress. We have already noted the internal inconsistencies in the philosophical background to the concept of primitivism as it was developed in Britain. The same inconsistencies, ironically enough, functioned inversely in America. Where in the former context they finally undermined the widely disseminated primitivistic sentiments to make room for new progressive ideas, now they threatened to undermine progress and lend inconvenient authority to primitivism. There seemed no way around it. The Indian had to be discredited: he was a nuisance, an obstacle. Unfortunately, because "natural goodness," besides supporting a concept of the noble savage, was also a necessary prerequisite for a theory of perfectibility which was a prerequisite for a theory of limitless progress, it was equally important, as Levin points out, that "Nature be relieved of responsibility for the Indian's failings." Pearce (1953) summarizes the dilemma faced by the American at this time:

> It was, in its simplest, most general terms, the problem of the relation of savage to civilized life. Savages were inextricably bound in what was to be called savagism. They might have a kind of good life in that state; for there were specifically savage virtues, natural virtues, even if there were not specifically noble savages. Yet one could not doubt that morality and virtue were everywhere essentially one and the same. How hold to a God-ordained moral absolute and to an assurance of common humanity, and still understand whatever good there might be in savage societies? How relate that good to the obviously greater good of civilized societies? How believe in two ideas of order? This was the special problem facing Americans who, from 1775 through the 1850s, tried to understand the Indians' place in American life.

The solution to this problem, as Pearce understands it, was found by combining a concept of cultural relativity with a theory of social evolution.

According to this view, different cultures could be considered "good" or "not so good" insofar as they allowed for "full realization of man's essential and absolute moral nature." Moreover, since "man realizes this nature as he progresses historically from a lesser to a greater good, from the simple to the complex, from savagism to civilization, [then] Westward American progress would...be understood to be reproducing this historical progression; and the savage would be understood as one who had not and somehow could not progress into the civilized, who would inevitably be destroyed by the civilized, the less good necessarily giving way to the greater" (Pearce). Bolstered by such "common sense" rationalizations as this, the American was enabled to believe that appropriation of Indian lands, removal, and even (regretfully, of course) the killing of recalcitrant natives were all fully justified—indeed, morally demanded—by the Grand Christian Idea of Progress as it might be (in Pearce's words) "conjectured back from empirical evidence" to God's own wishes.

One advantage of such a rationale was that it could easily be accommodated to the useful environmentalist views already popularized by such writers as Crèvecoeur. "Men are like plants," the latter says; "the goodness and flavour of the fruit proceeds from the peculiar soil and exposition in which they grow. We are nothing but what we derive from the air we breath, the climate we inhabit, the government we obey, the system of religion we profess, and the nature of our employment." Such a concept would support ideas as widely diverse as, for instance, the beliefs that eating wild meat leads to restlessness, that hot climates encourage "dissipation and pleasure," and that living near the sea, that "boisterous element," makes men more "bold and enterprising." It also, of course, lent itself to the salutary image of the sturdy farmer, drawing both virtue and sustenance from the earth he tills, and to the alternate—hopefully deterrent—vision of the irresponsible runaway degenerating in the wilderness.

More important to the developing idea of the savage, however, the environmentalist view allowed the proponents of progress to criticize specific elements of savage life without either suggesting that the savage was to *blame* for his unsavory customs or, in fact, having to attack the current sacred cow of primitivism as a general "idea" at all. This possibility would later invite such extremes as characterized the school of Schoolcraft (Zolla describes the latter's 1851 report as "a comprehensive and violent racist text" emphasizing unfairly the "static" and "infantile" aspects of Indian culture), but on the whole the writers who took advantage of the principle tended to be reassuringly moderate in their conclusions. "The Indian is essentially simple and undeveloped, living in an environment which demands that he concentrate all his energies on mere survival," says Robertson in his *History of America* (1777; summarized in Pearce, 1953). "He is 'naturally' independent. His passions are not as refined as they would be in a civilized society; rather they tend to the fierce and animal-like. He has little time or reason to think; his intellectual powers and attainments are few and limited." The impression to be gained from such statements was not particularly flattering to the subjects, but the tone of "scientific" objectivity ensured that the message would get through without unduly offending the romantic heart.

Counter to this, but equally usefully, environmentalism also supported the conscience-salving doctrine that the savage, thrust out of his traditional lands, would actually benefit in the long run from the civilizing influence of Christian culture. This comfortable view, as we have already noted, was a favorite of Jefferson's. In it, he often seemed to imply, would be found the solution to all Indian problems forever: assimilation. "When once you have property, you will want laws and magistrates to protect your property and persons, and to punish those among you who commit crimes," he told an Indian audience in 1808. "You will find that our laws are good for this purpose; you will wish to live under them, you will unite yourselves with us, and we shall all be Americans; you will mix with us by marriage, your blood will run in our veins, and will spread over this great island." Considering the current views of miscegenation, Jefferson's projection of ideal futurity was obviously a fantasy. This did not, however, prevent many post-Revolutionary romantic-progressives from using it to indulge vicariously their mutually exclusive cultural goals.

This brings us back to the more emotional aspects of the city/garden debate. Another advantageous corollary to the emerging theory of savagism was the fact that under the umbrella of cultural relativity it could accommodate a free and even enthusiastic discussion of savage virtues *without* allowing a toehold to creeping primitivism. The Indian could be admired for his "devotion to freedom and independence;...perseverence, dignity, and implacability; heroism and bravery in war; and...devotion to the tribe." His "celebrated eloquence," especially, could be acclaimed as "evidence of a kind of 'original genius' forever lost to high civilization" (Pearce, 1953). No matter how gratifying these ideas might seem to the romantic, however, they did not, and could not, contradict the basic assumption that the Indian's virtues were still specifically savage virtues, and as such inevitably inferior to civilized ones. There was, in fact, no real basis of comparison at all. Although the savage could be praised in terms of his *own* context, cross-references between cultures, as Pearce makes clear, were totally invalid because they would necessarily imply equality:

[J]udgment of the savage as being noble or ignoble is precluded. Savage life and civilized life are realms apart, separated by centuries of cultural history, or by entirely different environmental situations, most likely by both. Hence what is good for a savage is not necessarily good for a civilized man. The ideals of a savage society are built around the hunt and warfare; and its members can develop no further, no higher than their life will let them... The Indian is not a beast because he treats his women as he does; our saying that he is, is tantamount to our judging behavior in a savage society in terms of behavior in a civilized society. [On the other hand,] Even as what seem to us to be the Indian's inferior traits are the products of his immature and inhibited society, so are his superior traits. American writers noted again and again that the Indian's ability to bear tremendous physical pain stoically makes him neither better nor worse than the civilized man, but rather is simply a characteristic result of the natural ideals and aims of a warrior-dominated society... Savage virtues... like savage vices, are uniquely savage.

The end result of this relativism was to deflate the authority of "Indianness" even as it exculpated the Indian. In the early nineteenth century, as Louise Barnett points out, "all fictive Indians are fine physical specimens, proficient in wilderness skills, stoical, and given to figurative speech" *but* "none of these characteristics are moral, according to the special white formulation of good and bad for Indians."

For all its apparent new liberality, then, contemporary philosophy actually provided a built-in curb on the incipient more romanticized view of the Indian that began to emerge after the Revolution. Savagism was not, moreover, the *only* defense against the incursions of romantic sentiment at the disposal of the nineteenth-century pragmatist. An even more effective means of controlling the poetic-philosophic movement back to nature was the appearance in the latter part of the eighteenth century of a new symbolic version of *the* American. This figure, capable of deflecting and indulging all the primitivistic fantasies that might otherwise have collected around the Indian, was (in complete contradistinction to the eighteenth-century ideal) the frontier hero prototypically represented by Daniel Boone. Numerous critics have discussed Boone's significance as a cultural symbol, most notably Henry Nash Smith in his excellent study *Virgin Land: The American West as Symbol and Myth*. Some, like R.W.B. Lewis, have even gone so far as to claim that the Adamic role which, by and large, the Boone-figure fills is *the* symbolic correlative of American experience as a whole. Rather than making any detailed examination of his antecedents and incarnations, therefore, we will merely note here the extent to which the frontiersman, like the captive and the farmer of earlier phases, was popular primarily because he appeared to offer a resolution (aesthetic if not actual) of the emotional ambiguities most likely to emerge from the clash between the social realities and the psychological profile characteristic of the period.

We have identified the focal issue of post-Revolutionary America as the antithesis between the garden and the city. We have also pointed out the referents that gave such a considerable emotional weight to each of the alternatives, often at the same time. The backwoodsman, as unlikely as it may seem, somehow came to represent *both* in the American imagination. Boone, for instance, was acclaimed by contemporary writers variously as "the standard-bearer of civilization and refinement" and "the child of nature who fled into the wilderness before the advance of settlement" (Nash Smith). Obviously he could not have been both purveyor of and fugitive from the American progress westward, but a survey of biographical and quasi-biographical material indicates clearly how determined the public was not to relinquish either image.

The Boone-figure, in fact, like the noble savage in his British heyday, was forced by sheer public pressure to serve a wide variety of psycho-symbolic functions. Between 1800 and 1845, according to Slotkin, numerous distinct versions of the frontiersman emerged in different parts of the country, each answering to a different aspect of public needs. The west, for instance, gave birth to Davy Crockett, "who embodied the western ambition for self-improvement and the attainment of equality (equated with economic prosperity) and whose career reflected the concept of economics and politics as a hunt, in which he who bags the most and biggest prey is the best man." The west, however, Slotkin continues, "also developed the almost mystical image of the hunter delineated by Flint, as a myth-hero whose deeds of violence and destruction are deeds of love that lead him to a marriage with the wilderness." Slotkin's unravelling of the multiple strands of this legend makes fascinating reading. The main point, though, is that it was specifically the Protean capacity of the symbolic backwoodsman that made him such an effective vehicle for the essential ambiguousness of the American response during that period. Not only did the figure imply "a certain myth-scenario of interaction between themselves, their land, and the dark races belonging to their land," as Slotkin says, but it actually coalesced numerous different and even antithetical versions of that myth. The backwoodsman came variously to symbolize union with nature, primitive simplicity, democracy, unrestricted freedom, and so on *ad infinitum*, seeming to exemplify all those qualities that the American most wanted to emulate and/or indulge.

The fact that this view was a long way from reality was irrelevant, of course, but it is worth noticing the extent of the discrepancy. Arthur Moore's discussion of frontier life in all its crudeness and brutality (see section 3.3. below) represents only one side of the picture: even crudeness, from one angle of vision, could be rationalized according to the primitivist manifesto. What was—or should have been—much more disillusioning than those features that *separated* the frontiersman from the easterners, even though they might be negative distinctions, was the degree of *sameness* that would emerge at closer sight. As Samuel Goetzman explains it in his study of the Jacksonian Mountain Man, they "may have dreamed of 'Arcadia,' but when they turned to the task of settling the west as fast as possible, the former Mountain Men...brought with them all the aspects of an 'industrial,' mercantile and quasi-urban society. The opera house went up simultaneously with the ranch, and the Bank of Missouri was secured before the land was properly put into hay." Hardly a picture of glamorous eccentricity! Despite this, the myth remained untarnished. The Boone-figure was so successful in reconciling all the anomalies—the incompatible fantasies and the humdrum realities both—associated with his multiple role that he survived as a primary culture symbol well past the middle of the nineteenth century. Some of the ideas associated with him, in fact— like the regenerative effect of the frontier and the wilderness roots of democracy— not only persisted into the twentieth century but, under the auspices of such historians as Frederick Jackson Turner, became almost wholly institutionalized; part of the American's most cherished beliefs about himself and his country.

One point to note: this is the first period in which the representative type is not defined primarily in opposition to the Indian. In some aspects the frontiersman did, it is true, resemble the traditional Indian-fighter, and as such tended to perpetuate the satanic image. In another, more important sense, however, he could be seen as actually *competing* with the native as an image of primitivism. The Boone figure was, in fact, a kind of noble savage himself. Does this mean that the real savage had been superannuated, in effect, as a meaningful literary figure? The early nineteenth century in Europe saw the virtual death of the convention. Was this trend, like so many others, finally emulated—albeit slowly, and in a typical watered-down form—by the American literati of the period? Was the transfer of primitivistic fantasies to the white frontiersman a sign that the savage was about to be civilized into oblivion? Surprisingly enough, no. In fact, by diverting some of the more ambiguous aspects of noble savagery, the frontiersman may have helped ensure that the American Indian would not, or at least not immediately, become—like the European noble savage—such a trivialized and absurdly broad symbol that it would collapse under its own weight. Instead it was the Boone-figure himself who "collapsed."

This is not to imply that the symbolic frontiersman *disappeared*, of course. We have already mentioned his persistence in American culture. His emphasis changed, however, to the extent that he could only be seen as fully primitivistic by a considerable act of imagination. Although he continued to exhibit many of the external characteristics of the noble savage, and was still *formally* comprehended in this role, the attribution was, in fact, beyond a certain point meaningless. On the one hand, his function came to be increasingly that of a conventional pastoral mediator. Like Cooper's Leatherstocking (see section 3.4. below), his opposition to the city tended to be moral and instructive—relative—rather than absolute. In most cases, in fact, he seemed clearly subservient to progress. On the other hand, and partly because of this last transformation, he could no longer be seen as a "really" primitive figure. He had been tainted. Indeed, by the nineteenth century he had become almost a symbol *of* progress— at best a national idol like our retrospective Abe Lincoln, emerging from his log cabin to dedicate his frontier-bred skills and virtues to the service of the country; at worst, like a Walt Disney version of Davy Crockett, the epitome of the self-made man acting out the archetypal American success story.

What did all this mean with respect to the Indian? For one thing, as mentioned above, the popularity of his competitor may actually have helped preserve his mystique. The fact is—if we may jump ahead of the argument for a minute—by the time the neo-primitivist fad, aided and abetted by the upsurge in post-Revolutionary boosterism, would finally gather enough momentum to usher in a new and more critical stage in America's love/hate affair with the natural environment, the Daniel Boone-figure, to the detriment of his emotional authority, would already have lost most of his essential symbolic ties with nature. The symbolic associations of savagery, on the other hand, while hardly unequivocal, would still carry enough residual numen to make the native a potentially powerful literary icon. But more of this later. In the meantime we might merely note that the diffusing effect of the alternative vision tended to render the image of the Indian a peculiarly unstable one. During the period characterized by the garden/city antithesis as we have outlined it here—from the Revolution, that is, with diminishing intensity for the first half of the nineteenth century (at which time both garden *and* city symbols in some sense broke free of the traditional linkage to become enshrined as separate, inversely-authoritative but seemingly coeternal, emblematic expressions of different currents of American culture)—views of the Indian in fact varied as widely as the theory of savagism would permit. Sometimes he was set forth in primarily positive terms; at other times the brutal beast or demonic adversary of the Puritans reappeared.

The most popular fictional formulas of the day, according to Barnett, were updated and conventionalized versions of either the captivity story (now focusing more on the *rescue* of the captive heroine by the hero than on the ordeal itself) or the bloody saga of the Indian fighter *à la* Judge James Hall, but in spite of the negative implications of these vehicles most writers tended to mix *both* versions of the savage indiscriminately according to the logical or rhetorical needs of the moment. Even villains had by this time lost the wild man's physical repulsiveness. Indeed, as Barnett says, "If imposing physical attributes alone made a noble savage, few Indians in frontier romances would fail to qualify." As a result it is often hard to distinguish between pro-Indian and anti-Indian treatments, at least on the basis of style. The same holds to a large extent in non-fictional works as well. The historians Bancroft and Parkman, for instance, are popularly supposed to have presented antithetical views of the natives, the former romantic and the latter sceptical. Levin, however, examining the texts themselves, soon discredits the suggestion that their attitudes were either as simple or as consistent as this opinion might imply. "It is well known," he says,

> that Parkman, relying on his own experience of western Indians, set out to prove that the Indian was no fit subject for the romances in which some nineteenth-century fiction and poetry had cast him. But the difference between Parkman's attitude and that of other writers has been exaggerated. Even Bancroft's most laudatory language shows agreement with Parkman's contention that the Indian race was inferior. And Bancroft also used extremely uncomplimentary rhetoric when he described the Indian as an ally of reaction....
>
> The difference between Parkman's and Bancroft's treatment of the Indian is a difference of degree.

The early nineteenth-century literary Indian was thus on the whole a contradictory, almost motley figure. Still largely negative, he had at least one characteristic in common with the British noble savage. He became, in Fairchild's words, "a convenient example of whatever a writer may wish to prove."

For all his inhomogeneity, there are, on the other hand, at least a few relatively consistent attributes acquired by the savage during this period that should be at least mentioned here, since they are associated with the more complex role which was already making its first appearances on the American scene. In the first place, under the influence of a scientific theory of environmentalism, the Indian became more closely identified with "nature" than ever before. This meant that he would become increasingly understood in traditional primitivistic terms of "harmony" with his environment. At the same time, because nature, even in America, had by now been energized by both the aesthetic theories of the eighteenth century and the pantheistic tendencies of moderate (Wordsworth rather than Shelley) Romanticism, this relationship took on a stylized, almost emblematic quality. The two facets coalesced before mid-century to reinject the idea of savagery with at least some of the glamor it had shed when the wilderness reluctantly yielded up its terrors to burgeoning Yankee pragmatism. Did this also reinvest the Indian with his mythic authority? Yes and no. There was in fact one further development during this period that added an ironic twist to the newly intensified symbolic association between the savage and his setting. Paralleling the evolution of explicit public opinion that we have traced here, between the seventeenth and the nineteenth centuries the *covert* aspect of American attitudes towards nature also underwent a radical transformation. "For Bradford and Mather," says Slotkin, "the wilderness is the proto-renegade's 'strange bride' or a male captor-violator of female avatars of Christian culture. For Edwards nature is the male thunder god or the sweet spirit that murmurs to Sarah Pierrepont as she walks amid 'groves and fields.' " For Boone, the post-Revolutionary man, however, "the spirit of nature" is simply and unambiguously feminine, "and his relation to it is that of panther to deer, hunter to prey, sexual aggressor to coy, amenable victim." This observation—leaving aside the question of whether the victim in the long run was so much "amenable" as merely helpless—provides an interesting backdrop to President Jackson's Second Annual Message to the Nation in 1830:

> Humanity has often wept over the fate of the aborigines of this country, and Philanthropy has been long busily employed in devising means to avert it, but its progress has never for a moment been arrested, and one by one have many powerful tribes disappeared from the earth. To follow to the tomb the last of his race and to tread on the graves of extinct nations excite melancholy reflections. But true philanthropy reconciles the mind to these vicissitudes as it does to the extinction of one generation to make room for another... Philanthropy could not wish to see this continent restored to the condition in which it was found by our forefathers. What good man would prefer a country covered with forests and ranged by a few thousand savages to our extensive Republic, studded with cities, towns, and prosperous farms, embellished with all the improvements which art can devise or industry execute, occupied by more than 12,000 happy people, and filled with all the blessings of liberty, civilization, and religion?
>
> The present policy of the Government is but a continuation of the same progressive change by a milder process.

3.2 The Positive Response

In spite of the numerous reasons, physical and psychological, why negative versions would dominate the American imagination right up to the nineteenth century, positive images were never entirely eliminated from the overall public response. The emotional bias of the Puritans was closely related to the peculiarities of the Calvinist world-view. Starting with a different set of assumptions, even in the same inhospitable environment, it was quite possible to adopt an entirely different stance with respect to Indians. Thomas Morton, for instance, the black sheep of the Plymouth colony, was expelled from New England largely because of his intimacy with the natives. His settlement not only "traded with them, avoiding Plymouth regulations, [but] consorted and slept with them, violating Plymouth morality" (Slotkin).

The great divergence in attitude was possible only because of a total difference in orientation. "Where the Puritan saw the New World as a desert wilderness, like that through which Bunyan's Pilgrim travels, Morton," Slotkin tells us, "saw it as a new Arcadia, a land rich in the promise of spiritual and erotic fulfillment and renewal." Morton conceived this promise, moreover, in "overtly pagan terms... His metaphors are pagan-classical rather than spiritual... He [was] infinitely more attracted by the 'Canaanites' [as he calls them] than to the self-appointed 'Israelites' of New Plymouth." He was thus able to view the primitive Indians as "emblems of the innocent childhood of man." Clearly, then, if one were free from the religious predispositions that accentuated the alien aspect of the wilderness, the European image of the noble savage could continue to provide a symbolic correlative for certain aspects of experience.

Assorting oddly with the irreligious Morton, there was in addition at least one of the early Protestant sects whose basic assumptions encouraged an image of "good" if not noble savages. As Pearce describes it in his commentary in *Colonial American Writing*, the Quakers differed from the Puritans not in kind but merely in degree. It was a critical difference nonetheless. Bringing to its full potential the pietistic, almost neoplatonic potential in Protestantism, Quaker creed emphasized above all the possibility of "individual contact with divinity and...the faculty which was the means of that contact...the 'Inner Light.' " Quaker psychology, in other words, owed a considerable debt to the primitivistic doctrine of natural goodness. It is thus hardly surprising that the typical Quaker view of the Indian should tend to be very similar to that early British view which projected the savage primarily as simple, innocent, and childlike. The Quakers in America lived too close to the Indians to be totally blind to the more unsavory aspects of their lifestyle, but the general tone of their response was set by William Penn as early as 1683:

> [I]n Liberality they excell, nothing is too good for their friend; give them a fine Gun, Coat, or other thing, it may pass twenty hands, before it sticks; light of Heart, strong Affections, but soon spent; the most merry Creatures that live, Feast and Dance perpetually; they never have much, nor want much...and the Reason is, a little contents them: In this they are sufficiently revenged on us; if they are ignorant of our Pleasures, they are also free from our Pains.

The echo of Montaigne is quite noticeable here, overlaid with a mildly affectionate, almost paternal, indulgence.

Note that word "affectionate," though. Whatever we said above about differences of degree, here we hit on something that places the positive response in an entirely different category than the negative one. The Puritans were not merely mildly antipathetic, but almost hysterically hostile toward the Indians. Doctrinal factors notwithstanding, the reason for this considerable contrast in emotional component almost certainly has to do with the psychological, rather than the purely religious aspects of the situation. Or the purely intellectual. What we would seem to have on the surface is simply a divergence in preconception based on two different views of human nature. As Slotkin puts it, the "proponents of the good savage theory saw [the] hidden self as inherently good in its motivating principles and were willing to trust its expression when its passion had been curbed a bit by intellect. The proponents of the degeneracy theory regarded the intellect as weak in comparison with the forces of the hidden mind, which they considered the dark side of human nature, the source of its bestiality." Below the surface is a less rational stratum, however. The image of an internal threat is a disturbing one—especially for a people obsessed with a sense of unremitting spiritual danger. If one may find plenty of explanation for divergent *opinions* in the simple, obvious antithesis between exemplar and object lesson, when the Indian is seen as epitomizing not merely bestiality but an all too natural kind of human degradation there is also a concomitant fear of contamination. In the long run it was the fear, not the intellectual disagreement, which was responsible for the significant difference in emotional intensity between the positive and the negative views.

A similar element may have exerted a crucial influence in forming the distinctive attitudes of yet another group, the southerners. The fact that the typical Virginia gentleman was far less of a religious extremist with his aristocratic terms of reference and his neoclassical education certainly had *some* relevance to the fact that his image of the wilderness was less hag-ridden than the Puritan's, but it would be a mistake to overestimate the difference between their basic world views. If the Puritan was an extreme of one sort, Morton and the Quakers were no more representative of the general seventeenth-century religious ambience, and whatever part economic motives played in the settlement of Virginia, it should not be forgotten that even here the mercenary aspects of the venture were, at least "officially," subsidiary to the idea of a divine mission to civilize the New World. The Letters of Patent issued in 1606 for the colonizing of the area was, for instance, phrased in terms that the Puritans would both understand and applaud. In this document the King urged the furtherance of a work "which may, by the Providence of Almighty God, hereafter tend to the Glory of His Divine Majesty, in propagating of Christian Religion to such people, as yet live in darkness, and miserable ignorance of the true knowledge and worship of God, and may in time bring the Infidels and Savages living in those parts, to human civility and to a settled and quiet Government." The difference in basic assumptions was clearly, therefore, far less extreme than has retrospectively been supposed.

It can hardly be denied, on the other hand, that there was *in fact* a great contrast between the images of the Indian produced by the two groups. William Byrd, for instance, described the natives as "tall and well-proportion'd...Healthy & Strong, with Constitutions untainted by Lewdness, and not enfeebled by Luxury." Nor is this the "good but inferior" viewpoint developed later under the auspices of eighteenth-century cultural relativity. "Morals and all considered," he continues, "I can't think the Indians were much greater heathens than the first Adventurers." Elsewhere, to reinforce the comparison, he says of Christian colonists that they "were always engaged in Factions and Quarrels, [and] detested Work more than Famine." For this southerner at least, then, the Indian was not merely tolerable, but represented the kind of positive norm legitimized by classical literary primitivism.

What are we to make of this? If Byrd may be considered as typical at all, the gap between New England and Virginian viewpoints was obviously considerable. Even allowing for a diminution if not a dissipation of religious influence, a question must arise as to the reasons for such a marked divergence. At least part of the difference in response may perhaps be attributed to the contrast in climate. We have already examined the way the inhospitable New England winter and the barren, savage environs symbolically reinforced certain predispositions in the Puritan psychology. In Virginia, on the contrary, the answering echo found in the landscape invited another response entirely. In Virginia, in fact, the garden metaphor utilized by the early explorers *continued* to offer an imaginatively viable image of experience even at the same time as it was being replaced in New England by the wilderness. This did not mean that the southern response was entirely positive, of course. The garden, as we have seen, has two potential meanings. Neither of them, though—and this is the key point—invited the *fear* which was such a characteristic aspect of the Puritan reaction. Even the fact that the *physical* danger presented by the Indians' warlike propensities was greater, if anything, among the notoriously ferocious southeastern tribes than in the north was less intimidating here since the danger could be viewed as purely and manageably *human*, rather than supernatural. For a period of approximately fifty years following a massacre in 1622 that wiped out more than a third of the Virginia settlement the Indians were painted in purely negative terms, but, as Gary Nash points out, this reaction was quite understandable not merely in a psychological sense but also (as was at least a partial factor in the Puritans' more uniformly violent reaction) with respect to the pragmatic political necessities of the time: "This vocabulary of abuse reflects not only the rage of the decimated colony but an inner need to provide a justification for colonial policy for generations to come. Hereafter, the elimination of the Indians could be rationalized far more easily, for they were seen as vicious, cultureless, unreconstructable savages rather than merely as hostile and primitive men." Outside of—and even (relative to the Puritans) to some extent during—this particular episode, however, whether he was inclined to bemoan the seductiveness of the climate as an invitation to sloth and social instability, or whether, like Byrd, he frankly enjoyed its garden-like atmosphere, the Virginian's views were typically more *reasonable.*

If moderation was the keynote of the southern response, it must be remembered that this works both ways, compromising not just negative views but positive ones as well. Even Byrd's enthusiasm can easily be overstated. If the conventional noble savage appears in the pages of his book as an agreeable contrast with the lazy settlers, we are also given less salubrious glimpses of an "uncleanly People" whose skins were so crusted with "Winter's Soil" and "Bear's oyl" that "it requir'd a very strong appetite to approach them." And his recommendation that the colonists emulate the French in intermarrying with the natives was less symptomatic of an infatuation for the noble savage than based on his intuition for the politically advantageous gesture. Such a policy would be advisable, he said, first because it would offer the best means of "Converting these poor Infidels, and reclaiming them from barbarity"; second, as an encouragement to population growth; and thirdly (perhaps most importantly), because the Indians "would have less reason to Complain that the English took away their Land, if they had received it by way of Portion with their Daughters." On the other hand, if the southern responses tended to be more pragmatic than idealized, their images of the Indian were still considerably more attractive than those favored by the Puritans.

More than merely intrinsically interesting, these early responses forecast later developments in the symbolic savage's American career. Indeed, the several groups we have used to illustrate the varying influences counterbalancing the negative Puritan viewpoint collectively elucidate almost all the factors responsible for the generalized decrease in hostility towards the Indian which was discernible throughout the eighteenth century. On the one hand, as we might have expected, the process of secularization with its concomitant optimism and more encouraging view of human nature removed a great deal of the mythic stigma projected onto the savage by Calvinist concepts of degeneracy. On the other hand, after the various conditions responsible for the colonists' fear of the Indians were removed, the foundation was laid for a more objective assessment.

The most important of these "conditions" involved the degree to which the Indians were perceived as an actual physical threat to life and property at a given time. By the late eighteenth century the northern colonies had largely eradicated any real danger from this source by force, literally decimating some tribes in the process. The frontier in this part of the country had thus been pushed well to the west, and the Indian problems with it. In the less heavily populated regions to the south (even before the policy of forced removal was inaugurated under Jackson), the major tribes—the remnants of them that survived the early campaigns of extermination, the disease, and the cultural degeneration subsequent to the white man's influence—had been assimilated to an extent that may now seem surprising. The view of the Indian as uncivilizable which was such an intrinsic part of nineteenth-century political rationale has been widely promulgated by popular culture but, in fact, as LaFarge tells us, the "southern tribes radically changed their costume, and quickly took over cattle, slaves, and many arts. By the [early nineteenth century]...the Cherokees had a stable government under a written constitution, with a bicameral parliament, an alphabet for writing their language, printing presses, a newspaper, schools, and churches." The Indians here thus not only came to *seem* more "normal" in terms of white lifestyles but, acculturalized, actually *were* far less dangerous. Only in the western regions, where the aborigines still presented a very real danger to the white settlers, did images of the Indian in local literature continue to be both negative and extreme. Even here, however, white numbers, weaponry, and fighting expertise made the settlers feel far less vulnerable than the isolated early colonists had been, which made their response less hysterical in turn. In general, therefore, the Indians were no longer widely viewed as presenting much of a threat to the Americans, and the white response was consequently much more reasonable as a whole.

At the same time as the physical danger was lessening, the psychological threat was also diminished by the public's growing sense of familiarity with the wilderness and its inhabitants. "Because the social context of Indian-white relations was changing," says Nash, "the white community was far better disposed emotionally to see the Indians as another cultural group rather than simply as the enemy." As a result, from the middle of the eighteenth century such an enormous volume of travel literature, histories, and semi-scientific reports was published in related areas that by 1850 the Indian had lost most of his threatening aura of strangeness. John Bartram's *Observations* (1751); Jonathan Carver's *Travels Through the Interior* (1778); John Filson's *Kentucke* (1784); the Lewis and Clarke Expedition in the early nineteenth century; Henry M. Brackenridge's *Views of Louisiana* (1817); Edmund Dana's *Geographical Sketches* (1819); the expeditions of William Ashley and Jedediah Smith in the 1820s; Timothy Flint's *History and Geography of the Mississippi Valley* (1833); Irving's *Astoria* (1836); Thomas J. Farnham's *Travels in the Great Western Prairie* (1841); Josiah Gregg's *Commerce of the Prairies* (1844); Francis Parkman's *Oregon Trail* (1849); and George Bancroft's *History* (1834-76), to mention only a few, provided an abundance of support for the demythicization process. Admittedly, these sources as a group are far from demonstrating an unequivocally positive attitude toward the Indian. Indeed, though they do cover a wide spectrum of views, Brackenridge's conclusion that the "savage state, like the rude uncultivated waste, is contemplated to most advantage from a distance," is far more representative than William Bartram's Quaker sympathy. By denuding the savage of his fearful mystery, however, they cumulatively removed one of the greatest obstacles to his (at least symbolic) rehabilitation.

By the time the romantic impulse reached full bloom in America (several decades later than its popular peak to England), enough of the stigma had thus been removed from the Indian to make him a fit object for a moderate swing toward primitivism. Now that the conflict of cultures had been safely resolved by the virtual extermination of the red one there was time for what Slotkin calls "the reconciliation of the hunter and his prey—a flash of sympathy and fellow feeling that caps the climactic moment when the long hunt ends and the kill is achieved." More specifically, "With the gradual vanishing of the Indian population east of the Appalachians, it became possible to romanticize the Indian as a noble savage and to employ him as a symbol of American libertarianism and independent patriotism." Of course, as Slotkin himself adds, this "romantic tendency did not in any substantive way alter the policy of the nation...nor did it alter the fundamental conviction...that the Indians were a race doomed by constitutional and institutional weaknesses to diminution, assimilation, extinction, and replacement by the civilization of the whites. In literary terms, however, it became possible...like Cooper to [show the Indian as]...upright, moral, proud, and occasionally aristocratic."

Once the ground was laid, this new image quickly began to challenge (if hardly to supplant) the older, xenophobic conventions on a surprisingly broad front. Pragmatic realities notwithstanding, the literati were not the only ones who rallied to the bedside of the almost forgotten noble savage during this period. Indeed, as soon as the great American public considered itself safe from all the various threats that the Indian had formerly embodied as a social reality, the movement to rehabilitate him as a symbol became both fashionable and respectable too. Scientists, historians, politicians all hastened to espouse the popular cause. As early as 1790, for instance, Jedediah Morse in an essay on Indians in the *Encyclopedia* defended the natives vehemently against charges of being "perfidious, stupid, vain, effeminate, or in any way degenerate." "Such partial and detached views," he said, "were they even free from misrepresentation, are not the just grounds upon which to form an estimate of their character, their qualities good and bad (for they certainly possess both), and their way of life. The state of society among them, with all the circumstances of their condition, ought to be considered in connection, and in regard to their mutual influences." Here again is that cultural relativity we noted earlier, but whereas our previous focus was the extent to which the theory of savagery inevitably truncated attempts to present primitivism in the person of the Indian as any sort of *ultimate* standard, we now see clearly the other side of the coin: the provision of an orthodox vehicle for indulging the newly awakened *desire* to see the savage, in some terms at least, as noble again. In ironic contrast to the "official" policy cited by Slotkin, it was this desire which came increasingly throughout the first decades of the nineteenth century to set the tone for popular as well as literary views of the Indian.

We must not, on the other hand, overstate this trend. For all his undeniable appeal, the new American noble savage was not without considerable component ambiguity. Even leaving aside the coterminous negative tradition discussed in the previous section, the American experience had made it impossible for the Rousseauistic vision to be accommodated easily no matter how much the increasingly buoyant mood of the country may have inclined writers to do so. The transition from vituperation to celebration, in other words, was neither as sudden nor as smooth as the above outline might imply. Old habits die hard. Philip Freneau, often identified as the first American Romantic, provides a striking illustration of the lingering discomfort which even the most ardent proponents of sentimental primitivism were prone, in their unguarded moments, to reveal.

Freneau has been widely misunderstood by critics, and the "Romantic" label in itself is perhaps the major source of this difficulty. The reader, expecting the characteristics of a different tradition, may easily be led to read things into his work that are not really there. Albert Keiser, for instance, remarking (with apparent approval) that the "student of Freneau's Indian poems [will be] struck by the fact that the attitude of the poet is both romantic and realistic," attributes Freneau's vitality to that same dynamic tension between the ideal and the real with which critics have been apt to "explain" such writers as Crèvecoeur. "He looks upon the native as predominantly nature's nobleman, exhibiting all the qualities with which travellers and romancers were wont to invest the lord of the forest... When[, however,] in the Indian death songs [he] expresses the 'savage notions and romantic heroism' so 'horrible to the imagination,' the transition to realism has been made." Is this, though, an adequate analysis? Certainly it cannot simply be dismissed out of hand. Whether the two voices are as distinct as Keiser implies may be debated, but in a few places at least there *does* seem to be a doubleness in Freneau's apparent attitude toward the Indian that makes one wonder whether he is totally in control of his material. This, of course, is the problem. Even leaving aside the question of whether the resulting tension is an aesthetically pleasing one, there is ample evidence that the double vision invoked by Keiser, far from a literary strategy, relates primarily to an unresolved conflict in the writer's own mind. Indeed we might go so far as to say that the shift in tone has nothing whatsoever to do with a clash between Romanticism and realism; the active ingredients diagnostic of such a clash are simply not present in this case. The fact is, being almost wholly in the eighteenth-century tradition of Thompson through Gray, Freneau is Romantic only in the most vestigial sense. As for reality, his model is obviously not nature but art. So where does the "tension" come from? As with Crèvecoeur, if we look closely we will realize that those hints of ambivalence on which Keiser focuses owe much less to the juxtaposition of self-consciously "literary" material with a more naturalistic perspective than to the shadow of that other, less felicitous though no more realistic version of the savage which had been integrated into the American's symbolic vocabulary long before. Identifying the source of the discrepancy does not, admittedly, excuse the poet's apparent lack of critical awareness, but, in the light of the underlying anxieties that we have explored in the preceding sections, it does make his evasiveness—his fuzzyminded attempt, as Annette Kolodny describes it, to "preserve both competing landscapes...[by imposing] the identical pastoral labels on pioneers, farmers, and Indians alike"—somewhat more understandable.

The problem of control becomes even more pronounced in *Tomo-Cheeki, the Creek Indian in Philadelphia* (1790-95). Like Goldsmith's Lien-Chi-Altangi, the title figure of this book was intended to function primarily as a conventional vehicle for social criticism: the device, as Pearce (1953) describes it, of "a simple and wise foreign visitor who was at once critic of the bad society and standard for the good." Again his basic model owes more of a debt to the neo-classical or even the Renaissance pastoral tradition than to contemporary Romanticism. Unlike Goldsmith's urbane sage, however, Freneau's noble savage turns out to be disconcertingly more savage than noble. As Kolodny sees it, for Freneau, "the Indian *persona* provided a way of expressing what later became the religious and philosophical mediator between the world he had hoped for and the one he knew," and certainly this is the way the poet would have liked to see his conventional creation operating. On the basis of the text itself, however, we would have to deny that he succeeded in this conciliatory aim. Neither as remote from primitive nature as the eighteenth-century poet nor as immersed in it as the true Romantic, Freneau "found that he could not go all the way and posit an Indian society to which whites should go to school" (Pearce). Unfortunately, Freneau also refused to relinquish his sentimental attachment to primitivism. The result is an odd and uneven book where an ignoble savage is forced to play the symbolic role conventionally associated with a noble one.

The reassimilation of the noble savage into the American popular pantheon was not, then, accomplished without problems. What is important to note for present purposes, though, is that it *was* accomplished. In the end, as we might have predicted, the power of the popular imagination did prove equal to the power of the now unpopular misgivings. Writing only a couple of decades after Freneau, Washington Irving, for instance, would seem to have repressed or rationalized almost every trace of ambiguity that lingered along the underside of America's new primitivist fantasy. *The Sketchbook of Geoffrey Crayon* (1819-20) in fact stands as a kind of landmark. Although this collection still offers the usual token gesture of recognition to the native's negative qualities, particularly his lack of aptitude for the sort of virtuous delicacy and gentility which was the mark of civilization, the author's primary and avowed concern here is a sentimental vindication of the Indian: a discovery of the appealing human emotions hidden beneath his stoical facade; a defense of his retaliation against the whites for their profanation of his sacred burial grounds; an exoneration of his purported cruelty and barbarity; an indignant indictment of the treatment he had all too often received at the hands of the American settlers. Going even further than general apologetics, moreover, the essay "Philip of Pohanoket" presents King Philip as a recognizable if not wholly stereotypic variant of the noble savage standardized in the eighteenth century as a primary moral referent. Here, indeed—*despite* his uncharacteristic violence and warlike nature (the traditional noble savage, you will recall, was supposed to be simple and innocent)—is the noble savage that Freneau failed to grasp. Irving did not hesitate to take full advantage of the conventional associations either, using the Indian, far more successfully than Freneau, as an explicit foil to set off the flaws of civilization:

> In civilized life, where the happiness, and indeed almost the existence, of man depends so much upon the opinion of his fellow-men, he is constantly acting a studied part. The bold and peculiar traits of native character are refined away or softened down by the levelling influence of what is termed good breeding; and he practices so many petty deceptions and affects so many generous sentiments for the purposes of popularity that it is difficult to distinguish his real from his artificial character. The Indian, on the contrary, free from the restraints and refinements of polished life, and, in a great degree, a solitary and independent being, obeys the impulses of his inclination or the dictates of his judgment, and thus the attributes of his nature, being freely indulged, grow singly great and striking.

A Tour of the Prairies (1835) and *Astoria* (1836) commemorated Irving's experience on actual expeditions among the Indians, so one might expect them to be more realistic. The truth is, however, that despite the considerable amount of data he collected, and even in spite of his surprisingly acute capacity for factual observation, Irving's *interpretations* of his experience were strongly colored by his emotional bias. As Zolla says, "Irving does not change the ideas expressed in *The Sketch Book*. As always, experience does not modify the ideal pattern prepared to accommodate it; form, whether it be good or bad, prevails over substance." In apparent complete disregard for his own comments on the less salutary aspects of native sanitary habits and social behavior, in his *general* description and assessment of native character the author was almost monotonously laudatory. He was also quite unrelievedly literary—not only returning over and over again to those clichéed qualities of pride, independence, reverence, and lofty contempt for death prescribed by convention, but also more often than not relapsing into such hoary epithets as "shepherd of pastoral romance" or "prophet and dreamer." Irving's *intent*, characteristic of the new quasi-primitivistic impulses which had begun increasingly to animate American attitudes towards nature, was so determinedly sympathetic, in fact, that he was forced to deny the real Indian as strenuously as had his Puritan antagonists.

Again, then, it was subjective rather than objective experience that determined the conventional response. The demonic fantasies were in the end debunked not by reality but by counter-myth. The result, in a sense, far from clarifying American ideas of savagery was simply to obscure the matter further. Irving's brand of idealization, indeed, hardly represents the worst distortions and stereotyping suffered by the noble savage after he managed to capture the public imagination. Even from a purely "literary" point of view, the trend was not an entirely happy one. As with most literary fads, once the savage was taken to the lowest common denominator he lost almost all the vitality that made him a fad in the first place. The Indian drama in America furnishes a vivid example of this process. According to Keiser, though over fifty plays featuring a native hero were written or produced in the early nineteenth century, less than twenty have survived. Those few, moreover, indicate that the stage Indian—while immensely popular for a period—was a flimsy vehicle at best. Even John Augustus Stone's famous drama, *Metamora, or the Last of the Wampanoags* (1928), which played to enthusiastic audiences for two decades, was notable primarily for its overripe rhetoric and masterly manipulation of an unprecedented number of stock theatrical clichés. Consequently, once the novelty of the Indian drama began to pall, as Keiser says, "the obvious defects of the stage Indian, notably a sentimental idealization and a strained and bombastic speech, furnished clever burlesque the means to drive him from the stage." If nothing else, on the other hand, parody being an unmistakable sign of success, this is clear evidence that the noble savage as a conventional if not necessarily as a meaningful culture symbol, despite both his covert association with subversion and his concomitant fall from favor in Europe, did in fact achieve a triumphant comeback on the American scene within the first few decades of the nineteenth century.

There was, of course, more than a slight irony involved in this sudden upsurge of interest in the savage. Originally, as Pearce (1953) says, "Out of theory, wishful thinking, and reading in the theorizing and wishful thinking of travellers, there had been conceived the image of the Indian as the paradoxical man who was civilized because he was uncorrupted by civilization." In America, however, the precondition for the savage's symbolic rehabilitation was his physical defeat, and this in turn all too often meant that the only Indians left around to provide models for the painter and poet had already been so thoroughly debased as to make the attribution of "nobility" seem nothing so much as a nasty joke. Even Irving (1819-20), in spite of his sympathy, had to admit the degradation found among the "miserable hordes which infest the frontiers and hang on the skirts of the settlements...corrupted and enfeebled by the vices of society." The condition entailed for the enthusiastic what Dorothy Dondore calls "a rather amusing consequence." "It is easy," she says, "to draw inspiration from a bronze warrior of heroic mould, his sleek locks feather-helmed, his eye alert, his garb rich furs that he himself has trapped; but the same warrior dazed by bad whiskey, muddying some soldier's castoff finery, is a sadly different story." Different indeed, one would think! Fortunately the American's hold on his "noble" savage was not easily daunted. As we have already noted, American views of the Indian never were much bothered by reality, anyway. What is interesting to observe is the development during this period of certain classic mythopoeic strategies by means of which the nation would be able to protect its most cherished wishful misapprehensions for generations to come.

The keynote to these strategies is compartmentalization. One way to bypass the immediate savage for a more inspirational version was to dwell on the past, bringing him by association into the same category of vanished grandeur that dominated typically reverent views of the classical period. With this approach there would be no expectation of realism or contemporaneity to evoke in the reader's mind any embarrassing pictures of the Indian in his present state. The classical features that the noble savage already carried with him as a legacy from his European career made this transfer very easy to effect, and references to the Indian's "proud stoicism," "magnanimity," and Ciceronian oratory proliferated in current descriptions. Even early romantics like Irving drew largely on the Homeric model of noble manhood in portraying their heroic Indians. The real exemplification of this version of the noble savage, however, is found in William Gilmore Simms. And in this case at least, we may be sure that the resemblances are neither casual nor fortuitous.

Why? Even aside from the passive example one may infer from his novels, in an article entitled "Indian Literature and Art" published in *Views and Reviews in American Literature, History, and Fiction* (1846), Simms goes to some pains to make the classical connection explicit. "The Greeks sung by Homer," he says, "were neither more nor less than highwayman and pirates—the chiefs and demigods of the northern nations, honoured by Odin with highest places in Valhalla, were of the same kidney;—and both find their likeness in the hunter of the American forest—the dark, fierce, barbarian, Choctaw or Cherokee—whom we are apt to consider nothing more than the barbarian. But he too had his song, his romances and his deities—good and evil—even as the Hellenes and the Northmen; and his deeds were just as deserving as these, of their Saemund and Melesigenes." One must, of course, make some allowances for the bombast here. Taken out of context, indeed, the highly literary tone of such passages as this may lead us to suspect that what we are hearing is pure rhetoric, devoid of either substance or serious intent. It is evident from his writing as a whole, though, that Simms believed—or wanted to believe, at any rate—that the American Indian in his natural state *was* comparable to classical primitives in both type and value:

Regarded without prejudice, and through the medium even of what we most positively know of his virtues and his talents, and the North American Indian was as noble a specimen of crude humanity as we can find, from history, any aboriginal people to have been. There is not the slightest reason to suppose that he laboured under any intellectual deficiency. On the contrary the proofs are conclusive, that, compared with other nations—the early Romans before their amalgamation with the great Tuscan family; the Jews prior to the Egyptian captivity;—the German race to the time of Odoacer,—the Saxon, to the period of the Heptarchy, and the Norman tribes in the reign of Charlemagne; —he presented as high and sufficient proofs of susceptibility for improvement and education, as any, the very noblest stocks in our catalogue.

There is considerable evidence, then, that Simms really did intend the references to past models to function as a serious apologia for the Indian.

Might we not, on the other hand, be making too much of a simple stylistic device? Such backward looks as may be inferred from the popularity of this particular version of the savage *could* just signal a delayed response to the late eighteenth-century literary vogue for chronological primitivism. On the evidence of the oeuvre itself, though, there is good reason to believe that something more is involved here than colonial mimicry. If we compare, for instance, Ossian or even Gray to Simms, a significant difference in their treatments of similar material at once becomes evident. For the British the appealing traits of the archaic primitive were his passion and spontaneity. The Americans, in contrast, were with good reason somewhat leery of the more fiery side of savage nature, and the *kind* of primitive qualities they characteristically chose to emphasize, regardless of Simms's token references to the barbaric Norsemen, etc., were such as brought to mind the stern and stoic Roman soldier much more readily than any of the more exotic heroes of eighteenth-century primitivism like the Druid or the ranting Bard. One can, in fact, make a clear and almost complete separation—on the basis of both literary function and character traits—between the archaic savage of northern Europe exalted by the Ossianic cult and the more traditional "noble" one whose literary roots went back to a cosmopolitan Mediterranean culture which culminated in a far from archaic Rome. The latter was both more stylized and more idealistic. He also exhibited very specific moral associations. In England, partly *because* of these moral associations—which, in the context of more exotic fashions came to seem both outdated and dull—he had steadily lost ground over the eighteenth century. In nineteenth-century America, where the literary savage was struggling to become *respectable* rather than *exciting*, it was in contrast the "outdated" tradition to which writers would most often turn.

The figure who emerged from Simms's pages was thus painted in terms meant to appeal more to the reader's admiration than his sympathy, his reason than his sentiment. The American noble savage, in other words, was tailored specifically to *American* tastes. Wishful fantasies notwithstanding, he was also tailored to serve a more covert function almost diametrically opposed to the ostensible aims of his most enthusiastic supporters. Although the attribution of classical nobility was intended by Simms as a defense for the actual Indian, it was, in fact, more successful in hastening the compartmentalization process which would ultimately dissociate the literary noble savage completely from his degenerate real-life cousins. The result was necessarily to disenfranchise the American native to an even greater degree than formerly. While the classical treatment exalted the "idea" of savagism, it did so by placing it quite firmly in the past (note Simms's last quotation: "The American Indian *was* as noble a specimen...") where it could be appreciated dispassionately as one also appreciated, and mildly regretted, the glory that was Rome.

In this way, then, the noble savage and the modern Indian were progressively divorced, one from the other, in the public imagination. Judging by most fictional treatments, in fact, by the second quarter of the nineteenth century they were rapidly becoming perceived as almost two entirely different breeds. As such, by definition, they were not merely proof against but actually immune to the dangers of symbolic contamination. How did this work? Simms's novel *The Yemassee* (1835) might be seen as providing an almost paradigmatic demonstration of the phenomenon. Not only are the major Indian protagonists of this book, Chief Sanutee and his wife Matiwan, just about as highly idealized as contemporary conventions would allow but, more to the point, the portrait of classical virtue presented by this pair remains untarnished even after we have been confronted with the weakness and treachery of their son, a once proud warrior now irredeemably corrupted by the white man's rum into a vicious parody of "noble" savagery. Neither racial complicity nor the ironizing potential of a more realistic view is enough, in other words, to deflate Simms's romantic vision of primitive ideality. An improbable scenario? Here is where the above mentioned strategy comes in. The reader *accepts* this unnatural dissociation of savage "types" because, within the world of the book, conventional alignments carry more weight than natural ones. By means of both implicit and explicit literary associations the reference point for Sanutee and Matiwan is placed firmly in the past—not just their own past either, but a heroic past, a mythic past, a past long dead and gone. Occonestoga, on the other hand, speaks only for the present. Through his life he repudiates the past. On an imaginative level, therefore, there is no meaningful connection between the two generations that will allow the youth's degradation to reflect on his parents' stature in any way, except perhaps by magnifying it. Thus, though his defection is tragic for them, the tragedy has the remoteness—and also, fleetingly at least, in spite of Simms's unevenness, the grandeur—of those ritual tragedies built around gods and heroes far removed even from the long-ago poets who immortalized them. It is significant that we sympathize almost solely with the parents in this book, rather than with the son himself, who seems only to provide a foil and an occasion for demonstrating their nobility.

The classicization of the noble savage, whatever else it entailed, was thus remarkably effective as a distancing mechanism. Purged of his contemporaneous associations, the "good" Indian was in a sense purged of ambiguous reality altogether. Going far beyond literary effects, the social ramifications of this maneuver were considerable. If the remoteness facilitated more sympathetic treatment for the individual aborigine in books and plays, it paradoxically also helped rationalize a certain public callousness toward the *non*-fictive predicament of his race. The emotional association between the long-vanished classical civilizations and the fast-vanishing Indian culture made the fate of the latter seem, like the former, a mere trick of history, a regrettable circumstance far beyond the power or responsibility of the latterday individual. It's no wonder that the definitive savage produced by the nineteenth century (see chapter 3.4 below), though somewhat more complex than Simms's Homeric exemplar, would share many physical and mental characteristics with him.

Distance, then, was the key prerequisite for the imaginative rehabilitation of the native. Locating his primary emotional referents in the past was not the only way to achieve such distance, of course. Testifying vividly to the increasing incoherence of the popular mythology, another and in some ways conflicting version of the Indian emerged in the literature of the young republic right beside the classical model. If the one appealed to reason, the other appealed to sentiment. If the one exemplified classic virtue, the other spoke to romantic sensibility. And if the one discreetly ignored the Indian's deplorable current condition, choosing rather to focus on his heroic past, the other turned its attention to that decline itself and, rather than simply overlooking the associated wretchedness, transformed it into a pathetic, heart-rending appeal to the sensitive heart. The mood was elegiac, nostalgic. The Indian's fate was portrayed as sad, almost beautiful, but inevitable. Pearce (1953) outlines the characteristic approach:

> There is...a whole series of miscellaneous narrative and descriptive poems, ranging from the crude to the innocuously competent, which celebrate the death of the noble savage and the coming of civilization. The pattern of these poems is uniform enough itself to constitute a received way of imaging American relations with the Indians. The Indian is described for what he is, a noble savage. The coming of the white man is described for what it is, the introduction of agrarian civilization. And the Indian is shown dying or moving west, often with a vision of the great civilized life which is to come after him, occasionally with the hope that he himself can become civilized. The tone is now bitter, now melancholy. The end is said to be good.

There were numerous advantages to this approach. For one thing, since the unhappy destiny was presented as an unavoidable *fait accomplit*, the writer was freed from any necessity for patriotic rationalizing, and—taking it for granted that his readers would understand and share the relativistic theories that historically condemned even as they figuratively praised the principles of savagery—could concentrate on the most appealing, most positive aspects of the savage character. It was possible, in fact, as Pearce says, "to show that it was his very savage nobility which had brought him to his death." This is the tactic employed by Irving, for instance, in his essay on Philip of Pohanoket. "The fate of the brave and generous Canonchet," he says, "is worthy of particular mention: the last scene of his life is one of the noblest instances on record of Indian magnanimity." "Though repeated offers were made to him of his life on condition of submitting with his nation to the English, yet he rejected them with disdain." Here is the archetypal pattern of death before dishonor. Here too is primitive virtue *par excellence*. Lest the point be missed, Irving does not hesitate to magnify the redman's moral rectitude at the specific expense of his own "overcivilized" countrymen:

> So noble and unshaken a spirit, so true a fidelity to his cause and his friend might have touched the feelings of the generous and the brave; but Conanchet was an Indian, a being toward whom war had no courtesy, humanity no law, religion no compassion—he was condemned to die. The last words of him that are recorded are worthy the greatness of his soul. When sentence of death was passed upon him, he observed "that he liked it well, for he should die before his heart was soft, or he had spoken anything unworthy of himself."

Quite a change from Michael Wigglesworth's "hellish fiends"!

There is a catch, to be sure. For all the passion exuded by these panegyrics, we would be mistaken in supposing for a moment that even Irving "really" preferred Indian to white culture. Remember what we said above regarding the current theory of "savagism." Though subtler than in Simms's case, the critical distance between observer and object is still scrupulously maintained. The more "literary" the Indian became, indeed, the more complete his dissociation from reality. The more dissociated, on the other hand, the less he was perceived as presenting an emotional threat. This, finally, was what accomplished the last step in his symbolic conversion. The result? The above quotation says it all. Only a few generations removed from direct guilt the American was able to exploit the pathos of the Indian's death rather than, like the Puritan's, having to justify it. This meant, among other things, that the negative image of the bestial savage was no longer required. Was counterproductive, in fact. Already energized (albeit diffusely) by the new primitivism, the more noble the native could be made to seem the more useful he was as an emotional ploy. Irving, if early, was thus quite typical. In the first half of the nineteenth century, predictably enough, American writers produced a virtual orgy of tear-stained Indian death scenes. Equally predictably, the victims in these productions were invariably noble in every respect: in blood (they were always chiefs or the sons or daughters of chiefs), in appearance (they were always handsome if young, and venerable otherwise), and in demeanor. In the latter category more often than not it was the classical savage that set the standard, but the manipulation of all the elements together was definitely patterned after the late eighteenth-century sentimental school. As Dondore describes it, "the pictures of them [were] tinctured with the pathos of their passing," adding to "the idealization that had from the beginning surrounded...[the noble savage] with idyllic glamor" a "pensive comprehension" that gave it a new, "poignant," truly "romantic" air.

The thing that seems most remarkable when one looks back from a twentieth-century vantage point, is the skill with which the public of this time managed to sustain a stance that ranged from disinterested regret to sentimental self-indulgence for the fate of the poor savage while at the same time this fate was being visibly hastened by their own political leaders. Surely, one is tempted to ask, these touching renditions of the Indian death scene, not to mention the copious elegies to the fast-fading light of Indian culture, must have stirred at least a tiny pang in the public breast for their guilt by association, their sins at least of omission? There was, in fact, an undertone, an ambivalence, that is not recognized in the official version of the noble savage, and this, as we will see in section 3.4 was eventually to turn the Indian into a far more complex symbol. Judging by the popular literature and letters of the day, however, the average nineteenth-century American remained comfortably blind to the ethical discrepancies of the attempt to celebrate the all-out program of national expansion which was hastening the Indians' downfall at a headlong pace while simultaneously indulging a tearful sympathy for the poor Indian after he had regrettably been dispossessed. "Even though convinced of the necessity of their removal, my heart bled for them in their desolation and decline," said Jules Latrobe in the 1840s. And this summarizes the general public response of the period—an unquestioning acceptance of the inevitability of the Indians' decline ("their speedy disappearance from the earth appears as certain as though it were already sealed and accomplished," Latrobe said later) accompanied by a melancholy reflection on the sadness that this had to be so. Underlying the conventionally elegiac mood, meanwhile, one may sense a palpable smugness about the white ascendency which is the other side of Indian extinction. In life as in novels, in other words, the "tragedy" is both contained and countered by the obligatory happy ending. For all the heroine's delicate regrets, the hymeneal celebration is in no way overshadowed by the deaths of a few friendly natives.

Hypocritical? Certainly from a century's distance it seems so. Fortunately, nineteenth-century readers—and writers—were rarely forced to consider the ultimate implications of either their fictional strategies or their public policies. In exactly the same way that the eighteenth-century primitivists in England stubbornly embraced *all* the current notions that appealed to them, regardless of intellectual or emotional inconsistencies, the popular version of the noble savage which appeared widely in American literature in the first half of the nineteenth century implied just as much as the public wanted to see—and not one bothersome bit more.

In connection with the eighteenth-century primitivists, this might be an opportune moment to consider the question of *why* the noble savage, after a long history of negative responses and in the context of a continued pragmatic need to keep the Indian firmly in his place, suddenly emerged into popularity in America just at the time when he was fading out of sight in Europe. Part of it should undoubtedly be marked down to culture lag, but the influences that affected literary views of the Indian in American were far too complex and far-reaching to be adequately accounted for in terms of any mechanism as singular or as simplistic as this one. In spite of shared traditions and continued cross-fertilization, the American cultural environment differed in some important and very fundamental ways from that of Britain. This is obviously not the place to launch into a full-scale account of American culture history, but it is interesting and useful to consider at least a few of the currents which were related, at least indirectly, to the noble savage. Most important, it is interesting and useful to consider how given fashions in thought, transplanted, could take on a whole new coloration. Accident, indeed, accounts for more than we might normally be inclined to acknowledge. We have seen, for instance, how the noble savage developed in Europe out of characteristic Enlightenment ideas, such as the natural goodness of man. During the eighteenth century in America, residual negative images of the Indian, plus the pragmatic considerations of a colonial economy, tended to shift the primitivistic implications of the Enlightenment onto the less primitive but still "simple" figure of the farmer. Significantly, however, Enlightenment ideas lingered longer in America than in Europe. As a result—and this is the key point to note— when other conditions were ripe they were still "coincidentally" available in current terminology to add their weight to a late-burgeoning primitivism.

Why, on the other hand, *should* the Enlightenment linger this way in America? After all, as Curti points out, at least at first sight "colonial society [seems] a particularly uncongenial soil for the growth of the Enlightenment" if only because it tends to be dominated by agriculture rather than trade. Agriculture didn't *mean* the same thing in America as in Europe, though. For one thing, unlike Europe, America was not (in Curti's words) "glutted with feudal remains." The basis of agriculture in America was in fact "the small independent farmer or...the planter who as an exporter of staple crops was something of a business man." Especially in the context of Protestant traditions of social (if not moral) equality, the predominantly middle-class population produced by this economic situation was inherently amenable to the ideals of democracy and humanitarianism which were such significant elements of the Enlightenment. More to the point, its own historic experience inclined it not merely to tolerate but to *assume* upward mobility. Being themselves typically "dynamic, recruited from beneath and on the make," in other words, it was almost inevitable that social classes in America would be "better able to think in terms of social improvement than the traditionally static classes of long established privilege" (Curti). The increasingly visible national prosperity, moreover, made the doctrine of perfectability seem less wishful theory than accomplished fact. The American—as we have noted— was already committed to progress on every level that mattered. Add to this an innate optimism, a pioneer's pragmatism, and a Calvinistic faith in the rationality of God's universe, and it is easy to see why, despite its rural roots, America would be predisposed to many of the most central tenets of Enlightenment thought.

This, then, is at least part of our answer. Compatibility makes willing bedfellows. Is it enough, though, to explain the *durability* of the phenomenon?

Perhaps not. The fact is, however, that in addition to these positive reasons why the Enlightenment flourished in America in the first place, there are even stronger negative ones why it should have continued to do so long after it lost its hold on Europe. Indeed, there is ample basis for believing that America's *resistance* to certain types of influence may actually in the long run have played a greater part in confirming (if not catalyzing) her belated entry into the eighteenth-century mainstream than the aforementioned susceptibility. How? Quite aside from anything else, it is impossible to overstate the importance of the fact that the mythos of the young republic provided not merely an incentive to, but a defense against, the headier extremes of libertarian enthusiasm. If his traditional egalitarian bias inclined the American to some moderate degree of free-thinking, in other words, an equally ingrained conservatism deterred him from endorsing the more radical Enlightenment doctrines so wholeheartedly that he would feel the need, after the fact, for an equally sweeping recantation. This, of course, is what happened in Europe. There, in the bloody aftermath of the French Revolution, the public impulse toward self-exculpation found its most natural expression in a breastbeating repudiation of almost all Enlightenment ideals. It also, as mentioned earlier, found a natural scapegoat in its erstwhile hero, the primitive. And why not! "The image of the good savage," as Slotkin points out, "had expressed the Enlightenment's faith in the essential goodness and reasonableness of the natural man; but the savages of France, given freedom to express their will, proved passionate and bloody-minded." Under the circumstances it is hardly surprising that disillusionment should produce—among other things—a "European revulsion against the romanticization of the natural man." Across the Atlantic the case was quite different. Whether because their conversion was late or because it was lukewarm, the Americans by and large proved immune to this sort of backlash. While equally appalled by events in France, they consequently tended to blame not nature but their old enemy, a decadent Europe.

Which brings us to a problem. The difference between these reactions is clearly the difference between the self-righteous censure of a disapproving but dispassionate outsider and that more immediate, more emotional reaction of an involved individual which produces a "revulsion" against what is, essentially, the projected image of an idealized self. Yet how strange that the Americans— the original revolutionaries—should exhibit the first reaction while the technically guiltless British joined in the general European movement suggested by the second! One would think that having recently undergone a revolution themselves the Americans, for all their philosophical inhibitions, would feel a certain amount of complicity-by-association with the Jacobin cause. On the basis of their overt reactions, however, this clearly was not the case.

Perhaps it was because they did have a revolution, and because that revolution, in comparison with the French one, was in their own eyes so admirably conducted, so restrained and rational, that they felt quite justified in a moderate display of hand-washing horror. The truth was that the two revolutions—however one cares respectively to define them—were essentially two different kinds of movements. In some ways, moreover, it was the American, not the French, Revolution that fully realized Enlightenment ideas, and it was the British, not the Americans, who had been emotionally implicated in the extravagant, radical mood of "Jacobin rationalism." Martin Green defines this difference as the difference between Erasmian and Faustian cultures. It was because of a firm commitment to the former values, he says, that the Americans waged not Paine's but Jefferson's version of a revolution:

[The] striking fact about Jefferson [was that] he remained very much an eighteenth-century man, as much so as Washington and Adams. He is a liberal and not a radical hero. That very liberality of mind, that extraordinary range of interests and talents, that beautiful temperateness and health of temperament, prevented his making—in terms of a whole life—Paine's sort of unequivocal assertion. Not that Jefferson equivocates, but he balances, he combines.

In other words, Jefferson's temperament was, like that of the whole group to which he belonged, Erasmian. The Enlightenment as a whole was Erasmian; and so was the American Revolution, that part of it which finally triumphed. Those revolutionaries who did partake of the radical temperament were never effectively organized, and were edged out of those positions of power which they had held as soon as the fighting was over.

The smug certainty of their own Erasmian stance—the complacent conviction that they were free themselves from any taint of the "enthusiastic radicalism" of the Jacobins—meant that the "object lesson" of the French Revolution could be viewed as largely academic from the western side of the Atlantic.

This is not to imply that feelings of guilt did not exist at deeper levels of response, but such uncomfortable feelings tended in America to be quite deeply repressed (see section 3.3. below). It is also not to imply that there was no overt conservative reaction at all. The American could hold himself self-righteously aloof from many of the Jacobin atrocities, but when "violence was directed against property," *then*, as Curti notes, "American conservatives were stirred to wrath." American critics of the Revolution in fact cited the necessary connection between social stability and the security of property as a rhetorical justification for their conservative policies even more frequently than they made the standard appeal to humanitarian fears of bloodshed. For all its crass expediency from a modern perspective the argument was not lost on a predominantly middle-class audience. Briefly at least, in consequence, the reactionary mood had a palpable effect on the rhetoric if not the policies of the republic. The refrain, as Curti notes, invoked a return to traditional values. "Negatively the defense of the established pattern of economic, social, and political arrangements centered in an attack on the French Revolution and alleged Jacobinism at home; positively a case was made for institutionalism, aristocracy, the continued restriction of suffrage to substantial property owners, and revealed religion." Despite such appeals, on a broad scale the French example obviously failed to stimulate a desirable degree of consternation in the United States. As the trend toward Jacksonian democracy was soon to illustrate, for all the talk of "chaos, despotism, and horror," public opinion here was simply not sufficiently aroused for the conservative reaction to do much permanent damage to the general prestige of Enlightenment ideas.

The American, then, responded quite differently than his British brethren to the news of alarums in Europe. In the main, in fact, the bulk of the population—busy with nation-building—was affected not at all. Those who had opinions were by and large unable to translate them into action. Indeed, even among that relatively self-conscious minority who were inclined to retrench after the French Revolution, there was no consensus as to what direction the reaction should take. "The conflict," says Curti, "was not formal or sharply defined. Many substantial merchants and planters repudiated the political, social, and economic philosophy of the Enlightenment and the French Revolution without rejecting deistic and rationalistic ideas. Some clergymen and a great number of plain people," on the other hand, "accepted democratic ideas but rejected scepticism and rationalism in the religious realm." The lack of consensus made it difficult for reaction to find an appropriate vehicle on the political level—especially in the face of an increasingly optimistic mood throughout the country.

This last is a key point. In Europe the conservative backlash had been reinforced by economic disappointment. Faced with the widespread suffering that accompanied social breakdown, says Slotkin, the "postrevolutionary European writer could hardly help despairing of the Enlightenment's dream and deserting it for Burkean conservatism, Napoleonic despotism, or Romantic irrationalism." In the New World, however, the situation was entirely different. Recovery after the Revolution had been rapid. Industry was thriving. The population was increasing. Most important of all, "the availability of cheap land seemed to offer the hope that the American people could enjoy the progress derived from the awakened ambitions of middle and lower-class people without suffering a breakdown of the [democratic institutions]...which were the political and social legacies of the Age of Reason" (Slotkin). Practical results, in other words, spoke louder than any theory. Bolstered by so much visible evidence that his utopian schemes were *in fact* working, the American was unlikely to be either attracted by an anti-intellectualism that would undermine his vision of limitless progress or frightened by pessimistic prophecies of doom.

If it achieved little in changing the overall direction of American political development, on the other hand, the one thing the conservative reaction did accomplish was to reinforce American distaste for the more *extreme* aspects of eighteenth-century thought. Without repudiating the Enlightenment entirely there was an emphasis on the more down-to earth, pragmatic viewpoints it had spawned—like the Scottish school of "Common Sense." As Curti explains it, the "appeal of the Scottish philosophy lies in the fact that for the baffling subtleties of the philosophic idealism of Berkeley, the negations of Hume, and the quasi-materialism of Locke, it substituted a common-sense assurance of the validity of Christian morals and Christian principles generally. It was, in short, admirably suited to the needs of conservative-minded intellectuals recovering from the hysteria that deism and Jacobinism had aroused and from the vicissitudes of life in a period devoted primarily to the hardheaded tasks of consolidating the existing order and promoting commercial and industrial enterprises." So popular did this school of thought become in the new republic that—according to Boas in his account of "Romantic Philosophy in America"—at Princeton, "which became the headquarters of American philosophy, President Witherspoon took it upon himself to stamp out what remained of the idealism of Bishop Berkeley and apparently succeeded before the end of the eighteenth-century. His successors carried on the good work and, if we may judge at this distance, no young Princetonian was ever tempted to doubt the reality of the material world, the efficacy of common sense, or even the finality of authority."

The emphasis on Common Sense also tended to have a damping effect on Romanticism in America. There was, as we have noted, a great upsurge in popularity of what has subsequently come to be called "romantic" literature during the first half of the nineteenth century, but the philosophic core of true Romantic thought was largely ignored. This was probably related to a number of factors. For one thing, Romanticism as a *personal style*—the cult of the poet and of the personality which produced the Byronic figure as a type of the age—was associated with the dangerous events and opinions of the "other" Revolution. What was even worse, it was tainted with Europeanism. On top of that, the German idealistic philosophy which was so central to Coleridge and Wordsworth was anathema to American Common Sense, so this too—until Emerson's publication in 1836 of a small book entitled *Nature* signalled an almost imperceptible but ultimately crucial shift in the American intellectual orientation—was largely ignored. There was still, of course, a voracious public appetite for Romanticism, but for several decades this was satisfied with the appearance rather than the spirit of the Romantic age. Green, in fact, makes a discrimination between two different *kinds* of Romanticism—"the Faustian temperament's Romanticism being most often the significant kind, and the non-Faustian's merely decorative." And America, he says, "could swallow only the latter."

Thus, until the Transcendentalist school blossomed in the mid-century, and even beyond that for the vast majority of the American population, the Romantic upsurge in America was largely associated with "entertainment" rather than a serious-minded attempt at philosophic redefinition. Scott's romances were devoured with alacrity—according to Curti, "during the decade 1813-1823 five million volumes of the Waverly Novels issued from American presses"—as were those of his numerous imitators. The sentimental novel, gushing with sensibility, gentility, and didacticism, was ubiquitous. The gothic genre with its cavalcade of "incredible plots, bewildering spectacles of goblins, ghosts, and damsels in distress stalking or stumbling through somber dungeons and dilapidated castles" (Curti), reached heights of popularity in America that is never attained even in its British heyday, and the exotic tale—as in Irving—also found an enthusiastic audience.

The obvious point about all these productions is that they do not belong properly to Romanticism at all. The things that the Americans called Romantic, in fact, almost without exception were derived from the eighteenth-century, *pre*-Romantic period in England, being by and large products of Enlightenment ideas rather than of full-fledged Romantic philosophy. Even the accelerated back-to-nature movement that characterized the post-Revolutionary period focused primarily on a nature defined by the eighteenth century. Ideas of the sublime and picturesque continued to dominate popular literature well past the middle of the century. The noticeable split in American attitudes during this period, far from signalling a head-on collision between a new Romanticism and an older rationalism, was merely an intensification of the two-sidedness in Enlightenment philosophy which we saw in Chapter 2: natural wisdom vs. education, archaism vs. perfectability, primitivism vs. progress. The early nineteenth century in America could be seen as a period in which *both* of these possibilities gathered and maintained enough intellectual prestige and emotional appeal that each could hold the other in the momentary immobility of a balanced opposition.

The implications of all this for the noble savage were considerable, of course. The Enlightenment ideas that continued to dominate American culture well into the nineteenth century provided the same fertile ground for the growth of primitivism as had similar or even identical ideas during the eighteenth century in England. What is more, as mentioned above, while the American public had not been receptive to a positive version of the savage during the earlier period, they were now not only receptive but eager. Like the gothic novel and sentimentality, it was a "safe" kind of Romanticism, kept from extremes by the counterbalancing weight of rationalism. It might therefore be indulged without qualms. Indeed, there were other prevailing influences at that time which made the noble savage potentially one of the most popular cultural images of the period. To some extent, as we saw in the last chapter, the literary Indian suffered from competition with the romanticized frontiersman for the same audience, but there was still enough public interest to give him a prominent part in popular literature for several decades.

Among these other influences, one of the most important was the growth subsequent to the Revolution of a new national self-consciousness. As the founding fathers were all too well aware, political independence was only a first step *towards* freedom, not freedom itself. Before it could shake off its cultural dependence on Europe, the country had to develop a culture of its own. Hence the feverish concern with the development of a "national" literature addressed in varying ways by Brockden Brown, Simms, and Cooper. Hence also a radically new attitude towards the environment, a redefinition of America in terms of both time and space.

The spatial reorientation emerged from an attempt to pin down exactly what America meant, in contradistinction to a panAtlantic community, as a unique and separate unit. Nature, as we have seen, had always played a significant part in American self-images, and the American's attitude towards his environment tended to be more immediate and more complex than corresponding attitudes in Europe. Especially in later stages of settlement this relationship was an important source of positive reinforcement ("Because they had conquered nature, Americans came in time to think that they had created it" [Commager]). After the Revolution, consequently, it provided a primary means of combatting the young country's nagging feelings of self-doubt.

This sense of inadequacy was based mainly on general (though vehemently denied) assumptions about the ultimate superiority of European arts and letters. The opinions expressed by de Tocqueville about the cultural poverty and crudeness of style implied necessarily by democratic institutions were as widely believed in America as in Europe. The American public, in fact, was so deeply conditioned to consider its own provincial culture as second-rate, that even in the intensely patriotic post-Revolutionary period American writers found it hard to win an audience for their books, and the writers who did manage to make themselves heard tended largely, as Simms says in *Views and Reviews*, to "think after European models, draw their stimulus and provocation from European books, fashion themselves to European tastes, and look chiefly to the awards of European criticism." Even those same patriots who pleaded for a national literature, more often than not joined the general consensus in believing that American society was deficient in those elements—the variety of manners, the venerable sense of age and tradition, the polished style—which were central to conventional literary genres. Americans would thus, they felt, have to base her claim for recognition on something *different* from the traditional forms. And what better than nature to shore up the national honor.

In the first place, nature was one thing that America certainly had *more* of than Europe. And if American scenery, as Thomas Cole complained, was "destitute of the vestiges of antiquity" which would have made it picturesque, it did exhibit an incomparable grandeur and sublimity that were even more valuable because they were capable of opening up a vista to the future. Cooper, speaking through the persona of Cadwallader in his *Notions of the Americans*, expresses this view succinctly: when "you complain of the absence of association to give its secret, and perhaps greatest charm which such a sight is capable of inspiring," he says, "you complain unjustly. The moral feeling with which a man of sentiment and knowledge looks upon [the Eastern] Hemisphere is connected with his recollection; here it should be mingled with his Hopes." The brand of nature to be found in America, far from being *inferior* to the European style, was thus uniquely suited to the optimism of a new nation. As this rationale gained currency, a sense of "national pride in the rude native scene as contrasted to the effete... European civilization" (Sanford) became an increasingly important component of both official ideology and popular mythos. By the early nineteenth century, in fact, nature had become an almost obligatory fixture of American art and literature, serving not just as a subject but as a portmaneau metaphor. Displayed characteristically in the work of Bryant and Cole, as Sanford points out, it could be used as both "a moral symbol inspiring a reverential awe of deity" and "a symbol for permanence amidst change, a restorative and refuge from a frenetic, utilitarian civilization."

Above all, it became a symbol for growth and hope and futurity.

This last aspect of nature led by a natural process of association to other ideas which had even more significance for the development of a distinctive American point of view. Emphasis on the beneficent face of nature at the expense of her more threatening moods, for instance, brought the original dream of paradise once more to the fore of American thought, stimulating a sense of newness, of primeval innocence, of making a fresh start. The popularity of Edenic images was further reinforced by both the fact and the idea of the west during the great expansion that followed the Revolution. At the same time, the momentum achieved by this expansion was itself at least partly due to the new authority of such images. The myth, in other words, was a self-feeding one. It also had implications that went far beyond geography. Above and beyond its association with the actual westering movement, inasmuch as the paradisial ideal implied a specific attitude towards *time*, it modified not only the American's mythico-spatial terms of reference but also—in the long run more important—his sense of history.

The past, for America, meant Europe, and Europe meant not only an intimidating cultural superiority, but also corruption: political and social decadence. The myth of newness, as Sanford point out, was thus attractive not only for its celebration of the physical attributes of the country but even more because it lent credence to the vision of "a moral and spiritual rebirth" by which the country could be finally saved from the threatening past. This vision in turn implied earlier visions of rebirth, revitalized the idea that "success in taming the wilderness was tantamount to entering the kingdom of heaven on earth, and seemed to demonstrate a direct casual relationship between moral effort and material reward." In this way, the idea of a new paradise became inextricably interwoven with the idea of progress.

Progress, in turn, added the final ingredient to the recipe. With an unlimited future in sight the past became finally and totally irrelevant. As an unnecessary encumbrance it could thus be shed—along with the whole of European culture—just as (to use an image so familiar that it has become by now almost the archetypal emblem of American self-definition) the proverbial snake sloughs off his worn-out skin. This is the critical step. Where the past, as Baritz says, had been identified "with evil by the Puritans, and with intrigue and duplicity by the revolutionaries," the new republicans determined to deny it altogether. "The earth belongs to the living, not to the dead," said Thomas Jefferson. "We may consider each generation as a distinct nation," free from the influence of any other.

The new sense of time—or *timelessness*—implied a new kind of man, of course, for if America had no past, neither did the prototypical American. As a result, pioneering became a metaphor even more than an actual style of life; a general attitude that proclaimed spontaneity better than authority, practical experience more important than tradition. The nineteenth-century American, in fact, most often chose to embody his sense of self in an Adamic role. During this period, as R.W.B. Lewis illustrates amply, "the image contrived to embody the most fruitful contemporary ideas was that of the authentic American as a figure of heroic innocence and vast potentialities, poised at the start of a new history." Adam in Eden. A primitive fantasy indeed!

This obviously brings us back to the Boone figure we discussed in the last chapter. It also, however, brings us back to our old friend, the noble savage. Just as much as the frontiersman the Indian was an ideal primitivistic symbol: close to nature; uncorrupted by a tainted past; best of all, just about as authentically American as it was possible to get. It should hardly surprise us, then, to note that even during the peak of the Boone-cult the conventional image of the noble savage appeared with great frequency in American popular literature. His revitalized role was partly, no doubt, related to the general popularity of such semi-Romantic eighteenth-century genres as we discussed above, but even this brief outline reveals the extent to which trends in American thought during the post-Revolutionary era encouraged both primitivistic and patriotic ideas of a sort that would naturally find a symbolic correlative in an idealized version of the American Indian. And after the Boone figure began to diminish in prestige, or at least to change his symbolic associations—after American writers started to recognize, or if not to recognize at least to sense, that "the moral posture [the frontiersman] seemed to indorse was vulnerable in the extreme" (R.W.B. Lewis)—the image of the Indian began to gather a whole new set of associations, both less patriotic and more ambiguous, which enabled it to become, in a few limited cases at least, a cultural symbol of much greater depth and complexity than before.

This complex image marked a culminating point in the symbolic savage's career in America, and as such will be discussed separately in section 3.4, beginning on page 120. It would be misleading to suggest, however, that the more complex version ever *dominated* the literary response in the sense of replacing the earlier, conventional images that we have been examining. On the contrary, as Barnett's survey of Indian romances in *The Ignoble Savage* amply illustrates, the vast majority of noble savages to be found in the pages of American literature, even during the convention's peak of popularity, are simple, stereotyped, and largely distorted by conscious or unconscious didacticism. Longfellow's "The Song of Hiawatha" (1855), cited by Keiser as expressing "whatever is poetic and appealing in the primitive man of America," although both technically superior to, and more "literary" than, most contemporaneous "wilderness romances," provides a prime example of the popular (positive) view.

Typical of the more serious among his mid-nineteenth-century compeers, Longfellow professed to be greatly concerned with authenticity in his portrait of Indian life. In collecting background for his poem, consequently, he went to Schoolcraft's *Algic Researches* and *History, Conditions, and Prospects of the Indian Tribes of the U.S.*, generally considered during that period as among the most authoritative works ever published on the Indian. Even leaving aside Schoolcraft's own bias, however, at least from a twentieth-century perspective the loose manner in which the poet actually *uses* this material would seem to render the claim of "realism" a dubious if not outright preposterous one. Keiser excuses the distortions on the basis of "his artistic purpose of unity" and a "kind and delicate nature," but even this critic's desire to vindicate his subject cannot disguise the unjustified liberties that Longfellow took with his sources, and particularly with the myth cycle on which his story purports to be based. He eliminated incongruities and improprieties; he toned down the trickster elements that played so central a part in the Indian rendering; he even went so far as to conflate the legendary Algonquin culture-hero Manabozha with an historical Indian statesman transplanted from among the enemy Iroquois. If this weren't enough, he also took it upon himself to "clean up" any facts of native lifestyle that might offend "the esthetic sensibilities of [his] white reader" (Keiser). The result of all these excisions and revisions, whatever their value from an aesthetic point of view, is, of course, to obscure the "real" Indian almost entirely.

How, with his reiterated concern for accuracy of detail, could Longfellow rationalize such cavalier handling? The answer obviously has to do with his expectations, the vision of savagery that he brought to, and imposed upon, his work. Despite his *explicit* intent in the poem, in fact, Longfellow, like the vast majority of his countrymen, was concerned with the savage primarily insofar as he provided a valid referent for white experience. The theme of "Hiawatha" consequently has almost nothing to do with the Indian who is its ostensible model. Far from intrinsically interesting, indeed, the primitive protagonist functions almost solely as a conventional (pastoral) exemplar. A "spiritual halfbreed" mediating between society and solitude, agriculture and hunting, Longfellow's hero—as Slotkin points out—provides (far from lessons in "real" savagery) a moral touchstone to help the reader interpet his *own* American identity. Does it work? Even leaving aside the question of authenticity as irrelevant to the mythopoeic if not the purely literary function, we would have to say no. Inasmuch as he images the resolution of a fundamental experiential antithesis, Hiawatha has at least some of the attributes of a true mythic typos. Because, however, this resolution is purely pedagogic—and thus essentially *painless*—he lacks the inner tension that typically energizes such a figure. Longfellow's noble savage—like the majority (if not the best) of his literary brethren—is simple rather than complex, conventional rather than truly symbolic, a chauvinistic celebration of American unity rather than a viable image of the disturbing ambiguity implicit in the nation's inherent sense of self.

3.3 Mixed Feelings

This is where things get a little trickier. If, by the early nineteenth century the hitherto almost consensual negative view had come increasingly to be challenged by a new, more positive image of the Indian, the latter, as we have seen, was still in general no less and perhaps even more conventional than the former. Lest we be misled by the quantitative dominance of these relatively simplistic stereotypes, however, it should be noted that the symbolic savage we may *abstract from* specific literary contexts continued to demonstrate both ambiguousness and duplicity. Why? Again—or still— the key lies with current perceptions of nature. Despite the post-Revolutionary enthusiasm for "scenery" there is ample evidence in the communal oeuvre that the American's reconciliation with otherness was more apparent than real. Secularized, even domesticated, the landscape still remained subtly resistant to assimilation. This fact in itself was enough to rule out a wholly sanitized savage. Whatever else he might come to suggest, the iconic Indian, his organic/symbolic relationship with the wilderness reaffirmed rather than de-emphasized by nineteenth-century views of primitive culture, was almost guaranteed to localize the tensions inherent in this now covert but still unhealed breach.

The residual ambivalence is strikingly evident, for instance, in Robert Montgomery Bird's *Nick of the Woods*. Published in 1837, this otherwise conventional novel is distinguished by an extreme, unrealistic, and intolerant treatment of the Indian which would have been more characteristic of a seventeenth-century sermon. The modern reader may be inclined to rationalize Bird's attitude as merely reflecting a conditioned bias, but as our brief survey of trends in nineteenth-century American culture indicates, hostility so virulent was by this time fairly atypical. At least some of Bird's contemporaries, in fact, were as uncomfortable with his natives as we tend to be. The British novelist Harrison Ainsworth, for instance, in an introduction to an English edition of *Nick* accused Bird of "painting the Indians as black as possible in order to justify the vicious persecutions and robbery of lands they suffered at the hands of American pioneers." As we have seen, however, by the nineteenth century the Americans had plenty of ways to rationalize and/or compartmentalize their policies regarding Indians without for the most part having to resort to this rather clumsy kind of vituperation. Harrison's interpretation of Bird's motives betrays a lack of familiarity with current American modes of self-imaging.

Another possible explanation for Bird's satanic savage is suggested by his own preface to the second edition of the book. According to this, the writer merely wanted to correct the naive and misleading impression of the Indian which had recently been promulgated by numerous of his countrymen:

[T]he North American savage has never appeared to us the gallant and heroic personage he seems to others. The single fact that he wages war—systematic war—upon beings incapable of resistance or defense,—upon women and children, whom all other races in the world, no matter how barbarous, consent to spare—has hitherto been, and we suppose, to the end of our days will remain, a stumbling-block to our imagination: we look into the woods for the mighty warrior, "the feather-cinctured chief," rushing to meet his foe, and behold him retiring laden with the scalps of miserable squaws and their babes. Heroical? *Hoc verbum quid valeat, non vident.*

There is some question whether this preface, as an afterthought inspired directly by critical attacks on the original publication, was likely to have been an accurate analysis of either his true intentions or the creative process involved, but even leaving aside this problem we may still ask why, considering the general predispositions of the period, Bird objected so strenuously to the romanticization of the Indian; why, in fact, his own attempt to be more "realistic" was characterized by a bias so directly opposed to the prevailing view. Irving's "objective" descriptions of Indians were just as inaccurate as Bird's, for instance, but in his case the distortions were obviously influenced by increasingly popular and widespread beliefs and opinions about the subject matter. Irving, in other words, merely reflected the general trend in early nineteenth-century America toward a more mellowed attitude to the Indian. Bird, on the other hand, was swimming against the current, a maneuver which takes considerably more energy than simple conformity. This being the case, I think we are justified in looking further for an explanation of his attitude.

Another possibility, of course, is that Bird did *not* formulate his opinions in the same cultural environment as Irving. In the frontier regions, as we mentioned, bitterness toward the natives lingered far longer than it did in the east, largely because out there the danger of Indian attack was a present and continuing threat rather than a purely historical factor. Bird, having travelled extensively in the west, may well have absorbed these prejudices along with the local color. The trouble with this explanation is that it presupposes a degree of ignorance, either accidental or self-willed, to reinforce the bias, and there is ample evidence that Bird was far from ignorant about his subject matter. In fact, according to Cecil Williams, who introduced the 1939 edition of *Nick*, Bird "became one of the most assiduous students of Western historical and literary writing of the period." The certainty, therefore, that Bird must have been exposed to more reasonable points of view (indeed, some of his own earlier work such as *Oralloossa* and "The Colapeesa" displayed a more typical tendency to idealize the Indian) makes one suspect that there was something more involved here than simple ignorance or bigotry. The fact that Bird, knowing better, even went so far as to distort the historical basis of his novel in order to make Indian behavior appear more atrocious and Indian nature more inhuman may seem to imply—as with the more extreme Puritan response—an emotional reaction at odds with the conscious intent.

Before pursuing this line of thought too far, however, there is one further possibility that should be considered. To some extent the incongruity which we seem to find in Bird may simply result from a failure on the part of the reader to understand the implications of his literary technique, and the projection of inappropriate expectations upon the novel. A careful examination of the purely *literary* background to this book may therefore cast some useful light on the problem of Bird's Indians.

The first issue we need to resolve is the question of what exactly, in terms of literary "kinds," we are dealing with here. Traditionally, *Nick of the Woods* has been considered a "romance"—and with good reason. In basic structural elements, from the elaborate plot with its many reversals and harrowing escapes right through to the emphasis on both picturesque and sublime aspects of the natural landscape, this book appears to offer almost a textbook example of late eighteenth-early nineteenth-century genre conventions. Using Sir Walter Scott as a standard of comparison, it would seem, indeed, that Bird accepted and utilized nearly all of the most common and clichéed aspects of the "romantic" fiction of his day. Like Scott he sets his story in a period more or less historically remote from his audience. Also like Scott, moreover, he devotes considerable effort to reproducing with plausible authenticity the manners and speech appropriate to his setting. His careful and almost tedious delineation of such frontier characters as Colonel Bruce and Roaring Ralph Stackpole—thought by many critics to be "the original in polite fiction of the wild, lawless, half-horse, half-alligator species [of Mississippi riverman] known as 'a ring-tailed roarer from Salt River' " (Dahl)—is one example of this emphasis on historical and regional verisimilitude. Above all, the central characters of the book appear to align very closely with the stereotypes established by Scott. Roland is the colorless hero, exhibiting in the abstract all the virtues of ideal manhood, but without the slightest trace of individuality. Edith and Telie Doe, the triumphant blonde and defeated dark heroines respectively, represent the archetypal duality of feminine nature as conceived by the age of reason. Braxley is the inexplicable and mechanical personification of evil, while his henchman Abel Doe, a more humanized example of villainy, is, typically, the renegade who has betrayed the deepest bonds of both kinship and race. Completing the *dramatis personae*, finally, Nathan Slaughter is—in at least one aspect—what Perry Miller (1967) calls "the simple son of Nature" who "expounds the piety and craft of the woods, and ranges the benign forces of the primeval on the side of virtue, so that at last [the protagonist] can settle down to civilized monogamy" with his fair-haired bride. All very predictable!

Despite its fundamental conventionality, however, there are other elements in *Nick of the Woods* which, albeit subtly, militate against an unqualified romance classification. If nothing else, the brutality and bestiality of the Indians are made to seem even more of an artistic incongruity in the context of a tradition generally distinguished by its predilection for limpid moods and highly stylized forms. Although *Nick* does appear at first glance to be a more or less straightforward example of the romantic fictions turned out by the hundreds of imitators of Scott, in fact, on closer examination it *also* reveals a number of characteristics which point more readily to a related but quite distinct subset of this species. Those features, for example, collectively identified in Curtis Dahl's introduction to the 1967 College and University Press edition of the book as "strained melodrama"—"Ghostly voices, kidnapped babies, illegitimate heirs, stolen wills, vile machinations of a villain...to kill the hero and force the heroine into an abhorred marriage"—while hardly uncommon in the popular literature of that period, are trademarks in particular of the gothic novel. Most significant of all, the strange figure of Quaker/killer Nathan Slaughter—the locus of most of the supposedly supernatural phenomena in the book—shows evidence of a strategy almost always diagnostic of the latter genre. To be specific, although this character was clearly based on the "Indian-hater" of frontier legend popularized by such authors as Judge James Hall, Bird's careful attribution of schizophrenic symptoms to his villain was right in line with that convention favored by the Radcliffe school of gothic writers which dictated that once the reader was given the chance to indulge his appetite for the gruesome, the thrilling, and the fantastic, all paranormal manifestations had to be neatly explained away in naturalistic and preferably scientific terms. Whether or not the pseudo-psychological aspect of the book—a study of split personality and its relationship to physiological problems such as epilectic seizures—was, as Dahl claims, central to Dr. Bird's purpose in writing, the treatment is an interesting clue to the author's possible influences and ideas about the kind of fiction that he was producing.

Considering *Nick of the Woods* as a work in the gothic tradition rather than as a typical romance seems to eliminate or at least to mitigate the critical problems presented by Bird's Indians. As gothic stage props, they were meant to function primarily in symbolic terms. To complain about a lack of realism here is thus as pointless as criticizing that eighteenth-century European gothic classic, *The Monk*, for failing to give an historically accurate picture of the Roman Catholic Church. Realism was both incompatible with and irrelevant to the artistic necessities implied by the choice of genre. And if the objection is made that there was a considerable difference between the Indian and the stock figure of the mad monk who had at least the authority of folk tradition to justify the terms of his literary incarnation, it need only be pointed out that however much mellowing the American image of the Indian had undergone by the nineteenth century, the satanic savage of the Puritans was still embedded firmly enough in American culture to provide a perfect model for the role. Moreover, there had already been at least one other American writer—and a popular one with whose work the widely-read Bird was almost certainly familiar—who utilized the Indian in just such a manner.

In his preface to *Edgar Huntly*, published in 1799, Charles Brockden Brown explains his unusual material as a conscious, literary decision. The purpose of the novel, he says, is

...that of calling forth the passions and engaging the sympathy of the reader... Puerile superstition and exploded manners, Gothic castles and chimeras, are the materials usually employed for this end. The incidents of Indian hostility, and the perils of the western wilderness, are far more suitable; and for a native of America to overlook these would admit of no apology.

At the peak of post-Revolutionary fervor such a replacement of conventional European materials with native American ones as Brown suggests was an obvious and necessary step for the American writer to take. Aside from the patriotic motives, however, Brown was also perceptive enough to realize that the improbability of the settings and devices used by Radcliffe and Lewis, once detached from the traditions in which they found their roots, must inevitably present a stumbling block for the American reading public which could only be successfully eliminated through the substitution of symbols with a specifically American meaning. Turning to the historical fears and anxieties of his own people, Brown thus proposed to replace the haunted manor house and crumbling abbey with the forest and the cave. More to the point, instead of the insane priest or decadent baron he designated the Indian—already imbued with demonic qualities by the Manichaean imaginations of the Puritans—as the most appropriate New World embodiment of unnatural evil. In *Nick of the Woods*, then, Bird was simply following an established literary tradition.

Does this "explain" all the oddities we have noted? Actually, the Brown/ Bird version of the Indian implied considerably more than just the Americanization of a European genre. Quite above and beyond shifts in literary fashion, the fully developed American gothic, especially as it altered rather than merely imitating its European models, signalled some very important features of the American consciousness which produced it. As Leslie Fiedler notes in his classic study *Love and Death in the American Novel*, "The change of myth involves a profound change in meaning." The gothic Indian who appeared in American literature may therefore be seen as representing not just an aspect of the natural landscape, but also—as so often before in his multiplex American incarnations—a unique quality of the American mind. According to Fiedler, indeed, the two different gothic traditions, American and European, were almost paradigms for two divergent responses to social/political experience. The gothic in Europe, he says, developed its characteristic form at least partly as an expression of middle-class discontent with and suspicion of a decadent and amoral aristocracy. In nature-haunted America, on the other hand,

our novel of terror...(even before its founder has consciously shifted his political allegiances), is well on the way to becoming a Calvinist expose of natural human corruption rather than an enlightened attack on a debased ruling class or entrenched superstition. The European Gothic identified blackness with the super-ego and was therefore revolutionary in its implications; the American Gothic (at least as it followed the example of Brown) identified evil with the id and was therefore conservative at its deepest level of implication, whatever the intent of its authors.

The phenomenon noted here by Fiedler was obviously yet another manifestation of the early colonists' fear not so much of the wilderness but of the answering echoes that it found within their own minds. This fear of the darker, more unruly aspects of the human psyche lost its institutionalized structure once secularization divested it of its supernatural associations, but the persistence of the demonic savage in American literature whenever it could find a suitable vehicle testifies that the feelings involved were more generalized than their specific connection with the Puritans might suggest. Indeed, leaving aside for the moment the political implications of the situation, what we would seem to be dealing with here is *not*, strictly speaking, an historical phenomenon. Slotkin, like Fiedler, claims that the Indian in American mythology has *always* tended to function as a symbol of the libido. If this were so, it would certainly explain why, even after he no longer presented any "real" danger to his white antagonists, his literary incarnations continued to carry so many ambiguous undertones. For the civilized man the libido is virtually guaranteed to be ambiguous. On the one hand, as Slotkin points out, it is a reservoir of "sexual, conceptual, and creative energy." On the other it is the locus of violent passions and irrational behavior. But in *both* guises it is clearly ranged against "reason, the power of will, the socially-formed conscience." This is no more nor less than Moira internalized. The wilderness every man carries within him! The threat implicit in such a condition is a common source of tension in the literature produced by cultures of any significant degree of complexity, signalling as it does an inherent and largely irresolvable conflict between public values and private impulses. According to Slotkin's analysis, then, the American writer who projected a demonic image of nature in the person of the savage—no matter whether the latter appeared as bride, brother, or evil alien—was to some extent just responding normally to a universal human dilemma.

Taking a clue from Fiedler, however, we can carry this analysis one step further than Slotkin does. The gothic savage was not merely a new symbol for an old fear, but to some extent, as we have already seen, reflected an attempt to deal with a radical unbalancing of traditional experiential antitheses. Just to review some of our previous conclusions, in America, where the age-old controlled opposition between Moira and Themis was endangered by the overwhelming impact of unmediated nature, the threatening aspects of the libido became much more apparent than its promise. Even—or perhaps *especially*—the creative, beneficent side of nature was often seen as dangerous because, evoking as it did "the earliest period of childhood, unseparated from 'the exuberant bosom of the common mother' " (Rogin), it invited a submission, a surrender of the self-discipline that progress and civilization, the two prime referents of the great American Mission, required.

To what extent was this response rational, and what, if any, were its sources beyond a purely subjective level? Fiedler, as we have noted, suggests that there was a direct relationship between the American's fear of the wilderness and his particular political stance; Martin Green's analysis of the revolutionary spirit reinforces this kind of interpretation. During a revolutionary period, he says, when the Faustian mode predominates, sexual license and other unrestrained behavior is valued as a symbol of rebellion against entrenched institutions. After a revolution, however, there tends to be an equally violent revulsion against that sort of behavior and a corresponding emphasis on socially constructive virtues. From one point of view, the early colonists in America were, one and all, living in the aftermath of a revolution. Cromwell's ultimate act of rebellion—culminating in regicide—was only a prototype for the necessary repudiation of father and fatherland by every new immigrant to America. The American Revolution, in other words, merely re-enacted publically what had been a controlling factor in American emotional experience all along (see section 3.4.2). This being the case, it is hardly surprising that the eighteenth-century Americans, even the Fathers of the Revolution themselves, should have been

Erasmian—that is, conservative—rather than Faustian. Nor is it surprising that this stance would imply a fear of overt sexual behavior and of the libido from which it stems.

In complete contradistinction to this quirk of character, the country itself, with its unrestrained fertility and mythic overtones, had always seemed steeped in erotic associations. "Come boys, Virginia longs till we share the rest of her maidenhead," cries the Captain in the Renaissance play *Eastward Hoe* by Marston, Chapman, and Jonson, while John Donne describes his disrobing mistress as "America, [a] new-found-land" which invited his roving hands "before, behind, between, above, below." Here then, in this overtly conflicting vision, is at least part of the explanation for the ambivalence towards, indeed the outright fear of, nature which eventually produced the gothic savage. The libido was not only *hypothetically* dangerous, but in America, by pre-definition, it would *always* tend to run rampant if only it were given the slightest opportunity. Small wonder that the Puritans were horrified by Morton's sexual trafficking with the Indians. It reinforced what they feared and expected all along. The Indian, as an emblem of the most tempting aspects of nature, thus became a symbol for this largely unrecognized sexual fear. "These saints," said the contemporary William Byrd, "conceived the same Aversion to the Copper Complexion of the natives, with that of the first Adventurers to Virginia, who would, on no Terms, contract alliances with them, afraid perhaps, like the Jews of Old, lest they might be drawn into Idolatry by those Strange women."

There was one level, however, on which the revulsion against nature and libido was inspired not only by a deeply ingrained psychological orientation but also by objective observation. There was ample evidence available that the wilderness was in fact an evil influence on the European immigrants. Long before there had been time to develop a distinctively "American" character both Beverly and Byrd, as we have seen, commented on the sloth and apathy that overtook so many of the newcomers in their garden-like environment, and as the wilderness was pushed back further such writers as Crèvecoeur continued to make similar observations on the unfortunate effects of the wilderness setting. It was consequently very easy for the American to reinforce his conservative predispositions by making a factual correlation between the wilderness and viciousness. This correlation, as Curti points out, came to be all the more widely believed as the frontier became more of a reality than an idea:

Poets like William Blake, identifying the western country with pristine purity, thought of it as a blank tablet on which was to be penned a new chapter in man's history even more glorious than that being written on the Atlantic seaboard...[but] an increasing number of travelers expressed disillusionment with the meanness of the frontier. The French scientist Volney had been one of the first to do so. In the early years of the nineteenth century Englishmen, drawn to the West by curiosity and lust for adventure or by hope of gain, painted it in their travel books in the blackest hue. They dwelt on its unhealthfulness, its infertility, its poverty; they condemned its inhabitants for their ignorance, crudeness, downright bestiality, and wickedness.

In this way, then, the American's deep-seated fears of his unconscious drives were externalized, projected into concrete historical terms by his identification of the symbolically threatening wilderness with an observable social phenomenon. By the late eighteenth century, American fear of nature thus tended to be localized and rationalized into commonsense dicta largely devoid of hysterical overtones: "If the will and conscience, formed to facilitate the progressive thrust and the moral order of society, are...turned from their proper social objects and concerns," the average American of this period might claim, "social disintegration may follow" (Slotkin).

That the less rational substrata still lurked beneath the surface of American pragmatism may, however, be easily inferred from the recurrence of the demonic Indian in American literature, along with, to a lesser extent, his stylized antagonist, the Indian-hater, long after xenophobia was no longer considered to be a normal, socialized mode of response. The satanic savage in fact continues to be seen, at least sporadically, from the Puritans through Melville's Fedallah and Twain's Indian Joe to twentieth-century "horse opera." Bird's Indians may thus be understood as a manifestation of a generally submerged but persistent current in American thought. Less of a departure in purely literary terms than it may seem when viewed primarily in the context of romance conventions, *Nick of the Woods* is consequently still an interesting indicator of underlying emotional influences because the literary tradition to which it belongs is itself related to and inspired by those more covert levels of public response. Moreover, although Bird may have been inclined towards this tradition in the first place because he, as a southerner, was more deeply touched by racial-sexual fears than the average nineteenth-century American ("To the slave-holding south," says Slotkin, "there could be no question of the degeneracy inherent in any form of race mixing. Any figure who blended Indian and white traits would be automatically suspect."), the same fears were to some extent latent throughout American consciousness. The gothic savage was simply a displaced fragment of that dark underside of the human psyche which the American, with his feelings of helplessness and vulnerability in the face of overwhelming and incomprehensible nature forces, has *always* found so difficult to deal with.

The gothic savage in and by himself was, of course, no more complex than the classical savage or the romantic savage. He did represent a more deeply buried side of American experience during a period largely self-committed to progress, optimism and common sense, but if the fundamental ambiguity contained no more than this single term—the negative one—it would not have been likely to produce the kind of focal tensions characteristic of great literature. No matter how violent the reaction, however, Moira still had an undeniable appeal, and there were other currents in American history, even beyond the more or less obvious aesthetic and intellectual fashions cited above, which, coalescing sometime after the second decade of the nineteenth century, gave nature in general and the Indian in particular a symbolic depth and evocative power that they could scarcely have achieved in any other culture.

To some extent, admittedly, these currents were simply related to the general upswing in the popularity of nature stimulated by "Romanticism." For the most part, however—surprisingly enough—this particular influence proved a fairly minor one. Because, as we have already discussed, the Romantic impulse in America was channelled largely into *safe* outlets like a few basically trivial fictional forms, "moderate" or nostalgic primitivism, and a vogue for landscape emphasizing aesthetic taste more than spontaneous emotion, it actually helped domesticate and/or sublimate the more immediate aspects of nature rather than encouraging full receptivity to them. Views of nature produced under the direct auspices of American Romanticism thus tended to be highly stylized and, beyond the most superficial levels of response, emotionally neutral. A more important focus for the truly subversive potential of nature symbolism was therefore provided by two other elements which were influential if not fully recognized in American culture at this time: (1) the continued operation of a paradise myth as a controlling metaphor at a very deep psychological level, and (2) the simultaneous vision of a mutilated garden, with Adam self-impelled to his second and final fall away from nature.

We have already examined the influence of the paradise myth on early conceptions of America, but we have perhaps not yet given adequate recognition to either the ubiquitousness nor the full psychological significance of the various garden images, not just in America but in the whole cultural context from which the idea of America arose. In fact, as Mircea Eliade suggests in *The Eternal Return*, the complex of emotions embodied in such images may possibly be among the few constants of human nature. The underlying tenor to the metaphor, in other words, reverberates far beyond any particular time-specific incarnation. The key to this reverberation is not literary but psychological. As Charles Sanford summarizes in his own study of wilderness/paradise myths in Christian tradition, Edenic fantasies may be seen to serve a specific therapeutic function insofar as they have the capacity to mediate between human hopes and inhuman limitations.

Interested in discovering the main source of that collective faith, belief, or tradition which enabled tens of millions of men and women "for century after century, to endure great historical pressures without despairing, without committing suicide or falling into that spiritual aridity that always brings with it a relativistic or nihilistic view of history," [Eliade] investigates the myths of early...civilizations and finds that a common denominator...was the myth of eternal return. Everywhere—in ancient Mesopotamia and Syria, in India and Greece, among early Christians as well as among North American Indians—recurs the myth of a lost paradise together with an eschatological view of history in which the end of time reactualizes the beginning of time. Everywhere he finds a periodic confession of sins, a tendency toward purification, which reveals the nostalgia of "fallen man" for the lost paradise of mythical memory.

There is a sense, therefore, in which man *needs* to believe in the possibility of paradise regained, whether in time or in space. Hence the eagerness to recognize in a new found America a reality that fulfilled the dream. Hence also the reluctance wholly to relinquish that dream even after the experienced facts—as we have seen—failed to correspond with it.

This reluctance to give up on the wishful idyll, if not the only reason, was certainly high among the reasons why the American conquest of the west was such a feverish process. So strong was the will, or need, to believe, that even after the original experience of America betrayed the paradisial expectations the myth lost very little of its power as a motivating force, the focus for its constantly renewed promises being merely moved progressively further westward as larger areas were progressively demythicized by the inroads of civilization. If America as a whole were not the earthly paradise, surely the "West" would still prove to be. It was a potent hope. Unless we realize just *how* potent, indeed, the intensity of the pioneering movement in America will hardly seem credible. As Lewis Mumford points out:

[The] westward expansion of the pioneer was, without doubt, furthered by immediate causes, such as the migration of disbanded soldiers after the Revolution, endowed with land-warrants; but from the beginning, the movement was compulsive and almost neurotic; and as early as 1837 Peck's New Guide to the West recorded that "migration has become almost a habit." External matters of fact would perhaps account for the New England migration to Ohio: they cease to be relevant, however, when they are called upon to explain the succession of jumps which caused so many settlers to pull up stakes and move into Illinois—and then into Missouri—and so beyond, until finally the Pacific Coast brought the movement temporarily to an end. This restless search was something more than a prospecting of resources.

It was, in actuality, nothing less than a continued search for paradise.

The correlation was more than merely implicit. As in the reports of the early explorers, paradisial imagery was used by western travellers so widely in their descriptions that it became a commonplace. Dorothy Dondore lists an impressive number of enthusiasts who heaped superlatives upon the Mississippi River Valley during the nineteenth century (Americans and Europeans both, including such figures as Marryat, de Tocqueville, William Darby, James Caird, and Jacob Ferris) and then goes on to comment on the surprising conventionality and repetitiveness of the language characteristically used in their descriptions. "These are all, of course, mere variants of the crescendo of praise which, beginning with the first explorers of the valley, is repeated in different keys throughout its successive periods of ownership," she says. "So, too, the more extended descriptions re-echo notes early struck. The tribute 'a good poor man's country; for, in truth, the clusters are clusters of Eschol, the land foams with creamy milk, and the hollow trees trickle with wild honey' is only a slightly more orthodox conception of the mediaeval notion of the Earthly Paradise." Despite Curti's invocation of travel books which painted their object in "blackest hues," the west in fact (just like Virginia two centuries earlier) more often than not seems to have struck newcomers as not just vaguely but specifically Edenic, a land—as C.W. Dana puts it in a popular travelogue entitled, aptly, *The Garden of the World*—"where the wildest dreamer on the future of our race may one day see actualized a destiny far outreaching in splendor his most gorgeous visions."

Of all the western regions it was Kentucky which, in the minds of the public, seemed most strikingly to exemplify the promise of a New Eden. A century before even the first settlers arrived, this area had already been transformed by rumor into "something rich and strange," not merely "a magnificent forest enveloped in a blue haze but also a fabled garden interpenetrated with myth." Arthur K. Moore, in *The Frontier Mind*, claims, in fact, that this focal territory provided "the ground...upon which the frontier mind, ultimately the western mind, acquired [its] definite form...[and where] The forces which shaped the West converged...and fell into a perceptible pattern." The paradisial terms which typically dominated descriptions of Kentucky were not, moreover, purely decorative. In his history of the area Moore reveals how direct the relationship was between the garden imagery and the motives which drew colonists thither:

> The "flowery and enchanting fables" of enthusiasts and knaves, according to Thomas Ashe, produced the frenzied emigration to Kentucky. Oversimple to be sure, this explanation has a significant core of truth; for Imlay, among other knaves and enthusiasts, intensified the mythic connotations of the tramontane garden land. In other words, the primordial longing for the Earthly Paradise actualized as emigration to Kentucky to some extent as a consequence of *A Topographical Description* and similar accounts, which described the region in terms familiar to the tradition. It goes without saying that speculators exploited the myth. Many individuals in Europe and the East were seduced by the vision of paradise in Kentucky and hastened there without much concern for the realities of settlement. The solicitations of the speculators would have fallen on deaf ears, however, had people not been emotionally prepared at the end of the eighteenth century for the discovery of an Eden.

The primary inspiration for immigration was thus not so much the *actual* capacity which the American west displayed for providing a convincing facsimile of an earthly paradise as the need and/or desire of the immigrants to *believe* that they would find that paradise there.

So strong was the hold of the paradise myth on the American mind that it persisted in the public imagination in the face of numerous blatant contradictions. For many of the actual participants, unfortunately, the shock of confronting these contradictions had tragic consequences. They came to Kentucky expecting "abundance in all desirable things and boundless liberty for all, thus a new life immeasurably superior to that before and equal to the idyllic modes of existence after which the human race has always yearned" (Moore). They found instead a crude and often cruel reality. Mumford summarizes the ironic gap between the idea and the experience of pioneering:

> The vast gap between the hope of the Romantic Movement and the reality of the pioneer period is one of the most sardonic jests of history. On one side, the bucolic innocence of the Eighteenth Century, its belief in a fresh start, and its attempt to achieve a new culture. And over against it, the epic march of the covered wagon, leaving behind it deserted villages, bleak cities, depleted soils, and the sick and exhausted souls that engraved their epitaphs

in Mr. Masters' Spoon River Anthology. Against the genuine heroism and derring-do that accompanied this movement...must be set off the crudities of the pioneer's sexual life, his bestial swilling and drinking and bullying.

For the pioneers themselves, then, the garden was often full of snakes. And their reactions in turn provided more than enough reason for observers to become disillusioned as well. Indeed, those aspects of Kentucky which *did* live up to mythic expectations—its wildness, abundance, and lack of social restraints— were often just enough to bring out the worst in the newly arrived emigrants. Refusing to conform to the cultural program laid out for him, the real (as opposed to the legendary) Kentuckian behaved more often than not with the utmost profligacy—a poignant contrast with his much-touted mythic role. "Kentucky," Moore says, "was...something of a laboratory in which the noble savage of the primitivists had every opportunity to fulfill himself and thus disclose his actual quality—and fulfill himself he did, though not as the Enlightenment had anticipated." Instead of bringing out the natural nobility of human nature, in fact, the "American frontier...functioned as a catalyst to precipitate such barbaric modes of behavior as highly developed societies suppressed. European travellers...were appalled." In America itself, though— despite all the disillusioning evidence—the myth still hung on. For a while during the nineteenth century it seemed, indeed, as if the idealized version of the west would *never* be dislodged.

Whence, then, came the aforementioned ambiguity?

Again the problem was less deflation than diffusion. That the real Kentuckian emphatically and repeatedly repudiated by his behavior his romanticized portraits was less damaging to the coherence of the paradise myth than some of its own terms of reference. As we saw in our examination of the Boone figure, in fact, the authority of this myth was undercut by conceptual ambivalence right from its inception. Edwin Fussell attributes the problem to the paradox implicit in the shifting temporal/spatial associations of the term "frontier." "The American West," he says "is almost by definition indefinite and indefinable, or at least changing, pluralistic, and ambiguous in signification." This vagueness is never more apparent than in the American's tendency to vacillate between "an absolute meaning (location)" for the frontier, and an often incompatible "relative meaning (direction)." The semantic confusion in turn leads to confusion about the experiential referents of the word. As Fussel points out, those "exhilarating analogous progressions from East to West and from present to future [which underlay the American sense of mission] were surcharged with teleological nationalism cartographically advancing from right to left, Old World to New, reality to beatitude. Yet paradoxically the American West—as chaos, matrix, or embryo—was also 'earlier,' and therefore in the past." We thus have "radically divergent conceptions of the national destiny," as embodied in the "conflicting notions 'back' ('backwoodsman') and 'front' ('frontiersman')," reflecting "the antithetical regressive and progressive readings of the Westward Movement." The problem, in other words, comes back once again to the difficulty of sanctifying simultaneously both nature and civilization.

"Difficult" does not mean "impossible," of course. If here we come up against the same old conflict, we also find ample evidence—again—of the digestive powers of the popular imagination. In "The 'Garden' and the 'Workshop': Some European Conceptions and Preconceptions of America, 1830-1860," for instance, Marvin Fisher details the extent to which new immigrants to America—and, presumably, by extension, also immigrants moving from the east into the western regions—managed to accommodate "two seemingly distinct and somewhat contradictory sets of images" in their expectations: "(1) a surprisingly complete version of the 'myth of the garden,' and (2) an even more surprising faith in the ability of the machine to lead the individual American to the good life and...the nation to a position of eminence." Disagreeing with Nash Smith's conclusion that the agrarian myth (a domesticated version of the paradise myth) was discarded early in the nineteenth century because it was not comprehensive enough to offer adequate intellectual apparatus for interpreting post-industrial society, Fisher demonstrates the extent to which both "garden" and "workshop" were made to merge into a single, broad, explicitly paradisial image of felicity.

This merging of the two concepts was accomplished partly by the readiness of Americans, as Cheyfitz describes it, to violate the "fixed hierarchy" of language, seducing or coercing key words "into an ambiguous form." The use of a single vocabulary to describe divergent effects, whatever the intentions of the speaker, implies an essential identity between opposites. "[T]he coexistence of agricultural abundance with potential industrial abundance" (Fisher), both promising similar social and individual benefits, made it easy for Americans to consider both possibilities as manifestations of a single generalized prosperity. Such writers as Poussin and Martineau, moreover, painted the new "golden age of civilization" to be ushered in by technological expansion in almost identical terms as their contemporaries used for the primitive garden. Just as agrarian doctrine stressed the purifying or regenerative powers of nature, in fact, the progressives, too, stressed the social orderliness, the moral advantages, and the improvement to health which could be expected from industrialization. Such a viewpoint as this was facilitated by the fact that in America the existing factory towns, generally small, scattered, and located in rural settings, gave little indication of the wretchedness and squalor potential in a highly industrialized society like Britain. In general, though, as Fisher points out, it seems that the philosophical "inconsistencies which trouble contemporary historians and critics—[that is, the conflicts between]...the primitivism implied by the garden and the technological progress of the workshop myth—were not obvious to most observers in the nineteenth century." The paradise myth, far from being invalidated by the principles of progress, thus became a comprehensive, all-inclusive image for the American dream of happiness.

In spite of the way it tended to swallow conflicting social doctrines which might otherwise have challenged its authority, however, the paradise myth was usually used primarily in reference to "nature" in some guise or another. It was because progress entailed certain inevitable unpleasant consequences, in fact, that the garden symbol became so powerful throughout the nineteenth century. As Moore points out, it is "perhaps the consummate irony that at each step up from savagery the human race has regarded the fruits of progress with a degree of misgiving and often longed against reason for a return to a simpler condition." "Such inclinations toward the not-here and not-now," he continues, "doubtless originate as wish-fulfillment phantasies floating up from the suffering unconscious mind, though none reaches the level of expression without a more or less rational garment. *Men invariably invoke authority to cover their cultural retreats and seldom disclose as the true cause their own failure or disillusionment*" (italics added). The idea of perfectability, the image of a land offering limitless opportunity, the belief that prosperity was within reach of everyone: all these optimistic clichés put a great pressure on the individual to *succeed*. Failure and disillusionment were thus even more of a danger in an expanding society than in a static one where expectations were more realistic. And here is where the idea of an earthly paradise became so important, offering an externalized substitute to fill the inner emptiness of exploded dreams. The more that Eden retreated from the grasp, the more important the *idea* became that it was still out there waiting.

The frontier, then, precisely because it was not a fixed and final location but, for a time at least, seemed to recede indefinitely (enticingly) into the distance, provided a particularly appropriate point of reference for the Edenic myth in American imagination. As long as there was an area of free land somewhere, the hope of an earthly paradise needed not be totally relinquished. The frontier—the "West"—thus for many people became associated with all that was most meaningful in nature. Even beyond this, it collected so many more and deeper symbolic associations throughout the nineteenth century that many Americans came to believe that it actually represented some sort of epitome of what was meant by "American."

The almost exemplary illustration of this trend of thought is provided by Frederick Jackson Turner, who produced in 1893 a thesis about frontier society which was to be one of the most persuasive views of American history ever formulated. The interesting thing about Turner's thesis, however—and probably the single factor most responsible for its broad and immediate influence—was not its originality but, rather, the extent to which it summarized a view which had been gestating in the American imagination for more than half a century. In Turner's view it was the frontier alone—the free land, the earth itself—which, Anteus-like, imparted to American culture its distinctive strength and vitality.

Our early history is the study of European germs developing in an American environment. Too exclusive attention has been paid...to the Germanic origins, too little to the American factors. The frontier is the line of most rapid and effective Americanization. The wilderness masters the colonist. It finds him a European in dress, industries, tools, modes of travel, and thought... It strips off the garments of civilization and arrays him in the hunting shirt and the moccasin. Before long he has gone to planting Indian corn and plowing with a sharp stick; he shouts the war cry and takes the scalp in orthodox Indian fashion. In short, at the frontier the environment is at first too strong for the man. He must accept the conditions which it furnishes, or perish, and so he fits himself into the Indian clearings and follows the Indian trails. Little by little he transforms the wilderness, but the outcome is not the old Europe, not simply the development of Germanic germs... The fact is, that here is a new product.

Turner's theory is obviously related in basic principles to the environmentalist theories which had been a predominating element in American thought as far back as Crèvecoeur. What an immense distance there is between Turner's conclusions and Crèvecoeur's, though! In eighteenth-century America the frontier was seen as a corrupting influence. By Turner's time it had come to seem a central factor in the formation of the American character, the American intellect, the American way of life as a whole. By Turner's time, in fact, the more disturbing attributes of the wilderness had—on a public level anyway—been almost completely repressed. As a result, many of the beliefs which had been promulgated by eighteenth-century primitivists about the causal connections between nature and liberation re-emerged to become a key factor in American views of American history. Thus, according to Turner, one of the most important effects of the frontier was "the promotion of democracy." Indeed, in his view the frontier almost *created* democracy. How? "As has been indicated," says Turner, "the frontier is productive of individualism. Complex society is precipitated by the wilderness into a kind of primitive organization based on the family. The tendency is anti-social. It produces antipathy to control, and particularly to any direct control... The rise of democracy as an effective force in the nation came in with western preponderance under Jackson and William Henry Harrison, and it meant the triumph of the frontier."

From the distance of almost a century it is, of course, easy to discredit the Turner thesis on academic grounds. As history it is "too optimistic, too romantic, too provincial, and too nationalistic to be reliable" (Pierson). As science, on the other hand, it is simply implausible. Turner's emphasis on the useful qualities of resourcefulness and self-reliance purportedly fostered by frontier life invites "ironical contemplation," says Moore, because it is based on the palpably erroneous assumption "that man in a state of nature"—allowing that it is even reasonable to apply any such label to the European immigrants who largely comprised American pioneer stock—"could somehow create an adequate culture virtually from nothing." Without denying the validity of this criticism, it is nevertheless still possible to cite Turner's thesis as one of the most significant documents in modern historical thought, *not because it is an accurate account of events that actually took place but because it represents so well what most Americans liked to* think *took place*. What Turner produced, in other words, while perhaps bad history, was very good myth.

The *idea*—not the reality—of the frontier was thus one of the most important elements in the American world view. Paradoxically, it became more emotionally compelling as the reality played an increasingly smaller role in the American experience. This was the second element in the equation. The frontier was important first of all because its association with age-old symbols of rebirth and regeneration. It was important secondly because it was vanishing. Again Turner offers, by way of summary, a representative response:

[N]ever again will such gifts of free land offer themselves. For a moment, at the frontier, the bonds of custom are broken and unrestraint is triumphant. There is not *tabula rasa*. The stubborn American environment is there with its imperious summons to accept its conditions; the inherited ways of doing things are also there; and yet, in spite of environment, and in spite of custom, each frontier did indeed furnish a new field of opportunity, a gate of escape from the bondage of the past; and freshness, and confidence, and scorn of older society, impatience of its restraints and its ideas, and indifference to its lessons, have accompanied the frontier.

In just such terms as this the nineteenth-century American attitude towards nature, that purported touchstone of health and sanity, inevitably became touched with nostalgia.

Because the disappearance of the wilderness was as rapid as the need was great, on the other hand, nostalgia was only the lowest common denominator to this reaction. According to Simonson, for instance, in a book aptly called *The Closed Frontier*, the settlement of the west was *the* crucial event in American history, signalling as it did the replacement of optimism with pessimism, of idealism with existentialism, of a "limitless frontier" with a "wall." The decade—the 1890s—during which the American frontier was officially declared closed thus marked the dividing line between states of mind symbolically represented by Henry Adams as the "Virgin and Dynamo, or in more recent years [by] Henry Nash Smith's symbolic Garden and Desert." The traumatic transition, according to Simonson, was marked out by historians in a variety of suggestive terms. "Henry Steele Commager described this decade of the nineties as 'the watershed of American history.' Henry F. May called it 'the end of American innocence.' Van Wyck Brooks used the image of Indian Summer." The meaning implicit in all these terms, however, is that somehow a closed frontier—"the end of the Edenic myth and the illusions it fostered" (Simonson)—meant the loss of some element essential to America's health and happiness.

How did America react to this development? Actually, the closing of the frontier was not a single or sudden event. The sense of loss can be felt in American literature as far back as the 1820s. What was almost purely sentiment in Irving deepened in writers like Cooper into an intense (if confused) emotional reaction. This was not necessary bad, of course. It is possible, in fact, like Simonson, to see the shift as almost wholly positive—the Fortunate Fall that shattered Adam's childish illusions and offered him the mature self-knowledge which is the prerequisite of true tragedy. Unfortunately, the response to self-knowledge is not always—and indeed, not often—as positive as Simonson, with his invocation of a sadder but wiser existential hero, apparently would like to believe. Ideally, perhaps, the recognition of limitations *should* trigger some form of enlightenment, but in American literature it has more often led either to bitter cynicism or—more likely—to a fraudulent escapism which, denying knowledge of limitations, looks always and only backwards "to a time when the myth assured us no walls existed, to a time of perpetual youth and innocence" (Simonson). This general repudiation of the tragic mode would seem amply illustrated by the well publicized failure of classic American literature to move beyond adolescent fables and fixations in its treatment of, for instance, sexual passion, and the fact that—as critics such as Fiedler have pointed out—some of the greatest writers in America have been content to produce "boys' books" like *Huckleberry Finn*. The oddly involuted emotional tenor of such productions, with their "child-like innocence" and "regressive-erotic undertones" (Nance), may, on the other hand, be even more plausibly attributable to yet a third factor underlying the American's feelings about nature and the frontier: guilt.

The basic problem faced by the would-be pioneer was that his headlong quest for paradise entailed inevitable destruction of the same features that made the country seem paradisial in the first place. As Mumford puts it, the "return to Nature led, ironically, to a denatured environment." Nor was this development solely impersonal, a by-product of vast historical forces far beyond the understanding or the responsibility of the individual. There was an obvious and direct correlation between specific actions of the settlers and the despoilation of the wilderness:

> Whole forests of oak, beech, poplar, maple, and walnut, standing since Columbus, collapsed in a matter of years from girdling and deadening with fire. There was in the heart of the new race no more consideration for the trees than for the game until the best of both were gone; steel conquered the West but chilled the soul of the conquerer. This assault on nature, than which few more frightful spectacles could be imagined, owed much to sheer need, but something also to a compelling desire to destroy conspicuous specimens of the fauna and flora of the wilderness. The origin of this mad destructiveness may be in doubt, but there is no question about its effect. The Ohio Valley today has neither trees nor animals to recall adequately the splendor of the garden of the Indian which the white man found and used so profligately. [Moore]

Up to a certain point this process could be justified in terms of America's sense of mission. Before even the end of the eighteenth century the same reasoning that rationalized the sad necessity of sacrificing savagery to civilization—and often, indeed, in the same orations—was also being used to excuse, even to applaud, the inroads made by the pioneers on the forests. The "mighty forests must finally bow to human strength," said James Sullivan in 1795; "the hills and vallies, where [the Indian] has enjoyed the chase, shall be covered with cities and cultivated fields... His agonies, at first, seem to demand a tear from the eye of humanity; but when we reflect...that five hundred rational animals may enjoy life in plenty, and comfort, where only one Savage drags out a hungry existence, we shall be pleased with the perspective into futurity." By the mid-nineteenth century, in contrast, these phrases were starting to sound a little hollow.

Part of the reason why this celebration of national glory no longer glittered quite as brightly as in the early days of the new republic was probably the simple fact that the "mighty forests" were beginning to seem much more finite than they once had. Even more influential than this, however, was the increasing suspicion that the "heroic" pioneers, far from being mere innocent instruments of destiny, had—as Moore implies—wasted the natural resources with a shameful disregard for either sense or sentiment. The ugliness left everywhere in their wake was a rude shock to that majority of observers who had been nurtured on a romantic-aesthetic view of the westward movement, and the virtual disappearance of once-abundant wildlife was a sobering illustration to many Americans of the extent of their national irresponsibility. James Fenimore Cooper's portrait of a young settlement in *The Pioneers*, for instance, reveals a thoughtless profligacy so extreme that even the participants, or, at least, the few more thoughtful among them, had to recognize the ominous implications for posterity. The ugly and indiscriminating levelling of the forests and, especially, the wanton slaughter of wildlife ("So prodigious was the number of birds...[killed that] None pretended to collect the game, which lay scattered over the fields in such profusion as to cover the very ground with fluttering victims") emerge from Cooper's tale with a vividness that betrays his concern with more than simply literary effect. The pioneers who came seeking a garden, whether in the early eastern colonies or in the territories acquired later out west, invariably, in fact, seemed to turn what they found into a wasteland. A comment made by a local planter on the condition of Kentucky only a few decades after settlement is thus, as Moore points out, "somewhat amusing but rather tragic too, for it proclaims the vanity of paradisiacal myths": " 'Kentucky is morally and physically ruined,' " said the anonymous respondant. " 'We have been brought up to live without labour; all are demoralized. No man's word or judgment is to be taken for guidance and government of another. Deception is a trade, and all are rogues. The west has the scum of all the earth. Long ago it was said, when a man left other States, he has gone to hell, or Kentucky.' "

The gap between the pioneers' hopeful expectations and the ugly reality, distressing enough in any case, was, of course, made doubly distressing by the mythical context which shaped those expectations. As we may infer from such writings as Audubon's fondly retrospective *Ornithological Biography* (1831-39), with its ambivalent documentation of a landscape literally transformed by the spread of civilization and technology, even the intoxicating cry of "Progress" was not enough to exorcise from the American consciousness a desire for an archetypal garden which was both spiritual necessity *and* physical potential. In Europe, where the wilderness was long since gobbled up by agrarian and then industrial development, the ideal of nature and the vision of a beautiful but remote golden age of man could be transmitted as an imaginative possibility without ever implying an actual choice. In America, however, the natural paradise was eminently real—and its corruption was therefore not merely the consequence of some age-old fall from grace but the result, quite simply and clearly, of their own efforts. In a country where the myth of Eden had come to dominate both public and private aspirations, the suggestion of a second Fall was bound to haunt the imagination. In America, consequently, even after the wilderness was dying or dead, the guilt-ridden vision of a mutilated garden lingered indelibly on.

With these factors to complicate the emotional equation, it was no wonder that nineteenth-century attitudes towards nature were both ambivalent and compulsive. The wilderness was valuable: the wilderness was gone. That was the basic problem to be confronted. There were, to be sure, numerous ways to deal with this problem. One could, for instance, merely deny that the wilderness was valuable at all, and doubtless there were many individuals who had no trouble maintaining that stance. Unfortunately, during the nineteenth century so many national values, so many of the things that made America America, became associated at least indirectly with wild nature that it was hard to discredit it completely. Another possibility was to agree about nature's benefits but to deny that the reservoir had really dried up. This alternative could lead either to wish-fulfilling fantasies or to a re-internalization of the psychic landscape. On the one hand it would produce Melvillean south-sea romances, much science fiction, and all the untamed heroes of Wild West whom Henry Bamford Parkes called "Metamorphoses of Leatherstocking." On the other hand we have Emerson, belatedly perceiving that Romantic nature which only peripherally involved landscape, and identifying the wilderness with the mind; Whitman finding the whole world in his body; and Thoreau locating the symbolic west in his own back yard.

For many Americans, however, the myth was too firmly connected with *real* nature—an actual historical and geographical wilderness—to be reoriented easily. The spectrum of American literature is consequently dotted with figures like Huckleberry Finn and Hemingway's Nick Adams, who embody both the spiritual necessity of access to the natural world *and* the inescapable omnipresence of a wasteland society which more often than not denied this access to its inhabitants. The extent to which these two young men are explicitly associated with nature in the nature/society antithesis may, in fact, be taken as a paradigm of the national condition, for they are both unmistakable incarnations of that archetypal American protagonist whom R.W.B. Lewis calls "the American Adam": "a new kind of hero...an individual emancipated from history, happily bereft of ancestry, untouched and undefiled by the usual inheritances of family and race; an individual standing alone, self-reliant and self-propelling, ready to confront whatever awaiting him with the aid of his own unique and inherent resources... His moral position was prior to experience, and in his very newness he was fundamentally innocent." But was he, though? Is there not a fundamental point which Lewis has missed about the Adamic figure in American literature? Adam-as-victim is not merely related to but *identical with* Adam-the-despoiler.

Nor have attitudes *towards* the Adamic figure been as straightforward and simple as Lewis implies. In this particular mode—Adam-in-the-garden—he has not, in fact, been generally presented as a consistent, idealized self-image for the Americans: he *couldn't* be. In his posited intimate relationship with nature, on the one hand, he represents not only the beneficence of the garden (as if this weren't complicated enough with its mixed associations of love/need/loss/guilt) but also—and this takes us right back to the first half of this section and Robert Montgomery Bird—the disorderly to demonic face of wilderness. On the other hand, as the pioneer, he betrays the garden himself. What Lewis did not see, in fact, was that far from embracing the Adamic figure outright as a viable symbolic ego, the American writer has seemed most often to identify *both* aspects of the archetype (frequently confounding them in the process as if to obscure their more problematic implications) with anti-social elements that must be dispersed. Consequently, the true American Adam has most typically been cast out of the garden *by his own fellow Americans*—and the garden cast out with him. Although he is almost always defeated in some way, however—killed, or driven mad, or exiled, or, like Cooper's Leatherstocking, pushed westward beyond the frontier where his dangerous influence will be out of sight and mind—Adam's defeat has inevitably seemed more of a tragedy than a triumph, as if his conquerers felt in their hearts that rather than purging society of some subversive Lord of Misrule, they had cast out the very finest part of their own soul. And, of course, to a large extent they had. If a prelapserian Adam must always present too much of a threat to social integrity to be wholly embraced, the American has still, almost compulsively, continued to identify himself with Adamic values in a generalized sense, thus becoming his *own* betrayer, Adam-after-the-Fall. This is the irresolvable ambiguity lurking at the heart of much of America's finest and most powerful literature.

The complexity of this emotional response belies the common image of American culture poised somewhat uneasily between irreconcilable opposites. Marius Bewley sees the core conflict as a political tension "between tradition and progress, between democratic faith and disillusion, between the past and the present and the future; between Europe and America, liberalism and conservatism, aggressive acquisitive economics and benevolent wealth." For Leo Marx it is, more simply, the garden versus the machine. For dozens of other critics there have been dozens of other variations on this same basic theme. "American fiction," says Richard Chase, summarizing what has come to be almost a standard view, "has been shaped by the contradictions and not by the unities and harmonies of our culture." But while all these critics are *right*—these tensions, all of them, as we have seen, both energize and undermine the American's view of his world—they are also *wrong*. Their simplifications tend to falsify the pattern which emerges.

As we pointed out in relation to Crèvecoeur, the American is *not* simply poised between antithetical values. Set against the backdrop of a lost garden, each pole of his emotional spectrum has its own inner tensions. There are, in other words, conflicts within conflicts, and at every level these ultimately resist *all* attempts at resolution, if only because the terms of reference tend to shift and change whenever one tries to focus too closely on them. Chase senses something of this when he points out, speaking of the American novel, that "there are some literatures which take their form and tone from polarities, opposites, and irreconcilables, but are content to rest in and sustain them, or to resolve them into unities, if at all, only by special and limited means...[and] in oblique, morally equivocal ways." Even more revealing, however, is the suggestion that the prevailing ambivalence is symptomatic of not merely intellectual confusion but actual sickness of some kind. "American literature is schizophrenic," says James E. Miller. "It is held paralyzed between hope and despair, between the affirmative and the negative, between illusion and fact, between optimism and pessimism, between the ideal and the real." *Paralyzed!* Paralyzed because, among other things, the American could neither embrace nor reject, find nor forget the great white Leviathan, Nature; because, in Perry Miller's (1967) words, "as soon as the identification of virtue with Nature had become axiomatic, the awful suspicion dawned that America was assiduously erecting the barriers of artifice between its citizenry and the precious landscape." And what about that (according to the latter) "most embarrassing of questions—on which side does religion stand, on nature's or on civilization's?" No answer to this seems possible.

The sickness metaphor is thus a very appropriate one—but what kind of sickness was it? Homesickness? Lovesickness? Of all American writers it is Hemingway who perhaps best illuminates this complex matter of the American's emotional ill health, and its connection with nature. In the two-part story "Big Two-Hearted River" that concludes his seminal collection *In Our Time,* for instance, he gives a compelling portrait of the soul-sickness which, increasing throughout the last half of the nineteenth century, seemed finally to reach a climax after the First World War in what has come to be called "the lost generation."

At the beginning of the sketch, Nick Adams, returning after the war to the scene of his childhood, has just stepped off the train. The town, which represented society for the boy, has been devastated by fire and, like the world at large, truly transformed to a wasteland. The grasshoppers, sole inhabitants of this barren scene, have changed their natural bright colors to a dull, dead black, just as the natural emotional capacities of man have also been deadened and dulled in the modern world. As Nick passes through the desolation into the green of the woods beyond, he symbolically leaves the sterile world behind. His goal, much like that of the pioneer Kentuckians, is the river at the heart of the green land, a source of life and fertility, purification and spiritual rebirth.

We thus see that the sickness of modern America is *directly* related to his exile from the garden, and its only cure a return to that Edenic source. The green land, however, is no longer as easy to find as it once was. It takes a special kind of attitude and effort. From the moment that Nick reaches his campsite in this story, in fact, his actions take on the unmistakable overtones of a ritual, and we are given the impression that he is carefully following a prescribed pattern in which every detail is significant. He sets up his tent with the solemn air of a man arranging an altar. He prepares his food as if it were a sacrament. He goes through the motions of fishing slowly and formally, as though he were repeating the steps of a magic formula which, all requirements being perfectly fulfilled, will produce a prescribed and infallible result. Nothing must be neglected or rushed, or the spell will be broken: "He was really too hurried to eat breakfast, but he knew he must." The whole section has the tone of a ceremonial recitation. For the Hemingway hero, unlike the pioneer, the "West" is no longer simply there for the taking. He must, in a sense, recreate it out of his own faith and need.

In the end, the formula *is* successful for Nick. The terror is still there, in the background, but concentration on the simple, safe, physical actions demanded by the ritual holds it at bay—"His mind was starting to work [but] He knew he could choke it because he was tired enough." Eventually, of course, he must go back to the world; the river is only a temporary sanctuary with horror no further away than the swamp where "the sun did not come through" and fishing is a "tragic adventure." For the time being, however, until he is stronger, until the magic of the green world has healed his spirit, Nick will fish in the sun. "There were plenty of days coming when he could fish in the swamp."

The ritual reconciliation with nature works for many of Hemingway's soul-sick characters, in episodes as different as the trout-fishing interlude in *The Sun Also Rises* and Francis Macomber's climactic coming of age on an African safari. For many others, however, such a reconciliation is at best fragile, at worst an inaccessible dream. Even in Hemingway it tends to be frighteningly vulnerable, threatened at every moment by war, women, domestic obligations, or simply the obtuseness of one's less sensitive fellows. A great many of America's most thoughtful writers, "finding the myth of the open frontier fraudulent and the reality of...confinement too overwhelming to endure" (Simonson), are thus concerned with finding/creating a means of *mediating* between man and nature, ensuring (if only symbolically) the relationship which unaided he is apparently incapable of achieving. And this brings us back to the noble savage. If Nick Adams and Huckleberry Finn may be seen as representing the central protagonist of American literature and if the focal problem confronting him has been the necessity/impossibility of a reconciliation with the garden/wilderness, then the Indian obviously offers a comprehensive image of that multi-sided nature which establishes one of his primary terms of reference.

This is not to say that the Indian could become, like the captive, the farmer, the frontiersman, an image of *self* for the American, but he did provide an eminently suitable vehicle for an image of that all-important *otherness* represented by the landscape. For one thing, even above and beyond the causal connections posited by the environmentalists and the aesthetic connections suggested by literary primitivism, there was an obvious physical connection between the wilderness and the natives whose lifestyle had been dependent on it. The disappearance of the one necessarily entailed the disappearance of the other. Even more important, however, was the symbolic versatility achieved by the savage as he accumulated such a wide variety of different and often contradictory associations throughout American history. The satanic/innocent, fearful/tempting, bestial/noble savage was, in fact, one of the few symbolic vehicles which could ever be capable of encompassing the hydra-headed apparition that was nature for an American.

The next section will examine in detail the development of the savage's latest and perhaps most significant role, from Cooper through to Faulkner.

3.4 Cooper and the New Noble Savage

James Fenimore Cooper occupies a peculiar position in American letters, having attracted over the years extremes of both critical adulation and critical abuse. Without attempting to recapitulate this chequered history in any detail, we shall merely note that no single critic seems yet to have explained or explained away a continuing if erratic appeal which, especially in the light of his unquestionable flaws, seems strangely out of proportion. This failure is at least partly due to a tendency to see Cooper in undimensional terms—as a social critic, for instance, or as a romancer in the style of Scott—isolating the appropriate books or even parts of books, and ignoring the rest of the corpus as irrelevant. The fact is, however, that Cooper's major claim to our attention rests on the extent to which he resists such simplifications, his books embodying—often at the cost of inner coherence and stylistic control—much of the ambiguity and complexity typical of American culture as a whole.

It is surprising that this complexity has been largely overlooked or simply written off as artistic inconsistency. Two of the features most frequently discussed in Cooper criticism (both pro and con) from contemporary reviews right up to the present have been: (1) his unique (although ill-defined) quality of "Americanness," sometimes related to attitude, sometimes to subject matter, and (2) his connection with "nature." Parkman, for instance, sounds a typical note in his 1852 review: "Of all American writers, Cooper is the most original, the most thoroughly national. His genius drew aliment from the soil where God had planted it, and rose to a vigorous growth, rough and gnarled, but as strong as a mountain cedar. His volumes are a faithful mirror of that rude transatlantic nature, which to European eyes appears so strange and new... A genuine love of nature inspired the artist's pen; and they who cannot feel the efficacy of its strong picturing have neither heart nor mind for the grandeur of the outer world." Popular assumptions aside, this picture is muddied by the fact that, far from self-explanatory, such terms as "national" and "nature" are rendered by the American context not merely ambiguous but deceptive. And Cooper misses very little of their referential complexity.

Modern critics have been more analytical than Parkman, but not necessarily any more successful in avoiding the dangers of vagueness or oversimplification. In addition to (or perhaps, more accurately, as an elaboration of), the nature/ nationalism duo, during the last two decades discussions of Cooper's novels have most often focused upon (1) the balance of or conflict between antithetical values at the level of theme in his books, and (2) a generally mythic quality.

As we have already seen, the first of these approaches characterizes a popular critical view of American culture as a whole, and for that notable group of academics in quest of *the* definitive polarity by which the national consciousness may be explained (Bewley, Lewis, etc.), Cooper, as a key figure in American culture/history, seems not only to offer a prototypical embodiment of these tensions because he is so representatively American, but also to be so representative precisely because he does embody the characteristic American tensions. The second approach is also conveniently versatile. Few of the critics who use the terms "mythic" or "archetypal" are very clear about what qualities or structures they intend their adjectives to imply, but there seems to be a general feeling that it is again Cooper's representativeness, especially as evinced in his response to nature, which makes his work "something like" an American myth. Richard Chase, combining both approaches, is more explicit, suggesting that it was in expressing those typically American tensions that Cooper achieved his status as a myth-maker.

All this is very interesting, even illuminating, of course—but it can also be misleading, especially if the desire for final and comprehensive definition tempts one into reducing Cooper's exploration of ambivalence into either a simple dialogue or, worse, a closed-ended dialectic symbolically resolved in the "archetypal" figure of Leatherstocking. Used with due caution, however, the perspective offered by these related critical approaches can offer some useful insights into Cooper, particularly insofar as they help us to *appreciate* his complexity rather than simply rationalizing it out of existence.

If the surface is misleading, where then do we start? Actually, leaving rhetoric aside, one of the best keys to evaluating the various tensions, conflicts, and mythic oppositions in Cooper may be found in certain aspects of his style. Much, for instance, is signalled by his preference for a flight-and-pursuit plotline. This feature, due to its general association with sub-literary adventure fiction, has historically been viewed as denoting either frivolity or crass commercialism. We should be careful, however, not to let such habitual attributions mislead us in this case. For all its ubiquitousness in "popular" culture, there is nothing innately trivial about the chase convention. As Charles Brady points out, "Since Conrad endowed this particular pattern with a metaphysic, Kafka with a demonology, and Greene with a theology, it no longer requires defense as a significant esthetic device." *Qua* device, moreover, it has particular relevance to the American state of mind. Echoing the experience of both the captive and the Indian hunter, Cooper's version of the archetypal flight-and-pursuit situation with its characteristic recurrent reversals and inversions of roles and relations, provides a graphic correlative for the self-obsessed American psyche which, in quest of self-definition, and fluctuating between "fear and desire" (Clark), is simultaneously both hunter and hunted. It also points clearly to the focal concern with identity around which not only his "stories" but most of his major themes revolve.

More important than this relatively simple kind of foreshadowing, the principle of organization one may detect *behind* and *beyond* the narrative surface bespeaks not merely Cooper's thematic preoccupations but the characteristic *modality* of his vision. To his contemporaries this author's natural description most often seemed realistic. In somewhat surprising contrast, more recent critics tend to view his style as loosely but broadly symbolic, since different classes of events or objects (such as, for instance, weather and narrative incident, landscape and mental state) often seem to bear a more generalized relationship to one another than their purely naturalistic connections would imply. Although the latter group is undoubtedly correct in perceiving that the uneven and often disjointed quality of Cooper's writing becomes less obtrusive when one stops expecting a logical and orderly sequence of events, completely coherent and fully explained, they are, however, mistaken in replacing logical organization with the kind of structured semantic relationships governing such figures as extended metaphors. In the sense that a metaphor, even the most diffuse, implies two terms bound by some sort of mutual resemblance, such figures seldom have a significant organizational function at all in Cooper's work, since his more characteristic method is the multiple juxtaposition of elements whose interrelationships remain largely potential and problematical. Metaphorical resemblances may be inferred from the network, but the emphatic coexistence of alternate, often incompatible, terms and modes of relation affects the stability of these inferred metaphors to the extent that they shift, dissolve, even explode.

This is why it is a mistake to generalize too broadly from the polarities evident in Cooper's books. Even when one stops short of the comprehensive national dichotomies posited by Bewley *et al.*, the figure may be misleading. Consider, for example, the following statement by Kay Seymour House:

> [H]ead-on, no-quarter-given opposition enters many of Cooper's novels; no compromise is possible between the groups of squatters and landowners, Indians and whites, Dutch and Puritans, or even those who cherish privacy and those who snoop. The values of each group are absolutes; and where there is opposition, there must also be extinction. The manner of extinction may vary—the Indians die violently, while the Dutch and gentry are pressed to death like Giles Cory—but the result is the same, the end of something. A true synthesis of societies is impossible in Cooper's world; the best that society as a whole can achieve is the tolerant coexistence that a controlling disinterested gentry or maritime order makes possible.

House's observations here are quite unobjectionable, but her insistence on projecting the consequences (thematic or historical) of the proffered oppositions into a generalized condition tends to distort or at least to obscure Cooper's technique. Certainly this author is interested in antitheses. Certainly, too, he explores the possibilities and difficulties of reconciliation. The significant point about these explorations, though, is that *none* of the potential modes of group interaction put forth for our consideration is represented by Cooper as necessary *or* ideal according to either fictional or socio-historical reality. Quite counter to House's "must" and "impossible" and "absolutes," Cooper tacitly refuses to arbitrate the alternatives he invokes. Sidestepping both imputations of prejudice and accusations of inconsistency, as presented *in* the oeuvre itself the mode of any given interface (the interface between whites and Indians, for example) would rather appear to be both variable and dependent on the other interfaces energized in any particular fictional grouping.

The same principle of organization may be seen at work in Cooper's portrayal of action. More precisely, it may be inferred from the fact that what he portrays under the guise of action isn't really action at all. For all the conventional blood and thunder, we tend to see events in these novels not in process but as a discontinuous series of frozen tableaux; "periods of arrested motion, the chilling pause in, or sequel to, violence," as D.E.S. Maxwell describes them. In spite of—perhaps because of—Cooper's wordy and staccato play-by-play description, we do not for instance actually experience the fatal struggle between Uncas and Magua in *The Last of the Mohicans* as movement so much as we glimpse in rapid succession the taut figure poised to strike, the fall of a body, the plunge of a knife, and then, like a spent breath, the sudden relief of the action completed. Maxwell implies that this techique is an unfortunate one. "It is unnecessary to linger over the evasiveness of 'Happily he soon succeeded in disarming his adversary...' or the indolent visualization of 'the fierce and disappointed countenance of his foe, who fell sullenly and disappointed,' " he says. "Cooper's heart may have been in the action but his eye was defective...any excitement to be found in the action of the *Mohicans* is in fact supplied by the reader's own imagination with surprisingly small help from Cooper's—in these circumstances—curiously barren prose." The truth is, though, that the suggestiveness about which Maxwell complains is much more effective than explicit commentary. Indeed, Cooper's montage of still photos conveys even more vividly than filmic flow the dynamic quality of movement by capturing and intensifying those few timeless and emblematic moments of pure potentiality.

On a broader scale, the same technique is also turned to account for marshalling incidents of plot. Utilizing an arrangement similar to Henry James's "string of beads," Cooper deploys a series of discrete "scenes"—using the word in its original, graphic sense—along the minimal linear linkage of the conventional line of flight. Each of these foci tends to be emotionally isolated, detailed, concrete, and pre-eminently visual. Collectively they are not merely set within but represented by—*bodied forth as*—a series of clearings in the middle of a dense, shadowy forest.

Again, then, message and medium are mutually reflective in Cooper's text. Again, too, the approach is eminently effective for both underlining *and* delineating meaning. Even aside from the obvious moral implications that Ringe and others have pointed out—even aside from its implied conflation of time and space, fulfilling if only obliquely the American dream of immortality—the value of the iconic glade-in-the-wilderness is, according to Nevius, "both pictorial and psychological—pictorial by virtue of the heightened contrasts between light and shade, open space and interminable forest, and by virtue also of the frame it provided within which the elements of the picture could be composed and the action of the story arrested for a moment; psychological because it provided an exhilarating relief from the claustrophobic experience of the woods." It is also—and more important—*philosophical*. Frames not only contain but exclude. On a more covert level, therefore, Cooper's use of a dense, almost opaque natural landscape to insulate given groupings—given "scenes"—from extrinsic elements tends to deny—or at least deny the importance of—the normal causal or chronological connections between incidents. Since, moreover, elements of theme, character development, symbolic sub-structures, etc., all tend to be rooted in and revolve around these discrete scenes, the general impression of discontinuity carries over into other levels than that of plot. As a result, as we already pointed out, structural relationships of every kind are tenuous, shifting, absorbing potential signification like a sponge. Inconsistencies disappear, or at least are displaced in such a way that it is difficult to pinpoint with confidence any sensed discrepancy.

The evasiveness makes this author difficult to evaluate. It also makes him considerably more interesting. From the standpoint of myth at least, the advantage of his technique lies in its capacity to subsume widely diverse statements of belief or value *without* imposing any definitive conclusions about relative worth or forcing a narrow and unnatural synthesis of polarities. In an overt sense, Cooper (as we will see) often seems to insist upon specific resolutions to the ambiguities implicit in his fictional world, but other levels, other elements structurally juxtaposed with the authorial commentary and challenging this commentary in terms of both aesthetic and emotional weight, combine to offset if not undermine the monologic of conscious intent. If Cooper does provide an almost paradigmatic illustration of the national consciousness, it is in fact not so much his subject matter nor even his treatment of this subject matter that makes him so representative as the unique ability of his novels to *encapsulate untransformed* the full gamut of social and psychological facts that comprised his particular cultural ambience. The reason that so many critics, in basic agreement about the importance of "tensions" in Cooper's work, have disagreed about the precise sources of these tensions (political, social, aesthetic, racial, personal), might thus be the fact that the tensions are not so much *in* the work, as stimulated *by* the work in the context of the reader's own responses and recognitions. This is not to say that the books themselves contribute nothing to the dialogue. If only because he brought together all the problematic elements that we have been discussing in the foregoing chapters *without* falsifying them—indeed, without more than token attempts at reconciliation or interpretation—Cooper, perhaps more than any other writer of his day, succeeded in documenting the full complexity of American consciousness in the first half of the nineteenth century.

Nowhere is this more evident than in the single overriding theme we may infer behind the melodramatic action, the social/political parables, and the sententious authorial commentary of Cooper's novels. We have already said that two of Cooper's most characteristic literary concerns were nature and nationalism. To be more precise—taking a clue from his predilection for the flight-and-pursuit plotline—the two aspects coalesce in his exploration of man-in-nature as a means of finding and defining the American identity.

Appropriately enough, Cooper's most compelling portrait of this national obsession with self-definition is cumulatively conveyed through a kind of kinship myth which runs like a scarlet thread through the diffuse greenery of his novels. The strategy is not, to be sure, a unique one. Throughout the communal oeuvre, says Sundquist, the "tension between experiment and sacrament...is...refracted into the elements of a larger drama, one in which the family is not so much the 'real' family as the constellation of forces generated within a dramatic communal context." Cooper's version of this drama, however, manages not merely to embody but in a sense to defuse this tension. Again we come back to his structural techniques. The same pattern that dominates his presentation of plot segments is repeated in the network of relations between characters. In each book we are presented with a number of discrete personalities in more or less close juxtaposition, but the connections between them tend to be ambiguously defined. Sisters become brides, father figures turn up as lovers, guardians reveal themselves as usurpers. The whole *idea* of relationship becomes incredibly problematic. Indeed, even aside from those technical questions of kinship which are pivotal at the most superficial levels of narrative— the lost children or mates, the unrecognized heirs, the disguised or misplaced parents—the quest for identity in Cooper's novels is characteristically expressed as an extended exploration of familial roles: an attempt to discover and define the modes of relation appropriate to a self-appointed Adam.

What does this have to do with the subject at hand? Since this quest, in its classic form, takes place in a setting far removed from all conventional clues to social roles and relations, like the wilderness or the ocean, the problems of kinship become inextricably interwoven with the problems posed by the natural environment if only by simple contiguity. This association in turn intensifies the whole emotional dynamic of the books. In Cooper, as in his countrymen, feelings of guilt associated with the rape of nature tend to shade over into the less accessible guilt associated with filial rebellion. Since the American Adam was fatherless not merely by definition but by choice, the landscape, as we have noted, became an emotional substitute in the familial equation, replacing the "bad" father with the "good" mother. As the garden was progressively more mutilated, on the other hand, the feminine element also came to seem a threat to self-justification which needed, like Nobodaddy, to be purged, replaced, or discredited. We will examine the ramifications of this symbolic cross-fertilization in greater detail below (section 3.4.3.). In the meantime it is important to recognize the extent to which Cooper's oeuvre, superficially adventitious, depends upon the linked nature/kinship myths for both continuity and coherence.

Next question: how does our old friend the noble savage enter the picture? Precisely because he was *not* a protagonist in the ritual action, the Indian offered Cooper a versatile reference point for exploring the psycho-social and particularly the moral dimension of the American's existential dilemma. Not only are there numerous savages in Cooper, noble and otherwise, therefore, but they tend to play focal roles in the value structures of his novels. The savage, of varying face and hue, is, in fact, one of the most interesting inhabitants of Cooper's fictional world. More to the point, Cooper's attitude toward this iconic personage—which changed significantly over the years—is one of the most interesting elements in the "real" history that hovers behind the made-up stories, illuminating as it does with almost incomparable vividness the ambiguity, the instability, and the complexity of the American's attitude toward nature—*and* toward himself. It is this aspect specifically to which we will address ourselves in the following pages. Where to start? Notwithstanding what we said above about the dangers of partial views, Cooper's prolificity necessitates a certain amount of arbitrary bracketing. Although the corpus as a whole includes a good deal of conventional European-style historical fiction as well as social commentary, quasi-allegorical works, and outright satire, for the task at hand we find our most obvious point of departure in those books in which the man/nature relation is treated most explicitly—the five Leatherstocking novels plus a handful of other tales that fall into the category of "wilderness romances."

3.4.1 Quest for a Mediator

Cooper's first wilderness novel, *The Pioneers* (1823), was an historical study of the American settler's unmediated confrontation with raw nature. One of the most significant fictional treatments of the pioneering movement ever produced in America, this book documents with great perceptiveness and subtlety some of the most ambiguous aspects of the exercise in nation-building. It also documents the ambivalence of its contemporary auditors. Although there is an *apparent* resolution to the communal problems in the symbolic marriage of Elizabeth Temple and Oliver Effingham with its implications of the advent of a new and wiser order, the novel as a whole resists any such simplistic conclusions.

The resistance is hardly surprising. Reviewing the oeuvre we see that Cooper himself was far from consistent in what he said, let alone what he revealed, in his handling of this seminal and recurrent theme. He was fairly consistent, on the other hand, in what he *wanted* to believe. Foremost among his motives for writing was a desire to justify the young republic. And this meant justifying its history. To this end, in *Home as Found* (1838), the second of a pair of novels forming the chronological sequel to *The Pioneers*, Cooper goes out of his way to explain and defend frontier culture, describing the process of settlement itself in somewhat equivocal but unmistakably optimistic terms. The first years after a community is founded, he says, comprise "the pastoral age, or that of good fellowship" when the crudeness of external conditions is compensated for by the energy, social tolerance, and mutual aid of the fellow sufferers. This is unfortunately followed by a vulgar period of social climbing in which "we see the struggles for place, the heart-burnings and jealousies of contending families, and the influence of mere money." The third and final phase, however, looks forward to a time when "men and things [will] come within the control of more general and regular laws." If willy nilly he was forced to recognize its less salutary concomitants, then, Cooper's vision of pioneering was redeemed by his faith in futurity. Or was it?

During his later years, disillusioned by the social/political upheavals of the Jacksonian period and embittered by the hostility of a fickle public, Cooper began to express serious doubts about whether America was in fact going to reach the third stage. Directly in *The Redskins* (1848) and allegorically in *The Crater* (1847) he demonstrates how second stage vulgarity and ignorance might be able to impede realization of that admirable destiny. Even in his early books, moreover, there is ample evidence that he was less sanguine about the inevitability of progress than he liked to admit. There is also evidence that his retrospective assessment was not always as entirely roseate as his historical summation may suggest. During the period in which he wrote *Home as Found*, finding himself trapped in the throes of the "second stage," Cooper looked back at the early days through a haze of nostalgia, referring to the interlude as a "period of fun, toil, neighbourly feeling, and adventure." In 1823, however, his description of a young settlement was nowhere near as idealistic as this. The town of Templeton is characterized far less by good fellowship than by crudeness, not merely of lifestyle and personality, but of the environment itself. Descriptions of the physical setting in *The Pioneers*, significantly enough, return again and again to the destruction of the forests by the pioneers, emphasizing equally the *waste* and the *ugliness* of the phenomenon. Even more than the shock value of the highly dramatized pigeon shoot mentioned in the last chapter, this repetitous lament for the lost trees offsets whatever glamor the thriving young community may offer in other respects.

It also unbalances the whole moral dynamic on which the book is built.

Why? The problem as Cooper reveals it is *not* just a matter of simple ignorance on the part of the settlers. The figure of authority in this village, Judge Marmaduke Temple, is well aware of the implications of the widespread profligacy (" 'It grieves me to see the extravagance in this country' "; " 'We are stripping the forests as if a single year replaces what we destroy' "), but he is powerless to control it. His personal influence, apparently, is insufficient to convince even his closest associates (" 'You are always a little wild on such subjects,' " says cousin Richard), and as for the law which he administers, it seems a rather blunt instrument when for a single unimportant lapse it strikes down Leatherstocking (the one figure on the scene who demonstrates a consistently responsible attitude towards the community's natural resources), and yet remains completely incapable of preventing either the routine despoilation of the environment or more extreme abuses like forest fires and wholesale slaughter of wildlife. This, of course, is the crux of the matter, the point at which *The Pioneers* rises above the particular. If the educating influence of exemplary figures is doomed to fail in establishing just and proper social relations because it lacks the enforcing power of formal authority, and if formal authority, as codified into law, fails equally because it cannot operate on any but the most general and indiscriminating level, what then is the alternative? Personal morality? But even supposing the average person capable of moral judgment, the very conditions of a progressive society, to say nothing of the basic weakness of the human will, make it essential—as the aging Natty Bumppo himself comes to realize in *The Prairie*—that the more vulnerable elements be afforded the protection of the powerful and impartial institutions of law and order. The fact that this basic philosophical problem becomes most agonizingly acute in a frontier society where custom and tradition do not govern behavior to a normal extent is one of the major obstacles to a satisfactory resolution of the dilemma posed by *The Pioneers*. It also helps explain why Cooper's enthusiasm about the "pastoral age" had to be somewhat less than total.

The symbolic level of *The Pioneers* is even more inimical to the possibility of resolution than the overt theme. The symbolic "father" of the community is revealed as a technical usurper with no right to either his privileges or his obligations. Temple's position with regard to the Effingham interests may be satisfactorily "explained," but the symbolic taint remains, since this legal question—as the Leatherstocking reminds us—is an obvious analogue for the fundamental act of disinheriting the Indians. Other, more covert shadowings are equally damaging. The fact that his implicit alter ego, the senior Effingham, is a senile old man shut away from the realities of the world in a cave, for instance, goes far to suggest that the Judge's social optimism and faith in progress, however well-intentioned, are more than a little naive. Most telling of all, Temple's public impotence is both mirrored and underlined by an analogous failure to fulfill privately his most basic paternal responsibilities. For all his much advertised fatherly concern, it is left to the non-father, Leatherstocking, to provide not only moral guidance but physical protection for Elizabeth, saving her first from a panther and later from a forest fire. Striking a note which will increasingly dominate the tone of the series, paternal guidance is thus discredited as a trustworthy basis for social action. Even Judge Temple, one of the most enlightened members of the community, lacks the power either to control or to live in harmony with the forces of nature. But if parental guidance is inadequate, neither is the unaided child capable of dealing with these forces. The essential message the book gets across, in fact, seems to be that unmediated confrontations between man and nature must result in the destruction of one or the other. It is this assumption that must be understood as a background to all Cooper's later explorations of the subject.

The question of how access to nature should be regulated takes on even more ambiguity in the remaining novels of the Leatherstocking series, as it becomes obvious that Cooper not only deplored the *means*, but also shared the national doubts about whether, finally, that access was a good or bad thing as an *end*. As McWilliams describes it, in fact, Cooper's ambivalence echoes exactly the communal response that we have examined in the last few chapters.

In each of these novels, the neutral ground [between civilization and nature] releases both the bestiality and the piety in man. The frontier restores one man to Adamic purity but unleashes suppressed violence in another. Because success in the forest is solely dependent upon physical prowess and mental cunning, Cooper believes that the forest permits settlers to dismiss moral considerations. Yet he also considers the forest to be the source of individuality and true manliness. The forest evokes all of Cooper's yearnings for utter freedom, but also reveals his acute awareness of the inevitable perversion of freedom.

This, however, is where the next two Leatherstocking novels, *The Last of the Mohicans* and *The Prairie*, move, or seem to move, beyond the thematic equivocations of *The Pioneers*. For all their similarity of concern, in these two books Cooper actually in a sense *bypasses* the dilemma by offering, in the person of a rejuvenated Leatherstocking, a composite hero who could reconcile the best of both worlds. As the author explains in his "Preface to the Leatherstocking Tales," removed as he was "from nearly all the temptations of civilized life, placed in the best associations of that which is deemed savage, and favourably disposed by nature to improve such advantage," Leatherstocking seemed "a fit subject to represent the better qualities of both conditions"— that is, civilization and savage life—"without pushing either to extremes." Natty had functioned as a moral referent in *The Pioneers*, demonstrating a power quite out of proportion to the homely role in which he was cast. Natty, moreover, as it turned out, was ideally suited to play the protective, instructive role of the father without being implicated in real fatherhood. Might not Natty then be the mediator that both Cooper and his public were looking for?

Many readers, past and present, would answer this question in the affirmative. In Cooper's own day, Leatherstocking was viewed as "in some sort an epitome of American history" (Parkman), and over the years his symbolic stature has been augmented to the extent that it is now a critical commonplace to classify him as a mythic or archetypal figure. Brady, for example, illustrates the extremes achieved by this recent school of criticism, describing Leatherstocking in his article "Myth-Maker and Christian Romancer" variously as a "semi-divine hero," a "Herakles wrestling against death on behalf of a series of clean-cut young American Admetuses and their Alcestises," an "immortal both in a Keatsian sense and in the sense of numen," and a "young god...an embodied conscience for America." But was Leatherstocking really as completely successful in his symbolic function as such attributions would imply? Surely the internal inconsistencies—much like the inconsistencies in the public transformations of the Boone figure—must necessarily tend to undercut the emotional coherence of the role. Nash Smith, on the other hand, seems to think that the symbol attained its profundity not despite, but specifically *because of* Cooper's "genuine ambivalence":

The original hunter of *The Pioneers* (1823) clearly expresses subversive impulses. The character was conceived in terms of the antithesis between nature and civilization, between freedom and law, that has governed most American interpretations of the westward movement. Cooper was able to speak for his people on this theme because the forces at work within him clearly reproduced the patterns of thought and feeling that prevailed in the society at large. But he felt the problem more deeply than his contemporaries: he was at once more strongly devoted to the principle of social order and more vividly responsive to the ideas of nature and freedom in the Western forest.

While appreciating the undoubted literary enrichment achieved by Cooper's internalization of conflicting allegiances, one must also acknowledge—*contra* Smith—that the thin line of balance between the extremes is almost impossible to maintain. There is a considerable basis for believing, in fact, that rather than the reconciliation of opposites intended by the author, Natty Bumppo or the Leatherstocking simply represents a wavering of allegiance between the two mutually exclusive responses. If he does lean toward one side of the dichotomy more than the other, moreover, it is *not* toward the side of that nature which he was intended to mediate.

On the surface, to be sure, Natty Bumppo appears firmly committed to the primitivist camp. Described by his creator fairly consistently throughout the series as "a just-minded and pure man...untempted by unruly or ambitious desires, and left to follow the bias of his feelings, amid the solitary grandeur and ennobling influences of a sublime nature" (*Pathfinder*), he is equally emphatic in his indictment of "the waste and wickedness of the settlements and villages" (*Prairie*) and in celebrating the moral benefits of the wilderness:

He loved the woods for their freshness, their sublime solitudes, their vastness, and the impress that they everywhere bore of the divine hand of their creator. He seldom moved through them, without pausing to dwell onn some peculiar beauty that gave him pleasure, though seldom attempting to investigate the causes; and never did a day pass without his communing in spirit, and this, too, without the aid of forms or language, with the infinite source of all he saw, felt and beheld. Thus constituted, in a moral sense, and of a steadiness that no danger could appal, or any crisis disturb, it is not surprising that the hunter felt a pleasure at looking on the scene. [*Deerslayer*]

Quite counter to this is the fact that, for all his reiterated championship of nature, Natty's life is spent almost entirely in the direct service of white, Christian civilization and the values for which it stands.

Even more puzzling, for all his obvious superiority in terms of natural law and personal worth, the Leatherstocking is indicated as socially (and thus, for Cooper, *essentially*) inferior to the aristocratic young men and women who represent that civilization in the novels. In *The Prairie*, for instance, Middleton's quotation from his grandfather gives the reader a revealing glimpse at Cooper's real opinion of Natty: "In short, he was a noble shoot from the stock of human nature, *which could never attain its proper elevation and importance, for no other reason than because it grew in the forest*" (italics added). And Natty himself seems to agree with this opinion. As he describes his early adventures retrospectively in *The Pathfinder*, his typical attitude towards these representatives of the upper echelons of the traditional social hierarchy, in spite of their inadequacies on the level of practical action, apparently goes far beyond simple respect to seem almost worshipful: "I...have guided them through the forest, and seen them in their perils and in their gladness; but they were always too much above me to make me think of them as more than so many feeble ones I was bound to protect and defend." Natty's deference with regard to both birth and education, and his continual deprecation of his own claims to respect thus make it abundantly clear that Cooper was not proposing "natural" goodness as a *higher* standard than social position, but merely as a desirable adjunct to it. Judging by Cooper's characterization, Natty's role in the novels was simply that of a supporting actor, secondary in importance and relative at all times to the formal moral/emotional centrality of the conventionally genteel protagonists.

The problems do not stop here, either. An even greater obstacle to considering Natty as a primary exemplar is the extent to which his own stance may be seen as morally equivocal, perhaps even corrupt. In relation to the racial issue which, as we will see in greater detail below, provides a paradigmatic image of the nature problem in general, Porte claims that "Natty Bumppo was set by his creator in a condition of permanent tension, stretched between what might be called a submerged Manicheism, which sees the world in archetypally strict black and white terms, and a liberal rationality, that tends to insist on the complexity of moral questions and the consequent danger of simplistic views." Against this interpretation, however, it is possible to see Natty's moral position not as a dynamic balance between extremes at all but, rather, as a hypocritical refusal to confront the implications of either alternative. Zoellner, for instance, in "Conceptual Ambivalence in Cooper's Leatherstocking" goes so far as to classify Natty's characteristic response as "infantile regressiveness":

> This moral infantilism which glimmers fitfully beneath the rough-hewn surface of Leatherstocking relates him, not to the forthright heroes of epic and myth, but rather to such delicate moral blooms as Hawthorne's Donatello and Melville's Billy Budd. But even here there is a difference. Melville and Hawthorne precipitate their heroes, by a positive act, into the ambiguities and anomalies of the mature moral world: Donatello and Billy both commit murder. In contrast the crises which both characterize and determine Natty's moral nature are essentially negative, a mere withholding [from]...the temptations of a child-world full of simple blacks and whites; whatever wisdom Cooper may have Natty utter springs out of a system of moral imperatives essentially infantile. Yet Cooper's preoccupation with moral questions in the *Leatherstocking Tales* is not infantile: the other inhabitants of Natty's forest world, from Judge Temple to Judith Hutter, are morally complex, displaying a consequent maturity, in comparison to Natty, which constantly undercuts his attempts to develop into a dominant mythic archetype.

If Zoellner's analysis is correct, although Natty may be seen as exemplifying quite aptly the public emotional immaturity which was at least one element in the American consciousness of that period, he was far from the tutelary saint of Cooper's wishful imaginings. Even without the overt viciousness and vulgarity that reflected upon the historical frontiersman as a national hero, in fact, Leatherstocking was tainted by his inherent moral inadequacies. Natty Bumppo, as Zoellner points out, was stuck in "a moral never-never land, sterilely dissociated from both white [civilization] and red [nature], rather than mediating between them as is often suggested." Was Cooper blind to this flaw?

There is quite a bit of evidence that Cooper (the artist, if not the man) was perfectly aware not only of what House describes as "the impossibility of a Natty Bumppo in society" but of his symbolic impossibility as well, for we need not go as far as Zoellner to recognize the disturbing contradictions to Natty's nature. Perhaps the insistence that these contradictions comprise a flaw in Cooper's characterization, however, rests upon mistaken expectations on the part of the reader. It might, in fact, be very instructive to examine the extent to which Leatherstocking, more than either the traditional Boone figure *or* America's various literary Indians, resembles Rousseau's natural man— not, of course, the complete primitive whose only concerns were "Food, a female, and sleep," but the noble savage of his later writings who, as Fairchild notes, "is simply the highest common denominator of humanity—man stripped of all that differentiates one person from another, all that makes this man an Indian chief and that man an eighteenth century pawnbroker." The comparison is useful because the figure of Leatherstocking seems to have been misunderstood—retrospectively sentimentalized and oversimplified—in exactly the same ways as Rousseau's conception was transformed by the public imagination of his day.

In both cases, two points must be clearly understood. For one thing, the perfectly natural man has never existed. He was a symbolic ideal only. And insofar as he *was* real his virtues—as Rousseau was well aware—were purely negative ones. "Except for the redeeming gift of natural compassion, the life of natural man," says Fairchild, "is admirable only in that it is comparatively free from pain."

It is easy for natural man to exist... His mind is free from the problems of our complex civilization, because in the state of nature those problems do not exist. He is never disappointed, because he never undertakes anything. He has little to fear, because there is no reason for anyone to envy him. He is not jealous, because one woman is no better than another. He can see through other people, because his fellows have yet to learn deception. He is not unhappy because he has no ambitions; and he is not vicious, because he has never been taught what evil is.

Secondly, even to the extent that these negative virtues *may* be viewed as valuable, it must only be as a starting point, not as a final goal. "In natural man Rousseau discerns a germ of goodness, a moral sense," Fairchild explains. "This sense is older and deeper than reason, and in very simple stages of society it is in itself an adequate guide." *But*, he continues, "as man becomes confronted by more complex problems his moral sense needs the support of reason." The civilized man should, of course, beware "lest reason stifle his instinctive virtues instead of developing them." On the other hand, it should be remembered that the "savage has [only] the goodness of stupid innocence." The truly ideal man is thus one who "has retained the goodness of the savage, but has made it blossom into wise and strong-nerved virtue by means of art, science and philosophy."

Neither Rousseau's savage nor Cooper's Leatherstocking should therefore be taken as viable models in any ultimate sense, although they certainly may— and do—embody certain principles important for the development of a character (like Cooper's Middleton) who *can* epitomize the social ideal. The role of the noble savage is thus didactic, perhaps even exemplary, but does not invite *identification*. And so it is with Leatherstocking, at least in the early decades of his career. Cooper undoubtedly meant us to take Natty's moralizing about nature quite seriously, but however pleasant the wish-fulfillment fantasy about symbolic reconciliation may at moments seem, there are clear indications buried beneath the more obtrusive sentimental strata of the novels that our admiration was intended to stop far short of imitation.

Again covert content supports this interpretation. Bryon Davis, for instance, points out that in spite of Natty's impassioned indictments of "clearin's" and his recurrent lengthy paeans to the forest, it was more often than not an open spot such as the Glimmerglass "where an expansive view conveys the idea of God's majesty and man's creaturehood" that inspired in him the "sentiment half-poetic, half-religious" which animated such moral disquisitions. Nor are the anomalies limited to the verbal level. If, as mentioned above, our most characteristic visual after-impression of a Cooper novel evokes the image of a series of sunlit glades in the middle of the wilderness, this graphic representation also places Leatherstocking physically *in* those glades, huddled together with that handful of whites in whom Cooper incarnates variously the spirit of civilization, not—except for purposeful errands *on behalf of* those whites—in the surrounding forest.

To emphasize the community of these tiny groups, moreover, the forest is given a density and an inscrutability that make it seem both a physical and a psychic barrier. Admittedly, as Porte indicates, Cooper's description of landscape "often sounds more Augustan than Romantic, especially when he takes the trouble self-consciously to develop 'correct' views of nature in orotund periods, intoning with Burkean sweep," but even through the conventional style we sense a presence fully as mysterious and threatening as Bird's gothic wilderness. As Davis, for instance, describes it, the "forest is irregular, mysterious, and physical in an almost sexual sense...a place of danger and surprise, at one moment deathly silent and at the next swarming with murderous Indians...[like] the tenebrous painting of a Salvator Rosa." Far from the ordered English garden evoked by Cooper's prose, Cooper's forest is, in fact, quite unmistakably a nightmare forest like the forests of Crèvecoeur and Brown, populated less by flesh and blood savages than by "the phantoms of fears and anxieties" drawn from "the darker passages of the human imagination" (Philbrick).

What we have here is, of course, that same deep-seated symbolic antithesis we discussed earlier. What makes this version of the conflict even more complex than most, however, is that Cooper seems unable to make up his mind whether it is the natural or the cultivated paradise that Leatherstocking represents. In either case, he is clearly set in opposition to the wilderness. His purported function as a mediator *between* civilization and savagery is thus belied by the dynamics of the novels. The reconciliation Cooper flirts with in the first two books of the series is, in fact, an illusion. Perhaps this is why he was so ready to dispose of his celebrated frontiersman in *The Prairie*.

Many critics have seen the Leatherstocking's role in this pivotal third novel of the series as a "messianic" one, functioning as a symbolic redemption for the American public guilt. "Beset with... remorse" for the ruthless and criminal dispossession of the Indian, says Warren Walker (1962), Americans "were provided a measure of atonement in the spectacle of the white man, in the person of the frontiersman, being offered up on the same altar of progress with the red man and the buffalo." Alternately Natty may be seen as the spiritual representative of nature, and the novel as a whole as an elegy for the passing of the wilderness. At the same time, however, there is an air of futility and bitterness about the old trapper in this book that runs quite counter to his supposed symbolic aggrandizement. As Zoellner points out, in fact, "*The Prairie* is filled with scenes which Natty does not dominate as the mythic-epic hero should, scenes in which he hovers indecisively on the periphery of the action, passages in which he seems little more than a garrulous, retrospective old man, fast declining into a vapid and lonely senility."

Whichever of the two opposing views Cooper *intended* to present, both these aspects are implicit in the book, and the inconsistency inevitably colors our response to such statements as Natty's "I am without kith or kin in the wide world!... When I am gone there will be an end to my race." The old trapper's pronouncement of his ominous epitaph at the end of the book, acknowledging what the reader has known all along, that the pioneers will continue to pour westward over the prairie until not a mile remains uncharted, saddens us, to be sure. The tone is not, on the other hand, as completely unambiguous as critics like Walker seem to feel. To what extent, for instance, is Natty's kinless state a *cause* rather than a *result* of the destructive sterility of the westward movement? What does Natty offer as an alternative to the brutal Bushes who, if they bring their axes into the new country, also carry along with them the archetypal female—dark, mysterious, and beautiful—who may (figuratively) fecundate the barren land? Surely the author is at least half-aware of these problems. In spite of Natty's much emphasized sublimity, in fact, there are enough infelicities in the book—enough strain in the way Cooper works so hard at arranging absolutely everything for maximum aesthetic effect—to make us suspect that he felt few real regrets at sacrificing to artistic necessity a figure whose symbolic function turned out to be as dubious and hard to handle as his historical importance was short-lived. Whether this suspicion is justified or not, it seems probable that in killing off his old trapper Cooper was signalling his loss of faith in the fontiersman as mediator. His anxiety about the frontier itself unfortunately remained as strong as ever. This is no doubt why, as Leatherstocking grew increasingly recalcitrant, Cooper became increasingly obsessed with the moral and emotional significance of the "redskin."

Since Cooper's own time there has been a great deal of controversy about how far his Indians departed from reality—and whether the divergence was aesthetically if not historically justified. An anonymous reviewer in 1828 said that Cooper "described beings with feelings and opinions, such as never existed in our forests" (in Walker, 1955). And even the generally complimentary Parkman review of 1852 complained that Cooper's Indians were "for the most part either superficially or falsely drawn; while the long conversations which he puts into their mouths, are as truthless as they are tiresome." Cooper was not alone in misrepresenting the Indian during that period, of course. Vestigial Romanticism predisposed readers to place a high value on images of savage ideality. At the same time, however, the "ironic consequence of regarding the [heathen] Indian from a fundamental Christian point of view" made it difficult, as Fussell points out, for the American to see him as worthy of Christian charity at all. The Indian "was outside the purview of their ordinary religious obligation, too different from themselves to touch the conscience." Exacerbating the problem, there was simply insufficient data available for the public to be able to judge where fact ended and fantasy or bigotry began. As Curti says,

that the English, Dutch, and Germans did not achieve the same measure of racial and cultural fusion with the Indians as did the Spanish and the French had far-reaching consequences. For one thing it prevented [them] from understanding what great differences existed in the cultural levels and characteristics of the various tribes; in their eyes all red men were alike. Thus the white man's ideas of the Indians were warped by much misinformation, fancy, and prejudice. The Indian concept of the collective character of land ownership, for instance, did not make sense to a people rapidly becoming more [capitalistic]... By and large the whites understood little of Indian nature worship, of the poetical Indian love of the land as it was rather than as it might become under cultivation... Neither did the whites fully understand the Indian concept of passive submission to an irresistible fate, or the curiously dual behavior of the red man when he was with his own kind and when he was with the whites. The stoicism, the sober gloom, and occasionally the dignity attributed by the whites to the Indian did not always correspond to his actual behavior when he was with Indians.

Even after interior exploration made more hard data available, political and emotional motives tended to delay and distort the dissemination of that information. In a fascinating essay called "Myths That Hide the Indian," Oliver LaFarge reveals some astonishing discrepancies between the stereotyped images of the Indian as "savage" and the true state of the various Indian cultures in colonial times, many (in contradistinction to the myth of the primitive hunter) heavily agricultural, and some—like the southern tribes with their elaborate social structure or the politically sophisticated Iroquois—"well on the road toward civilization." Cooper's errors were thus quite typical and understandable.

Perhaps they seemed particularly glaring, however, because after the appearance of his early books he was often lauded as the first to paint a "true portrait" of the American aborigine.

Cooper's major problem lay in an unfortunate choice of source material, since he relied heavily on John Heckewelder's *History of the Indian Nations* for his information. According to Paul Wallace in "Cooper's Indians," Heckewelder, who had lived among the Delawares, was so sympathetic toward his subjects that "he allow[ed] his historical judgment to become unbalanced." This had unfortunate results for Cooper. Not only did he follow Heckewelder in projecting upon the Indian a rather ludicrous concept of gentility and natural courtesy, but he also picked up an idea (described by Walker as "patently artificial even to lay readers and painfully naive to anthropologists") that "the woods of America were divided between Indians of two sorts, the noble savage and the savage fiend, the former personified, with qualification, in the Lenni Lenape or Delawares...the latter, without qualification, in the 'Mingoes'...or Iroquois" (Wallace). Naive or not, on the other hand, there is some question whether Cooper's borrowed misinformation was as damaging to the integrity of his novels as his critics have claimed. Whatever its *historical* basis, the division of Indians into "good" and "bad" not only enriched the psycho-social functions of the Tales by deflecting some of the latent guilt feelings catalyzed by colonial expansion (Cooper's displacement of the Iroquois from their historical territories and alliances stemmed, says Clark, from a desire "to repress knowledge of their cultural attainments" and make it appear "that the patriarchal estate...[was] a wilderness before the arrival of the white man"), but also provided an effective literary correlative for the duality of the historical American attitude. From an aesthetic standpoint, then, Cooper's portrait of savage duality cannot be dismissed out of hand as a mistake. From an aesthetic standpoint, it is also unimportant that Cooper, as Arthur C. Parker complains, confused the Mahicans and Mohegans, mistook Uncas's filial relation to Chingachgook, mistranslated the latter's name, and lied about the two of them being the last of their tribe. The facts are irrelevant to either Cooper's intent or his achievement. As it happens, neither his good Indians nor even his bad Indians, as they appear individually in the novels, are quite as shallow and undimensional as Walker and Wallace imply, but if they were it still wouldn't matter too much: Cooper's Indians are more important as symbols than as realistic portraits in any case.

What are they symbolic *of*? It is for his noble savages in the classic and traditional sense that Cooper is best known—and for good reason. Although comprising a small proportion of his total cast of native characters, the type provides an imaginative core for his "idea" of the Indian in the early stages of his career. The romantic savage, playing his most memorable and characteristic roles in the books where he is sacrificed in the cause of progress, was not an original creation of Cooper's, to be sure. As mentioned in section 3.2, popular literature in the first few decades of the nineteenth century was littered with the most heart-rending savage deaths imaginable, and dozens of princely copper-skinned youths gave up their lives with a panache that somehow managed to combine the martial ardor of an Anthony with all the affecting delicacy of Richardson's Clarissa. Cooper's treatment did add a new emotional depth to the stock character, however. Fully aware of the implications of his actions, but impelled to doom by the demands of honor, his archetypal noble savage seems to sacrifice himself for the greater good in much the same way as the priest-kings of Frazer's *Golden Bough* were self-sacrificed in order to restore and safeguard the fertility of the land. Thus Uncas in *The Last of the Mohicans* dies not simply for love, but, symbolically at least, in order to guarantee the survival and perpetuation of the finest flower of white culture and civilization.

Symbolically too, Uncas's martyrdom may just possibly—like the death of the priest-king—effect that ritual mediation between man and nature that Cooper was looking for. The mythic overtones make such deaths not merely poignant but tragically commanding. More important, the aura carries over to—and in a sense aesthetically justifies—the racial death of which they are only emblems. The key to this justification was the victims' collaboration in their own fates, their resigned, almost grateful, acceptance of inevitability. "The pale-faces are masters of the earth, and the time of the redmen has not yet come again. My day has been too long," says the sage and ancient Tamenund— another easily recognizable figure from the noble savage convention—at the end of *The Last of the Mohicans*. And Tamenund's attitude guides our final response to Uncas's death as well. His reaction to the youth's disclosure of identity has such a note of incredulity that we are almost made to feel that it is unnatural for Uncas to be alive in these latter days, sole remnant of the heroic youth of an aging, outworn culture. "The arrow of Tamenund would not frighten the fawn; his arm is withered like the race; yet is Uncas before him as they went to battle against the palefaces," says Tamenund, wonderingly— "Tell me, ye Delawares, has Tamenund been a sleeper for a hundred winters?" Born too late to find his proper place in the great scheme of things, it seems appropriate that the young warrior should die.

This is so neat and pretty that we might almost suspect Cooper of subscribing to the simplistic national formula for Indian affairs. "The way to deal with the Indians was to root them out, and then bewail their disappearance in sentimental plays and novels," says Fussell of the popular mood. There is an almost neurotic intensity about *The Last of the Mohicans*, however, that offsets the conventional implications of the theme. Philbrick, for instance, points out the nightmare effects, the nearly pornographic obsession with violence, which underlay the surficially limpid fantasy. *The Last of the Mohicans*, he says, "can be regarded as...in some sense a rendering of the night journey... It is as if Cooper had projected the troubled tensions of his own imagination on his fictive screen." For the author anyway, aesthetic sleight of hand is obviously not enough to lay to rest all the problems implicit in his theme.

A good part of these problems stem from the fact that *Mohicans* echoes not merely classical tragedy or pagan myth but also, and quite specifically, the archetypal Romeo and Juliet story. The would-be lovers, Cora and Uncas, both die. According to plan, their deaths should be a signal for a reconciliation between feuding families which they represent. There is, moreover, at least a suggestion of this in the denouement of the book. Although Leatherstocking seems explicitly to deny the reconciliation fantasies implied by the joint obsequies—"when they spoke of the future prospects of Cora and Uncas, he shook his head, like one who knew the error of their simple creed"—his interchange with Chingachgook at the end of the book seems to hold out the hope of *some* kind of bond between the races. " 'No, no,' " answers Hawkeye. " 'The gifts of our colour may be different, but God has so placed us as to journey in the same path.' " And the novel ends with the two standing hand in hand over the grave. What kind of promise is there, though, in the union of childless men? " 'I have no kin, and I may also say, no people',' " Hawkeye himself points out to his friend. Whatever this conclusion implies on an aesthetic level, it is clear that we are not meant to see the embrace of Leatherstocking and Chingachgook as the symbolic beginning of a full-scale racial reconciliation.

We might ask, in fact, whether Cooper seriously entertains the vision of a white-red reconciliation at all. His responses to the possibility are far from consistent, whatever may appear on the surface. Expressed through the persona of Leatherstocking his formal philosophic views on the subject tend to be phrased in conventional eighteenth-century terms. As Porte summarizes it, "Natty affirms that 'natur' (human nature) is everywhere the same but that 'gifts' (habits and customs) are environmentally determined. On earth, he finely insists, we find 'different gifts but only one natur .' " Judging by Natty, then, Cooper is "committed to a kind of ethical relativism—influenced by...Enlightenment egalitarianism—that would tend ultimately to undermine the validity of making moral distinctions between races." The logical conclusion would thus seem to be that Indians and whites, if separate, were in Cooper's eyes at least equal.

Further to this, there is some indication that if the balance *were* to be tipped in any direction at all, the moral laurels were meant to go to the Indians. Some critics, in fact, complain that Cooper, unfairly weighing the case for primitivism, invariably made his white characters "helpless and...undignified," "absurd [and] incredible," in order to play up the Indian half of the antithesis (Dekker). This leaning towards the Indians may, on the other hand, be more apparent than real. While Cooper's good Indians, like Uncas, are to a certain extent presented as moral examples, embodying many of the finest human virtues of courage, endurance, pride, justice, and loyalty, and while Indian culture as a whole is often contrasted favorably with white civilization, especially in regard to use and misuse of natural resources, the author, whatever his articulated creed, gives little evidence of a belief that the Indians are even equal, let alone in any *essential* way superior to the whites. Natty's theory of "gifts" is belied by his evident pride in being "without a cross" and his subtle condescension towards Indians in general. When we examine his racial theory more closely, moreover, we realize that Cooper did not intend the relativity it sometimes seems to imply. "Whiteness" and "redness" are more often than not treated as absolute rather than contingent categories, and as for the contention that "gifts" are only skin deep, dependent upon "edication," this is contradicted by Natty himself: " 'As for the real natur' [of the races],' " he says, " 'it is my opinion that neither can actually get that of the other' " (*Pathfinder*). In the long run, as Porte points out, the distinction between red and white "is part of an archetypal distinction between good and evil on which the moral being of the American hero itself seems to depend."

The idea of reconciliation is further complicated by the sexual overtones that it carries. Some critics have attributed the ambiguities of Cooper's practice to a repressed fear of/desire for miscegenation. Others, like Dekker, claim that "criminality" was less of an obstacle to a Cora/Uncas marriage than the fact that they had nothing in common *except* sex. Rogin, departing significantly from both these views, asserts that sex was not an operative factor in the American myth of savagery at all. While blacks "represented sexual threat and temptation...the Indian was a fragment of the *self*, that primitive, oral part which was dangerously indolent and aggressive...[connected as it was with] the pre-ego state of undifferentiated bliss and rage" (italics added). That sex was, however, at least indirectly related to Cooper's repudiation of a multi-racial concept becomes more obvious in his next wilderness novel, *The Wept of Wish-Ton-Wish*—though not necessarily in the sense that the miscegenation theory suggests. Here again is the Romeo and Juliet motif. This time, moreover, there is a suggestion that the mediating role of the Indian is not merely symbolic, but represents a real historical possibility. Not only is an Indian boy assimilated for a time into a white household and then a female child of that household carried off into his wilderness environment in turn, but the cultural interchange is actually consummated in a marriage.

Does this signal a change of heart? Hardly. Before we even have time to consider the implications of his emblematic union Cooper carefully undercuts our sense of its viability. Despite this the denouement seems a peculiarly ambiguous one, as if the author were genuinely ambivalent on the matter of racial intercourse. To dispose of him neatly, Cooper propels Conanchet into Uncas's sacrificial role, but this time the ritual is given an ironic twist by an inversion of white/red identities—the Indians show both restraint and mercy in their conflict with the community, while the whites themselves become the bloodthirsty, vengeful savages—which imbues his act with a specifically Christian significance. As McWilliams points out, "Conanchet, the spiritual son of Mark Heathcote, is the Indian who obeys Mark's command of Christian justice. Content, the natural son of Mark Heathcote, is the white who disobeys his father's dearest principle. Conanchet's inherited impulse to revenge himself upon the Heathcotes has risen to an act of mercy. Content's Puritan piety, however, has degenerated into an expedient revenge." By sacrificing himself to save Submission, the archetypal Puritan with his burden of secret guilt, instead of for the conventionally idealized young heirs of civilization, Conanchet is thus the innocent scapegoat dying for the sins of his enemies. " 'Heathen,

heathen,' " says Submission, "moved nearly to tears by the loyalty of his guide, 'Many a Christian man might take lessons from thy faith.' "

The problem posed by Conanchet's death is not the only source of ambiguity in this novel's ending, either. In dealing with the half-breed child who, according to the mythic pattern which is invoked, should have embodied the promise of ultimate reconciliation, Cooper seems almost to lose control of his material. Is Narah-Mattah's death bed regression "to her childish fear of Indians as evil spirits," as House claims, a "failure of nerve on Cooper's part"? Is he simply sidestepping the issue when the "baby is...lost in the final action (except for the adjective 'stricken' applied to it), and the whole question of miscegenation is blotted out in a mother's tears"? I think the author's confusion is more radical than this. I also think that it is rooted less in the personal than in the public—that is, the conventional—dimension of his writing. While the romance form did indeed facilitate a kind of evasive maneuver by which "the dilemmas of [American] society" could be reduced "to the condensed and schematic oppositions of the dream," it was also, as Clark points out, continually undercut by its own subversive subtext, and particularly by the inherent tendency of myth to "deconstruct" itself. The reason Cooper is unable to deal honestly with this material is because it operates on more than one level and requires more than one single response.

As far as the straightforward sexual angle is concerned, Cooper offers too many faces of the Indian, good and bad, realistic and stylized, throughout his books for us to believe that he suffered from the kind of rabid racism which would make him incapable of seeing beyond a sexual threat. Consider, for instance, this passage from a later novel, *The Oak Openings*:

> The girl had now seen so much of the Indians as to regard them much as she did others, or with the discriminations and tastes, or distastes, with which we all regard our fellow-creatures, feeling no particular cause of estrangement. It is true that Margery would not have been very likely to fall in love with a young Indian, had one come in her way of suitable age and character; for her American notions on the subject of colour might have interposed difficulties; but, apart from the tender sentiments, she could see good and bad qualities in one of the aborigines, as well as in a white man.

While this is admittedly a long way from enthusiastic primitivism, it is hard to believe that anyone capable of such a dispassionate, *common sense* view of racial relations could have been susceptible—at any time—to the outright sexual paranoia implicit in the miscegenation theory. Indeed, insofar as there *was* a sexual element to Cooper's rejection of the Indian as a mediating figure, it was more likely based upon the fact that the Indian's sexuality had become, to the American imagination, a manifestation of or symbol for that generalized strangeness in savage culture by which Crèvecoeur was both attracted and repulsed; of the whole disorderly Moira face of the wilderness, in fact, which threatened the integrity of white Christian masculinity. Thus it is that Cooper's arch-villain Magua is characterized in terms of both "unnatural" passions *and* subversive opinions. As Porte points out, "Whites are abject to their wives, heartless to their servants, capitalists by nature (thus grasping and acquisitive), cowardly, deceitful, and rendered disgusting by their appetites and desires. Since these are for Cooper secret truths almost too terrible to be uttered, they are entrusted to the care of the darkest and most savage of all Cooper's savages."

The subversiveness of the savage was not *only* "terrible," however. Its greatest danger lay in the extent to which, like the subversiveness of the wilderness, it was also secretly enticing. The traditional sexual associations were, moreover, intensified by the general American myth of kinship. On the one hand, the white masculine ideal was a necessary adjunct to a strenuously patriarchal religion like Christianity. On the other hand it was simultaneously undermined by a political mythology that tacitly discredited the father (see section 3.4.2. below). The individual American, caught between these opposing emotional demands, was both required to honor his Father *and* impelled to repeat *in petto* that archetypal act of rebellion in order to prove that the original was indeed justified. The Indian, identified with the "female" principle of nature, was hence appealing as well as threatening; perhaps appealing *because* he was threatening. Even Magua, combining Iago's dedication to evil with Othello's depth of passion, has a compelling quality that makes him hard to dismiss. And in *Mercedes of Castile* the overtly sexual Indian maiden, Ozema, casts such a spell over the hero that without—seemingly—either his consent or comprehension she almost succeeds, like the "false bride" of the fairy tale, in usurping the place of the true, genteel white heroine. For Cooper as for Crèvecoeur, the lure of savagery apparently seemed almost too strong to be risked. The symbolic marriage between red and white was thus a perilous undertaking, especially from the point of view of social solidarity, because it was all too likely to entail the loss of white identity rather than facilitating a balanced fusion of the two. The Indianized idiot Whittal Ring in *The Wept of Wish-Ton-Wish* is offered as a horrible example of what a white/red reconciliation could imply.

This feeling of Cooper's makes it inevitable that the Indian's role in the myth of reconciliation must be severely circumscribed. While the *actual* sexual threat was fairly trivial, as the representative of an entire alien culture the Indian was just too much of an unknown quality for Cooper to feel easy about him. It was probably for similar reasons, moreover, that so many of the mothers in Cooper's novels, while praised effusively and *defined* as saintly, were carefully neutralized as influences at the level of action. A remarkably high percentage of them are dead before the story starts; the few remaining are generally so passive that they are capable of only negative effects. The feminine principle, in other words, while not tainted *a priori* like the traditional father, was too emotionally ambivalent to be manageable. And the Indian, his "feminine" sexuality/irrationality free even of that minimum control afforded by firmly rational social definition, had to be even *more* strictly censored by the displacement of his affective potential into "safe" because conventional roles.

On more overt levels of meaning in the novels, there is only the very faintest hint of a recognition that any other possibilities exist at all. Hard Heart in *The Prairie* achieves the same kind of tragic status as Uncas and Conanchet without even having to die, not only because as the self-proclaimed spiritual son of Leatherstocking he symbolically accepts the old trapper's fate—exile, childlessness, and a lonely death—as his own inheritance, but also because we are made to hear in the background the tacit but unmistakable approach of the relentless juggernaut that would inevitably make reconciliation a dead issue by killing off the alien element altogether. " 'Why should the Indian and the white do each other this violence?' " asks Submission. " 'The earth is large, and there is place for men of all colours and of all nations on its surface.' " Very nice—but the reader knows as well as Conanchet that it is a purely rhetorical gesture. " 'My [dead] father has found but little,' " is the sour reply of the latter.

In the end, whatever echoes of Romeo and Juliet we may think we hear in Cooper's legend of the noble savage, the resemblance is solely an ironic one. Beyond the level of wishful fantasy there is no real implication at all in these books that the two warring cultures, shocked into a realization of their blindness and bigotry, will ever like the Montagues and Capulets join hands in peace and equality. And this, of course, is why the deaths of Cooper's young Indian heroes must always be effected by the villains of their own race rather than by their formally defined white enemies. On behalf of his own countrymen, Cooper figuratively *repudiates the shared guilt* which is necessary in the Romeo and Juliet story to impel the final act of reconciliation.

3.4.2 Leatherstocking: Red and White

After *The Wept of Wish-Ton-Wish* Cooper did not write another wilderness novel for more than ten years. Perhaps he felt that symbolic savagery, white *or* red, was too problematic in itself to resolve the conflicting forces that divided his nation's consciousness. And when he did return to the forests with *The Pathfinder* in 1840, he claimed to have done so only in response to popular pressure. This mercenary motive was probably not, however, Cooper's only reason for reviving not merely the wilderness genre but Leatherstocking himself. The author's repatriation after almost a decade in Europe had been a traumatic experience. For a man to whom Jefferson had once seemed somewhat common, the crudities of Jacksonian democracy were a nightmare.

As we mentioned earlier, in fact, Cooper's whole faith in the destiny of America—the heartfelt belief that a rapid spread of education and refinement would soon usher her into that highly polished third stage of civilization—was severely shaken by the conditions he found throughout the country on his return. There is some question about how much his observations were prejudiced by personal considerations (see, for instance, Dorothy Waples) but, justified or not, Cooper's disillusionment with American society was obviously a central feature of his response during that period. It was probably this disillusionment that turned him once more towards the enticements of primitivism.

For all that they represent a "revival," in any case, Cooper's second group of wilderness novels reveals a quite different emphasis than the first. For one thing, his reaction to Jacksonian society made the primitivist vision more compelling, less purely academic somehow, and there is at least a hint in both the arcadian spring of *The Deerslayer* and Miles Wallingford's private kingdom in *The Crater* that the author was at moments carried away by his own wish-fulfilling fantasies. On the other hand, as the new democrats became his own private Jacobins, he recoiled from the irrational underside of primitivism. The Indian consequently became an even more ambiguous figure than before, and Cooper concentrated his hopes once more on that eighteenth-century child of nature, Natty Bumppo. The last two Leatherstocking tales thus form a focal point for the final decade.

One major change in these last two novels is that the author has apparently discarded the idea of making Leatherstocking a symbolic *mediator* between social man and nature, perhaps because American society at that time seemed to have degenerated beyond a point where it deserved redemption. Instead, Natty himself is brought to the center of the stage. Dropping the aristocratic hero and heroine completely, Cooper seems to offer this former servant as a potential focus for a *new* kind of society that will be close enough to nature, by definition, not to *require* mediation. Appropriately enough, Natty is young enough in both of the novels to be seen, at least theoretically, as a man with a future. For numerous reasons, however—and not entirely because we already know what Natty's fate is to be—the experiment is doomed to failure. Cooper's intuitions ruthlessly undercut his wishful thinking.

The most obvious problems revolve around the question of Natty's marriageability. If nothing else, on the most general level the author's failure to provide the backwoodsman with a mate reinforces the impression of his social inferiority. Any female of sufficient refinement and delicacy to claim consideration as a romantic heroine must in the end—even when, as in Mabel Dunham's case, her birth is sufficiently undistinguished as to admit the possibility of such an alliance—be seen as too refined and too delicate for Leatherstocking's humble station and personal uncouthness. Again Natty himself supports the conclusion. " 'I am but a poor ignorant woodsman,' " he says; " 'I'm too rude, and too old, and too wildlike to suit the fancy of such a young delicate girl.' "

In addition to the overt reiteration of subordination, the negative implications of Natty's bachelorhood are also echoed on the structural level of the books. According to traditional literary convention, a hero is usually defined in part by means of a symbolic marriage or betrothal, and since it is this character who always provides the final normative standard for such a book, the fact that Natty never really comes close to matrimony or, indeed, to any serious and reciprocated romantic relationship makes his normative function a very ambiguous one. Unmarried, as Ringe points out, Natty remains a kind of permanent prepubescent. Whether this is bad or good can be debated, but in either case, throughout the whole series, Natty's unmarried state is one of the most influential factors in determining our attitude toward him.

Cooper's shift of focus in the later novels brings the problem into particularly high relief. If Leatherstocking is to represent the moral basis for a new society, the symbolic marriage, as the smallest viable social group, is not merely a theoretical asset but a prerequisite for the success of his role. A celibate solitary can function as either a servant or a critic of established society, but he can hardly—even at an imaginative level—offer a replacement for it. Unmarried, Leatherstocking is both actually and figuratively sterile. So why did his author opt for celibacy? Miscalculation? A failure of nerve? Or are we missing some element in the aesthetic equation that sets our conventional reading at naught? A survey of the literature suggests that many critics have thought so. Brady and Porte, for instance, claim that the avoidance of sexual encounters was a necessary attribute of Natty's "mythic" role. Their conclusions, however, seem inconsistent with the terms of the very myths to which they allude. As a nature spirit—as Brady's "wood god" particularly, but even as a kind of unfallen Adam—surely Natty should have been associated with fertility rather than asceticism. The fact is, Natty is *not* the kind of wood god that many readers have supposed him to be. He is not a spirit of fertility, nor is he ever—appearances to the contrary—really young. As D.H. Lawrence senses, his "simplicity is the simplicity of age rather than of youth. He is race-old. All his reactions and impulses are fixed, static. Almost he is sexless, so race-old." No wonder "he does not give much for the temptations of sex." "His soul is alone, for ever alone." Here, then, is the nub of our uneasiness. As long as Leatherstocking's function is a subsidiary one this aspect of his character is not too much of a problem, but once he emerges in a primary role the conflict between past associations and present expectations is enough to interfere significantly with his moral/emotional authority.

The problem reaches a climax in *The Pathfinder*. Until this point, while Natty's celibacy has certainly been inconsistent with *traditional* nature myths, the contrast could actually be interpreted as a valid symbolic statement about nature's specific place in the American imagination. A lonely and childless man, from one point of view, provides the most appropriate correlative for a progressively denatured landscape. The conjunction is only convincing, however, when—like Chingachgook—the focal figure is denied his natural posterity by a stroke of fate, an incomprehensible and uncontrollable historical necessity. In the first three books, Natty's solitude could easily have been interpreted as something imposed upon him, but in *The Pathfinder* Cooper clearly demonstrates that it is not fate, nor even simple luck, but the man's own inadequacies that keep him single. In this process of revelation, moreover, the reader's admiration for Natty changes first to ridicule and finally to pity. The result? Natty's fall—his resounding defeat in the lists of love at the hands of a younger man—is not a tragic one, like the death of Uncas, but unintentionally comic. As such it loses all its potency as symbol. Instead, the stock situation makes Leatherstocking an easy target for pathos or scorn, neither exactly appropriate responses to a heroic role.

The reader might wonder whether Cooper was not aware of how this fumbled courtship would diminish the stature of his backwoodsman. Many of the ambiguities of his work, as we have seen, were related to deep-seated psychological/philosophical problems, but in this case the flawed characterization is clearly an artistic failure. A hero who is pitiful can hardly hold an audience's respect. Perhaps, however, the *reason* for this lapse in judgment may still be brought down to the specifics of the American's existential dilemma. To put it bluntly, Cooper is in a double bind. On the one hand, as Kaul points out, as "the complex of social behavior and institutions, or what might be called the image of actual society...becomes progressively less attractive," his impulse is to recommend Natty's own character and values more strongly, and "to make his successive escapes from civilization more and more readily endorsable." Unfortunately, as an essentially social being, the only *kind* of hero that Cooper can imagine is first and foremost a social hero, defined in terms of social values. Thus Natty cannot be a viable model unless he is symbolically socialized. Merely dropping the aristocratic characters out of the book is not enough. On the other hand, the more socialized he becomes—courting a refined young lady, engaging (albeit humbly) in the social life of a garrison, identifying himself as a functionary of that garrison, and thus participating at least symbolically in the destructive westward movement by aiding the agents of its advance—the more he loses the character that made him a meaningful symbol for Cooper in the first place.

The author's confusion is mirrored in the physical setting of the book. Throughout *The Pathfinder* the vastness and the obscurity of nature are emphasized more than any other feature. The first paragraph strikes a characteristic note:

> The sublimity connected with vastness is familiar to every eye. The most abstruse, the most far-reaching, perhaps the most chastened of the poet's thoughts crowd on the imagination as he gazes into the depths of the illimitable void. The expanse of ocean is seldom seen by the novice with indifference; and the mind, even in the obscurity of night, finds a parallel to that grandeur which seems inseparable from images that the senses cannot compass.

From this perspective the landscape tends to lose all definition. Unfathomable, it is merely an unrelieved diffuseness that swallows up all petty human concerns. Illimitable—notwithstanding "poetic thoughts"—it resists comprehension. Physically it is simply impervious. As "wilderness," untransformed by the civilized will—which is how it appears throughout this novel—the landscape is alien, recalcitrant, totally closed. Mere man—as Cooper emphasizes over and over again—can lose himself in it without making an impress on it at all.

By stressing this of all aspects, Cooper casts an ironic light on Leatherstocking's current avocation. As the "Pathfinder," he is explicitly in the service of progress, pitting himself against wild nature in much the same way as Andries Cohjens, the surveyer of *The Chainbearer*. The much insisted upon vastness of the forest, however, belittles his efforts before the fact, thus undermining the authority of the man himself. What exactly does he stand for in this book? More important, what is he capable of achieving? Despite the direct implications of his new name, even Leatherstocking seems unsure. "I rather pride myself in finding my way where there is no path than in finding it where there is," he says. And throughout the novel we get the impression that both Natty and his creator are thrashing about in some particularly dense moral woods.

Natty himself is bristling with contradictions. The author compares him with Adam before the fall, but then hastens to add that he was "certainly not without sin." He was "stern, stoical, masculine, and severe," yet revealed "a mind that was almost infantile in its simplicity and nature." Above all, it is in this book that the moral confusions noted by Zoellner seem to reach their most extreme. " 'Towns and settlements lead to sin,' " Natty says, and later, more vehemently adds: " 'The things they call improvements and betterments are undermining and effacing the land! The glorious works of God are daily cut down and destroyed, and the hand of man seems to be upraised in contempt of his mighty will.' " He reinforces these indictments of society, too, with frequent explicit references to the moral influence of the woods as the "true temple" where man can "stand face to face with [his] Master." What, then, are we to make of such statements as (on the same page with the "temple" reference) Natty's complaint that " 'the man that lives altogether in the woods and in company with his enemies or his prey gets to lose some of the feelin' of kind, in the end' "? What are we to think of the continual reiteration of his inferiority to the town-bred Mabel, and of his explicit identification, moreover, of this inferiority with his lack of civilized polish and education? To Natty, we are told at one point, "rank had little or no value," but elsewhere he gives full recognition to the fact that the apparent levelling effect of the woods is merely a temporary and artificial interruption to the social stratification of the settlements. Natty's deference to his social "superiors," allied with his constant self-denigration *because he was only a rude woodsman*, undercuts completely the moral schema that Cooper puts into his mouth.

What this all adds up to is that neither Natty nor Cooper in *The Pathfinder* seems to be quite sure who and what he is or represents. The idea that the weaknesses of the book are related to a groping after identity is, moreover, reinforced by a sententiously repetitious harping on racial gifts, as if a successful definition of race would lead to that successful definition of the symbolic "self" which was necessary to clarify those ultimate moral and social values that kept slipping away from Cooper's grasp. Like so many other elements in this novel, however, Cooper's treatment of the racial question is muddy. The multiplication of references merely multiplies the ambiguities. " 'It is the law with me to fight always like a white man and never like an Injun. The Sarpent, here, has his fashions, and I have mine.' " " 'A redskin has his notions and it is right that it should be so; and if they are not exactly the same as a Christian white man's, there is no harm in it.' " " 'Ever skin has its own natur', and every natur' has its own skin.' " " 'An Injun' knows how to hold his tongue; but we white folk fancy we are always wiser than our fellows.' " " 'My gifts are a white man's gifts, and not an Injun's.' " " 'I'm not a redskin born, and it is more a white man's gifts to fight openly than to lie in ambushment.' " " 'We are white men and cannot mangle a dead enemy; but it is honour in the eyes of a redskin to do so.' " " 'It was a gift of a pale-face.' " " 'They have their gifts, Mabel, and are not to be blamed for following them. Natur' is natur', though the different tribes have different ways of showing it. For my part, I am white and I endeavour to maintain white feelings.' " " 'Each colour has its gifts, and its laws, and its traditions.' "

"Natur' " and "gifts"!—it is clear, as Porte says, that Cooper is quite unsure whether these are hereditary or environmental, absolute or relative differences. The terms are used so loosely and inconsistently that they become virtually meaningless. At times, in fact, they seem to refer to something as trivial as skills or "knacks" (" 'The gifts of the lad are for the water, while mine are for the hunt and the trail' "), or even simply "moods" (" 'I have not felt it was my gift, this morning' "). Far from being the "Marcus Aurelius of the forest" that Zolla calls him, the Pathfinder consequently comes across as one of the most deranged individuals of American literature. He is deranged, moreover, specifically in that area where one should be most sure—in his self-consciousness; that is, literally, his consciousness of self. That a confusion of roles should be a major feature of Leatherstocking's abortive love affair is, in fact, a significant commentary on the book as a whole. Natty forgets (if he ever knew) his proper place, and from this error spring all the vulgarities and absurdities that detract from his ostensibly heroic stature. Mabel enlightens him finally. " 'When you are old you will come to our dwelling and let me be a daughter to you,' " she says at the end of the story. " 'You're more befitting to be my daughter than to be my wife, you are,' " is Natty's melancholy reply.

The Deerslayer, Cooper's last novel, contains many of the same moral ambiguities as *The Pathfinder*. Again we find the same confusing theory of "gifts." This time, indeed, the submerged racism comes right out of the closet. " 'I hold it wrong to mix colours, except in friendship and services,' " says the young Natty, glowing with self-satisfaction that he himself is "without a cross." Again, too, we find evidence of a great deal of ambivalence about nature. The book on the one hand contains not only some of Cooper's most memorable paeans to the morally beneficent and sensuously beautiful forest but also his most impassioned denunciations of the settlements. At the same time we once again find the Deerslayer undercutting the primitivistic platitudes he spouts so fervently with a reiterated sense of his own social inferiority. To make matters worse, Natty's basic moral inadequacies are underlined by an implicit (and obviously unintentional) parallel between his own florid moralizing and the religious mania of the simple-minded, half-crazed Hetty Hutter. Surprisingly enough, these ambiguities do not obtrude in the way that they do in *Pathfinder*. The reason for this is perhaps hinted in Chase's criticism of Marius Bewley for "assuming both that our writers have wanted to reconcile disunities by their art and their intelligence and this is what they *should* have wanted to do." "The fact is," says Chase, "that many of the best American novels achieve their very being, their energy and their form, from the perception and acceptance not of unities but of radical disunities." Writers such as Cooper, therefore, were great because, not in spite of the fact that they "proposed and accepted an imaginative world of radical, even irreconcilable contradictions." In *The Pathfinder*—and this is perhaps its greatest flaw—Cooper *was* apparently trying to resolve these contradictions, to thread his way through a moral wilderness. The aborted marriage motif, if aesthetically unsatisfying, is in fact a singularly appropriate correlative for his confused attempt at reconciliation. In *The Deerslayer*, however, he returns to his former technique of presentation, and the result is much more successful from both an aesthetic and an emotional point of view. Again the physical setting suggests the author's stance. Glimmerglass, in Kaul's words, is "Nature's unblemished mirror [which] functions physically as Natty's conscience does in a moral sense; it reflects back to man his true image of himself." Like the lake, Cooper in this book is content for the most part, as Ringe points out, to accept reality as "immanent," to reflect passively a cluster of morally energized but discontinuous events, without straining unduly to find any kind of "transcendent validation" for them.

This is not, of course, to suggest that there are not elements of conflict in this book. Conflict, moral and otherwise, provides a focus for both plot and theme. The first level of conflict is simply between the good guys and the bad guys—the whites and the Delawares against the satanic Mingoes. Here Cooper borrows the stylized savage of an earlier era to delineate the archetypal tension between good and evil, light and dark, life and death, that provides the basic dynamic of the book. This cosmic conflict provides a backdrop against which a second, more specifically American kind of struggle can be enacted: a struggle identified by David Noble as the conflict between "the myth of the West, Deerslayer, and the reality of the West, the Hutter family and Hurry Harry." It is here on this level that the question of Natty's symbolic status becomes most critical. In emotional terms Deerslayer carries the full weight of his author's approval and sympathy. Despite this, as the battle unfolds it becomes obvious that whatever he represents, he cannot and is not meant, ultimately, to win. For one thing, his roots are in the past rather than the future. As Noble points out, "Cooper...is aware that the myth is of European origin and he is aware that the myth must change in response to historical events." More explicitly, in McWilliams' words, "Natty Bumppo may represent Cooper's yearning for the free forest life, but the author of *The American Democrat* is a writer who recognizes, very clearly, that Deerslayer is an anachronism to which he is paying a nostalgic tribute." Natty is thus recognizably a wish-fulfilling fantasy, and one moreover which turns its back on the present and prospective reality of America. What is worse, from a practical point of view both the author and the reader know quite well that the style of action and attitude Natty demonstrates *just won't work.*

The problem goes back once more to the old law/justice dichotomy. It also involves the ambivalence of the wilderness as a field of action. "The forest is both the temple of God and an arena for slaughter, depending upon the man who enters it," says McWilliams. "To Natty Bumppo, the neutral ground is God's handiwork constantly subjected to the mutilation of settlement. To Tom Hutter or Hurry Harry, the forest is a mine waiting to be plundered. To more gentlemanly whites, it is a beautiful, unknown world in which they feel both exiled and incompetent." What basis can be found for clarifying and controlling such flawed responses as this list suggests? The law? But the law is back in the garrisons. It is thus powerless to prevent the injustices (kidnapping, murder) perpetrated out in an inaccessible wilderness. When it does attempt to enter this strange new field, moreover, the basic alienness of the surroundings prevents it from functioning properly. Harry's avaricious quest for scalps, the most unmoral act in the book, is ironically enough fully sanctioned in law, and the martial rescue party at the end far outdoes the Indian in its indiscriminating savagery.

But if the law is inadequate, what happens without it? This, as McWilliams points out, is a question that Cooper has already answered in his earlier books: "The absence of all law results in a massacre at Fort William Henry or the unchecked depradations of a Billy Kirby." What about other, extra-legal codes of morality, then? McWilliams answers that as well. "Stubborn adherence to the principle of revenge [*lex talionis*], Indian or white," he says, "starts a progressive chain of death or destruction which leaves little behind." On the other hand, "Those who attempt literally to practice Christian morality must be protected by ruthless force; if unprotected, their Christianity leads to madness or death." So what is left? The exemplary individual? Does Natty Bumppo offer a solution to the problem? Again, no. He may function idealistically as a model, but on the level of action he is as helpless as a Judge Temple.

The liberty from the law and the individualism for which Natty stood were feasible only if everyone in a frontier society could retain Natty's purity and moral conscience. The entire series has contradicted that possibility. In every frontier novel, the underlying conflict between Christian law and the law of revenge results in the triumph of bloodshed. Ironically, Cooper's great hero can do little to solve the problem of frontier lawlessness. Natty's greatness depends on his solitary independence, but his independence renders him ineffectual in solving social problems. Although Natty opens paths for the forces he most detests, he retreats from social injustice and refuses to make social decisions. He possesses an "unerring sense of justice" that is dependent solely upon a rifle and individual moral laws.

Natty, then, as we said before, if admirable is functionally impotent when it comes to the larger social issues.

In *The Deerslayer* the dilemma is pursued even one step further than it was in previous books. Not only is Natty's symbolic role undermined by the negative factor of his impotence but the question of his personal guilt as dramatized in this novel even reflects upon his value as a passive exemplar. How? One thing that tends to be obscured by his much insisted upon morality is that Natty, at least incidentally and perhaps—as D.H. Lawrence claims— essentially, is a killer. An "innocent" killer, perhaps, but still a killer. And it is in this book above all that we are forced to face up to this disturbing truth. In spite of Cooper's emphasis on the external compulsion and on the protagonist's great reluctance, the fact is that the slaying of the youth's first Indian—especially in the context of a frontier culture which not merely excused but glorified such acts as a kind of "racial eucharist" (Davis)—cannot be seen merely as a coming of age but, in Noble's words, necessarily implies a "loss of innocence."

Was this rather sinister sidelight to Natty's character another artistic lapse on the part of the author? Noble says that Cooper's treatment of the American myth in *The Deerslayer* was written "with the purpose of destroying rather than celebrating the American Adam." McWilliams goes even further. "*The Deerslayer* ends the series," he says, "because it has in effect killed the hero whose life it is initiating. The dark ending, together with Natty's inability to counteract the effects of an evil civil law, form a tacit admission that Natty was, after all, only a gleam of 'pure spirit.' " Perhaps, though, rather than illustrating a failure of the Leatherstocking's symbolic role, this book offers us a clarification of what that role truly was. In the earlier books, certainly, the author made a point of identifying Natty as a mediating link between man and nature but, as we have seen, this identification had many ambiguous aspects. In *The Pathfinder*, he changed his strategy, showing Natty not merely in the *service* of society but attempting to *become* society himself. Again, the emphasis was on reconciliation—and again the response was an ambivalent one. In *The Deerslayer*, however, there is some indication that Cooper has given up on this futile fantasy. This time, in fact, if the reader complains about a tension between incompatible aspects of Natty's role, it is possible that the problem is rooted in a discrepancy between the Deerslayer, as portrayed in the book, and the wood god/Christ figure whom his audience and perhaps even his creator would have *liked* him to be.

There are many indications in the text itself that these projected *umbra* provide a misleading perspective for understanding Cooper's final Leatherstocking. D.H. Lawrence intuited the truth, but he has been largely misunderstood as well. Critics who quote his interpretation of Cooper generally emphasize the famous description of the Leatherstocking novels as "the true myth of America" which goes backwards in time "from old age to golden youth," thus focusing on Natty's role as the noble young Adam, full of life and promise. Lawrence himself, though, saw through this delusive myth to a cold, static, sexless solitary whose greatest gift was for rejection. The book itself points in both directions. If Deerslayer *was* Adam, however, then his ritual killing *must* be seen as a fall. If the act was not a fall, then he was not the archetypal Innocent but something else entirely. Which view are we to take? In the climactic scene when Natty gratuitously shoots down the eagle merely to demonstrate his skill are we to believe his protestations of regret or his "glistening and delighted eyes"? Perhaps we may find the answer if, instead of focusing on Deerslayer's conformity to mythic patterns, we concentrate rather on the extent and the direction of his *divergence* from conventional roles.

There are, in fact, *two* potential myths that operate simultaneously in the structure of this novel. *Both* revolve around the possibilites of a symbolic marriage.

The first is a myth of culture. As Slotkin points out, when "Judith gives [Leatherstocking] Killdeer, a rifle of simple perfection in design and mythlike reputation for accuracy...[the event] marks his achievement of heroic stature (much as the armor of Hephaestos was given to Achilles on the eve of his battle with Hector)." It is thus a ritual occasion. It is a ritual occasion, moreover, with ample precedents. The point is an important one. To the extent that it yields formal echoes associating it with many pagan and Christian myths, "particularly the Arthurian legends of hero kings and knights receiving their legendary weapons from the Lady in the Lake," the incident in a sense becomes constrained by the logic of its precursors. The patterns if not the details of psychic development illuminated by the archaic forms, while far from determining Natty's response, thus provide important clues as to how that response should be interpreted. What are these patterns? According to tradition the hero, besides seeking worldly power also (and concomitantly) seeks the anima figure who will, as Slotkin describes it, "complete his half-formed identity." In terms of underlying theme, then, the "whole strain of this archetypal myth is toward some form of sexual union between the male and female principles." How does this relate to *The Deerslayer?* By association if nothing else the "psychological and emotional urges embodied in [this book]...seem to demand his marriage to Judith, his union with the anima." In refusing this marriage, Natty thus refuses the true goal of the quest.

It is a significant departure. When the prince in the fairy tale finds and marries the lost and/or disguised princess the event does not just provide an appropriate conclusion to/reward for his own private ordeal. It also symbolizes the union between temporal power (the King) and the higher wisdom/love (the Queen) which will restore order to society. The bride (a folk version of Robert Graves' White Goddess) may represent the darker side of the psyche but her ultimate role, in effecting balance, is a socially supportive one. As Slotkin points out, in fact, "the gift of the weapon itself signifies that the woman's function is to enable the predatory male to play the man's part." Leatherstocking's refusal to complete the ritual, therefore, clearly implies a repudiation of both the traditional mediating role of the hero *and* the potential society in which he should play his symbolically central part. Masculine power is henceforth to be dedicated only to solitary, asocial functions.

So much for the City of New Jerusalem.

So much, too, for the primitivistic fantasy that would *seem* to be its antithesis. A few chapters later Natty also rejects a marriage with nature, symbolized here as elsewhere by the Indian.

In this case the mythic parallel is with that redemptive murderer, Frazer's King of the Wood, who in turn can be traced to the fertility myths/rituals of dozens of primitive societies. It is easy to see the relevance of the pattern to the American experience. The one element common to all the various versions of this ritual was the mediation between man and the land both symbolically and in fact through the person of a single sacred priest/king. Because of his peculiar relation to nature, the health and fertility of this individual was essential to the health and fertility of his kingdom. Not only were his powers more potent than those of ordinary men, however. They were also, like the natural world, subject to a cycle of death and rebirth. In ritual terms, therefore, the priest/king had to die an annual death in order that renewal of his forces be effected. In some cases this ritual involved an actual sacrifice, the victim being replaced by a younger, stronger leader. In other cases his death was only symbolic; either it was enacted through banishment or, as in most of the later versions embodied in the Grail cycle, he was "healed" by the young hero, his resurrection being accomplished by proxy, as it were. In the prototypical case cited by Frazer, the priest/king in the grove at Nemi was slain by his own successor. In every case the result of the sacrifice was the re-establishment of a harmonious relationship between man and nature.

How does *Deerslayer* fit into this picture? The drama has an epilogue. Although, according to tradition, the critical succession was actually effected by that redemptive "murder" whereby the new priest/king could assume his predecessor's function as a mediator, the consummation of the ritual act was more often than not symbolized by a marriage with a queen who was, in Frazer's words, "no other than the Queen of heaven, the true wife of the sky-god"— the goddess of natural and human fertility. Again, therefore, the ritual comprised two aspects: death *and* life. Again, it was only by completing the cycle that the killer could become both saved and savior. Significantly enough, Cooper's version of the myth is a truncated one. Natty kills his Indian all right, and even ritually acknowledges the act by accepting from the victim the new name and identity of Hawkeye. He refuses, however, to follow out the ritual role by replacing his dead predecessor in ritual marriage. " 'Take the gun,' " says Rivenoak to the young captive; " 'go forth and shoot a deer,   and   bring the venison and lay it before the widow of Le Loup Cervier; feed her children; call yourself her husband. After which, your heart will no longer be Delaware but Huron; Le Sumach's ears will not hear the cries of her children; my people will count the proper number of warriors.' " No, no, answers Leatherstocking, rejecting both the wife and the tribal responsibility. " 'I may never marry; most likely Providence, in putting me up here in the woods, has intended I should live single, and without a lodge of my own.' " Leatherstocking, far from being a messianic mediator, thus repudiates both society *and* nature, thereby becoming not redemptive but simply a murderer. Indeed, as Slotkin points out, the "conclusion of the novel reveals that although his blending of Indian and Christian qualities makes him a hero and a kind of saint, it ultimately prevents him from playing his proper role in either the Indian or the Christian frame of reference."

To what extent does this circumstance weaken Cooper's story? Actually, judging by the ability of this fictional world not merely to convince but to compel, in this book at least, the discrepancies between Natty and his juxtaposed mythic models, rather than signalling a failure of control on the part of the author, would seem to have provided the means whereby he could transform neurosis into art. Far from a botched retailoring of traditional materials, in other words, despite or more likely precisely because of its illogic *The Deerslayer* is a *new* and specifically American myth. The young Natty Bumppo, moreover, as many critics have recognized (albeit without understanding the ramifications of the fact) comes close to epitomizing the new, archetypal American. We might go so far as to say, in fact, that this novel both reflects *and* resolves the iconic quest for kinship which comprised such a dominant and widely recurrent motif not just in Cooper's writing but in the post-Revolutionary consciousness of his whole country. More specifically, we might say that its hero represents the "long-lost heir" on whose identity the public anagnorisis in some sense must always depend.

Does this sound a little extravagant?

Familial modes in America are not quite what the official ideology would lead one to expect. Which is hardly surprising. The climactic event in the nation's development as an independent cultural entity was the break with Europe, symbolized as the break with paternal authority, and this single symbolic event continued to play a central, almost obsessive role in the American imagination long after the purely political reverberations had died away. We might ask, on the other hand, why this should have been so. As Geoffrey Gorer pointed out as far back as 1948 in his analysis of national character, *The American People*, "in nearly all other parts of the world and in many periods individuals have changed their country of allegiance and have seen their children acquire characteristics and adopt values which were alien to them." The reason the experience was so anomalously traumatic for the American, however, was that "in these other cases the numbers of immigrants were insignificant in proportion to the populations of their host countries, whereas in...the United States...they greatly outnumbered the older [residents]." In this country, then, the break with tradition, normally no more nor less than "a private solution to a personal problem," has from earliest times been a *communal* act, imbued with far-reaching significance by its public and recurrent nature.

The actual political Revolution whereby the break became official focused and exacerbated all the feelings related to the more generalized affective phenomenon. Because of the historical background, in fact, this political event was in a sense pre-colored—perhaps even predetermined—by a pattern of response already present in the American communal psyche. In return, the "individual rejection of the European father as...a moral authority, which every...American had to perform [symbolically], was given significance and emphasis by its similarity to the rejection of England by which America became an independent nation." Public and private experience thus echoed and reinforced one another in very striking fashion.

One consequence of this mythicization of filial rebellion was a unique attitude in America toward authority and toward the father-figure in whom it was embodied. In order to accomplish emotional independence, the Americans had first to discredit the past. Almost overnight, once the break was made, the "England of the textbooks"—as Gorer points out—"became a monster of oppression and tyranny." By this means

...the throwing off of the English allegiance was stripped of nearly all the ambivalence which had accompanied the historical act; to reject authority became a praiseworthy and specifically American act, and the sanctions of society were added to the individual motives for rejecting family authority personified in the father... Whether the individual father hindered or helped his children to become a different sort of person from what he was, was a question of minor importance; the making of an American demanded that the father should be rejected both as a model and as a source of authority. Father never knew best...

Here again the private response was echoed on a public level. "The typical American attitudes toward authority...remained substantially the same as those manifested by the framers of the American constitution: authority [was] inherently bad and dangerous." Americans distrusted the communal or symbolic father as much as the purely private one.

The other side of this picture was the concomitantly changed role of the mother in the American familial ideal. While the role of the father along with his moral influence was so greatly diminished, "the biological importance of the mother was to a great extent maintained. She might be as old-fashioned and tainted with European ideas as the father; but these drawbacks could not interfere with her provision of care and succor and food and love. The mother [thus]...became the dominant parent in the American family, almost, as it were, by default." Along with emotional dominance, however, the mother also necessarily inherited much of the father's traditional authoritarian role. As a result, according to Gorer, the "idiosyncratic feature of the American conscience" soon became the fact that it was embodied in woman. "Owing to the major role played by the mother in disciplining the child, in rewarding and punishing it, many more aspects of the mother than of the father [became] incorporated. Duty and Right Conduct [became] feminine figures."

These changes in familial roles naturally entailed a number of significant emotional consequences. Rogin's exemplary psycho-biography of Andrew Jackson (a "legendary" figure, driven by "infantile rage," who could be viewed as embodying both the "proud independence" and the hidden insecurities of the new nation) testifies vividly to the ambivalence felt by post-Revolutionary America about its real and symbolic progenitors. Pulling down the father-figure and asserting one's absolute autonomy is a heady experience, whether on a public or a private level, but it also leads to considerable concomitant anxiety, both guilt for the act accomplished and fear about an undefined future. The changed relation with the mother, on the other hand, is even more problematic because her ambiguities cannot be publically confirmed.

The fact that the rules for moral conduct are felt to emanate from a feminine source has been a source of considerable confusion to American men. They tend to resent such interference with their own behavior, and yet are unable to ignore it, since the insistent maternal conscience is part of their personality. This frequently leads them into seemingly contradictory behavior, and is a major source of the bewilderment which most non-Americans feel when confronted with American men.

A second result of this state of affairs is that all the niceties of masculine behavior—modesty, politeness, neatness, cleanliness—come to be regarded as concessions to feminine demands, and not good in themselves as part of the behavior of a proper man. As such they become irksome and are sloughed off—with relief but not without guilt—whenever a suitable occasion presents itself. [Gorer]

Considering all this it is hardly surprising that the maternal figure in the American imagination, for all its "official" sanctity, should in reality be ambivalent at best. At its worst, moreover, it represents an even greater source for extreme though largely indefinable anxieties than the discredited, accusatory father. "The clinging mother," Gorer says, "is the great emotional menace in American psychological life, the counterpart to the heavy domineering father in England and on the Continent." More to the point, "the fear of such vampirelike possession—the hidden fear that one may oneself have been so possessed—is one of the components in the very strong ambivalence American men feel toward women."

From this outline it is easy to see the remarkable extent to which Cooper's fictional treatment of familial roles (his impotent or threatening father figures, his saintly but neutralized mothers, the hasty and perfunctory way that he disposes of his young lovers the minute they marry and become potential parents themselves) echoes the largely unrecognized attitudes of his countrymen, but we might ask what the pattern has to do specifically with the young Leatherstocking. In fact, the relational model one may infer from such parental images has a considerable relevance to his mythic role—and vice versa. As we have already noted, the environment in America, in its double, mutually hostile, natural and man-made aspects, tends also to be associated in the American imagination with specific sexual characteristics. Represented iconographically by the dual symbols of Uncle Sam and the maternal figure of Liberty, the nation itself, as Gorer indicates, thus displays two different faces. The aggressive, dynamic, *progressive* aspect is masculine, while the spiritual, creative side and, especially, the land itself—Columbia—is feminine. Furthermore, while these attributes naturally intensify the problems of the American's response to his environment (mutilating the land obviously generates more anxiety if it is unconsciously associated with the mother), his relationship with the environment, as we suggested above, also reflects on his attitude toward the familial model in turn. One level of experience thus stands as a symbolic correlative for—indeed, perhaps cannot be totally compartmentalized from— the other. As a result of this complex cross-fertilization of emotional responses what we find in American literature and American culture—almost across the board—is a good deal of covert anxiety about both the familial roles *and* the natural elements with which they are symbolically linked.

Cooper, then, was no more than representative in his confusions. More to the point, he was amply motivated in his evasions. The fact is, whatever we might be tempted to conclude from his apparent primitivism—his implied claims about the relative potency of the natural versus the civilized man, Leatherstocking versus Judge Temple or the military—the subliminal signals given off by his books reveal that he was genuinely torn on the rack of the universal antithesis. It is true that in the immediate proximity of the Revolution he seemed, in contrast with contemporary writers, more overtly concerned with the paternal than the maternal role, but if we look closely it becomes clear that his endorsement of the feminine—especially as evinced by his tediously reiterated uxoriousness—is largely illusory. *The Last of the Mohicans* can in many ways be taken as paradigmatic. As Peck indicates, the movement of this book is a double one. [T]he first journey is a search for the father and a testing of the values he represents... The true object of [the second] journey is the eternal feminine, and its motions describe what Joseph L. Henderson, in his study of initiation patterns, calls the 'return to the Mother.' " *Both* of these journeys, however, clearly fail in their attempts to elucidate any ultimate standard of value. As is characteristic of Cooper's kinship quests, the former is betrayed by the father's failure to sustain his daughters through the proper exercise of his paternal role. The latter is undercut more covertly, but no less strongly, by the nightmare effects which attend the descent into the wilderness and, especially, by the final image of sterility, all the more poignant for its juxtaposition with the vital young lovers' deaths. This strategy is typical of Cooper. What the books—as opposed to the author—tell us, in other words, is that *neither* Moira *nor* Themis offers any sort of viable solution to the protagonists' agonized attempts at self-definition. In *Deerslayer* this message becomes *almost* explicit. As such it accounts for much of the book's both power and appeal. What makes the work mythic rather than merely mythlike, however, is the fact that it doesn't just *echo* the forms and fixations of the communal consciousness but translates them into something new. By first invoking and then violating a ritual pattern Cooper in a sense actually manages to reconcile the irreconcilable.

How does this work? In terms of the American kinship myth, as Gorer points out, "the moral rejection of authority...[implies that] the child should grow up without any authority at all." In practice this is obviously impossible. Leatherstocking, though, *appears* to realize the ideal both in his background (he is the child without visible parents) and in his self-appointed future (neither will he be a parent himself). The truncated myths that underline the story, moreover, show him making the identical choices, symbolically, in terms of his public role. Natty Bumppo will not commit himself to either feminine nature or masculine society. He will remain, as Lawrence says—and this is the key point here—"alone, and final in his race...stark, abstract, beyond emotion." Despite his macho trappings, then, Cooper's young frontiersman is actually none other than Emerson's "hermaphrodite" (Cheyfitz). Unsexed yet powerful, he is also the prototype for the American sense of self. Does the claim seem extreme? The full implications of Deerslayer's role are obscured both by other aspects of a busy book and by after-images of the Leatherstockings that Cooper created earlier. The character *and* his situation have stalked through the pages of many an American novel since Cooper's day, however. In some ways we get a more useful perspective on his achievement obliquely, by examining his literary descendents. William Faulkner, for instance, not only picked up but clarified the core conception of *The Deerslayer* in *Go Down Moses* a hundred years later.

Not only does "The Bear" utilize much of the same mythic underpinning as *The Deerslayer*, but Ike McCaslin, the main protagonist of the series of stories, was (as many critics have recognized) very similar to Leatherstocking in both his symbolic associations with the vanishing wilderness and his "deep-seated suspicion of civilization which has been present, if submerged, in American literature since its early times" (Brumm, 1960). In Faulkner, moreover, the emotional implications of the equation are accentuated even more than in Cooper. "His sorrow about the vanishing wilderness is as acute and more articulate than Cooper's," says Brumm, "and he comes to a conclusion which to my knowledge no European has ever drawn with such severity: at the root and beginning of civilization and all its achievements is rapacity, and civilized man has to bear the burden of this guilt always and everywhere." Faulkner's intentions in this book, however, have been misunderstood as widely as Cooper's Leatherstocking series, for neither of these writers is the simple-minded primitivist that blanket statements like this imply. Ike, like Natty, is a very deceptive character.

We have already discussed the King of the Wood: even a cursory glance at "The Bear" reveals unmistakable resemblances to the archaic pattern characteristic of this myth. The description of Ike's training, and especially of the archetypal quest which is its climax clearly makes the story a species of initiation ritual. Even without the specific parallel, Faulkner's choice of a bear for a focus of action is alone enough to signal a mythic dimension. As O'Connor says:

The bear, as Frazer and others have pointed out, has been treated reverently by primitive hunters. In seeing him walk upright, leave footprints much like a man's, sit up against a tree, and employ a wide range of facial expressions and yet belong to a non-human wilderness, these hunters must have thought the bear a kind of bridge between man as a rational and conscious creature and man as a physical creature dependent on and involved in that same mysterious nature. Obviously the bear almost begs to be treated as a symbol in stories dealing with man's relationship with nature, especially those stories that present the physical world and the creatures in it as sacramental.

The Bear, title figure of Faulkner's story, is thus an obvious choice for a ritual personification of nature. The bear represents only one side of nature, though: her wild and dangerous side. The other, beneficent side is represented (characteristically) by Sam Fathers, an old half-negro, half-Indian hunter who is Ike's moral/spiritual guide and woodcraft instructor. The bear and Sam, in other words, are both incarnations of the same two-faced natural principle, the wilderness, and of its human avatar/priest. To become the new "King of the Woods" Ike must, therefore, both *kill* the bear and *become* the teacher.

The earlier stages of the initiation are carried out successfully under Sam's tutelage. They culminate in the boy's ritual submission to the wilderness, leaving behind all the weapons and artificial appurtenances of his civilized life. He is rewarded for his trust by a glimpse of the ghostly stag which too is a spirit of nature. In achieving such an epiphany, he proves his worthiness to enter into the ultimate ritual battle. When that final moment comes, however, the ritual pattern is irretrievably broken. The Bear is killed—and so, appropriately enough, is Sam—but killed also is the dog Lion who, as "the spirit of bravery and courage" (O'Connor), symbolizes the best side of the quester/hunter. What is worse, the ritual murder itself is not accomplished by the initiate who has been ritually prepared as the priest/king's successor, but by Boon (note the provocative choice of name), an ignorant, unsanctified blunderer. Like Deerslayer, then, Ike breaks off the ritual before it is properly concluded.

What is implied by this truncation of the myth pattern? One is sure that Faulkner was quite aware of what he was doing, so one must examine the possibilities carefully. Most critics, unfortunately, have been too eager to identify the author's attitude with Ike's own point of view. The fact is, the juxtaposed ritual clearly indicates that Ike, far from being the "Christ-like figure" that O'Connor infers, is a self-appointed solitary, and ultimately sterile. The messianic function, in other words, exists only in Ike's self-image. It is a pose he assumes quite consciously, in fact—which alone might tend to make one suspect its authenticity. He repudiates his inheritance because it was tainted first by the dispossession of its original owners, the Indians, and then by the curse of slavery. He furthermore renounces all material possessions and takes up the trade of a carpenter. Like Leatherstocking, however, he remains willfully childless and dissociated. In "Delta Autumn," moreover, he reveals the shallowness of his proclaimed sympathy for the negroes by his inability to accept even the *idea* of a mixed marriage. Far from proving himself a fit symbol of renewed communal health and fertility, in the end, as Brumm points out, Ike, like Leatherstocking, "only establishes an example of refusal; he saves nobody but himself." As well, his failure in the ritual role marks the final irrevocable death of the wilderness. If only symbolically, then, Ike's ultimate function is a destructive rather than a creative one. By seeking selfishly to avoid the guilt instead of, like the King of the Wood, taking it upon himself, Ike loses any redemptive powers he might have had.

This brings us back to the mythic dimension that we earlier remarked as a characteristic of *The Deerslayer*. Again a similar pattern may be discerned in Faulkner's story. Again, too, the changes wrought by the retelling are instructive ones. Indeed, it is this final shared attribute which, more than anything else, illuminates the shape of Cooper's accomplishment. It also helps explain many of the critical problems posed by his work.

As has been amply illustrated by the work of theorists like Lévi-Strauss, a primary and necessary quality of myth is its ability to function on at least two levels, simultaneously serving both overt and covert aspects of the communal consciousness. In line with this definition, one of the most significant features of *The Deerslayer* and of the Leatherstocking series in general (well attested by widespread critical confusion about Natty's role) is its *duplicity*. And the same thing holds true of *Go Down Moses*. Superficially, for instance, both Natty and Ike *appear* to offer atonement for their countrymen's rape of the wilderness through their apparent self-identification with and consequent self-sacrifice for that ravaged nature. The sacrifical role, moreover, *seems* to offer a means of mediation. Whether as pagan wood god or Christian messiah, in fact, their implied functions on this level are redemptive ones, and therefore ultimately social in orientation.

Beyond this level, however, as we have seen, is a second level which answers to the American's submierged and subversive desire to *escape* from the anxieties of his uneasy moral position, to avoid rather than resolving inner contradictions. The orientation here, in opposition, is asocial or even anti-social. There are two possibilities offered. The first is a wish-fulfilling escape from time such as *The Deerslayer* appears to provide with its garden-like setting and its regression to a period pre-dating the inevitable national fall from grace. The second, more deeply buried still, is the exemplary figure of the real Leatherstocking—cold, competent, self-sufficient, and solitary: happily repudiating not only the threatening mother/father figures but also those even more dangerous seductions of human feeling and relation that could lead to responsibility and ultimate entrapment. This essential Leatherstocking, in complete contradistinction to the socially positive functions of his *overt* role, indulges vicariously the wish of the individual for the strength—the *power*— to be free of sex, to be free of history, to be free of all moral/emotional limitations.

In Faulkner the myth is carried a step further—a step which in a sense goes beyond myth, thus negating it. At the same time as he delineates the multiplex structure, Faulkner undercuts its capacity to function mythically by exposing the corruptness, the hypocrisy, that lies at its core. It is still possible for a reader to focus on the simple mythic Ike who dominates the surface, to be sure, and many critics have done so. But a closer examination must inevitably bring to light the sterile savior who lurks behind the mask, *mocking* the American's wishful delusions of a mediated reconciliation.

There is a kind of implicit anti-myth in the Cooper version too, of course, in that the vicarious participant in the subversive fantasy eventually punishes himself for his complicity by banishing the Leatherstocking alter ego like some archaic Lord of Misrule from his social purview. This aspect, however, is fairly deeply buried, and thus remains essentially inaccessible to spontaneous conscious recognition. It is *part* of the myth's duplicity rather than a criticism of it. This is why, perhaps, Faulkner's stories are great literature while Cooper's are American literature. The Leatherstocking novels, however—culminating in *The Deerslayer*—because they *are* less self-conscious and self-critical, contribute more, or at least more directly, to the American myth of identity.

Is this, then, the apotheosis of the noble savage in America?—from literary convention to myth in three easy centuries. The answer to this, strangely enough, is no. The transformations that Leatherstocking had to undergo to realize his full mythic potential simultaneously divested him of some of the most essential characteristics of noble savagery. For one thing, having repudiated nature as well as society in terms of ultimate commitment, Leatherstocking (whatever his superficial appearance and lifestyle) is no more truly primitive than Hurry Harry—if, indeed, he ever was. More important, however, is a fact that has emerged from our overview of numerous incarnations of this conventional figure. The noble savage, whatever his specific current attributes, never represents the central social consciousness. Rather he marks an external point of reference against which social man can judge/measure/define/indulge himself. The external point, moreover, is necessarily idealized, or at least abstracted. Once the savage becomes a focus—the "hero" or controlling consciousness of a novel, for instance—he therefore becomes too complex, too much of an individual, to function symbolically for the reader as a referential "otherness." At least within the confines of that book, in fact, society (and even when it is a morally ambiguous element, society, at least in its minimal form of "community," tends to comprise the symbolic "we" as opposed to the symbolic savage as "they") is relocated so that the "savage" who dominates the moral/emotional point of view, whatever his "formal" characteristics, now defines the social center. The early Leatherstocking *was* a species of noble savage (albeit, like Rousseau's own prototype, a problematic one). The later Leatherstocking, although he sheds some interesting sidelights on what can develop out of the convention, cannot technically be considered so.

3.4.3 The Last Mohican

If Cooper failed in his attempt to make Leatherstocking a convincing social hero, inadvertently creating instead a subversive myth, he still did not relinquish his desire to find a symbolic alternative to the crude realities of Jacksonian America. As mentioned earlier, on the other hand, this desire did not impel him very far towards primitivism. The white noble savage, Rousseau's child of nature, was as far as he would go during the last decade of his career, and even here his primitivistic tendencies were offset by his cautious, even cynical estimate of untutored human nature. However much he may have played with superficially primitivistic ideas, one suspects that Cooper was by this time quite convinced that too much "wilderness" was more likely to produce Hurry Harry than anything else. And if he seemed to turn his back on urban America during the period, to venture more and more often into the forests of his imagination, it was not in order to regain a state of nature but merely to find a *tabula rasa* where he could mold a society according to his own ideals.

Cooper's primary values during these years may, in fact, be inferred from his statement in *Wyandotte* that there is "a pleasure in diving into a virgin forest and commencing the labours of civilization, that has no exact parallel in any other human occupation." The bias evinced in this declaration is amply confirmed, moreover, by the fiction itself: the private empire-building or Robinson Crusoe fantasy forms an imaginative core to five out of his last eleven books. Cooper was not merely interested in but *smitten by* the vision of new beginnings. In the Littlepage trilogy and *The Crater*, to be sure, he uses the device for explicitly didactic purposes, but the loving care that he lavishes on the actual details of early development, the way he lingers over the creative aspects of pioneering, especially the dramatic image of the shipwrecked Mark Woolston literally *manufacturing* an idyllic kingdom out of nothing but fresh lava and bird dung, show that the concept intrigued and titillated the author quite apart from the petulent moral diatribes that he tacked on almost as an afterthought.

It is clear, then, that although Cooper was visibly disillusioned with his own society during this last period, his personal ideas were even more narrowly social—more unequivocally committed to the values of "civilization"—than before. As Dekker says, "the man who wrote [the later novels]...was one who could no longer tolerate moral ambivalence or uncertainty. The effect of his personal sufferings, which though chiefly mental were real and acute, was to radically contract the range of his sympathies." To this one might add that his imaginative flexibility was unfortunately narrowed too. The process is quite obvious in his progressive repudiation of his own earlier images of the Indian.

The crucial book in this regard, the one that reveals most clearly Cooper's deepest feelings about the savage during this period, is—appropriately enough— the one which yields the above-quoted encomium on the joys of pioneering. Even aside from its fable of domestication, *Wyandotte* is most notable as providing not merely an exploration of but a fictional correlative for the racial paranoia its author had at least *tried* to avoid in his earlier works, focusing as it does, to the detriment of all other features, on the Indian's essential alienness and mystery. The title character is an iconic figure embodying in a single self that fundamental doubleness the American has always imputed to the wilderness. To go one step further, indeed, this perhaps strangest of all Cooper's Indians might actually be said to incarnate the essential schizophrenia of Cooper's America. How? No simple monster, the Tuscarora, as Brady points out, is "an interesting composite of all the leading Cooper dichotomies and *personae* rolled into one: an outcast and hero, beset by clashing allegiances, with warring psychic doublets within his single personality." On the one hand he is Saucy Nick, the sly, degraded creature who fawns upon the whites, having long since sold both dignity and honor for the liquor which he craves. On the other hand he is Wyandotte, the noble savage, the archetypal warrior chief:

proud, honorable, and fearsome. Like Bird's Nathan Slaughter, the Indian-killing quaker, Nick/Wyandotte is an incredible amalgam of mutually exclusive psychic tendencies.

The idea *seems* absurd. Cooper's exploitation of the symbolic potential of the split personality is, however, surprisingly successful. On the level of characterization, for instance, the coexistence of incompatibilities is made plausible by Nick's own careful compartmentalization of the impossible antithesis which lies beneath his skin:

> "No man dare strike Wyandotte!" exclaimed the Indian, with energy. "No man—pale-face or red-skin—can give blow on back of Wyandotte, and see sun set!...Dat happen to Nick—Sassy Nick—poor, drunken Nick—to Wyandotte, nebber!"
>
> "I believe I begin to understand you now, Tuscarora, and am glad I have a chief and a warrior in my house, instead of a poor miserable outcast. Shall I have the pleasure of filling you a glass in honour of our old campaigns?"
>
> "Nick always dry—Wyandotte know no thirst. Nick beggar—ask for rum—pray for rum—t'ink of rum—talk of rum—laugh for rum—cry for rum. Wyandotte don't know rum when he see him. Wyandotte beg not' in; no, not his scalp."

Nick himself thus recognizes his dual role and distinguishes between the occasions and behavior appropriate to each persona.

On a thematic level, even more strikingly, the split is generalized by Cooper's skillful underlining, through graphic analogy, of its emblematic quality. The key passage of the book is the description of Nick's face in Chapter III. He "had painted a few days before, in a fit of caprice," Cooper tells us, "and...one half of his face was black and the other a deep red, while each of his eyes were surrounded with a circle of white, all of which had got to be a little confused in consequence of a night or two of orgies." The paint job, as House points out, is an externalization of Nick's own divided nature, using "red as a symbol of success, and black as a symbol of evil, death, or mourning," red as "the Chief Wyandotte half of the Indian...black...[as] the Nick half." Beyond this, however, and much more important, the colors also represent the opposed states of savagery and civilization which cannot be mixed without muddying. At this level, the "allegory" becomes somewhat more disquieting. Because it is an assumed mask, there is a strong suggestion that the task of discriminating among the antithetical possibilities is entirely incumbent upon the observer. This, in fact, is one of the primary issues of the book: the difficulty facing the white American when he tries to interpret the true meaning of the savage face of nature. The settlement at the Hutted Knoll may be understood as a microcosmic image of the nation as a whole, and the novel as presenting Cooper's far from sanguinary estimate of America's chances of dealing with this problem successfully.

There are four elements to the equation that he sets up here. The first is the colonists' vulnerability in the American environment. The Willoughbys' long and arduous trip though the wilderness to reach their patent, like the pilgrims' journey across the ocean, emphasizes the isolation of their situation, the extent to which they are cut off from both the comforts and the defences of civilization. The settlement itself, moreover, is located in another of those "clearings" that play such an important part in Cooper's fictional world, completely ringed in by the dense, impassive forest. Most dangerous of all, however, considering the omnipresence of this alien element, is the inadequacy of their own defenses. The "social" structures with which the settler attempts to shield himself *appear* quite formidable—the house, for example, "had a somber and goal-like air; there being nothing resembling a window visible; no aperture, indeed on either side of its outer faces"—but, in fact, as the rest of this quotation indicates, they are dangerously incomplete: it had no aperture *"but the open gateway,* of which the massive leaves were finished and placed against the adjacent walls, but which were not yet hung" (italics added). These unhung gates provide a focal image for the Willoughbys' vulnerability, just as the house itself, rigid and windowless, offers a correlative for the Captain's ethnocentric blindness and inability to adapt to/learn from the new environment.

The second factor, allied with this vulnerability, is the settlers' need to rely upon the very savage element that threatens them. In spite of his open scorn for and distrust of Nick, the Captain does not hesitate to call upon him frequently as a guide. It was Nick, in fact, who first discovered the site of the Captain's patent, and he who made possible the founding of the settlement there. The whites are thus forced to depend upon him, despite his alienness; *they are not capable of comprehending their environment without him.* In Chapter XXII the Captain even needs Nick to identify the footrpint of his own son, for in the wilderness the purely white, Christian modes of perception are inadequate for discriminating friend from foe. Appropriately enough, moreover, Nick is the only one able to sort out the shifting and ambiguous kinship relations which are central to the main love story, and to understand the vaguely guilt-ridden gropings toward conjugality of Maude and her "brother"-cum-lover, Robert Willoughby. "Nick had known her real father, and was present at his death. He was consequently acquainted with her actual position in the family...and what was of far more consequence in present emergencies, he had fathomed the depths of her heart, in a way our heroine could hardly be said to have done herself." Everything becomes changed and msyterious in the wilderness, in fact, and only Nick, a wilderness creature himself, is equipped to understand the signs. " 'Read book on ground,' " Nick advises his white listeners. " 'Two book always open before chief; one in sky, t' other on ground. Book in sky tell weather—snow, rain, wind, thunder, lightning...—book on ground tell what happen...Tuscarora read his book well as paleface read bible.' ". The paleface bible, as Nick knows, is a poor guide out here on the frontier.

The third, and even more significant aspect of the situation is the extent to which the whites—particularly as represented by Captain Willoughby—prove themselves incapable of understanding the savage nature on which they depend.

The Captain's first mistake is a stubborn adherence to an ethnocentrically narrow, white, Christian, and British moral perspective in dealing with the alien Indian. That there are other possible perspectives, responses, interpretations seems never to have occurred to him. He mistreats Nick, of course, but the real problem is less the mistreatment itself than the ignorance that causes it. "Captain Willoughby had been an English soldier, of the school of the last century," Cooper explains. "He was naturally a humane and just man, but he believed in the military axiom, that 'the most flogging regiments' were the best; and perhaps he was not in error, as regards the lower English character. It was a fatal error, however, to make in relation to an American savage; one who had formerly exercised the functions, and who had not lost all the feelings of a chief." Nor does the Captain seem capable of benefitting from experience. He remains totally impervious to the ambiguous aspects of the Indian's behavior (" 'If there be any change, Bob, it is in yourself. Nick has been Nick for thirty years.' "), because he sees only what he expects to see—a weak and witless rascal. It is this myopia that in the end dooms him.

Unhappily, at a moment when everything depended on the fidelity of the Tuscarora, the Captain had bethought himself of his old expedient for ensuring prompt obedience, and, by the way of a reminder, he made an allusion to his former mode of punishment. As Nick would have expressed it, "the old sores smarted"; the wavering purpose of thirty years was suddenly and fiercely revived, and the knife passed into the heart of the victim, with a rapidity that left no time for appeals to the tribunal of God's mercy.

This, Cooper implies, is the likely consequence (figuratively, at least) every time the white American is forced to confront nature on its own terms. The only alternative seems to be as quickly as possible to conquer, transform, eliminate the problematic element.

The realization Cooper seems to have reached at this point is, in fact, that savage nature is not relatively but absolutely alien—strange, inaccessible, and threatening. This is the fourth and final element of the equation. The Tuscarora's painted face is an emblem for Cooper of the Indian's divided nature. It is also, however, something more—a portent, an epiphany, a dream-image somehow conflating both riddle and solution. Reinforced by the story itself, it demonstrates that no matter how benign the mask may seem, *there is always another, more dangerous side ready to emerge.* As Nick, the Indian is weak, dependent, tractable, but even as Nick he is unpredictable, perhaps potentially treacherous. And as the chieftain Wyandotte he is even harder to assess. On the one hand, his nobility makes him admirable, and his honor (his gratitude to Mrs. Willoughby, for instance) makes him trustworthy. On the other hand, his pride and especially his *essentially* incomprehensible savageness makes him dangerous. In the end, moreover, it is this submerged but irradicable savageness that emerges, turning him—for the Captain anyway—into an implacable foe.

This fearsome incomprehensibility of the Indian is a dominant element of Cooper's last wilderness novels. In both *Afloat and Ashore* and *The Crater*, where he uses the attacks of warlike natives to represent all those irrational forces that beset the vulnerable individual or group cut off from civilization, the most fearsome aspect of these natives is again shown to be the impenetrable mystery of their savageness. "I was astonished at the intelligence that gleamed in the baboon-like face of Smudge," says Miles Wallingford in the former book— and indeed, his failure to judge the intentions or capacities of his antagonists is the cause of near-disaster. Miles's response, even *after* his forcible enlightenment, provides a vivid commentary on the white man's complete inability to see through the savage mask, or to empathize with savage nature:

As for Smudge, his eye was riveted on the struggling forms of his followers, in a manner to show that traces of human feeling are to be found, in some aspect or other, in every condition of life. I thought I could detect workings of the countenance of this being, indurated as his heart had become by a long life of savage ferocity, which denoted how keenly he felt the sudden destruction that had alighted on his tribe. He might have had sons and grandsons among those struggling wretches, on whom he was now gazing for the last time. If so, his self-command was almost miraculous; for while I could see that he felt, and felt intensely, not a sign of weakness escaped him. As the last head sunk from view I could see him shudder, a suppressed groan escaped him, then he turned his face toward the bulwarks, and stood immovable as one of the pines of his own forests, for a long time.

The Indian is thus too wholly alien for the white to comprehend him at all. His strangeness, his unpredictability, and his apparent immunity to the normal emotional needs and weaknesses of civilized man, moreover, make him— whatever his seeming stance—a dangerous potential adversary at all times. Like Smudge and his fellow tribesmen, like Nick/Wyandotte as well, he cannot be trusted simply because his thoughts and motives are always hidden from white observation.

During this last phase of Cooper's career, his earlier flirtation with primitivism seems to have virtually disappeared. The savage, *qua* savage, is portrayed as eternally and necessarily an enemy of civilized man, if only because their natures are unalterably irreconcilable. If, on the other hand, Cooper will no longer risk the wilderness, he does fantasize about assimilating the Indian into society; transforming him to the extent that he would no longer be mysterious, no longer *savage*. Thus it is that Susquesus in the Littlepage trilogy and especially in *The Redskins* takes over Leatherstocking's function as a servant of civilized values. He is given the *formal* attributes of the noble savage but the most essential aspects of his symbolic role are inverted. As Zolla points out, "No longer is he seen solely as representing the ideals of Libertinism— the propulsive force that will renew a faulty society. He [now] assumes certain qualities typical of conservatism, in order to put the...radicals to shame."

Zolla doesn't seem to sense the betrayal underlying this role reversal— the "failure of nerve," as House calls another instance of Cooper's moral retrogression—and indeed, as a purely mechanical device the use of the noble savage as a moral *deus ex machina* is at least moderately effective. Certainly the implicit irony of the situation, even if it were unintentional, is a refreshing change from the sententiousness and affectation of the rest of the book. In the context of Cooper's other, greater Indian characters, however, Susquesus cannot be seen as anything but a betrayal. Far from demonstrating the dignity and natural wisdom of a Tamenund, this noble savage, as Leslie Fiedler points out, has begun to act suspiciously like an Uncle Tom.

The thing is, Cooper doesn't seem to be able to believe any longer that there is any alternative. It's in these last few novels, in fact, that Warren Walker's complaints about "good" Indians and "bad" Indians seem most clearly justified precisely because Cooper now appears to be convinced that if an Indian is *not* "good"—purged of his savagery, in other words, and brought into the service of civilization—then he must *necessarily* be "bad." The dichotomy is seen in its ultimate form in *Oak Openings*. Here, as in *Wyandotte*, Cooper uses a single emblematic character to represent both poles of possibility; the result chronicles the author's final response to the problem of the American savage just as the earlier novel illustrated the crux of his ambivalence.

The similarities between the thematic structures of these two books are quite striking. Again we have the isolated outpost in the middle of the wilderness, with the representatives of white civilization surrounded by danger and reduced to dependence on that very savage nature which threatens them. Again too we have the figuratively schizophrenic Indian with his two names, Indian and white, Onoah and Peter. Onoah/Peter is a much less complex character than Wyandotte, however, for in *Oak Openings* the duality of the wilderness has split wide open. Rather than holding all diverse possibilities in dynamic psychological suspension, Onoah/Peter can only demonstrate first one and then the other of two mutually exclusive extremes.

At the beginning of the novel, Onoah/Peter is quite purely and simply the merciless and totally dedicated racial avenger. The "spirit of his people" has told him to slaughter the pale-faces, without respite or exception, and that is exactly what he sets himself to do. Known widely as Scalping Peter, Onoah-no-longer becomes an embodiment of the Puritans' worst nightmares. This is only the first phase in the metamorphosis, however. Subsequently this eminently conventional satanic savage is *converted*—rendering him as well an embodiment of the Puritans' fondest dreams. Your pale-face God, he tells the young bee-hunter, Bourdon, " 'has at last made himself heard' ":

"His whisper is so low that at first my ears did not hear him. They hear him now. When he spoke loudest it was with the tongue of the medicine-priest of your people. He was about to die. When we are about to die our voices become strong and clear. So do our eyes. We see what is before, and we see what is behind. We feel joy for what is before— we feel sorrow for what is behind. Your medicine priest spoke well. It sounded in my ears as if the Great Spirit himself was talking. They say it was His Son. I believe them. Blossom has read to me out of the good book of your people, and I find it is so. I feel like a child, and could sit down in my wigwam and weep."

The Great Spirit himself! A likely story! No less likely, though, than the "good Indian" himself. As this passage indicates, the transformation is almost appalling in its illogical abruptness and completeness. From black to white in an instant. Scalping Peter is gone; only Christian Peter remains, now fully resigned to the (deserved?) fate of his people and willingly subservient to a white Christian future. The result, of course, is an aesthetic disaster. As House points out, "the effect of conversion on Peter's fictional character is fatal." He becomes a Christian only by sacrificing totally his personal, savage integrity. He is civilized, but no longer a man. Onoah, the essentially Indian part of him—neither killer *nor* beggar—somehow gets lost in the shuffle. In Cooper's earlier version of this experience, Wyandotte/Nick, significantly enough, dropped dead at the moment of his confession to Robert Willoughby, the symbolic moment of completed conversion (" 'There was a wild smile gleaming on the face of the Indian; he grasped both hands of Willoughby in his own. He then muttered the words, "God forgive," his eyes rolled upwards at the clouds, and he fell dead on the grave of his victim' "), but poor Peter is forced to live on, a pitiful caricature of his former self. "Physically he was the man he ever had been...[but for] the obstinate confidence in himself and his traditions, which had once so much distinguished this chief, there was substituted an humble distrust of his own judgment, that rendered him singularly indisposed to rely on his personal views in any matter of conscience."

The portrait reveals such a distressing lack of critical judgment that we might well ask how Cooper could have been convinced by it. More to the point, quite beyond the artistic failure, we can hardly help reading into *Oak Openings* a serious moral failure as well. The formula used here seems smug and self-satisfied. As Dekker sees it, in fact, Cooper had become "what his earliest writings explicitly condemned—a zealous and bigoted Christian missionary." Why? In the pre-European phase, in Dekker's words, "in spite of his unclouded view of white American civilization he was nevertheless deeply troubled by the destruction of the aboriginal way of life—not to mention the destruction of the aboriginal Americans themselves. Now, ironically, when bitterly disillusioned with his fellow white Americans, he fell back without a qualm on the rationalizations of the *conquistadores*. It is difficult not to conclude that in his old age, as a result of his friction with 'fanatics' and 'demogogues,' Cooper had grown morally callous."

Is this all there was to it? Moral callousness? It seems unlikely, somehow. Even at his most obtuse and obnoxious, Cooper was still a complex and sensitive man. Dekker himself explains the worst lapses as a result of an intensified religious commitment consequent upon his bitter disillusionment with American society. Despite its surficial plausibility, however, this explanation is a little too facile. If we look at *Oak Openings* as a whole, in fact, we see that the religious conversion is only a subsidiary part of a much larger picture. We also notice that it functions more as a mechanism than an end in itself. Indeed, the real goal of the novel seems to be the total, comprehensive recreation of American civilization as a wish-fulfilling fantasy-land where all is peace and harmony and the lion lays down with the lamb.

What a change this represents from Cooper's earlier work—*The Pioneers*, for instance. As McWilliams puts it, "In 1823 the fringe of western civilization had been the barren desert of the prairie, but in 1842 Cooper finds the frontier to be a temple of fertility." The reason for the shift of perspective? According to McWilliams, Cooper was trying desperately to allay his "lifelong fears that Christian civilization had corrupted itself in the process of western settlement." He thus used the book to paint for himself the agrarian idyll that history now seemed to deny. Turning his back on the ugly realities, he built the novel around a natural setting which was more like a parkland than a wilderness even before the advent of settlement, and a hero who, appropriately enough, was no dubious primitive but—in McWilliams's words—a "middle-class white...who has steadfastly refused to kill in violation of his pacifist morality." Already half-molded to the needs of civilization, therefore, this particular wilderness and this particular hero could be assimilated, transformed, rather than being destroyed. At the end of the book, consequently, without any of that ugliness and conflict Cooper has previously recognized as the inevitable concomitants of settlement, we are shown an impressive panorama of "Fertile farms and efficient systems of transportation... Fenced fields surround[ing] neat villages." The author even includes a paean to the thresher as both harbinger and pinnacle of Progress.

Where does the Indian fit into this pretty picture? Well, this is where that unconvincing and arbitrary conversion comes in. The Indian could not be ignored—he was too potent a psychic symbol. He could also, on the other hand, not be let loose in the fictional universe without some means of *defusing* that potency. Defeated by history, the Indian became doubly dangerous as he seemed increasingly to body forth for his antagonists their most traumatic self-confusions. Even apart from his libidinal associations, his very existence, as Rogin points out, tended tacitly to undermine the idea that there was any firm and impermeable boundary "between self and environment." The Indian thus represented a kind of "intermediacy" that Cooper, like his countrymen—caught themselves between worlds, between orders—felt compelled either to assimilate or to deny. By the time *Oak Openings* came along the first possibility had ruled itself out. The only way that he could accommodate the Indian to his comforting schema, therefore, was to *divest* him of his essential savageness—to dissociate him from the dangerous "middle ground" with its lack of demarcation and potential for chaos (Clark). Religious conversion was merely a symbol of that desirable end.

Does this latterly falsification of his more complex early response signal a failure of Cooper's integrity as a moral critic and an artist? One has to conclude that it does. As House points out in her discussion of *Oak Openings*, in fact, with this final phase Cooper's vision seems to have become both dull and constricted. Repudiating his own perceptions and even his earlier, more subversive fantasies in favor of a mild, respectable, and comforting kind of escapism, he now appears to deny that element of duplicity which had always given his fictional world its richness. House summarizes the effect of this imaginative retrenchment:

> Cooper's final solution looks toward that time Whitman describes in "Passage to India," the time when "the true son of God shall absolutely fuse" man and nature. Yet...the ending of the book shuts out what Lawrence called "a great new area of consciousness, in which there is room for the red spirit too." It loses that marvellous sense of richness and complexity of human interdependence that Queequeg is aware of when he says, "It's a mutual, joint-stock world, in all meridians. We cannibals must help these Christians!" Consequently, even though *The Oak Openings* is Cooper's last statement on the Indian-white conflict, it is not true to his world as a whole.

Inadequate as this "last statement" may be, on the other hand, it is a mistake to separate it from the rest of the corpus. No single statement of Cooper's can be seen as a comprehensive or final summation of his response to a complex set of perceptions, and it is unfair to isolate certain aspects merely because they seem more or less appropriate or proper according to our own perceptions. Inasmuch as they invite juxtaposition, in fact, each version of Cooper's Indians adds a certain depth and shading to all the rest. Viewed cumulatively, moreover, his novels document the whole spectrum of possible responses (historically and affectively) to the idea of savagery in America, as well as the variety and diversity of symbolic savages variously implied by these responses. This is one reason why Cooper is a central figure in the history of the American noble savage. The other reason is that in spite of what has been revealed in this chapter about the ambiguousness and inadequacy of his various types of Indian characters, Cooper did in fact create a memorable, perhaps definitive noble savage for America. This was not, however, the romantic hero—Uncas, Hard Heart, or Conanchet—with his noble death, his dramatic moment of self-sacrifice, but the tragic figure who was forced to outlive that brief glorious spring: Chingachgook.

Actually, we see three images of Chingachgook in the Leatherstocking Tales, and all three must be held as a kind of mental triptych if we are to respond to the full depth and complexity of Cooper's conception. The fact is that the final noble savage is the one who stands suspended—impaled— at that crux in time between a lost heroic past and the slow, relentless, inundation of the future. In *The Deerslayer*, for instance, we see Chingachgook as his natural traditions and prospects dictated that he should have been: "a noble, tall, handsome, and athletic young Indian warrior," distinguished for his delicacy, dignity and natural courtesy; above all—like the fairy tale prince who has proved his worth by courageously rescuing his destined princess from the forces of evil—full of joy and the promise of a bright fulfilling future. This is the springtime Chingachgook, containing within himself entire the seeds of racial greatness.

Juxtaposed with this heroic image, unfortunately, is Indian John of *The Pioneers*, a motley figure who has somehow lost the strong-burning light of cultural identity which was embodied so beautifully in his younger self. "In common with all his people who dwelt within the influence of the Anglo-Americans, he had acquired new wants, and his dress was a mixture of his native and European fashions," says Cooper. Here, clearly, is the corrupted, denatured Indian described so vividly by Irving. Unlike the wretched creatures who wallowed indifferently in their own racial degradation, however, the aging Chingachgook is tragically aware of his unhappy state. "A profusion of long, black, coarse hair concealed his forehead, his crown, and even hung about his cheeks," Cooper tells us, "so as to convey the idea, to one who knew his present and former conditions, that he encouraged its abundance, as a willing veil, to hide the shame of a noble soul, mourning for glory once known."

What happened in between these two disparate pictures? Where did that glory go which seemed so sure in the hopeful morning of 1740? This is obviously not a simple case of a weak individual falling by the wayside. Chingachgook represented the *best* of his kind; the pitiful figure of Indian John may thus be seen as a paradigm for a general fate. Indeed, as Cooper points out, "war, time, disease, and want" had conspired to thin the numbers of his tribe until he was "the sole representative of this once-renowned family," and John himself parallels his decline with the general decline of his race:

"When John was young, eyesight was not straighter than his bullet. The Mingo squaws cried out at the sound of his rifle. The Mingo warriors were made squaws. When did he ever shoot twice!...But see," he said, raising his voice from the low, mournful tones in which he had spoken to a pitch of keen excitement, and stretching forth both hands—"they shake like a deer at the wolf's howl. Is John old? When was a Mohican a squaw, with seventy winters! No! the white man brings old age with him—rum is his tomahawk!"

"Why then do you use it, old man?" exclaimed the young hunter; "why will one, so noble by nature, aid the devices of the devil by making himself a beast!"

"Beast! Is John a beast?" replied the Indian, slowly; "Yes; you say no lie, child of the Fire-eater! John is a beast. The smokes were once few in these hills. The deer would lick the hand of a white man, and the birds rest on his head. They were strangers to him. My fathers came from the shores of the salt lake. They fled before rum... Then John was the man. But warriors and traders with light eyes followed them. One brought the long knife, and one brought the rum. They were more than the pines on the mountains; and they broke up the councils, and took the lands. The evil spirit was in their jugs, and they let him loose. Yes, yes—you say no lie, Young Eagle; John is a Christian beast."

John, then—his drunken befuddlement (like Oedipus's blindness) a bodying forth of what was always implicit—is not merely the shadow side but the nemesis of his younger self/selves.

Despite the invocation of Oedipus—despite, too, Cooper's efforts to convince his audience that what they are witnessing in John's case is a true fall from greatness—it is important, on the other hand, to recognize that neither the young nor the old Chingachgook can, by himself, be seen as a tragic figure. The first (apart from our melancholy knowledge of his later career) is a naive romantic image conceived with the shallow optimism of (second) adolescence; the latter (apart from our retroactive recognition of the heights from which he has fallen) is someone we can only pity and despise. The first, viewed contextually, has relevance only for the past; the latter represents a future in which all past is denied. Bracketed between the two in the reader's consciousness, however, at the crucial moment when that future diverges from the past, and thus containing both (and all) possibilities within himself, the Chingachgook of *The Last of the Mohicans* stands as one of Cooper's finest and most provocative creations. The title of the book itself underlines his symbolic stature. Many readers interpret the designation as a reference to Uncas, but in fact—as we know from *The Pioneers*—it is Chingachgook, not his son, who is the surviving member of his tribe. It is he, therefore, who dominates our final vision of the American noble savage.

Using a tridimensional Chingachgook as a point of reference, what features may be seen as characteristic of this final symbolic savage? The first point is that he is a totally isolated figure divorced by history from both future *and* past. Uncas's death is the key factor here. The younger man, with his climactic feat of heroism, does manage to fulfill his inherent destiny and prove himself as a warrior just as his father did/will in *The Deerslayer*. With Uncas, however, the natural and necessary succession is broken. His act, in other words, instead of confirming futurity through an appropriate symbolic marriage like his father's marriage to Hist, revolves around a nonmarriage, a symbolic impossibility that transforms it into a self-destructive gesture, futile instead of fertile.

At the same moment, moreover, that the tragedy of Uncas's fruitless death robs Chingachgook of his future—his posterity—the irony of the abortive sacrifice also robs him of his past. From this point on, the natural inherited pattern becomes an empty and meaningless one. In *The Pioneers*, consequently, when Indian John makes one final attempt to reclaim the heroic destiny which should have been his in the only possible way left open to him—by dying nobly—his own act, divorced from the historical context that would imbue it with proper meaning, is belittled, misunderstood, *denied* by his Christian auditors. " 'Farewell, Hawkeye,' " he says— " 'you shall go with the Fire-eater and the Young Eagle to the white man's heaven; but I shall go after my fathers.' " " 'The Lord in his mercy avert such a death from one who has been sealed with the sign of the cross!' cried the minister, in holy fervour."

In his death, as in his life, therefore, the noble savage is alone—except for Leatherstocking, of course. But Leatherstocking's sympathy merely underlines Chingachgook's essential isolation. We see clearly, in fact, that his white friend, while well-intentioned, is as far from real understanding as the more sophisticated whites. " 'He thinks, like all his people, that he is to be young ag'in, and to hunt, and be happy to the end of eternity,' " says Natty patronizingly, in an attempt to explain the Indian philosophy to the Reverend Grant. Indeed, *The Pioneers* undercuts seriously that illusive brotherly handshake at the end of *The Last of the Mohicans*, for the condition in which we find Indian John here indicates quite clearly that it is not merely the *bad* whites who destroy the Indian but the inevitable pernicious influence of *any* whites whatsoever. Even having the good and sympathetic Natty Bumppo for his lifelong companion has not prevented Chingachgook from succumbing to that predictable common fate. Which brings us to the second major feature of Cooper's noble savage—his impotence, his complete and utter powerlessness in the face of an absolutely pre-determined doom. *This figure is almost wholly without volition.* The fact has important ramifications. Stripped of free will, the Indian is not merely vulnerable but passive. Passive, he is anti-heroic by definition. More importance, his acquiescence, along with the perversion/ parody of his paradigmatically idealized role, transforms him from a potentially tragic figure into an ironic figure. This—the explicitly ironic undertone—is what strikes that note of modernity which, in combination with the continued relevance of the covert myth cumulatively contained in his work, has made Cooper, in spite of his clichéd plots and dated stylistic conventions, a surprisingly durable writer (the "line of filiation," says Ward, extends "from Cooper...to the best of American literature in our own time"), and his noble savage a surprisingly durable symbol.

The specific typos that endured was not, to be sure, the same as the conventional noble savage who, as we have seen, became in varying ways a positive referent in early nineteenth-century American literature, and who still appears quite centrally in Cooper's novels alongside his more fully developed cousin—for *that* noble savage both reached and passed his prime during the space of Cooper's own career. Again, in fact, we must emphasize the distinction between Uncas and his father. Uncas's death in 1826 might almost be seen as representing the demise of his literary as well as his historical race. The patient did, to be sure, linger on in attentuated form for a considerable period, but by the mid-nineteenth century the full-fledged "romantic" noble savage, at least as a "serious" literary character, had, as in Europe, almost disappeared. The problem was, it had been in large part his vaguely subversive associations with nature that made this noble savage into a literary fashion in the first place. In the process of institutionalization, unfortunately, he lost almost all the depth and ambiguity consequent upon such an association, becoming "respectable" to the extent that he was able to evoke only the most conventional of responses. At the same time, a progressively more cynical view of history made his pseudo-tragic posturing seem hopelessly vulgar and naive. In the context of America's lingering post-partum depression, the virtual disappearance of the wilderness—the final triumph of the machine over the garden, with its concomitant anxieties—came increasingly to discredit the simplistic views embodied in such complacently "literary" Indians as Hiawatha.

This last is the important point. In the long run the resurgence of an old, familiar ambivalence was just enough to precipitate the nation into a new stage in its fluctuating relationship with nature, a stage that made the symbolic Indian, as either mediator *or* model, redundant by and large. The fact is, the same years during which Cooper was first redeeming and then betraying the peculiarly American genre of the wilderness romance saw the emergence of two distinct reactions against the sentimentalization of nature that early nineteenth-century pseudo-romantic primitivism had sponsored. On the one hand, for example, there was Hawthorne, who flatly denied the moral efficacy of the wilderness altogether on the grounds that, as an essentially unhuman element, nature in the long run could only serve to cut one off from that all-important integration into the life of the community which was man's only possible protection against a spiritual isolation entailing the death of the soul. When the wilderness appears in Hawthorne, consequently, it is at best—when beautiful—a correlative for the unregenerate and thus dangerous instinctual self (as is generally the case in *The Scarlet Letter*); at worst—when desolate or nightmarish—a projection of the chaos, distortion, and despair of a self-isolated individual's mind. Does the formula sound familiar?

Even *more* inimical to the noble savage than Hawthorne's revival of Puritan nature paranoia was—somewhat ironically—the ardently pro-nature stance of the Transcendentalists, for this, while accepting at least as a starting point the ostensible *goal* of the primitivists, that is, some degree of reconciliation between the individual and phenomenal reality, implied that the *kind* of reconciliation to be sought, the *means* utilized to achieve that end, and the moral/philosophical ramifications of the experience itself were all quite different than they had been hithertofore. To Emerson, for instance, somewhat like the British Romantics, nature *qua* nature was relatively unimportant, being merely a mask for the spiritual ground—the "oversoul"—that he, the participating consciousness, the "naked eyeball," hoped, by comprehending in its fullness, not merely to *see* but actually to *assimilate*. Even more interesting, because in some ways more uniquely American, was Thoreau's less consistent response; a response incompatible with the conventional concept of mediated exchange not because nature was seen as any less valuable *or* because it was merely a symbolic code, but simply because of an assumption (subtly different from Emerson's) that the individual had to confront it as a fully real phenomenon *immediately* and *directly* for himself.

This is not to imply, of course, that nature for Thoreau does not have any of the same significatory function for which Emerson looks to—or through— it. Indeed, on at least one level, Thoreau, just like Emerson, does tend to view nature as primarily a means to an end. "Thoreau goes to Walden to live again in what he sees and, doing that, to fasten words again to visible things in a proper creation that is *his certificate of a renewed alliance with truth, being and God*" (italics added), says Benoit:

The nature of this certificate accounts for the peculiarly Oriental flavor of *Walden*. Abstraction, in alliance with technology, is a dominant characteristic of Western man. Symbolization, on the other hand, in alliance with nature, characterizes classic Eastern thought. In contrast with abstraction which tears away, symbolization gathers together (from the Greek word *symballein*, "to bring together"). Chinese, for example, gathers the idea to image and image to the idea in the exposed concealedness of the ideograph. Such symbolic language,

as Pound believed, is the exterior sign of man's harmony with himself and with the world...
[which] shows itself in the ideograph as the vestment or picture of its creatures' ideas. Such
a gathering of man with himself and man with the world is what Thoreau sought in going
to Walden.

The exercise sounds like an inspiring one, does it not? Unfortunately, as is
perhaps always the case, to the extent that it attends the *intrinsic* significance
of the phenomenon-as-ideograph rather than merely recreating it in the terms
of subjectivity, such an endeavor tends to run up against a complexity and
essential recalcitrance in nature that makes assimilation—at root,
humanization—an increasingly difficult task. "As he pores over the exposed
concealedness of the pond's nature, the gathering deepens and the language
becomes progressively more imaginative: ideas become more and more
inexplicable, not because they are abstruse, but because they become less and
less extricable from the images they join and which join them" (Benoit). This
is a crux that seems continually to be arising in Thoreau's willed relation
with the world, largely because, whatever else it may have connoted, nature
to him was real, diverse, mysterious—and as such imperfectly accessible, resisting
all his attempts either to enter wholly into it or to appropriate it to himself.

The problems entailed by Thoreau's peculiarly mixed attitudes and
experiences are examined by James McIntosh in a book entitled *Thoreau as
Romantic Naturalist: His Shifting Stance Toward Nature*. According to
McIntosh, at least part of the difficulty, actually exacerbated by such seemingly
positive aspects as Thoreau's basic self-honesty as well as (ironically) his genuine
love of and knowledge about the natural world in and by itself, was related
to that traditional American conflict between the demands of the "ego" and
the demands of the "other," an inability either to live with or to relinquish
the existential limitations of individuality. Whatever the reason, it is certainly
true, as McIntosh says, that "[d]espite all his efforts to love and explore it,
a residue of nature remains alien to him."

Like Goethe and Wordsworth he combines a powerful wish to love nature and even
to merge with it, with a consciousness, sometimes explicit, sometimes concealed, of separation.
Throughout this study the cutting edge of the argument is the idea that romantic self-
consciousness necessarily separates the romantic observer from nature, however he may regret
the separation. The understanding that "the poet's thought is one world, nature's is another,"
as Thoreau observed at the age of twenty-one, forces him to make the best of the separation,
or to pit himself against nature, or to lose the relation entirely... Throughout his meditative
life he is preoccupied with the questions, how close can I get to nature? if I get too close,
shall I be hurt or undermined? how can I discover an appropriate distance from which to
survey and use her? The uncertainties expressed in these shifting attitudes are the result of
his consciousness of separation. A "natural man" like one of Thoreau's lumberman or Indians
would hardly be bothered by such reservations.

This last sentence raises a rather interesting point. We said above that
Thoreau's orientation was inimical to the kind of function that the noble savage

implied, but McIntosh's comment here intimates that perhaps Thoreau *did* look to such a figure as the Indian for an exemplar after whom to re-model his own, not entirely satisfactory response. This is quite true. In fact, Thoreau was fascinated by Indians. Speculations about their history and culture play a significant part, for instance, throughout the whole of *A Week on the Concord and Merrimack Rivers* (not a day goes by without at least one reference), and, as Fiedler points out in *The Vanishing American*, Thoreau's speculations about emblematic incidents like Alexander Henry's captivity, which ended in an exemplary red/white friendship, and Hannah Dustin's, which ended in a bloody act of revenge, are thematically central in that work. Further than this, Thoreau had apparently intended for a number of years before his death to write a whole book about Indians, and his Journals are full of information gathered to that end. The significance this particular quest attained for him is perhaps hinted at by the fact that he died with the word "Indians" on his lips (something that has fascinated and tantalized critics and biographers ever since). In spite of all this, however, the savage eluded him. This is perhaps why that projected book remained at the stage of notes. One may perhaps speculate that at the same time as Thoreau's romantic urge to merge with nature made him admire (and perhaps envy) the native whose "natural" responsiveness purportedly facilitated the assimilation which white self-consciousness denied, that same self-consciousness—evidenced by his naturalist's and historian's passion for gathering and compiling factual details—made it impossible for him really to believe that this naively primitivistic vision held out any real promise with respect to his own difficulties in maintaining (at least in Transcendentalist terms) a wholly consistent stance. Just as Thoreau knew nature as phenomenon too well to be completely comfortable transforming it into something more ethereal, in other words, the painstakingly collected information that grew out of his fascination with Indians perhaps meant that he knew too much about the savage as human to be able to view him successfully as pure symbol any more.

This is perhaps what is *always* going to happen when nature exerts too great an appeal. A high enough estimation of its value and authority tends progressively to downvalue conventional indirect approaches, but direct confrontation either creates anxiety (by exposing the unreality of the ideal) or takes nature's value-generating numinousness away. This is why Cooper's noble savage, despite, and perhaps even *because of* the fact that he is stereotyped, artificial, and sentimentalized to a very high degree, may be seen as representing not merely a short-lived literary fashion but a critical element in the ongoing American quest for self-definition. The fact is that he facilitates a kind of displacement of affect that will allow his auditors *to straddle the fine line between too close and too closed.* The noble savage, in other words, functions not as a mediator but as a *buffer* between man and the land. The noble savage is thus—in function if not in form—a *necessary* rather than a *casual* component of the American myth.

This is not to imply that he does not suffer from—and sometimes almost disappear under—an accrued burden of triviality. To the extent that he seems to be rather easily implicated in somewhat simple-minded literary fads, indeed, the majority of his purely conventional guises will probably have fairly minimal aesthetic or emotional value, especially outside of the immediate cultural context that determines the features of any particular incarnation of the type. Today, for instance, even such relatively appealing figures as Uncas more often than not simply seem dated. Such reservations, on the other hand, while quantitatively justified, do not establish an absolute limitation applicable a priori to every member of the field. The Chingachgook version of the noble savage, for instance, with its greater maturity of conception and wider range of signification, is, as noted, capable—at least in the abstract—of striking a modern chord. This particular noble savage, in fact, establishes a number of normative features which in a sense come to comprise a set of definitive parameters for a mythic Indian still functioning (albeit diversely) as an important symbol and sometimes model in the communal consciousness of America to the present day. As we shall see.

4. The Noble Savage in the Modern Age

Chingachgook, then, was the first "modern" among literary Indians. If we look at developments in late nineteenth-early twentieth-century culture, we begin to realize the extent to which Cooper anticipated the public mood in creating his composite "survivor." Except for this single limited tradition, after mid-century the vogue for literary primitivism—in mainstream or "serious" literature, in any case—seemed to split in two, effectively negating itself in the process. The figures that emerged into prominence, whatever formal resemblances they may have displayed to more traditional roles, were thus in general either not noble (in the sense of being a positive moral referent) or not savage.

Melville was one of the last major American writers to use the traditional romantic associations of the aboriginal figure creatively, but even here there is a discernible difference in emphasis. For one thing, despite the recurrence of quasi-conventional natives in his books, Melville's fiction collectively works to deny the idea that there actually is any such thing as a "savage other." For Melville, as Louise Barnett points out, it is the civilized man as much as and perhaps more than the primitive who embodies the demonic side of life. "Far from subduing man's evil inclinations, civilization provides him with the technology to implement them far more effectively than the primitive aborigine can," she says. "The superiority in evil which writers of the frontier romance reserve for the aberrant white man, whether Indian hater, renegade, or melodramatic villain, Melville distributes among the race at large." Melville himself provides ample explicit support for this view in *Typee*:

> The term "Savage" is, I conceive, often misapplied, and indeed, when I consider the vices, cruelties, and enormities of every kind that spring up in the tainted atmosphere of a feverish civilization, I am inclined to think that so far as the relative wickedness of the parties is concerned, four or five Marquesan Islanders sent to the United States as Missionaries might be quite as useful as an equal number of Americans dispatched to the Islands in a similar capacity.

One must be careful not to jump to the wrong conclusions about passages like this, however. Whatever the quotation may imply out of context, Melville does *not*, like the true primitivist, follow up his indictment of civilization with a naive celebration of the natural state. There are good savages and bad savages, good and bad white men in Melville just as there were in Cooper, but *unlike* Cooper, and in clear opposition to the current theories of savagism, Melville's disposition of his symbolic counters implies that the essential distinction to be made within these categories is between the moral categories rather than between the color polarities of red and white. Indeed, concerning himself with a holistic vision of generalized "humanity" rather than an evaluation of relativistic human conditions, Melville resists the stereotypes even as he uses them. "What emerges from Melville's extended contemplation of civilization and savagery is a more generalized usage of the terms, a rejection of their automatic identification with particular races" (Barnett).

Another of Melville's usages which is even more important for the history of primitivism is a kind of *re*mythicizing process operating both against and concomitant with the basic demythicization invoked here by Barnett. Leo Marx describes the thematic center of *Typee* as "the process of discovering an equivalence between the exterior and the psychic landscapes." Tommo's confrontation on his idyllic island with the dangers of "cannibalism," he continues, is a double realization, not merely exposing the mysterious and threatening two-sidedness of nature, but also identifying "the ferocity of flesh-eating natives" explicitly with "a nameless aggressive force within himself." The natives in this book, both good and bad, thus seem to function primarily as externalizations of purely subjective phenomena. Melville, in other words, has used the conventional savage to represent not just abstract possibilities, but specifically psychic states. The shift is an interesting one. As Thorsley points out, in "retrospect it seems that this is perhaps the end toward which the myth of the Wild Man has been tending all along":

> For centuries the Wild Man has stood as the civilized man's projection upon the outside world of his own desires and values: both those which he would not hesitate to acknowledge—a longing for lost innocence and uninhibited and oblivious love, for instance—and also those darker impulses which he attempts to suppress or hide. This projection or externalization serves both to give an objective and extra-personal sanction to the civilized man's values, and also to transform his evil desires into something physical and external which he can control or even enslave. The final revenge of the Wild Man comes when...the myth becomes transparent, and civilized man is forced to recognize that the only source of evil, as well as the only sanction of value, is within himself.

By such means, then, the two-faced savage is transformed from objective to subjective, from "other" to "alter ego." As the wilderness with which he has traditionally been associated is progressively conquered and assimilated, he becomes, in Hayden White's words, "despatialized." Despatialization in turn triggers "a compensatory process of psychic interiorization." Psychic interiorization, finally, produces the defurbished native we are given by Melville. And not just in *Typee*. In *Moby-Dick*, for instance, as Henry Murray points out in his essay entitled " '*In Nome Diabole*,' " the essential action, despite its naturalistic trappings, clearly comprises a species of psychodrama in which the transpersonal realm of nature is represented not by the Indian but by the white whale. Set free from their conventional "meaning," the primitive figures of Queequeg, Tashtago, Daggoo, and Fedallah no longer simply personify aspects of the unknown. Rather, they illuminate, almost perforce, the multiple facets of man's *own* savage underside, from beneficent to satanic.

In one sense, this development gives the symbolic savage a greater profundity and broader resonance. In another sense, it merely undercuts the complexity he has accreted by virtue of his cultural/historical associations. Psychic fragments, both angelic and demonic, as "subcharacters" generated by a tacitly assumed universalized protagonist, inevitably suggest allegory even when the systematic intent is lacking; this association in turn tends to accentuate (at the expense of all other dimensions) their iconic aspect. As Angus Fletcher explains, by "splitting off...chips of composite character, the author is able to"—in some ways *must*—"treat them as pure, isolated, personified ideas." In this particular direction, therefore, the literary savage typically becomes even more narrowly stereotyped than before. In terms of onesidedness, there is little to choose between Wigglesworth's "hellish fiends" and Twain's Indian Joe: both incarnate unmitigated evil. Indeed, even the less simplistic Melvillean psycho-savage, because he is almost entirely interiorized, tends to become a *more* restrictive conception than the Puritan satanic savage, since the latter, as we have seen, operated as a symbol simultaneously on internal *and* external levels. For the Puritan the wilderness, while clearly connoting a state of mind or heart, was still and also an equally significant objective and external phenomenon as well—a *type* rather than a simple *metaphor* of mental experience. In Melville, however, the allegorical implications tend finally to drain the external landscape of all *except* its inner, psychic significance. Can the great whale exist meaningfully apart from his hunter? In posing this question the book is at once a criticism of and an ultimate surrender to the inevitability of an anthropomorphic view of nature. The Melvillean primitive, as an abstract entity like Thoreau's generalized "red face of man," is therefore in the end an intellectual rather than a moral symbol.

Moving in the other direction, after Cooper's day many of the qualities and functions of the noble savage are taken over first by blacks and then by various peasant types. Among the characteristics typically displayed by these figures in their conventional roles are (1) a simple, uncomplicated lifestyle close to nature, and (2) an innate nobility of character. The latter may be shown in two distinct (though not incompatible) ways. On the one hand, the emphasis may be on qualities like courage and endurance, as exemplified among the blacks by Faulkner's Dilthey (her designation in the appendix to *The Sound and the Fury* is simply "they endured") and among the peasants by Hemingway's Santiago in *The Old Man and the Sea*. On the other hand, the emphasis may be on the capacity for "true" feelings: the ideals of brotherhood, unaffected love, mutual aid. Twain's Jim is a prototypical figure in this category. The maturity and compassion that emerge from beneath his stereotypically childish demeanor in the course of *Huckleberry Finn* not only provide a striking foil for the corruption and hypocrisy of riverbank society, but also serve as the direct instrument of the young hero's moral enlightenment. Similarly, it is Hemingway's Spanish peasants who teach the educated Robert Jordan the true meaning of life in *For Whom the Bell Tolls*. One thing to note is that the specific ideological alignment is irrelevant. In both these latter cases the keynote is *caring*, not *doing*. More explicitly, in Steinbeck's *The Grapes of Wrath* it is the selfless love both actuating and underlying the burgeoning class consciousness of the dispossessed migrant workers, not the political expression of this consciousness, which provides the climactic recognition in the book. " 'I'll be ever'where—wherever you look,' " says the newly awakened Tom Joad. " 'Wherever they's a fight so hungry people can eat, I'll be there. Wherever they's a cop beatin' up a guy, I'll be there.' "

Tom Joad is, of course, as much of a moral exemplar as anything one might find in literature. And in this he is typical. Unlike the Melvillean savage, the blacks, peasants, and other disaffected ethnic types who comprise this class almost always have an explicit and conventional moral function. The particular standard they represent, moreover, is very similar to the double ideals of stoic self-discipline/spontaneous natural passion which during the eighteenth and early nineteenth century were variously located in the stock figure of the noble savage. They have one further characteristic, however, that the traditional noble savage did *not* have, and it is this, ironically, which allows them to take over so many of his functions in the twentieth century. As in Cooper's Chingachgook, involuntarily torn away from the heroic traditions, one of the most significant features of the peasant is that he is denied a tragic role. Far from self-reliant, in other words, he is by circumstance if not by definition, helpless, hamstrung, incapable of coercing either his environment or his fate. It is this impotence, quite specifically, that makes the non-savage primitive an appropriate model for man in a modern industrialized society.

Why? The fact is that while the early nineteenth century could still find a viable image of escape in dreams of heroic action, the modern American has more often than not viewed himself as being trapped and powerless in an increasingly alien world. Within the first few decades of the new century— soon after the official "closing" of the frontier—the city managed to establish a seemingly unequivocal ascendency in the American sense of self. By and large this was not, however, the "good" city, the City of New Jerusalem that the Puritans dreamed of, but a dehumanized and demonic City of Mammon. As such it betokened the negative side of the garden myth without invoking any positive opposing vision. "[W]hether delineating a blasted urban garden of ashes, a jungle-like Chicago, or a New York where 'jeweled doors' lead 'from hypercivilized Byzantine luxury straight into state of nature,' " says James Machor, "this century's imaginative writers repeatedly have conceived of America as a place where only an aberrant version of the ideal can obtain." *This city offered no "way out"!* The result? The wishful fantasy of a continual and continuing rebirth to eradicate the continuing failures of history remained just as strong, perhaps even stronger than it was in the days of the early republic. In this phase, indeed, so great was the emotional hold of the Adamic ideal that the garden image came almost to subsume the values of the good city as well. In twentieth-century literature, nostalgic visions of the true community, the small town in a boyhood's midwest, often assume many of the same symbolic overtones as the wilderness retreat. Pastoral and paradisial images collapse into one vague all-encompassing vision of "naturalness" to counter the "unnaturalness" associated with the demonic city. The new, comprehensive garden symbol thus usually includes not only the erstwhile antagonistic wilderness, but the rural landscape as well.

The surprising thing about this development in the American dream is not that it happened but that it *lasted*. Despite apparent public disillusionment, post-sixties popular ideology, as noted in the Introduction, has continued to enshrine the idea that somehow, some way, America *will* realize at last the promise of her original Adamic vision. Judging from the collective discourse accrued from both mass and elite sources, in fact, there is an almost indomitable determination on the part of Americans—a corollary, no doubt, to that "terrible desire" legitimized by the Eden myth to step out of time and "wash one's hands and those of future generations of the crimes committed in the name of America's foundation" (Callahan)—to deny, even in the face of repeated self-betrayals, that any betrayal is necessarily complete or irreversible. Sixties political unrest and 70s cynicism notwithstanding, the strength of American self-regard is amply illustrated in a collection of centennial essays on American culture and history called *An Almost Chosen People*. As Walter Nicgorski points out in his Afterword, notwithstanding an obvious general pessimism about many of the *specifics* of American society, almost all of the contributions to the volume "resonate with the suggestion that the American experience and the American responsibility are more than ordinarily significant for all mankind." Indeed, according to Nicgorski's co-editor, Ronald Weber, recent American disillusionment with the failure of the national dream is itself the strongest proof that the basis for that dream is still alive. "Only a moral people can be truly pained by moral failure," he points out. The half-apologetic optimism of the essays in this book gives vivid testimony to the continued relevance and representativeness of Jay Gatsby's example, painted by Fitzgerald more than half a century ago. "Gatsby believed in the green light, the orgiastic future that year by year recedes before us," says narrator Nick Carroway, pondering his own imaginative recreation of that enchanted moment when the Dutch sailors stood poised in wonder on the brink of the new continent. "It eluded us then, but that's no matter—tomorrow we will run faster, stretch out our arms farther... And one fine morning— / So we beat on, boats against the current, borne ceaselessly into the past."

The apparent persistence of this naive hope should not, on the other hand, mislead us about the true state of America's self-image in the twentieth century. There is ample evidence in the communal oeuvre that what the country *wants* to believe of itself is by no means necessarily determinate of, or even congruent with, what is actually perceived as a national reality, at least by the more thoughtful among its auditors. Developing concomitantly with the seemingly incurable hunger for the elusive Edenic ideal, consequently, is the despairing suspicion, especially within the intellectual community, that the garden is dead, the quest a futile one after all. By the 1960s, in fact, claims Raymond Olderman (1972), American literature, in contradistinction to the simplistic affirmations of folk culture, far from celebrating the Adam in his New World Garden "finds its controlling metaphor in the image of the waste land." We don't have to go as far as the 60s to see the burgeoning influence of this new vision. Despite, or perhaps even because of, the overt and evident authority of the paradisial dream in writers such as Hemingway, almost all the characteristics Olderman associates with the contemporary wasteland can be found at least embryonically in those post-First World War writers who have been labelled as the Lost Generation, three or four decades earlier.

John Dos Passos offers a prototypical illustration of these early versions of the America-as-wasteland theme, especially in his monolithic "documentary" novel, *U.S.A.*. This work uses a variety of narrative techniques ranging from the putative objectivity of news clippings to a series of purely subjective, semi-autobiographical, stream-of-consciousness Camera's Eye sections to present a comprehensive and panoramic view of American society as a whole. Each of the three volumes covers a different historical period, and each period is characterized by a different social phase. *The 42nd Parallel* reviews the years between 1900 and 1919, tracing the rise of big business and imperialism, and the consequent widening of the gap between the upper and lower classes. *1919* focuses on the war, emphasizing the discrepancy between the experience of the officer class and that of the common working man. This volume also delineates the failure of idealism, both in public and in private terms. The last volume, *The Big Money*, is a chronicle of moral decay. Post-war America is characterized by an unabashed pursuit of wealth, prestige, and power at the expense of political freedom, equality of economic opportunity, and human dignity, while social values disintegrate. Collectively and cumulatively, the picture that emerges is of a long, steady, downhill plunge from hope to hopelessness.

Each of the narrative strands contributes to a different aspect of this general movement. The Newsreel—a collage of snippets from newspapers, magazines, advertising, political speeches, and popular songs—uses an effect of randomness to suggest a cumulative analogue for the whole spectrum of public experience during the period covered, while at the same time manipulating its contents in order to ensure that the key features are brought into the highest relief possible. Lest the message be diluted by its distance, this choral refrain is both complemented and particularized by a series of public biographies delineating between them the national shift from optimism through cynicism to waste and corruption. This establishes both background background and tone. The "history" is then personalized through the stories of a dozen fictional characters implied to represent a cross-section of the society whose gross realty has been so amply and so carefully documented. As on other levels, the thrust of these stories is once again to reinforce the impression of a communal downfall: from dream to disaster, from ideals to avarice, from Moorehouse, the brilliant young man on his way up the ladder, to the hopeless, embittered wanderer of the "Vag" section with which the trilogy concludes. Implicit in this movement, however—and it is here most strikingly that Dos Passos presages the wasteland vision that later came to be such a dominant element in American literature— is the additional theme of the relationship of man to society, or, more specifically, the domination of man by bureaucracy. Each of Dos Passos' subjects can be defined according to his or her relationship with the capitalist establishment. There are those who accept the conditions of the machine-world and rise to success, and those who fight hopelessly against exploitation. When one looks more closely at the cast as a whole, though, it becomes apparent that in terms of happiness there is little to choose between victors and victims. "[H]owever much their aims may have differed," says Aldridge, "the destiny of both groups is the same: the rebels are defeated by the system and the tycoons are corrupted by it." Material discrepancies notwithstanding, the author's message is that in the long run *no-one* wins against the machine.

Rich losers and poor losers: these are the sole types whom Dos Passos would offer us as a microcosmic reflection of American society. This, of course, is one of the books' major flaws. As individuals these people are plausible, convincing, probably well founded in the social facts of the age, but obviously they are not, as a group, representative. America may have had a lot of problems in those years, but it was certainly not as unmitigatedly bad as Dos Passos implies. Among his "representative" lives we find not *one* person who achieves any reasonable degree of satisfaction or stability. And we see the same thing in the biographies. Nearly every figure portrayed in these sketches is either successful and corrupt, or enlightened but frustrated. They are also collectively much more atypical than the ostensively "objective" style of presentation tends to imply. Whole sections of society, as Michael Millgate points out, are left out of the picture entirely. Where, he asks, among these "desperate and unsettled lives full of arrivals and departures and casual love affairs...is the sense of the heavy underswell of American life, of the great mass of ordinary, relatively static, politically indifferent working—and middle-classes: scarcely anyone in *U.S.A.* has a home and family." Despite its *statistical* inaccuracy, however, Dos Passos' biased portrait still retains an important degree of verity. If we compare the world of *U.S.A.* to Olderman's description of the wasteland, in fact, we get the sense that at least on a symbolic level the experience of Dos Passos' Americans is far from as idiosyncratic as the empirical yardstick suggests:

In the waste land all energies are inverted and result in death and destruction instead of love, renewal, or fulfillment. Water, a symbol of fertility in a normal land, is fear, for it causes death by drowning instead of life and growth. Wastelanders are characterized by enervating and neurotic pettiness, physical and spiritual sterility and debilitation, inability to love, yearning and fear-ridden desires. They are sexually inadequate, divided by guilts, alienated, aimless, bored and rootless; they long for escape and for death. They are immersed in mercantilism and materialism; their lives are vain, artificial, and pointless. Close to being inert, they are helpless in the face of a total disintegration of values. Life constantly leads to a reduction of all human dignity; the wastelander becomes idealless and hopeless as he falls prey to false prophets. [1972]

In both tone and detail, this description characterizes the world of *U.S.A.* quite as much as the 50s and 60s novels to which it was directed.

The wasteland, then, has a longer history than recent doomsayers tend to imply. Despite his pessimism, on the other hand, it is important to note that Dos Passos' version is at least *potentially* more humane than its mid-century successors. Why? Because, unlike Olderman's subjects, Dos Passos' rage is fuelled by a vision of what society could be, *should* be, under a better political system. By the 50s, ideological certainties have shrivelled along with everything else. Abstracted into omnipresence, the infamous "machine" is now typically represented as a threat not just to happiness but to survival itself. Far from the Puritans' wilderness phobia, the American's paramount fear at mid-century is the fear of identity loss through mechanization. At mid-century, indeed, the image of Adam as automaton— *The Man in the Grey Flannel Suit*—is well on its way to becoming a consensual image both inside and outside the country. And after mid-century the sense of dehumanization only accelerates. More and more, "the world verifies [the] perception of America as *deus ex machina*," notes John F. Callahan in 1972, citing as evidence recent film versions of World War II. Whatever their country of origin and style of presentation, he continues, productions like the Japanese *Fires on the Plain*, German *The Bridge*, and Polish *Ashes and Diamonds* are well-nigh unanimous in their portrayal of American soldiers as "one-dimensional mechanical men." It wasn't merely the foreigner who was haunted by this image. Considering the frequency with which modern writers have utilized the condition of war as an analogue for the human condition as a whole, the robot-like soldier remarked upon by Callahan here may easily be taken to represent the new version of *the* American.

As in the trends already discussed, the roots to this development are well anchored in the past. War has played a very significant role in the American imagination throughout the entire twentieth century. Indeed, since the early days of the Republic, the phenomenon of war has seemed to exert a peculiar fascination for a nation whose actual military adventures—the Revolutionary War, the Indian wars, the Civil War—carry such ambiguous moral implications. Despite the quantitative precedents, on the other hand, recent war fiction would seem qualitatively to comprise almost a new species. Where earlier versions from Cooper's *The Spy* to Crane's *The Red Badge of Courage* almost always focused on the traditional and eminently pro-social theme of physical and moral testing, a quarter of a century later the formula has become much more complicated. Equally far from both eighteenth-century romance and nineteenth-century realism, it was not in the grand canvas but in private and often claustrophobic fables like e.e. cumming's *The Enormous Room* that twentieth-century writers found an adequate paradigm for an age which by its very nature *denied* the affirmative implications of Private Fleming's triumph over self, over fear. Where war for Stephen Crane was a kind of initiation rite, in other words, for cummings and for Hemingway and for so many others of that generation it epitomized alienation. It was also, judging by their books and poems and stories, viewed as a symptom of a much broader malaise. In Hemingway, typically enough, the brutality and meaninglessness of war serve not simply as a backdrop for some questing "hero" but as an analogue, both extended and explicit, for the brutality and hollowness of the whole modern world.

War, then, has come to "mean" something entirely different in the quarter century between Crane and Hemingway. Nor is this merely a matter of positive versus negative views. Even allowing that Crane's vision of war is hardly a celebratory one, the realignment of attitudes toward its moral effect is radical enough that one might be justified in concluding that the actual experience of war, and consequently the conventional thematic implications accrued to that experience in literature, is different not merely in degree but in kind before and after the First World War. The key to this change lies primarily in a shift of focus. In traditional war stories war might be either exalted as "glorious" or condemned as terrible, wasteful, brutalizing etc. In both these cases, however, it is the physical encounter itself that occupies the center of the stage. The modern emphasis, in contrast, is typically not on the battle itself but on the living conditions, the state of being, contingent on but peripheral to that encounter. The effect of this, ironically enough, is to diminish the thematic importance of the war as *event* even as its significance as *setting* is enhanced. In marked contrast to books like *The Red Badge of Courage*, it often strikes one in reading these war—or to be more precise, antiwar—novels (Faulkner's *A Fable* is an extreme but not untypical example), that the protagonist is less endangered by the "enemy" than he is by the military machine. As Walter Allen comments with regard to Dos Passos' *Three Soldiers*, in fact, in almost all major American war novels of the twentieth century it seems as though "the real target of [the author's] hatred is not the war at all: it is the United States Army, and the Army precisely because the inevitable circumstances of Army life impose an intolerable restriction on the rights of the individual being." Whatever may appear on the surface, then, it is evidently not the fearful potential of war for death and violence that is central to the power this particular metaphor exerts for the twentieth-century American (although as a background to the wasteland and symptomatic of its destructiveness this is certainly a contributary factor) so much as the threat of regimentation, of *compulsion*, that life in the army implies. Being turned into a robot is thought to be far worse, in other words, than simply being killed. "To the European," Allen goes on to point out, "this seems a very American attitude."

It is because of the felt relevance of this particular aspect of military experience that Joseph Heller's 1955 novel, *Catch 22*, despite its flaws as a literary work, has come to assume a certain centrality in retrospective overviews of contemporary American culture. Heller's Yossarian, as both rebel and victim, is in many ways the Huckleberry Finn of our time. The tone of the book— the black humor that characterizes Heller's attitude toward his material—also reflects an important aspect of the contemporary scene. In particular, however, it is because *Catch-22*, perhaps more than any other popular novel of the period, provides a vivid portrait of the wasteland world not merely in the general terms formulated by Eliot but in its most characteristic American form that the book seems to epitomize American experience in a particularly memorable way. Here, as in Dos Passos' novel, it is the army itself that is the real enemy of the GI.

The enemy in Heller's book is not simply the chaos of war, but also the deadly inhuman bureaucracy of the military-economic establishment which claims to be a stay against chaos while it threatens life more insidiously than battle itself. "The enemy is anybody who's going to get you killed, no matter *which* side he's on." Heller finds it confusing and difficult always to condemn the act of war—to say it was evil to fight against Hitler—but he is unqualified in his condemnation of the military institution that springs from the necessities of battle. The establishment that runs the war goes so far to destroy sanity and life and the human spirit that Heller finds war's greatest evil is its responsibility for the production of organized military inhumanity. *Catch-22* does not really deal with the chaos of war—although that is its persistent backdrop. The emphasis is never on battle, and even the antiwar theme is soft-pedaled when the question of relative morality involves choosing between life-negating war or life-negating bureaucracy. Heller deals instead with one real terror that haunts the novel of the sixties—the organized institution which in the name of reason, patriotism, and righteousness has seized control over man's life. [Olderman, 1972]

Catch-22 thus uses the military setting even more specifically than *A Farewell to Arms* to evoke the quality, the terror, of contemporary American life. So successful is the evocation, moreover, that the book (like Cooper's Leatherstocking novels before it) is now more often cited by popular reputation than it is actually read. Indeed the mysterious regulation designated "Catch-22" has long since entered the general currency of popular culture in America as an axiomatic expression, along with the Peter Principle and Murphy's Law, of the ultimate illogic—half humorous, half sinister—of the extensively bureaucratized society in which we all live. "If they don't get you coming, they get you going." "You can't fight City Hall." "You just can't win." This is the promise implicit in Dos Passos' machine-dominated social hierarchy carried to its inevitable conclusion.

What of the inhabitants of this particular setting? Doc Daneeka is representative, perhaps prototypical. Mistakenly declared dead, he is, despite his vociferous objections and the incontrovertible evidence of his physical presence, expunged not only from all official records but even from the memory of his wife. The wasteland deprives everyone of humanity, in one way or another. Even the "villains" in Heller's army lack real substance. They are victims of their own obsessions: rank, money, appearance. One-dimensional, inflicted with tunnel vision, they, like Dos Passos' "successes," apparently have no more freedom of initiative than the more obvious victims who are their pawns. When the fanatically entrepreneurial Milo Minderbinder contracts out to bomb his own side it is as much a betrayal of his own human potential as it is of the "friends" he injures in his attack. Similarly, the innocents in *Catch-22*—or, at least, those whose transgressions are relatively unspectacular—are as seriously undermined by their own inner flaws as they are brutalized by the external conditions of the war. As Olderman sums it up, in fact, these men are almost without exception "characterized by an enervating and neurotic pettiness...they are alienated, aimless, and bored. They long for escape and even death—almost everyone does either die or disappear. They are close to being inert and are helpless in the face of a total disintegration of values." The key characteristic of Heller's soldier, then, is above all, his *impotence*. Guilt and innocence are much less important points of reference in the book than a greater or lesser capacity for action. Yossarian's escape, the happy ending, is almost completely anomalous. The "real" wastelander, the emblematic figure who lurks at the heart of Heller's world, exemplifying with horrid aptness his comrades' omnipresent feelings of vulnerability—their constant sense of being hemmed in by unmanageable and incomprehensible forces—is the *totally* decapacitated individual, the "soldier in white":

[H]e was encased from head to toe in plaster and gauze. He had two useless legs and two useless arms...pinioned strangely in air by lead weights suspended darkly above him that never moved. Sewn into the bandages over the inside of both elbows were zippered lips through which he was fed clear fluid from a clear jar. A silent zinc pipe rose from the cement on his groin and was coupled to a slim rubber hose that carried waste from his kidneys and dripped it efficiently into a clear, stoppered jar on the floor. When the jar on the floor was full, the jar feeding his elbow was empty, and the two were simply switched quickly so that stuff could drip back into him. All they ever really saw of the soldier in white was a frayed black hole over his mouth.

The next question that arises is how typical Heller's characters really are with respect to modern American writing. Taken as a whole, the corpus yields numerous other stock figures who differ quite significantly not just in detail but in essential conception from the victimized robot-soldier we have been examining here; some of these will be discussed in greater detail later. In general, however, it is surprising how often the same general type does recur. As early as Dreiser's *An American Tragedy*, for instance, despite both the radical difference in tone and the shift of focus to private rather than public experience, we are offered a protagonist *essentially* identical to the more overtly bizarre personae who appear in Heller's novel more than half a century later. As Allen describes him, "Clyde Griffiths is, almost by definition, Wyndham Lewis's dumb ox, the passive victim of circumstances. Dreiser himself says that he was 'a soul that was not destined to grow up.' He is selfish—this Dreiser insists upon— and weak, incapable even, whatever his wishes may be, of any decisive action. Objectively he seems scarcely to deserve our pity. 'Why don't they kill the God-damned bastard and be done with him?' asks a spectator in the court-room; and this response to a creature who is characterized by 'the most feeble and blundering incapacity' is understandable. Clyde Griffiths," he concludes, "is everything a tragic hero is not."

The thing that Clyde Griffiths and the denizens of *Catch-22* have in common, of course, is the fact that they are all the helpless victims of a reality quite out of proportion to both what they deserve and what, in the specific terms of the American myth of justice and freedom, they are led to expect. This is the real essence of the modern American Adam—and herein lies the real American tragedy, a tragedy which, in Allen's words, is founded upon "the contrast between the promise of America, and indeed of its material pride and luxury, and the poverty in which so many millions of its people [live]...not merely a material poverty [but]...a poverty of values, a poverty of spirit." As we implied above, in other words, the nightmare world of the wasteland is not, strictly speaking, a symbolic *counter* to the abundant garden but, rather, a logical *consequence* of that overoptimistic dream, a shattering vision of discrepancy actually predicated upon the simultaneous affirmation of the myth. Dispossessed, the Adamic hero thus becomes the anti-hero. It is this anti-hero, in a variety of guises ranging all the way from a murderous Joe Christmas to weak, well-intentioned Willy Loman, who seems to dominate the roster of modern through contemporary American literary personnel.

What specifically, is an anti-hero? Michael Woolf explains:

[T]he heroic is an inappropriate concept in the context of contemporary culture. The concept of the anti-hero reflects the nature of our reality much more obviously. It recognizes a literary procedure in which the central character is seen to have no special powers that distinguish him from others; nor is he able to act as a dynamic factor in the evolution of a given fictional system. More precisely, anti-heroic fiction reflects a view of reality that grew out of recent historical experience, out of the realization that the individual's capacity to effect changes or to control the direction of his own experience was severely limited. The individual was revealed as powerless, buffeted by forces too massive, too nightmarish. Society no longer seemed to have an accessible logic, was no longer hospitable to man. The characteristic response was the creation of the character who acts or fails to act out of impulses deriving from the pressures of mass experience rather than from the moral direction of his will... He appears in two guises. One of his manifestations is as the comic figure jerking powerlessly through a set of circumstances framed by pressures quite external to him, beyond his control and, perhaps, his understanding. He also appears as an anguished figure, impotent in the face of a consistently inhospitable or mysterious reality. Very often he appears as a synthesis of these two positions—a comically impotent figure whose plight reflects a real sense of anguish.

The anti-hero—the new American Adam—is thus simply a generic name for the helpless and dehumanized robot-soldier who throughout the century, as we have seen, has haunted the American's sense of himself.

This brings us back to the neo-primitivism that we cited above. Whom better might one choose than the long-suffering and passive peasant to provide a correlative for the representative experience of the wasteland world, a world where even the exceptional man is all but completely denied the ego-affirming release of action? And if the real-life peasant would seem to be somewhat lacking in the glamor that made the noble savage during his heyday such an appealing referent, it is at least theoretically possible to infer from the qualities and circumstances associated with him a *new* standard of nobility, a new *kind* of primitivism appropriate to the ironic and deterministic universe that replaced in the American consciousness the romantic and heroic vision of the Republic's younger days. For the prototypical elucidation of such a standard we turn to the ethical-aesthetic code of behavior illuminated by Hemingway.

Hemingway's code is really only implicit in the novels themselves. In spite of the fact that it provides an essential background to his fictional world that must be felt, if not articulated, for the reader to make appropriate judgments, it is never clearly and comprehensively explained in any single fictional work. *Death in the Afternoon*, a semi-documentary treatise on bullfighting, may, on the other hand, be seen not merely as a "readers' guide" to the rest of the oeuvre but as a comprehensive moral parable for the twentieth century. Why? The key lies in the reverberatory nature of the subject itself. As a structured activity (falling somewhere between ritual drama and sport) wherein all rules, methods, and results are minutely predetermined, the bullfight offers a singularly appropriate symbol for a mechanistic modern society. At the same time, however, it *also* offers a tacit proof that determination need not imply defeat. Accepting the absolute fixity of condition, and operating within the narrow limits offered by such an arena, a man can still behave well, if not heroically. Like the old noble savage, moreover, the matador (a prototypical primitive in the *modern* sense) provides a perfect model for the proper response.

The phenomenon is worth examining in some detail. Beginning with fundamentals, on a pragmatic level the bullfight simply serves the same function as primitive religious ritual, providing a means of dealing emotionally with man's greatest and most terrifying enemy—his mortality. The bullfighter, in other words, demonstrates that defiance of death which for Hemingway is the only possible alternative to slavish and soul-destroying fear: by taking upon himself the act of killing, a man makes himself the master of mortality rather than its victim. As Hemingway explains:

> A great killer must love to kill; unless he feels it is the best thing he can do, unless he is conscious of its dignity and feels that it is its own reward, he will be incapable of the abnegation that is necessary in real killing. The truly great killer must have a sense of honor and a sense of glory far beyond that of the ordinary bullfighter. In other words he must be a simpler man. Also he must take pleasure in it, not simply as a trick of the wrist, eye, and managing of his left hand that he does better than other men, which is the simplest form of that pride and which he will naturally have as a simple man, but he must have a spiritual enjoyment of the moment of killing...the feeling of rebellion against death that comes from its administering. Once you accept the rule of death thou shalt not kill is an easily and naturally obeyed commandment. But when a man is still in rebellion against death he has pleasure in taking to himself one of the Godlike attributes; that of giving it. This is one of the most profound feelings in those men who enjoy killing.

The cathartic value thus found in killing also explains Hemingway's obsessive interest in blood sports, like hunting (the hunter, *qua* hunter, is a kind of primitive too)—but whereas hunting can never be more than a private enactment of the ritual (and therefore less emotionally satisfying than the intensification of response that takes place when a ritual is shared), the bullfight provides a public drama in which the spectators can participate vicariously in the matador's triumph over death. In order for this sharing to be possible and complete, there must obviously be a high degree of empathy developed between the bullfighter and his audience. For this reason his commitment to and domination of the ritual, the *means* by which he kills as well as the mere fact of his killing, are all-important. Here is where the code, the moral model, enters the picture.

What does this code entail? In the first place, and above all, of course, since any sign of fear would automatically negate the efficacy of the ritual, the bullfighter must display great courage—and not mere passive or stoic acceptance of risk, but positive, aggressive, absolutely gratuitous bravado in the face of danger. For equally obvious reasons, the bullfighter must also display great honor; if the encounter isn't "real," without trickery or fakery, it can hardly be cathartic. Popular assumptions aside, on the other hand, these traditional virtues are not enough in and by themselves to guarantee a satisfying performance. For slightly less obvious reasons, the perfect matador must also comport himself with style. This means, among other things, a high degree of self-consciousness and an even higher degree of control. Since the bullfight is not merely a sport in which the sole aim is the defeat of the bull—Hemingway continually refers to it as an "art" and a "tragedy"—and since the emotional impact is more important than the fact of the killing, it is up to the matador to make sure that his confrontation with the bull will be as dramatic as possible. The only way in which he can do this is to dominate his antagonist at all times and to manipulate each interchange for maximum visual appeal rather than rather merely reacting. The third required component to the performance, then, is authority. And the fourth is an intangible quality Hemingway calls grace:

> The danger incurred in a "quite" is so real, so controlled and selected by the man, and so apparent, and the slightest tricking or simulating of danger shows so clearly, that the modern quites in which the matadors rival with each other in invention and in seeing with what purity of line, how slowly, and how closely they can make the horns of the bull pass their waists, keeping him dominated and slowing the speed of his rush with the sweep of the cape controlled by their wrists; the whole hot bulk of the bull passing the man who looks down calmly where the horns almost touch, and sometimes do touch, his thighs while the bull's shoulders touch his chest, with no move of defense against the animal and no means of defense against the death that goes in by the horns except the slow movement of his arms and his judgment of distance; these passes are finer than any cape work of the past and as emotional as anything can ever be.

With this we have clearly gone far beyond practical considerations to an aesthetic standard which is an end in itself.

We have also come to the last major component of Hemingway's morality. Or perhaps it would be more accurate to call it his *amorality*. The success of the bullfight is based on linked criteria drawn from several *different* types of value system. If one takes the matador as a exemplar, one must also accept that "good form" is as important a component of character as integrity. This is exactly what Hemingway does assume. Superficially cynical, the stance is not without its existential justifications. Modern man cannot control his unnatural environment in the way that the bullfighter controls the natural power of the bull—indeed it is this very powerlessness that makes his vicarious identification with the ritual so important—but, taking inspiration from the bullfighter's example, he can control him*self*, thus creating the illusion (which is all-important if life itself is considered an artform) of being in control of his destiny. Extending this example into everyday existence, moreover—which is what Hemingway does in his novels—it is possible to infer from the matador an ideal of social conduct which will both affirm and facilitate this effect, combining a stoic acceptance of the pain that is inevitable in the modern wasteland, the courage to meet life (and death) joyously in spite of it, the sensitivity (not really so far from the natural "taste" displayed by Cooper's positive characters) to appreciate the aesthetic nuances of a social situation, and enough pride always to keep up a good face. Beyond this prescription, using the bullfight as a moral model also and finally emphasizes the importance of the ritual component in behavior at all times—man's helplessness in the ironic world and his consequent need for a mediating structure of sorts to govern his relationship with the environment.

Hemingway's "code," focusing on the means rather than the ends of action, thus offers a vivid image of what would seem to be the only "heroic" ideal appropriate to a limiting, restrictive, modern society. His matador (or soldier, or boxer, or big game hunter—all are variations on the same type) may, in fact be seen as the only kind of noble primitive realistically possible in the twentieth century. In contradistinction to the Melvillean psycho-symbol, however, this new conventional figure, while unquestionably noble, is no longer savage. And this, of course, comprises a difference of kind, not merely of degree. If he is not savage, then the new primitive inevitably loses much of the depth and flexibility of the traditional savage's symbolic associations. The bullfighter is obviously defined in *opposition to* nature rather than in *harmony with* it. Peasants and blacks, on the other hand, may easily represent the cultivated garden; some of them may even be related to the natural, paradisial garden, depending on their literary context. There is no way, however, that they can plausibly provide a meaningful correlative for the wilderness. Such a limitation is an unfortunate one, for the wilderness itself—dead and mutilated as now appears to be—has in many ways become an even more important issue for the twentieth-century American psyche than it was a hundred years earlier when the process of destruction was at least *imaginatively* reversible. All things considered, America would seem badly in need of a symbolic vehicle capable of comprehending all the ambiguous emotional ramifications of her loss.

And this brings us back to Chingachgook.

Alone among the nineteenth-century noble savages, Chingachgook, as mentioned above, was conceived in complex and ironic rather than simple romantic terms. This transformation, however, did not entail a loss of his traditional racial association with the wilderness. Appropriately enough, his death in *The Pioneers* is simultaneous with (not simply *caused by*: the connection is more mysterious) a climactic destruction of the forest by fire. Again there is a superb touch of irony in Cooper's arrangement of the scene. At the moment of his death, as if he actually *were* the fabled mediator of American wishful fantasies, there is a rainstorm that extinguishes the destructive blaze. As a result, although the "next day the woods, for many miles, were black and smoking... The pines and hemlocks still reared their heads proudly among the hills." The entire thrust of *The Pioneers*, however—the relentless sound of axes we hear so constantly in the background—convinces us that the respite, the ritual revitalization, is illusory. Indeed, it might be said that the real forest is already gone, so diminished is it by the settlers' activities. What is left is a hollow token of its former expanse and glory. " 'Woods!' " exclaims Leatherstocking, in response to Elizabeth's misguided enthusiasm—" 'Indeed! I doesn't call these woods, Madam Effingham, where I lose myself every day of my life in the clearings!' " Chingachgook's death, therefore, is the symbolic end of the wilderness, and Natty himself has no choice but to pack up and get out.

Chingachgook consequently has a *double* capacity. Inasmuch as he is the helpless victim, forced to act out an ironic reversal of his traditional heroic role, he offers a relevant standard for the twentieth century. Inasmuch, however, as his fate is not merely individual but mystically linked with the fate of the doomed wilderness, he achieves a symbolic stature which few of the ironic heroes of the twentieth century can match. Rather than being *merely* a victim, in other words, he is heir to a fate which, universalized, intimates if no longer actually promises a potential for rebirth. Thus, in Faulkner's "The Bear," it is Sam Fathers rather than Ike McCaslin who is the true heir to Cooper's noble savage. The parallels between Sam and Chingachgook in fact are even more striking than those between the false messiahs, Natty and Ike. Both of them, dwarfed by white civilization, take their meaning and identity from a long unbroken racial/cultural tradition, and gifted by this tradition with "natural" wisdom both attempt to demonstrate for their white "brothers" the true response required by the wilderness if that symbolic promise is to be realized; if they would be brothers not merely in wishful myth but in fact. Potential notwithstanding, on the other hand, both Sam and Chingachgook are finally childless, in spirit as in body. This being the case, the question inevitably arises as to whether, when they (along with the wilderness) finally die, the whole tradition that they represent necessarily dies with them.

Is there, then— and this is the essential problem that must be confronted here— *any* valid version of the noble savage to be found in American literature since Faulkner? If there is, he is certainly not a common type. This may, however, simply be because the action of the typical contemporary mainstream novel, growing as it does out of our now predominantly urban experience, has been largely shifted away from his home territory. The garden, or at least the values associated with it, is, as we said, still as much an object of human desire as it was in Cooper's day (Yossarian's flight to Switzerland is an exact experiential equivalent to Leatherstocking's migration to the prairies), but it is now rarely evoked as a real place, a felt presence. In Hemingway the garden, the Big Two-Hearted River, is still *there*, although it takes a long, arduous journey through a burned-out wasteland to reach it. In Fitzgerald's *The Great Gatsby*, similarly, the vision if not the reality of the "fresh, green breast of the new world" is still attainable in the quiet evening, out by the shore, although this sanctuary too may be achieved only by traversing a desolate valley of ashes. By Heller's time, however, it is no longer *difficult* to reach the garden; for most the journey is not considered a viable endeavor at all. The protagonist of the typical 50s or 60s novel is located *in* the city, and since, as Olderman points out, his is clearly a static rather than a dynamic situation ("Made passive by the fear of external forces, we are simply waiting—picketing and protesting perhaps, but waiting for a new revelation, for new alternatives"), there, except for a few anomalous exceptions, is where he inevitably stays. Outside of his daydreams, his nostalgic memories of a childhood that in most cases never really existed, this new Adam—like Ralph Ellison's *Invisible Man*, shut away even from the sunshine in his basement full of lightbulbs—is as far from nature as it is possible to get. Small wonder then that we find few Indians in these novels. Indeed, when one appears in such a setting it can only be by doing significant violence to his own essential nature. There is, as we have seen, a basic conceptual incompatibility between the savage and the city.

To say there are *few* Indians, noble or otherwise, is not, on the other hand, to say that there are none. Before considering the question any further, in fact, it would be useful to examine the one contemporary novel that might be said to speak from—and *for*— that same tradition of romantic/ironic primitivism we have identified with Chingachgook/Sam, Ken Kesey's *One Flew over the Cuckoo's Nest*. As Olderman summarizes:

> The tale takes place in the ward of an insane asylum where an iron-minded, frost-hearted Nurse rules by means of one twentieth-century version of brutality—mental and spiritual debilitation. Her patients are hopeless "Chronics" and "Vegetables," or they are "Acutes" who do not, according to McMurphy, seem "any crazier than the average asshole on the street." McMurphy comes to the asylum from a prison work farm. He has been a logger, a war hero, a gambler, and generally a happy, heavily muscled, self-made drifter and tough guy. A contest develops between McMurphy (whose initials R.P.M. urge us to note his power) and the Big Nurse (whose name, Ratched, tips us off about her mechanical nature as well as her offensive function as a "ball-cutter"). The implications of the contest deepen; it becomes a battle pitting the individual against all those things that make up the modern waste land, for the Nurse represents singly what the institution and its rules really are. The drama of the battle is intense, and the action seesaws as McMurphy gradually discovers he must give his strength to others in order to pry loose the Big Nurse's hold on their manhood. As they gain in health, McMurphy weakens, and his ultimate victory over the Big Nurse is a mixed one. He is lobotomized, a "castration of the frontal lobes," but he gives his lifeblood to Chief Bromden who breaks free and leaves behind the Nurse and the Institution not a destroyed power but a shrunken, silent, and temporarily short-circuited one. Beautifully structured, the novel provides us with both a brilliant version of our contemporary waste land and a successful Grail Knight, who frees the Fisher King and the human spirit for a single symbolic and transcendent moment of affirmation.

Olderman's synopsis of the plot and major themes is perhaps a little too slick to capture adequately the full texture of this book—its humor, for instance, or Kesey's deft, sensitive rendering of his minor characters—but even the bare bones of the narrative as outlined here should be enough to establish its relevance to the trends that we have been examining in this chapter. The setting truly is, as Olderman emphasizes, "a brilliant version of our contemporary waste land." The mental hospital is the ultimate institution where, to an even greater extent than in the army, an individual is denied both his identity and his rights. This particular institution, moreover, is simply a front for a society which is nothing more than a total, monolithic machine: the *Combine*, as Kesey calls it, evoking the vision of a gigantic harvester cutting its relentless swath through a field, levelling grain, flowers, small trapped animals, and processing each unit of its yield into a uniform, socially useful form. "All up the coast I could see the signs of what the Combine had accomplished since I was last through this country," says Kessey's narrator: "things like, for example—a *train* stopping at a station and laying a string of full-grown men in mirrored suits and machined hats, laying them like a hatch of identical insects, half-life things coming pht-pht-pht out of the last car, then hooting its electric whistle and moving on down the spoiled land to deposit another hatch." Here, obviously, is the American's nightmare of dehumanization taken to its furthest extreme. Here too is the explanation for the book's power. Personalities aside, it is clearly because the Big Nurse is an *agent* of the Combine rather than simply a hostile individual that the contest with McMurphy, as Olderman describes it, achieves its mythic dimension. Whatever else it may be or do, *One Flew over the Cuckoo's Nest* provides an almost classic expression of the world vision we have already shown to dominate twentieth-century modes of self-imaging. The point has some important ramifications for the question of whether the primitive exemplar continues to have any real relevance in this century. Because the fact is, beyond its fairly conventional treatment of the wasteland theme *One Flew Over the Cuckoo's Nest* not only contains—is actually narrated *by*— a character who may be cited as a noble savage, but can itself be read as a fable about the whole concept of noble savagery in the modern world.

We perhaps need to backtrack a bit before we can establish the self-evidence of these claims. For one thing, there are admittedly some difficulties with calling Chief Bromden a noble savage. Certainly as both an Indian dispossessed of his land *and* a mental patient dispossessed of his identity (his "voice"), Bromden exemplifies the Indian-as-victim-of-history even more clearly than Chingachgook/Sam. In our discussion of the last of the Mohicans above, however, we made the point that it is because Chingachgook combines within himself not only the fatality of a degraded old age but *also* the glorious promise of youth that he is able to attain the symbolic stature that he does. Similarly, Sam, as a relict of the dead past, claims not only our pity for his loneliness but also—and much more—our respect for his obvious power and insight into the secret ways of the world that are denied to us. This power and insight, moreover, give the old man an integrity, a sense of self, so intense and indestructible that it finally makes a mockery of our presumptuous pity. Unlike this composite prototype, however, Chief Bromden seems *only* victim, passive and impotent, to some extent by choice, and very little more. "Nobody complains about all the fog," he says. "I know why, now: as bad as it is, you can slip back in it and feel safe." Nor, without reaching substantially beyond the bounds of the book, can we get around this objection simply by imputing to him, by association, as it were, the "nobility" of his racial background. Like the huge Bromden himself (" 'I used to be big, but not no more' "), the narrator's father—a Columbia Chief whose name means The-Pine-That-Stands-Tallest-On-The-Mountain— has long since been psychologically "shrunk," diminished in his self-opinion to the extent that he is no longer capable of maintaining the heroic stance that his "conventional" position implies. Bromden describes the process to McMurphy.

> "Everybody worked on him because he was big, and wouldn't give in, and did like he pleased. Everybody worked on him just the way they're working on you."
> "They who, Chief?" he asked in a soft voice, suddenly serious.
> "The Combine. It worked on him for years. He was big enough to fight it for a while. It wanted us to live in inspected houses. It wanted to take the falls. It was even in the tribe, and they worked on him. In the town they beat him up in the alleys and cut his hair short once. Oh, the Combine's big—big. He fought it a long time till my mother [a shrewish white woman] made him too little to fight it any more and he gave up."
> ..."[In the end they forced the tribe to sell its land.] He said, What can you pay for the way a man lives? He said, What can you pay for what a man is? They didn't understand. Not even the tribe. They stood out in front of our door all holding those checks and they wanted him to tell them what to do now... But he was too little anymore. And he was too drunk, too. The Combine had whipped him."

It would thus seem clear that Bromden— at least as he presents himself throughout most of the book— cannot, without stretching the definition to an absurd degree, be considered noble in any conventional sense, either personally or vicariously, by virtue of his noble forebears. He doesn't even have a claim on nature any more.

Fortunately for our present theme, Bromden, as Olderman's outline hints, proves in the long run not to be the static character that he initially seems. Indeed, his transformation is started, albeit almost imperceptibly, the day that McMurphy arrives on the ward and his ebullient vitality begins to counter the deflating effects of the Combine. "I remember the fingers were thick and strong closing over mine," says Bromden, reminiscing about their introductory handshake, "and my hand commenced to feel peculiar and went to swelling up out there on my stick of an arm, like he was transmitting his own blood into it. It rang with blood and power. It blowed up near as big as his." And by the end of the book Bromden, finally "blowed up" by virtue of McMurphy's encouragement and self-sacrifice to a mental size commensurate with his gigantic physical stature, is able to break through the window and light out—typically enough—for the last frontier, Canada: the north.

What is the meaning of this fable? It is more individual, I think, than Olderman implies when he simply subsumes it under the general category of grail quests. McMurphy is a conventional hero, that is clear, and—so Kesey seems to suggest—we need real heroism more than ever in the world of the Combine in order to "drag us out of the fog." Unfortunately, this world being what it is, a hero, unlike (at least in some cases) the long suffering anti-hero, almost inevitably *has* to be defeated: killed, changed, purged, eradicated. In addition to the hero, therefore, our modern pantheon also requires a symbol of hope, an exemplary figure through whom we can vicariously, if not *win*, at least escape the trap, light out for the territories. And who better to play this role than our old friend the noble savage, associated as he is with concepts of both personal and political freedom.

Unfortunately— and this too is explicit in Kesey's fable—the noble savage has been so diminished now, so ironically deflated, that he is no longer part of our current symbolic vocabulary ready to use. We simply can't believe in him any more. Even if we ignore the obvious helplessness and degeneration of his real life counterpart, the facts of history suggest that he *must* be our enemy after all we have done to him; if not, his own morality, or at least his good sense, must be suspect. John Updike touches on this problem in *Rabbit Redux*. "The Lone Ranger is a white man, so law and order on the range will work to his benefit, but what about Tonto?" muses the novel's protagonist. "A Judas to his race, the more disinterested and lonely and heroic figure of virtue. When did he get his pay-off? Why was he faithful to the masked stranger? In the days of the war one never asked. Tonto was simply on 'the side of right.' It seemed a correct dream then, red and white together." Where, he ends up wondering, has the "side of right" gone now? And this is the question we inevitably have to ask ourselves these days with regard to our relationship with the Indian. Like Rabbit, there is a part of us which would still like to think of Tonto "as incorruptible, as above it all, like Jesus and Armstrong," but the only way it will ever be possible to regain the purity of this vision, to reinvoke the emotional power that was once invested in the literary Indian—and this, I think, is the climactic point of Kesey's fable—is for us, the White Man, to take it upon ourselves to *redeem* instead of being redeemed *by* him. Like McMurphy, in other words, we are called upon to invest our belief in the noble savage in order to blow him up "big" enough to provide for us the symbolic mediation, the image of hope and freedom, that now more than ever we still require.

Is this prescription— the question begs to be answered— one we have any chance of filling? Kesey, to be sure, not only describes but *demonstrates* his procedure for combatting the despair of the contemporary vision. Like a phoenix rising from the ashes of its own degradation, he creates a noble savage right before our eyes. Whether the achievement has any broader relevance for contemporary literature, however, remains to be seen. The fact is, despite Kesey's implicit plea that our faith would be its own reward, even above and beyond the superficial problem of setting there are a number of features—attitudes—

associated with the postmodern mainstream novel that would seem to preclude the noble savage, at least as incarnated in the figure of the Indian, from playing the kind of role that Kesey seems to claim that he should.

One of the most serious problems lies in the Indian's inherent association with the American westering myth. Why? In the context of the modern wasteland, the idea of a perpetually regainable paradise must seem at best a joke, at worst a tragic sham. In the context of this recognition, the only treatment it would seem to invite is satire. Instead of sturdy pioneers and hot-blooded Indians, therefore, what we get more often than not is something like Nathanial West's biting apocalyptic vision in *The Day of the Locust* of a Hollywood which, for all it looks like a papier maché fairyland, is nothing but a garbage dump of dreams, a place where bored and empty people, having spent their whole lives slaving away at dull jobs, "saving their pennies and dreaming of...leisure," come to die. The closest we are likely to come to a noble savage in *this* garden, despite its abundant sunshine, luscious fruit free for the picking, and beautiful, luxuriant flowers, is a pugilistic dwarf or a horny Mexican cock-fighter— or, only slightly more credibly, a family of brandy-loving Eskimos left over from an old movie, simulating the tastes of home with smoked salmon and maatjes herring from the Jewish delicatessen. Even the violence which, just as in the original myth, the original west, inevitably erupts here is only a grotesque reflection of the cathartic violence embodied in the archetypal encounter between red and white. In West's version—which ends, appropriately enough, with a real riot and an imaginary holocaust—the paradise has, in fact, clearly become a hell. The transformation seems an inevitable one when we consider what a snare and a delusion the westward quest has turned out to be for almost all the twentieth century's literary pilgrims, from Steinbeck's Okies to (ironically reversing the directional iconography of the original fable) James Herlihy's *Midnight Cowboy*.

Debunking the good west also debunks the good Indian, of course. Given such thorough discreditation-by-association, in fact, the only way our savage could retain even the faintest vestige of his erstwhile exemplary stature would be to divest himself of his historicity altogether. The only *kind* of divestiture that has seemed to suggest itself to most contemporary writers, unfortunately, is a stickily sentimental "Sir Walter Scottification" of pioneer life which, as Fiedler (1968) points out, is not merely puerile but—carrying as it does the tacit admission that the frontier is now merely "a source of nostalgia rather than [a wellspring of] hope"— covertly self-negating. As dishonest as it is hackneyed, therefore, the typical twentieth-century western romance, while *seeming* to salvage at least the rudiments of the primitivistic vision, has in fact, like its close cousin the nineteenth-century "Indian drama," tended to undermine the moral authority of its habitual personae even more firmly than before. Once co-opted by such retrogressive forms, the Indian begins to carry a distasteful aura of sentimentality along with him in whatever guise he may appear. This aura is alone enough to debar him *de facto* from most "serious" literature.

The good Indian, then, is a dead Indian. Does this mean that primitivism is dead as well? What if we look elsewhere for a noble savage, one who is not irrevocably tied to a discredited myth? There is no real reason, since the type is, at least in theory, defined functionally rather than in terms of race, why the noble savage has to be an Indian. There is certainly evidence the feeling has been shared by numerous other post-mid-century writers besides Kesey that the bureaucratization and mechanization of modern society make it more important than ever that we find some sort of symbolic means of renegotiating, at least imaginatively, our relationship with nature. An untainted noble savage, if we could find one, would therefore seem to be a very useful addition to the *dramatis personae* of the contemporary novel. The problem is that nature in the broad sense—as we have seen—evokes all sorts of conflicting emotions and ideas, and once the concept is detached from the westering myth which has structured American attitudes towards it for so long (as, it seems, it *must* be to regain its authority), it tends to become very fuzzy indeed. The direct man/nature relationship has thus proved difficult for contemporary writers to deal with.

An example of this is Updike's *The Centaur*. In this book the central protagonist, a highschool teacher, is juxtaposed, indeed *merged* (whether in his own vision, or simply in ours is never made clear) with a mythic creature who, exemplified in Chiron, son of Zeus, teacher of princes and heroes, is conventionally considered to represent the ultimate blending of man and beast, art and nature. The idea is an interesting one, and Updike's handling of it, especially in the opening chapter, is skillful enough that the reader is led to expect an unusually rich fictional experience. Unfortunately the book as a whole never really redeems this initial promise. A major ingredient in the failure is the fact that Updike, having hit upon a promising symbolic structure, doesn't seem to know what to do with it. Indeed, the mediating potential of Caldwell/Chiron is never exploited to any significant extent at all. One might almost suspect that the author is oblivious to this particular aspect of the myth were it not for the fact that he seems to emphasize the centaur's duality quite specifically in the beginning. "A creature combining the refinement and consideration of a man with...'the massive potency of a stallion,' " Vera/Venus describes him. He also seems, quite specifically, to be setting up the centaur in this first chapter to play precisely the mediating role between man and "other" that is suggested by his inherent duplicity. "[I]t was rumored that Zeus thought centaurs a dangerous middle-ground through which the gods might be transmuted into pure irrelevance," Caldwell/Chiron muses. After assembling all this elaborate apparatus, however, Updike does very little more with it. There is a loose opposition between nature and civilization set up between George's garden-loving wife and art-loving son, but even aside from the fact that this is a motif too minor even to be called a theme, Caldwell himself seems flatly alienated by nature rather than mediating it in any real way. " 'I hate Nature,' " he says vehemently at one point. " 'It reminds me of death. All Nature means to me is garbage and confusion and the stink of skunk.' "

It may be argued, I suppose, that Caldwell, as a centaur who has denied his bestial side, is meant simply to represent Everyman, whose "mixed" nature has been stunted by modern society, warped away from the compromise of the golden mean. Again, however, there is little in the book to suggest that this is the point Updike means to make; indeed, there is nothing—outside, perhaps, of his failure to respond to Vera's seduction, a failure which is morally ambivalent at best—to indicate that George is in any way a lesser man for his repudiation of his earthier self. One can only conclude (on the evidence that both the opening quotation and the first chapter focus on Chiron's wounding) that this whole elaborate fiction of the centaur alter ego is merely introduced to give some sort of mythic stature to the truism that life itself is a "wound" but if it is borne bravely one may be redeemed in the end by a noble death (the Epilogue—"Zeus had loved his old friend, and lifted him up, and set him among the stars"— is obviously meant to suggest Caldwell's eulogistic obituary previewed earlier in the book). Despite the promise of Updike's basic conception, there is certainly nothing here of our noble savage.

If Updike fails to give us a true primitive exemplar, it is possibly because he has no desire or intention to do so, of course: his focus for good or ill, is elsewhere. One would think, however, that the endeavor might be more likely to meet with success in the hands of a writer like Bellow, whose world view in general seems softer, perhaps even a little more "old-fashioned" than the postmodern norm. "Bellow asserts through his spokesman Herzog that one should not 'sneer at the term Romantic,' for Romanticism preserved 'the most generous ideas of mankind, during the greatest and most rapid of transformations, the most accelerated phase of the modern scientific and technical transformation,' " says Allan Chavkin. "The problem for Herzog, the contemporary romantic hero, is how to preserve humanist values in a period in which mass society has accelerated beyond the English Romantics' worst fears, thereby creating views of man that are fundamentally nihilistic." Any writer whose philosophical stance is as Chavkin describes it here—and I think we can agree with him on the basis of external evidence that in this particular at least, Herzog may be regarded as a spokesman for his author—might very well be expected to believe, along with those English Romantics celebrated by his protagonist, that nature is a beneficial influence and as such to be sought out by any means possible.

Confirming these expectations, in *Henderson the Rain King* Bellow does in fact give us what seems on the surface a genuine revival of the noble savage convention, not so much as American tradition would have it but as it flourished in Britain in the late eighteenth century. Feeling his life to be essentially meaningless, desperate to break out of the endless empty cycle of fear and desire, "more or less the same fear, more or less the same desire for thousands of generations," an ultra-civilized modern white man—easterner, Ivy-Leaguer, and millionaire—sets out on a quest to the most remote and primitive region of

Africa he can reach ("I wanted to see some places off the beaten track") where he meets and is instructed by a noble savage in the primitive arts and rituals that will enable him to become a better and more fulfilled individual ("There will never be anything but misery without high conduct. I knew that you went out from home in America because of a privation of high conduct," says his savage mentor).

Unfortunately, once one gets beyond the conventional premise, what this novel achieves is somewhat more ambiguous than the summary makes it sound. Certainly King Dahfu does seem, by virtue of both his position and his personal attributes—his size, his vitality, his classically dignified demeanor—ideally suited to play the role of noble savage. Further to this, the specific focus of his instruction, his advice to Henderson to "imitate or dramatize the behavior of lions," is quite in keeping with the noble savage's traditional function of bringing his civilized auditor in closer contact with nature. His explanation of this task, moreover, is framed in terms that echo very closely traditional views about the value of such a contact.

"You ask, what can she [the lioness] do for you? Many things. First she is unavoidable... And this is what you need, as you are an avoider. Oh, you have accomplished momentous avoidances. But she will change that. She will make consciousness to shine. She will burnish you. She will force the present moment upon you. Second, lions are experiencers. But not in haste. They experience with deliberate luxury. The poet says, 'The tigers of wrath are wiser than the horses of instruction.' Let us embrace lions also in the same view. Moreover, observe Atti. Contemplate her. How does she stride, how does she saunter, how does she lie or gaze or rest or breathe?... Then there are more subtle things, as how she leaves hints, or elicits caresses. But I cannot expect you to see this at first. She has much to teach you."

"Teach? You mean that she might change me."

"Excellent. Precisely. Change. You fled what you were. You did not believe you had to perish. Once more, and a last time, you tried the world. With a hope of alteration... You have rudiments of high character. You could be noble. Some parts may be so long-buried as to be classed dead. Is there any resurrectibility in them? This is where the change comes in."

Despite the apparent striking conventionality of these features, especially insofar as they emphasize through example and precept both the greater immediacy *and* the innate dignity of a life close to nature (by tradition the two major attributes of the noble savage), Bellow's version of the noble savage is undercut by a number of equally striking ambiguities revolving, ironically enough, around the same didactic function that seems at first to align the book so clearly with classical primitivism.

For one thing, the author does not necessarily encourage us to share Dahfu's opinion of his "cure." Henderson himself expresses profound doubts about the ultimate morality of the exercise that the King has proposed. "[W]hat could an animal do for me?" he asks. "Even supposing that an animal enjoys a natural blessing. We had our share of this creature-blessing until infancy ended. But now aren't we required to complete something else—project number two— the second blessing." Secondly, even if we ignore this quibble, even if the lion *is* adjudged an appropriate model and the formative powers of sympathetic identification accepted at least in theory, this very principle implies yet a further difficulty in that Henderson, it would seem, has already been extensively "formed" by sympathetic identification with a much less noble and more civilized animal, the pig. The seriousness of this second, more pragmatic problem is borne out by the fact that in the end the regimen does indeed fail.

Aggravating our suspicions, another and perhaps even more serious difficulty lies in the fact that underneath his affectations, the King is not really a savage at all. He is an educated man, devoted to science; more telling, his lion ritual, despite its seeming primitivism, is conceived specifically not in spiritual but in scientific terms. As Henderson explains it, "Briefly, he had a full scientific explanation of the way in which people were shaped. For him it was not enough that there might be disorders of the body that originated in the brain. *Everything* originated there." The whole quest, therefore, is fraught with paradox. While not exactly a parody of the concept of noble savagery (Dahfu is indubitably noble and at least generically a primitive), nor even a consistent inversion of the paradisial quest, *Henderson the Rain King* does seem to signal a certain confusion in Bellow's mind about what, exactly, nature is, and how it relates to civilization. Henderson puts his finger on the central enigma of the book: "It was just my luck to think I had found the conditions of life simplified so I could deal with them—finally! and then to end up in a ramshackle palace reading these advanced medical publications."

Henderson is not an isolated case in Bellow's corpus. Indeed, it seems as though this confusion of attitudes toward nature is a central characteristic of his work. What does this imply? Since Bellow, particularly in this aspect, seems to represent in a fairly significant way the temper of post-mid-century America, this question is an important one for us to confront. In doing so we might perhaps profitably turn to Robert Boyers's 1975 essay, "Nature and Social Reality in Bellow's *Sammler*."

Without going into too many details about this novel, the most relevant feature for the present discussion is the fact that one of its most numinous elements is the protagonist's encounter with and subsequent vision of a black criminal who, despite his urban affinities and impeccable Western dress, is, like Dahfu, attributed with a number of characteristics clearly reminiscent of the classic eighteenth-century noble savage: "The black man was a megalomaniac. But there was a certain—a certain princeliness. The clothing, the shades, the sumptuous colors, the barbarous-majestical manner. He was probably a mad spirit. But mad with an idea of noblesse." This man, as Boyers points out, is thus clearly intended by Bellow to stand as a "potent image of nature," having in common with Dahfu "the element of primary animal vitality." The problem is, he continues, despite the unusual emotional intensity associated with both of these figures, neither of them "is generated in a context that espouses the return to nature in any authoritative way [since] The emotional context in each case is clouded by guilt and by...self-consciousness." While the problem remains primarily an academic one in *Henderson*, this uncertainty in the author's approach necessarily affects our response to Sammler's black thief a great deal. The values he embodies as a real individual are a little dubious at best (he is obviously a crude and vicious character), and without some clear indication on the author's part as to his *fictional* significance, we inevitably wonder whether the numen that Bellow imputes to him is justified. As Boyers says, "Sammler suffers for this black man...not because he is a mere mortal who has fallen on bad times, but because the idea of noblesse he somehow incarnates has been wantonly soiled by those who have no real sense of what noblesse might mean for all of us. One is tempted, surely, to share Sammler's attitude, but it is a little hard to do so if one does not understand what it is he admires in the black man."

In Boyers's mind these difficulties seem directly connected with Bellow's view of nature. What, he asks, is in fact evoked by the concept nature in Sammler's mind? Judging by the incident of the black thief, "it is not the nature of trees and blue skies and tip-toes through the tulips, nor the nature of pastoral swains and woodland nymphs, to which Sammler is drawn. Like other protagonists in Bellow's fiction, he is at least partially drawn to the idea and image of nature red in tooth and claw." The nature he "looks upon in the guise of a handsome black thief" is thus not only "ruthless and sordid" but *"all the more attractive for being so"* (italics added). What Sammler seems to suspect, in fact, is that "the other nature, the nature one associates with the divine flow of things passively regarded, is not really the sort of thing one can rely upon in the modern world, much as one would like to... The nature to which Whitman and other American writers have delighted in yielding themselves to is here rejected as inadequate, for it is unrealistic in its trust and in its failure to discriminate between a sense of the universe and a sense of social fact."

There is nothing wrong with this, to be sure. Indeed, since the pastoral/ mystical view of nature associated with the romance of the west has been discredited, it seems quite reasonable that a contemporary writer should focus on a different aspect of nature than that to which Emerson and Thoreau addressed themselves. Furthermore, as it is now quite clearly and simply the oppressiveness and sterility of the city rather than the unruly wilderness against which the modern Romantic must set his vision of the garden, it is fully appropriate that it is the vitality rather than the beauty, the potency—even the danger— rather than the instructive nobility, that Bellow should choose to emphasize here. Unfortunately, as one might expect after *Henderson*, Bellow wants to cling to the other face of nature as well. "Sammler's gentler nature, the nature he identifies with the mystic affirmations of Eckhart (rather than with the...black thief)," Boyers points out, "is not really very different from Wordsworth's." To make things worse, nature for Sammler seems "at once an exhilarating idea, no matter how disparate his varying conceptions of it, and also a rather sickening notion laced with a kind of emotional excess he finds intolerable."

Just how serious is this confusion? According to Boyers, not very. What bothers him much more than the lack of any clear and consistent ideal associated with nature is the fact that Bellow fails to establish the relevance of his portmanteau romanticism to the modern world in any direct, realistic way. "Where he disappoints us is in his continuing incapacity to get beyond the realm of sentimental affirmation to a more acute apprehension of social reality," he says. "We are not inclined to demand of him that he abandon his ideas of nature but that he somehow manage to place them in the perspective in which they belong." Boyers's complaint, therefore, concerns not the substance of Bellow's ideas so much as the use he makes of them. As far as the conceptual confusion is concerned—the inconsistencies associated with nature itself, especially as revealed by Bellow's ambiguous noble savage—this, Boyers suggests, is perhaps inherent in the context out of which Bellow writes. Despite its lack of coherence, therefore, Bellow's vision of nature is perhaps fully appropriate to and revelatory of the condition of the modern age:

> What Bellow is giving us, in other words, and what Sammler sees, is a universe in which the very idea of nature has been altered, confused, deliberately turned around in such a way that it does not mean what it used to. And as the idea of nature has been willfully perverted, so is it difficult any longer to think of social reality in the customary ways. Obviously, to think of the one idea is in some sense to compare it to the other, and this has become more and more difficult to do. *The self has no secure home either in nature or in society, for neither constitutes a firm reality to which it can relate with confidence.* [italics added]

This last sentence would seem to underline a very important characteristic of contemporary America. As history inexorably turns the American dream into a nightmare, not merely specific formulations like the westering myth but almost *all* traditional assumptions about nature and society are undermined. Both the garden symbol and the city symbol, despite the potential desirability especially of the former in terms of traditional and persistent emotional connotations, thus tend to be cut loose from any firm standard of values and any consensually recognized fictional vehicle. This, of course, makes them even more unreliable as literary tools than they have been in the past, which is why, one suspects, so many novels written during the 60s and 70s seem, whatever their "formal" settings, to take place in a kind of No Place, a social vacuum, an abstracted landscape drained of almost all the fully realized sensual detail that would make it— in terms of "felt" presence—either city *or* garden. Since the minimum definition of the noble savage necessarily entails at least some sort of mediating function, there is obviously—Kesey notwithstanding— no real place for him in such a neutered landscape.

This seems to confirm our initial assessment of the contemporary situation. If, as we said, we survey mainstream literature of the decades following mid-century, the noble savage, not surprisingly in the light of the foregoing discussion, is conspicuous mainly for his absence. If he appears at all it is likely to be only as a minor character presented in either conventionally sentimentalized terms or, more likely, due to the stigma associated with the romanticized Indian, as a parodic version of the former. Barth's *The Sot-Weed Factor* is typical. The Indians in this pseudo-baroque picaresque fantasy are identified almost solely in terms of their primitive (i.e., squalid) lifestyle and their violent perverted sexuality. The book is interesting despite its stereotypes, however, if only because the stereotypes concerned are such classically *American* ones. "[M]ore than a pornographic joke," what Barth has achieved here, says Fiedler (1968),

is a counter-parable, an anti-stereotype of our beginnings in Virginia, in which Pocahontas' relationship to John Smith is portrayed not as an act of pure altruism and pity, but a sexual encounter so mechanical, so bestial, that it seems an assault rather than an act of love—and, therefore, a truer metaphor of our actual relations with the Indians than the pretty story so long celebrated in sentimental verse.

Here, then, rather than with a Chingachgook, despite all his "modern" ramifications, is where the twentieth-century vision of noble savagery seems to leave us.

5. The Noble Savage Rides Again

If the relations and attitudes associated with the noble savage are essentially incompatible with the assumptions that have become increasingly characteristic of twentieth-century mainstream literature, there are other aspects of verbal culture in which the conventional primitive might very well find himself more at home. By this I mean those specialized categories that John Cawelti labels "formula stories" but I prefer to call, more neutrally, *genre fiction*: westerns, gothics, science fiction, fantasy, murder-mysteries, and so on.

This type of material has traditionally presented a great deal of difficulty for critics, largely because of its identification with popular culture, a phenomenon which, from the time of its emergence along with the literate bourgeoisie in the eighteenth century, has been discredited by virtue of its genetic association with the processes of urbanization and industrialism, both—in the eyes of the aristocratic and conservative cultural establishment—totally inimical to humanism and, more important, to "art." As C.W.E. Bigsby describes it, "To those convinced of the vital centrality of traditional culture, popular culture...becomes evidence of a collapse of values and, by...extension, the cause of that collapse. Thus, in the nineteenth century, the novel, itself both a symbol of the emergence of a new middle class and a mirror of its activities, was despised as a frivolous and immoral distraction—indeed, in true puritan form, immoral because frivolous." From its inception, therefore, popular culture acquired a political dimension that inevitably colors any discussion of the subject and makes objectivity difficult even without getting down to specific cases. In Bigsby's words:

[T]he debate is concerned with far more than a consideration of aesthetics or descriptive accounts of technological models. It involves a clash of ideologies, philosophies and social and psychological theories. Popular culture is accordingly seen by turns as epiphanic and apocalyptic, as evidence of social cohesion and social dislocation, as proof of subversive energy and evidence of decadence. On the one hand the direct emotional appeal, the heightening of expression, the extremes of experience which we associate with popular culture are seen as serving identifiable psychological and sociological purposes, permitting the cathartic release of destructive passions and subversive feelings in a manner conducive to individual and social stability and hence, by extension, leading to the possibility of personal and public stasis: popular culture as adjustment syndrome. On the other hand, it is regarded as an expression of genuine needs not usually validated by a society which chooses to stress a view of man (rational, puritanical, socially-determined, innately moral) incompatible with an energetic emotionalism and an antinomian stance.

When Leslie Fiedler exalts popular culture as a vitalizing force, consequently, or Marcuse condemns it as "an instrument of repression because it stimulates a shared experience which has the power to de-emphasize real class differences and to assimilate cells of resistance" (Bigsby), these are both political judgments rather than literary ones. Indeed, it becomes almost impossible to talk about popular culture without invoking some such terms.

On top of this, even leaving aside the political considerations, there is an additional problem posed by the question of what, exactly, popular culture should be taken to include; what, in other words, it actually *is*. Again Bigsby indicates the extent of the problem:

> Part of the difficulty over the meaning of the term "popular culture" arises from the differing meanings attributable to the word "popular" itself, for as the OED makes evident it can mean both "intended for and suited to ordinary people," or "prevalent or current among, or accepted by, the people generally." The latter includes everyone; the former excludes all but the "ordinary." Hence popular culture is sometimes presented as that which appeals only to the commonality ("mass culture") or to the average ("middlebrow"), thus confirming the social fragmentation of society, and sometimes as a phenomenon cutting across class lines.

This semantic confusion not only makes it problematic as to whether any particular book, let alone *class* of literature, should be categorized as a product of popular culture, but also clouds the issue of what, in terms of either extrinsic function or intrinsic value, inclusion under the general title should imply.

In practice, of course, the problem is somewhat less acute than it seems in theory—classification by consensus is the rule—but this in itself leads to yet other complications. In general the American academic/literary-critical establishment has so broadly confounded *both* meanings of the word—popular as *widespread* versus popular as *ordinary*; quantitative versus qualitative—that more often than not popularity, or wide acceptance, is simply taken to be synonymous with minimal literary value. This institutionalized snobbishness goes all the way back to Matthew Arnold, whose seminal work, *Culture and Anarchy*, not only first conceptualized culture as a moral force associated with authority, tradition, and order, but also imbued the term with its present elitist implications by claiming that culture "does not try to teach down to the level of inferior classes." Arnold's dictum could simply be taken to mean that the masses just as much as the elite should have access to "the best that has been thought and known in the world"—that the common people, in other words, should be stimulated with the best art and literature available at any given time rather than fobbed off with an inferior product—but subsequent critics, most notably Eliot, Leavis, and the New Critics of the 30s, followed by the New York literary aristocracy of the 50s, have hardened this generalized project into a narrow prescription for canonical inclusion based on what Bigsby calls "a personal view of human values and exquisite form." In particular, as might be predicted from the original British and later European orientation of these influential schools of criticism (an orientation—and an influence—which, as Jeff Riggenbach pointed out a few years ago in a polemical article in *The Libertarian Review*, seem to reveal that the self-deprecating colonial mentality Emerson decried a century and a half ago in "The American Scholar" is still a dominant element in American culture), the type of fiction that has come to be accepted throughout most of the century as establishing the normative standard of literary merit—now that the novel has lived down its early disreputability—is characterized by generally ironic or pessimistic "realism" as opposed to naively optimistic and irresponsible "fantasy." ("[M]imetic literature tends toward the bringing of latent or hidden motives into the light of consciousness while escapist literature tends to construct new disguises or to confirm existing defenses against the confrontation of latent desires" [Cawelti].) As a result of this hardening, moreover—adding yet another ingredient to the confusion surrounding the concept of popular culture—any fiction that does not fall clearly on the approved side of this dichotomy is adjudged as sub-literary and hence, regardless of either its technical quality or its actual readership, as *a priori* "popular." The whole question of influence, quantitatively considered, becomes incredibly complicated. The apparent predominance of the wasteland as a controlling metaphor in contemporary novels does not necessarily, therefore, prove as much about American attitudes as might at first appear. As the "approved" vision it is merely the most visible in any academic study of literature.

This critical bias would seem to be a disadvantage under any circumstance (to rule out whole large categories of writing as not even worthy of consideration is obviously to narrow unduly the range of aesthetic experience available in literature), but it seems particularly inappropriate for a country in which, as has been more and more widely accepted since Richard Chase's influential examination of the subject in *The American Novel and Its Tradition* (1957), the most natural form of expression is apparently not the realistic novel of Leavis's "Great Tradition" (Eliot, James, Conrad) but the asocial and anti-realistic romance. For this, if for no other reason, it would seem to be not merely justifiable but extremely important that any survey of American cultural history should consider as evidence of national orientation both mainstream literature *and*, as the primary repository of the romance conventions largely disdained (although certainly covertly utilized) by the contemporary literary establishment, the body of writing that I have called *genre fiction* as well.

To accomplish the second part of this task, however, implies a number of practical problems even after the philosophical stigma is removed. Genre literature is *not* synonymous with "lowbrow" literature, but there is an almost ineradicable impression abroad that it is. One widespread expression of this prejudice is the popular axiom much bemoaned by science fiction fans that "if it's science fiction it can't be good; if it's good it can't be science fiction." Unfortunately this sort of assumption inevitably turns out to be a self-fulfilling prediction since the books properly belonging to the class which *are* widely accepted as having literary value—Huxley's *Brave new World* and Orwell's

1984 are the classic examples—are rarely labelled as science fiction by either the booksellers or the critics. The same thing applies to other categories. One would never, for instance, expect to find Graham Green's *Brighton Rock* nor Dostoyevsky's *Crime and Punishment* in the "Crime" or "Mystery" section of the public library—they are filed under "Literature"—but whatever else these books may be, they quite definitely belong to the same genre as Dashiell Hammett and Georges Simenon. The fact is—popular prejudice notwithstanding—within each of the genres cited above, as in mainstream literature itself, one can expect to find a fairly normal proportion of bad ("pulp"), mediocre ("bestsellers"), and outstanding ("literary") books. One *should*, therefore, be able to treat genre fiction by means of much the same critical methodology as any other literary group. In practice, unfortunately, this is not possible. Ironically enough, given the "popular" designation, most of these genres are still so poorly understood outside of their rather specialized readership (typically different in each case) that many people will be totally unfamiliar with the kind of conventional assumption that can simply be taken for granted in any discussion of mainstream literature. The lack of any such grounding naturally militates against a proper response to the material under consideration and, indeed, reversing the old adage, often goes to prove that unfamiliarity breeds contempt. Any critic who wants to deal with genre fiction is therefore put in the position of having to establish the broad parameters, the lowest common denominator, of each class before he can meaningfully examine the implications of the more aesthetically valuable *special* case. As a result of this necessity, especially in a limited context such as is offered by the present chapter, one is all too often reduced to talking about the genre as if it were an essentially homogeneous *set* (as Lévi-Strauss would deal with myth) rather than a discontinuous series of individual works which are alike in many of their underlying conventions vis-à-vis settings, plots, character types, specialized vocabulary, and characteristic themes, but not necessarily in the use that they make of these. It is only, therefore, with an acute awareness of the reservations that must inevitably arise that we can embark on this problematic endeavor.

Of all the classes of genre fiction, the one body of writing in which one would expect to find a viable noble savage surviving in the twentieth century is, of course, the western. If the Indian is denied a place in mainstream literature specifically because of his association with the discredited and sentimentalized westering myth, then surely he must play a central role in the fiction which, as heir apparent to Cooper's wilderness novels, seems by convention to be dedicated above all to a continuing celebration of the Adamic vision that myth implies. Despite our nostalgic memories of the "cowboy and Indian" stories of childhood Saturday matinees, however, the Indian appears in most westerns more as a token presence than as an individual. As in earlier stages the reason for this somewhat surprising fact can be traced to historical developments and their covert effects on cultural trends.

"[O]n June 30, 1834," Dee Brown tells us in his history of the American Indian, *Bury My Heart at Wounded Knee*, "Congress passed *An Act to Regulate Trade and Intercourse with the Indian Tribes and to Preserve Peace on the Frontiers.* All that part of the United States west of the Mississippi 'and not within the States of Missouri and Louisiana or the Territory of Arkansas' would be Indian country. No white persons would be permitted to settle in the Indian country. The military force of the United States would be employed in the apprehension of any white person who was found in violation of provisions of the act." Unfortunately, before these laws could be put into effect, "a new wave of white settlers swept westward and formed the territories of Wisconsin and Iowa." Even without the additional stimulus of gold discoveries in the west, white America, however conciliatory the rhetoric of the politicians, was committed to the neutralization of free Indian culture by any means possible from bribery to all-out war. The Indians themselves unknowingly contributed to their own downfall. Curiosity and avarice put them into the clutches of the white traders; once there, rotgut liquor, disease-ridden blankets, and a fast-growing dependency on the products of white technology all contributed to a weakening of their own cultural resources. Even after the threat of white aggression became more generally recognized, their traditions of democratic individualism made it difficult for the different tribes, even different members within the same tribe, to co-operate in combatting the well-organized invader. Desperation seemed to spawn resignation rather than defiance. The Ghost Dance cult, a pseudo-Christian religious movement that swept through the Plains Indians in 1890 under the inspired leadership of Wovaka, the Paiute "Messiah," reinforced this tendency toward passivity with its apocalyptic promise of impending divine intervention:

In the beginning, he said, God made the earth, and then sent the Christ to earth to teach the people, but white men had treated him badly, leaving scars on his body, and so he had gone back to heaven. Now he had returned to earth as an Indian, and he was to renew everything as it used to be and make it better.

In the next springtime, when the grass was knee high, the earth would be covered with new soil which would bury all the white men, and the new land would be covered with sweet grass and running water and trees. Great herds of buffalo and wild horses would come back. The Indians who danced the Ghost Dance would be taken up in the air and suspended there while a wave of new earth was passing, and then they would be set down among the ghosts of their ancestors on the new earth, where only the Indians would live. [Brown]

"Preaching nonviolence and brotherly love," Brown points out, he "called for no action by the Indians except to dance and sing." Ironically enough, it was this mass dancing which, striking the whites as an alien and thus threatening phenomenon, set off the chain of events that led to the disastrous battle of Wounded Knee in the winter of 1890 that marked the end of any real possibility for Indian independence in America.

What effect did this process have on public opinions of the Indian? On the surface the battle for possession of the western territories, a more widespread and concerted conflict than any since colonial days, naturally elicited a token revival of the old image of the satanic savage, and this did, to some extent, find its way into the western fiction of the time. Mark Twain, for instance, as Fiedler (1968) describes him, was "by instinct and conviction, an absolute Indian hater, consumed by the desire to destroy not merely real Indians, but any image of Indian life which stands between White Americans and a total commitment to genocide." Similarly, in the dime novels that proliferated during the period, Indian warfare is a staple of the western landscape in which the action was set. The violence of the reaction, however, was in general more apparent than real. Twain's aversion may have been a genuine one, but in most cases, as Cawelti points out, "the Indian has become an item of furniture rather than an opposing force."

The fact is, the odds were so clearly on the side of the whites in this last phase that the Americans in general were more concerned with rationalizing the morality of their behavior than in excoriating the enemy. As a result, by the mid-century, "the policy makers in Washington invented Manifest Destiny, a term which lifted land hunger to a lofty plane. The Europeans and their descendents were ordained by destiny to rule all of America. They were the dominant race and therefore responsible for the Indians—along with their lands, their forests, and their mineral wealth" (Brown). The effect of this American version of *noblesse oblige*, the white man's burden—an ultimate extension of the useful philosophy of savagism that we examined back in section 3.1.3 above— was to denude the Indian almost entirely of his mythic potency, positive *and* negative, replacing the fear and awe of initial contact with a demeaning paternalism which, whatever ambivalence it may have signalled covertly (to the extent that "Indian removal carried violence against symbolic childhood," says Rogin, the "fantasies of its perpetrators also expressed longings for death [to]...release them from worldly cares"), *ostensively* converted him from a symbol of wildness into a kind of domestic pet. As Donald Kaufmann describes it, "Sympathy for a so-called dying race made Sitting Bull popular enough to parade in Wild West Shows, a cross between a dignified warrior and a beloved freak. A few years later Geronimo, the last great Apache chieftain, surrendered to federal troops for the second time in 1886, and after taking up farming and Christianity, he became a celebrity, a special added attraction at the Omaha and St. Louis Expositions and at Theodore Roosevelt's inaugural parade." Concurrently, the fictional Indian came to be presented more and more often in the colorful but wholly specious terms of a side show exhibit, his conventional nobility or conventional fearsomeness now *entirely* conventional, with neither the profound simplicity of myth nor the subtle complexity of symbolic resonance to intimate that anything at all existed beneath the surface of his stereotyped role. In the popular imagination as in the field of serious literature, the Indian as a locus of real emotion to all intents and purposes finally disappeared.

On one level the development is quite understandable. On another, however, it raises a number of questions about the claims that were made in earlier sections of this book. During the last half of the nineteenth century a number of the conditions we cited as favoring the rise to popularity of the romantic savage actually became more highly visible ingredients in the cultural ambience than they were earlier. Increased familiarity with native customs, confidence in white military capacity, and, especially, removal of the subject from immediate view all combined to neutralize that initial resistance to the Indian inspired by fear. The reading public, largely based in the east, was, moreover, well enough insulated from any real confrontation with the wilderness that it displayed an increasingly voracious appetite for the vicarious excitements of literary adventuring in the west. Above all, even among those pragmatic masses openly disdainful of the "highbrow" maunderings of the Transcendentalists, the emotional, almost mystical authority of nature as a perceived correlative for America's national greatness became, as noted in Chapter 3.3. above, increasingly enhanced as the real frontier passed from promise into memory. Even if the more thoughtful American, deploring the complacent hypocrisy which accompanied the westward push, would have to perceive the "pseudo-tragic posturing" of the romanticized savage as a "hopelessly vulgar and naive" response to the destruction of the wilderness, from the point of view of the average citizen, blandly enthusiastic about the most incompatible elements of the national mission, the situation at the end of the century—if our earlier analysis was correct—would seem to favor an ideal of noble savagery even more than the earlier period.

Ironically, it was the very intensity of the nineteenth-century commitment to the garden myth, which peaked, as Simonson pointed out, with the closing of the frontier, that was itself largely responsible for the virtual disappearance not only from mainstream literature but also from popular culture of the Indian as nature symbol. The more that the irreconcilable conflict between the westward quest for the garden and the denatured landscape which was its inevitable consequence became forced into public recognition, the greater became the desire to rescue the myth by changing its terms of reference. This process of rationalization does not show up to any great extent in mainstream literature, where the emphasis, as we have seen, is on the shattering rather than the refurbishing of the dream. In the development of the western, however, we are given a vivid demonstration of the way that the westering myth was reoriented finally *away* from the values of the garden that had dominated it at least during Cooper's time.

The first step in this process was a de-emphasis of the symbolic setting on an existential border. "Cooper's image of the West as a place of encounter between civilization and nature gave way to the portrayal of the West as an open society where the intricacies of complex social institutions are unknown, where people are surrounded by loyal friends, where hearty individualists can give vent to their spontaneous urges, and where justice is done directly and without ambiguity." The immediate result of this simplification was, as Cawelti points out, a loss of "serious thematic significance." The western thus became "primarily a fictional embodiment of fantasies of transcendent heroism overcoming evil figures of authority." Going even beyond this moral retrenching and the retreat into formula, however, a second phase was entered soon after the turn of the century in which the westering myth actually came to be used, paradoxically enough, as a vehicle to advance the claims and values not of nature but of its traditional opponent, the idealized American city.

How does this work? Owen Wister's novel, *The Virginian*, which was a bestseller in the year of its publication, 1902, and for several years thereafter, offers a prototypical example. This book *seems*, initially, to be in the tradition of Cooper, since a central motif is the conventional opposition between east and west. When we examine Wister's treatment of this familiar material more carefully, however, we realize that this symbolic dichotomy does not, as in the past, represent the mutually exclusive poles of nature and civilization but, rather, *two* versions of civilization, one corrupt and effete, the other, reflecting the increasingly popular theory of frontierism codified by Frederick Jackson Turner, young, fresh, and vital. Nature is still a *factor* in the thematic opposition, but rather than offering any sort of symbolic ideal in its own right it is valued only insofar as it provides the kind of social *tabula rasa* that will favor the development of the ideal democratic community as represented in the person of Wister's hero:

> The Virginian is a new self-made man, but he is also a throwback to heroic types of the past like the medieval knight; he is a nascent entrepreneur and he marries a New England schoolteacher, but he is also a son of the old South and carries in his demeanor the chivalric ideals of the antebellum South; thus he represents a synthesis of the conflicting stereotypes of Cavalier and Yankee; he is a tough fearless killer, skilled in violence, and a gentle lover and friend; and, finally, he is a supreme individualist of unstained honor, and yet a dedicated agent of the community. [Cawelti]

As Cawelti puts it, in other words, "Wister [resolves] the old ambiguity between nature and civilization by presenting the West not as a set of natural values basically antithetical to civilization, but as a social environment in which the American dream could be born again."

In a number of important ways Wister's formula sets the pattern that dominates the western for the next half century. Like Wister, later writers—and filmmakers—tend to "portray the West as a distinctive moral and symbolic landscape with strong implications of regeneration or redemption for those protagonists who can respond to its challenge by recovering basic human and American values"; most of them, too, commonly structure their works around the thematic opposition (often embodied in a romance between an uncouth cowboy hero and a genteel eastern woman) between "the cultivated but enervated East and the vigorous, vital and democratic West" (Cawelti). On the other hand, as the real west becomes increasingly domesticated and the fictional west correspondingly idealized, there is also an apparent resurgence of genuine primitivism focused on nature. In Zane Grey, in particular—a writer who, as

Cawelti notes, was "not only the leading western writer but the single most popular author of the post-World War I era, with at least one book among the top best-sellers for almost ten years straight"—one typically finds an enthusiasm for scenery so intense (and so lushly over-written) that the western landscape inevitably comes once more to seem "symbolic of the transcendent religious and moral forces of the wilderness rather than, as in Wister's case, an environment for a certain kind of human culture." Nor is the imputed value of this landscape purely decorative or formal. In many of these later westerns the qualities that set the hero apart from the common run are qualities specifically imbibed through a quasi-mystical encounter with solitude and wild nature. As Max Westbrook explains:

> Some of the heroes I have in mind are actual mountaineers. Most are not. But all of them have at least a metaphorical home in the mountains, that is, a home elsewhere, removed from society and close to the gods. They have a home there in the sense that something happened which made them different. In the ancient and classical tradition of heroes, they have had a second birth, or an experience which changed them, and they can never be the same again. Basically this hero has seen God, or had a vision, or experienced the original creation. Nature, afterwards, is not a symbol of God. Nature is God's personal and immediate hand alive and at work.

We must be careful not to overestimate the significance of this apparent primitivism, though. What Westbrook's enthusiastic description obscures is the fact that however important the experience of nature may be for the education of the hero, its ultimate function, in transforming him—in Paul Zweig's terms— from an asocial *adventurer* (like Odysseus) into a specifically social *champion* (like Aeneas), is in the service of civilization. As Cawelti points out, "As Grey and Hart developed their conception of the hero...he shed his close ties with society and became the more mysterious and alienated figure of the heroic gunfighter or outlaw" *but*—and it is this *but* which is all important here— at the same time, "the Grey hero has a deep yearning to become part of society." As a result, the *anti*-primitivistic formula whereby the outlaw is socialized— "the domestication of the wild hero," as Cawelti phrases it—becomes a major theme of the western throughout the 20s and, increasingly conventionalized into a stereotyped escapist fantasy, the 30s as well.

This yoking together of logically incompatible elements would probably not be accomplished so easily if it were not that the basic ambiguities of the national experience had already long encouraged the American in the art of wishful reconciliation. Just as the nineteenth-century immigrant had no trouble subsuming both the garden myth and what Fisher calls the "workshop myth," primitivism and progress, under one comprehensive image of soon-to-be-accomplished national and personal prosperity, so the twentieth-century public, in responding to the western, had no trouble at all in overlooking the essential evasiveness of its characteristic vision; indeed probably responded all the more enthusiastically because the western did offer this illogical and oversimplified view of the promise *still* (or so it was suggested) implicit in the American west. The requisite paean to nature is thus able to retain a privileged position throughout the period as a trademark of the genre without for a moment obscuring the fact that the real focus of the story, just as in Wister's somewhat more straightforward presentation, is not the experience of the isolated desert or mountain camp but, quite simply, the realization of the democratic ideal of non-repressive order in the frontier town.

The Indian, inevitably, comes to seem increasingly irrelevant to such an eminently social vision. The token savagery required to stimulate the growth of personal awareness and social solidarity is amply provided by the white villains—the rustlers, the bank robbers, the land-grabbing cattle baron with his army of uncouth mercenaries. Aside from using him to add a bit of local color to the background, or perhaps even, in his standard gothic guise, to provide occasion for a token demonstration of white supremacy, the traditional twentieth-century western thus tends to ignore the Indian altogether.

It is not until the 40s and 50s that we find any significant new development in the western formula. The main ingredient in this change is the delayed realization, largely through a forced confrontation with the less easily romanticized violence associated with pre-War Europe and, of course, the War itself, not only that the "old" west is long past as an historical phenomenon but also that the values embodied in the "mythic" west are no longer appropriate to the modern world. Indeed, as Walter Van Tilburg Clark explains the genesis of his 1940 novel *The Oxbow Incident* (a story about a tragically misguided lynching party which, in its exposure of the dark reality at the heart of the heroic ideal of frontier justice, was not only the first but one of the finest of the new breed of westerns), it is these *same* values, so long enshrined in the American imagination, which themselves may be seen as responsible for that war:

> The book was written in 1937 and '38, when the whole world was getting increasingly worried about Hitler and the Nazis, and emotionally it stemmed from my part of this worrying. A number of the reviewers commented on the parallel when the book came out in 1940, saw it as something approaching an allegory of the unscrupulous and brutal Nazi methods, and as a warning against the dangers of temporizing and of hoping to oppose such a force with reason, argument and the democratic approach. They did not see, however, or at least I don't remember that any of them mentioned it (and that *did* scare me), although it was certainly obvious, the whole substance and surface of the story, that it was a kind of American Naziism that I was talking about. I had the parallel in mind, all right, but what I was most afraid of was not the German Nazis, or even the Bund, but that ever-present element in any society which can always be led to act the same way, to use authoritarian methods to oppose authoritarian methods.
>
> What I wanted to say was, "It can happen here. It has happened here, in minor but sufficiently indicative ways, a great many times." [quoted in Webb]

Viewed in such a light, the Turner thesis which had so long irradiated the American myth of the west acquired distinctly ominous overtones.

One of the most obvious results of this new and more realistic vision was a ritual casting out of the traditional frontier hero. Where before this charismatic figure was seen as being integrated *into*, indeed himself helping to *establish*, "the new pioneer society that [was] gradually evolving out of a more chaotic and lawless earlier era" (his "culminating act of violence is a final purging of the lawless men who prevent the new society from coming into existence"), he is now typically portrayed "as a somewhat archaic survival, driven by motives and values that are never quite in harmony with the new social order." Thus, as Cawelti sums it up, "the relation of the hero to the community tends to move in a reverse direction from that of the pre-1940s western. There the hero typically made the transition from outlawry to domestication. In the classic western, the hero increasingly moves toward isolation, separation and alienation."

An outstanding illustration of this movement described by Cawelti is provided by the 1953 film *Warlock* where we have *two* western heroes, one of the old variety, a gunslinger who is hired to protect the town from a lawless local gang, plus a new, more civilized version: the subsequently established sheriff whose primary task, as *legal* peacemaker, is to rid the community of its dangerously unpredictable and individualistic erstwhile champion. This process, as Frank McConnell points out, actually reflects a necessary stage in the establishment of the "city in the wilderness," signalling as it does the transition from the primitive shamanic to the socialized priestly authority:

> Scenario: if we wish to imagine the primal horde gathered at the verge of their assembly into a structured unit, a civilization, then the first person to organize them into a religious and law-abiding group will have been the mysterious figure of the shaman. The shaman (witch doctor, medicine man, crazed prophet or old man of the mountain) is the mediator, the voice of the divine, for the seminomadic society of man as hunter. Radically individualistic, erratic, even...schizophrenic, he represents the religious impulse, the impulse to law and social morality, in its most problematic state...
>
> With the organization of hunter groups into stable agrarian societies, however, and with the consequent formation of settled towns rather than portable, nonce villages, the shaman is displaced by his less dramatic, less energetic, but more predictable cousin, the priest. The priest—true pontifex, builder but not crosser of bridges to the Moral Imperative—is no longer the erratic voice of a divine order assumed to lie beyond human attempts at understanding or codification. Rather, he is the representative of an established, divinely revealed form of worship and uprightness—the Law.

The gunslinger and the lawman, McConnell continues, are figurative equivalents to these contrasting types of charismatic leaders. And like the shaman, once the civilizing process progresses beyond its most primitive stage, the anarchistic hero of the pre-40s western—while effective and even necessary in his time—becomes an anachronism which must be purged for the good of the social whole.

The ultimate result of this development was to split apart the precariously balanced elements of progressivism and primitivism in the western in a particularly interesting way. During the 50s, as might be expected, western films (the western novel having by now degenerated for the most part into subliterary pulp) were dominated by what McConnell calls "the priestly, town-centered film"—*My Darling Clementine, Gunfight at O.K. Corral,* and *High Noon*—starring such staunchly normative figures as Gary Cooper and Jimmy Stewart. Gone is even the limited primitivism of Zane Grey. Ironically, though, this socially affirmative vision was to break down after little more than a decade of ascendency—and for much the same reason that ushered it in. If social disenchantment during the 30s worked eventually to discredit the retrospective myth of the honorable individualist and the wholesome, self-regulating community of the west, the even greater social disenchantment and political polarization of the 60s undermined the 50s faith in the disinterested power of the law as well. In the new version of the western, as a result, "society is usually represented as weak and corrupt; its agencies—such as posses and armed forces—are given to impulsive and inefficient violence that is more likely to bring on further innocent suffering than to establish true justice" (Cawelti). More important, the gunslinger-outlaw suddenly becomes popular again *for the very same reason that he was rejected in the 40s*: his antisocial stance and confirmed opposition to civilized (that is, "eastern") values. From this development emerges two related but ultimately distinct western heroes. One—more of a revival than a new departure—is the inherently "good" individual (like John Wayne's *Chisum*) "who is able to overcome the outlaw's evil aggression and society's own endemic violence and corruption by superior ruthlessness and power of his own" (Cawelti). The other, coalescing in some quite important ways with the protagonist of contemporary mainstream literature, is the outlaw himself (*Butch Cassidy and the Sundance Kid*) who, despite his admitted criminality according to *law*, is more of a victim than a villain, a good-hearted picaro defeated in the end by the oppressive forces of society.

What has happened to the Indian in all this time? Interestingly enough, where the ostensibly primitive fantasies of the early western had no real place for the Indian, this latest development in the genre, while seemingly more "modern," has been generally conducive to a resurgence of interest in noble savagery. Moving from a covert affirmation of the values of the city to an overt condemnation of those same values, yet without being unduly constricted by the "realistic"—that is, anti-heroic—conventions governing the mainstream response, the new western lends itself to a revitalized and more genuine primitivism. The Indian, both as an individualist—like the outlaw—whose personalized and chivalric brand of violence is set in contrast to the more brutal, impersonal, institutionalized violence of modern society (the message, as Cawelti explains it, being that corporate violence "is more dangerous and evil than the acts of individual aggression implicit in the Indian or outlaw's way of life") and as an exemplar of a simpler, more harmonious lifestyle, close to nature, thus becomes a useful vehicle for social criticism.

As a result of this resurgent primitivism, we find a whole spate of individually slight but generically interesting novels appearing during the 60s— John Knowles' *Indian Summer*, Frank Water's *Man Who Killed Deer*, Jan Jordan's *Give Me Wind*, Reuben Bercovitch's *Odette*, and Francis Dave's *Cherokee Woman*, for example—which purportedly elucidate Indian culture. "This new fiction," says John McAleer, "much of it written by non-Indians, is remote from nineteenth-century narratives of noble savage and skulking redskin...the prevailing emphasis is as limpid as Hiawatha's gaze—the lifeways of the Indian offer a sane alternative to the chaos of contemporary modes of living." Unfortunately, despite McAleer's enthusiasm for what he views as a new departure, most of the writing in this mode tends to be both conventional and sentimentalized. In Kaufman's words, "To feed this new white escapism, American writers worked over a backlog of Indian stereotypes—uncanny woodsmanship, super-coolness, stoic mysticism and so on—and turned them sunny-side-up for a readership despairing of city ways."

Even in the more thoughtful products of this neo-primitivistic impulse, moreover, a serious problem is implied by the author's—and by extension the reader's—supposed point of view. "The striking thing about the more recent Indian westerns is that they move beyond sympathy for the plight of individuals toward an attempt at a reconstruction of the Indian experience itself," says Cawelti. "Their central plot device has been the story of the white man who becomes an Indian or who, through his experiences, becomes identified with the Indian perspective in the clash between white and Indian... It is through his involvement with the Indians and their way of life that the hero is regenerated." Without disagreeing that what these books *attempt* to do is essentially what Cawelti has outlined here, however, one must note that the presumptive sense of identification is almost inevitably undermined by the same well-intentioned sympathy which motivated the writer in the first place, inasmuch as it necessarily evokes a superior and subtly patronizing stance that diminishes its object even as it propagandizes on his behalf. The prototypical example of this formula is found in Thomas Berger's *Little Big Man*; here the problem of viewpoint actually becomes a major motif. Throughout the book the protagonist harps on the paradox that when he is with the whites he inevitably ends up identifying emotionally with the Indians but when he is with the Indians he always seems to feel perversely white. The fact is, though, that Jack Crabbe's touted biculturalism is patently specious. His experience and response certainly serve to indict the white man's historical dishonesty and viciousness, both directly and indirectly (and our institutionalized guilt feelings help to reinforce this level of the book), but in the long run none of the moral outrage evoked on the Indian's behalf is anywhere near as damning as the narrator's casually superior jokes at the expense of the Indian's childish vanity, illogic, and—especially—dirt. Ultimately we have to agree with Fiedler (1968), who concludes—in response to a reviewer's claim that the book ranks with *The Big Sky* and *The Oxbow Incident*—that "it has neither the moral earnestness of the latter nor the easy realism of the former, only a desire to demonstrate how, for all its pathos and danger, the West was and remains essentially *funny.*" Villainy being more likely to command respect than victimization, the Indian, in these kinds of situational comparisons, inevitably seems to come off second-best.

This last statement points up the real ambiguity of this most recent version of the noble savage. The question to be considered is not simply whether the revitalized literary Indian is a positive symbol or not, but what, specifically, he is symbolic *of.* Fiedler (1968), as we noted in the Introduction, claims that the sense of identification that emerged in the 60s was an all-encompassing one: in adopting native dress and customs the hippy signals his fall "not merely out of Europe, but out of the Europeanized West, into an aboriginal and archaic America." Kaufmann, however, offers a radically different interpretation of the same phenomenon:

> Blacks, with a media boost, had also eclipsed Indians as to the racial lifestyle to be emulated by white youth. Woodstock Nation was strictly a black and white show, despite Abbie Hoffman's philosophical aside: "It's a nation of alienated young people which we carry around in our minds just as the Sioux Indians carried around the Sioux nation in their minds." Asserting group sovereignty by alluding to Indian tribalism might have seemed appropriate then, when the Woodstock Nation, during its high moment, seemed to have universal overtones. No doubt there was scattered evidence of Indian presence—an overlap in hippie clothing that included moccasins, beads, leather accessories, and headbands. But the overall record that led to Woodstock showed little direct Indian influence. When "alienated young people" yearned for transcendence from Western abstractness, they went directly to the third World for their mystical messages, not to the American Indian who, at best, remained a Third World refugee stuck on the wrong continent. Some at Woodstock knew their Zen, but few, the religion of the Sioux.

If Kaufmann is right, and a retrospective consideration of the period suggests that he is, then it is quite possible that the apparent resurgence of primitivism— seemingly as easily satisfied by the emulation of urban black culture or the ancient civilizations of the Orient as concerned to recover the authentically "savage" lifestyle of the American native—was perhaps not such a straightforward phenomenon as it initially seemed. Certainly there *was* an increase of interest in native culture and history during the 60s. A closer examination of the products of this interest, however, reveals that such visions of noble savagery as were associated with the hippie movement, as Kaufmann implies, typically floated quite free of actual Indians, while serious attempts to deal with the Indian *qua* Indian generally placed him in quite a different, less "romantic" role.

We find a striking example of this development in Thomas Sanchez's *Rabbit Boss* (1972), one of the more successful Indian novels to come out of the period. This book, serially juxtaposing the experiences of four generations of Washo Indians, can be seen from one point of view as presenting a more compact version of Cooper's cumulative savage. Where it differs from Cooper quite radically, however, is in its truncation of the full experiential spectrum that endows Chingachgook with his significance. Where the earlier Indian, as we have said, is seen as poised on the brink between a hopeful past and a hopeless future, this later one, like Kesey's untransformed Chief Bromden, is presented *only* in terms of his long downhill slide. The moment at which the book opens, significantly enough, is the moment when the white man appears on the scene. Setting the tone for the entire story, moreover, is the specific form in which Sanchez images forth this initial encounter. Gayabuc, a Washo brave hunting in the Donner Pass for meat to celebrate the birth of his son, is a witness to a horrifying act of cannibalism by a party of snow-bound whites which so shocks and fascinates him that he is thrown violently and irreversibly out of harmony with his past. So powerful is the white man's influence, it seems, that the vulnerable Indian culture can be infected by his madness even before direct contact is made. Aside from its symbolic condemnation of white morality, the major effect of this scene is to underline the Indian's impotence in the face of history. Having *already* fallen out of his timeless Eden at the opening of the story, his potential for ideality is by definition gone.

To point out that Sanchez's Indian lacks at least part of the generic attributes of Cooper's prototypical noble savage is not, however, to suggest that he does not have a significant connection with primitivism. Indeed the white/red dichotomy in the book is translated quite specifically into the traditional terms of the opposition between civilization and nature. Since the Indian has already begun to degenerate at the beginning of the book (the Washo brave not only fails to complete the post-birth ritual for his son, but as a result of his obsession with the terrible "medicine" of the white man, is "as dead" to his wife, an alien in his own community, from that moment hence), we are never given the chance to see the pattern of native life in its original purity, but it is made obvious throughout the book by means of memories, myths, and surviving rituals (like the male and female puberty rites) that the heart and basis of this life was a conservative's reverent responsiveness to the natural cycle. The white man, on the other hand, is repeatedly characterized, in terms consistent with our first brutal view of him, as a killer and a waster. Sanchez's vision of a California sportsmen's annual "charity" deer hunt, for instance, is fully as shocking as Cooper's famous descriptions of similar phenomena in *The Pioneers*, especially in its use of the archery motif to underline its discontinuity with the tacitly juxtaposed Indian model.

"DEER!" They were running everywhere, the arrows catching their bodies and tossing them to the ground. The fawns moving their young legs with the incomplete muscle of their short days, trying to match the stride of the does in front, stumbling on the loose rock, sliding down into manzanita and climbing up again on the shaking of their young legs to catch an arrow in the thigh or breaking free and running in the path of their mother, until they sprawled over her dead body as she dropped before them with the feather lanced sticks sunk in her hide.

[Then]...coming out into [the ridge] from all sides was the blaze of red caps, running across the open space were the bucks, herded together, charging the length of the meadow, trying to break the advancing lines, the brown bulk of their bodies moving swiftly as the arrows thudded into their flesh, dropping them quivering to the grass.

As the dispossessed and fugitive Joe Birdsong, last of the Washos, perceives in the moment of his death, in fact, paralleling his grandfather's vision at that equally deadly moment of first contact, the white man is, above all, an agent of destruction. "He killed all the birds out of the Sky and fished up all the Fish out of the waters. He tore the hide from the mountains and stole the power from the rivers. The White beast was a flesheater... The flesheater always devours his own children. The flesheater eats himself."

Despite the author's emphasis on this racial disparity, however, the image of the "good" Indian does not appear to be intended as exemplary in any normal sense of the word. As presented here, the message seems to be that there never was—and could never be—any real alternative to those results which did in fact obtain. The white man's power is so strong, so irresistible (this is a fact that weighs equally on every member of the subject family), it seems inevitable, and even right, that the Indian should give way in the face of his advance. Such circumstances do not invite imitation. Sanchez underlines the deterministic implications of this historical perspective, moreover, by his choice of the Washo as vehicle for his theme. Unlike the Sioux or Commanche who, having put up a good fight against white domination, can be admired for their courage and ferocity—mythicized in terms of what-might-have-been—even as one recognizes the finality of their defeat, the Washo, an exceptionally meek group of Indians—peace-loving, primitive, lacking any sort of political structure whatsoever—seem to have put up no resistance to the invaders at all, taking the first opportunity possible to become beggars and scavengers living on the fringes of the white community. Nor do the particular members of the clan singled out for our attention mitigate this impression of *fatality*. The second generation representative chosen by Sanchez, for instance, is not, as might be expected, Gayabuc's first-born, an angry young cynic whose loss of his arm and his innocence in the white man's war has turned him into a bitter opponent of Indian dependency, but Captain Rex, a drunken opportunist who exploits his people in return for the white man's token "badge" and meager favor. The third, perhaps even more damaging to our expectations of nobility, is Hallelujah Bob, a half-crazed Indian evangelist whose final vision of desolation closes off the future for the Washos just as surely as it closes the book. "The dreams have deserted us," he says:

We are as empty as the day Coyote molded the Earth. There is no power for tomorrow. Tomorrow will kill us because we cannot go out to meet it. We walk along roads humped with cold clots of Frogs run over by the cars passing us. The forests are smoking with fire. All along the road leading down from the Mountain House the flames of trees join the Sky. The forests are burning. There is no way to save the tres. We turn around and look back. America is a burning house. The dreams are dead. We do not have the power to dream another day.

These are not noble savages. They do not have the vitality to teach us how to live. What they are is victims. What they teach us is simply how to die.

If, in the light of this generalized pessimism, we have any further doubts about the relation of these Indians to our conventional expectations, the author also emphasizes his point quite overtly by making his last Washo somewhat more self-aware. Joe Birdsong explicitly disclaims the noble savage role in *all* its variations, evidently viewing this patronizing projection of white wishful thinking as yet another injustice perpetrated on his people, yet another way that the Indian's individuality and true nature are stolen from him, transforming him into a comfortable caricature more socially acceptable, more easily domesticated by his generally (when convenient) well-intentioned but fastidious white neighbor. Joe recognizes all the stereotypes but simply refuses to react, in either confirmation or denial, to something so alien to his sense of self. " 'I bet you could educate hell out of us along those lines, hey Joe,' " hoots a jovial hunter, enraptured by his own lascivious vision of the mythic potency of the Indian. " 'I guess so,' " Joe replies expressionlessly, his flat tone deflating the proffered cameraderie as effectively as a slap in the face. Nor is it only the insulting stereotypes that he rejects. He is equally uncooperative in response to the ranger's impassioned ecology speech, with its smug self-congratulatory undertones. Stung by Joe's lack of appreciation, the man is finally reduced to uncomprehending anger. " 'You're not listening to a word I'm saying, are you?' " he says accusingly. " 'No.' " " 'You could care less whether you live or die, whether nature lives or dies.' " " 'Right.' " " 'You know Birdsong, I don't see one damn thing noble in your situation.' " " 'Neither do I.' " Joe, as he wearily tells his hopefully Indian-militant brother-in-law, knows better than to believe the false promise—false for everyone concerned—implicit in the noble savage role.

"Felix," Birdsong interrupted. "Why is it every Sunday you go on about how Indians are the last hope. You tell me the same thing week after week, year after year, you never even bother to change the words around a little, and you go over to Truckee and tell it to those people at the meetin's and they tell it back to you again and back and forth it goes, you all tellin each other how if *they* don't recognize you as an organization *they* will come to ruin just like that place in history called Rome, because you're the last hope. You keep pumping yourselves up about being the last hope and all the while *they* keep goin on like they always been, without you, and all the time no closer to that Rome place than when *they* was tearin the mountains down for gold and silver or rippin the trees from everywhere to put up houses. *They* didn't need you then and *they* don't need you now, and if *they* do reach that place like Rome there won't be no redman alive to see it."

Far from reincarnating the noble savage, Sanchez's novel thus seems specifically intended to discredit the ideas that he represents—as, indeed, must any serious treatment of the Indians these days. One problem is that the noble savage, as we said before, is by definition an external referent, a *foil* for the center of consciousness or symbolic ego in a book. Once we focus directly on a character, our attention—*his* perceived complexity—is inevitably inconsistent with, and destructive of, the narrow abstraction of the simplistic conventional conception. Even beyond this formal problem, moreover, the Indian is by now too deeply involved in the American's complex sense of his national history to be easily amenable to literary stereotyping such as the conventional response implies. As long as he was a cypher, compartmentalized well away from the public perception of relevant social reality, he could still serve a minimal conventional function in the western, positive or negative, but as soon as there is a revived emotional commitment to real primitivism—a condition which one might expect to *favor* the re-emergence of a literary type that generated so much numen in its prime—the consequent recognition of the Indian as both a real individual *and* a member of an alien culture ironically enough makes it impossible for the serious writer to exploit his purely literary function, to use him as a means to an end. If such a thing as an authentic modern noble savage does exit in the American imagination, then, we must expect to find him not in either a survival or a revival of old discredited modes like the western, but in a new context where his conventional function—which is already problematic enough by virtue of its associations with an ambivalent nature—will not be encumbered by too many extrinsic preconceptions and inconsistencies. It is for this reason that we now turn to the most "modern" of popular genres, science fiction.

5.1 From the City to the Stars

"[S]cience fiction writers and critics have been trying without success for forty years to define science fiction, because each of them has been talking about his own idea of what the field ought to be, never about what it is," says Damon Knight, citing half a dozen conflicting opinions by some of the field's more eminent practitioners to prove his point. This lack of an adequate, consensual, exclusive definition does not really pose a problem, however, as long as we are more concerned to achieve a descriptive overview of a literary phenomenon in its most general sense than to evaluate individual works in relation to some theoretical norm. With such an end in view, in fact, there would seem to be more of a danger of limiting our perspective unduly than the reverse. The *popular* definition of science fiction, if one can judge by the diverse material sold under that category in bookstores, has come to subsume a considerable body of writing which would not be acceptable in terms of almost *any* of the classic prescriptions. There has been some attempt to accommodate this development—proposing a change of name, for instance, to science fantasy (in recognition of the substantial adventure/romance/"inner space" component) or speculative fiction (to allow for a more significant "literary" dimension)—but in general both the purist (out of snobbishness) and the omnivorous (due to inertia) among its readership have resisted this sort of ploy. In the present study we will sidestep as far as possible this controversy, including in our examination as many as possible of the major literary types popularly associated with the genre whether strictly canonical or not, and labelling the entire phenomenon—for convenience—simply SF.

It is possible to trace the roots of different aspects of SF back to a whole variety of early satirists and fantasists—Sir Thomas More, Voltaire, Cyrano de Bergerac, Swift, Poe, Lewis Carroll: the list is both long and diverse. In its true modern sense, however, SF developed out of the late Victorian period in Britain, and pre-eminently from the work of H.G. Wells. In particular, American SF—at least through its classic period, up to the mid-40s—was dominated by that aspect of Wells's vision we might call "technological optimism." Essentially this is an affirmation of the values of the city in their purest and most extreme form. Even more fundamentally, however, technological optimism—showing the influence of Darwin and T.H. Huxley— is based on a *negative* view of the garden. It thus implies a violent distrust of nature, "the belief that the cosmic process is an amoral force which man must check if there is to be any human progress" (Hillegas). Indeed, as Wells himself describes it through Urthred, the spokesman of his utopian novel, *Men Like Gods*, nature is above all else an enemy to man:

> "These Earthlings do not yet dare to see what our Mother Nature is. At the back of their minds is still the desire to abandon themselves to her. They do not see that except for our eyes and wills, she is purposeless and blind. She is not awful, she is horrible. She takes no heed to our standards, nor to any standards of excellence. She made us by accident; all her children are bastards—undesired; she will cherish or expose them, pet or starve or torment without rhyme or reason. She does not heed, she does not care. She will lift us up to power and intelligence, or debase us to the mean feebleness of the rabbit or the slimy white filthiness of a thousand of her parasitic inventions. There must be good in her because she made all that is good in us—but also there is endless evil. Do not your Earthlings see the dirt of her, the cruelty, the insane indignity?"

In American SF, as might be expected, the antiprimitivist strain so evident in Wells is rarely this overt, but it is the natural corollary to this negative perception of nature—the belief that it is, specifically, the products of civilization which alone stand between man and total ruin—that becomes, more than anything else, the primary characteristic of the field.

What is involved here is more than a minor environmental bias. Technological optimism implies a distinct, total world view. If idealization of the garden enhances the importance of emotional and, to some extent, aesthetic capacities, once the continuing progress of civilization comes to be perceived as all-important, in Wymer's words, the "major function of man...the operation for which he is most prized is his capacity to know and engage constantly in the quest for knowledge." By extension, and more important, however, such a project also encourages "the belief that the universe is essentially knowable and that progress, the growth of knowledge, is its fundamental law." "This," Wymer continues, "is essentially an Enlightenment world view, modified somewhat by the nineteenth-century discoverers of geologic time, evolutionary theory, and astronomical distance so that the idea of progress is expanded to a grander scale, while satisfaction, almost religious awe, is achieved through the consciousness of partaking in the universal process." It's easy to see how such a view would fit in with the American sense of national mission. Bolstered by the lingering authority of Enlightenment ideas in American culture, an exaggerated respect for the power of rationality has always been a major ingredient in the national ideal.

In terms of its integration into literature, on the other hand, the philosophical ramifications of technological optimism were largely abandoned (at least for a time) in favor of its more tangible consequences. As Thomas Clareson puts it, "If SF elevates reason, then it celebrates science and the scientific method with an almost mystic fervor." A substantial part of the impulse behind SF, therefore, was simply the desire to demonstrate, following in Wells's footsteps, that technology offered a universal panacea for the world's ills:

> The plain message physical science has for the world at large is this, that were our political and social and moral devices only as well contrived to their ends as a linotype machine, an antiseptic operating plant, or an electric tram-car, there need now at the present moment be no appreciable toil in the world, and only the smallest fraction of the pain, the fear, and the anxiety that now makes human life so doubtful in its value. There is more than enough for everyone alive. Science stands, a too competent servant, behind her wrangling underbred masters, holding out resources, devices, and remedies they are too stupid to use. And on its material side a modern Utopia must needs present these gifts as taken, and show a world that is really abolishing the need of labour, abolishing the last base reason for anyone's servitude or inferiority. [from *A Modern Utopia*]

SF's major subject thus came to be a depiction of a futuristic world in which science's purportedly enormous potential had been realized, and the technological utopia was widely assumed, even when not treated explicitly, as a standard setting, regardless of the individual plot.

In the beginning this project was typically approached in rather simplistic terms. This was partly because Hugo Gernsback, the man who in 1926 established *Amazing Stories*, the first publication devoted exclusively to science fiction, was less concerned than Wells with either the social implications or even the strict scientific versimilitude of his material. "As a popular entertainer," says Samuel Delaney, "he was just as interested in the possible as he was in the probable."

> In his own novel, *Ralph 124C41*, there is the chaste ghost of a love interest, but it vanishes amidst a host of marvelous gadgets. His use of behavior went only so far as it showed what things could do. Most of the objects were socially beneficial. When they were not, they were in the hands of the criminals that Ralph triumphed over. But there was none of the socially functional logic in which Wells indulged. *Since this is scientifically infeasible, it would not be socially beneficial to discuss what might come out of it.* The logic behind Gernsback's view of SF, which persists today, is rather: *Even though current technology claims this is impossible, if we were to achieve it, look at what marvels might result.*

In consequence of this orientation in one of the prime movers of the genre, early SF tended to be heavily weighted toward what Isaac Asimov calls "gadget science fiction": "story after story came out in which that stock character, the irascible, eccentric (or even mad) scientist explained his inventions and discoveries in interminable double-talk."

Another, and perhaps ultimately more important determinant in shaping early SF, however, was the nature of the audience. "Most of the readers and many of the writers were in their teens," Asimov points out, and while their enthusiasm for technological marvels had no bounds, their taste in literary vehicles was somewhat less than sophisticated. Under such circumstances, "it was not reasonable to expect many stories containing social and economic complexities to be written, and even less reasonable to expect the few that were to be appreciated." More typical of the period, in fact, were stories revolving around the "epic individual who is the hallmark of primitive literature; the hero of infinite resource and infinite daring." The only significant thing that distinguished this corpus from more conventional brands of adolescent fantasy was that the "d'Artagnan sword and the Hickok six-shooter...[had been replaced with] raygun and spaceship." Along with gadgetry, then, from 1926 to 1938, the period that Asimov calls the "Gernsback Era," SF was dominated by "adventure science fiction."

Fortunately this adolescent orientation did not last. In 1938 the period often referred to as the "Golden Age" of science fiction was ushered in almost single-handedly by John W. Campbell who, in that year, became editor of the influential *Astounding Stories* magazine. In contrast to Gernsback, Campbell's preference was for what Asimov calls "social science fiction": *"that branch of literature which is concerned with the impact of scientific advance upon human beings."* As a result, SF quickly began to mature in two important ways. First, it became more realistic in terms of story and characterization. Campbell, in Asimov's words, "de-emphasized the nonhuman and nonsocial... Science fiction became more than a personal battle between an all-good hero and an all-bad villain. The mad scientist, the irascible old scientist, the beautiful daughter of a scientist, the cardboard menace from alien worlds, the robot who is a Frankenstein monster—all were discarded. In their place [he] wanted businessmen, spaceship crewmen, young engineers, robots that were logical machines." Secondly, it became more realistic in terms of its intellectual content. "Campbell also brought to the field an increasing rigor as far as scientific background was concerned"; he demanded that a story "must be coherent with the life we know in the sense that it does not contradict that which we know to be uncontradictable." These two factors together transformed the genre from primarily juvenile pulp into a more serious literature of ideas, directed toward adults, and gave it the characteristics most generally associated with it today. Classic SF in this sense may thus be summed up reasonably accurately in terms of Theodore Sturgeon's 1952 definition to the effect that a "good science-fiction story is a story about human beings, with a human problem, and a human solution, which would not have happened at all without its science content."

So far the genre, by definition progressive if not overtly anti-primitivistic, does not seem to present a particularly fertile field for the development of a noble savage. However, after the mid-40s (1945, with the bombing of Hiroshima, was the key date, Asimov claims), a growing disenchantment with scientific advancement came increasingly to diminish the glitter of Wells's technological paradise. More and more frequently thenceforth the futuristic setting one encountered in an American SF story was not a utopia but what has come to be called a *dystopia* instead. This development breaks down into three different aspects. In literary terms the prototypes for these aspects may again be found in early work by British writers: Forster, Huxley, and Orwell.

The first stage in the development of the dystopic vision was characterized simply by an unfocused ambivalence toward the products of science cumulatively considered. The single most important factor catalyzing this backlash, ironically, was probably the one that *should* have made technological optimism more respectable. As the *power* that Wells claimed for science came to be accepted more and more widely not as a fantasy but as fully feasible, in other words, it also came to seem increasingly threatening to the public in general. This response obviously triggers some kind of vicious circle. Science is viewed as fearsome because it is incomprehensible and incomprehensible because it is fearsome. Modern man, as Patricia Warrick points out, thus "tends to reject...technology at the same time as he increasingly comes to rely on it. A split personality results—a condition described in Robert M. Pirsig's *Zen and the Art of Motorcycle Maintenance* (1974). Even as man uses technology, he refuses to give it his care, attention and concern." And in the long run this willful ignorance naturally exacerbates the sense of threat—especially in America, where technologization has been maximal—by making the public feel that it lacks any significant control over a major component of its environment.

One of the most highly visible symptoms of this feeling of vulnerability was the proliferation of SF and even mainstream stories and novels focusing on some aspect of atomic war in the late 40s and 50s. The Bomb seemed to objectify the more generalized threat of science in a particularly potent fashion. More often than not, moreover, this fiction seems less cautionary than prophetic in tone. Walter Miller's *A Canticle for Leibowitz* (1959), though by literary standards clearly superior to most of its ilk, is quite characteristic in its implication that given man's greed and foolishness on the one hand and science's dangerous potential on the other, destruction is *always* going to be the end product of the civilizing process. Showing a full cycle, beginning in the immediate aftermath of one atomic war and ending, after man has painfully raised himself out of a state of primitivism once more, on the brink of another, Miller asserts that it is only by keeping a firm hold on spiritual values—in this case, as represented by the Church—that humanity has any chance at all, and even here the promise is only the negative one implied by the act of running away. In this particular subgenre, ambivalence toward science seems to become an all-out phobia.

Of somewhat greater interest than the multitudinous post-atomsmash stories, on the other hand, are those works which elucidate the loss-of-control theme in a more subtle but more profoundly disturbing way. "[F]ear of not being in full control...is experienced as acute anxiety, as a threat to one's very self, as a sense of helplessness and loss of identity...where there is a dread that the basic underlying character of reality is negative, frightful, or meaningless," says J. Norman King. "The 'man-eating' or man-destroying machine is the symbolic representation of such anxiety." Early versions of this motif show up in mad-robot or gadget-gone-wrong stories. The ultimate expression of anti-technological feelings, however, is the story where human existence is endangered not by machines but by Machine.

The prototype for this mode is E.M. Forster's "The Machine Stops" (1909), a story set in a world where the entire human population lives in a gigantic human hive in which the individual's every need—from physical comfort to mental stimulation—is provided for by an elaborate system of automatic servo-mechanisms. Man has actually integrated himself *into* the machine, created a mechanical womb upon which he is totally dependent for survival. Needless to say, the outcome—as implied in the title—is catastrophe.

This particular conception—Wells's technological utopia taken to its ultimate and most dangerous extreme—was not a popular one in early or even classic American SF, but in the less optimistic atmosphere of the 50s and 60s, stimulated and refined by developments in computer technology, the world-machine becomes a staple of the field. This later version, however, typically emphasizes a slightly different aspect of the dangers associated with universal mechanization than Forster did. In Forster's story it is *overdependence* that is the primary villain. Because man allows himself to rely utterly on artificial life support systems, he becomes both physically and mentally enfeebled, unable to get along on his own if ever this support is removed—which, because (as Forster viewed it) technology is ultimately untrustworthy, will inevitably happen in the end. In the typical American machine story, in contrast, it is not generally a systematic breakdown that provides a focus for anti-technological fears (the machine by now is omnipotent, invulnerable), but, rather, the loss of individual freedom which total automation—even total automation designed to maximize human comfort and happiness in every possible way—necessarily implies. Indeed, in Ira Levin's novel *The Perfect Day* (1970), a classic example of the type, Forster's formula is in a sense inverted—his *cause* of catastrophe becomes a *cure*—since the protagonist himself instigates a breakdown of the world-machine ("Unicomp") as the only way to give back to the coddled and drugged population the freedom to be *unhappy* without which one cannot, it is implied, be fully human.

This brings us to a second aspect of the SF dystopia. Particularly in America, postwar fear of technology itself quickly becomes subsumed and even superceded by the fear of a technologically-supported authoritarianism which, no matter how benevolent, inevitably destroys the quality of human life. What makes this shift an especially distressing one is that the broader focus makes the source of danger seem more diffuse and inescapable. When a real machine is invoked in a story the mechanization of man seems a relative (and thus correctable) condition directly linked to specific environmental factors, rather than an absolute one. As Mark Hillegas points out with respect to Vonnegut's *Player Piano* (1952), a novel that features yet another version of the staple world-machine (an electronic brain called *Epicac XIV*), "since the machine is never bothered by reason-clouding emotion, it is not surprising that its decisions often result in the non-human use of human beings, in the quantification of human problems." Stories where there is *no* actual machine to blame, however, imply that science is not a cause but merely a symptom of the social distemper; the problem lies in the fundamental nature of the modern world view. Since the War a delayed assertion of Romantic against Enlightenment values in America has shifted emphasis somewhat away from the mechanical model of the world (with its disastrous dissociation of spirit and matter, meaning and event) to a more organic one. As long as the progressive and empirical stance continues to dominate our thinking, however, this shift is only a relative one. As Wymer points out, "whether one's metaphor for man and the universe is based on Newtonian physics or quantum mechanics, the metaphor is still mechanical. Whether man is a cog in a clock or a subatomic particle, he is still an object, not a human being." The dystopic vision thus embraces not merely the technological aspects of modern society, but also—and to an even greater extent—the social processes of bureaucratization and standardization that seem an inevitable consequence of large-scale technology.

Once more the prototypical literary treatment of this theme is found in a British work, Aldous Huxley's *Brave New World* (1932). Like Wells's utopic vision earlier, the social conditions depicted in this novel become very much a standard *donnée* of the post-war SF setting. In particular, American dystopic fiction has been fixated on that one aspect of Huxley's world which seems most horrible to a nation of would-be individualists: the concept of total social control. Huxley sums up the main features of what has since become such a familiar nightmare in his Introduction to the 1946 edition of the book:

> A really efficient totalitarian state would be one in which the all-powerful executive of political bosses and their army of managers control a population of slaves who do not have to be coerced, because they love their servitude. To make them love it is the task assigned, in present-day totalitarian states, to ministries of propaganda, newspaper editors, and schoolteachers. But their methods are still crude and unscientific...
>
> The love of servitude cannot be established except as the result of a deep, personal revolution. We require, among others, the following discoveries and inventions. First, a greatly improved technique of suggestion... Second, a fully developed science of human differences, enabling government managers to assign any given individual to his or her proper place in the social and economic hierarchy... Third...a substitute for alcohol and the other narcotics, something at once less harmful but more pleasure-giving than gin or heroin. And fourth...a foolproof system of eugenics, designed to standardize the human product.

Again, predictably, subsequent American versions improve on the British model, finding negative implications in the projection far beyond those that Huxley fixes upon. Different authors emphasize different aspects of this consensual near-futuristic community. Robert Sheckley's *The Status Civilization* (1960) "describes a world which, frightened by the powers of destruction science has given it, becomes static and conformist" (Hillegas). In Ray Bradbury's *Fahrenheit 451* (1953), it is anti-intellectualism, as exemplified in state-sponsored book-burning, which is central. Clifford Simak's "How-2" (1954) emphasizes the desperate boredom of a world where technology robs the individual of any significant function. In Robert Taylor's "A Sense of Beauty" (1968), progressively advancing civilization and the subsequent sophistication deprives man first of his capacity for emotion and finally of his aesthetic sense as well. Kate Wilhelm's award-winning novel *Where Late the Sweet Birds Sang* (1977) demonstrates the distortion and eventual breakdown of personality that occur as a result of large-scale cloning. Above all, there are numerous books and stories—going all the way back to Wells's *The Time Machine* (1895), with its vision of a degenerate posterity—based on the idea, simply, that the lack of challenge offered by the highly artificial environment will eventually diminish *all* man's innate capacities:

> [A] man's spirit stagnates and he loses personal identity when all challenge is removed, when hedonism prevails, when all disturbing thoughts are carefully shielded, and when anonymous conformity reigns. Pleasure, comfort, security, ease, all destroy—or at least put to sleep—the most deeply creative forces in man, who must either grow in the face of these challenges or wither. Such works give flesh to two very deep and polar human drives: toward familiarity, security, and certainty on the one hand; toward exploration, new growth, and risk on the other. The tension between them is set forth with particular clarity in Asimov's *The End of Eternity* (1955). A society, engineered to ensure "safety and security, moderation, nothing in excess, no risks without overwhelming certainty of adequate return," produces as its end result only "a loss of purpose, a sense of futility, a feeling of hopelessness." The reason given is that triumph and disaster are of a pair. "It is in the meeting of great tests that mankind can most successfully rise to great heights. Out of danger and restless insecurity comes the force that pushes mankind to newer and loftier conquest." [King]

In this second phase, then, technology is viewed as dangerous not merely because it is inhuman, *de*-humanizing, but because its coddling of a creature that evolved through adversity must inevitably have debilitating side effects. A plausible enough conclusion given SF's penchant for a nineteenth-century world view. To focus too exclusively on the commonsensical rationalizations for technophobia, whatever their scientific defensibility, is, however, to miss the twist that distinguishes the American response from that of even the most committed British social Darwinist. For all its ritual recitation of the diverse and multifarious ills connected with the Brave New World phenomenon, American dystopic fiction in fact focuses its attention—its anxiety—not on the results but at a much more fundamental level, on the inherently evil (or so it is perceived) *process* of standardization. The American fears the machine-world not for what it does but for what it *is*. Frank Herbert, discussing his 1968 novel *Santaroga Barrier*, ponders the implications of this attitude:

> Why is it...that most people detect something sinister in...a process to produce humans who would behave in a predictable, although "socially beneficial" way? Behavioral control and happiness appear to be inextricably linked in the contemporary social engineering field. Most humans feel, however, that such tampering would not produce happiness, but would force us into new crises.
>
> We have always distrusted Machiavelli.
>
> Is it the coldness? The manipulation of humans by humans? Is it the inevitable separation into the *users* and the *used*, the abject seekers after help and the all-knowing helpers?
>
> The character, Gilbert Dasein, sees the common identity of Santaroga thusly:

"In there behind the facade, Santaroga did something to its people. They lost personal identity and became masks for something that was the same in all of them...a one-pointedness...such that every Santarogan became an extension of every other Santarogan." [1974b]

The fear implicit in the basic American dystopic vision, therefore, would ultimately seem to be the fear of uniformity in and by itself. Herbert cites public reaction to American psychologist B.F. Skinner's purportedly utopian treatise, *Walden Two*, as an example of this. Skinner's book, ironically, was intended as a serious blueprint for social engineering. The conditioned and regulated community it depicts, however, was perceived by many people to be fully as negative, and as threatening, as the intentionally dystopic societies invoked by SF. Why? Remember, says Herbert, "that Thomas More, the author who gave us the *Utopia*...conceived his paradise in the form of the army—as does Skinner." "Ask people who have served in a branch of the military if they judged that a Utopian existence."

With this latest version of dystopia we appear to be moving very close to the wasteland vision that we noted as a predominant feature of contemporary mainstream literature. This convergence no doubt explains at least partially why SF, having for the most part left naive technological optimism behind by the 60s, became not only far more popular, attracting a vastly larger readership than the relatively small and specialized group of fans who supported it during its classic period, but also respectable enough that by the early 70s it was being taught (albeit generally in a token fashion) at an increasing number of universities. SF shares with mainstream literature one further feature, moreover, in its characteristic movement toward the third phase of dystopic vision, a phase in which frustration becomes outright paranoia. In Raymond Olderman's (1972) words, "When a man of the sixties feels he has lost control of his own life, when he thinks no single individual can influence large public events, when he feels he can no longer cope with the irrationality of public and private affairs, when he yearns for some transcendent explanation and meaning, he begins to find patterns in the accidents of fortune—mysteries in the indifference of fact. Or, perhaps, he does discover the devil." It is at this moment the view of the wasteland as Institution gives way to a view of the wasteland as Conspiracy. From imperviousness to hostility, from passive to active negativity—exactly the same thing happens in the SF dystopia. Here, in fact, the process is exacerbated by the natural tendency of the progressive, conquest-oriented world view implied by science to emphasize, as Wymer says, "the stereotypically masculine virtues of mastery, control, power, and a personal superiority which is accompanied by imperialistic kinds of attitudes varying from contempt to paternalism toward the lower orders." A preoccupation with wielding power naturally lends itself with special ease to its opposite, a strong sense of the immanence of victimization.

Again a British novel provides both our fictional prototype and its essential rationale. As the author of that novel, George Orwell, points out in an essay on "Wells, Hitler, and the World State," it is *Nineteen Eighty-Four*, not Wells's

Modern Utopia, which is the logical outcome of the authoritarian technological state. In Hillegas' words:

> Orwell noted that Wells was too sane and rational to understand Hitler, nationalism, and militarism. Similarly, the Wellsian vision of a great World State where men have joined together to apply reason and the scientific method to human problems, where men no longer derive pleasure from violence and power, is unrealistic. Given human nature and the managerial revolution, we should rather look forward to something like *Nineteenth Eighty-Four*, where an elite of talent pursues power for its own sake and the image of the future is "a boot stamping on a human face forever."

Nineteen Eighty-four, with its use of conditioning, surveillance, and, ultimately, violence to exploit a captive working population (the essential hypocrisy of Big Brother's ostensible benevolence is aptly epitomized by the image of the torture chamber in the cellar of the Ministry of Love), proved an attractive model for American SF. The Americans, indeed, have gone considerably further than Orwell in illuminating the horrors of the totalitarian society. F.M. Busby's *Rissa Kerguelen* (1976), for instance, is set in a world where the majority of the population have, through fraud and coercion, been made into welfare slaves. The stark living conditions, gruelling labor, and total lack of personal freedom, dignity, or individuality characteristic of this class are in striking contrast to the increasingly decadent luxury in which the ruling Committee maintains itself. This book, a fairly stereotyped example of post-mid-century trends, also points up one additional feature, however, which, typically American as it seems to be, is not presupposed by Orwell's model. In American dystopic fiction of this sort the power tends not to be in the hands of a political elite (the government proper is more often than not a mere auxilliary, a tool of the power-mongers rather than a *source* of power), but, rather, is associated with big business and the corporate elite. The classic early examples of this are Frederick Pohl and C.M. Kornbluth's *The Space Merchants* (1953) and *Gladiator-at-Law* (1955), where monolithic competing corporations, their sole motive and rule of conduct being the objective of maximizing sales by any means possible (control and manipulation of the communications media is naturally a primary aspect of their strategy), literally make their own laws, impervious to any concept of disinterested justice and with a total disregard for the rights—even the lives—of individuals.

By the 60s the dominant focus of SF had thus, in a sense, moved to almost the opposite end of the spectrum from Wells's technological optimism. There were, of course, still a significant number of writers—Isaac Asimov and Larry Niven, for instance, would be among the best known of these—who continued to work in traditional modes, celebrating the potentials of scientific progress and the values of the city. Indeed, between 1955 and 1962 James Blish produced what might be called the ultimate urban fantasy. Collected in 1970 under the title of *Cities in Flight*, this series comprises a four-volume saga based on the idea of lifting entire cities—genuine old-earth cities like New York and Chicago, not artificial ones—into space with anti-gravity devices and sending them perambulating merrily around the galaxy exchanging their technological know-how for raw materials like so many hard-headed Yankee traders. In some ways, though, Blish might be said to mark the end of an era. This sort of vision was coming to seem increasingly old-fashioned. By the end of the decade, in fact, rather than imitating their own elders, young American SF writers were more likely to show the influence of the British-based New Wave, a group whose terms of reference, besides an emphasis on technical experimentation and a more self-consciously "literary" style, were formulated in explicit revolt against the optimism of traditional "scientific" science fiction. "Slanted against the idea of progress and all the works of private enterprise," Jack Williamson says, "New Wave fiction magnified all the ugliness around us: of war and racism, of filth and crime and drugs and pollution. Its forecast futures were nightmares of overpopulation, mechanized oppression and universal frustration." If the American response was generally far less extreme, far less virulent than the British one, by the late 60s the dystopic vision was nevertheless a predominant motif. Although technological optimism never disappears completely, in fact, chances are that a typical book of this period would probably have something in common with *Three For Tomorrow*, a 1969 collection of novellas by Robert Silverberg, Roger Zelazny, and, ironically, the pre-eminent city-celebrator, James Blish, in which—as the cover blurb informs us—we find not one but three dystopias: "A world in which the credit card is king, and debt has enslaved all humanity...a giant data bank controls the lives of every man and woman...land, air and water have reached the final disaster level of pollution."

One consequence of this shift is that in the context of the anti-progressive dystopic vision it becomes possible to invoke primitivistic values once again. Indeed, from one point of view the possibility has always been at least hinted at in the conventional stance of SF. The city, an icon of rationality, stands, as Gary Wolfe says, "in the midst of the unknown just as humanity exists in the wilderness of space and time...its wonder [coming] not only from the implication of the waste beyond, but also from the awe at what might be accomplished with human knowledge." This prescription, however, might just as well be reversed. Every symbol inevitably implies its opposite. If, in Norman King's words, in "the ultrarefined city civilization, all that is above, below, and outside the confines of automated and artificial paradise is shunned through a lack of interest that masks a subtle fear," it is equally true that the "waste," the wilderness, *is* out there, waiting. When the time comes, therefore, that the "supremely rational" city, "like the supremely rational structure of science itself...threatens to overwhelm the individual" (Wolfe), this same wilderness, transformed back into the garden, suggests an obvious means of escape. In SF, moreover, there is no "realistic" bias, as there is in the mainstream, to prevent writers from overtly invoking the garden in this particular way. Indeed, as Herbert (1974b) points out, the development seems almost inevitable. As "reality" becomes increasingly unpleasant, we "turn to science fiction for the temporary illusion, for the *prediction* that once again we will enter into the blissful universe of godlike order." This capacity to provide a symbolic relief from the generalized sense of entrapment—a significant divergence from the mainstream—is undoubtedly the other and perhaps more important factor behind the increased popularity of SF in the last two decades. "In a time when most high literature, for all its freedom in language and form, was ironizing myths of the Past rather than releasing archetypes of the Future," says Fiedler, "inadvertent and styleless as a dream...[SF] released, *without knowing it*, images born in the sleep of men torn by love and fear of a technology they could scarcely understand, much less control" (1975). The American public may feel a strong sense of identity with the vision of victims in a wasteland, but as a corrective to this corrosive vision it also evidently requires, at least covertly, a note of hope.

The garden symbol does not, to be sure, emerge all at once, or unambiguously. In early and especially British versions even the dystopic vision was strongly aligned with the values of the city. In Huxley's *Brave New World* a savage is used as a naive foil/observer—a function traditional to pseudo-primitivistic satire—in order to set the shortcomings of that particular reality in the highest relief possible. The Reservation which is the savage's home, however, is not by any means depicted in paradisial terms; existence there is physically crude, emotionally brutalizing, and, in either intellectual or aesthetic terms, minimal. As Huxley himself describes it, "The Savage is offered only two alternatives, an insane life in Utopia, or the life of a primitive in an Indian village, a life more human in some respects, but in others hardly less queer and abnormal." If Huxley *were* to offer an ideal alternative to his dystopic city, moreover, it would not, he tells us, be formulated in terms of a return to primitivism but, quite specifically, as exemplifying a different but still quite eminently *civilized* attitude toward life:

> If I were now to rewrite the book, I would offer to the Savage a third alternative. Between the utopian and the primitive horns of his dilemma would lie the possibility of sanity... In this community economics would be decentralist and Henry-Georgian, politics Kropotkinesque and cooperative. Science and technology would be used as though, like the Sabbath, they had been made for man, not (as at present and still more so in the Brave New World) as though man were to be adapted and enslaved to them. Religion would be the conscious and intelligent pursuit of man's Final End, the unitive knowledge of the immanent Tao or Logos, the transcendent Godhead of Brahman. And the prevailing philosophy of life would be a kind of Higher Utilitarianism, in which the Greatest Happiness principle would be secondary to the Final End principle. ["Introduction," *Brave New World*, 1946]

The ideal of the garden, in this version, is still a long way away.

Other early versions make the garden somewhat less unattractive than Huxley's Reservation but, setting up an even greater obstacle, demonstrate that the natural environment is inimical to denatured latterday man. In "A Story of Days to Come" Wells establishes what is to be a familiar pattern in dystopic fiction, first in using the love of the two central characters, Elizabeth and Denton, as a contrast with the "oppressive tyranny" of life in the giant city, and secondly in inducing these young lovers to escape to freedom outside the wall. Despite the hopeful implications of this escape, however, Wells's protagonists are not allowed to find peace in their rural sanctuary. The garden, the author intimates, is not a *real* alternative, but merely a naive and unrealistic dream. Enfeebled by civilized life, the pair are unable to cope with nature's harsher manifestations, like the wild dogs, and are consequently forced to retreat back into the city again. This is only a slightly less dramatic version of the fate of Forster's cityfolk, who die when they are decanted from the machine.

In America, on the other hand, the situation even in earlier periods tends to be perceived in slightly different terms. The usual early SF city is still the familiar locus of an "inside/outside" opposition, but "outside" isn't quite so alien as the British version characteristically makes it appear. Here, as we have seen amply demonstrated, feelings about nature are rarely unmixed, so even at the peak of technological optimism a sneaking nostalgia for the garden is very close to the surface. As far back as the early 50s, therefore, we find such affectionate offerings as Algis Budrys' "Riya's Foundling" (1953), where nature is stereotypically rendered as a friendly alien being—herbivorous, ruminant, mammalian, not very intelligent, but with an indomitable maternal instinct (the central facet of her entire personality) which suits perfectly her role on a ravaged earth as adoptive mother at the War Orphans's Relocation Farm. Indeed even as radically different an approach as Philip Jose Farmer's good-natured satire on American mother-worship—a story, aptly entitled "Mother" (1953), in which a spaceshipwrecked, mother-fixated musician is ingested into the "womb" of an alien organism where he lives happily ever after "in the darkness, in the moistness, safe and warm, well fed, much loved"—demonstrates indirectly the persistence of the positive "Mother Nature" image in the American mind: As a consequence of this undercurrent, the typical American version of the dystopic fable, rather than following the Wells-Forster pattern right to the end, would probably be something like Richard Stockham's 1954 story "The Valley," where not only is the garden—a tiny oasis of life in a dead and mutilated world—offered as a *symbolic* alternative to the sterile city, but the fleeing lovers actually do find safety and happiness there:

> They ran down the gentle slope, feeling the patches of green touch their feet, smelling a new freshness in the air. And coming to that little spring, they stood beside it and watched the crystal water that trickled along the valley floor and lost itself around the bend. They saw a furry, little animal scurry away and heard the twitter of a bird and saw it resting on a slim bending branch. They heard the buzz of a bee, saw it light on a pale flower at their feet and work at the sweetness inside.
> Mary knelt down and drank from the spring...
> "We can *live* here, Michael!"
> Slowly he looked all around until his sight stopped at the bottom of a hill. "We'll build our house just beyond those rocks. We'll dig and plant and you'll have the child!"
> "Yes!" she said. "Oh yes!"

The wishfulfilling Adam-and-Eve fantasy instanced by this sentimental finale has been characterized by Frank Herbert as the "cliché of clichés" in the SF field. The fact is, though, the general vision implicit in Stockham's conclusion—in striking contrast to Wells's and Huxley's jaundiced views of nature—has proven so appealing to the American that it might be seen as representing not merely a persistent feature but, in this country at least, one of the genre's most basic and important themes. So persuasive is the dream of Paradise Regained in America, indeed, that despite the *quantitative* emphasis on the city during SF's early and middle years, the idea of a futuristic Eden, typically counterpointing as it does the technological disaster of both Bomb and dystopia stories, often seems to be presented as a motive and ultimate justification for simply abandoning rather than trying to heal modern civilization; in some cases actually hurrying the preliminary catastrophe along. Because of the Edenic implications of its aftermath, in other words, somewhere along the line even the atomsmash becomes perceived as a promise rather than a threat. "[T]he reason world catastrophe stories...are so popular," says Sam Moskowitz in his introduction to a 1969 anthology, "is that they vicariously release the individual from the responsibilities of family, law and conscience. They mark the demise of everything that binds, inhibits or restrains... The doom may be horrible but it symbolizes an end to the old order and 'escape'.... All the old laws are gone and the reader, identifying with one of the survivors, can wipe the slate clean and start over again." For this if for no other reason, in American SF, even relatively early, the opposition between city and garden is not merely formal but *real*.

To say that the garden is early evoked as an alternative, however, is not to imply that the attitudes towards nature revealed by American SF during most of its development are anything like enthusiastic primitivism. Even after the turn to dystopia in 1945, in fact, the garden, despite its consensual appeal, often tends to be treated in a very ambiguous way. In F. L. Wallace's "Student Body" (1953), for instance, nature is presented as a relentless opponent to man. Pioneers on a virgin planet encounter a fast mutating "omnimal" which, negating all attempts at defense, comes at them in increasingly formidable forms from insects through rats to tigers. Even as late as the 60s we still find a substantial number of stories—like Ted Thomas's "The Doctor" (1967), a time travelling tale in which an altruistic doctor's mistreatment at the hands of ignorant stone-age savages gives a somewhat less than celebratory view of the primitive state—that express an ambivalent view of the garden at best.

Aside from such more or less individualistic responses as these, perhaps the greatest counter to the primitivistic impulse during the 50s and, decreasingly, the 60s, is an apparent resurgence of the colonial American's identification of nature with identity loss, possibly for reasons similar to those which underlay the earlier reaction, that is, the guilty sense that the influence of the wilderness is subversive and dangerous to the ultrarational masculine orientation (Themis) of the "official" ideology of the time. In any case, a survey of short fiction from this period soon reveals, if nothing else, the mixed feelings that the

American has typically associated with this idea. Many of the stories utilizing the identity-loss theme are simply and unambiguously negative, of course. The sinister alien hive-mind that wants to absorb the human race is another well-worn staple of the field. There are numerous treatments, however, that take a subtler approach to the theme, and these, it seems probable, are most representative of the attitudes that actually prevail.

One typical version of this latter group is Philip K. Dick's "Piper in the Woods" (1953), a story in which a party of explorers on an asteroid, purportedly under a mysterious compulsion emanating from some elusive "wild" version of the planetoid's primitive aborigines, develop the neurotic conviction that they are plants. In terms that can't help but remind us of Crèvecoeur, the psychologist brought in to deal with the problem claims that this delusion is merely a reaction to the anxiety engendered by the unfamiliar situation combined with the naturally disruptive influence of the primitive lifestyle:

"Each of the Garrison crew sees the natives and *unconsciously* thinks of his own early life, when he was a child, when *he* had no worries, no responsibilities, before he joined modern society. A baby lying in the sun.

"But he can't admit this to himself! He can't admit that he might *want* to live like the natives, to die and sleep all day. So he invents The Pipers, the idea of a mysterious group living in the woods who trap him, lead him into their kind of life. Then he can blame *them*, not himself. They 'teach' him to become a part of the woods."

Despite this valiant attempt at demythicization, however, we are left in the end with the unmistakable impression that there is indeed some sort of unnatural influence—a "dreadful charm"—exerted by nature here that lures men away from their duty and undermines the strength of their commitment to a civilized identity, a civilized role. This almost seems like the Puritans' seige mentality all over again.

A similar point is made by Poul Anderson's "Call Me Joe" (1957), although since the process of naturalization is here personalized it comes across in a significantly different way. In this story a crippled telepath who, as part of an interplanetary exploration team, is "operating" a bio-engineered centaur-like pseudocreature on the surface of Jupiter, is so enchanted by the freedom and vitality experienced vicariously during his sessions as puppetmaster that in the end he gives up all connection with his human body up in the satellite (and thus, by extension, all connection with civilization itself) to merge completely with the beast. "Joe" (the new joint identity), is clearly happy with his choice—but after all, so were the plant men of Dick's more explicitly cautionary tale. Even aside from the question of the morality of Angelsey's "desertion" of his own kind, this later story, notwithstanding its generally more positive tone, makes it quite clear that this kind of happiness is achieved only at considerable human cost.

The problem here, as for the Puritans, goes far beyond the pragmatic one of maintaining communal integrity in the face of a seductive and disruptive environment. The real fly in the ointment—the reason that Edward Anglesey is initially so disturbed by his unrecognized subversive impulse that he keeps blowing out tubes on his psionic transmitter; the fact that turns official disapproval in to personal fear—is once again the American's obsession with individuality that inevitably makes any sort of contact with the alien "other" suspect. George R.R. Martin's prize-winning story, "A Song for Lya" (1975), illuminates (rather than merely expressing) the full conceptual ambivalence of this characteristic American stance. Far in the future (the galaxy has long since been explored and settled) two humans, both telepaths, having come to an ancient city to investigate a strange religious cult, are faced with the possibility of a life-in-death Union (through absorption into a blob-like organism) that epitomizes perfect love, total understanding, assured immortality. One of the two—significantly enough, the woman—despairing of the imperfect contact which is alone possible to the isolated individual (" 'I'm here and you're there and we can touch and make love and talk, but we're still apart' "), chooses to take this step. The other, however, even with the added incentive of regaining his beloved partner, resists the temptation with all his strength (" 'I was struggling, fighting it, battling back against the sea of sucking love' "). It is his explanation for *why* he rejected the proffered apotheosis, however, which—encapsulating as it does what seems to me to be the essence of the American's resistance to nature—really focuses the significance of Martin's parable:

Lya whom I could still have. Whom I could have now. It would be easy, so easy. A slow stroll in a darkened cave, a short sleep. Then Lya with me for eternity, in me, sharing me, being me, and I her. Loving and knowing more of each other than men can ever do. Union and Joy, and no darkness again, ever. God. If I believed that...why did I tell Lya no?

Maybe because I'm not sure. Maybe I still hope, for something still greater and more loving than the Union, for the God they told me of so long ago. Maybe I'm taking a risk, because part of me still believes. But if I'm wrong...then the darkness, and the pain...

But maybe it's something else... For man is more than Shkeen [the alien cultists], somehow; there are men like Dino and Gourlay as well as Lya and Gustaffson, men who fear love and Union as much as they crave it. A dichotomy, then. Man has two primal urges, and the Shkeen only one? If so, perhaps there is a human answer, to reach and join and not be alone, and yet to still be men.

I do not envy Valcarenghi. He cries behind his wall, I think, and noone knows, not even he. And noone will ever know, and in the end he'll always be alone in smiling pain. No, I do not envy Dino.

Yet there is something of him in me, Lya, as well as much of you. And that is why I ran, though I loved you.

The American, in other words, has traditionally been caught between his masculine egocentricity and his desire for mystical dissolution—and in most cases, if it comes down to a clear choice, it is his egocentricity that wins. Indeed, if we take the meeting between man and alien in Damon Knight's "Stranger Station" (1957) to be a kind of paradigm for the actual encounter between man and nature in America, it would seem that the mutilation of the wilderness was not an accidental or anomalous act at all, but, in terms of the American psyche, a foregone conclusion from the moment he arrived. *"When...two alien cultures meet, the stronger must transform the other with love or hate,"* proclaims Knight's protagonist. Unfortunately, he—the archetypal American, agonized by the thought of *any* transformation, good *or* bad—would rather *destroy* than give in to alien altruism, regardless of the gifts of love, of knowledge, of immortality even, that he also destroys with his hatred.

It may be misleading, of course, to talk about *the* American like this as if there had never been any other kind of response. The parallels to be observed between certain aspects of 50s SF and the Puritan world view discussed above would suggest that there is *something* about this particular attitude that gives it a tendency to recur, and we will examine the implications of this possibility in the next chapter. In the meantime, however, it must be noted that despite both the initial resistance and the persistent ambivalence we have observed, there *was* finally, in the 60s (as might have been expected in the context of the cultural trends that we touched on briefly in the first section of this chapter), a basic shift toward overt primitivism in American SF.

The one factor probably more responsible for this shift than anything else was the increase in awareness of nature that took place during the 60s as America gradually became ecology-conscious. SF, in fact, preceded and probably contributed to this particular trend. A conditioned sensitivity to developments in the sciences along with a dystopic enthusiasm for doommongering meant that SF writers picked up on the pollution scare long before it became a public issue. Indeed, as early as 1943, P. Schuyler Miller could write a story ("The Cave"; see section 5.2.1 below) that perfectly exemplifies modern views of the egotistic and anthropocentric perspective that sets man so inevitably in conflict with other life forms. By the late 60s, when the public concern peaked, consequently, literally hundreds of novels, stories and theme-linked collections of stories on ecology-related topics had appeared. Indeed, reflecting what seems to be a real sense of mission (SF, ever since Wells, has always been particularly drawn to the missionary stance), the ecology dystopia became perhaps the most dominant form of the period. The motivation, so it was commonly claimed, was not merely the escapist function of traditional disaster tales, either, but specifically didactic. "By the questions asked, by the alternatives displayed for your consideration, such science fiction represents a metaphor of history and sometimes a preview of reality," says Frank Herbert in his introduction to an anthology called *The Wounded Planet*. By extrapolating from the current situation, in other words, SF writers claimed to provide a cautionary glimpse at what unmodified behavior could bring. Blish's "We All Die Naked" (1969) is fairly representative of the species. This story shows a world choked with garbage: air pollution is not only a major health hazard (respirators are mandatory) but has also created a greenhouse effect which has partially melted the icecaps, flooding most of the world; this in turn, exacerbated by geological disturbances induced by indiscriminate underground disposal of liquid wastes, has unbalanced the isostatic balance of the earth's crust and introduced radical irregularities into the planetary rotation. The ultimate result of this process—*the seeds of which are already planted*, says the SF writer—is obviously extinction for the human race.

Ecology SF naturally influenced the consensual image of the man/nature relation as it became a more fashionable mode. A lot of its energy was simply devoted to misanthropic diatribes on human behavior, of course. Man is commonly presented as at best ignorant, at worst a spoiler who will by his very nature upset *any* ecological system that he encounters. Both the culpability and the destructiveness of his actions tend to become exaggerated throughout the period, moreover. In Paul Ash's "Big Sword" (1958), for instance, though human misunderstanding of an alien ecological system *almost* destroys an intelligent culture (they want to cut down the sacred tree on which the young "podlings" mature), in the end the Terran exploration team not only discovers its mistake but helps the tribe improve its lot by reforesting a desert that cuts them off from others of their kind. Sydney J. Van Scyoc's "Mnarra Mobilis" (1973), in contrast, shows that interplanetary colonists are quite prepared to eradicate any species that interferes with the welfare of their imported terran crops, even if this means that the entire planet is sterilized of native life as a result. The other side of this negative view of "civilized" behavior, however, is an increasingly positive view of nature itself. As we said of the American westering myth during an earlier period, an awareness of decreased accessibility automatically intensifies the sense of *need*. A typical response to this sense in late 60s SF is the image of nature as a beautiful doomed woman: a *Mother* in Howard Fast's "The Wound" (1969), where oil exploration by means of atomic percussion probes destroys the earth's inner integrity; a *Mistress* in James Tiptree's "The Last Flight of Dr. Ain" (1969), where a scientist deliberately releases an incurable plague to kill off mankind before it finishes killing the earth (" 'Oh my girl! Oh Beautiful, you won't die. I won't let you die. I tell you girl, it's over...' "). Gone, it seems, is the ambivalence: nature is pre-eminently desirable again.

Interestingly enough, the primitivistic trend in 60s SF was also accompanied by a greatly increased interest in the mind sciences, or *psionics*: telepathy, telekinesis, clairvoyance, etc. On the surface this phenomenon may seem to run counter to the primitivism, since in earlier SF such powers were traditionally associated with advanced stages of evolution (British writer Arthur C. Clarke's *Childhood's End* provides the prototype for this motif). If we examine the later and especially American treatments more closely, however, there is ample evidence that *psi* and primitivism aren't quite so far apart in their conventional associations as it may at first seem. For one thing, even back before the telepathy story became an SF staple, mental powers were normally set in explicit opposition to technology. A classic example is Theodore Cogswell's "The Wall Around the World" (1953) where the human race is split into two completely segregated cultures, one based on technology, the other on "magic," the message—as explained by the young protagonist's teacher-guide—being that the two will simply not coexist.

"Do you remember what I said to you in my office that day—that Man can't follow two paths at once, that Mind and Nature are bound to conflict? That's true, but it's also false. You can have both, but it takes two worlds to do it.

"Outside, where you're going, is the world of machines. It's a good world, too. But the men who live there saw a long time ago that they were paying a price for it; that control over Nature meant that the forces of the Mind were neglected, for the machine is a thing of logic and reason, but miracles aren't. Not yet. So they built the Wall and they placed people within it and gave them such books and such laws as would ensure development of the powers of the Mind. At least they hoped it would work that way—and it did."

Cogswell confuses the issue by identifying technology with "Nature" (a characteristic of the mechanistic world-view), but the implication is nevertheless clear. Once the essential irreconcilability of these two terms of reference becomes more widely accepted, consequently, the powers of the mind are almost automatically associated with the values of the garden.

As a result of this dichotomization, we tend to find quite a few stories during the 60s asserting in different ways the belief that only if man is *freed* from the psychologically crippling influence of contemporary technological society can mental powers ever develop "normally." Fast's "The First Men" (1960) is a fairly typical illustration of this approach. Citing the example of feral children becoming, past a certain age, ineducable due to their conditioned image of themselves as animals, this story relates how a group of children, experimentally isolated as babies, develop—*naturally*, as it were—the power to enter into a telepathic gestalt. Two in particular of the points made by Fast were subsequently to become conventional features of the new *psi*-fiction fad. The first is that the power of mind-link is based on *love* ("Only the unspoiled devotion of mother for helpless child can approximate the love that binds them together—yet here it is also different, deeper even than that"); the second that it has a beneficial effect on human behavior ("Before the transformation took place, there was sufficient of the children's petulance and anger and annoyance— but after it took place, we never again heard a voice raised in anger or annoyance"). The development of *psi* powers, then, is associated directly with those same oddly assorted qualities of immediacy (passion) and mystical transcendence (serenity) that have traditionally been imputed to communion with nature. It would seem, in fact, that the identity-loss theme of the 50s and the *psi* theme of the 60s are simply negative and positive views of the same experiential phenomenon. The celebration of man's purported psionic potential during the 60s was thus probably an important factor in stimulating the primitivistic impulse as a whole.

The end result of these various developments is that by the end of the 60s a new version of the garden/city opposition has emerged. After this period, for one thing, in terms of sympathy or center of consciousness the movement is almost always away from the city; often right from the beginning we are on the outside, looking in. M.A. Foster's *The Gamesplayers of Zan* (1977), which, interestingly enough, is almost an inversion of Huxley's schema (the sane and simple lifestyle of a group of telepathically-gifted mutants on a relatively primitive reservation is depicted as an absolute alternative rather than merely a corrective or foil for the paranoid technological dystopia on the other side of the fence), presents its story almost solely through the eyes of the simpler of the two cultures involved. This shift in perspective is not only formal but confirms the polarization of *value* away from the omnipotent city of the early progressive and transitional-ambivalent modes, draining it both of felt reality (now it is this pole of the dichotomy, rather than the garden, which is simply cited as a conventional counter) and of symbolic authority. In this respect Harry Harrison's *Deathworld* (1960) provides a striking early prototype for the vision which came to dominate before the end of the decade. Here, in fact, the primitivistic mythos can be seen in its most explicit and overt form.

At the centre of Harrison's novel is the concept of an entire planetary ecology which is organically unified, self-modifying, and *psi*-sensitive. In such a world as this, nature invariably responds in kind. Man's attitude thus becomes a very important factor in determining what he finds in his environment. Two possibilities are illustrated. On the one hand is the highly technological and militaristic culture of the "junkmen," which is in constant life-and-death conflict with a hostile wilderness; on the other are the primitive communities of "grubbers" out in the woods who, because they project positive instead of negative feelings, are actually able to domesticate those same natural phenomena which the city-dwellers find so lethal. In the course of the book it becomes clear, moreover, that nature simply cannot be beaten in the end. The *only* way for the city-dwellers to survive is to become grubbers, give up their pathological hate. The city must be abandoned for the garden. American SF has certainly come a long way since those early imitations of Wells.

One interesting point to note here, since we are concerned in this entire study to establish certain aspects of American culture as unique responses to the unique experience of this country, is that British SF, starting from the same place—indeed, providing most of the original impetus for the development of the genre—does not follow the same pattern vis-à-vis the progress/primitivism debate as American SF does. Nature has never seemed to hold quite the same attraction for British writers as it does for their American counterparts, and indeed in terms reminiscent of Wells has continued to be presented more often than not in contemporary SF as inimical to human survival. One particularly striking evidence of the divergence between the two countries is provided by their different approaches to the disaster story. Where in American SF (at least until recently) the crisis is most typically man-made and technological in origin, in Britain, as Blish points out, we commonly find that "peculiar...type which might be dubbed the one-lung catastrophe, pioneered by, of all people, Conan Doyle...[in which] the world is drowned, parched, hit by a comet, smothered by volcanic gas, sterilized by the Van Allen belts, or otherwise revisited by some version of Noah's Fludde." In terms of British conventions, in other words, it has usually been nature rather than man which is a threat.

Even in the later, more sophisticated British SF that appeared while America was busy climbing on the primitivist bandwagon, nature, if not ignored completely, tends to be imaged in morally neutral terms. In many of Brian Aldiss's intriguing novels, for instance— *Starship* (1958) and *Hothouse* (1962) are prime examples—nature, especially as associated with evolutionary processes, is shown to be a blind, irresistible force oblivious to the puny destinies of men. Richard Adams's *Shardik* (1974)—although fantasy rather than SF proper—is interesting in this regard, insofar as it seems to offer a particularly British view in its allegory of the way man himself mythologizes an essentially alien and impervious nature (in this case a great bear). Adams's view of this process is not a simple, negative one. It is true that the bear-god is shown as both dangerous and unpredictable, resisting the euphemizing tendency of the myth. It is also true, however, that Adams seems to insist that the myth itself is important nevertheless. If man betrays it (if he uses it cynically for political ends), he not only destroys nature but also suffers himself; if he affirms it—which is what the protagonist Kelderek does through his transmogrification of Shardik's death into a mystical event—the joyful vision thus achieved, stimulating human awareness of the *human* condition, can liberate the entire community from its own worst self. In both cases, though, it is the human capacity to inject meaning into nature rather than any of nature's intrinsic qualities which is the source of any benefit received.

The American tendency to impute special regenerative powers to nature is thus just not an important element in the typical British view. Missing almost completely, in fact—with noticeable effect on the concerns of the genre—is the wishfulfilling Adamic fantasy of the U.S. Many of those early after-the-flood stories certainly carry some implication of Adam and Eve in their treatment of survivors, to be sure, but more often than not, in sharp contrast to the American version where the result is the establishment of a new, ideal community, in the British catastrophe, as Blish says, often "everybody gives up and nobody survives." And even if a few individuals do muddle through, their situation—denied the supports of civilized society—is definitely seen as desperate rather than ideal. There is evidently no faith and not very much interest in the Edenic dream over there.

Both British and American SF share the dystopic vision of the world, but— and here is the significant difference between the two countries—where America fantasizes an escape back into the simple, orderly, natural environment of the garden, the British have traditionally envisioned progressing forward beyond nature altogether; where the American SF writer invokes a heroic and old-fashioned young Adam to *redeem* society, his British alter ego seems rather to suggest that anarchism and nihilism provide the most plausible response to such a world. As British critic Peter Nicholls pointed out (disapprovingly) in 1976, "the portrayal of a fragmenting and decaying world whose moral values are totally inadequate to the task of saving it, has produced some of the most compelling science fiction of the last decade":

I would produce three compelling but in some ways distasteful novels as my prime documents here. They are *Crash* by J.G. Ballard, *Barefoot in the Head* by Brian Aldiss, and *The English Assassin* by Michael Moorcock...[T]hese books are very different in tone, but they have some features in common. The first is a very heavy emphasis on things—objects and places, clothes, cars, advertisements, guns, records, together with a diminishment of focus on character. It is as if character were coming to be seen as definable only in terms of environment and life style. All three books are [also] notably cool and unimpassioned... Indeed, the Monster of Anarchy is characterized above all by his cool. He saunters laconically through landscapes pitted and scarred by the stigmata of self-destruction, resting occasionally in the Garden of Gesthemane, asking and expecting no advice or assistance from any quarter, human or godly. He fucks a lot, and does so most cheerfully when surrounded by the detritus of destruction, the crashed car, the dully gleaming carbine slung over the shoulder, the empty syringe lying on the toilet floor.

As may be inferred from this rather bleak description, the late-60s British and American SF heroes are alike at least to the extent that they are both formally anti-social and self-reliant. Here, however, the resemblance ends. The British Monster of Anarchy is not merely an out-law, but an agent of dis-order as well. It is *un*naturalness, essentially, that he represents. The American Adam, in contrast, draws his legitimacy from an alignment with nature that makes him a natural moralist; in the long run he can always be trusted to do the "right" thing.

It seems clear, therefore, that the primitivistic impulse we have traced in the foregoing pages is a characteristic of American culture rather than SF in general. As we have seen, though, SF turned out to be an eminently suitable vehicle for the garden myth, once the cultural context became conducive to a revival of the Adamic mode. As Richard McKenna's story, "Hunter Come Home" (1964), aptly illustrates, in fact, the conventions of the field, as they developed in America, were particularly susceptible to a radical re-interpretation that inverted their original meanings. Indeed, as a kind of summary of our observations, "Hunter, Come Home" itself might be taken as an analogue for the historical process that took place as well as a prime example of the genre norms twenty years after the war.

The setting of this story is another one of those worlds where the entire ecology comprises a unified biomass only superficially differentiated into separate life forms. An exploration team from the planet Mordin is trying to eradicate this native life in order that (in a typical benighted masculine fashion which might be taken to represent the "classic" SF view) they can establish a hunting preserve to stock with the giant carnivores now becoming extinct on their home world. Their battle against the *phytos* is made extremely difficult, however, by the fact that the organism keeps self-mutating to combat the increasingly extreme measures that they use against it. In the end their attack backfires (you can't beat nature!); an experiment in bio-engineering lets loose a deadly plague. The aggressors die; the passive and peaceful *phytos* survive.

This is only half the story, however. The new primitivistic vision is represented here *positively* too. The young protagonist of "Hunter, Come Home"—a low-caste worker who is despised because he hasn't been able to buy himself an opportunity for the ritual kill without which no Mordin male is considered a man—is emotionally caught between a desire to emulate his macho companions and his love for a gentle ecologist who opposes the Mordin Plan. In the end he chooses to die with her in exile rather than finish his life violently, fighting nature, like the rest of the team. Having made the decision to embrace nature, though, it turns out that Roy no longer has to die. He—along with Midori, his chosen Eve—is absorbed into the biomass: *remade*, immortal and immune to the plague.

This, of course, is in symbolic terms the ultimate transformation implicit in the American yearning for Eden. Roy himself, typically enough, initially reacts with some ambivalence, expressing the traditional doubts of the American individualist about identity-loss, loss of initiative, *submission* in any form. " '[A]ll I wanted was to kill it,' " he says. " 'Now it's done this for me...I want to love it back and I can't. Not now. Not after. I just *can't*... [M]e. Tamed. A pet. A parasite. I *can't*, Midori.' " McKenna/Midori has the perfect answer for him, though: in the American version of Genesis one can have the best of *all* possible worlds. Man can merge with nature *without* giving up his ascendency, his special niche in the scheme of things. Even better, in a total denial of history, man now actually becomes in some sense the *savior* of the garden that he formerly betrayed.

"Roy. Listen to me." She was in front of him again, but he would not open his eyes. "This life emerged with infinite potentialities. It mastered its environment using only the tiniest part of them," she said. "It never split up, to fight itself and evolve that way. So it lay dreaming. It might have dreamed forever."

"Only we came, you mean? With *Thanasis* [the organic assassin]?"

"Yes. We forced it to changes, genetic recombination, rises in temperatures and process speeds. Whatever happened at one point could be duplicated everywhere, because it is all one. One year to it is like millions of years of Earthly evolution. It raised itself to a new level... [Then] we *wakened* it...I think we focus its awareness, somehow, serve it as a symbol system, a form giver... It is a great and holy mystery, Roy. Only through us can it know its own beauty and wonder."

This, surely, is the ultimate version of the American's Great Escape!

5.2 The Adaptable Alien

The next question that arises is whether we are likely to find a noble savage in this new literary garden. The primitivistic corollary to dystopia would presumably *allow* for the emergence of such a figure, since the noble savage has generally been associated with primitivism in the past, but perhaps in this particular case the turn to nature is so wholehearted that (as in genuine rather than decorative Romanticism) a mediating structure is neither necessary nor desired. Certainly stories like McKenna's seem to imply that the relation can and should be personal and direct. "Hunter, Come Home" is a fairly late version, though, which, as we have seen, did not suddenly appear full-blown. And if the idea of noble savagery seems to assort somewhat ill with the technological orientation that spawned the modern dystopic vision, peripheral to the main line of development but still properly an influential element in early SF is another tradition out of which, when the time is ripe, a noble savage does in fact emerge.

"It will be appropriate," says Robert Scholes, "...at least as a beginning, to see the tradition that leads to modern science fiction as a special case of romance, for this tradition always insists upon a radical discontinuity between its world and the world of human experience" (1975). In the classic form of the genre such a *dérangement* is achieved through displacement into a future which is full of extrapolated scientific marvels. This, however, was only the latest development in a formula which reveals a close kinship with SF even in its more generalized variants. In Scholes's words, "In its simplest and most ancient form [the] discontinuity is objectified as another world, a different place: Heaven, Hell, Eden, Fairyland, Utopia, The Moon, Atlantis, Lilliput." Many of SF's early precursors were thus explorations not of another time but simply of another space.

From its inception SF consequently showed a strong affinity for the ancient motif of the imaginary journey. In the late nineteenth and early twentieth centuries, for instance, such fantastic voyages as appeared in fiction tended to reflect the same interest in science that informed Wells's futuristic vision, while many putative "scientific" romances adopted in return the conventional journey form. Despite the objection of latter-day purists that most of the imaginary journeys turned out during this period are pure fantasy, in fact, insofar as geology and archeology are just as scientific as physics, the two strains could be said to converge in some of the most popular fiction of the time. As Clareson describes it,

...in both Britain and America, during those years between the 1870s and the 1930s, by far the most popular kind of imaginary voyage took the form of the so-called "lost race" novel. Most simply, that type of story reflected the impact of three interrelated areas upon the literary and public imaginations of the period: first, the renewed vigor of the explorations which sought to map the interiors of Africa, Asia and South America, as well, of course, as both polar regions; secondly, the cumulative impact of geological discoveries and theories which expanded the past almost immeasurably and populated it with such creatures as Tyrannosaurus Rex, Pithecanthropus Erectus, and Neanderthal Man; and finally, the impact of archaeological discoveries and theories which—from the valley of the Indus to the depths of Africa and Pre-Columbian America—raised civilizations in the past more spectacular and mysterious than legendary El Dorado or the Kingdom of Prester John.

The pseudo-primitivistic "lost race" novel, therefore—ranging from Rider Haggard's *She* (1887) and *King Solomon's Mines* (1885), through Conan Doyle's *The Lost World* (1912), to James Hilton's *Lost Horizon* (1933)—was at bottom as much a celebration of the advancement of human knowledge as the SF interplanetary voyage was. Indeed, demonstrating vividly this fundamental compatibility is the extent to which early SF writers were able to adopt many of the features of the Haggard/Doyle/Hilton formula, along with characteristics of the related more-muscular Kiplingesque adventure tale, and integrate them into their ostensibly more radical excursions virtually unchanged. "Lifting elements 'from every sort of adventure fiction—Spanish Main, Western, Oriental soldier-of-fortune, South Sea beachcomber, French Foreign Legion, and California and Alaskan Gold Rush'...the writers proceeded to 'fill in the map behind the explorers'—taming, as it were, the strangeness of space into the familiarity of the frontier," says Paul Carter, quoting from Alexei and Cory Panshin. "Dreadful, hackneyed pulp stories appeared, purportedly taking place near spaceports on Mercury or Jupiter or Mars, which could just as well have been set in Asian port cities like Shanghai or Singapore or Saigon. And the authors clung to these Arab and Indian and Chinese 'interplanetary' settings as long as they could." The relationship between the earthly imaginary voyage and the space voyage of early SF was thus not merely secondary but direct.

Insofar as the space voyage, as a specialized kind of imaginary journey, was brought to maturity primarily as an American form, however, it soon began to reveal an emphasis that set it apart in some important respects from its British progenitors. As Clareson points out, "in the early years at least, the 'lost race' novel was little more than a modification of the traditional utopia," and even in twentieth-century versions, its protagonist typically finds an "ideal society" in the course of his quest. In common with the classic didactic pastoral romance, many of these utopic visions appear to support the pseudo-primitivistic tenet "that a perfect society can exist only when man lives close to nature," but, again as in the pastoral, the ultimate orientation is clearly pro-civilization nevertheless. In the American SF version, in contrast, there is increasing evidence that the primary interest is more in the discovery of *uncivilized* regions than in the rediscovery of ancient wisdom; indeed that the space voyage just as much as the cowboy saga represents an attempt, specifically, to recapitulate the frontier conditions of America's own past. So strong is this association, in fact, that the alien worlds of early SF are often described in terms reminiscent of the classic western landscape not merely in spirit but in detail. The prototypical example of this is Edgar Rice Burroughs' *A Princess of Mars* (1917), where an American westerner, in character and background much like Wister's Virginian, ducks into a cave to escape from hostile Indians and is miraculously transported to Mars:

As [Burroughs'] transplanted hero looks more closely at that strange and weird landscape, it takes on familiarity. "I seemed to be lying in a deep, circular basin, along the outer verge of which I could distinguish the irregularities of low hills." It is high noon, and the dry solar heat on his nude body reminds him of the Arizona desert he has so abruptly left. "Here and there were slight outcroppings of quartz-bearing rock which glistened in the sunlight." As he begins to explore, moving awkwardly in the lighter Martian gravity, the environment again becomes strange. But John Carter's initial impression—that Mars is a place not so very different from Arizona—has decisively influenced all subsequent interplanetary fiction. When Americans land on another world, it seems, they expect it to resemble the American West. [Carter]

Displaying such resemblances as these, it seems clear that the interplanetary voyage, whatever formal futuristic trappings it may carry along with it, actually has a significant backward-looking strain. It is possible, though, that the implications of this are not quite as simple as the conventional echoes might make us think. The space opera is not "just another" version of the horse opera. It goes *further* than the western; develops yet another aspect of the myth.

In the above pages we noted a number of motives in connection with the American's apparently persistent obsession with the pioneering experience. Underlying the whole, of course, is the universal desire to regain the innocence of an archaic past that Eliade refers to in *The Eternal Return*. Beyond this, however, are, as we noted, a number of associations that are more specifically American than Eliade's archetypal Edenic urge. For instance, one of the most basic reasons, especially during the days of the young republic, but with periodic revivals right up to recent times, that the westering process has appealed to American writers so much is simply its association with a *patriotic* impulse which expresses itself in two ultimately irreconcilable but traditionally interrelated forms: first, a celebration of the American landscape, and second, a celebration of the prowess exhibited by the nation in carving a civilization out of this untamed land. Next, developing subsequent to this and revealing slightly more subversive undertones, is the *nostalgic* impulse—celebrating the individualistic lifestyle characteristic of the frontier condition—that came to dominate, especially in popular genres such as the western, as the actual business of nation-carving receded into the past. Finally, growing out of a sense of national guilt and anxiety that intensified as the wilderness itself disappeared, providing Americans with "a way of protesting a power to which [they had] already...capitulated" (Douglas), is the *sentimental* impulse. Coexisting with other modes almost right from the beginning, this was realized perhaps most fully in such escapist fantasies as the Adam-and-Eve story of SF, which would symbolically recreate (undo) history by providing a vision of the garden still intact.

Subsuming and to some extent surpassing all of these varying conceptions, however, is the motive that seems fundamental to the interplanetary romance. Carrying the process described by Mumford to its logical extreme, essentially what has happened here—probably because of the American's unhappy recognition that it is impossible for *any* reality to measure up to his idyllic expectations of either a perfect city *or* a perfect garden—is that the goal-orientation of the original westering myth has been replaced with an emphasis solely on the *means* to its end. The SF formula, as Gary Wolfe points out, "may be summarized somewhat as follows: the known exists in opposition to the unknown, with a barrier of some sort separating them. The barrier is crossed, and the unknown becomes the known. But the crossing of the barrier reveals new problems, and this sets the stage for a further opposition of known and unknown. This barrier is crossed, yet another opposition is set up, and so on." The advantage of SF, in other words is the fact that it offers an *indefinitely receding frontier*. The pioneering experience, the eternally enticing process of *becoming* as opposed to the ofttimes disappointing state of *being*, may consequently be presented as a perpetual condition rather than a transition stage. "As Mars ceased to be a suitable place to build a little house on the prairie," says Carter, "the dream moved on out through the stars. Somewhere, away in the Greater Magellanic Cloud or at the Galactic Rim, there may still be clean air and elbow room—in short, a West."

The identification of spacefaring with perpetual pioneering characteristic of this particular strain of SF has some important implications for our noble savage. On the one hand the space voyage does open up the possibility of regenerating the primitive in the new guise of an extraterrestrial being. On the other hand, the conventions of interplanetary adventuring meant that the alien encountered was probably *not* going to be noble, not at least until a much later phase. The problem is that many of the anti-primitivistic elements of the original westward movement, and especially of its standard-bearer, the frontiersman, are necessarily characteristic of space "westering" as well. The pioneer, insofar as his role places him in direct conflict with the natural environment, whether on earth or elsewhere, is—despite the ostensibly primitivistic stance that he often assumes—an agent of progress, and as such ultimately an enemy of savagery of any kind. SF strengthens this association, moreover, through its necessary connection with hardware. It has long since become a critical cliché that the spaceship is the ultimate phallus, but the implication of masculine aggression in stories of interplanetary exploration is too obvious to ignore. As Clareson points out of this newest version of the imaginary journey, when "their use of the past did not answer their questions nor solve their problems...they created a new, erotic escapism. Their narratives became increasingly a proving ground for the protagonists' masculinity: survival in a hostile world." As long as the space pioneer is set forth in such ultramasculine terms as these, the primitive native, associated with the nature the hero is trying to conquer, must needs be nothing more than the villain who provides occasion for his demonstration of Terran—that is, American— superiority. "In Space Opera," says Kingsley Amis, "Mars takes the place of Arizona with a few physical alterations, the hero totes a blaster instead of a six-gun, bad men are replaced by bad aliens looking just like bad men with green skins and perhaps a perfunctory sixth digit, and Indians turn up in the revised form of what are technically known as bug-eyed monsters...BEMs."

Most of the aliens who appear in early SF, then, are as unequivocally negative as the demonic savages that the Puritan encountered in the American woods. In Gernsback's time the danger is usually quite direct and preeminently physical. The alien, as Amis implies, is usually either a grotesque "creature" of some kind or a brutal, bloodthirsty warrior (more often than not repilian, insectoid, or crustacean, as if to emphasize its absolute distance from man) which the protagonist must fight in order to protect either himself or, more likely, some innocent female who just happens to be on hand. During Campbell's era, there is a bit more of an attempt to avoid the BEM stereotype, and even a few minor excursions into alien psychology, but outside of the occasional cute alien pet or kooky comic character the extraterrestrial—probably at least partly due to wartime xenophobia—is still viewed as sinister in the great majority of cases. In Anthony Boucher's "Expedition" (1943) the earth, typically enough, is threatened with an invasion by giant insects who consider killing to be the ultimate aesthetic act.

During the later 40s and the 50s the threat associated with the alien tends to become an increasingly subtle one—indeed, from around 1948 to 1953, peaking in 1951, there actually seems to be a brief hiatus or at least a fairly radical softening of xenophobia, possibly as an aftereffect of the end of the war— but it by no means disappears. C. L. Moore's "Shambleau" (1951), for example, presents the prototypical SF equivalent to Crèvecoeur's seductive savage in its depiction of a medusa-like creature that hypnotizes humans into finding unimaginable delight in its degrading and unnatural embrace in order that it may "feed" off their life force. Other characteristic enemy aliens of the period include the agent of the hive mind mentioned above (Isaac Asimov's "Misbegotten Missionary" [1950] is a good example of this) and—stimulated by the political situation—the "alien among us": the counterfeit human who represents the threat of invasion from within (Alan E. Nourse's 1952 story, "Counterfeit," and Don Seigel's 1956 film, *Invasion of the Bodysnatchers*, illustrate the norms of this mode).

With this last item we have gone considerably past the simple equation alien=nature=enemy, to be sure. Indeed, once we get at all beyond the simplistic physical encounters of space opera, the alien—like the Indian before him— tends to become a catchall scapegoat, his specific associations varying with the political wind. Looking at 40s and 50s SF, in fact, one might easily suspect that one of the most attractive aspects of the genre was that it offered the American a chance to escape from the moral and political complexities of the modern world by presenting a simplified, Manichaean version of reality; displacing, like the Puritan before him, all evil into an accessible and easily identifiable external "other." Even after the turn away from technological optimism and the abandonment of space opera for more complex kinds of journeyings, therefore, it was difficult for the alien to escape the negative connotations that had been imputed to him earlier. Fortunately there were counterinfluences at work which led, if not directly, at least eventually to a rehabilitated savage, capable of playing a variety of conventional and not so conventional roles.

The first and most obvious of these influences was the increasing hold of the dystopic vision. Even with politically-inspired xenophobia added to the American's normal ambivalence toward nature, a few years after the war distrust of technology was becoming so widespread it was inevitable that there should be signs of an at least *relative* rise in the authority of Moira in SF. During the 50s, as a result, a significant number of books and stories appeared which stressed the benefits of a good working relationship with nature, often by means of a partnership between man and some other life form. Murray Leinster's "Exploration Team" (1956) is typical of these, especially insofar as the anti-technological bias is here made an explicit part of the theme. In this story, set on a planet with particularly deadly wildlife, an opposition is set up between two modes of exploration supported on the one hand by animal assistants (a team of mutated grizzlies) and on the other by robots. The former, being less fragile and more flexible, naturally prove by far the most effective, just as the protagonist, an American-style individualist, claims. In a manner strikingly reminiscent of the early twentieth-century western with its important west versus east, cowboy versus tenderfoot motif, the impressively equipped "official" survey party has to be rescued in the end by the lone hero and his bears. The pattern becomes a familiar one. In Andre Norton's Azor novels, (*The Beast-Master* [1959)]; *Lord of Thunder* [1962]), for instance, we find exactly the same kind of situation: the hero with his telepathically-linked beast-team (eagle, meercat, and dune-cat) can solve problems and overcome obstacles easily where a conventionally armed and equipped individual is helpless. Technology is clearly not Wells's perfect servant any more.

We may be making too much of this vestigial primitivism, however; the alien-as-noble-savage is obviously still a long way away. For one thing, as in the western, the primitive *style* of the space pioneer in stories like these is combined with an ultra-masculine *intent*. The "alien" here is clearly a tool rather than an exemplar. The turn to nature thus appears at this point to concern only means, not ends. This seems to be all the more true when we note that with a few important exceptions by far the majority of "helpful" aliens that turn up in mid-50s SF are non- or only marginally sapient; closer to animals (albeit superior ones) than to potentially "noble" (but more threatening) intelligent beings. John Hancock's "Exiled From Space" (1951) is perhaps more typical of that decade in that the clever aliens in the story are enemies; the only good alien is a pet. Judging by the field as a whole, in fact, it would seem that the American is not really looking seriously for an external referent during this period no matter what the occasional more positive glimpse of nature might imply. The focus for the most part is inwards, man-centered, anthropomorphic in its dealings with the "other." Indeed, in the early 50s as in the chauvinistic 40s, a universe inhabited totally by humanoids is the most common arrangement to find.

The non-human extraterrestrials that do appear in this phase, moreover—sapients and non-sapients both—tend, if presented sympathetically at all, to be much less strange, much less *alien*, in both biological and psychological terms, than the traditional giant insect or BEM. Even Gordon Dickson's Ursine Hokas and L. Sprague de Camp's dinosaur-like Viagens—notable exceptions to the non-sapience rule cited above—are essentially humanized under the skin. To the extent that such creatures are anthropomorphized, they are, of course, no longer "other" in any meaningful way. The "true" *(bad)* alien, in contrast—like Cooper's later savages—is viewed as *absolutely* different; impossible *by definition* for man to assimilate. It is quite likely, therefore, that James Schmitz's "Grandpa" (1955), an early version of the ecology story, provides a more important clue to the prevailing mood of the period vis-à-vis nature than any of these affectionate renderings of the alien/animal-helper do. In this story an exploration team discovers that a seemingly benign and even useful organism—a large mobile "raft" which can be maneuvered with blasts from a laser gun to provide transportation up and down the waterways of the planet—

can turn out to be extremely dangerous under different circumstances (during certain periods of the year it becomes host to a hostile symbiote that changes its behavior patterns). The true alien—as opposed to the anthropomorphized extraterrestrial—should thus always be feared, simply because it *is* alien. Though the appearance of the alien/animal-helper in 50s SF does indicate that there is some realignment of attitudes towards nature, it would seem that it is a tentative and partial shift at best.

Having said all this, we must note that the picture that emerges of an overwhelmingly anthropocentric literature, while reasonably accurate in a quantitative sense, is on another level not entirely true.

Anthropomorphizing is one way of denying otherness, yes, but the process also has the effect, ultimately, of breaking down resistance to what really is alien by making it seem familiar and, if not physically "safe" in every case, at least more acceptable—more *manageable*—in conceptual terms. This is what happens in the 50s. In contrast with attitudes toward science during the same period, as the alien becomes less incomprehensible, he becomes less fearsome too. Useful field assistants are part of this process, to be sure, but more significant are some of the *unconscious* adjustments that are taking place underneath.

A striking example of this kind of covert reorientation can be seen in the treatment of such movie monsters of the decade (the horror film clearly being a sub-species of SF, if not always acceptable to the purists as fulfilling prescriptive definitions of the genre) as *The Creature from the Black Lagoon* (1956). Here, in this typically American version of the beauty and the Beast fable, the monster, unlike the traditional BEM, shifts from "other" to "ego"; despite his physical strangeness he is clearly a psychic projection of the protagonists' own inner needs:

> I do not mean to identify the Creature as that shibboleth of critical oversimplification, a "phallic symbol." He is much more than a sublimation, he is a realization of the psychic violence of the phallus itself. He is a *gill-man*, a man-fish, a dweller in the aboriginal bath of the world's youth, a rigid swimmer in the generative fluid. I have mentioned that he is one of the most recognizable and memorable of monsters. And surely part of the reason for this is that his makeup is exactly in tune with his deep-structure function in the plot: to put it simply, his now famous head looks like a penis. And his behavior in the film, an ambiguous meld of canniness and sheerly instinctual reaction, is not symbol as much as it is a hieroglyph, an icon for the infinitely variable but single-minded urging of the libido. [McConnell]

The significance of this cannot be overestimated. It is not just a matter of making the creature more sympathetic—indeed, being identified with subversive impulses, it is in some ways more fearsome even than before—but of normalizing it, establishing significant connections with it that tend to undermine the sense of impregnable psychic integrity characteristic of xenophobia.

The extent to which *Creature* is a departure from established norms can be gauged more easily if we compare it to an earlier version of the same fable, *King Kong* (1933). Both of these movies exploit a similar base situation—a dangerous subhuman creature fascinated by the beauty of a human female—but where *Creature* is clearly a psychodrama of sorts, the earlier film, in celebrating the doublesidedness of nature ("masculine" brute strength and violence juxtaposed with the "feminine" gentleness and sensitivity which are also displayed by the beast), may simply be seen as a conventional variation on a classic pastoral theme. The giant ape, in other words, is simply a personification of natural forces, and the story as a whole illustrates the absolute incompatibility of man with nature in both its hostile *and* its loving guises. *King Kong*, whatever formal sympathy it may invoke for the ape, thus ultimately reaffirms the boundary between ego and other. *Creature*, on the other hand, covertly works to break this boundary down. The whole film, as Gary Wolfe describes it, appears to revolve around a series of barriers symbolic of the known/unknown interface:

> First, there is the barrier of time, established when we learn that the creature is an anachronism apparently produced by some ancient aberration of the laws of evolution. Secondly, there is the barrier whose crossing provides the suspense in the early sequences of the film, that of the frontier of civilization... Third, there is the all-too-familiar barrier between darkness and light, in this case represented not only by day and night (as it is in almost all horror films), but also by the contrast between the shadowy depths of the lagoon itself and its sunlit, mirror-like surface. Related to this, and highly important to the film's visual structure, is the barrier represented by the surface of the water in the lagoon, with the human community represented as the crew of a boat which rests on the surface while the underwater world...is the realm of the creature, or the unknown.

The integrity of *all* these barriers is undermined, however, by the fact that the last, emblematic barrier mentioned by Wolfe, unlike the more literal barriers in *King Kong* (the thick fog that hides his island; the wooden palisade that the natives construct to separate themselves from the beast), is by definition a permeable one. Above all, reinforcing the implications of the creature's grotesque near-humanity, the relation between the two sides of this barrier is called into question by the fact that the water world, as mirror, is in an important sense merely a reflection of the sunlit world above. Even in the mid-50s, when the alien is characteristically portrayed in his most dangerous and repulsive form, therefore, covert levels of implication seem to be preparing him for a more significantly referential role.

It was not, as it turned out, this subversive undercurrent that finally catalyzed the radical shift in attitude toward the SF alien which took place sometime before the 60s. The more profound kind of assimilation barely hinted at in *The Creature From the Black Lagoon* does surface later, along with all its associated ambivalence, but in the meantime another element emerges into prominence by means of which the alien is *domesticated* rather than transformed.

This latter development is perhaps a predictable one. If, as we said above, space voyaging is commonly an analogue for the westering movement, then it seems inevitable that any change in public perception of the original phenomenon—such as crystallized in the 60s with the growth of ecology consciousness—should also affect the conventions in terms of which SF recreates the frontier. If, in space opera, the alien tends to be conceptualized most easily in terms of Indian-as-savage, with only a minor reorientation he is equipped to play the role of Indian-as-victim equally well. The potential, indeed, is there right from the beginning. The Americans, exhilarated by visions of their own masculine prowess and technological wizardry, chose for a long time to de-emphasize this aspect of the metaphor, but the same material, read from only a slightly different perspective, yields a picture of interplanetary colonization quite different from the conventional self-congratulatory saga of the brave space pioneer. We find a particularly striking early demonstration of this "different picture" in British author Olaf Stapleton's *First and Last Man* (1930). It is worth quoting at some length, I think, in order that the full impact of the parallels between fact and fiction—parallels not only in the kind of physical process involved, but also, more interestingly, in the attitudes and responses of the participants—may be appreciated.

It was hoped, of course, that in colonizing Venus mankind would be able to accommodate itself without seriously interfering with the native population. But this proved impossible for two reasons. In the first place, the natives seemed determined to destroy the invaders even if they should destroy themselves in the process. Titanic explosions were engineered, which caused the invaders serious damage, but also strewed the ocean surface with thousands of dead Venerians. Secondly, it was found that, as electrolysis poured more and more free oxygen into the atmosphere, the ocean absorbed some of the potent element back into itself by solution; and this dissolved oxygen had a disastrous effect upon the oceanic organisms—Man dared not stop the process of electrolysis until the atmosphere had become as rich in oxygen as his native air. Long before this state was reached, it was already clear that the Venerians were beginning to feel the effects of the poison, and that in a few thousand years, at most, they would be exterminated. It was therefore determined to put them out of their misery as quickly as possible...

This vast slaughter influenced the mind of the fifth human species in two opposite directions, now flinging it into despair, now rousing it to grave elation. For on the one hand the horror of the slaughter produced a haunting guiltiness in all men's minds, an unreasoning disgust with humanity for having been driven to murder in order to save itself...

On the other hand a very different mood sometimes sprang from the same...sources. After all, the failure of science was a challenge to be gladly accepted; it opened up a wealth of possibilities hitherto unimagined. Even the unalterable distress of the past constituted a challenge; for in some strange manner the present and future, it was said, must transfigure the past. As for the murder of Venerian life, it was, indeed, terrible, but right. It had been committed without hate; indeed, rather in love. For as the navy proceeded with its relentless work, it had gathered much insight into the life of the natives, and had learned to admire, even in a sense to love, while it killed.

Stapleton's "future history," with its thinly disguised recapitulation of past history, reads as one of the most biting indictments of the ruthless opportunism and hypocritical sentimentality characteristic of imperialism to be found in literature. Just as the Americans used the allegorical potential of SF to relive their moment of national glory, here, largely due to Stapleton's flat documentary style, unallayed by either authorial rhetoric or characters inviting identification, the same associations achieve an exactly opposite effect. There are numerous early American accounts of the interplanetary colonization process that superficially sound very similar to Stapleton's except that they lack entirely the ironic undertone which makes the excerpt from *First and Last Man* so devastating. In such books as Henry Kuttner's *Fury* (1947) the heroism displayed by the intrepid pioneers in their battle to defoliate the landscape and exterminate the wildlife is not only obviously *meant* to be taken straight, but the emotional tone—the enthusiastic boosterism—is such as to ensure that this is the impression the reader will probably carry away. The underside of the vision is always *there*, waiting, however. Once disillusionment with the westering myth sets in, the latent irony that emerges in Stapleton scenario soon begins to insinuate itself retrospectively into the interplanetary pioneering saga as a whole, discrediting entirely the naive gusto of space opera and stimulating a general trend to rehabilitate the otherwordly as well as the Terran aborigine as an appropriate act of symbolic expiation for (and repudiation of) the national sins. By the late 50s, the sympathetic image of the alien-as-Indian-as-victim consequently becomes a staple component of SF, taking over from all the various traditional versions of the extraterrestrial to provide one of the most resilient stereotypes in the field.

It is at this point that the noble savage, first as a simple didactic referent, then as a symbolic mediator, and finally as an actual ego-model, becomes possible in American SF.

5.2.1 The Exemplary "Other"

Even before the general rehabilitation of the alien, the one positive role in which an extraterrestrial might (and often did) appear in American SF was an ecological exemplar. In the last section we mentioned P. Schuyler Miller's story "The Cave" (1943). Here, in this early Mars tale, we find a prototypical version of the alien who, in explicit contrast to egotistical man, lives according to a strict law of interspecies cooperation. Ironically, although not surprisingly considering the prevailing attitude of the period, this harmony, far from eighteenth-century "benevolence," is both conceived and described in explicitly *anti*-primitivistic terms. For all that it lacks the standard encomium on landscape, however, like the classic pastoral fable "The Cave" can be read first and foremost as an indictment of pioneer individualism. It is a cornerstone of Martian philosophy, says Miller, that "all living things—all *grekka*—are brothers." Why? *Because to believe otherwise would be fatally foolish.* "Millions of years of unceasing struggle with the forces of an inclement environment on a swiftly maturing and rapidly dying planet have ingrained in the native Martian race, greenlanders and drylanders alike," the conviction that if *any* is to survive, each must be oath-bound to aid every other, be he friend or enemy, "whenever the latter is clearly losing out in a battle with Nature." This is obviously a cautionary message to *un*cooperative humanity.

The plot of the story focuses on a cave in which a number of Martian life forms, from half a dozen small reptiles and mammals through to a humanoid native and a deadly carnivorous *zek*, have taken shelter from a storm. Normally the members of this group would be mutually hostile, but, as the protagonist (the Martian tribesman) recognizes, being all *grekka*, they "knew the law and the brotherhood, and they would keep the truce as long as the storm lasted." When an Earthman blunders into the gathering, however, the very fact that he is an unknown quantity disturbs the natural balance ensured by this age-old and incontrovertible mutual understanding. "What puzzled the young *grak*...was whether man—specifically Harrigan—was *grekka*. If he was, he was an innate member of the brotherhood of living things and subject to its laws. If he wasn't, then he could only be a personification or extension of the inimical First Principle Himself, and hence an inherent enemy." How can this critical question be resolved? Simple. By trial and error. *Harringan's* error. Though the group accepts him provisionally at first, in the end—as we might expect from his own attitude ("Harrigan, of course, knew absolutely nothing of all this. It would probably not have mattered if he had. What some damned animal thought about the Universe was nothing to him.")—he breaks the Law and is killed by the *zek*.

> The matter of water lay at the very root of the law by which all *grekka*—all living things— existed. It was the thing which all must have, which none, under the law, could withhold from another. Without it there could be no life. With it every living thing was given strength to battle on against the eternal foe.
>
> The man had brought water to the cave. Under the law all *grekka* must share in it according to their need. But when the *zek* had gone to take its share, the man had tried to kill it. By that small thing he revealed himself—no *grak*, but one of His evil things. So he had died.

The human is condemned, in other words, by his own obtuseness, his insensitivity, his failure to recognize the rights of any other form of life.

Here in the narrator of this story is perhaps the first real noble alien in American SF. Despite its exemplary demonstration of brotherly cooperation, though, one peculiar characteristic that sets Miller's narrative apart from full-blown versions of the ecology tale is the *relativity* of its didactic message. The prospector here is not condemned as essentially bad (although the association with Evil made through the young tribesman certainly does nudge the story in that direction) so much as merely misguided. In this, of course, Miller was no more than typical of his era. During this particular stage, human self-obsession tends to be criticized (if at all) primarily because it is disfunctional rather than because it is immoral.

The point comes across more clearly in a similar story that appeared a few years later. In Poul Anderson's "Duel on Syrtis" (1951) we again have an opposition between a Martian native and an Earthman, in this case a gamehunter who is pursuing him. Again, too, there is an environmental association. This time, indeed, behind the native's ecological awareness is not merely a pragmatic behavioral precept governing his interrelations with other animals but, reflecting the trends that we have noted elsewhere, a mystical bond with the whole of nature: "The enormous oneness of life on Mars, drawn together against the cruel environment, stirred in his blood...*You do not fight alone*, whispered the desert. *You fight for all Mars, and we are with you.*" Thanks largely to this new, overt animism, the connection between the Martian's nature-harmony and the human's downfall is made even more explicitly here than it was in Miller's story. Thorn bushes impeded the man's hound, a cliffside vine entangles his hunting hawk, a snake jumps up and pulls aside his gun when he aims. Despite the augmented primitivistic echoes, however, the man himself is still not portrayed as a particularly negative character. Indeed, though the pursued native is indubitably noble, in many ways the hunter seems so too. He is not vicious. He is not even crude and ignorant like Miller's protagonist. According to Anderson he is merely acting according to his own nature ("His ancestors had fought under one name or another—viking, Crusador, mercenary, rebel, patriot, whatever was fashionable at the moment. Struggle was in his blood, and in these degenerate days there was little to struggle against save what he hunted"). Notwithstanding our sympathy for the Martian, in fact, the hunter's fairness, his acceptance of risk, his wholehearted respect for his quarry, give the exercise—as in Hemingway's bullfight—a special kind of legitimacy. The point we are left with, consequently, seems to be an argument that although man's lack of responsiveness to the environment is unquestionably a *weakness*, it is in some ways intrinsic to his identity as a man.

This is a point that comes up with some frequency in early 50s SF. Even in that small minority of stories which give us a positive alien (and despite the general anthropocentricity noted above there are always a few, especially early in the decade), there seems to be a reluctance to condemn human flaws in any absolute way simply because they *are* human, good or bad. We might note a similarity to Cooper's qualified primitivism here, but the phenomenon goes even further than that. In Lawrence Manning's "Good-bye, Ilha" (1952), for instance, an ultra-civilized, ultra-rational alien is so infatuated with the crude, youthful vitality of a Terran exploration team that despite his decision that their savagery is such that they cannot be allowed to stay on the planet ("you must not risk our entire civilization merely because I have taken a liking to these monsters—and it is a real risk, for they are truly dangerous"), he himself resolves to go into exile with them. The idea that the gift of laughter is at once the mark and the justification of humanity is one that turns up time and again.

Even more revealing, perhaps, is Frank M. Robinson's "The Fire and the Sword" (1951), where the discovery of an entire culture of noble aliens leads, ironically, to disaster for the human observers sent to study it—simply because of their own sense of racial inferiority. The message in this story—and in a sense it is an explicit anti-noble savage fable—is that man, being stuck with a full slate of innate imperfections can only become unhappy and frustrated when confronted with what for him is an unattainable ideal.

"The environment is perfection, and so are the people, or at least as near to perfection as it's possible to get. An intelligent people who have as much technology as they desire, living simply with themselves and each other. A fluke of nature, perhaps. No criminals, no insane, no neurotics. A perfect cultural pattern. Tunpesh is a paradise. You didn't want to leave, neither did I, and neither did Pendleton."

Templin turned on him. "So it was paradise. Would it have been criminal if I had stayed there? Who would it have hurt?"

"It would have hurt you," Eckert said gravely. "Because the Tunpeshans would never have accepted you. We're too different, Ray. We're too aggressive, too pushy, too persistent. We're not—perfect. You see, no matter how long we stayed there, we would never have fit in."

From one point of view, this story might very well be a critique of America's whole historical obsession with ideality. In fact, however, what it does present is a late and unusual version of the pioneer mentality. Keep moving on. The quest is more important than the prize. More indirectly: the crudeness of mankind being appropriate to the frontier condition, it is better to accept our flaws than to hunger after an inhuman perfection. At this time, in fact, America was determinedly self-referencing; whether complacently or despairingly (depending on the writer's temperament), most SF appeared to *deny* the ultimate relevance of any such external referent as the noble savage might represent.

It is not until the alien-as-good-Indian stereotype becomes more widely established—along with the primitivistic trends that in part inspired it—that we notice much of a change. Clifton and Apostolides' "We're Civilized" (1953), an early version of the dispossession theme, is still primarily a cautionary tale (Earthmen who fail to recognize the cultural integrity of the Martians are themselves subsequently dispossessed by a superior race), but by the late 50s it is the *ethic* of the pioneering process that has become a focal concern. A number of stories during this later period, moreover, explicitly attack exactly the anthropocentric assumptions that we have been examining. In both Poul Anderson's "Sister Planet" (1959) and H. Beam Piper's *Little Fuzzy* (1962), for instance, the problem of recognizing alien forms of intelligence, alien behavioral norms, alien values as qualitatively equivalent, if different, becomes a major theme. The later book is rather too sentimental to make its point very powerfully. The "fuzzies" are small, cute, furry creatures who, despite their toolmaking abilities and quick learning capacities, are almost denied sapience because they don't appear to have any language. The seriousness of the question is obscured, however, by the overt villainy of the anti-fuzzy faction (a corporation that will lose its planetary charter if it is proven that there are sapient natives on the scene), and then sidestepped altogether when it turns out that the fuzzies do communicate normally after all, at an ultra high frequency. The fuzzies, in other words, are no real threat to anthropomorphic definitions. In Anderson's story, though, the limitations of anthropomorphizing are presented in a much more serious way. The protagonist, convinced that the friendly dolphin-like creatures encountered on Venus are intelligent, but equally convinced that the strangeness, the *unhumanness* of their culture will prevent this from being realized (they have no technology, they are not aggressive, they would rather play than work), decides—after much soul-searching, of course—to destroy their underwater community as a warning, so they (unlike the Indians) will not co-operate in their own exploitation and thus hasten their own cultural demise. "Sister Planet," aside from its implication (similar to Piper's book) that greed will always give the human entrepreneur a motive for failing to recognize aliens as intelligent beings with equal rights, leaves the question open whether it is *ever* possible for even a disinterested observer to respond to "otherness" *except* in anthropomorphic terms. The conceptual vocabulary that would make comprehension, let alone communication feasible is just lacking, it seems.

In the light of these problems, one might wonder if it is possible for an alien to become a noble savage—defined specifically in terms of referential function—at all. The aliens in the first story cited here, being anthropomorphized, are accessible but—inevitability perhaps—inferior. Like the Indian himself in many traditional presentations, they are, in other words, though sapient, closer to children than to adults. In Anderson's story, in contrast, the problem is just the opposite. The aliens are simply *too* alien to provide a referent of any real relevance. In both cases, moreover, they are presented primarily in terms of victimization. They serve a didactic function all right, but only in the negative sense that their very existence stimulates negative behavior in man which the reader, recognizing, is henceforth supposed to eschew. This, unfortunately, does nothing for the alien's own moral authority. If his association with the Indian has made him more sympathetic, there is in fact a very real question whether the historical-symbolic identification with defeat concomitantly acquired is not such a dominant element that it virtually eliminates the possibility of any more positive role. Theoretically the alien is not, like the Indian, diminished by the inevitably of degeneration entailed by a real historical existence (on a fresh planet there is always the chance that the whites might behave differently or even that the Indians might beat the pioneers), but it is possible that the metaphoric bond is as strong a determinant and as much of a limitation as the deflating shadow cast by reality. The felt immanence of national experience that energizes the new image of the extraterrestrial, in other words, possibly also constricts this image even before the fact.

Is this inevitable? Zenna Henderson's "Things" (1960), although constructed around a situation that cannot help but evoke the stereotyped encounter between red and white in America, fights against our sense of *déja vu* at least insofar as the one native whose greed and curiosity opens the door to the invader is repudiated definitively by his tribe.

"But see!" cried Deci. "With these strange things our coveti can rule all the valley and beyond and beyond!"

"Why?"

"Why?" echoed Deci. "To take all we want. To labor no more save to ask and receive. To have power—"

"Why?" Veti's eyes still questioned. "We have enough. We are not hungry. We are clothed against the changing seasons. We work when work is needed. We play when work is done. Why do we need more?"

. . .

"All change is not progress," rumbled Tefu, his hands hiding his blindness.

"Like it or not," shouted Deci. "Tomorrow the Strangers come! You have your choice, all of you!" His arm circled the crowd. "Keep to your homes like Pegu or come forward with your devi and find me a power, a richness—"

"Or move the coveti again," said Dobi. "Away from betrayal and foolish greed. We have a third choice."

Deci caught his breath.

"Veti?" his whisper pled. "Veti? We do not need the rest of the coveti..."

. . .

So knowing Deci dead the coveti turned from him. There was for memory of him only an uncertainty to Veti's feet and a wondering shock in Veti's eyes as she turned with the others to prepare to move the coveti.

The wind came and poured over the dust and the things and Deci.

And Deci lay waiting for his own breath to stop.

Unfortunately the escape hinted at in this finale is undercut by what, inevitably, we bring to the story from elsewhere. There is too strong an echo of Simms here. Matawan and Sanutee disowned their foolish son, too, and while this repudiation preserved their own integrity, it did not in the end do their race any good. Where one is vulnerable, all are vulnerable. Henderson's natives themselves seem to sense the ultimate futility of their flight. " 'Benefits!' spat Dobi. 'Death!' His foot spurned the weapon in the dust. 'Madness!' The flask gurgled as it moved. 'Vanity!' Dust clouded across the mirror and streaked the shining fabric. 'For such you have betrayed us to death.' "

What of stories where the historical association is less explicit? The problem is a lack of consensus about what, outside of his identification with the Indian, the new exemplary alien should represent. In a few stories there is an attempt to equate *reason* with nature, but the success of this is debatable, partly because of the conflicting association of rationality with science but more particularly because of the weight of those things to which it is *opposed*. James Blish's *A Case of Conscience* (1958) provides a striking case in point. In this novel Earthmen are confronted with what appears to be a truly paradisial planet (" 'the closest correspondence is to the Earth in its pre-Adamic period, before the coming of the first glaciers' ") populated by a race of aliens who are about as noble as it would be possible to be (" 'There are no criminals, no deviates, no aberrations of any kind. The people are not standardized—our own very bad and partial answer to the ethical dilemma—but instead are highly individual. They choose their own life courses without constraint—yet somehow no antisocial act of any kind is ever committed.' "). So what could possibly be wrong? " '[Y]our Lithian is a creature of logic,' " says Blish's most sympathetic protagonist, a xenobiologist who is also a Jesuit priest. " 'Unlike Earthmen of all stripes, he has no gods, no myths, no legends. He has no belief in the supernatural—or, as we're calling it in our barbarous jargon these days, the "paranormal." He has no traditions. He has no tabus. He has no faiths, except for an impersonal belief that he and his lot are indefinitely improvable. He is as rational as a machine.' " Even if we are not likely to agree with Father Ruiz-Sanchez that goodness without grace, being a theological impossibility, is a sign of Satanic influence (the Great Tempter tempting humans to doubt the necessity of divine intervention), there are a number of items on this list which we are accustomed to consider as among the more admirable, or at least interesting, aspects of humanity.

Blish never really succeeds in solving the problem he has posed. A young Lithian comes to earth and grows up to be a notable troublemaker, but whether this is because he is by nature demonic or whether he has been unbalanced by an insane environment is not entirely clear. Also not clear is how we are to interpret the ending. Lithia is destroyed in an immense explosion, but the author does not finally specify whether we are to believe that this is the result of Ruiz-Sanchez's exorcism or to blame the nuclear experimentation that his associate is carrying on there. At the conclusion of the book, consequently, far from enlightened we are simply left wondering: Who really is the devil here? In Harry Harrison's somewhat similar story, "The Streets of Ashekelon" (1962), there would seem to be no question—perhaps because of the increased authority that primitivism picked up during those few intervening years. A missionary corrupts a community of "rational" natives by introducing them (against the advice of the local trader, an atheist and their friend) not only to God but to sin. In attempting to recreate the crucifixion as a mistaken act of faith, these erstwhile innocents are actually able to recreate only the Fall (" 'Then we will not be saved? We will not become pure?' " " 'You were pure,' Garth said, in a voice somewhere between a sob and a laugh. 'That's the horrible ugly dirty part of it. You were pure. Now you are...' " " 'Murderers,' Itin said, and the water ran down from his lowered head and streamed away into the darkness."). Harrison's *ostensibly* less ambiguous treatment does not answer the questions raised by Blish, however, so much as it merely ignores them. And these questions are critical ones. The early 60s vision of the noble alien, to the extent that it does manage to escape from the more simplistic aspects of the Indian stereotype, seems to revolve around the problem of what "innocence" and "reason" and "natural" really imply. Before the noble alien can become a truly effective literary symbol, his character—rather than merely borrowing from the conventions of the past—has to be substantially redefined. Human enough to seem relevant but strange enough to represent otherness, aligned with nature but not too blatantly victimized, sharing the Indian's *potential* nobility but not his *actual* weakness, the exemplary extraterrestrial must walk a fine line.

One of the most interesting and certainly the best known putative noble savage figures of the decade is not, strictly speaking, an alien at all. Michael Valentine Smith, the "Man from Mars" of Robert Heinlein's *Stranger in a Strange Land* (1961) is, like Cooper's Leatherstocking, a link between two different worlds. An Earthman by genetic inheritance, through a fluke of history he was born and brought up in complete isolation from his own kind on Mars. This is not, to be sure, the same sort of dichotomy that Leatherstocking incarnates, and although Heinlein utilizes it in much the same way to set up thematic oppositions, there is a valid question about whether, in fact, Smith *can* properly be categorized as the kind of "primitive" hero that noble savagery implies. Even leaving aside the objection we have raised in the past that a central protagonist is generally too complex to play such a formal referential role (this particular protagonist, in fact, is developed more as a *type* than an individual in spite of his thematic centrality in the book), it must be admitted that Smith does not exhibit any obvious connections or sympathies with what we have traditionally considered to be the realm of nature. Indeed, in practical terms, despite his initial ignorance of earthly ways and *apparent* helplessness, he turns out to be a relatively sophisticated, highly educated, *advanced* human being. So how, we might ask, can this expatriate earthling, for all his demonstrable nobility, be considered a *savage* in any way?

There are two reasons for making this identification. The first is the author's attitude. Heinlein's Martians are themselves mixed figures. Although the masculine adults without a doubt epitomize civilization with their enormous wisdom and vast powers, the young female nymphs spend the first few years of their lives in a total state of nature which only the fittest survive. Martian life is therefore more "natural" than its Terran counterpart—and this, for a Social Darwinist like Heinlein, means more "reasonable" as well. Coming from such a background, consequently, young Smith could be considered to represent some kind of standard of naturalness simply by association. More important than Heinlein's own ostensible primitivism, however, Michael Valentine Smith can be considered a valid noble savage figure because he demonstrates right down the line those qualities that exemplify *what 1960s counter culture considered "nature" to be.* Indeed, the reason *Stranger in a Strange Land* was so enormously popular among young people in the 60s was that it not only focused a lot of their anti-social energies into a form compatible with their primitivistic leanings, but provided a wish-fulfilling fantasy tailored specifically to satisfy the diverse urgings of the new hippy mythos. The 60s version of the noble savage, around whom this fantasy revolves, might thus be summarized as follows:

Mental. The most striking thing about Smith is his extraordinary mental powers. He is capable of the whole gamut of popular psi talents and a few more besides: telekinesis, teleportation, levitation, astral projection, interdimensional displacement, clairvoyance, and so on. We have already noted that these phenomena tend, in the 60s, to be associated with "nature." The attractive aspect of Heinlein's conception is the extent to which it simultaneously reinforces and democratizes this prejudice. *Anyone*, it is implied, is capable of Smith's virtual omnipotence. It is only a matter of countering the psychically crippling influence of modern society and releasing *natural* aptitudes. The dream of being invulnerable is, of course, a common basis for fantasy, and Heinlein provides a way for his readers to indulge this vicariously while yet repudiating the tainted masculine powers of militarism and technology (an important consideration during the 60s). To Smith, guns carry an essential "wrongness"; he responds instinctively by making them go "away." As the triumph of the natural over the unnatural, this is one of the most significant acts in the book.

Physical. Body and mind are totally interdependent in Heinlein's view; Michael's body, therefore, will do or be whatever he wants it to do or be. In one sense this is the old idea of "harmony" between the physical and the mental, Moira and Themis. On another level, it simply represents a different aspect of the wishful dream: control over what is normally beyond control; even, it is implied, an ultimate escape from the limitations of mortality. To whatever end, however, Heinlein's conception of his protagonist clearly gives an important place to good animal health and vitality, especially insofar as these offer a primary means of combatting (denying, transcending) any unnatural repression or distortion of physical forces, whether by psychic stunting, by external coercion, or even by age. Above and beyond this, Smith's happy fatalism and patient responsiveness offer an effective counter to the stress- and anxiety-related ills of normal twentieth-century existence ("He...simply waited in a fashion which may be described as 'patient' only because human language does not embrace Martian attitudes. He held still with quiet happiness because his brother had said that he would return. He was prepared to wait, without moving, without doing anything, for several years."). From the point of view of Heinlein's readers this passiveness offers not only a satisfactory rationalization of their own social ineffectuality but also an emblematic expression of their essential superiority to the goal-oriented, ulcer-ridden aggressors of the corporate elite. "Coolness" is health.

Social. The fundamental rule for social interaction embodied by Smith is tolerance. Dangerously warped individuals must, for the good of the whole, be done away with—destroyed, not imprisoned, which is unnatural ("Killing a man may be necessary. Confining him is an offense against his integrity.")— but short of this extremity, virtually anything goes. The two primary areas in which this principle is demonstrated in *Stranger* are religion and sex. As far as the former is concerned, the basic tenet is that every individual is himself divine ("Thou art God!"), so any religion expressing a sense of the sacral nature of human life (which, according to the book, would be all the traditional ones plus a number of others normally dismissed as "cults") is consonant with every other. With respect to sex, the attitude is very similar. Any sexual act—singular, plural, or sequential—is good as long as it is performed with love. Since love is, or should be, the basic social cement, in fact, the rule would seem to be the more the better. Beyond these two basics, Heinlein's idea of utopia would seem to imply some sort of tribal unit governed internally by communistic sharing of all real and emotional property but externally by as much competitiveness as the individuals enjoy. There is a considerable (apparently approving) emphasis on the "carnie" concept of conning the "marks," in fact. Heinlein is against the corporation, but clearly favors capitalism of the most extreme and fundamental kind. It is easy to see how this combination paves the way for the communal lifestyle and cottage industry with which so many young people experimented in the 60s.

Moral. This last element is in a sense prior to all the rest, since it provides a philosophical justification not only for everything Smith does but also for everything he might do. Apparently based on a theory of innate moral capacity and natural goodness not significantly different from that which was so enthusiastically embraced back in the eighteenth century, *Stranger in a Strange Land* seems to insist that the noble savage—the wholly natural individual—will instinctively "grok" (a verb which, as "drink," "know," "love," "understand," etc., seems to entail a kind of total comprehension through sympathetic identification something like Buber's I-Thou relation) the rightness or wrongness of any situation, and automatically act morally in response to this perception. In practice it seems to offer a blanket justification for any behavior based on a sincere conviction. The key to this philosophy is a conception of "innocence" which has nothing to do with either knowledge or performance but only motivation. One may even commit murder—which, in fact, Smith does, frequently and without qualm—and still be innocent, as long as the act is neither malicious nor undisciplined nor self-interested. Heinlein underlines what he means in using the word "innocent" in this context—and incidentally demonstrates the book's debt to classic primitivism—by comparing Smith to a poisonous snake: harmless as long as he isn't threatened; deadly when provoked; but in either case, since he acts only according to his nature (which is, of course, by definition divine), totally without sin or shame or guilt.

In many ways *Stranger in a Strange Land* represents the same kind of cultural norm for its period that Cooper's Leatherstocking tales do for his. Interestingly, Heinlein is just as flawed as a writer as Cooper was. His early books lean toward the clichés of space opera; his later ones are propaganda only thinly disguised as fiction. In both cases his characterization is minimal; his plots stereotyped; his ideas hackneyed, inconsistent, and far too obtrusive. But this is perhaps to be unfair to Heinlein. He has the storyteller's talent of rising above his technique. And in *Stranger,* by some strange osmosis, he hit upon a combination that reflects with particular vividness the covert hopes and concerns of the young people of the day. Again as in Cooper's case, Heinlein's achievement seems to have been at least partly unintentional. Heinlein's politics (old-style American conservatism) are in many ways quite at odds with those of the group who responded so enthusiastically to his book, but Michael Valentine Smith—like Natty Bumppo; indeed, like most mythic figures—subsumes so many incompatible elements from passiveness to powerfulness, capitalism to communism, prominiscuity to exclusiveness, tolerance to moral infallibility, that he apparently *reconciles* many of the most bothersome cultural conflicts of his time.

There is one further point we should note about *Stranger in a Strange Land* that has considerable significance for our study as a whole. In our examination of past literature we noted, with respect to both eighteenth-century Britain and nineteenth-century America, that there was a tendency for the noble savage figure, as it gathered authority, to change from a mere conventional counter to the excesses of civilization (used primarily satirically), to an exemplary figure representing certain positive attitudes and behavioral norms associated with nature (used didactically), to a charismatic figure who actually appears to effect the mediation which earlier was only a referential abstraction; from a formal role (static, emotionally neutral) to a cultural symbol (dynamic, emotionally energized) or even—especially in America—a *myth*. It was this latter stage which saw the development of both the Last of the Mohicans type and the exiled frontiersman in nineteenth-century American literature, sacrificial victims on the altar of progress, scapegoats for the national guilt. It is this stage, too, that *Stranger in a Strange Land* represents. Smith's Christ-like apotheosis focuses psychic energy in the same way as those earlier ritual purgations, but with the additional advantage of being truly rather than only nominally self-impelled, and thus free of public guilt. This is not the end, though. In the earlier period, the noble savage disappeared almost as soon as he acquired this kind of numen, as if he had been given too great a weight of significance to bear. Cooper tried to go one step beyond symbolic mediation to use him as a serious moral model—the natural next step—but in spite of his charismatic appeal, the young Leatherstocking, as we noted, was implicated in too many morally ambiguous but socially immanent issues having to do with racism and the progress/primitivism debate to be able to carry off this focal role with total success. In SF, however, where it is at least *theoretically* possible to achieve an overt displacement to a morally neutral arena without sacrificing covert associations, the noble savage should be able to combine both his conventional and charismatic functions to become a true effectuator where he was only a passive exemplar before. And he does.

The book that best exemplifies this new development in the noble savage is one which, significantly, was almost as much of a cult favorite in the late 60s as Heinlein's was slightly earlier: Frank Herbert's *Dune* (1965), a novel of adventure set in the far future against a background of galactic feudalism on a desert planet called Arrakis. Without going into the complexities of either the plot or the political background to the book (both of which are intriguing and skillfully handled; Herbert has all Heinlein's storytelling ability, plus a far greater technical proficiency and imaginative reach), we can simply say that this novel is a form of the classic *bildungsroman*, the education of a king. And this is where the noble savage comes in. Conventional modes of training a young prince in weaponry, politics, diplomacy, and the courtly arts are not neglected, but most of this aspect of Paul Atreides' education is simply assumed, completed before the beginning of the book. The one element that makes the difference between a well-endowed but not particularly extraordinary young nobleman and the great charismatic political/religious leader, Muad'Dib, is a sojourn in the wilderness which, like both the Hebrews' archetypal pilgrimage and Christ's later ordeal, both releases and restructures the seeds of greatness in the boy, transforming him into a very special kind of man.

The tutelary genii of Paul Atreides' initiation are the Fremen, the desert nomads who live in the most savage regions of a planet which, in terms of both climate and geography, is inhospitable as a whole. After Paul's father, the ruling Duke of Arrakis, is deposed and killed in a coup by a feudal competitor, the boy and his mother take refuge with these people, and it is to a significant extent the lessons learned from their way of life which, added to Paul's own considerable powers, give him the personal resources to win back his birthright— and more—in the end. On the simplest level it is the desert itself, an environment harsh and demanding to an extreme, that stimulates Paul's development of the superior capacities he needs to survive. It is the Freman, however, who offers him the specific behavioral model that proves so effective not only in the immediate context of the Arrakeen desert but in the political arena at large.

What qualities does this model imply? As in Heinlein's noble savage there are strong associations with older conventions but some of the emphases are new. The Freman is not the gay and innocent eighteenth-century child of nature, but the hardy barbarian of earlier, sterner climes. The first things Paul acquires from Freman culture, therefore, are basic survival traits such as conservatism (every drop of moisture must be conserved in a desert environment: "water discipline," which presupposes discipline, care, and restraint on *every* level, is consequently the most basic law of the land), alertness (in an ultra-hostile environment one must be totally sensitized to his surroundings; to be surprised is to be dead), subtlety (one cannot battle the storm but one can learn to flow *with* it, attaining one's goal in a roundabout way), decisiveness (hesitation kills), loyalty (the tribe is only as strong as its weakest member), and that ruthlessness which is only the other side of perfect justice. Aside from anything else, therefore, what Paul learns from the Freman is how to be a *survivor*, which means, in that environment, a superb fighting and killing machine.

If this were all, of course, the Freman would be no different than the pioneer, battling *against* nature instead of living in harmony with it, and thus could not exemplify mediation in any real sense. There is, however, a second aspect of Paul's desert experience, again given focus by Freman culture, that is ultimately far more important to him than the martial skills he acquires. In a way that the traditional noble savage was never quite able to manage, the Freman reconciles the conflict between the masculine and feminine modes. He is not only nature's *master*, in other words, but—more importantly—her *servant* as well. The ultimate goal of the whole Freman culture, in fact, is to transform Arrakis into a paradise, not by wrenching it out of its natural rhythms but by working *with* those rhythms; using the insights provided by a visiting empire ecologist to become an intrinsic *part* of the ecological system, influencing it lovingly, gently, patiently from within. This goal necessitates not only such traditional attributes as a reverence for and a responsiveness to the processes of nature, but an extraordinary breadth and depth of vision capable of encompassing complex and shifting ecological relationships on a planetary scale. " 'A planet's life is a vast, tightly interwoven fabric. Vegetation and animal changes will be determined at first by the raw physical forces we manipulate. As they establish themselves...our changes will become controlling influences in their own right—and we will have to deal with them, too!' " The second level of Paul's desert education, then, is a lesson in the necessity of and means for transcending the egocentric perspective to view (and manipulate) all phenomena *systematically*, regardless of the context—an obvious advantage for one who would be a ruler.

Finally, going beyond the specific physical and intellectual insights offered by his primitive mentors, Paul also experiences in the desert environment a kind of spiritual growth that would be impossible anywhere else. In an immediate sense his transformation into a prophet—the triggering of his paranormal abilities—seems simply the result of a coincidental and unforeseen reaction, due to a peculiar genetic inheritance, to the drug that the Freman use in their religious rituals. In a larger sense, however, his birth into awareness is made to appear an intrinsic part of the desert experience as a whole. This may be partly because of our conventional coupling of *psi* powers with primitivism in the context of SF. It is also, however, due to Herbert's skillful manipulation of covert cultural associations throughout his book. As Scholes (1975) points out, "The imaginary sands of Dune owe a good deal to the real sands of Arabia, and somewhere behind this novel stands T.E. Lawrence's *Seven Pillars of Wisdom*, in which Lawrence speculated on the curious propensity of the semitic geography for producing prophets and mystics." The allusion to Lawrence is a critical one, inasmuch as it suggests what is undoubtedly a major element in Herbert's success in making Paul's experience convincing. As Scholes intimates, it is not merely the real, historical desert culture that Dune suggests to us but the *mythic* desert, the desert that we see through the eyes of past visionaries from the Old Testament prophets to Lawrence himself. "Lawrence's desert is as far from England as...Grendel's cave from Hrothgar's brightly lit halls," says Paul Zweig. "The desert is 'elsewhere,' it is the essential elsewhere, and the desert traveller, like the archaic adventurer, is for Lawrence a traveller between the worlds." The Freman, imbued with this legendary stature—and this mythic capacity—by the multiple echoes in Herbert's novel, hence seems to us the true mediator between "ego" and "other," making the mystical apotheosis *accessible* for Paul.

The thing that *Dune* doesn't do is offer us one, single, memorable noble savage who lives beyond the pages of the book the way Chingachgook does. "The Freman" is an abstraction, although some of the individual Fremen in the book—like Stilgar; first Paul's mentor, then his lieutenant—are compelling figures in their own right. Perhaps it is because they are *too* credible as individuals that they lose—*qua* individuals—some of their potential archetypal power. Or perhaps it is only because where Cooper's "heroes" are nonentities who detract not at all from the charisma of the referential figures, Paul Atreides is such a complex, forceful, and enormously fascinating character himself that he is bound to dominate the book. In many ways, though, even as an abstraction, the Freman is still one of the most successful noble savages in American literature. Certainly insofar as Herbert has been able to balance masculine aggression and feminine sensitivity in his exemplary culture, combining them into a force that works *with* nature, nurturing *and* controlling it simultaneously, his version of primitivism is both an emotional and an aesthetic success. Interestingly enough, however, in another of his novels Herbert takes the opposite approach to his primitivist model, and renders the noble savage in as much individual detail as we could ever ask.

Soul Catcher (1972) is not in fact, strictly speaking, SF, but if we assume that the protagonist of the book is not simply insane—that the experience depicted is meant to be taken as real, objective—the fantasy element sets it off from both mainstream literature and the Indian-western genre. In any case, here, finally, is a literary Indian who, if any, might be Chingachgook's spiritual heir. Indeed it is as if the *real* Indian so lovingly delineated in all those 60s novels—the domesticated, integrated, *white* Indian of today—were suddenly and quite literally transformed, as Clark Kent is transformed into Superman, back into the *mythic* Indian, the noble savage, who vanished as *possibility* as the wagon trains rolled across the plains. The idea is an appealing one. As Herbert has handled it, avoiding the pitfalls of either sentimental cosiness or ironic detachment, it makes a compelling little book.

To put it simply, Charles Hobuhet is an Indian college student who is stung by a spirit bee (*Soul Catcher*), transformed into a shaman, and commanded to a ritual act which will effect the psychic renewal of his people. "He heard the message of Tamanawis, the greatest of spirits, as a drumbeat matching the beat of his heart: 'You must find a white. You must find a total innocent. You must kill an innocent of the whites. Let your deed fall upon this world. Let your deed be a single heavy hand which clutches the heart. The whites must feel it. They must hear it. An innocent for all of our innocents.' " Melodramatic? To be sure. And in the beginning (such is Herbert's sure touch) we are allowed to be as sceptical as we wish. Despite this scepticism, however, like his own people who come after him prepared to scoff and denigrate, like the boy himself who is his chosen victim (the 13-year-old son of a diplomat), throughout the course of the book as we get to know *Katsuk* (Hobuhet's new identity)—a spare, controlled, underplayed characterization with just the right mixture of the ordinary and the uncanny—we find ourselves coming to accept Herbert's noble savage at his own valuation. Having reaching this point of willingly suspending our disbelief, we then find that the novel offers us a classic demonstration of the exemplary function of the noble savage as ideally it should be. The young victim must be brought to the proper awareness if he is to be a fitting sacrifice—it is no mere murder that the ritual requires— and in watching the process of education we see exactly that release from egotism for which we have looked to the noble savage all along.

Katsuk marks the beginning of the ritual journey with a promise that illuminates the full potentiality of his role:

"I want to go back now," says the boy.

Katsuk shook his head. "We all want to go back, Innocent Hoquat. We want the place where we can deal with our revelation and weep and punish our senses uselessly. Your talk and your world sours me. You have only words...I will give you back your own knowledge of what the universe knows. I will make you know and feel. You really will understand. You will be surprised. What you learn will be what you thought you already knew."

"Please, can't we go now?"

"You wish to run away. You think there is no place within you to receive what I will give you. But it will be driven into your heart by the thing itself...Hoquat, I promise you this: you will see directly through to the thing at its beginning. You will hear the wilderness without names. You will feel colors and shapes and the temper of this world... I will fill you with fear and awe."

The boy, of course, doesn't at this point understand anything that his captor is talking about. He isn't even aware that he is lacking. Revealing the definitive characteristic of his race, he clings desperately to individuality. "The madman had called him Hoquat [white man], had forced him to answer to that name. More than anything else, this concentrated a core of fury in [him]... He thought: *My name is David. David, not Hoquat.*" This, then, is where it starts: the precondition—the predicament—that the ritual must counter. Just as much as his Puritan ancestors, David-not-Hoquat resists vigorously the subversive suggestions of Moira. Fortunately or unfortunately he lacks the socio-religious bulwarks with which those ancestors protected their precious integrity. It is consequently inevitable that as he gradually realizes the full extent of his helplessness he will become more receptive to Katsuk's influence.

The first lessons are pragmatic ones:

"Why are you trembling?" Katsuk asked.

"I...I'm cold."

"...Are you hungry?"

"Y-yes."

"Then I will teach you how to live in my land. Many things are provided here to sustain us—roots, sweet ants, fat grubs, flowers, bulbs, leaves. You will learn these things and become a man of the woods."

"A w-woodsman?"

Katsuk shook his head from side to side. "A man of the woods. That is much different."

Note that here David's only conception of how to approach the wilderness is based on the idea of the pioneer. Learning the difference between a woodsman and man of the woods is in a sense a prerequisite to everything else he must learn. It is also, however, only a beginning. As his experience starts to show some effects, we realize that the full transformation required by the ritual is by no means a simple one.

There was a new grace in things the boy did. He was fitting himself into this life. When it was time for silence, he was silent. When it was time to drink, he drank. Hunger came upon him in its proper order. The spirit of the wilderness had seeped into him, beginning to say that it was right for such a one to be here. The rightness of it had not yet become complete, though. This was still a hoquat lad. The cells of his flesh whispered rebellion and rejection of the earth around him. At any moment he might strike out and become once more the total alien to this place. The thing lay in delicate balance.

Katsuk imagined himself as a person who adjusted that balance. The boy must not demand food before its time. Thirst must be quenched only in the rhythm of thirst. The shattering intrusion of a voice must be prevented by willing it not to happen.

Willing it not to happen! The implications of a statement like this are considerable. And not merely because of the power it assumes. Entailed if not wholly predetermined by the monologic of the myth, Katsuk's function will obviously be satisfied by nothing less than a total reorientation of attitude. Certainly it is more than a matter of Leatherstocking teaching a few woodcraft tricks to the tenderfoot. " 'You need to know how to live that you may die correctly,' " he tells the boy. To *live*. No mean chore for a child of *this* parentage. Why? The white man, says Katsuk, has isolated himself in an artificial universe that obscures all natural answers. His condition is hence one of constant paradox. "In terms of the flesh, you whites act upon fragmented beliefs. You fall therefrom into loneliness and violence. You do not support your fellows, yet complain of being unsupported. You scream for freedom while rationalizing your own self-imposed limitations. You exist in constant tension between tyranny and victimization." Here is where the *real* lesson starts. It is only by recognizing his own complicity in such wrongheadedness that David can begin to free himself of its tyranny. Its power to delude. By what means does Katsuk trigger this all-important recognition? Once he is detached from all that is familiar it is only a matter of time before the boy, almost of himself, loses his grip on the white man's sense of separateness that prevents him from accepting his role as a member of his race.

"I care!" Katsuk touched his chest. "They came into our land—*our* land! They cut the underbrush to decorate their flower arrangements. They pile the logs high that should be left as trees. They take fish for sport that should feed our families. All the while, these hoquat do the one thing we must not forgive: They remain complacent in their evil. They are so satisfied that they are doing right. Damn these fiends!"

"Some of them were born here," Ish protested. "They love this land."

"Ahhh," Katsuk sighed. "They love our land even while they kill it and us upon the land."

Guilt filled David. He thought: *I am Hoquat.*

Renewed by his epiphany, David finally does become capable of the true woodsman's attitude: resigned, responsive, submitting to the rhythms of the earth. On a superficial — intellectual — level he still expresses reservations, but it is obvious that on a more profound level he has changed.

David felt no special worry. It was a time for storing up memories. A wonderful curiosity drove him. This would end in time and he would have a glorious adventure to tell. He would be a hero to his friends—kidnapped by a wild Indian! Katsuk was wild, of course...and insane. But there were limits to his insanity.

The light on the stranded logs had become like sunshine on autumn grass. David watched Katsuk and the hypnotic flow of the river. He came to the decision this might be one of the happiest days of his life: Nothing was demanded of him; he had been cold, now he was warm; he had been hungry and had eaten... Soon, they would eat again.

In the end, the boy chooses to stay with his mentor when he might have escaped. Awakened to a whole new set of possibilities under Katsuk's influence, he submits to his captivity, to his ritual role, *voluntarily*.

What does it mean for us, this odd apotheosis? Actually, what Herbert has done in this book is simply to redeem the Indian from his historical defeat and degradation by giving him a credible symbolic victory, thus, like Kesey, "blowing him up" to the stature that should rightfully be his. As we watch the emotional growth of the young victim, consequently, we ourselves are also *educated*, coaxed into the attitude that the symbolic mediation offered by this archetypal figure (in whatever incarnation) requires if it is to work any magic.

The spirits had summoned him to perform an artistic act. It would be a refinement of blood revenge, a supreme example to be appreciated by this entire world. His own people would understand this much of it. His own people had blood revenge locked into their history. They would be stirred in their innermost being. They would recognize why it had been done in the ancient way—a mark upon raw earth, an incantation, a bow untouched by steel, a death arrow with a stone head, the down of sea ducks sprinkled upon the victim. They would see the circle and this would lead them to the other meanings within this act.

What of the hoquat, though? Their primitive times lay farther back, although they were more violent. They had hidden their own violence from their surface awareness and might not recognize Katsuk's ritual. Realization would seep upward from the spirit side, though. The very nature of the Innocent's death could not be denied.

Realization does seep up—and more. It is not a purely intellectual exercise— nor are we, as in *Dune*, simply observers of the mediated transformation. Through our participation in the fictional experience, there is a sense in which we too *become* the victim; his death is thus an act, not just an event. As in the past, submission to nature is annihilation, but this time it seems just and proper, a welcome escape from the prison of our white man's isolation. Guided, as we should be, by the noble savage—no longer scapegoat but effectuator— we cathartically relinquish our kernelled sense of self.

5.2.2 The "Other" as "Ego"

Despite the apparent success of Herbert and a few others, the 60s noble savage, like those of the past, contained the seeds of his own demise. The directness and intensity of the confrontation with nature demanded by this most recent revival of primitivism unfortunately served to highlight the ambiguities that relation has always implied. Indeed, the same years that brought Katsuk to maturity also saw, as if in reaction, the birth of a countertrend that tended to discredit all the expectations that such a ritual mediation, fictional or real, necessarily represents.

One of the most serious problems that came to the fore during this period involved the fantasied redemption of the meeting between red and white. Honest reflection made it increasingly clear that the SF writer's attempt to retain the Indian's exemplary association with nature without the degrading effect of his victimization was in a very significant sense fraudulent. Both the Freman and Katsuk are anomalies. Their transcendence of history, their apparent successful reconciliation of masculine aggression (control over nature) with feminine passiveness (submission to nature) only works aesthetically because in both cases the action is raised to a mythical level due to the primacy of a specifically religious motif. The evasiveness, perhaps even dishonesty, of this technique (inasmuch as we are asked to accept these fables as containing a valid reflection of human experience, and resolving—albeit symbolically—real human problems) is even more blatant in *Stranger in a Strange Land*, where the mythic pattern, whatever the details, is explicitly Christian in outline. As Scholes (1975) points out with respect to C.S. Lewis's Christian allegories, such a formula works on us "because we are preconditioned to be moved by that particular material, with its legend of a redemptive sacrifice—preconditioned by our particular cultural heritage rather than by the shape of the work itself. In other words, this kind of allegory is leading its readers toward a stock response based on a pre-established and rigidly codified set of values." There is nothing *necessarily* wrong with utilizing the power of such a response to energize a fictional experience, of course, but at least in the case of *Stranger*, where the values we are asked to ratify are in many ways in specific opposition to the values of the original myth, one may perhaps legitimately complain that the conditioned reaction simply blunts our critical faculties, such that we overlook the inconsistencies and even the sinister undertones that would tend to undermine Heinlein's vision from a more objective point of view. Even when the mythic superstructure is a more legitimate one (placed "in the service of a metaphysic which is entirely responsible to modern conditions of being because its perspective is broader than the Christian perspective—because finally it takes the world more seriously than the Judeo-Christian tradition has ever allowed it to be taken" [Scholes]), the mere fact that the credibility of the implied reconciliation depends largely on the *discontinuity* between the real and fictional worlds means that the message is ultimately "false," that the resolution just won't work on a more naturalistic plane.

The most notable exploration of this problem is Ursula LeGuin's *The Word for World is Forest*. This beautifully crafted novella (which won a Hugo award in 1973) offers us yet another encounter between Earthmen and a race of extraterrestrials who would seem to be classic noble savages (in the traditional—that is, child of nature—rather than the 1960s sense). In contrast to the earlier more optimistic visions, here, however, the distance between the two, as in xenophobic 40s and 50s versions (although with inverted moral/emotional implications), is shown to be absolute and impossible to bridge. Modern and primitive man are not only different, the book implies, but profoundly incompatible in several very important ways.

The first and most visible difference, as might be expected, has to do with environment. The "creechies," as the Earthmen call them, are identified above all with the fecund life of the forest, secret and diverse:

All the colors of rust and sunset, brown-reds and pale greens, changed ceaselessly in the long leaves as the wind blew. The roots of the cooper willows, thick and ridged, were moss-green down by the running water, which like the wind moved slowly with many soft eddies and seeming pauses, held back by rocks, roots, hanging and fallen leaves. No way was clear, no light unbroken, in the forest. Into wind, water, sunlight, starlight, there always entered leaf and branch, bole and root, the shadowy, the complex. Little paths ran under the branches, around the boles, over the roots; they did not go straight but yielded to every obstacle, devious as nerves.

The humans, on the other hand, are both temperamentally unsuited and socially unprepared to deal with this environment. They feel "oppressed and uneasy in the forest, stifled by its endless crowd and incoherence of trunks, branches, leaves in the perpetual greenish or brownish twilight. The mass and jumble of various competitive lives all pushing and swelling upwards towards light, the silence made up of many little meaningless noises, the total vegetable indifference to the presence of mind, all this...troubled [them]." The human vision of felicity is thus by necessity diametrically opposed to the natives' feeling for their home. "Cleaned up and cleaned out, the dark forests cut down for open fields of grain, the primeval murk and savagery and ignorance wiped out, it would be a paradise, a real Eden," says one of the invaders. " 'I watched the trees fall and saw the world cut open and left to rot,' " is the Athshean's reply. This difference is not superficial but basic. It implies something critical about the nature of the human race. As the title of the book indicates, *Athshe*, the native word for world, means forest, whereas Earth, *Terra*, means not only the planet but the soil. There is no reconciliation of these conceptions, any more than there is a reconciliation of the living and the dead. "Terran man was clay, red dust. Athshean man was branch and root."

From the environmental difference stem other differences, moreover, which are just as important and just as deep. First and foremost—exactly as we would expect in terms of traditional primitivistic conventions—the Athsheans are in much closer touch with the spiritual side of existence; indeed they exercise continuing conscious control over their dreams. This practice has a number of implications. For one thing it means that they are in far greater control of their own psyches than humans can possibly be, defusing conflicts and restructuring ambiguities even as they come into existence. More important, the juxtaposition of dream-time and real-time gives the whole of lived experience an order and a significance impossible when the objective world is only an inert "other." To the Athsheans, therefore, human compartmentalization of disparate aspects of experience—displacement, projection, sublimation, and all the other Freudian mechanisms of self-delusion—is the ultimate act of self-destruction, the ultimate insanity. As Selver, the native protagonist in the book, says, "If the yumens are men they are men unfit or untaught to dream and to act as men. Therefore they go about in torment killing and destroying, driven by the gods within whom they will not set free but try to uproot and destroy. If they are men they are evil men, having denied their own gods, afraid to see their own faces in the dark."

Beyond the question of dreaming properly, the most telling difference between humans and Athsheans turns out in the end to be the physical one. Again the *terms* of divergence are tied to a traditional aspect of the noble savage's role: his exemplification if not of outright pacifism at least of a *relatively* peaceable mode of existence. Athsheans are not vegetarians, but (except in rare cases of psychosis) they never kill their own kind. Indeed, like a number of Terran animals (i.e., wolves) they have anti-aggression mechanisms built right in on an instinctive level. An Athshean could, theoretically, fight (although it is almost unthinkable that he would want to) in a battle between equals, but if either opponent adopted a submissive posture, exposing his throat, the other would be incapable of striking another blow. As a result, among the Athsheans, aggression is channelled into singing contests. The energy that might otherwise express itself in violence, in other words, is diverted into aesthetic ends.

Humans just don't function this way. Davidson, one of the two major human protagonists in the book, for instance, is totally obsessed with violence. Even when he isn't behaving aggressively (which happens at the slightest excuse), he dreams of doing so:

Just take up a hopper over one of the deforested areas and catch a mess of creechies there, with their damned bows and arrows, and start dropping firejelly cans and watch them run around and burn. It would be all right. It made his belly churn a little to imagine it, just like when he thought about making a woman... The fact is, the only time a man is really and entirely a man is when he's just had a woman or just killed another man.

It may be argued that LeGuin has weighted her case unfairly by focusing on such an extreme type—Davidson is a fanatical chauvinist (race, sex, country, self), as well as a sadistic bully—but being realistic, this is a kind of man whom pioneering often attracts. Besides, as LeGuin demonstrates, the rest of the humans are almost as despicable as Davidson and the few of his ilk if only for their sins of omission. All of them acquiesce in the enslavement and exploitation of the natives. In Athshean terms such behavior should have been impossible. Since the Athsheans are so much smaller and weaker than the humans, they *should* have evoked a protective stance. As the book emphasizes, however, the colonists here exhibit an almost opposite reaction to what both reason and nature would suggest. LeGuin's delineation of this psychological phenomenon is fully credible. As Fiedler points out in *Freaks*, especially where the institutionalized familial model is an ambiguous one, physical vulnerability can often stimulate outright aggression in man. "Not only the terms 'Dwarf' and 'Midget,' but all names used for men and women below normal height reflect our ambivalence toward the very young and the very old, our children and our parents." The colonists' behavior on Athshe, besides being objectively unethical, thus casts some very disquieting reflections on the emotional health of the modern American whom they must be taken to represent.

Here, then, it seems, we have yet another version of the stereotyped alien-as-Indian-as-victim and American-as-pioneer-as-villain theme. LeGuin goes beyond this conventional portrait of colonial aggression, however, to test yet another facet of the myth. Traditional primitivism emphasizes the static, timeless quality of life in the garden, probably because of its explicit connection with the Christian conception of the pre-lapserian state. In reality nature is never truly static. Neither are primitive cultures, since their prime necessity is to *adapt*. The Athshean culture, in giving such a central place to dreaming, provides a particularly effective mechanism for mediating change. One of the functions of the dreamer is to give a sense of coherence and continuity to experience by naturalizing—bringing to life—the archetypes of communal response. The Pursuer, the Friend who has no face, the Aspen-Leaf Woman who walks in the forest of dreams, the Gatekeeper, the Snake, the Lyreplayer, the Carver, and the Hunter are therefore not only symbols, but actual *roles* which emerge from dream-time when required so that gods may walk on the earth. Lyubov, the colony anthropologist, is the only Terran in the book to suspect what this might mean.

Sha'ab meant god, or numinous entity, or powerful being; it also meant something quite different...translator.

It was almost too pat, too apposite.

Were the two meanings connected?...If the god was a translator, what did he translate? Selver was indeed a gifted interpreter, but that gift had found expression only through the fortuity of a truly foreign language having been brought into his world. Was a *sha'ab* one who translated the language of dream and philosophy...into everyday speech? But all Dreamers could do that. Might he then be one who could translate into waking life the central experience of vision... A link: one who could speak aloud the perceptions of the subconscious. To "speak" that tongue is to act. To do a new thing. To change or to be changed, radically, from the root. For the root is the dream.

And the translator is the god.

After the coming of the humans, the dreams change. Selver dreams of giants walking across the forest followed by "moving things made of polished iron" that knocked down the trees, but he also dreams of a burning city. Selver hence becomes a god. "Selver had brought a new word into the language of his people. He had done a new deed. The word, the deed, murder. Only a god could lead so great a newcomer as Death across the bridge between the worlds."

Following their new god, the formerly meek and passive Athsheans rise up in vast numbers against the humans, and vanquish them utterly.

So the story doesn't have the same ending as all those others after all. But what does this different ending imply? Certainly in LeGuin's treatment it is not the vindication that it might seem from a simplistic point of view. The fact is that the change catalyzed in the Athsheans, while it might enable

them to survive, also in a sense cuts them off absolutely from what they have
been.

> "Sometimes a god comes," Selver said. "He brings a new way to do a thing, or a new
> thing to be done. A new kind of singing, or a new kind of death. He brings this across
> the bridge between the dream-time and the world-time. When he has done this, it is done.
> You cannot take things that exist in the world and try to drive them back inside the dream
> with walls and pretenses. That is insanity. What is, is. There is no use pretending, now,
> that we do not know how to kill one another."

The Freman notwithstanding, the only way that the noble savage can be rescued
from his fate, in other words, is by giving up some of the essential qualities
that define his nature. Organized aggression (as opposed to the spontaneous
and individual acts of violence characteristic of primitive cultures) transform
him at least vestigially into the entity he is trying to defeat. It was possible
for a while to evade this recognition (one of the features of the myth is that
anything can happen), but the more direct, the more immediate the confrontation
with nature becomes, the more clearly the ambiguities stand out. After LeGuin
the difficulty has become explicit.

Since we can't alter our noble savage without corrupting him, it seems
obvious, then, that if we really do want the experience that he represents, we
ourselves will have to change. Unfortunately this seems very difficult for the
American, even imaginatively, to do. His ethnocentricity is so ingrained, in
fact, that it seems almost impervious to will. The perspective is simply *assumed*
in almost every facet of life, a fixed feature of his response to otherness whether
he likes it or not. As if in oblique expiation of this unpalatable fact, the white
man's inherent racial myopia itself becomes a recurrent motif in SF almost
before the 60s noble savage reaches his prime. As an interesting complement
to our foregoing examination of the Athshe "victory," LeGuin's "Mazes" (1971),
for instance, makes clear—in a subtler but equally poignant way than the later
novel—the extent to which even the most well-intentioned Westerner necessarily
engineers his own defeat. This story is written from the point of view of an
alien who is undergoing psychological testing in an earth laboratory. The subject
is a highly intelligent creature who desperately *wants* to communicate, but
because its racial language is kinetic rather than verbal, the human observer—
with his anthropomorphic expectations—fails to recognize what its behavior
implies; indeed, draws an entirely opposite conclusion from it, since the dancing
interferes with the alien's "efficient" running of the standard mazes. In the
end, as the alien is dying (unable to tell its dietary needs), *it* has begun to
have some glimmerings of comprehension that might eventually help transcend
the communications gap, but the *human* is apparently totally incapable of
the kind of leap of empathy that even this vestigial understanding requires.

> I had become accustomed to its great size, and to the angular character of its limb positions,
> which at first had seemed to be saying a steady stream of incoherent and mispronounced
> phrases, until I realized that they were strictly purposive movements. Now I saw something

a little beyond that in its position. There were no words, yet there was communication. I saw, as it stood watching me, a clear signification of angry sadness—as clear as the Sembrian Stance. There was the same lax immobility, the bentness, the assertion of defeat. Never a word came clear, and yet it told me that it was filled with resentment, pity, impatience, and frustration. It told me it was sick of torturing me, and wanted me to help it. I am sure I understood it. I tried to answer. I tried to say "What is it you want of me?..." But I was too weak to speak clearly, and it did not understand. It has never understood.

Following hard on the heels of optimistic 60s primitivism, the vision of an agonized failure on the part of questing humans to make *any* meaningful contact beyond themselves is something that seemed to haunt 70s SF.

In some ways, to be sure, this could seem simply a retreat back to the stance of the 50s, implying that the primitivistic trends of the 60s merely signalled an anomalous, short-term interruption to an otherwise fairly consistent set of genre conventions. Although there is a common emphasis on anthropomorphism in both periods, however, the mood of the fiction—the response to the observed phenomenon—is significantly different in each case. In the 50s man's "uniqueness," even when this was displayed in terms of such negative (and thus formally regrettable) behavior as the motiveless aggression of the Earthman in Damon Knight's "Stranger Station," was dealt with in a tone that ranged from muted complacency to outright enthusiastic self-congratulation. Man is different, man is special, man is *better*, seemed to be the implicit refrain. Human incompatibility with other species was by and large seen primarily as evidence of the indomitable spirit which would carry us out into space and give us mastery over the universe. In the better fiction of the early to mid-70s, however, this aspect of the human condition—in the context of the renewed paradisial expectations that emerged during the 60s—seem to have been interpreted more often as isolation than uniqueness, a crippling lack rather than a valuable gift.

There is thus a strong sense in much 70s SF that man is a prisoner of his own base nature—along with an equally strong sense of distress at the results that this nature entails. Michael Bishop's "Blooded on Arachne" (1975), for instance, involves an initiation rite on a distant but human-colonized planet in which the young candidate, to survive, has to prey upon the young of an indigenous species. The protagonist of the story does, as one would expect, opt finally for self-protection, but rather than feeling triumphant, as his 50s counterpart undoubtedly would, he is heartsick and scarred by the experience. (" 'I'll outlive all of you!' He was sixteen. But he was crying. He wept for himself and the spider whose legs he had pulled away. Sej had as much as told Ethan that the Stalking Widows were intelligent creatures, sentient in the manner of man—or in a manner totally their own, at least. And he, Ethan Dedicos, had cruelly hurt one of their people.") In Joseph Greene's "Encounter with a Carnivor" (1975), similarly, a Terran scout is faced with a situation in which, to protect his own race's interests in a competition to salvage some potentially valuable equipment from a wrecked alien spacecraft, he has to shoot his former partner, a female warrior from a psychologically if not technologically primitive species of felines. In spite of the fact that he has come to love this fierce and vital creature during their association, he does carry out his racial duty—but not without the most heart-wrenching regrets. In the early 70s man's very success, in other words, has seemingly come to imply both moral failure and emotional loss.

What makes this failure even more disquieting is that even as the myth of reconciliation is breaking down, a confusion of identities between "ego" and "other" also seems to be taking place. This is not a totally new departure, of course; there is a long tradition in literature that the savage, the untamed landscape, is really located within. In terms, specifically, of SF progenitors, Robert Louis Stevenson's *Dr. Jekyll and Mr. Hyde* (1866) is the prototypical exploration of this theme. Even in Wells's *The Island of Dr. Moreau* (1866), where the beasts are clearly derived from animal stock, a human parallel is implied repeatedly throughout the book. Indeed, when Moreau's artificially created humanoids begin to revert, one by one, to their original savage state, the narrator himself insists upon the extent to which their battle against degradation mimics the human condition. "A strange persuasion came upon me that, save for the grossness of the line, the grotesqueness of the forms, I had here before me the whole balance of human life in miniature, the whole interplay of instinct, reason, and fate, in its simplest form." The covert identification with the monster that emerged as a reaction to "official" xenophobia in the 50s, especially on the part of the primarily teenaged audience for SF books and films, reinvigorated this tradition and established it as a minor but persistent undercurrent to the contemporary SF vision.

On the other hand, from the perspective of the 80s it is evident that this trend towards a more sympathetic view of the monster was not quite what, in the context of 60s primitivism, it may have seemed. Rehabilitating the bestial could easily be interpreted as part of the general quest for a new, viable noble savage. Neither at that time nor later, however, is there any indication that the savage nature implied by the monster—whether objective or subjective— is in any essential way different from the brutal, frightening, *destructive* nature that the bestial alter ego represented for Stevenson and Wells. The sympathetic monster does, probably, help to break down xenophobic resistence to the *idea* of the alien as we claimed above, but it is not itself drafted into the service of the garden. The noble savage that *does* eventually emerge is, in fact, as we have seen, essentially human. If the monster remains undomesticated, however, this is far from rendering him irrelevant. Reversing expectations, one notable consequence of the early 70s reaction to the primitivistic vision is that, increasingly, the human becomes monstrous. As it turns out, the pathetic beast enslaved by his own violent nature more often than not is *us*. (This is at least one of the messages embedded in that long-running late-70s television series, *The Incredible Hulk*, in which the hero, himself a scientist, dedicated to the cause of progress and rationality, is caught in a freak radiation accident as a result of which he now changes periodically—and involuntarily—into a brutish creature driven by instinct to acts of violence and destruction.)

Meanwhile, the token alien, the "good" primitive, becomes the locus of the kind of sympathetic identification normally inspired by the "ego" rather than the "other." In *The Word for World is Forest*, for instance, the reader is clearly alienated by his formal alter, the human villain, and emotionally aligned with the technical alien, not just in terms of the pity or admiration traditionally evoked by the noble savage in his various referential roles, but to the extent of accepting him as the symbolic ego of that particular fictional world.

This development has some important effects. In the first place, in the more thoughtful SF of the period, the relation between man and nature, as represented by the noble savage equivalent, typically becomes extremely ambiguous, not just in moral/emotional terms, as in LeGuin's novel, but even on a purely phenomenal basis. One of the most interesting explorations of this problem—indeed one of the finest SF books to come out of its decade—is Gene Wolfe's *The Fifth Head of Cerberus* (1972). It is impossible to do justice to the richness and subtlety of this set of three linked novellas in précis, but two things are basic: one is the question of identity (indeed, of *identifiability*) and the other is the relation between modern man and the primitive. In the last section, a Terran anthropologist, John V. Marsch, has come to the colony planet of Sainte Anne to try to find out what happened to the legendary aborigines (if they ever existed), reputed on the one hand to be magical shape-changers and on the other simply sub-human beggars and thieves. In line with this objective he goes on a journey into the mountains with a youth who may (or may not) himself be a descendent of these natives; after several years, "he" reappears alone. Our only access to Marsch's experience is through a disordered and incomplete collection of his journal entries, taped interviews, interrogation transcripts, letters, and "fictional" fragments compiled after he is subsequently arrested on Sainte Anne's sister planet Sainte Croix as a spy. The one thing that does emerge from this collage with any certainty is that "Marsch" underwent some sort of transforming experience in the mountains, but what this involved is unclear. As Pamela Sargent says in her Afterword to the 1976 edition of the book, the "authorities begin to have doubts about who Marsch is, and Marsch himself is unsure of his identity. Has the mysterious boy taken his place, so expertly imitating him that he is sure, at times, that he is Marsch? or has Marsch so fallen under the spell of the culture he seeks that his mind has become unhinged? Is it Marsch who died in the wilderness? One cannot be absolutely sure." This is obviously related to the identity-loss theme traditional to SF, but here it is debatable just who devoured whom.

The possibilities suggested by this novella become even more provocative when considered in the light of the second section in the book, " 'A Story,' by John V. Marsch," which purports to reconstruct the aboriginal experience, just before the coming of man. The credibility of this whole fragment is cast into doubt by its ostensible authorship, of course, but we cannot be any means dismiss it on that basis since for all we know Marsch (if, indeed, he *is* Marsch), despite his apparent instability, may have gathered evidence for this interpretation during those three lost years which may or may not have been spent with the surviving "Free People" in the mountains. In any case, this story claims that in the pre-invasion period there were *two* groups of sapients on the planet. One was a race of primitive humanoids; the other a more mysterious species called the Shadow-Children who at least in part seem to be non-corporeal, a kind of ghost. The real surprise, however, is the fact that these Shadow-Children claim (sometimes) that rather than being indigenous, they represent the survivors of an earlier expedition from earth. After they arrived on Sainte Anne, so the story goes, the true natives assumed human semblance and they themselves began to lose their human form. If this is true, it has the additional implication that the second expedition might have been "replaced" by the shape-changing aborigines as well. The Free People dispossessed by the colonists were thus perhaps no other than the colonists themselves.

If we assume, at least provisionally, that this version of history is accurate, there is a further question raised by " 'A Story' " about whether the human reversion to primitivism was ultimately a beneficial development or a change for the worse. The humanoid natives see the Shadow-Children as grotesque and deformed (" *'Your bones are bent and weak and your faces ill; you run from men and the light'* "), but to themselves they are tall and strong and " 'wrapped in terrible glory.' " " 'Long ago in our home, before a fool struck fire, we were so—roaming without whatever may be named save the sun, the night, and each other,' " one of them tells the shaman, Sandwalker. " 'Now we are so again, for we are gods, and things made by hands do not concern us.' " Which view is the true view? Is the return to nature a return to divinity (as the Edenic dream would have it) or simply the degradation it seemed to Wells? This has been the primitivist dilemma all along. In the mood of much post-60s SF, Wolfe's haunting little book appears to exacerbate the problem rather than attempting any resolution.

Simple confusion is not the only consequence of the post-60s reaction, either. The failure of the mythic reconciliation inspires considerable anxiety as well, all the more so if the alienated element is seen as part of the self rather than clearly "other." Michael Bishop (who, though lacking both Wolfe's poetic vision and LeGuin's power to evoke with complete credibility an extraordinary range of different cultural realities and alien personalities, is nevertheless one of the more interesting and important writers of the 70s) illuminates this aspect of the situation in his novel *A Funeral for the Eyes of Fire* (1975). The setting for this story is a planet named, significantly enough, Trope (meaning a figurative or metaphorical expression, a kind of riddle), the home of a race of humanoids who—lacking mouths (they communicate subverbally, by a form of telepathy) but endowed with strange jewel-like eyes with mystical powers of vision—are obviously meant to represent the essential nature of man himself: the reality of the spirit stripped of the delusory power of the word. The Tropeman's experience is therefore a comment on the reality that underlines the apparent coherence of the human experience as a whole. Early in the novel one of the characters relates a folktale which is a variant on the archetypal "divided self" motif—in this case the story of Loki, who, in casting out his better side, or Conscience (personified in typical mythic fashion as a twin), becomes an *absolutely* evil man—and this folktale, as we might expect, gives us a clue to the book's primary theme. Like Loki—by analogy, like man himself—Trope is divided into two mutually exclusive factions, a dominant, highly civilized, urban culture devoted to technological advancement and rationality, and a primitive religious sect called the Ouemartsee, who eschew all technology and embrace a simple, communal, agrarian lifestyle. The progressive and the primitive components, in other words, are totally at odds. In exemplary contrast to the embedded folk version, however, the situation on modern Trope is such that it is the savage, or natural, aspect which is repressed and denied.

Bishop does not stop here. There is, at least figuratively, an attempt in the book to reconcile these two disparate factions into a whole. It turns out that Elgran Vrai, the Magistrate of Trope, the high priest of logic, is himself a kind of Jekyll and Hyde. For one thing he has evaded the successive personality erasures undergone by the normal Tropeman as a kind of ritual repudiation of his own (primitive) past. More significantly, it is revealed that he is actually the spiritual heir to the Ouemartsee messiah, Aerthu, who disappeared mysteriously many years ago. It is a custom on Trope for a son to inherit the eyes (thus the "vision") of his father upon the latter's death. Elgran Vrai, formerly Gelvri, had repudiated his birthright, however, because his birth-father was a criminal. Subsequently, as a young soldier, he met the outlaw Aerthu and killed him secretly after—at the man's own urging—agreeing to accept both the gift of his eyes and the moral mission that went along with them. Elgran Vrai, therefore, is secretly the appointed mediator who, as the American has often wished of the noble savage, will effect reconciliation of the unnaturally divided population. His is a message of hope:

> One's birth-parent need not be the creature out of whom one is physically born ... nor must one embrace everything that his birth-parent, real or adopted, stands for. Gelvri was a Tropeman, not an Ouemartsee, but he had an understanding that bridged the chasm between the two and he hoped that through that understanding there might develop a reconciliation, a union. Gelvri became Elgran Vrai, Sixth Magistrate of all Trope, without renouncing either his former self or the understanding he had acquired. He did not completely comprehend the process by which he had reached this pinnacle, but he hoped that one day he could externalize the reconciliation working within him and extend it to the lopsidedly warring factions of the Tropean state. A rational, humane solution—for Gelvri, as Elgran Vrai, believed rationality and humaneness tautologies, different names for the same thing.

Unfortunately, Gelvri's dream—like the fantasy that invokes a noble savage to reconcile the American with his own inner landscape—turns out to be illusory. Obviously in practical terms rationality and humaneness are *not* the same thing. On a quest to the Ouemartsee community to try to establish some sort of basis for communication, Elgran Vrai finds himself the unwitting cause of a massacre. After he commits suicide his role is taken over by his deputy Foutliff who, fanatically hostile toward these reminders of his own primitive past, exiles the Ouemartsee to another planet where they will become slaves.

As a novel, *A Funeral for the Eyes of Fire* is somewhat too labored to be totally successful. As a simultaneous criticism of and elegy for the primitivistic fantasy, however, it is very effective. The most poignant aspect of Bishop's vision is his recognition that criticisms are not ultimately going to change the circumstances in any way. The American will continue, at least at intervals, to dream of the garden, and continue as well to suffer the disillusionment and pain of *failing* to reconcile through this dream the conflicting elements of his own mixed nature. In *Funeral*, for instance, the Earthman who has been not only an observer of the incident on Trope but also, albeit as an innocent pawn, partly responsible for its disastrous outcome, refusing to take the obvious lesson from Elgran Vrai's experience, still clings to what the reader recognizes as naive and irresponsible optimism, proclaiming near the end of the book (having decided to go into exile along with the dispossessed Ouemartsee) that the idyll is still possible—in the future: *"one day, when I have emancipated both Ouemartsee and myself, when we have raised our sister as an independent and beautifully unique human being, then perhaps we'll return to Earth and find a place where no monumental domes sprout out of the wilderness like pernicious toadstools. In that place we'll stop, and build a temple, and live out our independent selves in the reflections of one another's eyes."*

Bishop's vision here of painfully juxtaposed hope and denial of hope in many ways exemplifies the 70s vision of the American experience. Not just, as LeGuin would have it, that the fantasied reconciliation is impossible, nor even, as Wolfe intimates, that the nature we fail to save may be our own: the real tragedy in the failure of the American dream lies in the fact that the American seems doomed to keep dreaming it. Another of Bishop's stories, "Death and Designation Among the Asadi" (1973), perhaps illuminates the condition even more trenchantly than his novel does. In this odd, intricate tale a xeno-anthropologist (who has a sentimental fixation on the vanished pygmies of Earth) is so anxious to establish some sort of meaningful relationship with a tribe of primitive aliens that he literally drives himself mad when he fails. Like, it would seem, the wishfully primitivistic American, the researcher here apparently only has two alternatives for interpreting his experience: either the Asadi behavior adds up to something horrible and perverse or it doesn't have any comprehensible meaning, in human terms, at all—and he, with his wistful dreams of pygmies, is not able to live with either of these.

It would be misleading, of course, to imply that 70s SF is full of this sort of anguished confrontation with the American's apparent inability to verify in himself his nation's most cherished myth. Bishop's response is significant, as we said, in that it exemplifies a certain kind of recognition that *underlies* recent developments in the genre, but it cannot be said that it is typical in quantitative terms. There are, after all, other, more comfortable ways to respond to disillusionment. This is exactly what James Tiptree's "The Psychologist Who Wouldn't Do Awful Things to Rats" (1976) is about. This story, which initially seeks to utilize the old nature=good, science=bad dichotomy as a fundamental thematic opposition, concerns a psychology graduate student who is sickened by the cruelty of conventional experimental work (" 'Testing animals to destruction' ") and wants instead, to the disgust of his supervisor, to approach his subjects holistically. Drunk one night in the lab after being threatened with dismissal he has a vision of the mystical King Rat of medieval legend who has come to redeem, so he feels, all the victims of such an inhumane system, including him.

> He dares a quick look back and sees them. They are coming. The dim way behind is filled with quiet beasts, moving together rank on rank... And they are not only the beasts of his miserable lab, he realizes, but a torrent of others—he has glimpsed goats, turtles, a cow, racoons, skunks, an opposum and what appeared as a small monkey riding on a limping spaniel...
>
> My God, it is everything, he thinks. It is Hamlin in reverse; all the abused ones, the gentle ones, are leaving the world. He risks another glance back and thinks he can see a human child too and maybe an old person among the throng, all measuredly, silently moving together in the dimness. An endless host going, going out at last, going away. And he is feeling their emanation, the gentleness of it, the unspeaking warmth. He is happier than he has ever been in his life.
>
> "You're taking us away," he says to the King-Beast beside him. "The ones who can't cut it. We're all leaving for good, isn't that it?"

Suddenly, at the height of his elation, however, Lipsitz realizes the tragic truth. It has been a delusion, this feeling of brotherhood. He is a *man*, an aggressor. The escape is not for him. "He understands now, understands with searing grief that it really is the souls of things, and perhaps himself that are passing, going away forever. They have stood it as long as they can and now they are leaving. The pain has culminated in this, that they leave us—leave me, leave me behind in a clockwork Cartesian world in which nothing will mean anything forever." Here again is the failure of the dream.

Does Lipsitz sit around agonizing about the inherent taint that bars him from the garden, though? Not at all. Behaving in far more typical human fashion, the first thing he does when he wakes up in the morning is to deny that he ever believed the myth in the first place. Pushing aside for once and for all his sentimental reservations about his work, he chloroforms all his cherished rat families and starts to design a method for introducing electric stimulators into horses to make them run faster.

This is very much the reaction we find in 70s SF as a whole. For every LeGuin or Wolfe or Bishop who confronts and illuminates the real ambiguities of the primitivist vision, there are dozens of writers who simply jump on the anti-primitivist bandwagon and, rather than focusing on the human failure, devote themselves to debunking the promise implicit in the myth itself. Indeed, the anti-Edenic fable becomes one of the most popular forms of the decade. We're not missing anything at all, they assert: there's probably nothing out there we'd want anyway. Robert Silverberg's "Sundance" (1969), for instance, suggests that an obsession with the fate of the Indian can distort one's perspective so much that the whole of nature becomes quite unjustifiably irradiated with sentimental value, and guilt experienced where no guilt is due. In Tiptree's "The Milk of Paradise" (1972) a space-wrecked youngster's vision of the "noble savages" who fostered him is so idyllic that it makes it impossible for him to adjust to human society after he is rescued. Later it turns out that this vision was telepathically induced: in reality his idealized aliens are ugly slug-like things living in squalid mud hovels. In Barry Malzborg's "Opening Fire" (1973), a xenophobe is deliberately included in a spaceship's crew to counter their tendency to be overly sympathetic and trusting with aliens; bigotry becomes a survival trait. Phyllis MacLennon's "Thus Love Betrays Us" (1972) is an allegory of man's relation with nature. In the beginning nature is fearsome because it is alien; man invents a mediator, by anthropomorphizing an aborigine; the mediator betrays him because his beneficience is illusory; man turns against nature in revenge and becomes a killer. In Alexei and Cory Panshin's "Lady Sunshine and the Magoon of Beatus" (1975) the search for True Earth reveals that man heals nature rather than vice versa. In Kate Wilhelm's "Planet Story" (1975) an exploration party finds a "perfect" planet which turns out to be a deathtrap with an undetectable menace. In Ward Moore's "With Mingled Feelings of Anticipation and Apprehension the Emigrants Leave Their Native Earth for a Far-Off Destination" (1975) an unscrupulous government uses the lie of a paradisial New Earth to seduce its excess population out into space, where they will die. There is a lingering wistful note in many of these stories— after all, the writers would not likely protest so hard if they were not themselves aware of the emotional authority that the myth continues to wield—but on the whole they demonstrate vividly the extent of the 70s reaction against the perceived naiveté of the decade before.

The new noble savage was thus repudiated almost at the same instant that he was proclaimed.

5.3 Birth of a Champion

We know that the arcologies are little pathetic islands on the earth; that the carefully controlled life-support systems and the little humming beehives of activity are useless because the world has been destroyed, milked dry, ravaged. We know what's out there, outside the domes. We know that Genetics took over because men had ruined their bodies. Organs were failing in childhood. But medicine marched on. Artificial hearts, lungs, kidneys, livers, until finally a man was completely artificial by law, at age thirty-five. Totaled. And since nobody used his legs, confined to a super wheelchair...Let him dream for several hours a day to satisfy whatever human need for relaxation was left. Set timetables for life. [And at the prescheduled moment]... A button pressed, an office filled with odorless gas... All very clean and neat.

Here, again, is the staple SF dystopia. In Richard Posner's "Vacation" (1973), however, the conventional formula has been changed in a few significant ways. Despite tradition, there is no garden outside the domed communities in this story—only dry wind and killing heat and air too thin to breathe. The only escape from this city, therefore, is an escape into dreams of love and heroism and freedom. Or into death.

The movement of Posner's story parallels a critical development that took place in American popular literature in the early 70s. Confronted with what seemed to be evidence of an inexorable decay in national security and morality (Vietnam, pollution, Watergate) and, perhaps even more important, unable—due to their erstwhile optimistic idealism and demands for self-responsibility ("Do your own thing!")—to dissociate themselves from the phenomenon, much of the same readership and even many of the same writers responsible for the burgeoning popularity of SF during the 60s, apparently disillusioned with the failure once more of their old Edenic dream, turned away from the concerns of the genre to the simpler illusions of fantasy.

Fantasy is not a new or entirely separate genre, to be sure. Inasmuch as the science content and the extrapolative logic conventionally required is minimal or absent in much SF, their functions being replaced by invocations of the marvellous, fantasy has always been a component of all but the most hard-line SF novels and stories. A minor strain of "pure" fantasy, moreover, has always existed alongside the conventional core of the field. In 1939, for instance, Joseph Campbell, the dean of "scientific" science fiction, launched a companion magazine to *Astounding* called *Unknown* which exploited that element of black romance derived largely from Poe and Lovecraft. As Carter describes it,

> Although the new publication dealt not in rocketships and ray guns but in witches and vampires, it was quickly apparent that the two magazines had heavily overlapping constituencies. The paradox was not lost on alert readers (and writers): "The Jekyll-science-fictionist stands for experimental truth, for logic, for *proof*. The Hyde-nocturnal-seeker exists in frank fear of the dark, in the world of dreams...of witches'-brew, of curses, of Kismet. Fantasy fiction," concluded Seymour Kapetansky, "has bred the most illogical double-track mind in history," able to enjoy both the brisk technological forecasts of *Astounding* and the sinister revenants in *Unknown*.

This undercurrent was subsequently given new impetus and a new direction by the tremendous popularity of J.S. Tolkien's epic fantasy-romance in the 60s (yet another distinguished British progenitor). When appetites demanded a relief from the increasingly ambiguous visions of SF in the early 70s, therefore, there were already appropriate models at hand.

The shift of interest to the fantasy component did not merely signal a minor diversion, however. Since that time not only has a substantial amount of pure fantasy appeared in both new and traditional modes to the extent, indeed, that by the end of the 70s, judging by the selection available in the SF sections of bookstores, it had come to rival or even dominate (quantitatively) the older-style offerings, but SF itself (as many of the more recent examples cited in the last section imply) has in the past decade given much freer reign to its covert fantasy element as well. As Donald Wollheim observes in the introduction to a 1978 anthology, "the line between the two categories [has] become very smudged and shadowy in recent years and...what might have been labelled fantasy in the past can now find acceptance from confirmed science fiction addicts without much questioning." Fantasy, in fact, turned out to be the representative mode of the 70s. This marks a significant change in the public mood.

Why the shift? Alexei and Cory Panshin would claim that SF was too repressive. In the Wellsian romance, they say, "The Golden Age of the past is replaced by a vision of future perfection. Spirits become alien beings. Magic is replaced by science-beyond-science. Sorcerers become scientists." Unfortunately, whatever novelty the fable gains by means of these transformations is more than offset by a loss of profundity. "[T]he symbolic vocabulary of the new reaction...is not as sensitive and flexible as the old vocabulary of fantasy was. Magic has subtleties that super-scientific power or even psi-power do not have. Sorcerers have moral overtones that scientists do not have. There is a dimension in *Faust* that cannot be duplicated in the symbols available in *Frankenstein*." The appeal of fantasy—the reason why it has attracted so many erstwhile SF fans in the last decade—is thus, according to the Panshins, quite simply its capacity for "consciousness-expanding." Olderman would seem to agree. Fantasy, he says in his discussion of Peter Beagle's *The Last Unicorn*, conveys the sense of wonder essential to joyful existence: the main message of the allegory is that "there is magic in being human."

Fantasy *can*, and of course often *does* operate in this way, but there is some indication with respect at least to the 70s that both of these optimistic assessments are somewhat wide of the mark. Olderman and, to a large extent, the Panshins too are talking here about the *forerunners* of the real 70s fantasy revival: works that seemed specifically to grow out of and express the hopeful romanticism of the 60s. "The rediscovery of wonder in the world may ultimately be the best our decade can offer as a substitute for a truly accepted mythology to move us out of the waste land," says the former, making this connection explicit. "The sixties seem ripe for such a rediscovery; Tolkien has been gobbled up with a great deal of enthusiasm, and the atmosphere of the late sixties in particular is filled with 'flower children' and lectures on the false values that lead us to exist without wonder." Considering how ephemeral were the movements to which Olderman refers here, one must obviously take his inferences about their effects with a grain of salt. Indeed, if we review the phenomenon in the light of both concurrent and subsequent developments in SF, it seems highly likely that it was less the liberating, mind-expanding, wonder-inducing potential of fantasy which made it so popular in the 70s than that very feature the Panshins imputed to SF: the restrictiveness of the mode.

Scholes hints at such an interpretation when he points out that "A world in which values are clear (with heroes and heroines, villains and villainnesses), and action is fast and furious, has extraordinary appeal for people enmeshed in lives of muddled complexity." *A world in which values are clear*: this is the key phrase. As SF matured, as it confronted more honestly the implications of its own Adamic vision, the world view it expressed became increasingly ambiguous and complex. At the same time, however, the varied apocalyptic hopes of the 60s were foundering finally on the pettiness of Watergate and the apparent vulnerability of the economy and the bad sportsmanship of the winners in the Vietnam war; the social vision was becoming more complex and ambiguous too. Reacting in both fear and disillusionment, the erstwhile rebels now turned to literature not for enlightenment but for escape. Hence the turn to forms of fantasy, and in particular the heroic romance. As Zweig explains it,

> Adventure...is clearly a form of "experiential transcendence." In the midst of action, each move is dense with the weight of a lifetime, and is a lifetime, blazing with momentary intensity. Action fuses the moment into a separate whole, its parts powerfully compressed and interrelated, as in a dream. It is no surprise, therefore, that...[there] has been...a renewed fascination with adventure. The declining popularity of detective novels among the young is one evidence for the change. Whereas an older generation found its pleasure in the proposition that mysteries are puzzles which can be solved by "ratiocination," the young today show a marked preference for...versions of romance, in which the mysteries exist not to be explained, but to be vanquished.

Fantasy, in other words, is appealing not because it offers new possibilities or even new answers, but because it creates the illusion of a world where both the problems and the solutions are of the clear-cut, uncomplicated, and old-fashioned kind which can be comprehended without either moral confusion or emotional ambivalence. "There is no hint of existential darkness in Odysseus' plight," Zweig points out: "he is simply a man with enemies." An enemy without is much easier to combat than an enemy within.

It is not merely the relative straightforwardness of the fictional situation that makes fantasy attractive in such a situation, either. The very *forms* in which it tends to find expression—derivative, formal, familiar—allow the illusion of confrontation while all the time reassuring us that the risk is strictly controlled. Literary formulas, as Cawelti points out, "are at once highly ordered and conventional and yet are permeated with the symbols of danger, uncertainty, violence and sex. In reading or viewing a formulaic work, we confront the ultimate excitements of love and death, but in such a way that our basic sense of security and order is intensified rather than disrupted, because, first of all, we know that this is an imaginary rather than a real experience, and, second, because the excitement and uncertainty are ultimately controlled and limited by the familiar world of the formulaic structure." Fantasy can consequently indulge both the anarchic dream of freedom and personal power which is necessary to provide a relief from the feelings of impotence engendered by the modern setting *and*—what is perhaps more important in the 70s—the desire spawned by moral uncertainty for an assurance of ultimate order and meaning. Regardless of its specific plot, in other words, fantasy, simply by association, tends to express covertly what the Roses call the Deuteronomic view of history:

"There is a standard of virtue; a Force acts to reward those who abide by the standard and to condemn those who violate it... Good men win; bad men lose." This, judging at least from the response in the marketplace, is the preferred view in the 70s. Interestingly, it is George R. R. Martin's *Dying of the Light* (1977), itself properly SF rather than fantasy, which offers one of the most interesting explorations of this shift.

In this book representives of three diverse cultures come together on a wild, dying planet out beyond the fringes of galactic civilization. The center of consciousness is Dirk T'Larien, an interstellar academic whose values and outlook come close to the mid-70s norm: he is a man of reason, a proponent of "liberal" morality, a sceptic and a sentimentalist together. Confronting Dirk are two different models for determining his behavior on this world. One— embodied in Arkin Ruark, the Kimdissi researcher—is the epitome of gentleness, sanity, and peace. The other is the heroic culture of High Kavalaan, an explosive mixture combining the superstitions and passions of a primitive, warlike race; the extreme clannishness characteristic of feudal socio-political organization; the highly ritualized interactive modes implied by the *code duello*; and, of course, the violence inherent in all three. In the beginning of the book, consistent with his background (which is also ours), Dirk is predisposed towards the former. The Kavalar behavior seems to him both abnormal and disgusting. By the end of the book, however, he has completely reversed himself.

This is not the whole story. If it were, it would *be* a fantasy rather than exploring the psychology *behind* such modes. It is made clear in this book that the reason for Dirk's change of heart—and here is where the real significance of Martin's vision lies—is only peripherally related to his predictable realization that those individuals who represent his alternatives are not entirely what they first appear. The enlightened Ruark, as conventions would lead us to expect, is revealed as a coward and, what is worse, a traitor who sells out friend and foe alike in order only to secure his own safety. The other side of the picture is not quite so simple, though. Even the exemplary bound-pair of Ironjade warriors, Jaan Vikary and Garse Janecek, are, despite their spotless honor and demonstrations of *noblesse oblige*, discredited from a twentieth-century perspective by their adherence to a code that not only glorifies killing but also proclaims all out-caste individuals (which includes all women and all members of other races) as either "property" or animals. And the other Kavalars are a crude and brutal crew who spend much of their time in the book hunting down innocent aliens for "sport." Dick's conversion is not rational, therefore, but results purely and simply from growing fascination with the heroic vision itself—the *same* kind of illogical attraction that fantasy seems to exert as a literary form.

The transition is gradual. Early in the book he refuses absolutely to be implicated in what he sees as a degrading game, rejecting the Ironjade offer of a protective association with their clan. Not long after this, however, he is evidently so flattered by the trust that Jaan, addressing him now as an equal, demonstrates by naming him *keth* (friend/ally) that he is extremely reluctant to take Ruark's "rational" advice and back down from a duel that he has inadvertently instigated, thus leaving his Ironjade sponsors holding the bag. He does so finally (at this point his civilized conditioning still holds), but feels ashamed and guilty afterwards about his choice. And when, later, the Ironjades are in trouble, he volunteers to take on an almost hopeless mission to help them, seemingly desperate to make up for that earlier betrayal of a code he purports not to believe in, even at the risk of his life.

> "If this is some idiot move to make yourself a hero in my eyes, it isn't going to work," she said, putting her hands on her hips.
>
> He smiled. "What this is, Gwen, is some idiot move to make myself a hero in *my* eyes. Your eyes...your eyes aren't important anymore."
>
> "Why then?"
>
> He hefted the rifle uncertainly. "I don't know," he admitted. "Maybe because I like Jaan, and owe him. Because I want to make it up to him for running out after he'd trusted me and named me *keth*."
>
> "Dirk," she began.
>
> He waved her quiet. "I know... but that isn't all. Maybe I just want to get Ruark. Maybe it's because Kryne Lamia had more suicides than any other Festival city, and I'm one of them. You can pick your own motive, Gwen. All of the above."

As this excerpt implies, it is ultimately impossible to find a logical reason for the appeal of the glorious/hateful archaic code that the Ironjades represent. What we are left with after we follow Dirk's somehow fully credible change of attitude throughout the book (Martin's effective balancing of the emotional authority of sympathetic and realistic characters with the symbolic authority of their romantic/heroic literary associations provides us with a convincing demonstration of a fairly complex phenomenon), is consequently the conclusion that the desire, simply, to identify oneself with a heroic vision of life is much stronger than the dictates of common sense. Dirk's existence was rational but empty before he came to Worlorn; his emotions blunted, his values vague. On Worlorn existence is deadly but exhilarating. The presence of death gives some sense of purpose to life. In the end, when he goes willingly to the duel that he will undoubtedly lose, although there is a slight hint of ironic detachment in the author's treatment, he himself is undoubtedly far happier than he was at his earlier escape. "Dirk grinned the way Garse would have grinned, tossed the hair back out of his eyes, and went to him. No starlight ran down his blade as he lifted it and reached out to touch Bretan's. The wind was blowing. It was very cold."

In both this story and "A Song for Lya" discussed above, Martin shows a fine sensitivity to the ambiguities of response that underlie popular fictional patterns of different kinds. *Dying of the Light*, with its analysis of the psychology of fantasy, aside from being an exciting story in itself, may consequently be seen as a kind of parable illuminating an important aspect of the 70s mood.

What does this turn to fantasy imply for our major theme? Perhaps we should define more carefully what we mean by fantasy before attempting to answer this question. To start with, we are not, in general, talking about surrealism, symbolism, the macabre, southern grotesque, or private flights of fancy such as we find in 60s mainstream writers like Pynchon and Barthelme. Although genre fiction is by no means devoid of this kind of experimentation, especially in those writers associated with the New Wave of the late 60s-early 70s, that sub-species of SF usually designated as fantasy comprises primarily a small number of predominantly conventional or formulaic modes of romance.

In the earlier stages of the revival, because of the influence of Tolkien, the field was largely dominated by those kinds of imaginative excursion linked either by derivation or association with such traditional species as myth, legend, fairy-tale, and chivalric romance. Indeed, when the boom first occurred in the early 70s in order to meet the demand American publishers reprinted a great many works by late-Victorian to early modern British medievalists and fantasists such as George MacDonald, William Morris, and Lord Dunsany, and until more native writers caught up with the trend, this kind of material played a central role in establishing at least the initial character of 70s fantasy in the United States. A major component of the species is what Boyer and Zahorski call "high fantasy"; their description consequently provides a good basis for approaching the field.

The fairy tale and the myth-based tale are both set, entirely or in part, in a secondary world—that of faerie or the otherworld where gods and men mingle. Magic is the prime ingredient in the one, while the supernatural feats of the gods or their agents predominate in the other...

High fantasy has a number of other unique characteristics that accompany—indeed are integral to—its other-world setting and causality. The characters...often are imposing figures who, with unearthly powers, inspire wonder or fear, or often both: dragon kings, elves, dryads, demon princesses. High fantasy deals prominently with archetypal figures, motifs, and themes such as the temptress, death and renewal, and the spiritual quest, with its demands for courage and selflessness. And, finally, the style of high fantasy is a fittingly elevated one, characteristically working through imagery and metaphor to evoke its imaginary world.

This, then, in the immediate context of Tolkien, is the normative model for early contemporary American fantasy: archaic, conservative, and highly stylized. So pervasive was its influence in the initial stages of the fantasy-fad, in fact, that American fantasists tended to turn to Britain not only for examples of form but for source material as well. Arthurian legends, for instance, have seemed to exert a particular fascination on this side of the Atlantic, and during the last couple of decades there have been literally dozens of American fantasies given to the specific retelling of different aspects of the Grail Cycle and hundreds to the manufacture of less specifically founded but conventionally similar kinds of romance. Even when the connections are less explicit than those evoked by the recent gaggle of Gawains, Parsivals, and—especially—Merlins, moreover, the British associations tend to be strikingly obvious in a great majority of the fantasies written in this mode. In Katherine Kurtz's popular Deryni novels, for instance, the social context, the characters, and the themes—i.e., the ideal of kingship; the legitimate use of power—are all, typically enough, modelled quite closely on what has come to be a consensual (popular) view of England at the time of the crusades.

On the other hand, quantitatively speaking at least, American fantasy does tend to be somewhat less "high" than the above description would have it. In comparison with its late Victorian-early modern forebears, contemporary fantasy as a whole, even at the hands of such British practitioners as Tolkien, generally exhibits more individual characters and a more fully realized setting than the traditional version would dictate, and American writers in particular have inclined to democratize and humanize their visions. Often, indeed, in American fantasies the level of private thought and emotion—a level which is barely suggested in the highly stylized older forms—rivals or even surpasses in interest the public quests that provide the superstructures of these books. For this reason, and also in order to make room for those homelier species allied to the animal fable and the (real or facsimile) folk tale, we will label this body of fiction collectively not as "high" but as "pastoral" fantasy.

Despite its initial popularity the pastoral mode is not, however, the only, or even (ultimately) the dominant species of fantasy to be found in American bookstores during this decade. Another sub-group of the genre, in some ways diametrically opposed to the first, is what we might call heroic-barbaric fantasy. The hallmark of this species is the affirmation of personal prowess—physical strength and martial skills—rather than magic, the masculine mode rather than the feminine, as the determinant of value and the source of power.

Unlike the British-generated pastoral, the prototype for heroic-barbaric fantasy in its purest form is found in Robert E. Howard's American saga of Conan the Cimmerian, written back in the 30s (at the height of the "adventure SF" era) but—as intimated in Chapter 1—reissued, augmented, and amply imitated during the 70s. According to this model the setting is usually a primitive but unspecified (earthly or otherworldly) past. Most of the action takes place in relatively "civilized" southern regions suggestive of the ancient Middle East or North Africa, but the hero himself is typically a "barbarian" from harsher northern climes. A superb natural warrior, his most important identifying characteristics are physical. According to the formula he is *always*—like Lin Carter's "Thongor the Mighty"—big, heavily muscled, and conspicuously dangerous. He is also very much the sexual animal. "Beneath the cloak he was half-naked, his bronze body thewed like a young gladiator. Black and thick as a *vandar's* mane, his unshorn hair blew from broad shoulders, framing his stern, impassive face, strong-jawed, clean-shaven, grimly expressionless. Under scowling black brows his strange gold eyes blazed with sullen, lion-like fires." Other, non-physical features are less lovingly detailed. Poul Anderson's description of Conan would do justice to almost any of the breed:

Conan is [not] much...of an individual. His characteristics are few and obvious. Fearless in battle, though prone to superstitious terrors, he is a moody soul, his mirth rare and crude. He is unflinchingly loyal to friends, unrelentingly fierce to enemies. He picks up some knowledge of tactics, but seems innocent of all strategic concepts, and is handicapped (I should think) by such peculiar prejudices as his belief that the bow is an unmanly weapon.

Until rather late in life, he looks on women immaturely, as mere toys, and shows no particular interest in starting a family... Conan possesses a rough chivalry, and is not at all sadistic; but neither does he ever seem to think that the men he cuts down in such wholesale lots are human, too. This, with much else, betrays his limited intelligence...

But when we have thus delineated Conan, what remains is still good. He *is* brave, honest in his own fashion, steadfast, vaguely conscious of *noblesse oblige*. Once his juvenile-delinquent phase has been outgrown, he does his dogged best. You can like him, even if you wouldn't invite him to dinner.

If Martin's Ironjade warriors represent what one might *wish* to believe of the archaic hero, the prototypical barbarian who actually dominates the genre, judging by this description, implies a singularly adolescent view of what heroism and leadership comprise. Even when it resists its natural tendency to degenerate into thinly disguised sado-masochism (as exemplified by John Norman's seemingly endless and blatantly erotic Gor series, fixated as it is on the image of the adoring slavegirl, the erstwhile haughty princess degraded and enchained by her barbaric captor), the pure heroic-barbaric fantasy consequently lends itself less to *serious* (even according to the standards of "popular" genres) fiction than to pulp. The home-grown barbaric hero demands a certain amount of recognition, however, because he exemplifies, albeit in an extreme form, a number of values and attitudes, a code of behavior, which, in contrast to the somewhat less simplistic conventions of the traditional pastoral mode, tends at least by the late 70s to dominate American fantasy as a whole.

As a consequence of this influence, although the largest and most popular body of fantasy fiction in this country, loosely labelled sword and sorcery, is in terms of conventions located somewhere on the spectrum *between* the pastoral and heroic-barbaric poles, much of it takes its attitudinal stance from and models its heroes after the latter. Fritz Leiber's Nehwon stories offer a classic example of the species. At first it may appear that his two heroes simply reconcile in their separate persons the two opposing modes. Fafhrd, on the one hand, is in generic terms clearly a Conan-type. As Leiber himself describes it in his Introduction to *Swords and Deviltry* (1970), his "origins were easy to perceive in his near seven-foot height and limber-looking ranginess, his hammered ornaments and huge longsword: he was clearly a barbarian from the Cold Waste North." The Gray Mouser's antecedents, on the other hand, "were more cryptic and hardly to be deduced from his childlike stature, gray garb, mouse-skin hood shadowing flat swart face, and deceptively dainty rapier; but somewhere about him was the suggestions of cities and the south." The fact is, before he became an itinerant swordsman, Mouser was a sorcerer's apprentice. The Barbarian and the Magician: what we seem to have here is an exemplary illustration of the heroic and the pastoral paired. In practice, however, Mouser, just as much as Fafhrd, despite his early associations, now lives less by the power of sorcery than by his masculine prowess and (here is one place sword and sorcery typically differs slightly from the more blatantly anti-intellectual heroic-barbaric fantasy) his wits. In pastoral the goal of the hero is usually some sort of enlightenment: the villain is rarely if ever defeated by strength alone. The focus of sword and sorcery, as in heroic-barbaric fantasy, is, in contrast, quite specifically the military contest and the kind of victory that can be won by trial of arms. Magic may, and often does, enter into the picture in one way or another (unlike the pure Conan-type, both Fafhrd and the Gray Mouser have patron sorcerers), but because of the masculine orientation it is rarely a principle tool of the hero himself.

In addition to the two basic modes of pastoral and heroic-barbaric, there is yet one other category of fantasy in America which is in formal opposition to but borrows aspects from both of the others. In this last mode, usually called medieval futurism, technology (in theory anyway) replaces both magic and the primitive martial arts. The futuristic orientation of SF, in other words, is (somewhat paradoxically) combined with the social structure and patterns of behavior of archaic romance. We have seen it before—this is where fantasy and SF most clearly overlap—but without really examining the phenomenon for what it is. In Carter's words,

> [T]he...space opera tradition, socially regressive though it was, seems downright enlightened by comparison with the antiquated political forms typical of more recent interstellar fiction. Writers—even very good writers—have seemed unable to conceive of galactic society except in terms of absolutism and/or feudalism.
>
> "Cordwainer Smith" (Paul Linebarger), for example, whose work in the 1960s won deservedly high esteem, has his Lords of the Instrumentality, among whom "Mister and Owner" is a highly honorific form of address; his arbitrary forms of justice; his "under-people." Even so supposedly advanced a world as that portrayed in Frank Herbert's *Dune*...is a curiously old-fashioned place. The planet exists in a cosmos of squabbling barons and dukes, while its own native people resemble the nomads of Arabia Deserta just prior to the advent of Islam... In such a future universe, starships and lasers do have their place, but upon the world of Dune it is important to be able to strum a nine-stringed *baliset* and to swing a sword.

The question arises, of course, as to why such a peculiar vision of the future should emerge in the U.S. "Donald Wollheim in his personal history of science fiction, *The Universe Makers*, traces the beginnings of that consensus future history to Asimov's *Foundation* stories," says James Gunn, but other writers like Edmond Hamilton, Doc Smith, and Robert Heinlein could equally well be singled out as important contributors to the developing vision. "In the [SF] ghetto...as the stories and ideas passed, so to speak, from hand to hand, they were refined and added to like an oral epic until general agreement was reached—no one was bound to it, but through most stories ran the same general assumptions about what was likely to happen." The feudal future was, in other words, a kind of communal invention. Tracing its roots does not, however, explain the *popularity* of medieval futurism. Even if we stipulate a man-dominated universe, surely there are more plausible forms for it to take.

At least part of the impetus must be the lingering influence of that peculiar nineteenth-century version of chronological primitivism which, especially as codified by Ruskin, redirected British nostalgia from the ancient Celts and Britons to the Middle Ages. Such a vision as this may seem incompatible with

American democracy but, in fact, the feudal social model is better able than almost any other to provide an illusion of stability to counter the anxieties of a fast-moving technological society, while the chivalric code appears to foster the same ideal of individual action that the American has always revered. The concept becomes even more gratifying in the context of SF. Normally, as Scholes (1975) points out, "Legendary time has two stages, a 'then' and a 'now.' Then, there were giants in the earth, or a paradise inhabited by man. Now, men are smaller and the conditions of existence are more constricting." By projecting the nostalgic dream—in this case the medieval model— into the future (which the pastoral mode, implicated in the convention of "Once upon a time," does not do), SF implies that the vision is a real possibility rather than merely a wishful ideal.

Here, then, is our answer. The 70s mood, for all those reasons outlined above, was particularly amenable to the idea of a simpler but more heroic feudal future; the medieval trappings in turn lent themselves to—indeed, seemed to demand—the fictional conventions of romance. Insofar as it leans toward medieval futurism, 70s SF consequently overlaps with and tends to turn into fantasy. How, in that case, can we discriminate between the two modes? It must be admitted that this is a difficult point—indeed it is here, if anywhere, that we find a justification for Wollheim's statement quoted above that the line has become very "smudged and shadowy" of late. To a large extent classification must depend very much on the intangibilities of the author's stance and tone. James Schmitz's *The Witches of Karres* (1966), despite the fact that its focus is a race of paranormally gifted individuals actually labelled as "witches" by popular consensus, is quite clearly SF. Andre Norton's Witchworld series, on the other hand, despite its pseudo-scientific explanation that the setting is a planet governed by different natural laws than earth, to which a group of Terrans were accidentally teleported some time in the past, is just as clearly fantasy.

In other cases the distinction is not quite so easy to make, though. When hard-core "scientific" SF writer Larry Niven turned to a more romantic mode (and this in itself is a significant indicator of the 70s trend), he produced a book called *The Magic Goes Away* (1978) in which *subject matter* (plot, characters, setting) is unambiguously aligned with the conventions of pastoral fantasy. His concept of "magic" as a natural (and therefore exhaustible) energy at one time latent in the earth is logical and rigorously consistent enough in its presentation, however, that from another point of view the book satisfies the most stringent prescriptions of classic SF. And what about something like Poul Anderson's *The High Crusade* (1975)? This book, in which a group of fourteenth-century Englishmen almost by accident capture a spaceship from extraterrestrial invaders and transport themselves to the aliens' home planet where, pitting primitive vitality against scientific sophistication, they blunder their way into interstellar domination, provides a hilarious demonstration of the contemporary consensual view that feudalism is the most logical and most effective form for interstellar government to take:

The ins and outs of what happened are too complex, too various from world to world, for this paltry record. But in essence, on each inhabited planet, the Wersgorix had destroyed whatever original civilization existed. Now the Wersgor system in turn was toppled. Into this vacuum—irreligion, anarchy, banditry, famine, the ever-present menace of a blueface return, the necessity of training the natives themselves to eke out our thin garrison—Sir Roger stepped. He had a solution to these problems, one hammered out in Europe during those not dissimilar centuries after Rome fell: the feudal system.

To which of the two categories of medieval futurism, however, does the book actually belong? The hardware implies one thing; the lack of conventional verisimilitude another. Indeed, in this particular case—since both fantasy *and* SF, for different reasons, tend to take themselves too seriously to be fully comfortable with the comic muse—it could be either, neither, or both.

The fact is, in the long run such distinctions don't really matter too much. All the categories we have listed here tend to overlap in any case. The enormously popular late-70s film *Star Wars*, for instance, is fairly typical inasmuch as although it *appears* to be technology-oriented, with the protagonists using laser beams instead of swords, jet fighters instead of battlehorses, robots instead of animal-helpers, the code of values it exemplifies and the emphasis on personal combat are strictly chivalric/heroic, while the semi-religious conception of a supernatural *Force* energizing cosmic reality is quite in keeping with the magic-oriented pastoral mode. As this example demonstrates, in fact, notwithstanding its literary origins, medieval futurism in general seems closer in *mood* to fantasy than SF. We will simply say, therefore, that at least in 70s versions medieval futurism is basically a class of fantasy the conventions of which have often been borrowed by SF. The entire geography of contemporary fantasy may consequently be presented in the following graphic form. The American norm would be somewhere slightly above and to the right of center.

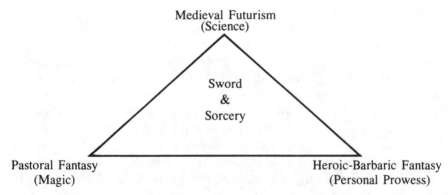

What of the noble savage in this context? What role does nature play? Let's us look at pastoral first. Traditionally the fairy-tale type of story is not only plot-oriented but, since it deals with *patterned* rather than *specific* action, lacks a strong sense of setting altogether. In recent, more complex versions, on the other hand—like Tolkien's *Lord of the Rings*— there does seem to be a general association between naturalness and Good, unnaturalness and Evil. Even here, however, if we look more closely we will realize that the archetypal conflict underlying the conventional quest motif is not, in fact, the nature/civilization, garden/city opposition that we have been tracing throughout this study but something at right angles to it, usually indicated as a conflict between Light and Dark, Order (or Law or Pattern) and Chaos. Nature can be on either or both sides of this dichotomy. Inasmuch as the basic vision is a pastoral and ultimately pagan one, there is a tendency for it to be perceived as a wholesome influence, but inasmuch as the entire field also has strong conventional associations with the specifically Christian chivalric romance, there is something of a distrust of the natural as well. Nature, in other words, can be seen as exemplifying the Law, or it can be seen as a disorderly element. A certain ambivalence is built in.

Even the question of magic becomes an ambiguous one. From one point of view it can be identified with a channeling of natural forces, but (unlike the typical psi powers of SF) it can also be—and more often is—presented as an *art* which requires great dedication and years of practice. Indeed, despite the pastoral setting, the vantage point in the Tolkien-type fantasy, with its medieval vision of social order, its emphasis on the prerogatives and obligations of birth, its celebration of the mystical power of royalty, is quite clearly that of civilization. Animal-helpers or other elemental creatures often turn up in pastoral fantasy but in most cases, largely on the basis of conventional symbolic associations, they simply function as *agents* of one or the other side in the conflict (as the eagles are good and the wolves bad in Tolkien) rather than representing any sort of moral authority in their own right. Any such creature which *does* exhibit a higher degree of autonomy and authority, as do Tolkien's Ents (the tree elementals) and Tom Bombadill, is usually (in traditional versions anyway) indicated quite specifically as morally neutral, essentially indifferent to man, dangerous or beneficial only insofar as his "natural" purposes oppose or parallel human endeavors.

The situation tends to be slightly different in American versions, although the divergence is obscured to some extent by the difficulty that many writers in the mode have had in escaping Tolkien's influence. In a few of the earlier and better American pastoral fantasies, however, there is at least a hint of the old garden/city theme. Evangeline Walton's beautiful and sensitive rendering of the Celtic myth *The Children of Llyr* (1971), for instance, deals with the period of mythic/historical conflict in Britain between the ways of the matriarchal ("natural") Old Tribes and the more warlike, patriarchal New Tribes. The theme of nature versus civilization is not treated explicitly in the book, but it is certainly implicit in the structural framework; the "moral" of the story, as voiced by the druid Math, also suggests a certain association with the conventions of that theme (" 'The Island of the Mighty will have many kings now, but none will reign in peace, and none will found a dynasty. And in the end fair-haired invaders will sweep over all and subject us all—New Tribes and Old alike. Bran might have prevented that had he not given away his sister and the Cauldren, that symbol of the cup within her body—the power of birth and rebirth, the power of woman. Now for ages women will be as beasts of the field and we men will rule, and practice war, our art.' ''). The most explicit and most effective fantasy treatment of the native American garden myth, however, is Ursula LeGuin's juvenile Earthsea trilogy (1968-71).

"What Earthsea represents, through its world of islands and waterways," in Scholes's (1975) words, "is the universe as a dynamic, balanced system, not subject to the capricious miracles of any deity, but only to the natural laws of its own working, which include a role for magic and for powers other than human, but only as aspects of the great Balance or Equilibrium, which is the order of this cosmos." The education of the young wizard, Ged, is thus a kind of ecology fable—more explicit than *Dune*, but based on the same essential vision of reality—demonstrating the appropriate attitude for peaceful coexistence with the natural world. The first lesson (countering the unloving and destructive manipulations of science) is that one must *know* what one would control: " 'A mage can control only what is near him, what he can name exactly and wholly.' '' The second, and more important, concerns the law of reciprocity.

[A] jewel...glittered on Ged's palm... The Old Master murmured one word, "*Tolk*, and there lay [a] pebble, no jewel but a rough grey bit of rock...[H]e took it and held it out on his own hand. "This is a rock; *tolk* in the True Speech," he said, looking mildly up at Ged now. "A bit of the stone of which Roke Island is made... It is itself. It is part of the world. By the Illusion-Change you can make it look like a diamond... But that is mere seeming. Illusion fools the beholder's sense... But it does not change the thing. To change this rock into a jewel, you must change its true name. And to do that, my son, even to so small a scrap of the world, is to change the world. It can be done...and you will learn it, when you are ready to learn it. But you must not change one thing, one pebble, one grain of sand, until you know what good and evil will follow on that act.

Ged's own experience drives home this message. In his youthful arrogance, unconsidering of consequences, he trespasses against the natural order by calling up a demonic creature from the world of the dead, and this transgression, sending its inexorable ripples down into the future as the fall of a pebble spreads disturbance over the surface of a pond, ultimately endangers the health of the whole world. In the end it is only by an act of self-sacrifice equal to the original act of self-indulgence that Balance can be restored.

LeGuin's fantasy is a product of the 60s, of course. It does not, in fact, invoke a noble savage, since its exemplary function has to do with direct rather than mediated experience, with man's duty to nature rather than nature's gifts to man, but in terms of its general sympathies it is aligned with the same world view from which the 60s noble savage emerged. By the mid-70s, however, despite the conventional bias and the distancing effect of the conventional form, even pastoral fantasy begins to show, at least covertly, the influence of the anti-primitivist reaction we observed above. In Patricia McKillop's *The Forgotten Beasts of Eld* (1974), for instance, a central motif is the inhumanity of nature versus the humanizing influence of love. A young sorceress living alone in a mountain garden has at her command all the virtues of nature, exemplified in her entourage of legendary beasts: beautiful, powerful, and wise. To become truly *human*, however, she must trade her invulnerability for pain, freedom for bondage; come down out of her mountain fastness and risk herself with her own kind. Perhaps even more indicative of the peculiarities of this period, however, is Stephen Donaldson's late-70s trilogy, *The Chronicles of Thomas Covenant the Unbeliever.*

On the surface this epic fantasy is very much in the tradition of Tolkien. Set in a basically earthlike but far more vital otherworld or elsewhere, it focuses on the heroic attempts of human and a few allied races to combat the encroaching (and corrupting) powers of chaos which threaten the whole creation with desolation. On a second level Donaldson introduces a variation that places the series quite specifically in the American tradition. A key figure in this cosmic struggle is Thomas Covenant, a man who has been miraculously transported to this faerie setting from 1970s earth. Most significantly, Covenant is made a leper—presumably to connote the unwholesomeness of the modern condition itself. The message seems obvious. If he can transcend his cynical disbelief, the "land" can cure him; he in turn may then redeem the Land. Whatever the ultra-conventional structure leads us to expect, however, this is not, in fact, how the story actually turns out.

For a long time, there is nothing in Donaldson's fantasy to challenge our conditioned response. Reinforcing and clarifying genre expectations, the people of the Land are depicted in terms of almost stereotyped 60s exemplars. Bound by an Oath of Peace, their entire culture is dedicated to nurturing, preserving, and studying nature. In return, nature gifts them with a number of semi-mystical powers; they are able to release and use the efficacy inherent in such natural elements as earth and stone and wood. The keynote of this culture is harmony. Existence for these people has a healthy coherence that Covenant's life totally lacks. Despite the apparently blatant implications of this instructive and much belabored contrast, though, the triumph of Good over Evil at the end of the trilogy does not—as the conventional allegory would seem to suggest—depend on the protagonist's willingness to give up his bitter egocentrism and affirm their "natural," holistic approach to life. Suddenly, in the third book of the series, the author reveals that the earth-bond itself is as much a weakness as it is a strength. "When the first new Lords, and all the Land with them, had taken the Oath, articulated their highest ideal and deepest commitment by forswearing all violent, destructive passions, all human instincts for murder and ravage and contempt—when they had bound themselves with the Oath, they had unwittingly numbed themselves to the basic vitality of the Old Lords' power." In the climactic battle between Covenant and the archvillain, Lord Foul—violating all our expectations—it is consequently *not* a newfound power of love that gives the Earthman victory but, rather, his very resistance *against* the relinquishment of his isolation and sense of self. " 'The Land and Unbelief,' " the Despiser jeers at him. " 'You poor, deranged soul! You cannot have both. They preclude each other.' " "But Covenant knew better; after all that he had been through, he knew better. Only by affirming them both, accepting both poles of the contradiction, keeping them both whole, balanced, only by steering himself not between them but with them, could he preserve them both, preserve both the Land and himself, find the place where the parallel lines of his impossible dilemma met." The one thing that makes this impossible reconciliation possible, according to Donaldson's non-traditional view, is, quite simply, self-assertion. " 'I'm outside the Law. It doesn't control wild magic— it doesn't control me,' " Covenant tells his opponent: " 'it's my will that makes the difference.' " Covenant's triumph over Evil, in other words, lies in a complete and utter egocentricity that *denies* the ultimate power of nature over man, for Evil *or* Good.

> [H]is Unbelief enabled him. He knew more completely than any native of the Land could have known that Lord Foul was not unbeatable. In this manifestation, Despite had no absolute reality of existence. The people of the Land would have failed in the face of Despite because they were convinced of it. Covenant was not. He was not overwhelmed; he did not believe that he had to fail. Lord Foul was only an externalized part of himself— not an immortal, not a god. Triumph was possible.

What apparently starts out as simply another ecology fable, utilizing the same symbolic associations and the same pastoral conventions that LeGuin and other 60s fantasists harnessed so effectively to the service of nature, thus turns out to be nothing less than a celebration of the efficacy of good old-fashioned American self-confidence and rugged individualism.

The result is not an entirely happy one. Whether because Donaldson's specifically modern, relativistic philosophy (" 'This demand for absolute answers is dangerous' ") cannot coexist—either logically or aesthetically—with the implied absolutes of the conventional form, or simply because his protagonist is so unsympathetic, so irritating with his whining self-pity and endlessly reiterated repudiations, that we resist the author's attempt to establish him as an exemplar, one cannot be sure, but if nothing else the experiment (an interesting one for all its flaws) demonstrates that even the pastoral fantasy— where, if anywhere, we might have expected to find the noble savage surviving— tends to reflect the reactionary 70s mood.

What of the other categories? There is a sense in which the barbarian is a kind of noble savage, inasmuch as he comes out of the primitive north to prey upon the effete and citified cultures of the south. To the extent that he epitomizes masculine aggression, however, he, like the pioneer (whom he resembles, temperamentally), must be seen as gaining his definition through *opposition* to nature. There is no superadded ecological fable in barbaric-heroic fantasy, as there is in *Dune*, to obscure this basic fact. We see the true situation quite clearly in that most famous progenitor of the heroic-barbaric mode, *Tarzan of the Apes* (1912). Edgar Rice Burroughs leaves no doubt in our mind that for all he exemplifies the savagery of the jungle, Tarzan is a *man*, using his wilderness training primarily as a weapon *against* his putative brothers, the beasts. "His strange life had left him neither morose nor bloodthirsty. That he joyed in killing, and that he killed with a joyous laugh upon his handsome lips betokened no innate cruelty. He killed for food most often, but, being a man, he sometimes killed for pleasure, a thing which no other animal does." Burroughs' Tarzan, in fact, is not so much *of* the jungle as he is merely *in* it. Indeed, for all that Jane Porter is initially horrified by his table manners ("She saw him eating with his hands, tearing his food like a beast of prey, and wiping his greasy fingers upon his thighs. She shuddered.") Tarzan's essential nature obviously owes less to his environment than to his instincts, his blood, his birth. "It was a stately and gallant little compliment performed with the grace and dignity of utter unselfconsciousness of self," Burroughs tells us of Tarzan's first spontaneous salute to Jane's beauty. "It was the hallmark of his aristocratic birth, the natural outcropping of many generations of fine breeding, an hereditary instinct of graciousness which a lifetime of uncouth and savage training and environment could not eradicate." As McConnell comments of the early film version, therefore, despite any appearances to the contrary, the "garden here...is not the pastoral of Oz...and Tarzan is its master, not its complacent dreamer and pilgrim. One is tempted to call this a picture of *homo cartesianus*," he continues. Far from being a primitive, the "implication of Tarzan's alert but assured stance is that he is lord of the jungle through his Promethean, innately civilized consciousness."

There is thus a lie at the heart of Burroughs' vision. This particular noble savage is none else than a savage noble. The idea that a child raised by apes would turn out that way is, of course, absurd in any case (this is one of the aspects of the Tarzan story which, along with the whole naive concept of what "primitive" behavior actually comprises, draws fire in Philip Jose Farmer's satirical and mildly pornographic *Lord Tyger* [1970]), but even if we were to stipulate this *donnée*, the Tarzan figure—indeed the barbaric hero as a type—obviously expresses the desire for *control* more than the dream of *reconciliation*. The dominance of this particular type in 70s genre fiction is consequently a strong indicator of the covert as well as the overt changes that were taking place in America's public temper over a period that saw the moral authority of nature, as a generalized symbol, give way to the personal authority of the charismatic hero himself.

What do these changes imply in psycho-social terms? Theoretically the shift *could* be a positive one. Contemporary America, complains Joe McGinniss, no longer produces heroes. Why? Because contemporary America is epitomized by mediocrity. "The current utopian ideal being touted by people as politically diverse (on the surface, but not underneath) as President Richard M. Nixon and Senator Edward M. Kennedy goes as follows," said Frank Herbert in 1974: "no deeds of passion allowed, no geniuses, no criminals, no imaginative creators of the new. Satisfaction may be gained only in carefully limited social interactions, in living off the great works of the past. There must be limits to any excitement. Drug yourself into a placid 'norm.' Moderation is the key... In a word, you can be a Bozo, but little else." In such a world as this, the example of the archaic warrior—a fictional version of Nietzsche's superman—would seem to be a healthy counter to life-denying complacency. As we said with respect to Hemingway's matador, in fact, in "the epic struggle of 'great men' seeking to humanize the inhuman, the highest level of the struggle occurs when men contend with death, refusing to acknowledge the modern world's humiliating conception of 'natural death,' an externally imposed impersonal limit to the accomplishments of the will" (Zweig). Hence the continuing importance of an old-fashioned physical (rather than simply moral) heroic ideal:

> Nietzsche did not intend to prescribe warfare, or even individual combat, as the "healthiest" human activity. He meant to offer combat as a model for the more complex activities of culture. In terms of epic contention, he meant to propose an agonistic vision of culture, and of life itself. Nietzsche's philosophy restores the adventurer to the place he had occupied in traditional cultures: no longer an outcast or a criminal, but, like Odysseus or Gilgamesh, a source of values, expressing the essentially human adventure of man engaged in the economy of a struggle which is the world.

Does modern fantasy, on the other hand, actually provide this kind of example? The myths that Zweig cites here exhibit an emotional depth and complexity that the conventional American fantasy just doesn't have. For one thing, Greek tragedy is by and large devoted to the demonstration "that all human greatness contains the seeds of disaster, and is a disaster; that the most vigorous aims of men are transgressions which must be punished. Greatness is the disease. To be a man to the fullest is to deserve, along with immortality in song, the bitterness of punishment." In the more simplistic romance conventions, where being a hero for the most part *means* being a winner, heroism does not demonstrate this kind of two-sidedness, though. The risk is illusory. As such it offers a poor correlation for Nietzsche's existential struggle. It would seem, in fact, that the appeal of the modernday fantasy hero is less that he challenges death (or Evil, or what have you) than that he is able to *beat* it.

Is this bad? if nothing else the image of the invulnerable, all-powerful hero provides an effective compensatory fantasy to offset the frustrations, the feelings of impotence, entailed by modern life. The need for this kind of compensation is undoubtedly why SF, as Thomas Disch points out, tends to be full of "powerless individuals, of ambiguous antecedents, rising to positions of commanding importance. Often they become world saviours." One of the most important functions of such fiction, in other words, is to provide a subversive vision of reality which ostensibly *denies* the helplessness of the average individual. "[The]he chief advantage of the ruling classes, their wealth and the power it provides, is dealt with in most science fiction by simply denying its importance. Power results from personal virtue or the magic of machines" (Disch). Fantasy, however, does not generally work in quite this way. The fantasy hero, especially in America, where he gains much of his character from the conventions of the heroic-barbaric mode, is *not* just an alter ego for the reader, a regular guy who just happened to get the breaks. As Joanna Russ points out, he is, rather, quite clearly an exceptional individual; an individual who—*as we consciously recognize*—appears to give the lie to both existential limitations and the human norm:

> The real He-Man is invulnerable. He has no weaknesses. Sexually he is super-potent. He does exactly what he pleases, everywhere and at all times. He is absolutely self-sufficient. He depends on nobody, for this would be a weakness. Toward women he is possessive, protective and patronizing; to men he gives orders. He is never frightened by anything or for any reason; he is never indecisive; and he always wins.
>
> In short, he is an alien monster, just as I said.
>
> The trouble with this creature—the megalith with the beetling eyebrows—is the trouble with all mythologies. It's not that he doesn't exist, because everybody *knows* he doesn't exist. I don't think there's a single sane man on earth who could seriously and honestly say: Yes, I am all that...I have no weaknesses whatsoever...Everybody obeys me—and so forth. We all know that such a person is impossible. We don't really believe that he exists.
>
> But we do believe that somehow—despite what we actually know about other people and ourselves—that he *ought* to exist, or that he's in some sense ideal.

So what's wrong with this? In fact, quite a bit. Russ here is particularly concerned about the sexist implications ("This is an ideal that is *by definition* absolutely closed to me. I can pretend to be Cleopatra but I can't very well pretend to be Anthony."), but even beyond this rather specialized complaint, it seems evident that the modern fantasy hero evokes a response which is not, ultimately, a healthy one. In the early stages of the noble savage convention, writers generally emphasize the extent to which their literary models can facilitate (whether by example or by symbolic mediation) a better relation between man and his environment; in later stages the attempt to improve this relation becomes even more direct. Heroic fantasy, however, changes not merely the base values of this primitivistic vision but also the stance. The ideal of self-education as a means to an end disappears; despite the emphasis on action *in* the fantasy, the individual observing this action—the reader himself—becomes essentially passive.

How? Such a development was always potential even in more traditional kinds of romance. The corollary to fantasy's happy facility of convincing us, through its formal echoes, that everything is going to come out all right is the further implication that the pattern *cannot* be changed, even if we would. In fairy tales, for instance, as one of Peter Beagle's magical characters explains,

> "The swineherd cannot already be wed to the princess when he embarks on his adventures, nor can the boy knock at the witch's door when she is away on vacation. The wicked uncle cannot be found out and foiled before he does something wicked. Things must happen when it is time for them to happen. Quests may not simply be abandoned; prophecies may not be left to rot like unpicked fruit; unicorns may go unrescued for a long time, but not forever. The happy ending cannot come in the middle of the story." [from *The last Unicorn*]

The feeling is even stronger, moreover, when the conventions are those of myth, which, because it carries a certain religious-cum-historical authority, often gives the impression of *pre*scribing rather than merely transcribing reality. Roger Zelazny's novels are particularly notable for this effect. In *This Immortal* (1966) the mythic patterns of an archaic past—both beasts and heroes—are mysteriously reasserting themselves in a ravaged, post-atomsmash Greece. In *Lord of Light* (1967), similarly, the power of the archetype seemingly transforms what is a purely arbitrary and cynical recreation of the conditions of mythic India by a group of technologically advanced invaders who style themselves as "gods" into the genuine spiritual reality associated with—catalyzed by—the original Buddha. As a result, in "spite of its updating process and historical setting, there is an underlying assumption—perhaps it is Zelazny's, perhaps it is built into the body of myth that he uses—that nothing really changes, that the gods never really die or alter, that what man does is basically irrelevant" (Lois & Stephen Rose). The Roses go on from this observation to object that the presence of such a viewpoint is a flaw in Zelazny, causing frustration in the reader of his books ("This hardly does justice to either human or divine freedom"), but the fact is, what Zelazny demonstrates overtly is a covert pattern in 70s fantasy as a whole. Alexei and Cory Panshin's *Earth Magic* (1978) is typical in this respect. In this book, which opposes two contrasting cultures, one based on the masculine power of arms and the other on the feminine power of magic, the young protagonist is given no opportunity whatsoever to decide for himself where to place his allegiance. He is simply *chosen* by the goddess, and throughout the story, against his will, stripped entirely of his own identity (rank, family, race, even name) to become totally her worshipper and her tool.

Even at best, such a view presents certain problems. As Zweig points out in his discussion of Nietzsche, the "notion of a rational world order, crowned and supported by 'Providence' (belief that 'law,' moral or scientific, will prevail, is a form of belief in Providence), weakens the human faculty of reason, by encouraging a passive attitude." If the perceived world order is *un*rational, as many mythic versions would have it (*vide* the Panshin novel, for instance), the situation is even worse. It is in terms not of reason, however, but of morality that the passiveness encouraged by fantasy may be most deplored. As Disch says, "The moral limitations of a literature built on such premises should be immediately apparent. Evil is seen as intrinsically external, a blackness ranged against the unvaried whites of heroism. Unhappy endings are the outcome of occasional cold equations, not of flawed human nature." Most important, the individual himself need accept no responsibility or blame.

When the charismatic hero enters the picture, the problems become even more acute. Unlike the noble savage, this figure, distanced as he is from all that is "ordinary," operates less as a model than as a messiah. Our felt relationship with him, consequently, is vertical rather than horizontal. Attributes and instrumentalities aside, the hint of hierarchy—invoking as it does the whole weight of what Tobin calls the "genealogical imperative"—is enough in itself to make this particular heroic typos an extremely ambivalent one. After the excesses of the 60s, as after the excesses of the 20s, it was almost inevitable that Americans would be attracted by the image of a Christ-like avenger capable of combatting not merely the bad guys but their own "insidious moral decline" (Hoppenstand). In the context of a political tradition condemning paternalism, however, and especially in the aftermath of the specifically anti-establishment, anti-authoritarian youth movements of the previous decade, the idea of acquiescence—of delegating completely both responsibility and choice—was bound also to evoke a certain amount of covert guilt.

Even aside from this general consideration, the fantasy tale itself is usually framed in such a way as to play up the more equivocal aspects of its own subtext. For one thing, there is often a strong (if subliminal) indication that the basis of our affective investment in the fantasy hero is essentially and specifically sexual. This holds not only where—as in the case of Tarzan and Jane—a "real" liaison is involved, but in almost *any* instance where the hero's masculine prowess has erotic undertones. Whatever parents and educators may say about the "bad examples" offered by this type of fictional experience, in other words, the average, uncritical reader, simply in automatic reaction to the hero's flaunted male dominance, tends unconsciously to assume the submissive attitude exemplified in Jane. "Presently Tarzan took to the trees, and Jane, wondering that she felt no fear, began to realize that in many respects she had never felt more secure in her whole life than now as she lay in the arms of this strong, wild creature, being borne, God alone knew where or to what fate, deeper and deeper into the savage fastness of the untamed forest." "She could not analyze her feelings, nor did she wish to attempt it. She was satisfied to feel the safety of those strong arms, and to leave her future to fate." In a political/cultural ambience as overtly masculine as the reactionary 70s appeared to be, our readiness to identify with/participate in this kind of response must be seen as signalling a rather disquieting public schizophrenia. It also signals a clear and present threat to democracy. No matter what its apparent validation, the fact is that unquestioning acceptance is dangerous. It is built on the illusion—if not the outright lie—that might is right, will *always* be right, for no other reason than the fact that it *is* might.

Naive? Certainly. As Zweig points out, there is a fundamental semantic confusion involved.

Why do we say that Odysseus is a hero? As a leader of men he is a remarkable failure. He is neither virtuous nor loyal, and he is a compulsive liar...

The problem, I think, lies in our use of the word "hero," which has overlapping meanings. In literature it [simply] refers to the central character in a story... In our usual parlance, however, the word has a wider meaning with moral overtones. By hero, we tend to mean a heightened man who, more than other men, possesses qualities of courage, loyalty, resourcefulness, charisma, above all, selflessness. He is an example of right behavior; the sort of man who risks his life to protect a society's values, sacrificing his personal needs for those of the community. Virgil's Aeneas is a hero, in this sense of the word. He devotes his warrior skills, his pleasures, and finally his life to the historical destiny of founding Rome...

There is...[however], another sort of heightened man who bulks large in the popular imagination... He is not "loyal," not a model of right behavior. Quite the contrary, he fascinates because he undermines the expected order. He possesses the qualities of the "hero"... But he is the opposite of selfless. He is hungry, "heightened," not as an example, but as a presence, a phenomenon of sheer energy... One thinks of criminals like Dillinger, or the old Hollywood stars, who thrilled us because they were such grandiosely bad examples in their private lives. These heightened men get too much pleasure out of their lives. We do not want our sons to be like them, yet they hold our attention. We perceive them as rebels and violators, encroaching on forbidden territory.

The American, judging by his taste in fantasy, tends to assume that his heroes are, at least in ultimate terms, members of the first of these two classes. Oh, not so much in the sense that they are expected to be explicitly law-abiding (the outlaw, after all, has become almost institutionalized as a national ideal), but in the sense that they are trusted to do the "right thing" in the end. Such trust, however, is foolhardy. If either of Zweig's prototypes can be said to represent the American hero, it is certainly *not* Aeneas. Take our oh-so-charismatic barbarian, for instance. At best he is self-seeking, deceitful Odysseus; at worst (and it's not a big jump, unfortunately) he is Achilles: unstable, irrational, dangerous—above all, as Zweig points out, "brutally antisocial."

That this sinister potential has from the beginning been just as strong in SF/fantasy as the eminently social vision of the clean-jawed young astronaut is amply demonstrated in an unusual novel by Norman Spinrad. The "alternate history" depicted by *The Iron Dream* (1972) is one in which Adolf Hitler moves to America and becomes a successful SF writer, winning both critical and popular acclaim for his award-winning futuristic fantasy, *Lord of the Swastika*. The implications of Spinrad's book are particularly disturbing in retrospect, since the fantasy boom of the 70s has tended to emphasize exactly those ambiguous aspects of the genre around which *The Iron Dream* revolves. Spinrad's basic aim here is to satirize the fiction by showing how it reflects a disreputable reality. The real danger now would seem to be the possibility that reality will come to reflect a disreputable fiction. The fantasy Hitler *did* invent was much more devastating than the ones he *might* have invented as a SF writer.

Is it possible that these ambiguities, as obvious as they are, have not occurred to the readers of heroic fantasy? If so, it certainly hasn't affected the popularity of the species. Indeed, fantasy seems to be addictive in a way even beyond most genre fiction. Western fans and murder-mystery fans may read voraciously in their specialties, but to a large extent, assuming a certain minimum level of skill and conventional consistency, one book is much like another. An Agatha Christie lover will usually enjoy equally Margery Allingham or Ngaio Marsh, and outside of the obligatory detective and his cohorts (who tend to comprise a kind of collective *deus ex machina* rather than being real people in any case) it is rare for individual characters or settings to recur. Fantasy readers *and* writers, however, seem to have a particular hunger for the illusion that their favorite fictional worlds are "true." This means, for one thing, that the settings and cultures involved are typically delineated, both in the stories themselves and by means of such additional support materials as "historical" appendices, maps, and glossaries, in incredible detail. More important, it accounts for the fact that an attractive, fully realized fantasy world almost always tends to expand far beyond individual stories. Both readers and writers apparently want to return to these settings, again and again. As many of the above references certify, fantasy (both better-quality and pulp) is thus very often produced in *sets* of three, four, or even more. Anne McCaffrey's Pern novels (*Dragonflight, Dragonquest,* etc.) are up to seven now; Philip Jose Farmer's World of Tiers series and Roger Zelazny's Amber series include five volumes apiece; Marion Zimmer Bradley's Darkover tales are well into double figures, with no necessary end in sight.

Interestingly enough, all four of the popular fantasy series in this list feature some version of a wish-fulfilling dream of power. The first suggests the possibility of mastery over and total rapport with a *dragon,* a creature which—augmenting its already considerable mythic authority—is here endowed with the power to transcend the limitations of both time and space. The second posits a super-science capable not only of bestowing personal immortality but of actually creating new universes to order. The third is based on the premise that phenomenal reality, comprising a continuous series of dimensionally-parallel alternate "worlds," was originally created and may be changed by an act of will and imagination. The last gives us a "lost" colony on a world where interaction with alien life forms stimulated—in a few of the original settlers—the development of hereditary telepathic/telekinetic talents. Even *more* interesting, considering the foregoing discussion is the fact that in every one of these cases, the fantasied power is available *only* to a small, exclusive elite rather than being in any way democratically allotted or accessible. In McCaffrey's books the candidates are selected arbitrarily by the dragons themselves on the basis, apparently, of some mystical sympathy perceived at the moment of birth. In Farmer's fantasy, the super-science is in the hands of a small group of ultra-civilized (but morally degenerate) "Lords." In Zelazny's and Bradley's novels it is quite simply noble blood that does the trick. This increasingly exclusive conception of power, apparently grafting the elitism of high fantasy onto the putatively more democratic qualifications of the barbarian, leads ultimately to that *nonpareil* of American heroic fantasy, Superman—a figure originally conceived in the 30s but, with some interesting political implications, recently revived:

The quintessential myth of omniscience and power in the folklore of the thirties is represented...by the corpuscular space detective, Superman... Since he is virtually immortal and can move away in defiance of gravity from the mean city streets and the life of Clark Kent, he enjoys a more glossy appeal than the...[merely human heroes] with their strange fears and limitations. Thinking never occurs to Superman; it is just not necessary for the success of his missions and could probably interfere with their execution. Leo Gurko capsulates this adequately: "Superman is sublimely indifferent, a condition in some ways more devastating than outright repudiation. He is, like Tarzan and most other factitiously primitive figures, a symbol of pure motor action, whose profound attraction lies in that very fact! To create personages who are free of the responsibilities of mind and have conquered the terrors of Nature is to provide a measure of release for oneself."

Superman appeared in 1938... The timing of his arrival was welcome in a society soon to be jittered by a radio version of H.G. Wells's *War of the Worlds* and threats of holocaust from European power devils... [As] an exotic descendent of Paul Bunyan, Pecos Bill, Jack London's Buck and Tarzan...[he] occupies the heroic position of cosmic pioneer who liberates the mythology of picaresque folklore by . . . argu[ing] against self-limitation and understanding. He, and his pop-culture progenies, Batman, Wonder Woman, Captain Marvel and Kid Eternity, are metaphors of a dream of limitless and juvenile power which gives access to the politicization of myth and the proposition "that 'evil' is a formulated conquerable enemy unable to resist American magic." [Melling; closing quote from Eric Mottram]

Once the hero becomes *absolutely* powerful, of course, he is no longer so much hero as god. And in many ways this exacerbates the problems indicated above. Whatever the Superman legend may imply (this typos, says Eco, is by definition "profoundly kind, moral, faithful to human and natural laws, and therefore . . . [uses] his powers only to the end of good"), gods are *not* necessarily benevolent. Look at the example of the Greeks. As we have already noted, however, vulnerability has never inspired the Americans (*unlike* the Greeks) to rise to tragedy. In this regard, in fact, it is interesting to note that the same period that made the film version of *Superman* a blockbuster hit, also—in both pulp fiction and popular movies—saw a significant revival of the gothic mode. It is this phenomenon, if any, which provides an outlet for covert anxiety about the superhero's intentions, especially insofar as the vehicle it offers is so strikingly consistent with the fatalism engendered by the whole heroic mode. The gothic, in fact, is a kind of inversion of the heroic fantasy proper. As Zweig describes it, the "opposite side of the satanism of the nineteenth-century Romantics is the dream of helplessness which emerges in the Gothic novel . . . Gothic novels, therefore, do not tell stories of adventure; they tell stories that long for adventure. Their situations call for adventurous exploits which fail miserably. The flood of Gothic anxiety results from actions not accomplished, deflated by ineptitude, heroes crushed helplessly by dark powers." We can thus perhaps see heroic fantasy and gothic horror as being the two sides of the essential 70s vision.

Where does this leave America? There is some indication to be found in late-70s, early-80s popular culture that the reaction goes even further than the relative passiveness implied by the heroic mode. As J. Norman King points out, "where conditions seem unchanging and unchangeable by human hands, man's fulfillment tends to be portrayed either in terms of an intervention from without by a force greater than man or in terms of the removal of man from his earthly realm." If we reverse this, we might say that the dominance of a *deus ex machina* motif in any period probably signals a certain resignation about the human lot. From this point of view, it is interesting to note that in a decade in which the SF alien is generally quite ambiguous, there is something of a counter-trend to be noticed, especially in popular modes of entertainment like movies and television, which invokes an immanent contact with a god-like, ultra-civilized, technologically superior, and (hopefully) ethically impeccable super-alien. *Close Encounters of the Third Kind*, one of the most popular films of 1978, is a prototype here. King ponders the implications of this phenomenon:

Reflecting upon such references to alien intelligences in science fiction and, in a broader context including the flying saucer phenomenon, Robert Plank observes that such imagined beings are expected generally to come either to save or to destroy us. He concludes that, from a psychological vantage point, such a relationship bears an uncanny resemblance to the love-hate Oedipal attitude of the small child to his father as perceived by that child. It reflects the childish wish for a "daddy" who will either punish us and get it over with or take care of us and make everything better. This view, which contains a great deal of validity, is essentially an adaptation of Freud's interpretation of belief in God as the illusion that our parents run the universe for our benefit, thus exemplifying a refusal to face the harshness of reality. A crucial element here is the association of the alien with a deity-figure.

From the ambiguous super-lover of heroic fantasy we thus move to the ultimate father-figure for a modern age. For a nation in which symbolic fatherhood connotes so many conflicting emotions (reverence-resentment-fear-guilt: the whole Major Molineaux syndrome), the development is a provocative one to say the least. Perhaps, however, it is merely the predictable corollary to contemporary fantasy's predilection for a Deuteronomic view of life. If the 70s reader feels a certain anxiety about his inability to live up to his 60s program for self-improvement and public enlightenment (his failure to make good the example of the noble savage), he has a strong incentive for rationalizing his dependence on an authoritarian father. "The biblical doctrine of justification by faith, properly perceived as forgiveness in the face of failure to meet *legitimate* demands, is Christianity's way of suggesting a means of freeing man from his predicament of guilt fed by the failure to do what he knows he should do," explain Lois and Stephen Rose. Similarly, it is secular faith, conditioned by the resurgent hero-worship of the 70s, that works to relieve contemporary anxieties by rehabilitating the father figure that eighteenth-century rationality dethroned.

It will be interesting to see what, in a political as well as a literary sense, the rest of the 80s will bring. Is Ronald Reagan a fluke, or will paternalistic leadership become the rule? Whatever else happens, it seems likely that the noble savage will disappear from the scene for a time. Even leaving aside the question of nature, paradoxically enough, as the active hero implies a passive auditor, the savage, being essentially passive himself, demands from the reader a more active participation. Judging from developments in genre fiction, this is not, evidently, what the post-70s American wants. The new alignment that will characterize the garden/city myth of the 80s is hence perhaps hinted at in Marvin Kaye and Parke Godwin's SF-cum-fantasy novel *The Masters of Solitude* (1979) where, despite their richer emotional lives, their enjoyment of nature, their physical vitality, the rural primitives of the book—typically enough, telepathic—are trying to find a way to get *into* the heavily protected, self-contained machine-city where, they hope, they will be able to find the scientific knowledge necessary to defeat a spreading plague. Once again the pattern has evidently inverted. Recent versions of the space-westering tale, too, seem to be undergoing a process of alteration. In a 1979 anthology edited by Jerry Pournelle, aptly named *The Endless Frontier*, space pioneers, rather than questing after a new, green, garden-planet where they can despoil Eden all over again, work to build their own space communities, totally artificial machine-cities hollowed out of lifeless asteroids or floating free in space. Pournelle's selection is far from anomalous. The same faith in/excitement about the wonders of science can be detected in book after book, movie after movie, produced during the last half-dozen years. As Lemieux puts it, "SF is now *technology's 'chanson de geste.'* " There is only one plausible explanation for such a development. Somewhere along the line—about the same time, no doubt, as they decided they wanted a president equipped to simulate "the classic hero of the Old West" (Hankins)—Americans shifted right back to technological optimism again.

6. Summary and Conclusions

Despite the apparent incompatibility between the characteristically ironic twentieth-century world view and the optimistic stance implied by "romantic" primitivism, the noble savage evidently lived—and died—again in American genre fiction during the last few decades. The most pressing question raised by this phenomenon is what the revival implies about American culture as a whole.

The simplest way to answer this question is to suppose that the operative links are the genetic ones; that the noble savage appeared at this time and in this context because of an essential sympathy between his own conventional associations and the assumptions underlying genre fiction as a class, rather than because of any specific historico-cultural factors implying special relevance for this particular age. What is the common element on which such compatibility as this might be based? Like primitivism in general, genre fiction, as we implied above, is commonly thought to express an "escapist" impulse. "The romance form," says Patrick Brantlinger, "always shadows forth a regressive journey inward and backward, through childlike states of mind, threatening the dissolution of the adult ego, while the novel form resists and punishes such dissolution, and also invokes higher principles of socialization and adult moral growth." Scholes (1975) denies the imputation of irresponsibility hinted at here, claiming that the sublimative function of literature is just as natural—and as necessary to human health—as is sleeping and dreaming (which in a fashion it resembles). He too, however, relates this function with the attempt to avoid unpleasant realities (sublimative fiction, "is connected to our actual existence precisely by offering us relief from its problems and pressures"). Cawelti is even more specific about the nature of the avoidance strategies by which such modes allow the reader to "escape." First, he says, formula stories "affirm existing interests and attitudes by presenting an imaginary world that is aligned with these interests and attitudes." Secondly, they "resolve tensions and ambiguities resulting from the conflicting interests of different groups within the culture or from ambiguous attitudes toward particular values. The action of a formula story will tend to move from an expression of tension of this sort to a harmonization of these conflicts." Thirdly, formulas "enable the audience to explore in fantasy the boundary between the permitted and the forbidden and to experience in a carefully controlled way the possibility of stepping across this boundary." Leaving aside the debate whether a taste for such varieties of wish fulfillment is or is not ultimately reprehensible ("the regressive nature of the romance form triggers feelings of guilt which have led to the devaluation of the form itself," says Brantlinger—but it is interesting to note how closely

Cawelti's program aligns with what is held to be a primary function of myth), it would seem reasonable to speculate that both the increased popularity of genres like SF during the last two decades *and* the tendency for such fiction to subsume the nostalgic fantasies that have always formed a substratum to the folk consciousness in America were a direct result of the predominance of the unpleasant wasteland image that Olderman remarks in mainstream literature of the period. To be more specific, the high degree of anxiety entailed by such a bleak vision simply stimulated an upsurge in and confluence of all available conventional vehicles for providing psychic relief.

The most obvious flaw in this neat solution is founded in the possibility that the status and function of "regressive" modes in America are not quite what the classic pattern outlined by Brantlinger might suggest. For one thing, what are we to make of the fact that for much of its history America's mainstream as well as "popular" literature seems to have been dominated by these very modes? As pointed out above, for instance, it has become almost a critical commonplace that it is the romance—the form Chase describes as being "less committed to the immediate rendition of reality than the novel," having in common with "the mythic, allegorical, and symbolistic forms" a "tendency to plunge into the underside of consciousness" and "to abandon moral questions or to ignore the spectacle of man in society"—which, *despite* the articulated preferences of the more internationally oriented literary establishment, comprises in an important sense *the* American form. One might not wish to grant the full degree of homogeneity that Chase's thesis implies, but there is obviously considerable evidence in the corpus itself to support at least a modified version of his view. Nicholaus Mills, for one, objects strenuously to the misleadingly broad generalizations about national differences typically entailed by such approaches, but even he has to admit a *relative* predominance in America of a kind of literary practice quite contrary to the traditional emphases and assumptions of the novel ("certain ideational or visionary concerns...[are made] superior to or situationally transcendent of the social context in which they appear") with the result that ostensibly comparable works—like Scott's Waverly novels and Cooper's Leatherstocking Tales, for instance—"for all their historical and poetic similarities," ultimately "seem to face in opposite directions: in the one case forward; in the other backward." This, of course, would normally be considered one of the fundamental distinctions between the novel and the romance. The point may thus be made that the American does seem to have an atypical propensity for the regressive form.

What exactly does this mean, though? On the simplest level—taken at face value—the preference would merely seem to imply that the American has historically been more prone than his European counterpart, while mouthing conventional slogans about the paramount importance of a social perspective, to indulge himself in *anti*-social dreams—and many aspects of American literary history would seem to suggest that this is in fact the case. If nothing else, there is the problem of the missing background. As noted in the Introduction, though it was commonplace during the nineteenth century for writers to lament that America offered neither the historical associations nor the social diversity necessary to provide good raw material for literature, the *practice* of these same writers—their preference for and preoccupation with specifically ahistoric fictional fantasy worlds—clearly undercuts the seriousness of their critique. Clark claims that the "rhetorical strategy of defining a society by the absence of negative features is characteristic of the utopian vision." From at least one point of view, then, the chorus of complaints about the "thin texture" of American culture may "be seen as a peculiar affirmation of the Edenic myth." Given the extreme disparity in this case between saying and doing, on the other hand, it is difficult to avoid the suspicion that the absenting of society from literature, far from covertly affirmative, was in fact symptomatic of an unwholesome bent in American consciousness as a whole. Indeed, if we were to take evinced tastes at face value, we would probably have to conclude that the country's moral fibre actually *was* undermined, just as Crevecoeur feared, by too much wilderness: Moira unrestrained by Themis. Other factors, however, suggest that the situation was somewhat more complicated that this.

What are they? Well, for one thing, we must not forget that American ideology, as already noted, differs from European in numerous important respects. This, among other things, alters significantly the public if not the private connnotations of romance. The view of the functions (and value) of so-called regressive modes that we have been examining in the last few pages is, at least partially, based on extrinsic assumptions about what, ideally, the relation between an individual and his social context should be. It is, in fact, quite specifically a European perspective we invoke when we stipulate that the "serious" (that is, typically pessimistic) mainstream novel expresses the official ethos of society, considering the naively cheerful romance to be by extension basically subversive, countering or at least short-circuiting the moral concerns of the modern secular state. As a summary of *American* attitudes, therefore, the model is somewhat inadequate. If we look more directly at the situation in this country, it becomes evident that the relationship between progressive and regressive visions here, compared to Europe, is in a sense actually reversed. Due to the terms of her founding, in other words, the *official* stance in America is very close to what would be considered subversive elsewhere. Its (ambivalent) ratification of masculine aggression notwithstanding, the party line in this country, as we have already observed, has always been quite amenable to, and indeed to some extent entails, the wish-fulfilling dream of cutting loose from historical necessity and social limitation, of moral and personal election; in short, of *escape*.

The assumptions of the seventeenth-century New England Calvinist differ as night from day from the assumptions of the late eighteenth-century rational, radical American deist. Yet they both have deeply in common the millennialistic self-imagery that was prepared for the New World by centuries of European imagination which transmogrified into the Christian contexts of Paradise regained and the City on the Hill the older Classical contexts of the Lost Golden Age...[to project a vision] of America as a special and new redemptive force in history...

So, too, although the nineteenth century, with its Romantic Transcendentalism, differed as much from either of the two preceding centuries as they did from each other, it, too, replaced culturally exhausted language and concepts in order to forge new ones to express the continuing idea of America as a special symbol...

...[T]he [subsequent] debasement and popularization of the millennialistic strain of many centuries of self-image is the political substratum upon which the critical edifices of the literary marketplace were built... Our materialistic insistence upon actualities turns the millennialistic strain into something like this: the visible actualities and necessities of common life are Reality; the success of historical process is proved in successful marketplace identity. American Reality is cheerful, fulfilling, good and, in all those terms, expansively and expandingly progressive. In sum what *is* is millennium realized or in the state of being very rapidly realized, and to question the unstated assumption that American society and bourgeois values are perfectability in process was un-Christian, un-American, and unmanly. [Stern]

As this passage implies, in whatever terms it was expressed, optimism—a sense of national exclusiveness and special privilege—was built into America's official ideology right from the start. Add to this the promise seemingly inherent in the physical realities of the American environment—the fact that, in Poirier's (1966) words, this was "the only time in history men could, with the prospect of a new continent, actually believe in their power at last to create an environment congenial to an ideal self"—and it seems very likely that the purportedly subversive romance form, with its implied regressive tendencies, far from signalling a mass defection on the part of American writers, *merely reflected the socially codified concerns and beliefs of the social ambience out of which they wrote.*

It is easy to see how this rather peculiar situation could affect the inherited attitudes that govern American literary expression even today. In particular, it throws a rather interesting light on the phenomenon of genre fiction with which we opened this discussion a few pages back. At the very least, we would seem to be dealing with a divided consciousness here. From one point of view, it's the mainstream novel with its obsession with the wasteland that represents the exemplary response and the optimistic romance-related genre fiction that's morally reprehensible; from another it's the ostensibly "realistic" stance that subverts the approved national vision with its perversely negativistic bias. As Stern says of the nineteenth century, "Since one assumption was that mundane American life in fact *was* good, [it was felt that] the gloomy and the morbid were not reflections of actualities, but were merely unpatriotic and disturbing reflections of what the literary marketplace called 'subjective' in the artist's imagination." From this latter perspective it's a mode like classic SF, its broad apocalyptic assumptions balanced both by social positivism and by a reassuring verisimilitude in detail, which expresses the authentic American self-image far better than the modern or contemporary mainstream novel—as described in chapter 4—possibly could. The burgeoning of genre fiction in the 60s and 70s thus cannot simply be written off as signalling a communal "escapist" impulse brought on by the unpleasant social and political realities of that particular time. Such a motive undoubtedly does enter into the picture to some extent, but the recent development may just as easily be seen simply as the *reassertion* of an attitude that has played a dominant part in America's national consciousness all along.

We find ample support for this interpretation if we re-examine what happened in mainstream literature during the period that the SF/fantasy boom was going on. Far from reaffirming the formal divergence between cognitive and sublimative functions (which is what one would expect it to do in the context of a resurgence of "popular" modes designed explicitly to satisfy the latter), mainstream fiction in the last two decades has in many ways demonstrated a propensity to *converge* with the purportedly sub-literary types.

At first this convergence takes place only on the level of *form*, as if to disguise the urge that it represents (in the context of modern scepticism and despair, the optimistic fantasy seems too puerile to embrace openly; the idyllic vision—which Honig, somewhat loosely, calls "pastoral"—is "acceptable only embarrassedly, in paradoxical, effete, or otherwise limited terms—as say, a joke"). Further, the explicit intentions are to a large extent reversed. When Kurt Vonnegut uses a time-travel motif in *Slaughterhouse V*, or William Burroughs employs the conventions of the alien-invader story in *Nova Express*, or—less extremely—Walker Percy invokes the disaster tale in *Love in the Ruins* the intention is clearly not, as in "straight" SF, to make the fantastic plausible but, rather, to underline the fact that the plausible is fantastic. As Olderman (1972) stresses in his study of the 60s novel, in fact, one of the major impulses behind contemporary fiction seems to have been the perception that modern American society is more absurd than anything one could possibly invent.

On the other hand, even as the parody of the popular genres is used to convey a very serious criticism of the quality of twentieth-century life, almost imperceptibly the usage begins to betray a covert desire (implicit in the parodic model but running entirely counter to the ostensible ideational thrust of the elaborated version) not for confrontation but, quite simply, for denial of absurdity. As Olderman points out, for instance, while a "cartoon version of identity provides the inevitable joke aimed at our sacred ideas of identity...it also contains an intimation of secret yearnings toward the comic book hero's control over human events." Surreptitiously, therefore, the mainstream novel begins to affirm the simplistic vision which its overt stance is formulated expressly to discredit. As a result of this camouflaged reorientation, the groundwork is laid for the novel during the 70s to invoke, albeit still obliquely, a generally more positive view of life. The philosophic assumptions embedded in genre fiction gradually start to be appropriated into more serious literary expression along with the purely formal aspects that have been borrowed in the past.

The first perceptible shift is in the imputed mimetic dimension; the implicit attitudes expressed by literary works about the relationship between the fiction and real life. In the 60s the retreat from naturalism into convoluted or fragmentary forms, pseudo-surrealism, apocalyptic fable, and idiosyncratic symbolism by writers as different as Isaac Bashevis Singer, Donald Barthelme, and Jerzy Kosinski, as well as (challenging as it does all fixed standards for "truth") the subjectivization of fact itself by the autobiographical "journalism" of Norman Mailer and Tom Wolfe, and even more by the journalistic fiction of Truman Capote, testifies to the felt lack of significant structure, the irrationality and incoherence imputed to human experience as a whole. It's as if, as Zweig points out, the most a writer can do, lacking an informative context, is to present the "disruptive moments, flashes of illuminating intensity...unruly and momentary, not casting a new light over what has been lived, but compressing life itself into [their] absoluteness, and bursting." Such fiction as this thus simultaneously exposes and reinforces our sense of the discontinuity of life.

As a secondary effect, however, the lack of attempted verisimilitude, the self-consciousness of the rhetoric, and the obtrusiveness of stylistic invention in such works all tend, as Woolfe points out, "to thrust the reader out of the fictional reality rather than enlist him in it; to emphasize that the novel is an artifact," not an imitation of life but merely a "fantastic manipulation of form." The result is that we draw from these fictions the tacit assertion that life is *not* so disturbing and disorderly even at the same time as the incongruous juxtapositions would seem to assure us that it *is* As Olderman puts it, "While the subject of these novels reminds us that fact and fiction are blurred and that reality is hopelessly indefinable, the fable form paradoxically assures us through its radical contrivances that *there is some difference between fact and fiction*" (italics added). In some cases the implication of this underlined discrepancy, as in the work of William Gass, is to devalue what is real with respect to what the artist can create ("the contrast between the world of symbols— a world of beauty, permanence and order—and the world of the flesh, which must inevitably decay and dissemble, is invoked in virtually everything Gass has ever written," says Larry McCaffery); more often, considering the inhospitality of so many fictional worlds, especially during the 60s, it works to console us that perhaps "ordinary" life is not really so bad.

At the same time as the existential chasm is displaced from a location *within* life to the interface *between* life and art, other aspects of the increasingly fabulous form adopted by 60s writers undercut the seriousness of their messages in yet other ways. Transforming personal trauma with black humor (offsetting pain with our delight in the absurd) allows the reader to detach himself not merely from the fictional experience but even from the answering echoes that might be evoked in the vicissitudes of his own life. The same thing happens on a broader scale when writers recreate history in a specifically fantastic-cum-comic form. Ishmael Reed's novel of the Civil War, *Flight to Canada*, is a striking example of this particular mode. In comingling past events and present culture, confounding historical incident and fictional stereotype, deflating Abraham Lincoln while redeeming Simon Legree, Reed does not emphasize the grotesqueness of reality so much as he displaces the object of his vision into a realm of fantasy where it need no longer incite either our identification or our concern. Obviously utilized to demonstrate the *continuity* of ethical problems like racism, the culpability of the present with respect to the past, this kind of maneuver, whatever its overt intentions, ends up rehabilitating the erstwhile troublesome real world by purging it figuratively of the elements that are most likely to disturb. If history is a fable, in other words, it need not be regretted at all. "Why *not* call that world a black joke?" Olderman asks—"a place where killers slap each other around with fable-feathered pillows, or jokers play patty-cake with big, very deadly weapons; a place where all of us, including the author, are dark vaudevillians, killer clowns." Why not, indeed! It can only help us convince ourselves that all the danger is up on the stage.

Even the *language* of fabulation adopted by so many post-60s writers tends to add to this effect. The assumed ingenuousness of the narrative voice in E. L. Doctorow's *Ragtime*, for instance—simple declarative sentences, one after the other, without rhetorical structure or dramatic accent or, indeed, any apparent exercise of deliberation or selectivity at all—is reminiscent not so much of childishness as of naive recitation of a culturally primitive kind. The effect of the book, on the basis of style alone, is therefore not only to free the author of any imputations of authority that might suggest he should or could arbitrate the possible meanings inherent in event, but also, through the archaic echoes, to mythicize the subject matter, transforming history as felt experience into history as exemplar, and in doing so to distance the reader from any disquieting sense of immediacy that the incidents recounted (which are, after all, distilled from American culture at no very distant time) may have otherwise evoked. Unlike Dos Passos, whom he has been held to resemble in terms of both subject matter and technique, Doctorow, in other words, not only challenges our faith in the factuality of so-called historic documentation by mixing impressionistic and objectively verifiable material seemingly inextricably, but also, even more effectively than Reed, by utilizing a verbal style suggestive of folk forms, works to minimize its personal importance for us as either reflection or moral model. Such a strategy ultimately diminishes the authority (and thus the threat) of both the past itself—indeed, any sort of "public" reality ordinarily verified for us by means of our vicarious spectatorship through written and other media— *and* the aesthetic vehicle. One might therefore say that the crucial development that took place in mainstream literature coming out of the 60s was the transformation (as a secondary effect of the adaptation of styles and structures culled from the romance-related modes of genre fiction) of literature-as-history, which is *directly* and personally relevant, into a merely *formally* relevant facsimile of myth.

The eventual consequence of this development is the emergence in 70s fiction (which, without deserting the fabular mode, typically eschews the more apocalyptic visions that 60s novelists borrowed from SF) of an attitude strikingly reminiscent of the response implied by conventional fantasy during the same decade. Already in the 60s there seemed to be a trend towards passivity even above and beyond what the conventional helplessness of the anti-hero would imply. As Thomas Hartshorne points out in his examination of the decline of the political mode throughout the sixties, "while Heller preaches the ethic of action, involvement and responsibility, Vonnegut preaches the ethic of passivity, tolerance, and love"; "while Heller offers instruction in how we may achieve solutions to our problems, Vonnegut offers perspectives on how we may learn to live tolerably in a world we cannot change." Developments in the 70s go beyond this to ensure that the entire focus is shortened—the unanswerable questions of cosmic import are no longer asked at all. In Olderman's words, the "fabulous world of the fable...unlike the irony used in the fifties...somehow transcends the absurdities it acknowledges without rancor, and makes possible an affirmation of life without the necessity of Meaning."

Robert Coover's *Pricksongs & Descants* provides an instructive early illustration of the orientation of the new decade. The most important point to note about this book is that its narrators "seek to illuminate reality, not transcend or change it" (Wineapple). As Coover himself describes it in his Introduction to "Seven Exemplary Fictions," although a writer's re-examination of "familiar mythic or historical forms" has the power to "conduct the reader...to the real, away from mystification to clarification, away from magic to maturity, away from mystery to revelation," it does so most effectively not by "naturalizing" the myth, not in fact by transforming the *terms* of the reality-as-given at all (historical necessity is the controvertible fact from which one always begins), but simply by grappling with those terms until they relinquish—spontaneously, as it were—the kernel of meaning that is hidden within. Coover's own application of this tenet is the best possible demonstration of the validity of the approach. He manages to transform utterly the assorted fairy tales and bible stories that he chooses to retell in *Pricksongs* without for one moment challenging our sense of the propriety, the inevitability, the *instransigence*, of event or result. By simply wrenching them out of context, approaching them from an unaccustomed angle of vision (the story of Jesus told from Joseph's point of view; the Hansel and Gretel story as lived experience rather than simply narrated event), he simultaneously affirms their predictability and their *différance*. At the same time he *con*firms both the integrity of fiction and the coherence of life as lived. As Wineapple points out, "When Granny, the aged Beauty who married the Beast in 'The Door: A Prologue of Sorts,' declares that her beast never became a prince and that she loves him, all legends aside, anyway, she asserts with Coover that in fiction and in spite of it, beasts remain beasts and death remains death. Notwithstanding that, love, laughter, and the imagination remain."

As in the fantasy realm, therefore, the world evoked by Coover's book is clearly deterministic as to content. The writer's serene acquiescence to this determinism—standing in for the reader's—implies, however, that the limitation need not be regretted unduly; it does not negate the possibility of meaning in human if not absolute terms. Coover does not, to be sure, go so far as fantasy in suggesting that what *is*, is—simply by virtue of some assumed but unspecified providential meaning—ultimately and inevitably *right*. In the end, though, the effect is somewhat the same. By merely stipulating event as *donnée*, unchallengeable, the reader is spared the necessity of contemplating the inevitable discrepancies between experience and *any* extrinsic explanatory structure that might be invoked to give it form. At the same time we are reassured covertly by the familiarity (preserved intact by Coover's restraint) of the traditional fabular forms.

Mainstream and popular modes of fiction thus grew much closer together during the early years of the 70s—to the extent, in fact, that it became impossible to draw a firm line between the two. Kurt Vonnegut has always considered himself a mainstream writer, for instance, but he is thought to write science fiction at least by afficionados of that field. Samuel Delaney's intriguing 1974 novel, *Dhalgren*, on the other hand, while explicitly identified as science fiction by both the author and the booksellers, is not merely a *qualitative* equivalent to "literature" so-called, but fully consonant with the *concerns* of the mainstream in terms of subject matter (a quasi-apocalyptic view of the deterioration of "reality" in the modern urban environment), technique (experimental, poetic, personal) and themes (the circular structure, reinforced by the elusiveness and often surreality of the experience presented, poses the question of the evidential status of subjective data). The popularity of genre fiction during both the 60s and the 70s did not, it would therefore seem, merely signal a localized upsurge in the escapist impulse on the part of the American public but, rather, a *general* reorientation (perhaps stimulated by the Europeanization of the mainstream that took place over the previous forty years) of the entire spectrum of American literature *back* to a more natural stance.

Next question: if genre fiction *in general* simply represents a special and perhaps extreme expression of trends inherent in the national character as a whole, what shall we say of the new noble savage who, regardless of the broader associations of his vehicle, would in himself seem, on the basis at least of our survey in the last section, to be more specifically and narrowly historically based? An interesting possibility touched upon earlier is that the revival in the 60s was catalyzed by a fortuitous recurrence of some of the same cultural factors responsible for his popularity in the early nineteenth century. Supporting this is the fact that one may detect a surprising number of at least general parallels between the psycho-social climates of the two periods. Both the Revolution and the Vietnam War triggered deep-seated anxieties about the moral bases for American conduct; both fragmented communities along quasi-familial lines in such a way as to stimulate considerable guilt; both called forth lofty (and conflicting) aspirations which were almost simultaneously undercut by the pragmatic realities of a commitment to progress; most important for the subject at hand, both put a great deal of pressure on the individual to question the dictates of tradition and create, as it were, a new identity for himself. The overlap was not limited merely to background factors, either. As an *after*-effect of the country's brief flirtations with "revolutionary" morality during each of these two periods, both, as if in expiation, saw, first, a considerable upsurge in the popularity of evangelical/fundamentalist religions, and second— somewhat later—an even more considerable upsurge of jingoism. With all this it is hardly surprising that fashions in popular thought should also have developed in similar directions.

The *problem* with such an explanation is that for all its eminent plausibility it makes the whole phenomenon sound a little too coincidental. It is a mistake in the first place to assume, simply on the basis that there *is* a demonstrable parallel, that these two periods comprise some sort of special case. Although the years 1810-40 and 1965-75 did, admittedly, see the *fullest* development of the noble savage in American literature, there is ample evidence that the urges with which he is both intrinsically and extrinsically associated recur much more widely than the special-case theory would admit. Hemingway's matador, for instance, while quite different from the traditional savage in both background and symbolic associations, nevertheless suggests a similar mediating function and indeed a similar world view. Certainly Hemingway's nostalgia for the lost garden, as noted above, is just as intense and somewhat less ambivalent than Cooper's or any of his contemporaries'. Nor was this writer exceptional. If the late 20s, early 30s were hardly noted for rampant primitivism, one can still infer a strong if subtle *relative* bias from, for instance, the pastoral preoccupations of what Patricke Johns-Heine and Hans Gerth call "mass periodical fiction":

Our analysis [of popular magazines from 1921 to 1940] points to certain striking changes in hero models and themes. Let us take the success story for instance...

...In the first period (1920s) the reward symbol is typically that of social ascent and its basis is a specific achievement. By the thirties, however, the predominant reward symbol is what we describe as recognition or deference from others. Its characteristic basis is moral virtue which is rewarded by love and esteem from others, sometimes even by a tangible reward; but never does it result in upward mobility marked by "wealth," "success," "status"...

As for locale, there is no mistaking that the farm and with it the small town is exalted as representative of a whole way of life. It is significant that the typical conflict within the story is between the essential human goodness of small-town types as opposed to a metropolitan moneyed elite: unpretentiousness against pretentiousness, and littleness versus power. In short, those values lacking in the metropolis are the ones capitalized upon in the depiction of small-town or farm life, and the latter become personifications of good while the city remains the vessel of evil.

Here's that same old dialectic again. Here, too, virtually unchanged for the passage of years, is Leatherstocking's indictment of the wickedness of the settlements. The message is clear. If the noble savage himself does not always materialize, the attitudes characteristically associated with him are just as persistent, if not as *consistent*, as the more general impulses implicit in the romance mode. What we are dealing with, then, is no isolated instance of cultural recurrence but a cyclic or quasi-cyclic phenomenon: a tendency toward repetition based on certain *constant* factors in the American mind that produces what is clearly, for all its surficial diverseness of effect, a profoundly conservative bias in modes of communal expression.

This bias—the American's habit of returning over and over to the same formulaic solutions, the same stock of imagery, the same hoary plots and themes—has been noticed before, of course. One of the more widely accepted of current views associates it with a kind of cultural retrogression. Philip Rahv, for instance, examining (as an antagonist) the phenomenon of recurrent primitivism (rooted, he claims, in "the fear of history and freedom, of change and making choices"), attributes this feature explicitly to Romanticism and to what he views as a direct corollary of the Romantic sensibility, a preoccupation with myth. Rahv notwithstanding, however, while some of the characteristics of Romanticism certainly reinforced and in a sense *confirmed* the bent of American culture, the seeds for those aspects of communal character most directly responsible for the developments we have been exploring here—particularly if one considers not merely the primitivistic face but also the other facets of the cyclic process, alternate and opposite, with which it is inextricably linked— were planted long before Romanticism came into bloom. The key to the whole phenomenon, in fact, goes back to the Puritans' tendency to view the world— and themselves—in terms of a cosmic drama. Inheriting this propensity both to simplify and to magnify experience, Americans ever since have had a compulsion to mythicize themselves and their country in every respect. This is undoubtedly why so many of the nation's better writers have exhibited an intense fascination with the possibilities offered by myth, primitivistic or otherwise, for informing literary expression. Even more important, it explains why such interest commonly reveals itself less in terms of traditional usages— employing mythic parallels to universalize private experience, for instance— than in an attempt to vivify myth, to make it into a tool for actually *creating* significance, for transforming the merely universal into something unique. The concern of the American writer, in other words, is more likely to be the dynamic mythopoeic *process* than the simple significatory function of given mythic forms. How does this work? According to Richardson, Melville's *Moby-Dick* provides a prototypical illustration of the mode:

In *Moby-Dick* we find. . .[an] interest in how myth originates, [although] the story never abandons the realistic level. . . Instead of our being given an abstract and mythical allegory, we are shown, by means of the thoroughly real figures of Ahab and the white whale, not only how myths arise but how they come to be believed by ordinary people like us. In the figure of Moby-Dick, Melville shows how a real creature becomes a legend, a symbol, a scapegoat, and finally a visible symbol of the god-like in nature. In the figure of Ahab, Melville traces and makes us accept the evolution of a plain old whale-hunter into a heroic quest-figure of Promethean proportions. In both cases, Melville not only provides a reasonable explanation of how this change happens, but he compels us ourselves to believe in these grand creations of the mythic imagination.

This novel, then, comprises not merely an exercise in but a demonstration *of* mythopoesis. And Moby-Dick is far from exceptional. More to the point, so is the *project* it sets itself to portray. More interesting by far than such purely "literary" phenomena, in fact, is the apparent desire of many Americans—

judging by both "high" and popular culture—not merely to create, but actually to *live* a myth.

It is Thoreau who provides the exemplary instance here. The mythic framework to *Walden* is much more than merely formal. There is considerable evidence that Thoreau actually *believed* the myth that he expresses in this work. This is perhaps not generally enough recognized. As Richardson points out, "The impression is sometimes left by criticism—not just of Thoreau—that myth is a literary ingredient which can be taken up, shrewdly used, and set down again. We are reluctant to believe that a modern writer such as Thoreau could have been religiously committed to myth. It is all very well to use it for metaphor, but to take it seriously seems almost past crediting." Taking myth seriously is, however, almost a national pasttime in the United States. (Could the misapprehension White cites be another case of imported critical theory being applied, inappropriately, to native materials?) Certainly in Thoreau's mind it was the experiential dimension of *Walden* that was ultimately important; the essay, in a sense, only documented the *transfiguration of self* that was at the center of that dimension. "Beyond the rational assumptions of what he lived for in his self-exile from society," claims Stein, "he descried in Carew's 'heroic virtue' the instinctive motivation behind his conduct. As a consequence he spent seven years rewriting his journals in order to give them the 'signifying' form that would recapture the mythic implications of his transformative experiences in the woods."

Questions of form aside, the *stance* Stein infers here is not an unusual one. The mythic element in much American literature, in fact, far from signalling a cerebral or aesthetic strategy only, proclaims itself as a fully serious do-it-yourself manual for the conduct of life. The mere presence of such an element tends to earn such literature the "Romantic" label no matter what other features it may exhibit, but in reality the affiliation is not determinative at all. Indeed, lest our example be misleading, we must emphasize that the tendency toward mythicization has less to do with the Romantic vision *per se* than with that original and continuing sense of mission Stern detects among Americans since colonial times, and their concomitant propensity to sacralize the whole of life. The advent of Romanticism merely exacerbated quirks of perspective that laid the groundwork for the American character long before. What quirks? If Americans were temperamentally indisposed to comprehend or approve the more mystical aspects of Germanic philosophy, they *were* equipped (by virtue of an inherited bent for typological thinking) to transmute the symbols of ideality into "real" life, to connect—nay, *confound*—them with purely pragmatic phenomena such that (like Turner's version of the westering movement) they would come in the popular mind to define the actual and historical rather than the merely mythical parameters of the American experience. Out of this marriage between the Puritan and the Romantic emerged the peculiar modes of response that still characterize the American consciousness today. Two features in particular are central: the need to believe in the efficacy of the individual will and the need to believe that there is a meaningful reality "out there"— *the cyclic character of American culture is predicated on the interaction of these.*

Let's examine this a little more closely. Abstractions aside, what exactly is it that we are talking about here? Taking the second element first, what we have is simply the psychological ground for those wish-fulfilling paradisial dreams we have been examining throughout the whole of this book. Both the garden *and* the city, in other words, are expressions of the American's desire to visualize his field of action in terms that lend value and coherence to both public and private experience. For the Puritan the whole world was irradiated with significance—everything was part of an all-encompassing cosmic design— and there has been a hunger in the country for this kind of comprehensive vision ever since. Given as much, it's easy to see the attraction that Romanticism exerted, even for pragmatists such as the Americans generally were. Calvinism, while heroic enough on a public level, was inimical to the individualism that the Adamic vision had come to imply. Rationalism, on the other hand, did not accord well with the American's need for ideality—indeed, since his paradisial expectations, in *whatever* terms they were imaged, considered as a blanket prescription for comprehending diverse experience were *not* reasonable, it could only emphasize irritating discrepancies he would much prefer to overlook. Romanticism, however, once it was translated into sensible terms, appeared to solve that problem by not only positing a unified, meaningful world but by making the individual himself the key to the value that this world could be made to yield. In the Romantic's eyes, as Peckham describes it, the "universe is alive, not dead; living and growing, not a perfect machine; it speaks to us directly through the creative mind." It was therefore in a sense almost irrelevant that the Romantic vision was based on nature (as we have noted, the city symbol exerted a quite comparable authority in America's historical development, so almost any idyllic formulation could have found— and indeed did find—an answering echo there); the important feature was its capacity to give moral significance and an appearance of *order* to a universe which rationalism had divested of its old hierarchical and unchanging form. No matter that this appearance—especially separated from the philosophical idealism which had originally justified and informed it—was largely delusory: Romantic theory authorized the formulation (something the average reader was quite willing to take on faith) while Romantic practice provided models which, even drained of metaphysical implications, continued to reinforce the *impression* of a coherent world. It is significant, says Northrop Frye, that in "popular speech...the word 'romantic' implies a sentimentalized or rose-colored view of reality. This vulgar [usage]...may throw some light on the intensity with which the romantic poets sought to defy external reality by creating a uniformity of tone and mood. The establishing of this uniformity, and the careful excluding of anything that would dispel it...is, psychologically, akin to magic...[in so far as it bespeaks] an effort to maintain a self-consistent idealized world without the intrusions of realism or irony."

That the American's need for coherence was stronger than his need for any specific *kind* of value casts light on some of the developments we have delineated in recent literature, particularly those species we have called genre fiction. By the 60s, as we have noted, it had begun to seem as though there were no coherence left at all. Even back in the era of the Lost Generation—the era that first formulated the wasteland metaphor—meaning was still conceivable, if conspicuously absent from the contemporary scene. As Clinton Burhaus points out, comparing Hemingway and Vonnegut, despite Hemingway's essentially pessimistic view of *society*, his "characters can and do transcend the conditions which hurt and destroy them: in an empty and indifferently maleficent universe, they confront the human condition directly and by living fully within it find or create meaning, order, and beauty." This is because, Burhaus continues, "Hemingway's vision and his art, in all their greatness, look backward to a time still able to evoke and sustain them: he has something of the harmony with nature of the Romantics, a largely positivistic epistemology, much of the concept of character of the realists, and much of the subject matter of the naturalists. He is, then, in most respects a thinker and artist with his roots in the nineteenth century." By Vonnegut's time, however, this positivistic underpinning had largely dissolved: the devastations of the moment are not offset by even the implied possibility that there once was, or ever could be, a better world. In "most novels of the sixties," says Olderman, "there is not only a sense that the world is an inverted mad waste land where only radical and violent responses can prove a man's humanity, but also an intensified fear that there are no distinctions between fact and fiction, sanity and insanity, and worst of all between good and evil. There is no ordinary recognizable reality, and man, bereft of any standard to measure either his world or himself, finds that survival is the most he can hope for in coping with his waste land."

How does one respond to such a situation? It all depends. The existentialist, if he is honest, simply *confirms* the tragedy of human isolation, eschewing the falsification of idealistic double-vision. This is where Kafka, for instance, differs most strikingly from the Romantics—*and* from the Americans. In Furst's words, his "dream-vision does not stand side by side with reality; the two are fused, the 'real' world, as we know it, has disappeared and we are left to confront the world of Kafka's visions. There is no escape, as from the Romantic realm of fantasy, because there is only *one* world, that of Kafka's subjective nightmarish vision" (1972). *No escape!* It is in his equivocation about this particular feature of the dystopia that the contemporary American writer, for all his ostensible kinship with the existentialists, and for all the terrifying absurdity of his background vision, seems most to cling to his Romantic roots. He *must* have an alternative. If the fantasy world is horrifying he must be assured that real life is still secure; if real life is unpleasant and incomprehensible, he needs to invoke a transcendent ideal.

This is why, of course, science fiction found such fertile soil in American culture after the war, carrying with it as it does vague but reassuring intimations of a better world: "the memory on the one hand of the innocence of a childhood lost beyond recall, and on the other...the precognition of a state of grace equally beyond present reach" (Ash). It also might explain the almost monopoly of irony as (up to the late 70s at least) *the* contemporary American mode. It may seem that irony would be inconsistent with Romantic idealism, but in fact it is simply the other side of the coin. Irony, like common Romantic strategies, unites opposites, symbolically transcending the existential gap. In "accumulat[ing] and condens[ing] meanings with the force of poetic imagery" (Honig), it not only juxtaposes but actually yokes dissimilars. Such yoking is, to be sure, merely a rhetorical device. More important, as Honig points out, it is employed to point up incongruence (moral or emotional) underlying likeness, rather than to establish a congruence (spiritual or metaphysical) beyond apparent diversity. It is nevertheless possible that for the American writer, disturbed by the thought of randomness and lacking any better means of unifying his fragmented perception, ironic juxtaposition—as with the functional inversion of more radically discontinuous forms noted earlier—is conjunctive even at the moment of disjunction. It thus actually consoles by cutting both ways.

The American, then, *will* have his ordered universe, one way or the other. If it is a necessary ingredient, on the other hand, ideality is not enough in itself to ensure an adequate mythos. The second of the defining factors cited above concerns our need to believe in the possibility of heroism (in a personal sense) no matter how inimical to such a concept the field of action may be. This particular wish is less defensible than the first from the Puritan point of view, but regardless of the transindividualistic orientation sanctified in "official" ideology, the habit of dramatizing *roles* could not help but encourage the individuals playing those roles eventually to start dramatizing them*selves*. The pioneer experience, reinforced by political democratization, strengthened that habit, and Romanticism, with its glorification of the power of the individual imagination added the finishing touch to the mix. The result was, by the nineteenth century, a virtually unanimous view which held heroic individualism to be not merely a privilege but a duty. This same view, moreover, as Mailer indicates in an essay aptly entitled "Superman Comes to the Supermarket," has *continued* to dominate if not always the official ideology then certainly at least the popular assumptions that provide a substratum to American culture, right up to the present day:

America was...the country in which the dynamic myth of the Renaissance—that every man was potentially extraordinary—knew its most passionate persistence. America was the land where people...believed in heroes: George Washington; Billy the Kid; Lincoln, Jefferson; Mark Twain, Jack London, Hemingway; Joe Louis, Dempsey, Gentleman Jim; America believed in athletes, rum-runners, aviators; even lovers, by the time Valentino died. It was a country which had grown by the leap of one hero past another—is there a county in all of our ground which does not have its legendary figure? And when the West was filled, the expansion turned inward, became part of an agitated, overexcited, superheated dream life. The film studios threw up their searchlights as the frontier was finally sealed, and the romantic possibilities of the old conquest of land turned into a vertical myth, trapped within the skull, of a new kind of heroic life, each choosing his own archetype of a neo-renaissance man, be it Barrymore, Cagney, Flynn, Bogart, Brando or Sinatra, but it was almost as if there were no peace unless one could fight well, kill well (if always with honor), love well and love many, be cool, be daring, be dashing, be wild, be wily, be resourceful, be a brave gun. And this myth, that each of us was born to be free, to wander, to have adventure and to grow on the waves of the violent, the perfumed, and the unexpected, had a force which could not be tamed no matter how the nation's regulators...would brick-in the modern life with hygiene upon sanity and middle brow homily over platitude; the myth would not die.

Despite Mailer's testimonial to its persistence, on the other hand, we must surely question whether, on anything but the most superficial level, the belief in individual efficacy, in freedom, that the heroic myth enshrines can still be maintained in an increasingly deterministic world. Certain features of Romanticism—in particular the emphasis on self-assertion and emotional liberation as paramount goals in and by themselves, plus an alternate world view that engrandizes the embattled individual simply for his refusal to submit— personalize and even in a sense interiorize the concept of heroic action to an extent that, theoretically, *should* re-open the possibility for such action even in the delimiting context of the wasteland. In Chapter 4, above, however, we noted that the hero had in fact given way to the anti-hero, at least in mainstream American literature. Either we missed something then, or we cannot claim after all that a *consistent* facet of the American psyche is belief in the heroic myth. Ihab Hassan would claim that the old heroic ideal has indeed given way to something else. In his view there is no doubt that it is the existentialist anti-hero—whether rebel or victim—who best represents the characteristic consciousness of the contemporary scene.

"The archetype of the inevitably ironic," Frye states, "is Adam, human nature under sentence of death. At the other pole is the incongruous irony of human life, in which all attempts to transfer guilt to a victim give that victim something of the dignity of innocence. The archetype of the incongruously ironic is Christ, the perfectly innocent victim excluded from human society." Between Adam and Christ, between inevitable and incongruous irony, lies the figure of Job, a would-be rebel whose failure, unlike that of Prometheus, is more bitter or absurd than tragic. He it is, in his self-taught irony, who represents better than Adam or Christ the archetype of existential man.

Is Hassan right, though, in imposing his essentially European model (again) on a specifically American object? Certainly his existentialist does seem to share many important features with the protagonists (leaving aside the question whether they are heroes or anti-heroes) we have observed increasingly in American fiction since the war. Despite the similarities of both condition and stance, on the other hand, there would seem to be something about the American protagonist that Hassan has missed; something that we too stopped just short of recognizing in our chapter above. In the existentialist's world, according to Hassan, there are *"no accepted norms of feeling or conduct to which the hero may appeal"* (italics added). This, however, is an admission that the American, as was pointed out in the Introduction, tries most strenuously to resist. Far from identifying himself with either Job's failure *or* Prometheus's guilt, the contemporary American protagonist in fact continues, albeit covertly and incongruously, to measure himself against either Adam or Christ.

Lilian Furst (1976), explicitly comparing the Romantic hero with the existentialist version, perhaps puts her finger on the source of Hassan's mistake. The truth is, in his later or *negative* phase, the Romantic hero—"self-conscious, paralyzed by guilt, and essentially in rebellion against his own background" (as Victor Brombert describes him)—is very similar to the anti-hero, enough certainly to explain recent trends in confounding the two modes. Despite these similarities, however, if we examine the phenomenon more closely we will realize that there are some important distinctions to be made between the two. For one thing, as Furst points out, in "contrast...to his twentieth-century counterpart, who accepts the hopelessness of his life with an ironic smile for the very reason that he already stands beyond hope, the Romantic hero, at least at the outset, still tends to cherish certain dreams." Like the American, in other words, the Romantic hero clings to the hope that "salvation may come from communion with the beauties of nature, from the true love of a fine woman, from commitment to art." Nor is this all. Signalling an even more significant divergence than his discrepant faith in transindividualistic meaning is the Romantic hero's attitude toward *himself.*

In [the] devolution from hero to anti-hero one further element plays a crucial role, namely irony and more specifically self-irony. Irony, as Lionel Trilling has succinctly defined it, is the capacity "to establish a disconnection between the speaker and his interlocutor, or between the speaker and that which is being spoken about, or even between the speaker and himself." It is particularly in this last sense...that irony is, in my view, one of the acid tests of the anti-hero. His alienation has progressed so far as to breed a genuine detachment not only from his world but also from himself. Often admittedly his self-mockery has the bitterest flavor; nonetheless its very presence denotes an ability to stand back from his own problems and...to rise above them by seeing them from a point outside himself...

This most advanced, quintessential stage of anti-heroism remains by and large foreign to the Romantic hero. He is still too filled with the certainty of himself to engage in a fundamental questioning of his own ego. The world could be, and was, exposed to a radical reassessment by the Romantic generation, but that revaluation was always undertaken from the *terra firma* of a total faith in the subjective.

Despite what we may have accepted above as a provisional explanation, it is here, I think, in Romantic tradition rather than in the existentialist fold, that we find our typical American "hero," with his ultimately hopeful view of the *inner* man at the very least.

This attribution would certainly help to make sense of some of the incongruities of contemporary American fiction. Even after the wasteland becomes a generally stipulated contextual metaphor, a great many American protagonists continue to exhibit a buoyancy, an optimism, a capacity for self-confirmation almost absurdly inconsistent with the hopeless terms in which their situations are painted. The vitality and resilience of Bellow's characters seem quite disproportionate to the trials they undergo. Augie March, for instance, is the classic innocent of eighteenth-century tradition who is neither corrupted nor discouraged despite the obstacles that beset his picaresque quest and even despite the failure of his dreams. Salinger's first major story, as Gross points out, "may end with the suicide of his central figure, but the stories that follow form an elaborate explanation of that suicide—a movement away from suicide to experience of joy." We have already noted the anomaly represented by Yossarian's escape in a fictional world that would seem more properly represented by the totally incapacitated "soldier in white." Yossarian, in Woolfe's words, "insists upon the value of his life even though he knows that the conditions of the war render life valueless... He is mad...because he represents values that are no longer credible within the fiction." The ending superadded to Heller's book would thus seem predicated more upon the author's own inarticulated faith than on any logic to be inferred from the fictional world in itself.

Heller's response is in a very real sense an exemplary one. Even among the blacks—who should, one would think, have the most reason for asserting a pessimistic view—one commonly finds "heroes who through their idealistic convictions feel they cannot only reform the forces of authority in America but also reassert that idealism which has always been the redemptive figure in the complex texture of American life" (Gross). Ellison's *The Invisible Man* is a prime example. As Olderman (1972) sums it up, this book concludes "with the narrator underground, discovering that he has been invisible because he has allowed himself to be invisible... But despite the chaos of a riot going on above him, and despite a world that has rejected him entirely...[he] makes an existential leap that carries him to responsibility, and then right up out of his hole." As endings go, this is about as heartening as one could get. It is also, unfortunately, somewhat less than convincing. The problem, as Gross points out, is the enormous unresolved "disparity between the Negro's experiences and what the Negro says about his experiences." Far from rationalizing any "leap," *The Invisible Man*, taken in its *own* terms, would seem to offer us very little hope for its groping protagonist. More important, again in Gross's words, "this hopelessness is *true*, this bewilderment amidst violence provides the great strength and truth of the novel" (italics added). So why the about-face, the last-minute bandaid solution? A failure of nerve? Perhaps. But remember Yossarian. If Ellison's optimistic coda seems somewhat facile from the worm's-eye view of the ironist, it *is* perfectly consonant with the American's propensity for the heroic mode. The protagonists of a great many contemporary American novels, even above and beyond their demonstrations of that quality of "radical innocence" Hassan identifies with a "denial of death," seem determined to wrench some positive meaning out of life itself. The result, as Robert Merrill points out, is covertly to render even the blackest of American fabular fiction "a good deal more optimistic than modern fiction is usually alleged to be."

This, of course, takes us right back to Stern's explication of American millennialism again. When rebirth becomes a way of life—when tradition is exorcised along with the past—the community must provide itself with alternate means of defining the polarities of ego and other. Self-orphaned, it also must provide a well-structured stopgap against the ever-threatening encroachments of chaos and despair. Hence the above mentioned resilience of the American dream. Far from idle or indulgent, in a historyless nation the reiterated image of an ideal self in an ideal world becomes a crucial part of social adaptation. When any given context, literary or cultural, denies the viability of such images, the public imagination, desperate to perpetuate its own self-creation, simply shifts its focus elsewhere: stealing vehicles from the past, putting new messages into old bottles, inventing "popular" modes to complement (and counter) established conventions. And always seeking to balance the hunger for ideality with the wishful vision of heroism. Robert Coover (who seems to "express" the shift into the 70s in much the same way that Heller, Bellows, and Vonnegut between them express the developing public mood from the 50s through the 60s) illuminates the phenomenon in *The Universal Baseball Association, Inc., J. Henry Waugh, Prop.*

Henry Waugh is a middle-aged accountant who gratifies his own need for significant order by inventing a "baseball game" which he plays according to a complex system of calculations night after night, keeping detailed and meticulous records, until he has completed the equivalent of more than fifty seasons of play. Though he says himself that the game "was not a message, but an event," the terms of his relationship to his "Association" make it obvious that it serves both a structuring *and* a significatory function in his life. It is not merely the ideal of *order* that is served by Henry's hobby, however, but— as time goes on—the ideal of *heroism* too. Where once it was primarily the statistics, the complex cumulative pattern of results that intrigued Henry, as the Association gradually comes to life—comes, indeed, to dominate and even swallow up mundane reality—it is his fascination with *personality* that begins to come to the fore. "Henry was always careful about names," Coover notes, "for they were what gave the league its sense of fulfillment and failure, its emotion. The dice and charts and other paraphernalia were only the mechanics of the drama, not the drama itself. Names had to be chosen, therefore, that could bear the whole weight of perpetuity."

Unfortunately, this secondary function of the game becomes so important to Henry that he almost loses his grip on the first. The involvement is suddenly too personal, too intense to be kept under control. Why? "Henry approaches his own aging with growing apprehension," Wineapple says. It is in response to this apprehension that he becomes obsessed with the possibility that he might be able to achieve at least a kind of second-hand "immortality" by identifying himself with "the incredible pitching career of the young Damon Rutherford" as he moves ever closer to "the perfection of absolute zero—a no hit game." There is, sadly, a fatal flaw in the wishful fantasy. As so often happens in "real" life, fate refuses to cooperate. To the obvious detriment of

Henry's vicarious aspirations, the brilliant young rookie is "killed" by an unlucky role of the dice—and Henry, in an irrational act of revenge that has near-disastrous results for the future of the game, manipulates the dice to "kill" also the pitcher who threw the fatal ball. " 'You know, Lou,' " Henry says to one of his friends early in the book, " 'you can take history or leave it, but if you take it you have to accept certain assumptions or ground rules about what's left in and what's left out.' " In the end the game's transindividualistic integrity reasserts itself (significantly, like American literature as a whole, it becomes transmogrified from historical event into something very like a myth), but for a while, so caught up is Henry by his wishful vision of heroism, that he breaks his own most treasured rule, thus endangering—cheapening—the entire significatory function of the game.

Order and heroism! If *The Universal Baseball Association* illuminates the *power* of the American's two deepest urges, it also demonstrates vividly the *problems* that this particular doubling can imply. Some of the most disturbing conflicts in American literature as in American public life can be distilled down to the basic desire—and the difficulty—of being both *good* and *great*. It doesn't seem as though there should be any *necessary* antagonism between these two, but in fact, if we think about Henry Waugh's baseball game we will realize that the antagonism is subtle but acute. Affirming a coherent moral context implies that one will view himself as part of a larger schema and behave solely according to the mores legitimized by that schema. One always and only, in other words, plays by the rules. A hero on the other hand is conventionally viewed as above all rules. This is an important part of his terms of reference. Like Nietzsche's superman, his legitimacy comes entirely from within himself. The orientations implied by these two ideals are therefore in some very important ways not only incompatible but mutually exclusive. To make matters worse, implicated as they are in America's chequered social history they are also irreparably *internally* flawed. In addition to their extrinsic conflicts, that is, each mode, taken in isolation, contains the seeds of its own decay.

How does this work? We have noted throughout this book the essential incompatibility of the two emblematic ideals most frequently invoked by the American, the garden and the city. Similar—and similarly unresolvable—difficulties arise with respect to heroism as well. One source of these is the attempt to apply the same standards to both public and private levels of experience. The American identifies himself in a very direct way with his country (a tendency which is reinforced by his idealistic bent), so it is important to him that he should be able to celebrate national as well as personal success. The emergence of the late 70s superhero, for instance, was connected in a very real way with public perceptions of international politics. "The Superhero was no bully, but you could push him only so far," says Hankins. "America was getting shoved around and needed a return to the no-nonsense, don't-cross-that-line nation of the past." In real life, unfortunately, the conditions conducive respectively to individual and to national greatness are bound to conflict, the one implying minimal government regulation, the other a strong, centralized locus of power; the one stressing spontaneity and immediacy, the other strategy and co-ordination; the one viewing action as an end in itself, the other making action the means to an end. Quite contra the implications of the wishful myth, then, the concept of heroism, in theory a variable, perhaps even a blanket term, in practice is almost inevitably going to catalyze the age-old conflict between public and private interests, public and private values. In the specific context of America it also catalyzes a whole host of quasi-institutionalized philosophical problems going all the way back to the Calvinistic world vision. Quite beyond traditional antitheses, in any culture where "freedom" is so loudly touted and so careful regulated, the heroic stance is almost impossible to define, let alone to maintain.

What is heroism, anyway? If it implies omnipotence it is obviously impossible, given the conditions of human life, to achieve. The individual is always going to be beaten sometime, if only by death. If it implies perfection— perfect courage, perfect wisdom, perfect love—then this is even more obviously an impossible dream. Even if the heroic mode is interiorized, any expectation that both control and intensity can be attained more than momentarily is doomed to disappointment. As Furst says of Novalis's *Heinrich von Ofterdingen* and Coleridge's *Kubla Khan*, both brilliant expressions of the Romantic vision, both fragmented, "their incompleteness suggests that it was impossible to sustain the Romantic elevation of reality through the imagination." Especially if— as is almost inevitably the case in America—we insist that he is also *good*, to the extent that he is realistically drawn the hero, it would seem, cannot possibly live up to either our hopes or his own ideals. The result? Logically, the only product we might expect to emerge from this collision between wish and must is Furst's post-Romantic anti-hero: manic, solipsistic, self-destructive, inert with despair. Unfortunately, the anti-hero is not an acceptable alternative on this side of the Atlantic. "Logic" notwithstanding, he does not gratify the American's need to be reassured of the feasibility of *positive* heroism.

A nice dilemma, isn't it? One way to sidestep if not resolve the bind is to release the hero from his impossible moral obligations. What we end up with more often than not if we do this, however, is a satanic figure like Melville's Ahab—a destructive rather than a socially positive force. If, on the other hand, we respond to the difficulty simply by making the hero less realistic—freeing him not of moral obligations but of the human limitations that militate against his success—this opens up all those problems of relativity that we came up against in our discussion of barbaric fantasy in the last chapter. *Too* strong, *too* charismatic, the hero tends to become less of an alter ego than an authority figure—and as such ultimately a threat to the reader's own wishfully heroic sense of *self*. Even only half perceived, this threat engenders a good deal of covert uneasiness in the American public at large. And some not so covert. Naive forms tend to gloss over the problem—the illusion of tension-management is, after all, their stock in trade—but some of America's greatest fiction deals directly with the dangers that the hunger for heroism entails. Again *Moby-Dick* springs to mind. "Much of the tension in Melville's work," says Gross, "grows out of his fear of power: power controls the significant figures of his novels and stories; power lurks behind the most innocent of his tales when it is not directly manifest; and the number of victims that groan behind the heavy weight of authority is...legion." What about the possibility of simply redefining heroism, making it both less fearsome and more accessible to the average man: *democratizing* it, as it were? This is a strategy that has frequently appealed in the past. The results, unfortunately, have in general only gone to prove that the concept of heroism and the concept of democracy (which properly belongs to the realm of "social" ideality) are mutually antagonistic not merely in practice but at root.

Again the nineteenth century provides our best example. In his early work Emerson defines the hero explicitly as a moral idealist rather than an activist— "the secular man who...can establish a harmony between himself and Nature," as Gross puts it—thus stipulating a norm of heroism which, being based on attitude rather than on effect, can and *should* be practiced by the common as easily as by the unusually advantaged man ("I embrace the common, I explore and sit at the feet of the familiar, the low," he says in "The American Scholar"). When he actually comes to illustrate his vision of democratic heroism in *Representative Men*, however, the exemplars he chooses—Plato, Swedenborg, Montaigne, Shakespeare, Napoleon, and Goethe—are, in Gross's words, common "only in so far as they have achieved what we [all] desire to achieve." Why the discrepancy? One problem, and a ticklish one, is that the very idea of heroism has about it something archaic and dark which will neither settle for commonality *nor* rest comfortably with the bloodless triumphs of the moral realm. As Emerson himself admits, "There is somewhat not philosophical in heroism; there is something not holy in it; it seems not to know that other souls are of one texture with it; it has pride; it is the extreme of individual nature" ("Heroism"). Heroism, in other words, is *by nature* archaic! The only way to sanitize it, therefore, is to relinquish the dream of private transcendence and bring the hero firmly into the social fold. As Emerson himself does. In *English Traits* his emphasis, as Gross points out, is "on the practical and not the ideal traits of the people, on their authority in the world and not their idealism." In *The Conduct of Life* the reaction is even more extreme. "The tone of these essays is patronizing, the attitude toward the common person condescending. Whereas the early work concentrated upon the moral virtues that stem from self-reliance, the later essays...are guides to practical success." We may, of course, simply attribute this rightward shift to the writer's advancing age. There is considerable evidence, however, that *whenever* the American attempts to rationalize the equally unsatisfactory possibilities of the hero as victim and the hero as villain, unless he gives up the idyllic vision of social harmony and moral coherence he is almost always forced, whether through sentimentalization (denying discrepancy) or through conservative retrenchment, to recast if not recant the base terms of his definition.

Many writers, to be sure, *do* choose to relinquish or—more commonly—compartmentalize the values associated with ideality, especially during periods when the authority of the garden is high. The regressive feminine orientations of Moira clash even more violently with the aggressive masculine traits traditionally imputed to the hero than does the social-consciousness of Themis with his individualism. This is the real reason why there are so many curiously isolated figures like Deerslayer. To avoid the discrepancies entailed when he is related too directly to an idealized moral context, no matter what kind, the American hero is more often than not depicted as in a sense totally *alone* on the stage.

[In American] romances the individual is defined not, as in the novels of Dickens, Flaubert, or Tolstoy, by his complex interrelationships with others who represent various social classes and their values. Instead he is defined by his relations to characters representing the contending forces in his own psyche or the alternative commitments of belief, value and action available to him. The most significant relationships in the American romance, are those between the representative hero and characters who embody unfallen innocence or innate corruption, primitive purity or civilized guilt, intellectual isolation or passionate community. Consequently the characters in the romance tend to reflect the allegorical bias of their origins and are seldom drawn with the inclusive roundness and realism of those in novels of society. [Hoffman]

Heroism thus *may* be affirmed in American fiction, as may social ideality—but only one at a time. Feidelson designates Emerson and Melville as the exemplary proponents of opposing but reciprocal symbolic modes ("Emerson embodied the monistic phase of symbolism, the sweeping sense of poetic fusion; Melville lived in a universe of paradox and knew the struggle to implement the claims of symbolic imagination"); implicit in this polarity are also these writers' differential relations to the ideality/heroism debate. Emerson, his eye on the unifying function of the "oversoul," is unable to condone a satisfactorily heroic hero; Melville brings alive the possibilities (and the problems) of the heroic stance but only at the price of exacerbating the sense of alienation between man and the transpersonal realm. Since the average American would prefer to believe that *both* of these positions can be held simultaneously, however, *neither*, alone, provides a stable basis for national self-definition.

Here is where we come to the *cyclic* response (using the term loosely to denote recurrence but not necessarily symmetry) that we mentioned above. At least since the Revolution confirmed and intensified certain propensities that already existed in the national character, American attitudes may in fact be seen as alternating between four unstable modes. These modes are identified, in terms of predominant mood and/or value system, with the four aspects of the nature/society opposition examined above. Each relates to the other three respectively as *alternate* (a philosophical opposition between divergent visions of "good," as in the Edenic Garden and the City of New Jerusalem), *inverse* (representing positive and negative, idyllic and demonic aspects of the same vision, as in the Garden and the Wilderness), and *complement* (where the positive aspect of one vision is reinforced through juxtaposition with the negative aspect of its alternate, as in the Garden and the World-Machine). Each implies a different attitude with respect to action (pure on the idyllic level, mixed or ambivalent on the demonic). This in turn suggests, first, a different kind of *hero*, and secondly, a different kind of *mediator* or *model* to exemplify the proper response in that mode. The whole complex of relations may be imaged in terms of the following schema:

THE UNSTABLE MODES OF AMERICAN CULTURE

	Primitivistic	*Progressivistic*
Idyllic		
	GARDEN	**CITY OF NEW JERUSALEM**
	Noble Savage	Soldier/Policeman
	(Submission)	(Assertion)
	SAINT	CHAMPION

modes
of
heroism

	ANTI-HERO	ADVENTURER
	Madman (Passive)	Pioneer (Active)
	Criminal (Active)	Captive (Passive)
	WORLD-MACHINE	**WILDERNESS**
Demonic		

We note that our old friend, the noble savage, along with his foil, the frontiersman or pioneer, appears prominently on this diagram. If we examine more closely the *dynamic* aspect of the schema we will perhaps finally understand why he keeps popping out of the hat the way he does. The key, it turns out, lies less with his historic than his formal associations. I have said that these modes are unstable. This is because each, in the context of the others, and especially in the context of America's mutually antagonistic and internally inconsistent urges toward heroism *and* ideality, tends either to invert or to slide over into complementary modes.

Let's begin with the city. It seems unnecessary to review its entire value system and covert associations, so we will merely stipulate that it is forward-looking, pro-technological, authority-oriented, and—at least in a token sense—social. The model here is the man in uniform, the soldier or the policeman who not only epitomizes good citizenship in his service to the state, but in his heroic aspect as *Champion* actively defends the values of his masters from both extrinsic and intrinsic threats. Paradoxically, he is also the key to the city's moral vulnerability. Inasmuch as he is necessarily regimented, subordinated to an impersonal collectivity, with only a slightly different emphasis the soldier—as we noted in chapter 4—becomes a victim rather than a defender of society, and the City of New Jerusalem takes on its demonic aspect of the World-Machine. So strong is the tendency to inversion here, in fact, that the American—with considerable concomitant anxiety—shifts back and forth along this particular axis all the time.

We have seen the demonic city at its most extreme in the dystopic SF of the decades following the Second World War. The mode doesn't have to take this specific form, though: any "city" wherein authority becomes perceived as monolithic, oppressive, and detrimental to individual well-being is, metaphorically at least, a kind of machine. Here we find two models. One is the madman who, as the ultimate victim, doomed (by virtue of his inability or refusal to comprehend or manipulate his social environment) "to massive introspection, to incarceration, to futile suicide, to impotent isolation, or to some comparable fate that reveals the unreality of [his] aspirations" (Woolf), represents the passive mode. Paired with him is the criminal, representing the active response.

Not all fictional criminals belong in this category, to be sure. In the City of New Jerusalem the criminal represents a destructive element which must, quite righteously, be purged. When he is set in the context of the "bad" world-machine, however, the criminal becomes in effect "good." This does not happen all at once. In the earlier stages of recoil, the literary portrait usually just betrays a covert admiration for the criminal's demonic vitality without condoning the values he represents. This strategy, which can be traced all the way back to the original gothic (in Lewis's eighteenth-century classic *The Monk*, as Zweig says, "although we feel for Agnes and Antonia, we are forced to admire the torrential genius of the monk Ambrosio...[whose] vast egotism persuades him that a desire creates its own legitimacy"), is the one most often employed in 30s gangster films where, in Cawelti's words, "beneath the moralistic surface of the story...[we can sense] a burning resentment against respectable society and a fascination with the untrammeled and amoral aggressiveness of a Little Caesar or a Scarface." There is a further stage, though, in which, as we intimated in our discussion of westerns, the criminal's values are actually shown to be less reprehensible than society's own. This is typically *not* a case—as in the traditional figure of Robin Hood—where the imputation of criminality is proved to be unjust in the end (such evasiveness is generally more characteristic of the transition stage), but an actual celebration of criminality itself. This particular kind of anti-hero is exemplary *because*, not in spite of, his lawlessness, in other words. Examples would include 60s versions of Bonnie and Clyde or, as cited above, Butch Cassidy and the Sundance Kid.

Like almost all the symbolic figures in the American pantheon, however, the criminal tends to be equivocal too. Indeed, in several American genres the cops and robbers almost seem to merge. The hard-boiled detective—as in the work of Hammett, Chandler, and Spillane—despite his *formal* alignment with the policeman as a protector of the innocent often finds himself working outside and even *against* the law. Similarly, although coming from the other direction, the more recent figure of the Enforcer often behaves more morally—indeed, even more legally—than the corrupt "official" agents of justice do. As Cawelti says in his discussion of a 1964 Don Siegel film, *The Killers*

...despite his savagery and ruthlessness, it is clear that the Enforcer is the hero of this story, and there is at least a suggestion of heroic accomplishment when he is killed while destroying the crooked businessman. The basis of our admiration for the Enforcer in this case...lies in our response to his professionalism, his lack of hypocrisy, and his willingness to risk everything to achieve his ends. It is also important that we respond to his affection and loyalty for the young killer who is his partner. Their loyalty and comradeship in danger stand out against the complex deceit and betrayal that characterizes most other characters in the film and thus becomes an expression of the Enforcer's code.

In some versions of the Enforcer—like, for instance, John D. MacDonald's Travis McGee, a chivalric mercenary who describes his extra-legal activity (provocatively) as "salvage" business—the moral authority of the maverick becomes so extensively legitimized that it almost seems as if he defends the values of the true city more vigorously than the compromised police.

The blurring that takes place along this particular axis reinforces the American's tendency to mythicize what he cannot rationalize. It also reinforces his ambivalence. As in his multiple and often irreconcilable images of nature as arena or temple, schoolroom or treasure trove, he is unsure, ultimately, whether the city is good or bad. Any provisional alignment with either mode, therefore, is always liable—overtly or covertly—to flip over to reveal the inverse. The same thing happens, of course, on the other oblique axis too. The noble savage and the frontiersman, as noted above, frequently affect each other's characteristics and even—insofar as both can be seen to mediate between fort and forest—play out certain aspects of each other's roles. This tendency for opposites to merge is one of the major reasons why it is difficult for the American to maintain a consistent stance. The other is that there is a certain amount of "leakage" between complementary modes too.

It's easy to see how this would happen between the wilderness and the city. The two have been paired as opponents, mutually antagonistic but also *mutually reinforcing*, as long as America has existed. There is, further, as we have seen, an ambivalence in the pioneer's role that makes him not merely the anti-social semi-savage but an agent of progress as well. Periods emphasizing one of these modes, therefore, tend to emphasize both. What of the garden/world-machine alignment, though? In our study of SF we observed that there is *in fact* a compatibility between the two such that the dystopic vision leads to primitivism as an after-effect. It is difficult, though, to see how the criminal and the noble savage can so easily be made to coexist. The link here is through the *attitudes* that each of these modes implies.

Although they tend to be treated differently in fiction, the madman and the criminal, the captive and the pioneer, are actually twinned aspects of the same basic roles. Passive and active respectively, they exemplify alternate responses, but since the controlling vision is the same for each member of a given pair, *both* of these responses are always immanent at any moment in time. The criminal, therefore, is not merely aggressor but also victim; not merely powerful but impotent—helplessly manipulated by forces (including his own violence) ultimately beyond his control.

Passiveness, or submission, however, is the noble savage's identifying response. This is why the heroic ideal associated with him is the *Saint*. The savage, moreover, inasmuch as he tends to divest himself of his nobility and slip down the axis to merge with the aggressive figure of his antagonist, the pioneer, has a subversive or schizophrenic underside that *embraces* even while opposing or redeeming the violence that the criminal represents. As Hassan implies in his discussion of the rebel/victim, in fact, these two modes are not ultimately antagonistic at all, no matter what, in superficial terms, may seem to be the case.

The saint and the criminal stand back to back on either side of the demonic. Both are protestants, both victims. But pure violence, like the demonic, has no reality in the public realm, the domain of action. Pure violence, as we shall repeatedly observe in modern fiction, seems almost the ultimate form of introspection. That the saint and the criminal, the suppliant and the psychopath—they are conjoined in the recent literature of hipsterism and in such enduring figures as Green's Pinkie and Faulkner's Christmas—partake of violence compulsively is no surprise. For untrammelled violence is not an act, it is merely a state; it is the experience of world negation. As Miss Arendt saw, the saint and the criminal are both lonely figures: "...the one being for, the other against, all men; they, therefore, remain outside the pale of human intercourse and are, politically, marginal figures who usually enter the historical scene in times of corruption, disintegration, and political bankruptcy."

Just as much as between the city and the wilderness there thus tends to be a potential for confluence between these two modes.

Why, on the other hand, *should* the perspective slip out of gear in this way? Mere potential does not entail cause. Even leaving aside the kind of *intrinsic* ambiguities we have noted, the tendency to move, say, from the world-machine to the garden is reinforced strongly by the urge to ideality that we discussed above. There is always a desire to make such formally demonic figures as the criminal and the pioneer more unequivocal, in other words; to co-opt them to the service of their idyllic complement—in effect to make them *good*. Countering this is the pull of heroism which, by setting the individual at odds with his ideal environment, whatever it may be, has a natural affinity for the demonic modes. Then, too, there are the coeternal attractions of the alternatives, each undercutting the other implicitly every moment they are juxtaposed. Up and down. Diagonally across. The fact is, there is very little to encourage or even to permit equilibrium in the American cultural mix. "Mythophilia," as Puetz says, "is in constant danger of turning into mythoclasm." All it takes is a little frustration, a dash of disappointment, a little pressure from world events, to tip the balance at any given time.

This situation explains much about the apparently chaotic course of recent history. It also suggests a number of important considerations that must be borne in mind if one is to successfully elucidate *any* expressive activity in

America, from politics to literature. Given both the instability and the repetitiveness of modal responses in this country, its culture must somehow be viewed as both dynamic *and* homogeneous. This dual perspective can only be achieved if individual phenomena are viewed *contextually*, as the concomitants to an ongoing process of reorientation consonant with and catalyzed by the events and influences that dominate the scene at any given time in society at large. How, in practice, can we carry out such an ambitious project? Actually, it need not be as difficult as it sounds. Any of the modal exemplars cited here (or their functional equivalents) may be considered as cultural markers. As such they may also be considered as cultural *indicators*. Signalling recurrences, they also provide a key to valid analogues. Signalling analogues they open up the whole question of what might be expected to recur. The relations one may posit between their differential career profiles and the relative authority of different attitudes and value systems at any given time is, in other words, direct enough to provide an excellent critical tool for elucidating not merely isolated cases but those far-reaching social/political *trends* which, especially from a contemporaneous perspective, often seem ambiguous or obscure. "The more we know about the conditions under which the attitudes of people have been set," says Hook, "the more intelligently we can go about the task of [dealing with] them." Tracing the rise and fall of the noble savage in genre fiction does not merely add a footnote to the history of American primitivism but actually offers a vantage point from which to survey and identify the characteristic features of the ever-revolving national mood.

Just for interest's sake, let's go back to that vantage point briefly before we close to see if we can put together some sort of picture of where, exactly, the country stands now, as it moves deeper into the 80s. At the end of the last chapter, judging by developments in SF, it looked as though we were entering a period dominated by the values of the city again. Even leaving aside the political swing to the right, this prognostication would seem to be born out by developments in other facets of the literary field. No outstanding soldier-heroes have turned up yet (apart from pop-cult caricatures like "Rambo"), but as we observed in our examination of the development of the 60s noble savage, the exemplary figure for any period takes a while to reach maturity— to cast off the stigma that he has accrued during the dominance of other modes. Even without the presence of a notable socially sanctioned champion, in any case, there are other signs strongly indicative of such a shift. As Cummins pointed out in a 1979 review, for one thing, the apocalyptic novel of the 60s and early 70s had by the end of the decade apparently been edged out by the "domestic"—that is, typically family-centered—novel of "familiar reality." Going far beyond a change of subject matter, this new emphasis bespeaks an entirely different, more socialized, and ultimately positive (if not optimistic) view of life.

Terrible things happen in the novels of the Domestics. Death itself is a major theme. The final scene of *Nickel Mountain* takes place in a cemetery; the first chapter of *Beyond the Bedroom Wall* (after the Prelude) describes in exquisite detail how a man prepares his father's body for burial; Margaret Ridpath is dead when her novel begins; T. S. Garp dies before his ends. Many others die, naturally and abnormally. Still others suffer pain and mutilation. In *Garp*, in a single accident, one child is killed, another is blinded, and their mother bites off the penis of her lover. The Domestics do not assume a safe and tranquil world.

However, unlike the terrors of the Apocalyptics, those of the Domestics are not intended as evidence of human helplessness and loss of control, the inability of the individual to confront his life. On the contrary, the characters of the Domestics not only stand up to death and disaster, they transcend the very worst that can happen to human beings.

Ultimately, and most significantly, in this transcendence the works of the Domestics become affirmations in a sense that is unusual in American literature. The fiction of all but a few of our greatest writers is pessimistic. Usually, affirmation can be found only in the cheap happiness of popular fiction, which titillates with superficial threats overcome at no real cost. But the Domestics inflict pains that cut to the core of their characters, that can exact the price of their own lives or of those most valuable to them. Yet they endure and triumph. The strength of their affirmation is intensified profoundly by the price they have paid.

This is quite a radical departure. If Cummins was right in his analysis of the current mood, then aside from anything else it would mean that despite the continuing boom in fantasy fiction, literary fashions in general were beginning in the late 70s to revert *away* from the romance all the way back to the "straight" (i.e. European) novel—impressive evidence for a resurgence in the authority of the idyllic city which, being *socially*-oriented in a way quite unlike any of the other modes, is the only environment in which it is likely to thrive. But *was* he right?—that is the question. Was that flurry of domestic fiction really as significant as he implies? It's hard to recognize trends while we're still in the middle of them. Samples are too small. Digestion-time is too short. Fortunately, the same movement seems to be confirmed if, rather than merely trying to establish a quantitative dominance by counting and categorizing new releases, we look at the metafictional implications of the cumulative corpus of the last decade.

The major aesthetic debate in the 70s was between two views exemplified by John Gardner and William Gass, the former advancing the claim of "moral fiction"—fiction that presents "valid models for imitation, eternal verities worth keeping in mind, and a benevolent vision of the possible which can inspire and incite human beings toward virtue"; the latter proclaiming the autonomy of the aesthetic object and assuming what Sukenik calls a "hermetic" stance. Without attempting to arbitrate or even review these arguments in any detail, we are forced to conclude, in the light of the apparent recent modal reorientation, that during the 80s it will probably be Gardner's view that prevails. Riggenbach claimed in 1980 that Gardner, like Howe and other members of the New York literary establishment, was, by virtue of outdated preconceptions, simply out of touch with much of the better writing that had appeared during recent years. If one looks at Riggenbach's own list, however, one notes that most of his candidates for canonization are 60s-oriented, in terms of actual genesis, or cultic associations, or membership in one of the classes of genre fiction (primitivistic SF and pastoral fantasy) which declined soon after that decade. McCaffery, similarly, dismisses Gardner on the basis that he is "operating from certain optimistic or humanistic premises that many modern writers, scientists, and philosophers have decided to abandon," but in many ways Gass's quasi-formalist stance, which he seems to support, is—at least in the American context—even more out of date. For our particular purposes, argument like this is ultimately irrelevant in any case. Certainly it has no evidentiary status. Neither approval nor disapproval of a cultural trend is going to affect its historicity. If we put aside the rather acrimonious *prescriptive* element that seems invariably to preoccupy the antagonists in this kind of debate and consider the covert messages conveyed by the fiction itself, however, we may possibly get a much better picture of what *is*, if not what should be.

With respect to normative views of the role of literature vis-à-vis both truth value and moral function we can, I think, actually discern a fairly clear trend over the last few decades. In the late 50s, early 60s it was generally held that literature did, in fact, in some sense mirror reality. If expression became increasingly incoherent and bizarre, this was a feature predicated on the disorderliness of the existential world. With the trend towards fabular forms in the later 60s, however, there was, as noted above, a tendency to deny art the possibility of an even peripherally mimetic role. Art and life simply did not coincide. One effect of this that we mentioned was in the long run to distance the reader from the anxiety entailed by the apocalyptic vision. Another, however, had very important ramifications for the artist's assumptions about what his task properly implied.

In the practice of Mailer, Wolfe, Capote *et al.*, the creative act, being in effect denuded of both its ultimate aesthetic dimension and its responsibility to fact, was, simply, *expression*, the only ordering principle being the observer's consciousness, the only hero—indeed, in a sense the only subject—the writer himself. This seems a long way from Gass's hermeticism, but in fact there is one principle that underlies both approaches. The author is considered free from any obligation to measure his project against anything extrinsic to itself. This is not entirely an irresponsible stance. On the one hand it *can* lead to indulgence; art, in theory, can be anything from private catharsis to a game. On the other hand, if mimesis is impossible—whether because of the *a priori* illusory nature of the aesthetic act, the inadequacy (degeneration) of available fictional forms, or the recalcitrance, irrelevance, and incomprehensibility of reality itself—the artist is unethical to suggest, even implicitly, that the world can be explained, or clarified, or organized in any overt sense by means of his work.

The increased authority of this view throughout the 60s is one of the major reasons for the ambivalent narrative tone of many of the later novels of the decade, suggesting, as it does, a willed detachment far more profound than can possibly be explained by the conventional passiveness of the anti-heroic stance. As intimated above, literature of this period clearly reveals a reluctance on the part of writers to suggest answers or offer solutions on even the most basic and immediate levels; a reluctance, even more—despite the covert associations of the apocalyptic mode—to take a moral stand of any sort (Vonnegut, as Hartshorne points out, is particularly notable for this latter effect: "His universe is one in which the basic rule is moral relativism. There are no villains in *Slaughterhouse V* or indeed in any of his other works. Of course he has moral values, but...he does not feel that the lines between good and evil can be drawn with absolute precision. Further, he feels that those who draw such lines are likely only to cause suffering in the long run. He attacks all pretensions to dominance, mastery, and control based on convictions of righteous certitude"). The retrenchment does not stop here, however. Above and beyond the repudiation of moral commitment there is even a sense that the more intangible ordering function of the aesthetic dimension of art (Wallace Stevens's jar on a hill, giving point and significance to the entire surrounding wilderness) has itself been pushed back to the level of the most limited and private transaction. This, at least, is the implication of Gass's novels, which not only (in McCaffery's words) focus on "characters seeking refuge in their own artistic constructions because of their inability to deal with the world directly," but also intimate that any attempt to make the fiction and the reality converge is likely to be disastrous. In *Omensetter's Luck*, for instance, both Henry Pimber and the Reverend Jethro Furber attempt literally to transform "lucky" Brackett Omensetter into a character more consonant with the terms of their own private dramas, the former needing a hero, the latter a demonic opponent. The effect of these fictions, irreconcilable as they are either with each other or with Omensetter as he appears to himself, is not enrichment but, rather, madness. Furber's paranoia almost gets Omensetter killed; Pimber, disillusioned by the deflation of his vision, simply kills himself. Vonnegut would at least allow that the "harmless illusions" of art, like those of Bokonism, the synthetic religion of *Cat's Cradle*, while certainly (and self-admittedly) untrue, can still comfort their auditors, but for Gass, it would seem, art is— and should be—like Barthelme's balloon, mysterious, self-referencing, and asocial; ultimately without any explicit public dimension at all.

Some people found the balloon "interesting." As a response this seemed inadequate to the immensity of the balloon, the suddenness of its appearance over the city; on the other hand, in the absence of hysteria or other societally-induced anxiety, it must be judged a calm, "mature" one. There was a certain amount of initial argumentation about the "meaning" of the balloon; this subsided, because we have learned not to insist on meanings, and they are rarely even looked for now, except in cases involving the simplest, safest phenomena. It was agreed that since the meaning of the balloon could never be known absolutely, extended discussion was pointless, or at least less purposeful than the activities of those who, for example, hung green and blue paper lanterns from the warm gray underside, in certain streets, or seized the occasion to write messages on the surface, announcing their availability for the performance of unnatural acts.

A stance like this cannot be sustained, of course—especially in America. Bleak as the 60s vision was, one might very well welcome a mode that would facilitate some degree of detachment, but the suspension required by this aesthetic not only of disbelief but of belief as well—the denial of our old expectations of mimesis, of relevance, of spiritual if not historic truth, without any proffered replacement via the more formal and inexplicit kind of order embedded in the romance—is offensive to the American's need for at least some *appearance* of coherence in his world. Early in the 70s, consequently, an almost imperceptible change occurs which in a sense ultimately ushers in a new fiction as well as a new decade.

It may be true generally that when the novel "contracts into poetic form it confesses its inability to share widely in the affairs of this world" (Hassan). On the other hand, in the specific context of American culture, as form becomes both more artificial and more significant, and especially as it assumes some of the tacit sententiousness of the sources from which it has borrowed, it begins to call attention to itself *as* form. "That is perhaps the most significant difference between fiction in the sixties and fiction in the seventies," says Ronald Sukenik. "The latter has dropped the sixties' sense of irony about the form, its guilty conscience about the validity of the novel, its self-parody and self-consciousness. That self-consciousness has become, in the seventies, a more acute consciousness about the medium and its options." This is a particularly crucial development because an increased awareness of the aesthetic component in literature necessarily calls attention to the artist as artificer. This leads on the one hand to the technical experimentation of such writers as Steve Katz, Peter Matthiesson, George Chambers, and Raymond Federman. Conversely, by emphasizing the hieratic element, it also makes art more public again. The writer, no longer viewed as wholly autonomous nor his expression as merely self-reflexive, is pressured towards a questioning of what has in fact become once more a social role.

If we think back to Coover, we can see how such a shift might take place: Coover's artist, as we infer from the apparently limitless variability of such stories as "The Babysitter," has a considerable discretion within his fictional world. Firmly countering the ostensible implications of absolute aesthetic autonomy, however, Coover also demonstrates the extent to which the artist is *limited* by his creative endeavor. This limitation is more than simply a responsibility to *fact*. We noted above that Coover accepted the rule of history as a basic *donnée*, but this "rule" is not nearly as simple as one might think. It does not, for instance, mean that an extrinsic pattern is *imposed* on the work. Quite the opposite, in fact. Being limited by history means above all that the artist is limited by the integrity and tendency toward self-realization of his creation. "I have brought two sisters to this invented island," says the narrator of "The Magic Poker," seemingly claiming complete responsibility for the authorial act. "It is indeed I who burdens them with curiosity and history, appetite and rhetoric. If they have names and griefs, I have provided them." Later, however, we discover the true state of affairs: this writer is as much manipulated *by* as manipulator *of* his work.

> I am disappearing. You have no doubt noticed. Yes, and by some no doubt calculable formula of event and pagination. But before we drift apart to a distance beyond the reach of confessions (though I warn you: like Zeno's turtle, I am with you always), listen: it's just as I feared, my invented island is like the old Dahlberg place on Jackfish Island up on Rainy Lake, people say, and I wonder: can it be happening? Someone tells me: I understand somebody bought the place recently and plans to fix it up, maybe put a resort there or something. On *my* island? Extraordinary!—and yet it seems possible. I look on a map: yes, there's Rainy Lake, there's Jackfish Island. Who invented this map? Well, I must have, surely. And the Dahlbergs, too, of course, and the people who told me about them. Yes, and perhaps tomorrow I will invent Chicago and Jesus Christ and the history of the moon. Just as I have invented you, dear reader, while lying here in the afternoon sun, bedded deeply in the bluegreen grass like an old iron poker...

Art is *not* merely illusion, then—or at least no more so than mundane reality. As with Henry Waugh's baseball game (and Henry is not just an author, but in some sense God: JHWH, Jehovah Himself), it takes on a life of its own that actually subsumes rather than simply mirroring reality. Art and life are continuous, in other words. And as a result—this is the critical point—the writer cannot betray one without betraying the other too. It is in this sense that the writer is limited by history. Being thus limited—through *intrinsic* rather than extrinsic factors—he is constrained, just as the traditional "mimetic" artist is, to accept the social truths of his environment (the established outlines of the retold fairy tales and myths in *Pricksongs & Descants*) and align his fiction with those truths in some meaningful way. Like the magician in "The Hat Act" the writer can manipulate his material quite sensationally, but if he goes one small step beyond the allowable degree of variance to challenge the fundamental rules, the creation is invalidated. In the magician's case, his assistant is killed. So much for the touted freedom of God!

Coover is not, of course, a "domestic." In many ways his fables of the aesthetic act would seem to have more in common with Gass than Gardner. For all the games he plays, however, in playing with, and thus tacitly *recognizing*, the relation between art and life, he opens up the possibility—indeed, perhaps even implies the necessity—of the kind of moral fiction, fiction written to explore if not to celebrate the explicitly social concerns of the idyllic city, that Gardner talks about. By the mid-70s, moreover, judging from a review by Raymond Olderman, something very like Gardner's aesthetic stance had already come to dominate the American fiction scene:

> The underlying metaphysic of most fiction in this period converts all questions concerning fact and fiction into questions of reality's levels or dimensions. Therefore, what we call fact and what we call fiction are—even in their clearest distinction—considered to be simply two dimensions of reality. They are related to each other in the same way an event is related to interpretation. Neither is quite real without the other, yet neither is more illusory than the other since both are real in their effect on humans...

...In the early Seventies, *fictions* meant simply all systems of metaphoric meaning. According to this definition, all systems or patterns which exist to explain reality and experience are fictions—myths and science are fictions. The search for new fictions meant simply the search for some explanations that partake of both myth and science, and also restore our sense of contact with reality. This definition remains implicit in the current meaning of the search for new fictions, but currently *fiction* means something more like *model* than myth. In 1974-76, then, the search for new fictions becomes a search for actual models which can *embody* contact with reality.

The last sentence here says it all. Somewhere in that five-year span, art became rededicated to the service of Themis again.

The results of this realignment were not, to be sure, as homogeneous as Olderman's summary may seem to imply. Different writers—different segments of the population—responded in vastly different ways to the revival of social consciousness. What is undeniable, though, is how many of the cultural developments of the last decade, despite an incredible diversity of both ends and means, collectively testify to the omnipresence of the new orientation. Most significant was the resanctification of discredited "masculine" modes of action. Long before the end of the 70s, despite a lingering uneasiness about the institutional side to military experience, affirmative or at least traditionally heroic versions of the war story in fiction and film had begun to challenge the anti-war stereotypes that dominated the previous decade. They also challenged the anti-intellectual stereotypes that had dominated recent war stories. Coppola's *Apocalypse Now* drew heavily on Conrad's *Heart of Darkness* for its controlling metaphor, while Cimino's *The Deer Hunter* provocatively enough transformed the vet-as-villain theme into an up-dated version of the captivity tale (Hellman). Fashions were transformed during this period too. The natural look died a natural death sometime around 1978. Earth tones lost ground to electric pastels. Art deco was revived, along with pre-war clothes, comics, and politics. Teenagers traded in their love beads for credit cards and designer jeans. Hair got shorter. Cars got bigger. The mystic warrior of *Star Wars I* was superceded as romantic hero by the anti-social rogue in *Star Wars II*, and the anti-social rogue definitively domesticated in *Star Wars III*. Art began edging back toward representation. Poetry began edging back to "story" (Perloff). *The Waltons* was one of the longest running and most frequently cloned TV shows of its decade. The mid-70s mainstream concern with spirituality was reflected in late-70s genre and pulp fiction through a proliferation of (usually sensationalized) religious themes and motifs. The new disaster tales—like *Jaws* and *Earthquake*—looked to nature for a villain. Ursula Leguin turned from pastoral fantasy to an exploration of socio-political reality in *The Dispossessed*.. Soap opera hit prime time, along with the lives of the rich and famous. *Roots* started a boom in the genealogy business. Woody Allen's urban comedies of manners, their satire (as tends to be the case in America) increasingly softened with sentiment, became both popular and critical successes. The movie version of *Dune* borrowed its sets from Jules Verne and its costumes from *The Student Prince*. Neo-medievalism was out. Technology, on the other hand, came back with a vengeance. And not just in SF. TV heroes acquired helicopters and super-cars. Middle America gobbled up home computers. Kids went crazy over toys called "transformers" that seemed to merge man with machine. Science was evidently no longer a dirty word. Neither, for that matter, was artifice. Within mere years of Woodstock, popular music had already begun to spurn "folksy" sincerity in favor of self-parody, unabashed theatrics, and big-city sophistication. Postmodern architects were starting to design skyscrapers that looked like giant Greek temples or Egyptian tombs. Most salient of all, perhaps, the newest version of the "Indian" bestseller, Ruth Beebe Hill's *Manta Yo*, was a limpid, deodorized fantasy in which the main native hero, far from the stereotypic brave with his bow and arrow, was an artist, an intellectual, and a moralist. *All* of these, despite their disparity, substantiate a resurgence of the city mode in fairly obvious ways.

We might also include in this list of symptoms the high visibility (in terms of both numbers and popular success) of women writers during this decade, since it seems likely that these prospered as a group of least partly because the sex's traditional temperamental bent for a primarily humanistic vision accorded well with the period's predominant mood. Back in 1975 Fossum lauded Joyce Carol Oates, for instance, for not having allowed her sense of reality and moral vision to be undermined by the 60s literary extravagance and pessimism even at the height of the craze ("she has not turned to parody or black comedy...she has not violated the conventional structures of language... Nor has she so lost faith in the power of realistic narrative that she feels compelled to undergird it with...mythical dimensions...[Instead] she brilliantly illumines our struggle to understand the world and ourselves."), while Jennifer Brady's more recent comments about Joan Didion stress very much the same kinds of basic concerns. Interestingly enough, Brady relates Didion's stance to the archetypally masculine pioneering myth, claiming that while she deplores and disagrees with Turner's theory of the value of unbridled individualism, she finds in the frontier condition a meaningful metaphor inasmuch as "for the pioneers to survive, they had to recognize and uphold the primal loyalties due to each other as blood kin." Invocations of naturalness notwithstanding, this is an emphasis *much* more suggestive of the Puritan's city-oriented view than of the heroic stance entailed by the wilderness mode.

This, of course, brings us back to the "domestics" again—and it does seem, adding considerable weight to Cummins' observations, that a domestic orientation, using the word in its widest sense, is a dominant feature of the age. If we think about it in retrospect, quite counter to all those critics like Gass who continue to fight a holding action against a trend they view as regressive, it doesn't even seem particularly surprising that such a development should occur. As in the special case of the genre fiction, which reached a high level of complexity and moral seriousness in the early 70s and then, in reaction, retreated from the anxieties that its confrontations aroused, American culture in general, having experienced a kind of revolution in the 60s, could almost inevitably be expected (according to Martin Green) to go through a period of conservative backlash such as this. "After a time of disruptive insight comes the rigors of specific change, a period that requires the soul to pay close attention to daily life," says Olderman (1979). "The characters in the fiction published between 1974 and 1976 are in such a period. They are the people who fell to earth after The Thing that Happened in the Sixties." The tendency toward and the direction of such a reaction, moreover, is strongly influenced by the dynamic entailed by the four unstable modes, especially—since the original social phenomenon was associated both with individualism and with the garden—the urge toward social idealism. In the light of such influence, it is only natural that late 70s, early 80s fiction should have concerned itself far less with cosmic issues than with the structuring of social relations, the attainment or regulation of personal and political power, the reconciliation of religious with secular aims, and of personal with public needs, the solution of problems posed by marriage, lifestyle, education, business, child-raising, work, and information overload. And this is exactly what did happen. As Olderman puts it, the questions that preoccupied American writers during the recent period are quite specifically post-apocalyptic: "What are to be the new social and spiritual arrangements now that the old ones are completely shattered?" What Olderman doesn't go on to say is that the new models are to a large extent simply older ones revamped and reconfirmed.

With this in mind, it is interesting to return to the questions of genealogy that we abandoned in our Introduction. If we rethink current history from a syntactical viewpoint, it becomes clear that political trends as much as literary fashions are determined by, rather than responsible for, the much commented upon post-60s paradigm shift. Like everything else in the United States the "cultural contradictions of capitalism" are in fact resolved sequentially. Actually, considering Bell's explication in the light of the foregoing analysis, it becomes clear that the apparent dichotomization of American society between economic necessities and cultural propensities is neither as simple nor as "fateful" as he implies. "The characteristic style of industrialism is based on the principles of economics and economizing," he says: "on efficiency, least cost, maximization, optimization, and functional rationality. Yet this is the very style that is in conflict with the advanced cultural trends of the Western world, for modernist culture emphasizes anti-cognitive and anti-intellectual modes which look longingly toward a return to instinctual sources of expression. The one emphasizes functional rationality, technocratic decision making, and meritocratic rewards; the other, apocalyptic moods and anti-rational modes of behavior." References to the "Western world" notwithstanding, what Bell has just described here is the difference between the 80s and the 60s, other- and inner-directed. Far from portending breakdown, therefore, the endemic conflict he attributes to the 70s only indicates the continued vitality of a *fundamentally* dualistic tradition. The 70s, as Noam Chomsky points out, was a decade of "organized forgetting," during which it was "the responsibility of the system of ideological control and propaganda to...return the domestic population to a proper state of apathy." Why? Not simply as a retreat from unpleasant realities, but as a prelude to transition. Allison Graham talks about a "remake culture." Like the goddess in the fountain, America in fact remakes herself constantly. Like Lévi-Strauss's bricoleur (1969), she does so entirely out of recycled materials. *Here* is the "lost center" Bell laments; the glue, the tradition, that holds it all together, not despite but *by means of* those very elements—the discontinuity, the compartmentalization, the short memory— to which *he* imputes the "break up" of culture-sustaining discourse.

Americans, then, are not merely inclined toward but *programmed for* face-changing. In the last half-century alone we have progressed from a city mode (40s), to a world-machine mode (50s), to a garden mode (60s), to a wilderness mode (70s), and now back to the city again. For each of these periods we have rewritten our political agenda, our social priorities, and even our moral standards. How do we get away with it? To the critic, and especially to the outsider, the capacity for unblushing revisionism seems naive if not hypocritical. For the community at large, however, the mechanism provides an all-important means of "managing" those inner contradictions that otherwise surely *would* precipitate the apocalypse so long and so gleefully predicated. It also—and largely coincidentally, considering the archaic roots of the base dichotomy— gives the country a tremendous advantage over traditional societies of *any* stripe when it comes to exploiting the potential of what Berman calls modernization. Bourgeois society, he says, has a vested interest "not merely in change but in crisis and chaos."

"Uninterrupted disturbance, everlasting uncertainty and agitation," instead of subverting this society, actually serve to strengthen it. Catastrophes are transformed into lucrative opportunities for redevelopment and renewal; disintegration works as a mobilizing and hence an integrating force. The one specter that really haunts the modern ruling class, and that really endangers the world it has created in its image, is the one thing that traditional elites (and, for that matter, traditional masses) have always yearned for: prolonged social stability. In this world, stability can only mean entropy, slow death, while our sense of progress and growth is our only way of knowing for sure that we are alive. To say that our society is falling apart is only to say that it is alive and well. [1982]

To the dismay of many, "alive and well" is exactly what the United States, with its myth of newness, its institutionalization of periodicy, would seem designed to remain.

7. Afterword:
The Noble Savage at Last

In January 1983, says Leo Ribuffo, President Reagan hailed "the flowering of the man-made miracle of high technology" as the universal panacea for all America's ills. It seems obvious from the foregoing overview that Reagan is far from alone in this belief. Despite the current vociferousness of the peace movement, despite the ongoing debate over the environment, despite such pronouncements as Wilson McWilliams' that "in 1980 the engine of progress, sputtering for a long time, finally broke down," despite the fact, too, that Christopher Lasch is still talking about America's loss of "selfhood" (1984), the covert messages of culture clearly suggest that both the technophobes and the pessimists are out of step with the public mood. They also hammer home the message that the new noble savage is once more well and truly defunct. Before the garden can even begin to regain its erstwhile ascendency, our city-centered vantage point on reality will have to slip down into the demonic realm again. It's only a matter of time, I'm sure. But for the moment, for good or ill, nature is simply not an operative symbol in the cultural mix. Interestingly enough, this is exactly the outcome that John Gardner predicted when he wrote his own implicitly city-oriented noble savage tale, *Grendel*, back in 1971.

The original legend from which Gardner drew his material is already a myth of socialization since, like the classic American western, it concerns the making of a champion from an irresponsible and asocial adventurer. "Just as Beowulf kills Grendel and his dragon mother," says Zweig, "he must tame the Grendel in himself which is both the source of his valor and the limits of his humanity." While retaining this level of implication Gardner, however, gives the basic movement more point by making his novel an allegory for the progression, archetypal and historical both, of mankind from nature to art. Complicating matters even more, instead of granting his audience the ethnocentric detachment faciliated by the original heroic form, he uses the monster as his centre of consciousness, humanizing and in a sense ennobling him, in order to illuminate the full complexity and moral ambiguousness of the psychic trauma which this pattern of development entails. A number of critics, indeed, have been so moved by the sufferings of the bestial narrator that they become fixated on the noble savage aspect of his role. To make too much of this particular level, however, is to miss the fable's clear contention that—regrettable as it may seem—humanity in its drive toward civilization could countenance no other outcome to the fundamental conflict that the battle with Grendel represents than that which actually occurs.

In the earlier sections of the book the relationship between Grendel and the humans is very similar to what the primitivistic myth would lead us to expect. Grendel may be savage, but he behaves *naturally* He is, moreover, capable at this point in the story of many of what we would consider to be civilized feelings: pity, an impulse toward friendship, a love of truth, susceptibility to beauty, respect for wisdom. The semi-civilized humans, on the other hand— as Grendel notes with great disgust—are more violent, more irrational, more *bestial* than beasts. "I was sickened, if only at the waste of it," he says of their constant warring; "no wolf was so vicious to other wolves." What Gardner sets up here, in fact, is none other than the conventional situation whereby a barbaric spokesman is utilized didactically to point up the flaws of the social state. Unlike the classic satire, however, Gardner's vision does not rest with this conventional dynamic. Something happens; something changes the situation for both Grendel and us. An artist suddenly appears on the scene, and after he sings his song—transforming Hrothgar's grubby little war into epic event—nothing can ever be quite the same again.

What was he? The man had changed the world, had torn up the past by its thick, gnarled roots and had transmuted it, and they, who knew the truth, remembered it in his way— and so did I.

I crossed the moors in a queer panic, like a creature half insane. I knew the truth. *It was a late spring. Every sheep and goat had its wobbly twins. A man said, "I'll steal their gold and burn their meadhall!" and another man said, "Do it now!"* I remember the ragged men fighting each other till the snow was red slush, whining in winter, the shriek of people and animals burning, the whip-slashed oxen in the mire, the scattered battle-leavings: wolf-torn corpses, falcons fat with blood. Yet I remembered, as if it had happened, great Scyld, of whose kingdom no trace remained, and his farsighted son, of whose grater kingdom no trace remained. And the stars overhead were alive with the promise of Hrothgar's vast power, his universal peace. The moors their axes had stripped of trees glowed silver in the moonlight and the yellow lights of peasant huts were like scattered jewels on the ravendark cloak of a king. I was so filled with sorrow and tenderness I could hardly have found it in my heart to snatch a pig!

This development is fatal to our noble savage. As the archetypal primitive, his psychic existence is predicated upon a coherent relation between himself and nature. The literally *un*natural transformative power of art, however, by interposing itself between man and the phenomenal world fragments experience in a way that threatens the wholesomeness of this bond. And Grendel knows it. He flees, "torn apart by poetry." "I gnashed my teeth and clutched the sides of my head as if to heal the split, but I couldn't." The moment is the beginning of his end.

The conquest is not achieved all at once, of course, nor, told from Grendel's own perspective is the moral/emotional dimension of the contest nearly as simple as the legendary context would imply. Grendel repudiates the singer's vision not merely because it is alien but because it is an affront to his entire moral being. No matter how attractive and persuasive his pictures may be (and this is an element that even Grendel, despite his resistance, is quite capable of recognizing), they simply aren't true—not in any *natural* sense. The particular *kind* of untruth they represent, moreover, by glamorizing mankind works to subvert everything that he himself is. No more nor less in actuality than man's own savage underself (" 'You *are* mankind, or man's condition,' " says the dragon: " 'inseparable as the mountain-climber and the mountain' "), Grendel is alienated and degraded by the song; made to feel a quite unnatural guilt and shame.

With all this counting against it, what does art—civilization—offer that would excuse or justify Grendel's death? Grendel himself, supported by the ultra-rationalistic dragon, insists that since the song is a lie its effect is an illusion; it doesn't really have any power to change. Indeed, by creating illusion it can only ultimately have a destructive effect, undercutting one's sense of reality and self-sufficiency by promising beautiful, impossible things ("I knew what I knew, the mindless, mechanical bruteness of things, and when the harper's lure drew my mind away to hopeful dreams, the dark of what was and always was reached out and snatched my feet"). Despite Grendel's protestations, however, and even despite our realization that on one level he is absolutely right—the song *is* a falsification—we gradually become aware that in fact it does, for good or ill, have a transformative effect. Grendel himself is confirmed in his beastliness by the singer's vision of him. The violence and irrationality— the unhumanness—that characterizes his nature in the view of the song is not merely *imputed*; as time goes on, it *is*. In the end, moreover, Grendel is finally defeated by none else than the very transformative power of art that he denies. The self-defined hero, no longer the helpless prey of an invulnerable nature's dumb recalcitrance to change, uses *words* to defeat the monster—words first of all to drag Grendel into *time* (the final nemesis of the primitive; the final and definitive triumph of art); more words to redefine his reality in more accessible terms:

> *Grendel, Grendel! You make the world by whispers, second by second. Are you blind to that? Whether you make it a grave or a garden of roses is not the point. Feel the wall: is it not hard?* He smashes me against it, breaks open my forehead. *Hard, yes! observe the hardness, write it down in careful runes. Now sing of walls! Sing!*
>
> I howl.
> *Sing!*
> "I'm singing!"
> *Sing words! Sing raving hymns!*
> "You're crazy. Ow!"
> *Sing!*
> "I sing of walls," I howl. "Horray for the hardness of walls!"
> *Terrible*, he whispers. *Terrible*. He laughs and lets out fire.
> "You're crazy," I say. "If you think I created that wall that cracked my head, you're a fucking lunatic."
> *Sing walls*, he hisses.
> I have no choice.

Convinced to the last that his antagonist is insane to believe that the imagination could actually modify fact, Grendel—once immune to human weapons—is nevertheless defeated by the vision of his own doomed mortality that the civilized hero so insistently projects.

It is not by any means an unequivocal victory that the social hero wins here, to be sure—even aside from the dubious morality of his victimization of the enemy that in his racial pride he has himself created, Grendel's dying words (" 'Poor Grendel's had an accident... *So may you all* ' ") remind us of what we know all too well: that all the poetry and heroic sagas in the world will not prevent brute nature from overtaking man at the last, less well prepared, perhaps, due to his estrangement from his primitive roots. In Gardner's telling, however, it is a victory that was predictable and perhaps necessary as soon as the possibility of art, of self-consciousness first arose. All we can do now is to use its considerable power for worthy ends.

And the noble savage? Gardner would undoubtedly say that he is a childish fantasy we should long since have discarded as irrelevant to *human* (i.e. civilized) reality. The instability of the American psyche, however, suggests that he *will* probably turn up again. In any case, whatever his future prognostications, it seems fairly clear that for the moment at least, the American noble savage has, like Grendel, been defeated by art.

Selected Bibliography:
Secondary Sources Cited

Abrahams, Roger D. 1977. "Contradicting Bell," *American Journal of Sociology*, 83.
Abrams, M.H. 1973. *Natural Supernaturalism: Tradition and Revolution in Romantic Literature*. N.Y.: Norton.
Anderson, Perry. 1984. "Modernity and Revolution," *New Left Review*, 144 (March/April).
Aldridge, John W. 1958. *After the Lost Generation: A Critical Study of the Writers of Two Wars*. N.Y.: Noonday Press.
Allen, Walter. 1964. *Tradition and Dream: The English and American Novel from the Twenties to Our Time*. London: Phoenix House.
Amis, Kingsley. 1977. "The Situation Today" *in* Knight.
Anderson, Poul. 1979. "The Art of Robert Ervin Howard" *in* L. Sprague de Camp, ed., *The Blade of Conan*. N.Y.: Ace.
Ash, Brian. 1975. *Faces of the Future—The Lessons of Science Fiction*. N.Y.: Toplinger.
Azimov, Isaac. 1977. "Social Science Fiction" *in* Knight.
Babbit, Irving. 1919. *Rousseau and Romanticism*. Boston & N.Y.: Houghton Mifflin.
Baritz, Loren. 1964. *City on a Hill: A History of Ideas and Myths in America*. N.Y.: Wiley.
Barnett, Louise. 1975. *The Ignoble Savage: American Literary Racism, 1790-1890*. Westport & London: Greenwood.
Battan, Jesse. 1983. "The 'New Narcissism' in Twentieth-Century America: The Shadow and Substance of Social Change," *Journal of Social History*, 17 (Winter).
Bell, Daniel. 1978. *The Cultural Contradictions of Capitalism*. N.Y.: Basic Books.
Benoit, Raymond. 1973. *Single Nature's Double Name: The Collectedness of the Conflicting in British and American Romanticism*. The Hague: Mouton.
Berman, Marshall. 1984. "The Sign in the Street: a response to Perry Anderson," *New Left Review*, 144 (March/April).
——— 1982. *All That Is Solid Melts Into Air: The Experience of Modernity*. N.Y.: Simon & Schuster.
Bewley, Marius. 1963. *The Eccentric Design: Form in the Classic American Novel*. N.Y.: Columbia U. Press
Bigsby, C.W.E., ed. 1976. *Approaches to Popular Culture*. London: Edward Arnold.
Blish, James (under the pseudonym William Atheling, Jr.). 1970. *More Issues at Hand: Critical Studies in Contemporary Science Fiction*. Chicago: Advent.
Boas, George, ed. 1940. *Romanticism in America*. Baltimore: Johns Hopkins.
Boyer, Robert H., and Zahorski, Kenneth J., intro. and eds. 1978. *The Fantastic Imagination II: An Anthology of High Fantasy*. N.Y.: Avon.
Boyers, Robert. 1975. "Nature and Social Reality in Bellow's *Sammler*," *Salmagundi*, 30.
Brady, Charles A. 1963. "Myth-Maker and Christian Romancer" *in* Gardiner.

Brady, Jennifer. 1975. "Points West, Then and Now: The Fiction of Joan Didion," *Contemporary Literature*, 20, 4.

Brantlinger, Patrick. 1975. "Romances, Novels and Psychoanalysis," *Criticism*, 17.

Bretnor, Reginald, ed. 1974. *Science Fiction, Today and Tomorrow*. Baltimore: Penguin.

Brombert, Victor. 1964 *The Intellectual Hero: Studies in the French Novel, 1880-1955*. Chicago: U. Chicago Press.

Brown, Dee. 1972. *Bury My Heart at Wounded Knee: An Indian History of the American West*. N.Y.: Bantam.

Browne, Ray B., and Fishwick, Marshall, W. 1983. *The Hero in Transition*. Bowling Green: Popular Press.

Brumm, Ursula. 1963. "Wilderness and Civilization: A Note on William Faulkner" *in* Hoffman and Vickery.

———— 1970 *American Thought and Religious Typology*, trans. John Hoogland. New Brunswick, N.J.: Rutgers U. Press.

Burhaus, Clinton. 1975. "Hemingway and Vonnegut: Diminishing Vision in a Dying Age." *Modern Fiction Studies*, 21, 2.

Callahan, John F. 1972. *The Illusions of a Nation: Myth and History in the Novels of F. Scott Fitzgerald*. Urbana: Illinois U. Press.

Carter, Paul. 1977. *The Creation of Tomorrow: Fifty Years of Magazine Science Fiction*. N.Y.: Columbia U. Press.

Cawelti, John. 1976. *Adventure, Mystery and Romance: Formula Stories as Art and Popular Culture*. Chicago: Chicago U. Press.

Chase, Richard. 1957. *The American Novel and Its Tradition*. N.Y.: Doubleday.

————, ed. 1962. *Melville: A Collection of Critical Essays*. Englewood Cliffs, N.J.: Prentice-Hall.

Chavkin, Allan. 1979. "Bellow's Alternative to the Wasteland: Romantic Theme and Form in *Herzog*," *Studies in the Novel*, 11, 3.

Cheyfitz, Eric. 1981. *The Trans-Parent: Sexual Politics in the Language of Emerson*. Baltimore & London: Johns Hopkins.

Chomsky, Noam. 1982. *Towards a New Cold War*. N.Y.: Pantheon.

Clareson, Thomas, ed. 1977. *Many Futures Many Worlds: Theme and Form in Science Fiction*. Kent State U. Press.

Clecak, Peter. 1977. "Culture and Politics in the Sixties," *Dissent*, 24.

Clough, Wilson O. 1964. *The Necessary Earth: Nature and Solitude in American Literature*. Austin: U. Texas Press.

Cohen, Abner. 1976. *The Two Dimensional Man: An Essay on the anthropology of power and symbolism in complex society*. Berkeley & L.A.: U. California Press.

Comfort, Alex. 1970. "The Ideology of Romanticism" *in* Gleckner and Enscoe.

Commager, Henry Steele. 1973. "The Search for a Usable Past" *in* Cords and Gerster.

Cords, Nicholas, and Gerster, Patrick, eds. 1973. *Myth and the American Experience*. N.Y.

Cummins, Walter. 1979. "Inventing Memories: Apocalyptics and Domestics," *The Literary Review*, 23, 1.

Cunningham, Mary E., ed. 1954. *James Fenimore Cooper: A Reappraisal*. Cooperstown: N.Y. State Historical Assoc'n.

Curti, Merle. 1951. *The Growth of American Thought*, 2nd edition. N.Y.: Harper.

Dahl, Curtis. 1967. "Introduction" to Robert Montgomery Bird, *Nick of the Woods*. New Haven: College & University Press.

Davis, David Brion. 1955. "*The Deerslayer*: A Democratic Knight in the Wilderness" *in* Walker.

Dekker, George. 1967. *James Fenimore Cooper, the Novelist*. London: Routledge & Kegan Paul.

Delaney, Samuel. 1977. "Critical Methods: Speculative Fiction" *in* Clareson.

Dickstein, Morris. 1977. *Gates of Eden: American Culture in the Sixties.* N.Y.: Basic Books.

Disch, Thomas. 1978. "The Embarrassments of Science Fiction" *in* Nicholls.

Dondore, Dorothy. 1926. *The Prairie and the Making of Middle America.* Cedar Rapids: Torch.

Douglas, Ann. 1977. *The Feminization of American Culture.* N.Y.: Knopf.

Dudley, Edward, and Novak, Maximillian, eds. 1972. *The Wild Man Within: An Image in Western Thought from the Renaissance to Romanticism.* Pittsburgh: U. Pittsburgh Press.

Fairchild, Hoxey. 1928. *The Noble Savage: A Study in Romantic Naturalism.* N.Y.: Columbia U. Press.

Feidelson, Charles, Jr. 1953. *Symbolism and American Literature.* N.Y.: Oxford.

Fiedler, Leslie. 1962. *Love and Death in the American Novel.* Cleveland & N.Y.: Meridian.

———— 1968. *The Return of the Vanishing American.* N.Y.: Stein & Day.

———— ed. and intro. 1975. *In Dreams Awake.* N.Y.: Laurel.

———— 1978. *Freaks: Myths and Images of the Secret Self.* N.Y.: Simon & Schuster.

Fisher, Marvin. 1961. "The 'Garden' and the 'Workshop,' " *New England Quarterly,* 34, 3.

Flacks, Richard. 1980. *In* "A Look at Christopher Lasch's Look at America," *Center Magazine,* 13 (July/August).

Fletcher, Angus. 1964. *Allegory: The Theory of a Symbolic Mode.* Ithica & London: Cornell U. Press.

Fossum, Robert H. 1975. "Only Control: The Novels of Joyce Carol Oates," *Studies in the Novel,* 7.

Foster, Hal, ed. 1983. *The Anti-Aesthetic: Essays on Postmodern Culture.* Port Townsend, Wash.: Bay Press.

Frazer, Sir James George. 1961. *The Golden Bough: A Study of Magic and Religion.* London: Macmillan.

Frye, Northrop. 1970. "The Drunken Boat: The Revolutionary Element in Romanticism" *in* Gleckner and Enscoe.

Fuller, Peter. 1980. *Art and Psychoanalysis.* London, G.B.: Writers & Readers Co-Op.

Furst, Lilian R. 1969. *Romanticism.* London: Methuen.

———— 1972. "Kafka and the Romantic Imagination" *in* McRobbie.

———— 1976. "The Hero, Or Is He an Anti-Hero?," *Studies in the Literary Imagination,* 9, 1.

Fussell, Edwin S. 1965. *Frontier: American Literature and the American West.* Princeton: Princeton U. Press.

Gardiner, G., ed. 1963. *American Classics Reconsidered: A Christian Appraisal* N.Y.: Scribners.

Gardner, John. 1978. *On Moral Fiction.* N.Y.: Basic Books.

Garvin, Harry R., ed. 1980. *Romanticism, Modernism, Postmodernism.* Lewisburg: Bucknell U. Press.

Gleckner, Robert F., and Enscoe, Gerald, eds. 1970. *Romanticism: Points of View.* Englewood Cliffs, N.J.: Prentice-Hall.

Glicksberg, Charles I. 1974. "Experimental Fiction: Innovation versus Form," *Center Review,* 18.

Goetzman, Samuel. 1970. "The Mountain Man as Jacksonian Man" *in* Cords and Gerster.

Gorer, Geoffrey. 1948. *The American People: A Study in National Character.* N.Y.: Norton.

Graham, Allison. 1984. "History, Nostalgia, and the Criminality of Popular Culture," *Georgia Review,* 38, 2.

Green, Martin. 1972. *Cities of Light and Sons of the Morning: A Cultural Psychology for an Age of Revolution.* Boston: Little, Brown.

Gross, Theodore L. 1971. *The Heroic Ideal in American Literature.* N.Y. & London: Free Press-Collier Macmillan.

Hall, Edward T. 1977. *Beyond Culture*. N.Y.: Anchor.

Hankins, Sarah Russell. 1983. "Archetypal Alloy: Reagan's Rhetorical Image" *in* Browne and Fishwick.

Harbison, Robert. 1977. *Eccentric Spaces*. N.Y.: Knopf.

Hartshorne, Thomas. 1979. "From *Catch-22* to *Slaughterhouse V*: The Decline of the Political Mode," *South Atlantic Quarterly*, 78, 1.

Hassan, Ihab, 1961. *Radical Innocence: Studies in the Contemporary American Novel*. Princeton, N.J.: Princeton U. Press.

Hellman, John. 1982 "Vietnam and the Hollywood Genre Film; Inversions of American Mythology in *The Deer Hunter* and *Apocalypse Now*," *American Quarterly*, 34, 4.

Herbert, Frank. 1974a. "Introduction" *in* Roger Elwood and Virginia Kidd, eds., *The Wounded Planet*. N.Y.: Bantam.

——— 1974b. "Science Fiction and a World in Crisis" *in* Bretnor.

Hillegas, Mark R. 1967. *The Future as Nightmare: H.G. Wells and the Anti-Utopians*.N.Y.: Oxford U. Press.

Hoffman, Daniel. 1961. *Form and Fable in American Fiction*. N.Y.: Oxford.

Hoffman, Frederick, and Vickery, Olga, eds. 1963. *William Faulkner, Three Decades of Criticism*. N.Y.: Harbinger.

Honig, Edwin. 1959. *Dark Conceit: The Making of Allegory*. Evanston, Il: Northwestern U. Press.

Hook, Sidney. 1955. *The Hero in History: A Study in Limitation and Possibility*. N.Y.: Beacon Hill.

House, Kay Seymour. 1965. *Cooper's Americans*. Columbus: Ohio State U. Press.

Jameson, Fredric. 1983. "Postmodernism and Consumer Society" *in* Foster.

Johns-Heine, Patricke, and Gerth, Hans. 1957. "Values in Mass Periodical Fiction, 1920-1940" *in* Rosenberg and White.

Jones, Howard Mumford. 1965. *The Frontier in American Fiction*. Jerusalem.

Kaufman, Donald L. 1974-75. "The Indian as Media Hand-Me-Down," *Colorado Quarterly*, 23.

Kaul, A.N. 1963. *The American Vision: Actual and Ideal Society in Nineteenth-Century Fiction*. New Haven: Yale U. Press.

Keiser, Albert. 1933. *The Indian in American Literature*. N.Y.: Oxford U. Press.

Kermode, Frank. 1967. *The Sense of an Ending: Studies in the Theory of Fiction*. N.Y. & London: Oxford U. Press.

King, J. Norman. 1977. "Theology, SF, and Man's Future Orientation" *in* Clareson.

Knight, Damon, ed. 1977. *Turning Points: Essays on the Art of Science Fiction*, N.Y.: Harper & Row.

Kolodny, Annette. 1975. *The Lay of the Land: Metaphor as Experience and History in American Life and Letters*. Chapel Hill: U. of N. Carolina Press.

Kristeva, Julia. 1980. "Postmodernism?" in Garvin.

Kumar, Krishan. 1978. *Prophecy and Progress: The Sociology of Industrial and Post-Industrial Society*. Harmondsworth, G.B.: Penguin.

LaFarge, Oliver. 1973. "Myths That Hide the Indian" *in* Cords and Gerster.

Lasch, Christopher. 1979. *The Culture of Narcissism: American life in an Age of Diminishing Expectations*. N.Y.: Warner.

——— 1984. "1984: Are We There?" *Salmagundi*, 65.

Lawrence, D.H. 1964. *Studies in Classic American Literature*. N.Y.: Viking.

Lemieux, Jacques. 1985. "Utopias and Social Relations in American Science Fiction, 1950-80," trans. Ronald Rosenthall, *SF Studies*, 12.

Levin, David. 1959. *History as Romantic Art: Bancroft, Prescott, Motley, and Parkman*. Stanford: Stanford U. Press.

Lévi-Strauss, Claud. 1966. *The Savage Mind.* Chicago: U. Chicago Press.

———— 1969. *The Raw and the Cooked: Introduction to a Science of Mythology,* trans. John and Doreen Weightman. N.Y.: Harper & Row.

Lewis, Merrill, and Lee, L. L., eds. 1977. *The Westering Experience in American Literature: Bicentennial Essays.* Bellingham: W. Washington U. Press.

Lewis, R.W.B. 1955. *The American Adam: Innocence, Tragedy and Tradition in the Nineteenth Century.* Chicago & London: U. Chicago Press.

Lovejoy, Arthur O., and Boas, George. 1935. *A Documentary History of Primitivism and Related Ideas.* Baltimore: Johns Hopkins.

Lucie-Smith, Edward. 1975. *Late Modern: The Visual Arts since 1945.* N.Y. & London: Oxford.

Machor, James L. 1982. "Pastoralism and the American Urban Ideal: Hawthorne, Whitman, and the Literary Pattern," *American Literature,* 54, 3.

Mailer, Norman. 1963. *The Presidential Papers.* N.Y.: Putnam.

Martin, Clare. 1981. *A Sociology of Contemporary Cultural Change.* Oxford, G.B.: Basil Blackwell.

Marx, Leo. 1964. *The Machine in the Garden: Technology and the Pastoral Ideal in America.* London & Oxford: Oxford U. Press.

Maxwell, D.E.S. 1965. *American Fiction: The Intellectual Background.* London: Routledge & Kegan Paul.

McAleer, John. 1976. "The Red Man Rediscovered," *Transcendental Quarterly,* 30.

McCaffery, Larry. 1979. "The Gass-Gardner Debate: Showdown on Main Street," *The Literary Review,* 23, 1.

McConnell, Frank. 1975. *The Spoken Seen: Film and the Romantic Imagination.* Baltimore & London: Johns Hopkins.

McGinniss, Joe. 1976. *Heroes.* N.Y.: Viking.

McGregor, Gaile. 1985. *The Wacousta Syndrome: Explorations in the Canadian Langscape.* Toronto: U. Toronto Press.

———— 1986. "A View from the Fort: Erving Goffman as Canadian," *Canadian Review of Sociology & Anthropology,* 23, 4.

McIntosh, James. 1974. *Thoreau as Romantic Naturalist: His Shifting Stance Toward Nature.* Ithica & London: Cornell U. Press.

McRobbie, Kenneth, ed. 1972. *Chaos and Form: History and Literature: Ideas and Relationships.* Winnipeg: U. Manitoba Press.

McWilliams, John P. 1972. *Political Justice in a Republic: James Fenimore Cooper's America.* Berkeley: U. California Press.

McWilliams, Wilson Carey. 1983. "Politics" *in* Ribuffo.

Melling, Philip. 1976. "American Culture in the Thirties: Ideology, Myth, Genre" *in* Bigsby.

Meltzer, Bernard, Petras, John, and Reynolds, Larry T. 1975. *Symbolic Interactionism: Genesis, varieties, and criticism.* London & Boston: Routledge & Kegan Paul.

Merrill, Robert. 1984. "John Gardner's *Grendel* and the Interpretation of Modern Fables," *American Literature,* 56, 2.

Miller, James E., Jr. 1964. "Uncharted Interiors: The American Romantics Revisited," *Emerson Society Quarterly,* 35.

Miller, Perry. 1956. *Errand into the Wilderness.* Cambridge: Belknap

———— 1967. *Nature's Nation.* Cambridge: Belknap.

Millgate, Michael. 1964. *American Social Fiction: James to Cozzens.* Edinburgh & London: Oliver & Boyd, 1964.

Mills, Nicholaus. 1973. *American and English Fiction in the Nineteenth Century: An Antigenre Critique and Comparison.* Bloomington: Indiana U. Press.

Moore, Arthur K. 1957. *The Frontier Mind: A Cultural Analysis of the Kentucky Frontiersman.* Lexington: U. Kentucky Press.

Moskowitz, Sam. 1969. "Introduction" to *Other Worlds Other Times*. N.Y.: Manor Books.

Mumford, Lewis. 1968. *The Golden Day: A Study in American Literature and Culture*. N.Y.: Dover.

Murray, Henry. 1962. " '*In Nome Diabole*' " *in* Chase.

Nance, William L. 1975. "Eden, Oedipus, and Rebirth in American Fiction," *Arizona Quarterly*, 31.

Nash, Gary. 1972. "The Image of the Indian in the Southern Colonial Mind" *in* Dudley and Novak.

Nevius, Blake. 1976. *Cooper's Landscapes: An Essay on the Picturesque Vision*: Berkeley: U. California Press.

Nicgorski, Walter, and Ronald, Weber, eds. 1976. *An Almost Chosen People: The Moral Aspirations of Americans*. Notre Dame & London: U. Notre Dame Press.

Nicholls, Peter, ed. 1978. *Explorations of the Marvellous: The Science and the Fiction in Science Fiction*. Glasgow, G.B.: Fontana.

Noble, David W. 1964. "Cooper, Leatherstocking, and the Death of the American Adam," *American Quarterly*, 16, 3.

O'Connor, William Van. 1960. "The Wilderness Theme in Faulkner's 'The Bear' " *in* Hoffman and Vickery.

Olderman, Raymond. 1972. *Beyond the Wasteland: A Study of the American Novel in the Nineteenth-Sixties*. New Haven & London: Yale U. Press.

———— 1978. "American Fiction 1974-1976: The People Who Fell to Earth," *Contemporary Literature*, 19, 4.

Panshin, Alexei and Cory. 1974. "Science Fiction, New Trends and Old" *in* Bretnor.

Parker, Arthur C. 1954. "Sources and Range of Cooper's Indian Lore" *in* Cunningham.

Parkes, Henry Bamford. 1957. "Metamorphoses of Leatherstocking" *in* Rahv.

Pearce, Roy Harvey. 1953. *The Savages of America: A Study of the Indian and the Idea of Civilization*. Baltimore: Johns Hopkins.

———— 1957. *The Continuity of American Poetry*. Princeton, N.J.: Princeton U. Press.

————, ed. 1969. *Colonial American Writing*, 2nd ed. N.Y.: Holt, Rinehart & Winston.

Peck, Daniel H. 1977. *A World by Itself: The Pastoral Moment in Cooper's Fiction*. New Haven: Yale U. Press.

Peckham, Morse. 1970. "Toward a Theory of Romanticism" *in* Gleckner and Enscoe.

Perloff, Marjorie, 1982. "From Image to Action: The Return of Story in Postmodern Poetry," *Contemporary Literature*, 23, 4.

Philbrick, Thomas. 1970-71. "*The Last of the Mohicans* and the Sounds of Discord," *American Literature*, 62.

Pierson, George Wilson. 1972. "The Frontier and American Institutions: A Criticism of the Turner Theory" *in* Taylor.

Poirier, Richard. 1966. *A World Elsewhere: The Place of Style in American Literature*. N.Y.: Oxford U. Press.

———— 1971. *The Performing Self: Compositions and Decompositions in the Languages of Contemporary Life*. N.Y.: Oxford Press.

Porte, Joel. 1968. *The Romance in America: Studies in Cooper, Poe, Hawthorne, Melville and James*. Middletown, CT: Wesleyan U. Press.

Puetz, Manfred. 1977. "Imagination and Self-Definition," *Partisan Review*, 14.

Rahv, Philip, ed. 1957. *Literature in America*. N.Y.: Meridian.

———— 1961. "The Myth and the Powerhouse" *in* Vickery.

Ribuffo, Leo, ed. 1983. *Contemporary America*, special issue of *American Quarterly*, 35, 1/2.

Richardson, Robert. 1978. *Myth and Literature in the American Rennaissance*. Bloomington: Indiana U. Press.

Riesman, David, *et al.* 1953. *The Lonely Crowd: A Study of the Changing American Character*. Garden City, N.Y.: Doubleday Anchor.

Riggenbach, Jeff. 1980. "The National Letters," *Libertarian Review* (March).

Ringe, Donald A. 1971. *The Pictorial Mode: Space and Time in the Art of Bryant, Irving and Cooper*. Lexington: U. Kentucky Press.

Robinson, Paul A. 1969. *The Freudian Left: Wilhelm Reich, Geza Roheim, Herbert Marcuse*. N.Y.: Harper & Row.

Rogin, Michael Paul. 1975. *Fathers and Children: Andrew Jackson and the Subjection of the American Indian*. N.Y.: Knopf.

Rose, Lois and Stephen. 1970. *The Shattered Ring* Richmond: John Knox Press.

Rosenberg, Bernard, and White, David Manning, eds. 1957. *Mass Culture: The Popular Arts in America*. N.Y.: Free Press.

Ruland, Richard. 1976. *America in Modern European Literature: From Image to Metaphor*. N.Y.: N.Y.U. Press.

Russ, Joanna. 1977. "Alien Monsters" *in* Knight.

Sale, Roger. 1978. "The Golden Age of the American Novel," *Ploughshares*, 4, 3.

Sanford, Charles L. 1961. *The Quest for Paradise: Europe and the American Moral Imagination*. Urbana: U. Illinois Press.

Sargent, Pamela. 1976. "Afterword" to Gene Wolfe, *The Fifth Head of Cerberus*. N.Y.: Ace.

Scholes, Robert. 1975. *Structural Fabulation: An Essay on Fiction of the Future*. Notre Dame & London: U. Notre Dame Press.

———— 1976. "As the Wall Crumbles" *in* James Gunn, ed., *Nebula Award Stories Ten*. N.Y.: Berkeley.

Sennett, Richard. 1978. *The Fall of Public Man*. N.Y.: Vintage.

Simonson, Harold. 1970. *The Closed Frontier*. N.Y.

Slotkin, Richard. 1973. *Regeneration through Violence: The Mythology of the American Frontier, 1600-1860*. Middletown, CT: Wesleyan U. Press.

Smith, Henry Nash. 1950. *Virgin Land: The American West as Symbol and Myth*. N.Y.: Vintage.

Smith, Timothy. 1979. "Righteousness and Hope: Christian Holiness and the Millennial Vision in America, 1800-1900," *American Quarterly*, 31, 1.

Stone, Albert E. 1963. "Introduction" to Hector St. John de Crevecoeur, *Letters from an American Farmer*. Toronto: Signet.

Stein, William Bysshe. 1961. "*Walden*: The Wisdom of the Centaur" *in* Vickery.

Stern, Milton R. 1977. "American Values and Romantic Fiction," *Studies in American Fiction*, 5, 1.

Stout, Janis. 1976. *Sodoms in Eden: The City in American Fiction Before 1860*. Westport, CT: Greenwood.

Sukenik, Ronald. 1977. "Fiction in the Seventies: Ten Digressions on Ten Digressions," *Studies in American Fiction*, 5, 1.

Sundquist, Eric J. 1979. *Home as Found: Authority and Genealogy in Nineteenth-Century Literature*. Baltimore & London: Johns Hopkins.

Symcox, Geoffrey. 1972. "The Wild Man's Return" *in* Dudley and Novak.

Taylor, George Rogers, ed. 1972. *The Turner Thesis: Concerning the Role of the Frontier in American History*. Boston: Heath.

Thorsley, Peter. 1972. "The Wild Man's Revenge" *in* Dudley and Novak.

Tobin, Patricia. 1978. *Time and the Novel: The Genealogical Imperative*. Princeton, N.J.: Princeton U. Press.

Vickery, John B., ed. 1961. *Myth and Literature: Contemporary Theory and Practice*. Lincoln: U. Nebraska Press.

Walker, Warren S., ed. 1955. *Leatherstocking and the Critics*. Chicago: Scott, Foreman.

_____ 1962. *James Fenimore Cooper: An Introduction and Interpretation*. N.Y.: Barnes & Noble.

Wallace, Paul. 1954. "Cooper's Indians" *in* Cunningham.

Waples, Dorothy, 1938. *The Whig Myth of James Fenimore Cooper*. New Haven: Yale U. Press.

Ward, John Williams. 1969. *Red, White and Blue: Men, Books, and Ideas in American Culture*. N.Y.: Oxford U. Press.

Warrick, Patricia. 1977. "Images of the Man-Machine Intelligence Relationship in Science Fiction" *in* Clareson.

Wasserman, Earl. 1970. "The English Romantics: The Grounds of Knowledge" *in* Gleckner and Enscoe.

Webb, Walter Prescott. 1960. "Afterword" to Walter Van Tilburg Clark, *The Ox-Bow Incident*. N.Y. Signet.

Westbrook, Max. 1977. "Mountain Home: The Hero in the American West" *in* Lewis and Lee.

White, Hayden, 1972. "The Forms of Wildness" *in* Dudley and Novak.

_____ 1974. "Structuralism and Popular Culture," *Journal of Popular Culture*, 7.

Whitney, Lois. 1934. *Primitivism and the Idea of Progress in English Popular Literature of the Eighteenth Century*. Baltimore: Johns Hopkins.

Williams, Cecil. 1939. "Introduction" to Robert Montgomery Bird, *Nick of the Woods*. N.Y.: 1939.

Williams, George H. 1962. *Wilderness and Paradise in Christian Thought*. N.Y.: Harper.

Williams, Raymond. 1975. *The Country and the City*. St. Albans, G.B.: Paladin.

Williamson, Jack. 1974. "Science Fiction, Teaching, and Criticism" *in* Bretnor.

Wineapple, Brenda. 1979. "Robert Coover's Playing Fields," *Iowa Review*, 10, 3.

Wolfe, Gary. 1977. "The Known and the Unknown" *in* Clareson.

Wollheim, Donald. 1978. "Introduction" to *The 1978 Annual World's Best SF*. N.Y.: Daw.

Woolf, Michael. 1976. "The Madman as Hero in Contemporary American Fiction," *Journal of American Studies*, 10.

Wymer. 1977. "Perception and Value in Science Fiction" *in* Clareson.

Zoellner, R.H. 1960. "Conceptual Ambivalence in Cooper's Leatherstocking," *American Literature*, 31.

Zolla, Elemire. 1973. *The Writer and the Shaman, A Morphology of the American Indian*, trans. Roland Rosenthal. N.Y.: Harcourt Brace.

Zweig, Paul. 1974. *The Adventurer*. N.Y.: Basic Books.